HIKING THE MOJAVE DESERT

The Natural and Cultural Heritage of Mojave National Preserve

Michel Digonnet

First printing: May 2013
Second printing: January 2014
Second edition: August 2021

Maps, illustrations, and book design by the author

Photographs by the author, unless otherwise specified

Volume Editor: Susan Cole

Cover Designer: Karen Frankel

Published in Palo Alto, California

Printed and bound in the United States of America

Front cover: Sunset over one of the estimated 1.3 million Joshua trees that perished in the August 2020 Dome Fire, Ivanpah Mountains

Back cover: Miner's cabin, Death Valley Mine, Mid Hills

Mound cactus, Castle Peaks, Providence Mountains

Library of Congress Control Number: 2021902778

ISBN: 978-0-9659178-4-1

To David Gilmour,
Nick Mason,
Roger Waters,
and Richard Wright.

Life would not be the same

By the same author:

Hiking Death Valley (Second edition)
Hiking Western Death Valley National Park
Mojave Desert Peaks
Hiking Joshua Tree (in preparation)

WARNING

Many of the hikes suggested in this book are potentially dangerous. They involve hours of strenuous physical activity across often rugged terrain, with no water, little to no shade, in a hot desert. They should be attempted only by hikers in excellent physical condition, with prior experience in desert hiking and good route-finding skills. Although many of the dangers of specific routes are mentioned in the text, all of them cannot possibly be covered. The information contained in this book should not be considered a substitute for common sense. The author declines all responsibilities for any injuries, physical or otherwise, anyone might sustain while hiking any of the routes suggested herein.

ACKNOWLEDGMENTS

I would like first to thank my wife Susan Cole for letting me take the time to research and write yet another book, which took much of my sparse free time away from her. I am also indebted to her for reviewing the manuscript. Michael Closson deserves a big thank you for helping us during the review of this manuscript.

I am indebted to Karen Frankel for designing the book cover, and for her assistance in selecting some of the photographs and graphic art that went into the book.

I want to acknowledge the few brave friends and relatives who accompanied me on some of my hikes in the eastern Mojave Desert, including Jérémie Mathon, Nike and Jeff Weintraub, my mother, and Susan, who often patiently waited for my invariably late returns. I wish to thank Scott Chopin for identifying from photographs the wrecks of vintage automobiles stranded in the preserve, which helped me date a few historic sites; and Larry Vredenburgh for kindly letting me use historic photographs from his personal collection.

Several staff members of the Mojave National Preserve have provided information that I would otherwise have had great difficulty locating. I thank Ted Weasma, the preserve's Geologist and Mining Examiner, for his valuable input on the preserve's geology and mining history, and for helping identify the location of a few lesser known historic mines, in particular the Perseverance Mine and a few properties on Alaska Hill, on Old Dad Mountain, and in New Trail Canyon. I thank David Moore, GIS Data Manager and Planner, for sharing detailed maps of wilderness and private-property boundaries, and for clarifying the legal status of old backcountry roads. Annie Kearns, Lands Specialist, helped me locate the Brannigan Mine and the current owners of the Bonanza King Mine. Park Ranger Michael Glore was very helpful on a number of occasions in providing miscellaneous information about the preserve and its regulations.

I would like to thank Chief of Interpretation Linda Slater for organizing and coordinating the review of the manuscript by NPS staff, and for providing the answers to numerous questions, regarding park policies in particular. Finally, I acknowledge Park Ranger Phillip Gomez for the useful comments he provided on the manuscript, especially regarding the history of the park.

A very special thank you goes to Jim Andre, Director of the Sweeney Granite Mountains Desert Research Center, for sharing his encyclopedic knowledge of the Mojave Desert flora, and for identifying many of the less common plants that I ran across.

For this second edition, I would like to express my appreciation to Karen Frankel for the cover design and her eye for artful details. I thank Barbara Michel, Park Guide at Mojave National Preserve, for her precious help in identifying areas described in this book that were affected by the Dome Fire, at a time when the pandemic prevented me from traveling to the park. I would also like to acknowledge Jonathan Wheeler for writing a quick Python code that automatically updated the index for this second edition and saved me a few weeks of tedious work. And of course a big thank you to my wife Susan for helping me with the big words.

TABLE OF CONTENTS

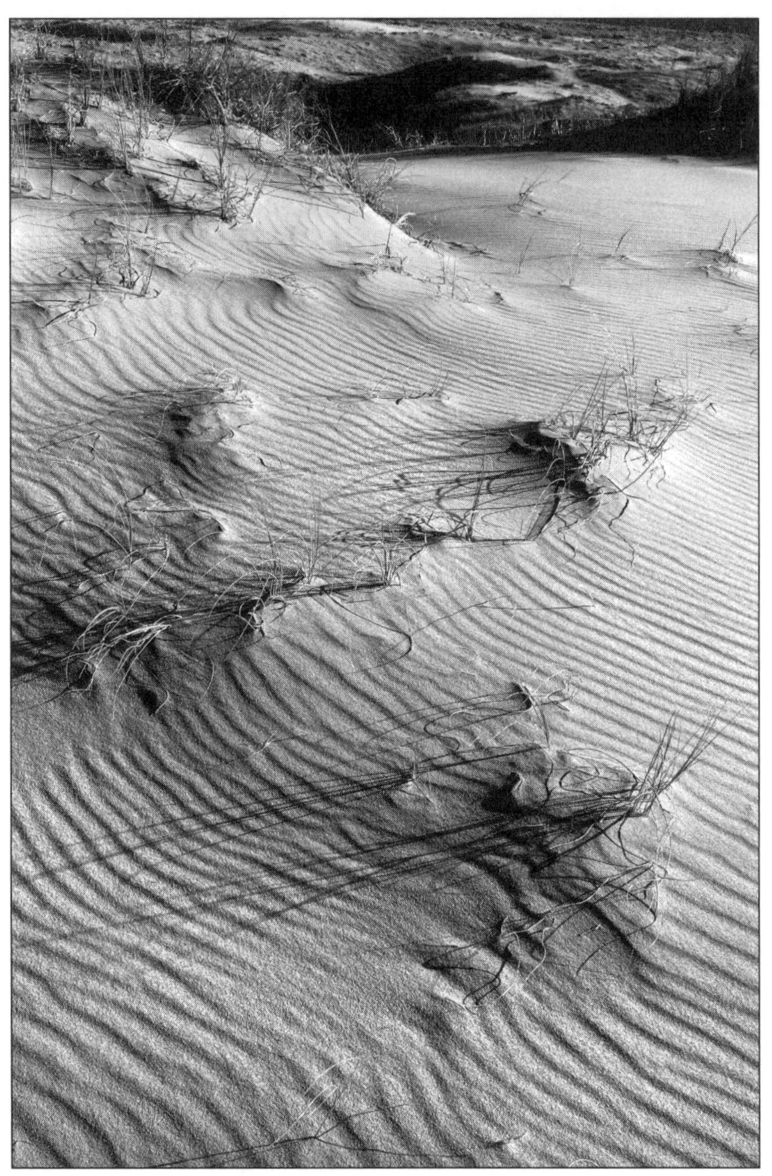

Ripples and grass, Kelso Dunes

FOREWORD

Human beings have traveled through the eastern Mojave Desert since ancient times, yet over the centuries few are the hardy souls who dwelled in it for very long. The isolation, the temperature extremes, the lack of water, and the daunting harshness of the land all conspired to make it a dreaded place shunned by most. Native Americans had only a few quasi-permanent settlements here, centered around the rare springs that carried sufficient water. The scarcity of resources forced them to be on the move much of the time. California-bound settlers saw in the Mojave Desert a perilous barrier that they crossed hurriedly, like a malevolent sea. Miners generally did not stay long either; most mining ventures survived only a handful of years. Later on, engineers came to build pipelines, power lines, railroads and freeways, and they left too. Even the homesteaders who bravely tried to eke out a living in the high desert found it too inhospitable and eventually moved on.

Today, nearly two decades after this area was protected as Mojave National Preserve, this mind-set still prevails. The eastern Mojave Desert is used mostly as a throughway, be it by freight trains rumbling along endless railways, by compressed natural gas flowing through buried pipelines, by high-voltage electrons surfing power lines, or by the swelling ranks of humans whizzing by on the interstates. The majority of drivers who actually enter the preserve use it as a convenient shortcut to get someplace else. Like the electrons and the freight, they never touch the land. In any given year, less than 70,000 people stop by the preserve's visitor center. The eastern Mojave Desert is still, after all these years, a place known by very few.

This is not for lack of magnificence. Part of the Basin and Range Province, the preserve is a grand celebration of this stunning region, a beautiful slice of fractured planetary crust suffused with vastness, beauty, silence, and intoxicating freedom. It is a land of impossible contrasts, where majestic mountain ranges rise thousands of feet above wide-open valleys, fiercely hot in summer and bone-chilling in winter, ignored by rain for months but occasionally pelted by violent thunderstorms. It is a place with luminous basins and shadowy canyons, cacti and evergreens, lifeless salt flats and profusions of wildflowers, forlorn wastelands and astoundingly colorful landscapes. When it comes to the great outdoors, size matters, and size is undoubtedly one of the preserve's most crucial assets. The third largest national park unit in the country outside of Alaska, Mojave National Preserve protects 1.6 million acres of land, a number that swells to 2.2 million when including surrounding wilderness areas. This immensity holds an immeasurable treasure of natural and cultural resources. The geological record spans some 1.8 billion years of Earth's history, represented by a wild range of sedimentary, igneous, and metamorphic rocks. They crop out generously as volcanic tablelands, cinder volcanoes, granite boulders and domes, sand dunes, salt flats, and limestone cliffs. Over much of this unforgiving region, cacti, yuccas, and chollas rule with undisputed authority—their unconventional gardens grace huge areas. Yet the high mountains are sprinkled with shady juniper and pine, oaks and manzanita thrive in remote canyons, and a few summits are home to rare groves of maple and white fir. In spite of the hardship, wildlife is surprisingly diverse. Hardly a day goes by without spotting a rabbit, a lizard, or a bird; you might even run across a mule deer, a bighorn sheep, or a mountain lion. Because the preserve was created relatively recently, its human history is also particularly rich. Native Americans, homesteaders, cattlemen, and miners have all left their marks. The backcountry is rife with abandoned mines and mills, rock art, derelict corrals, and the cabins of long-forgotten miners.

Mojave National Preserve holds remarkable landscapes, in which each element has its meaning and poetry, and an infinite number of stories to tell. Half a lifetime of wanderings has taught me that to best discover, appreciate, and learn about this complex minutia, there is no substitute for walking. This book is an invitation to desert lovers to explore this tremendous wilderness. Come and climb a grueling peak, scramble up heaps of boulders, slush across oceans of sand, stroll through sweeping forests of Joshua trees, hike up rugged canyons, visit caves and desert streams, or simply bounce along some of the preserve's 1,100 miles of primitive roads. In part because the preserve is eclipsed by even greater parks, in part because of our propensity to seek the best first, you will likely be alone. With the exception of a few popular destinations, I have encountered here fewer hikers than rattlesnakes. For some of us, choosing this over better publicized parks means trading up—trading the most spectacular for greater solitude, and for the heightened sense of mystery and ownership that comes from exploring rarely visited places. Take advantage of this incredible opportunity we still have, on a planet teeming with billions, to get lost, body and soul, in a mighty territory, and to trek one more time just beyond the point of no return—and back.

Cafe Claude, San Francisco, California
August 25, 2012

About This Book

General Organization

This book is divided into twelve parts. The first part provides background information about the preserve, including general natural features, facilities, weather, and road conditions. Parts 2 and 3 are devoted to the natural history and human history, respectively. Part 4 covers safety tips, regulations, and ethics. The remaining eight parts describe hikes in specific geographic areas, arranged generally from west to east and north to south: Kelso Basin, Clark Mountain Range, Ivanpah Mountains, New York Mountains, Mid Hills, Providence Mountains, Granite Mountains, and Lanfair Valley. Each part begins with a general introduction that includes an overview of the area's main features (location, access and backcountry roads, geology, hiking, etc.), summary tables of suggested road trips and hikes, and a shaded-relief map. The rest of each part contains individual hiking destinations, organized in the same cardinal order. At the end of the book, the index of destinations provides a quick reference to what the preserve has to offer, and to the places I found most special and exciting.

To avoid potential ambiguities, this chapter explains the purpose of these subsections, the definitions that were used, and the assumptions that were made.

Tables of Suggested Hikes

For out-and-back hikes the distance that is listed is the *one-way* distance, and the elevation change is the *one-way* elevation gain *plus* loss (since you will climb the elevation loss on your return), which is the same as the *total* elevation gain on the round-trip hike. For loop hikes, the figures listed are the *total* distance and again the total elevation gain. All elevation figures account for small local elevation changes.

Organization of Individual Driving/Hiking Area Descriptions

Each individual area description contains six common sections: a summary of highlights, three sections titled "General Information," "Location and Access," and "Route Description," a distance and elevation chart, and a map. When warranted, additional sections are included, such as "Geology" or "History."

About "General Information." This section provides a synopsis of the most important facts about the hikes / road trips. It includes the following entries.

Road status mentions first whether the hike is done on a road, a trail, or cross-country, then the type of road that gives driving access to the area (paved graded, or primitive), and the vehicle requirement (standard-clearance, high clearance (HC), or four-wheel drive (4WD)).

Hikes: The next entry lists the distance, elevation change, and difficulty of the main hike(s) in the area. For out-and-back hikes, distances and elevations are one-way figures from the starting point defined by mile 0 in the chart. For loop hikes, the figures listed are the total distance and the *total* elevation change (ups *plus* downs). All elevation figures account for elevation changes that may not appear in the chart.

Difficulty rates the overall hiking difficulty (this is often the only place where the level of difficulty is mentioned). Importantly, ratings assume that the entire hike, usually round-trip, is done in one day (breaking up a long hike into a two-day backpacking trip usually lowers its difficulty). They also assume cool to warm weather. In very hot weather, the difficulty of hiking anywhere worsens considerably, and these ratings underestimate the difficulty.

The following scale is used:

- Very easy: a fairly short stroll on nearly level terrain.
- Easy: involves relatively short distances, easy walking on gentle grades, and no obstacles that cannot be dealt with by easily walking around them; accessible to most people.
- Moderate: a longer hike (3-6 miles), with steeper grades and / or a few obstacles; anyone in reasonably good shape should pass this level.
- Difficult: steep grades (500–1,000 feet per mile) over moderate distances (~6 miles), rough terrain, uneasy footing, and / or obstructions to bypass or climb. Good physical condition is imperative.
- Strenuous: implies much of the way a combination of several of the following: steep grades (1,000 feet per mile or more) over long

TOPOGRAPHIC MAP LEGEND			
(66)	Highways/Paved roads		Contour line
= = = = =	Unpaved road (2WD)		Contour line (every fifth line)
- - - - -	4WD-HC road	3200	Elevation, in feet
--------	Hiking trail		Wash
....	Cross-country route		Broad gravel or sand wash
–––––	State border		Wash distributary
	Preserve boundary		Fall/Boulder jam/Chockstone
◄ To Baker (25 mi)	Mileage from edge of map		Sand dunes
			Natural bridge/Arch
	Pass		Summit
	Gate		Grotto
	Manmade structure		Pond/Lake
	Ruin		Spring
	Grave		Well
	Campground		Water tank
	Ranger station		Mine adit
	Picnic area		Collapsed adit
	Guzzler		Mine shaft
	Corral		Open pit/Surface mine
		x	Prospect
-N-	North Star		Windmill
		•S	Starting point of a hike

distances (about 8 miles or more), large rocks in washes, high falls to climb or circumvent, and very steep and rough terrain; requires excellent physical condition and recent practice.

This scale is subjective. However, I did my best to use this scale consistently throughout this and other books. So even if you disagree with it, use it as a relative scale: just calibrate it against your own scale and adjust it accordingly. For example, you may decide after trying a few hikes that what I call moderate is usually easy for you.

USGS topographic maps lists the USGS 7.5' maps that cover the entire hiking/driving area. When several maps are required, the most useful maps are identified with an asterisk.

Maps indicates, in this order, the page location of:

(1) the main contour map(s) for the hike, marked by an asterisk;

(2) in some cases, other contour maps (no asterisk) showing the area in relation to adjacent areas;

(3) the shaded-relief map of the area's general location, in italics.

About "Location and Access." This section gives driving directions to the starting point of a hike. They are meant to be clear enough without consulting a map. The type of road is also mentioned, and the vehicle requirement for unpaved roads, *assuming dry weather*. Vehicle requirement is a *very subjective* topic, and it reflects *only* my own experience. I tend to be tolerant of rocks and bushes scraping my car and consider that to get there, a few bumps here and there are worth it. Not everyone feels this way. *So be aware that on most of the preserve's primitive roads that I claim can be driven with a passenger vehicle, the NPS recommends a four-wheel-drive vehicle. If you have little experience driving desert roads with a passenger car, follow their recommendations instead of mine.*

About "Route Description." This is the main section. It describes the natural features, main attractions, and challenges of the hike and/or drive. When necessary, route finding and specific difficulties encountered along the hike are discussed. Unless otherwise specified all cardinal directions are referenced to the true north (North Star). Only in a few stated instances does it refer to the magnetic north. The magnetic declination is 12.5° east in the western and central parts of the preserve, and 12° east in the eastern part.

About the Distance and Elevation Charts. Each description contains a chart of key features along the route, their elevations, and their distance from the starting point (mile 0). For features reached by a side trip, the one-way distance from the preceding entry is shown in parentheses. For example, under New Trail Canyon, the New Trail Mine is 0.5 mile from the main line of travel (the canyon wash), up the New Trail Mine Road, and the distance is indicated as (0.5). The next entry, Revenue Copper Mine, is 0.6 mile further than the New Trail Mine, and it is shown as (1.1). The distance to the next entry (the side canyon to the Bullion Mine) is again measured from the starting point of the hike, assuming you did *not* take the side trip to the New Trail Mine.

About the Maps. Each description includes a topographic map of either the entire area or the most important portion of it (only the Mojave Road does not have a topo map, because it covers such a large area). All maps were hand drawn from USGS topographic maps. North (North Star) is parallel to one edge of the map. Although not as densely contoured as USGS maps, they are accurate enough for most hikes. However, on more extensive hikes, especially requiring orienteering, they should not be used as a substitute for USGS maps.

■

— 1 —

The Preserve At A Glance

A Desert Legacy

Mojave National Preserve covers 1.6 million acres of desert land in southeastern California, the equivalent of an area of about 50 by 50 miles. Administered by the National Park Service (NPS), it is the third largest desert park in the country. Most of it is bound by Interstate 15 to the north and Interstate 40 to the south, roughly from Baker east to the Nevada border. A smaller separate section is located north of Interstate 15, in the Clark Mountain Range. This huge track of land is surrounded on all sides by thousands of square miles of largely uninhabited desert, much of it preserved in a patchwork of wilderness areas, much of the rest *de facto* wilderness. Including these surrounding lands, the preserve sits at the heart of nearly three million protected acres. This is desert parkland at its best, not hemmed in by spreading cities like less fortunate parks but isolated in the midst of a considerably larger, mostly wild region, with room to roam and breathe stretching further than the eye can see.

The preserve's uncontested star is the beautiful alignment of high mountains that slices right through its core. Made of four contiguous ranges—from north to south the New York Mountains, Mid Hills, Providence Mountains, and Granite Mountains—this dividing backbone holds some of the region's most remote and spectacular scenery. Almost all of the preserve is part of the Great Basin and drains towards inland dry lakes with no outlet to the sea—Bristol Lake to the south, Soda Lake near the western edge of the preserve, Silver Lake to the northwest, Shadow Valley to the north, and Ivanpah Lake to the northeast. Only a very small portion of it, the southeastern side of the New

York Mountains, drains to the sea by rolling off gradually over Lanfair Valley's huge alluvial fans toward the Colorado River and ultimately the Sea of Cortez. From the approximate middle of this mountainous core, a second string of mountains—from north to south the Clark Mountain Range, Mescal Range, and Ivanpah Mountains—forms a 25-mile-long divide between Shadow Valley to the west and Ivanpah Valley to the east. The rest of the preserve is punctuated with some two dozen smaller isolated mountains.

With elevations ranging from about 930 feet at Soda Lake to 7,930 feet at the top of Clark Mountain, the preserve contains an extraordinary variety of terrains, geological features, flora, and fauna. It has limestone caves and granite canyons, cliff-bound mountains and deep valleys, conifer woodlands, Joshua tree forests, springs and desert creeks. It is the home of the famous Kelso Dunes, of the 25-mile sweep of sand known as the Devils Playground, of an extensive field of recent cinder cones, and of Cima Dome, a surprisingly symmetric granitic swell that boasted until recently the world's largest Joshua tree forest. Most of these features are still little known, yet as striking and exciting as comparable features in other desert parks. Many natural and man-made features are either unique or rare. Little Cowhole Mountain offers a slippery ascent up sand-inundated slopes. The awe-inspiring pit of the Vulcan Mine is one of a kind in the National Park Service. The Mojave Road, which traverses the entire preserve from east to west, is one of the longest primitive roads in the contiguous states that crosses no human habitations. In a good year, the spring flower displays are unbelievably profuse and colorful.

The geological diversity is equally remarkable, with sedimentary, intrusive, and volcanic rocks all well represented and collectively spanning over 1.8 billion years of Earth's history. This profusion has bred a wider assortment of formations and geological features than most desert parks, from volcanic mesas to lava tubes, extensive fields of granitic boulders, fossils and petrified wood, salt playas, young cinder cones, extensive eolian deposits, limestone mountains, and spectacular rock displays. Only the desert seems to produce such sheer mineral exuberance.

Another one of the preserve's unique assets is its vegetation. Hundreds of square miles, mostly around the mid to high elevations, are covered with Joshua trees and magnificent desert gardens. More than two dozen species of cactus, yucca, and agave thrive throughout the preserve. They weave an endless tapestry, never reproduced twice. This attribute alone makes the eastern Mojave Desert one of the greatest natural treasures in the American West.

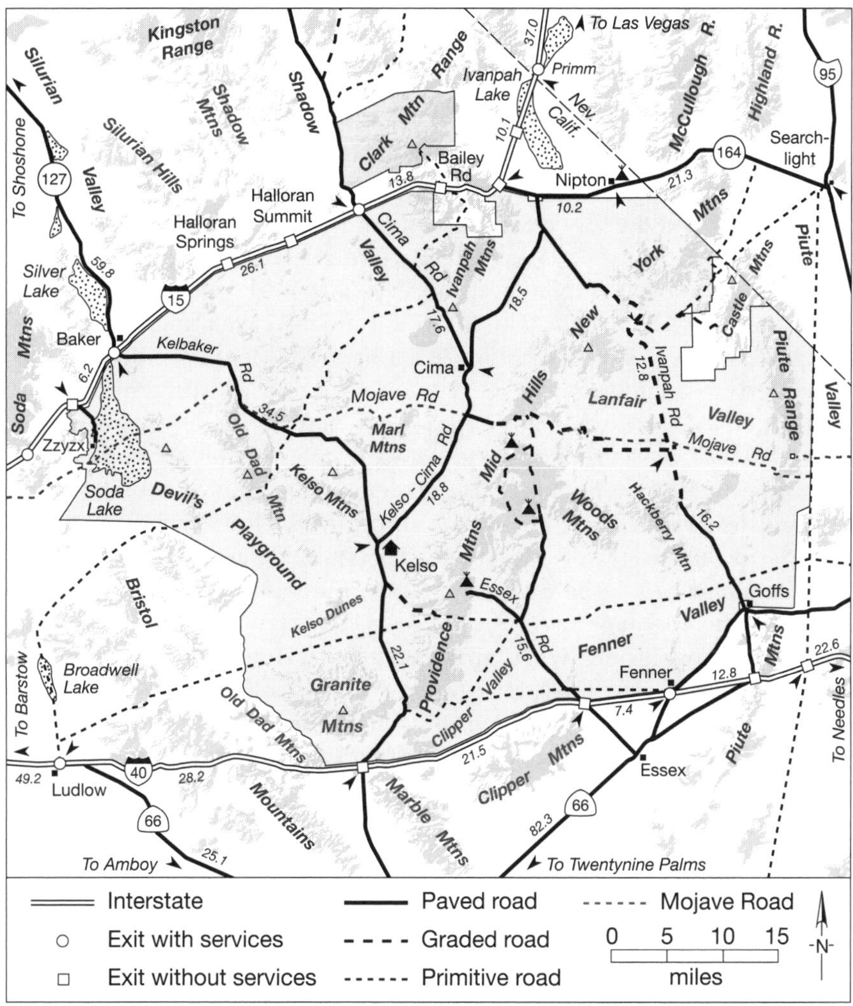

It is remarkable that in spite of this abundance of scenic splendors, and of the relative proximity to major urban centers, Mojave National Preserve gets so few visitors a year—probably less than 200,000. As it is, most of them are travelers who use the preserve's paved roads as a shortcut to somewhere else. Other than at a half a dozen well-advertised places, like the Kelso Dunes, Mitchell Caverns, and Teutonia Peak Trail, I have not crossed paths with a single hiker. Encounters on backcountry roads are also infrequent. This guarantee of solitude, combined with the largely undeveloped vastness, are the most important features of the preserve.

Unlike many popular national parks, where increasing visitation has forced the imposition of stringent restrictions on camping, in Mojave National Preserve camping regulations are still considerably more lax. In addition to a few park-maintained campgrounds, literally hundreds of primitive camp sites are sprinkled throughout the preserve. At the end of a tiring day in the wild, it is nice to be able to find a place to spend the night without having to drive long distances.

Compared to most parks, which were generally created a century or so ago, the Mojave National Preserve is a fairly recent addition to our national park system. This part of the desert was first set aside as the East Mojave National Scenic Area in 1980. Most of it became the Mojave National Preserve in 1994 as part of the California Desert Protection Act. Humans have had more time to develop this region before it was preserved, and the area's human history is particularly rich. Ranchers, miners, homesteaders, engineers, and of course Native Americans before them, all saw an opportunity to harvest something here, and they have all left something behind. Petroglyphs decorate boulders and cliffs at many locations. A railroad and two power lines and buried pipelines traverse the preserve. A few areas are still used for ranching. Others were annexed by academic institutions for research purposes. Historic mines and mining-related structures abound. A few gold mines were still active until the 1990s. The Mojave National Preserve therefore gives visitors a unique opportunity to take a look at active and deactivated ranches, railways, and homesteads, which are not represented in other NPS units on such a scale.

Campgrounds and Other Facilities

A distinguishing charm of the preserve is its dearth of facilities. There are no hotels or motels, no gas stations or garages, no grocery stores, and no public showers. This is the way a desert should be—remote, left to its own devices, uncluttered by manmade contraptions. Unlike in other parks in danger of turning into theme parks, when they have not crossed this line already, here nature is not fragmented by service-oriented communities. You cannot be tempted by modern comforts. At the end of the day you just drive or walk somewhere to set up camp, eat, and sleep, and in the morning the desert is right at your doorstep waiting for you. This unbroken contact with nature provides a much richer experience. Coupled with the low visitation, this is one of the preserve's most outstanding features.

The preserve does have, however, a few amenities. There is a visitor center at the Kelso Depot and an information center at Hole-in-the-Wall. There is a campground at Hole-in-the-Wall, rather exposed to

Cowhole Mountain from the Devils Playground

heat and wind but centrally located, as well as the Black Canyon Group and Equestrian Campground. In the warm season the Mid Hills Campground is much more pleasant, being located at higher elevation and shaded by large pine and juniper, many of which survived the 2005 fire. The Providence Mountains State Recreation Area also has a charming high-elevation campground, although the SRA is closed at the time of this writing. The rail siding at Cima boasts a tiny store, open intermittently, that offers a very limited supply of groceries, most of it basic and not all entirely fit for human consumption. The Kelso Depot serves sandwiches and selected drinks at limited hours. Tap water is available at all campgrounds, at the visitor and information centers, and at the Hole-in-the-Wall picnic area. At the time of this writing, the only public telephone is at Hole-in-the-Wall (phone cards and free calls to operator only), at Cima, and at the SRA.

And that's it. For other amenities, you will have to drive to one of the small gateway communities: Fenner and Ludlow along Interstate 40, Nipton to the north, or the Cima Road exit and Baker on Interstate 15. If you are in the middle of the preserve, it can take quite a while to drive there and back. So if you are planning on visiting for more than a day, make every effort to be self-sufficient for the duration of your stay

Kelso Depot

so you won't have to waste fun time and fuel driving in and out of the preserve. Load up on food, water, and gas. In the summer, bring plenty of ice to keep your food from spoiling.

Kelso. As you drive toward Kelso, what betrays the town from some distance is its slender twin water towers soaring about 100 feet like silver smokestacks. Next you will see its low spread of greenery, then its distinctive two-story depot and scatter of houses. First opened in October 2005 after extensive renovations (see *Railroad History*), the former railroad depot is the preserve's primary visitor center (open every day except Christmas Day, from 9 a.m. to 5 p.m.). In many ways, including its historical significance, this is a perfect place for a first contact with the area. With its cream-colored walls, red-tiled gabled roof, and long arcade wrapped around three sides, the depot was designed to mimic the style of California's Spanish missions. The recessed second story is lined with windows in teel frames capped by bright-red awnings. A green lawn shaded by stately date palms adds a soothing mood to this welcoming oasis. In pre-air-conditioning days, summer passengers waited for the Union Pacific train under the cool arched colonnade facing the tracks. On a hot day, the building still offers the only deep shade for miles around. It is an inviting place to

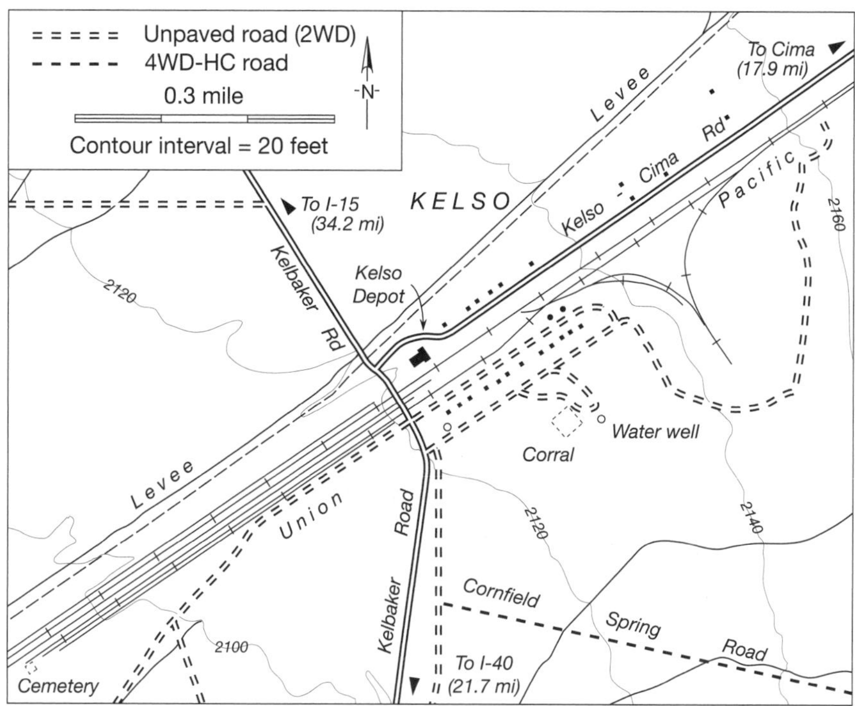

revel in the stillness of the desert while admiring the improbable mountains rising in the distance.

Generously distributed among the depot's many historic rooms, the Visitor Center is one of the most unusual in the NPS. The spacious high-ceilinged room you first walk into is the old Beanery, the elegant diner that fed train passengers and local workers for decades. Restored to its 1924 splendor, it is filled by a sprawling U-shaped counter lined with sparkling stools. A wide hallway leads off to former dormitories. A wing has been converted into a natural and human history museum; another one has a bookstore. At the end of the hallway is the baggage room and the restored ticket and telegraph office. From the main room, a graceful stairway climbs to the second floor, formerly a suite of dormitory rooms for rail workers and train crews. A couple of rooms are furnished as they looked in the 1920s–1940s. Others contain exhibits on the local mining, transportation, and ranching history. A stairway drops to the basement, which once served as a recreation and community center. The space now features the work of local artists, highlighting the preserve's historical and natural heritage. The beauty of this visitor center lies as much in the learning experience as in the setting in which you learn. The depot is an integral part of the education

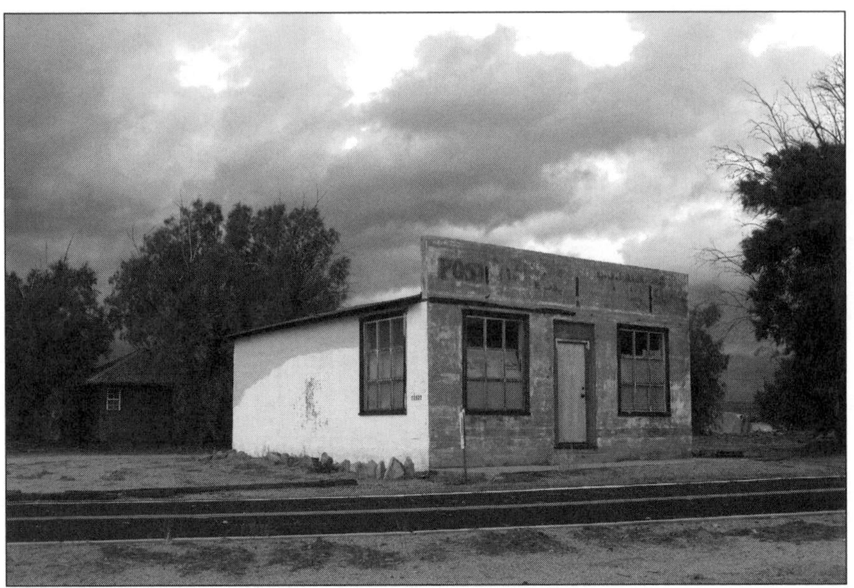

Old post office building at Kelso

process, a seamless juxtaposition of historic and present-day elements. After a 24-year hiatus, the Beanery reopened in 2009, so you can now enjoy a cold sandwich or a cool or warm drink in the same space as travelers of yesteryear. If you hang around long enough, you may find yourself transported back to another time, imagining some of the aging building's dramas, or waiting for a train to come to a screeching stop in billowing clouds of steam.

To get a feel for Kelso's past, take a stroll along the Kelso-Cima Road. The former post office is the first of several historic buildings, in various states of disrepair, strung along the road. After 0.5 mile you can cross the tracks and return on the graded road paralleling the tracks. Some of the houses under tall cottonwoods are former homes from Kelso's glory days, now the residences of mostly railroad employees. In 2009 15 people lived here, less than 1% of the historic peak. Water is still stored in the same magnificent twin towers, which are owned by Union Pacific. Many birds are attracted by the well-watered gardens. Doves and hawks often perch on the high-voltage line by the tracks. Turkey vultures spiral lazily overhead. In the spring you might spot a finch or an oriole. The dirt road soon crosses the Kelbaker Road and continues along the screen of salt cedar that lines the tracks. Tens of miles of these shaggy trees were planted decades ago to keep dust off the tracks. After 0.5 mile you will come to the

Telephone Numbers (760 area code) and Email Addresses			
Emergency		***Restaurants***	
24 hours	911	Whistle Stop Oasis, Nipton	856-1045
Fire Department	911		oasis@nipton.com
California Highway Patrol	256-1727		
		Visitor centers/Information	
Towing services and tire repair		Kelso Depot	252-6108
Brothers Towing, Ludlow	733-4400	Hole-in-the-Wall Info. Ctr.	252-6104
Rasor Road Towing	733-4347		928-2572
Stateline Serv., Cima Rd exit	856-2215	Mojave River Valley Museum,	
	(800) 442-2434	Barstow	256-5452
All Star Mobile Repair, Daggett/Baker		Hunting regulations	928-2586
	(866) 993-9977	Providence Mtns SRA	928-2586
		MNP HQ, Barstow	252-6100
Lodging		Preserve website	www.nps.gov/moja
Ludlow Motel	733-4463		
Hotel Nipton	856-2335	***Campgrounds***	
	hotel@nipton.com	Black Canyon Group and Equestrian	
		Campgr. reserv.	928-2572 or 252-6104

town cemetery, tucked between the tracks and the trees. A freight train will likely rumble by while you amble around town. On average about a dozen come by every day. Deafening beasts of steel, inching their way along as they drag an inconceivable number of cars, they are an integral part of Kelso's charm.

Hole-in-the-Wall Information Center. Named after the dramatic honeycombed rocks that drape the surrounding volcanic cliffs, this information center is a good stop while visiting this colorful area. The large ranch-style wooden building offers basic orientation, maps, books, a short film about the preserve, as well as candy bars, tap water, toilets, and the usual assortment of indispensable souvenirs. The staff is knowledgeable about the area and can give you useful tips about road conditions and places to see. The center is open 9 a.m. to 4 p.m. Wednesday through Sunday in winter (October–April). It is also open in summer (May–September), usually Friday through Sunday, as staffing permits. Saturday evening ranger talks and Sunday morning guided nature walks are often available in the fall and spring. Open hours tend to change from year to year depending on staff availability. Call ahead to verify hours.

	Restaurant	Groceries/food	Lodging	Campground	Gas station	Tire repair	Towing	Public phone	Water
Afton Road exit				✓					
Baker	✓	✓	✓	✓	✓	✓	✓	✓	✓
Cima		✓						✓	✓
Cima Road exit		✓			✓	✓	✓	✓	✓
Fenner	✓	✓			✓			✓	✓
Hole-in-the-Wall		✓		✓				✓	✓
Kelso	✓	✓							✓
Ludlow	✓	✓	✓		✓	✓	✓	✓	✓
Nipton	✓	✓	✓	✓					✓
Providence Mtns SRA				✓				✓	✓
Rasor Road exit		✓		✓	✓	✓	✓	✓	✓

Gateway Towns

Baker. If you are in the western half of the preserve and in critical need of Americana, Baker is your closest bet. Once an isolated desert outpost, Baker has been thoroughly transmogrified by Interstate 15. Today, it is an overgrown facility stretched thin along three closely spaced freeway exits. It features the generic outcrop of fast-food culprits, as well as a few restaurants, a grocery store, two motels, and several gas stations. At their prime, which was decades ago, the motels offered not much more than a fourth grader's idea of luxury. Located along the freeway, they are also quite noisy. Except perhaps on the hottest and coldest nights, the open desert is a better deal.

Nipton. Of the countless towns that rose and fell throughout the eastern Mojave Desert, Nipton is the last one standing. Located on the preserve's northern boundary, it has the only bed and breakfast in the region, and the only restaurant worthy of the name. If it is too cold or too hot for you to camp, or if you are craving a hot meal, think Nipton.

Nipton started quite modestly, in the second half of the 19th century, as a mere road crossing. One road connected the silver mines around Clark Mountain to the Colorado River. The other one linked

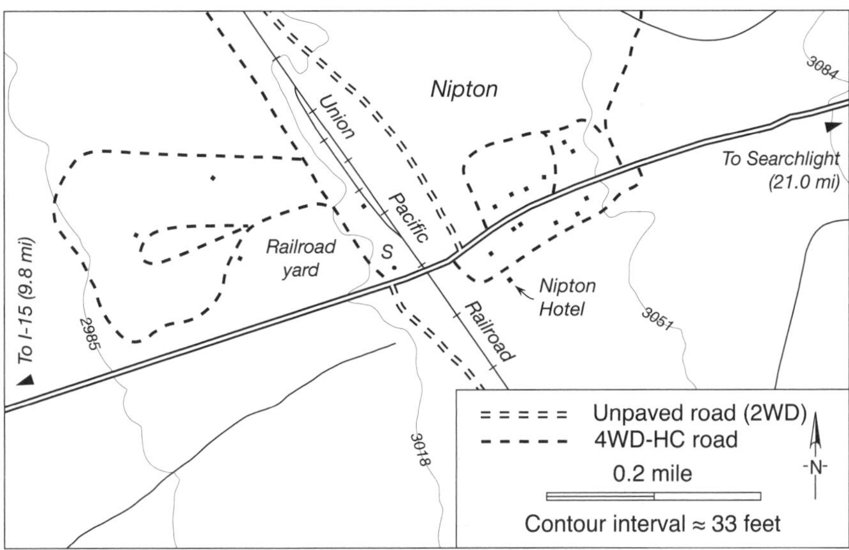

the Goodsprings Mining District in the Spring Mountains to Goffs on the Santa Fe Railroad. For years it was likely nothing more than a camping spot for wagon drivers on their way through. The town was first put on the map in the late 1890s by a gold strike just over the state line, around the southern tip of the McCullough Range. To support the miners, a small camp, named Nippeno after the district's main claim, was established at the crossroad in 1900. The extension of the California Eastern Railway into Ivanpah Valley in 1902 brought in additional business, but nothing did as much for its welfare as the arrival of the San Pedro, Los Angeles & Salt Lake Railroad in December 1904. A hotel—the predecessor of Hotel Nipton—was built around then, and for many years it faithfully served the railroad. Nippeno Camp was renamed Nipton in 1921. It was an active rendezvous point under the reign of Harry Trehearne, a miner from England, and his wife, who took the town under their wings and developed it until the late 1940s. The town was purchased in 1984 by the Freeman family, who revamped it and opened the bed and breakfast in the old Hotel Nipton.

Most visitors come to Nipton to see its old adobe hotel. The handsome one-level ranch-style building has an inviting front facade and a shaded wrap-around porch. The beautiful manicured rock and cactus garden fronting the hotel is known as the Garden of Mystery. It was built by "Big John" Silvera, Deputy Sheriff of Searchlight, in 1930-1931. Silvera made a similar garden for Rex Bell, a western movie star who became Lieutenant Governor of Nevada in the 1950s, at his Walking

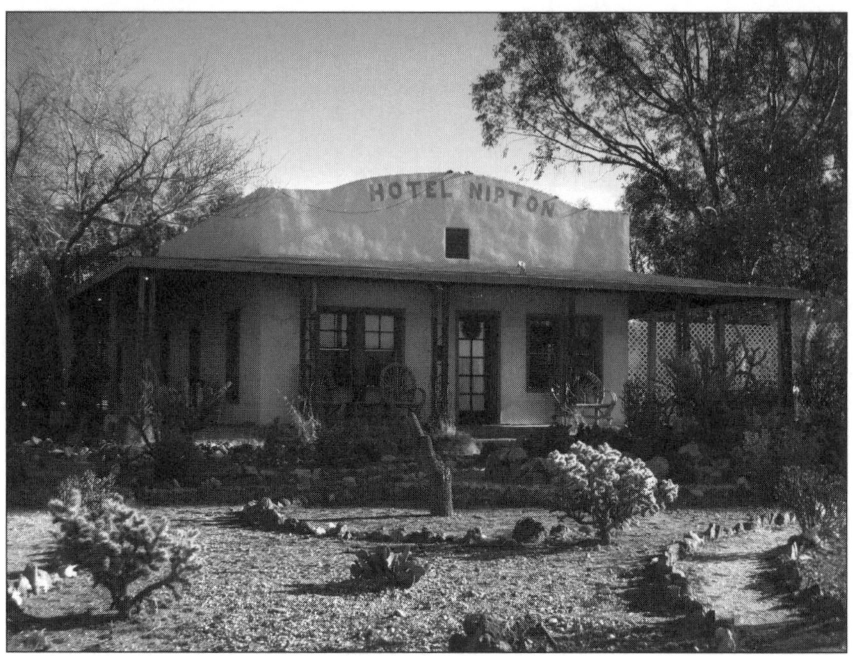

Hotel Nipton in winter

Box Ranch a few miles east of Nipton. The adjacent Nipton Trading Post is the descendant of Trehearne's general store. This western bazaar garners eclectic souvenirs, many not-so-subtle shades of tacky, others minor gems, including Native crafts and blue fluorite crystals from the nearby Lucky Dutchman Mine. It has a unique library on the local history, with hard-to-find publications. It sells groceries, sandwiches, snacks, cold drinks, ice, propane, and basic supplies.

Hotel Nipton has five cozy rooms just large enough for a twin or a double bed, with two communal bathrooms. The spacious central sitting room is decorated in Old-West style, with plush armchairs and antique museum cases brimming with early 20th century memorabilia. Historic photographs and binders full of archival articles recount forgotten events of the local history. In this vast desert, someone thought it best to erect the hotel right along the tracks. Every time a train comes along at night, which can be many, it feels like it is running right through your room. Before each train arrival, a loud bell comes alive at the rail crossing to warn imaginary car traffic and to wake you up in the unlikely event you sleep through the show. On any winter night, Hotel Nipton is still a far cry more comfortable than the frigid outdoors. You can also rent one of the Eco-Lodge Tented Cabins, which are heated with a wood-burning stove. Guests can use the grounds' picnic areas, barbecues, outdoor hot tubs, and 24-hour laundromat.

The Whistle Stop Oasis, adjoining the hotel, doubles up as the town's bar and restaurant. Like the rest of Nipton, it is likely to provide a memorable experience. On my first winter visit, the heater was out of order. It was so cold that customers could see their breaths and kept their coats and hats on while they gobbled down their dinner. But the food is good and the servings are copious. The restaurant and hotel are run by different businesses, so being a hotel guest does not imply the restaurant will be open for dinner. Let someone know you are planning to have dinner. Drop-ins are welcome.

Nipton made headlines in 2017 when an Arizona cannabis company bought the town with plans to convert it into a pot-friendly, solar-powered paradise. The new owner renovated buildings, installed teepees, and deployed public art that befits the desert like a fish a bicycle. The marijuana-retreat idea apparently went up in smoke, and the ownership reverted to the Freemans. As of 2021 Nipton is back on the market, so if you ever dreamt of owning a whole town, albeit slightly run-down, now is your chance...

Even if you have no intention to stay here, Nipton is a funky community well worth a visit. Improbable oasis pinned against an immense desert valley, it comes from a different place and time. Its aging buildings are the last breed of a defunct era. The weather is equally out of this world. In the summer, the ground is hot enough to cook an egg. In the winter an inch of ice crusts the hotel's outdoor tubs. The town is composed of about two dozen houses positioned randomly along a two-lane byway, under shaggy old eucalyptus trees. Cabins made of retired railroad cars and wood planks over 100 years old are mixed with more recent residences built with materials as disparate as corrugated iron, red brick, and concrete. Although a few historic structures are tiptoeing on the edge of oblivion, many are still in decent shape, and some have been renovated. The Nippeno House and the Hermitage House are rented as artist's studios. The trailer park hosts antiquated specimens that may not have been moved since the 1970s. As is often the case with owners of properties in the wild, some Nipton inhabitants take great pride in keeping their immediate surroundings a glorious mess. Mind-boggling odds and ends vie for space across hard-packed ground too degraded for native plants to reclaim their turf. Part of Nipton's charm is this whirlpool of antiques. Part of it is the railroad, still active after all these years, which connects the decayed town to its roots through a mysterious string of remote sidings only train drivers get to see.

Fenner and Ludlow. Unlike Interstate 15, whose exits have been turned into food-chain strips to tap business out of the endless stream of vehicles between Los Angeles and Las Vegas, Interstate 40 supports less traffic, and its exits are undeveloped except for Fenner and Ludlow. Fenner has a large convenience store that serves microwaved hamburgers and the likes, and a gas station. Ludlow is a little larger. Its buildings date back to the days when Highway 66 was the only artery connecting Los Angeles to Needles, and its old facilities still reflect the spirit of this pre-freeway era. Besides its two gas stations and their attendant mini-markets, it has an old Dairy Queen and a run-down motel. The grand prize goes to the funky A-frame coffee shop, in which waitresses wearing dresses from the 1930s serve hamburgers and other basic fare in an Old-West decor that I did not think still existed on this side of southern Utah. Several of the town's historic buildings are still standing along Highway 66 east of town.

Weather

The accompanying table lists the mean minimum and mean maximum temperatures (in °F) for every month of the year at Zzyzx, which is near the lowest (and generally warmest) point, and at three mountain locations in and around the preserve. First-time visitors are often surprised that winters here are so cold. Winter daytime temperature is commonly in the 30s or 40s at mid elevations, and lower up in the mountains. The temperature often dips below freezing at night. In late December I have found ice sheets on Piute Creek, at only 3,000 feet. Snow blankets the highest summits almost every year, usually off and on between December and March, although a cold wet front can dump snow later in the year. I have stepped in snow at Kokoweef, in New Trail Canyon, and even at the cinder cones, which can turn completely white. So it can be unpleasantly cold when hiking in winter. The only exception is the floodplain of Soda Lake, which lies below 1,000 feet and is noticeably warmer—although not always warm enough.

The eastern Mojave Desert is generally a little cooler in summer than other North American deserts. It is of course all relative. On a hot summer day, Baker's claim to fame—the world's largest thermometer—looms along Interstate 15 like a bad omen, proudly displaying temperatures exceeding 120°F. The lower desert is then true to its image, filled with burning air. Fortunately, at higher elevations in the mountainous interior temperatures are usually noticeably lower. I have often hiked around 5,000 feet in July in temperatures that did not reach three digits. In the summer, the temperature drops by about 4°F per 1,000 feet of elevation gain up to around 5,000 feet. The rate is a

Average high and low temperatures (°F) around the preserve								
	Zzyzx (950 feet)		Mountain Pass (4,650 feet)		Mitchell Caverns (4,310 feet)		Granite Mountains (4,200 feet)	
	Low	High	Low	High	Low	High	Low	High
January	34	61	30	50	38	54	36	50
February	40	69	32	54	40	56	38	54
March	46	74	36	59	43	61	41	59
April	53	83	41	66	48	69	48	68
May	61	93	50	76	57	79	54	75
June	70	103	59	87	66	88	63	85
July	77	109	66	93	72	94	67	90
August	75	107	64	90	70	91	66	89
September	68	100	57	84	65	85	61	83
October	55	87	46	72	56	75	52	73
November	43	73	36	59	45	62	41	59
December	34	62	30	51	38	54	34	50

little higher at higher elevations. This rule of thumb is useful to estimate the mean temperature at the highest elevations. So visiting here in the summer is not as treacherous as elsewhere.

The transition from fall to winter can be surprisingly swift. In just a few weeks, the temperature drops markedly and the days get noticeably shorter. It takes a long time for the Earth to release the phenomenal solar energy it has stored during the summer, which pushes fall later in the year. This planet-wide effect is exacerbated in the desert by both the more intense summer heat intake and the large temperature difference between seasons. An old timer who lived 80 miles to the east near Kingman once told me that in the fall he sometimes switched from air-conditioning his cabin one day to heating it the next.

It does not rain often in the preserve. In the six years I visited here to research this book I saw rain a few times, and it was often no more than a half-day drizzle. The average annual precipitation is 3.4 inches—about a cup—at Zzyzx, nearly three times as much—9 inches—at the Sweeney Granite Mountains Desert Research Center, and between 10 and 12 inches (almost all in the form of rain) at Mountain Pass. The wettest period is December through March; it receives 40%–50% of the total rainfall, depending on the location. The moisture comes from the Pacific Northwest, and comparatively little reaches the Mojave Desert because much of it is blocked off by the Sierra Nevada and the San Bernardino Mountains. There is a spike of rainfall in July, August, and September from thunderstorms originating in the Gulf of Mexico and the Gulf of California, which can be violent. The driest month is June. Any time of year, weeks can go by without a drop of rain.

If rain is not likely to affect your visit, wind is. High winds are common year-round, especially in winter and spring when storms cross the desert. They can be particularly strong and annoying in February and March. Compared to the northern Mojave Desert, where the long valleys act as wind tunnels, storms do not often degenerate into serious sand storms (except in the Devils Playground), but milder (though still unpleasant) dust storms seem to be more common. Also, it is not unusual for high winds to persist for a few days, often throughout the preserve. It can make hiking tedious and take much of the fun out of sleeping outdoors.

Best Seasons to Visit

For most people, the best season to visit the desert is early spring, which is when the blooming season is in full swing (although not every year is a banner year for flowering plants). I cannot overemphasize how magical the spring flower show can be. The sight of square miles of bright wildflowers engages our attention with an intensity that greatly magnifies our enjoyment of the landscape. No other season even begins to provide the sheer euphoria of witnessing such unconventional beauty. In the spring, the days are also longer, so they tend to be more action-packed.

Early fall offers similar advantages, minus the flowers, which are by then reduced to a smaller pulse of late bloomers, mostly at higher elevations. The days also tend to be clear and not as windy as in the spring. The Indian Summer period is particularly nice because days are also very warm. This is the second best time to visit.

As for the rest of the year, your own preference for cold or hot weather is your best guide. Most Americans prefer freezing temperatures to 100-degree heat. A downside of winter is that days are very short. I personally will gladly trade a cold winter day for a long, sizzling summer day. Since more than 50% of Mojave National Preserve lies above 3,000 feet, even on the hottest summer day there are plenty of high-elevation places to enjoy comfortable temperatures. In winter the only escape from a brutal cold snap is the not-so-great indoors.

During the three peak tourist seasons—Easter, Thanksgiving, and the last week of the year—the preserve does receive increased visitation, yet still so low that it is not a good reason not to come here then.

Desert tortoise, Clark Mountain Range

Driving in the Preserve

A good fraction of Mojave National Preserve can be viewed and accessed from good paved or graded roads. However, most of the interesting backcountry sites are reached by primitive roads, which total more than 1,100 miles. Many of these roads are in decent enough shape that they do not require a vehicle with special clearance or power, more so than in Death Valley National Park, for example. If you have a little experience with driving on primitive desert roads, you should be able to get fairly close to many destinations with a standard car. For each destination featured in the text, I indicate whether the access roads can be driven with a standard-clearance vehicle. These estimations are subjective. They depend on your skills, your determination, and your willingness to take your car on a rough road where it might sustain some damage, cosmetic or mechanical. Be aware that you may not make it, regardless of what I wrote.

The road conditions mentioned in this book assume dry weather. A strong rainstorm can quickly turn a perfectly good dirt road into an impracticable mess. So if you are driving a passenger car on a primitive road and it starts pouring, turn around right away.

Although a standard vehicle will do in many cases, for driving much of the preserve's primitive roads it is safer to use a more rugged vehicle. On relatively level rocky roads, and roads with a high crown, good clearance is generally more essential than power. Four-wheel-drive sedans often don't fair much better than normal vehicles because their clearance is only marginally higher. On rocky uphill roads, which are often slippery, you will likely need four-wheel drive as well.

The one area where driving should not be taken casually is the preserve's southwestern quadrant, from roughly the Marl Mountains west

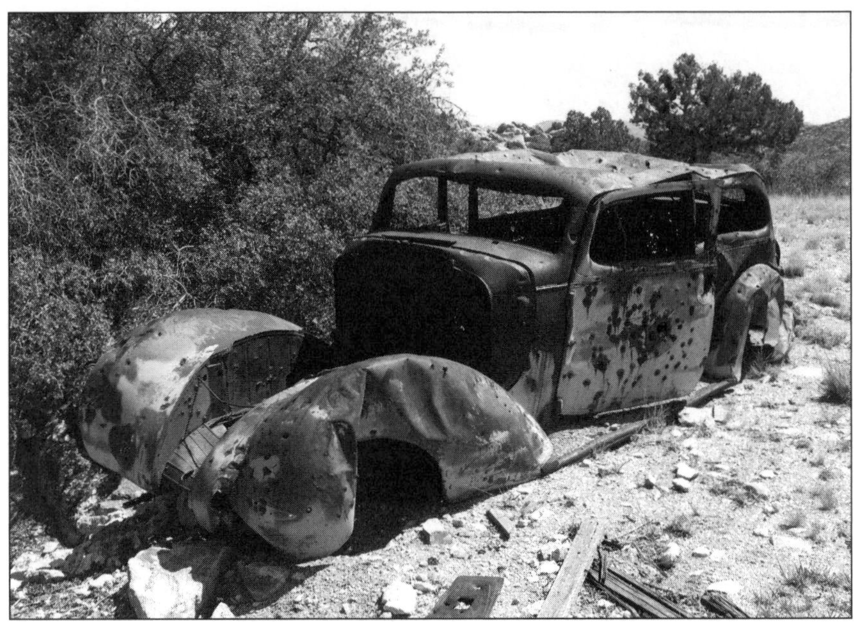

Desert casualty

to Soda Lake and south to the Kelso Dunes. This region, which includes the Devils Playground, is permeated with deep soft sand. Many local roads require nothing short of a sturdy, high-clearance, four-wheel-drive vehicle with wide tires. Venturing on these treacherous roads with the wrong vehicle can be a recipe for disaster. Bring a shovel and boards or strips of carpet, should you need to attempt getting your vehicle unstuck. Travel with another vehicle, and make sure only one vehicle proceeds at a time through a suspicious area.

This vast, inhospitable, and potentially dangerous desert, especially its backcountry, is infrequently visited. If you get stranded far from a main road, it could be days before someone happens to drive by and rescues you. Your only options might be to wait a long time for help or walk back to civilization, which could put your life and the life of your passengers at risk. If you are not sure you can walk your party out to safety, don't come here with a wimpy vehicle, or don't venture off well-traveled roads. Either way, bear in mind that getting there and back is a good part of the fun. Be careful, and look at it as an adventure.

▪

— 2 —

NATURAL HISTORY

Geology

The eastern Mojave Desert's spectacular scenery was created by a tumultuous geologic past that spans more than 1.8 billion years. The area witnessed extended sedimentation, glaciations, faulting, continental collisions, erosion, metamorphism, and devastating eruptions. It was flooded and seared, stretched and broken, uplifted and eroded. The end result is a remarkably diverse topography of mountains, domes, plateaus, canyons, dunes, valleys, fans, playas, and volcanoes, made of just about every kind of rocks the Earth ever generated. Many more studies are needed to unravel the entangled events that led to today's landscape. But by scrutinizing the evidence, on scales ranging from atoms to tectonic plates, geologists have already managed to transform this distant time of mystery into a familiar place of wonder. This is a brief synthesis of what they think happened.

Proterozoic: Metamorphism. The continental crust under the Mojave Desert is composed mainly of rocks from the Early Proterozoic. Our vision of that far-off era is still hazy, but we know that it was a period of repeated igneous activity. The area was intruded by magma several times between 1.76 and 1.1 billion years ago. The most notable event was a turbulent mountain-building episode called the Ivanpah orogeny that took place between 1.71 and 1.695 billion years ago. It involved intense faulting, folding, and metamorphism. Existing rocks as well as granitoids implanted concurrently were subjected to elevated temperatures and pressures deep in the crust, which altered them to gneiss and migmatite. Today these ancient rocks are exposed extensively in the northern New York Mountains, and on the east side of Clark Mountain and the Ivanpah Mountains. They represent the most complete sequence of Proterozoic rocks in California. Smaller exposures outcrop in the Bobcat Hills–Vontrigger Hills area, on the south side of Hackberry Mountain, and east of Tungsten Flat and Signal Hill.

Paleozoic: Sedimentation. Between the Middle Proterozoic and Early Triassic, North America occupied the western edge of Pangaea. The shore of the supercontinent then passed near the southern tip of Nevada, and much of the preserve was submerged. Thick layers of sediments accumulated at the bottom of the ocean, on top of what would become California and western Nevada. As the shoreline shifted with fault movements, the sediments changed. When the eastern Mojave was close to shore, as in much of the Late Proterozoic, sediments were predominantly gravel, sand, and mud washed down from the continent. Compressed by the weight of subsequent sediments, these deposits became the quartzites and shales of all the formations between the Johnnie and the Carrara formations. After a period of transition in the Early to Middle Cambrian, the depositional environment deepened; marine organisms became the main sediments. They eventually formed the dolomite and limestone strata that dominate the Paleozoic units between the Bonanza King and Bird Spring formations.

As an aggregate, these sedimentary rocks reached several miles in thickness. The ocean was able to accommodate such a staggering heap only because its bottom was sinking along fault lines, like a rift valley. These same formations were concurrently deposited up and down Pangaea's coast. Today, from the western Mojave to Death Valley and western Nevada, entire ranges are made of sequences of this long stratigraphic record. In the preserve, many of the Paleozoic rocks were more intensely abused by later erosion and faulting, and they are not represented as extensively. They outcrop over comparably small areas on Clark Mountain, on Cowhole Mountain, in the central Providence Mountains, and in the Ivanpah, New York, and Old Dad mountains.

Mesozoic: Plutonism. From the Early Permian into the Mesozoic, the depositional environment gradually switched back to shallower waters. The earliest Mesozoic rocks (Silver Lake Formation) record this gradual transition from marine to non-marine sediments. Around the end of the Triassic, after more than 850 million years, the ocean finally withdrew and the Mojave Desert dried up. The next formation, the Aztec Sandstone, reflects a completely different world. Made of arenite and sandstone, it was likely formed in a poorly drained region of sand dunes and silt pans. This was the Jurassic, prime time for dinosauria. Dinosaurs barely made it to what little of California existed then, but they did roam the Aztec sandscape. In the Mescal Range, this formation holds trackways of a flying dinosaur called pterosaur, and of coelurosaurs, a feathered bipedal dinosaur about the size of an ostrich.

The rest of the Mesozoic legacy is composed entirely of intrusive formations, a mosaic of some 30 waves of plutonism. The stratigraphic column on page 31 lists the most important events. The origin of this activity can be traced to the Late Triassic, when the sea floor started subducting eastward beneath the continent. As the subducting plate ground against the continent's underbelly and was shoved deep down, it melted into large reservoirs of magma. The phenomenal friction launched a series of compression waves through the continental margin, which folded and faulted the Paleozoic and Proterozoic strata. The magma's lighter components found a way up through these faults and erupted. By Early Jurassic, volcanism was rampant.

In Middle Jurassic to Early Cretaceous, after volcanic activities eased up, the remaining magma slowly cooled down underground and crystallized into enormous bubbles of granitic rocks. The largest of these batholiths produced California's 400-mile-long Sierra Nevada. Many smaller orogenies occurred east of it, clear across Nevada to Idaho. One of the largest orogenies in the eastern Mojave Desert was the Teutonia batholith. Comprised of six individual plutons formed between 92 and 100 million years ago, it originally covered more than 500 square miles, underlying the future Kelso and New York mountains, and Cima Dome. Another main intrusion was the Mid Hills Adamellite, about 93 million years of age. Comparable in exposed area, it lies at the core of the central mountains, from the southern New York Mountains to the northern Providence Mountains.

The preserve is dotted with many smaller granitoids, anything from diorite to monzonite, syenite, gabbro, good old granite, and a lexicon of tongue-twisting intermediate compositions. Several of them have been named after the single, limited locality where they outcrop, like Live Oak Canyon Granodiorite. They are found mostly in the Granite Mountains and in the southern Providence and Ivanpah mountains. These batholiths, large and small, delivered many of the rich metal deposits mined in the 19th and 20th centuries.

Cenozoic: Volcanism and Tectonism. After the last magma crystallization, the preserve probably formed an upland for at least 55 million years, into the Late Eocene or Early Oligocene. During this time erosion removed much of the older rocks overlying the Mesozoic

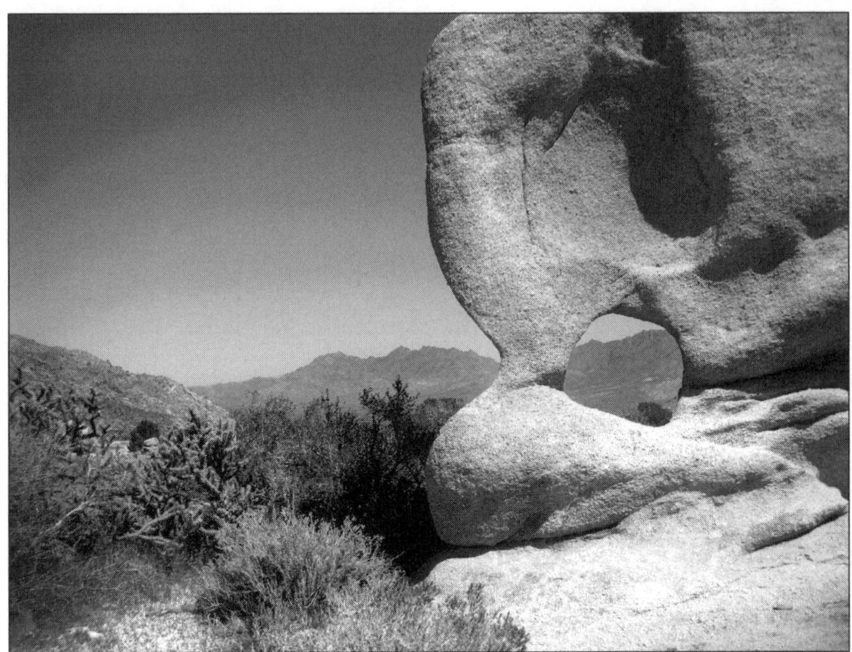

Arch in Cretaceous porphyritic monzogranite, Granite Mountains

batholiths, which led to the formation of pediment surfaces over large areas of the preserve. These pediments ultimately became part of the modern topographical expression of the preserve, in particular Cima Dome. In the Early Miocene, 20 million years ago, the preserve was a region of subdued relief dotted with shallow lakes, inhabited by many species of mammals, birds, and other wildlife.

The event responsible for the demise of this lasting quiescence was again the onset of tectonic movements. As a result of the collision of land masses at the continent's edge, over much of the Southwest the continental crust started to stretch. This east-west to northeast-southwest extension thinned and fractured the crust into fault-bound blocks the size of mountains. For the next few million years, pushed around by tectonic forces these blocks would tilt, rise, or sink, to become the landscape of long parallel mountains of today's Basin and Range.

During this time, magma found again pathways through the faulted crust and rose to the surface, which triggered intermittent outbursts of volcanism. The first eruption that hit the Mojave Desert occurred about 18.5 million years ago. Originating from a huge volcano thought to be located in southern Nevada, it was so violent that it makes all historic eruptions look like fireworks. In a short time—weeks, perhaps

STRATIGRAPHIC COLUMNS LEGEND			
———	Comformable formations	□ 900 ft	Thickness of formation
---------	Uncomformability	(*Corals*)	Main fossils
....	Unknown comformability	QM	Quartz monzonite
L	Late	MG	Monzogranite
M	Middle	MD	Monzodiorite
E	Early	GD	Granodiorite
?	Approximate age	*	Stratigraphic equivalent

only days—it smothered under thick ash flows a huge swath of land that stretched from Barstow to the western edge of the Grand Canyon. Upon reaching the ground, the hot ash welded together and became the Peach Springs Tuff, a formation that is still a prominent regional landmark today. In the preserve it is exposed only very locally, particularly around Wild Horse Mesa. A few hundred thousand years later intense outpourings produced the Hackberry Spring Volcanics, interlayered flows and domes of lava, ash, trachyte, and rhyolite, which later became Hackberry Mountain. About 17.8 million years ago other major eruptions rocked the area. This time the smoking gun was much closer, in the middle of the Woods Mountains. Over less than 100,000 years, three particularly violent ash falls locally covered much of the previous flows and built a thick plateau of welded ash known as Wild Horse Mesa Tuff. One of the preserve's most colorful, this formation is well exposed at Hole-in-the-Wall, in the western Woods Mountains, on Hackberry Mountain, and in the Blind Hills. It is also responsible for several of the preserve's iconic mesas, such as Table Mountain and Wild Horse Mesa after which it was named. About 100,000 years later, the old Wild Horse Mesa caldera was plugged by a hodgepodge of rhyolitic lava flows and other pyroclastics, the future core of Tortoise Shell Mountain.

Throughout the rest of the Miocene to the Pleistocene, about 10 more outbursts spewed cubic miles of molten rock onto the east Mojave and periodically obscured the planet's atmosphere with ash and dust. Several other mountains in the preserve's eastern section were spawned by Miocene volcanism. The Piute Range's stark bluffs and the spires crowning the New York and Castle mountains are volcanic materials that erupted between the Peach Springs and Wild Horse Mesa events. Neatly bedded rhyolite air-fall tuff and thin rhyolite flows created the striking banded slopes of Van Winkle Mountain.

Extensional deformation continued through this period of volcanism, then gradually diminished between 14 and 11 million years ago.

Era	EPOCH		AGE Million years	FORMATION	LITHOLOGY
CENOZOIC	Pleistocene		2.6	Basalt cinder deposits and lava flows	• Phreatic eruption of loose basalt-scoria, consolidated pyroclastic breccia, and tuffaceous conglomerate • Alkali basalt & hawaiite flows
	Pliocene	L			
		E	5.3		
	Miocene	L	10.0	Basalt flows	• Alkali basalt and olivine andesite lava flows
		M	11.6	Tortoise Shell Mtn Rhyolite	• Rhyolite lava flows and plugs, interbedded pyroclastics
		E	17.8	Wild Horse Mesa Tuff	• Layered, mostly welded sanidine rhyolite ash-flow tuff with abundant sanidine phenocrysts □ 1,050 ft
			18.5	Hackberry Spring Volcanics	• Interlayered lava flows, domes, ash flows, and dikes and plugs of trachyte, trachydacite, and rhyolite
			23.0	Peach Springs Tuff	• Welded rhyolite ash-flow tuff with conspicuous sanidine, minor sphene, and variable biotite and hornblende
	Oligocene	L	30.0		
		E	33.9		
	Eocene	L	41.2		
		M	47.8		
		E	56.0		
	Paleocene	L	61.6		
		E	66.0		

ERA	EPOCH		AGE Million years	FORMATION	LITHOLOGY
MESOZOIC	Cretaceous	L	66.0		
				? Porphyritic MG	• Light-gray biotite MG
				? Granodiorite	• Hornblende-biotite GD
				? Porphyritic GD	• Light-colored biotite GD & MG
				Mid Hills Adam.	• Light-tan leucocratic MG
			93	Kessler Spr. Adam.	• White porphyritic MG & MD
		E	100	Live Oak Cyn GD	• Equigranular granodiorite
				Teutonia Adam.	• Biotite monzogranite
				Black Cyn Hornblende Gabbro	• Medium-grained black hornblende gabbro
				Rock Spring MD	• Porphyritic hornblende-biotite MD, QM, and quartz MD
				? Granitoid Rocks of Cowhole Mtn	• Monzogranite, QM, and quartz monzodiorite
				? Sands Granite	• Pink coarse-grained granite
	Jurassic	L	145	Granite of Tough Nut Spr.	• Syenogranite & monzogranite
				Ivanpah Granite	• Porphyritic biotite syenogranite
				Quartz syenite of Winston Basin	• Coarse-grained granitoids
		M	163	Fountain Pk Rhyolite	• Dark-pink granite & rhyodacite
				QM of Goldstone	• Dark medium-grained QM
				? Syenogranite of Quail Spring	• Dark hornblende-biotite syenogranite
		E	174	? Mesocratic Rocks of Colton Hills	• Suite of granitoids
			200	? Striped Mtn Pluton	• Hornblende diorite
			201	? Aztec Sandstone	• Red, yellow, or buff quartz arenite and sandstone □ >2,700 ft
	Triassic	L		? Triassic volcanics (Soda Mountain Formation*)	• Highly altered & calcified tuff • Altered flows and flow breccia of andesite and dacite □ >5,000 ft
		M	237		• Siltstone, limestone, and conglomerate (*Gastropods*) □ 750 ft
		E	247 252	? Silver Lake Form.	

	EPOCH		AGE Million years	FORMATION	LITHOLOGY
PALEOZOIC	Permian	L	252		
			259		
		E	276		
	Pennsyl.		299	Bird Spring Formation	• Thick-bedded, middle-gray, cherty, sandy, and pure limestone • *Fusilinids, gastropods, brachiopods, crinoids, corals, echinoid, bryozoans* □ 2,400 ft
	Mississip.		323		
			333	Monte Cristo Limestone	• Massive pure, coarse limestone, with chert in lower part • *Crinoids, corals* □ 1,100 ft
	Devonian	L	359	Sultan Limestone	• Medium-bedded, interlayered limestone and dolomite • *Corals, stromatoporoids* □ 700 ft
		M	383		
		E	393		
	Silurian	L	419	Missing formation(s)	
		E	433		• Massive dolomite (black) □ 900 ft
	Ordovician	L	444	Ely Springs Dolomite*	• Dolomite with some limestone (*Gastropods*) • Shale (thin beds) • Dolomite (*Gastropods*) □ 2,600 ft
		M	458		
		E	470	Pogonip Group*	• Shale (*Gastropods*) • Mostly black/light 100-ft bands of dolomite □ 2,000–3,000 ft
	Cambrian	L	485	Nopah Formation	• Mostly thick beds of algal lime-stone and dolomite □ 1,000 ft
		M	497	Bonanza King F.	• Limestone, shale, silt beds • *Trilobite trash beds* □ 1,200 ft
		E	521	Carrara Formation	• Quartzite, mostly massive and granulated □ 215 ft
				Zabriskie Quartzite	• Dolomite • Quartzite, shale, quartzite beds □ 1,500 ft
			541	Wood Cyn Form.	

	EPOCH		AGE Million years	FORMATION	LITHOLOGY
PRECAMBRIAN	Proterozoic	L	541 580	Stirling Quartzite	• Quartzite, shale □ 4,900 ft
			615	Johnnie Formation	• Mostly shale (*stromatolites*) □ 2,400 ft
			635	Noonday Dolomite	• Dolomite & limestone (*stromatolites*) □ 500–2,000 ft
			? 720	Kingston Peak Formation	• Sandstone and siltstone • Limestone • Diamictite (*stromatolites, oncolites, microbiota*) □ 1,600–9,000 ft
			1,000		
		M	1,400	Granitoids	• Granite, syenite, shonkinite, and carbonatite
			1,600		
		E	1,680	Granitoids	• Granite, granodiorite, & diorite
			1,710	Granitoids	• Biotite-granite gneiss
			1,760	Granitoids and gneiss	• Pyroxene diorite, quartz diorite, augen gneiss, granitoid gneiss, migmatite, and amphibolite
			2,500		

The eastern Mojave Desert's typical physiography of high ranges separated by deep basins was by then essentially in place. The region has received only minor additions since then. Cima volcanic field's cinder cones were created between 7.6 million years ago and recent times by intermittent cinder and basaltic lava eruptions. During the last Ice Age, Soda Lake was flooded by runoffs from the Mojave River, which funneled water all the way from the San Bernardino Mountains. The Soda Lake playa had a pluvial lake several times in the last 22,000 years. At least twice, the lake reached its high stand and overflowed into Silver Lake to form Lake Mohave. It was then 20–40 feet deep and 20 miles long, and covered about 75 square miles. It last dried out about 8,700 years ago. The Devils Playground and the Kelso Dunes are also a recent addition. This complex dune field was blown in by westerly winds from the dry bed of the Mojave River over the last 25,000 years. All this time erosion has been tirelessly shaping the landscape, gnawing at the mountains and filling the basins, once again evening out the score.

Plants of the Eastern Mojave Desert

Plant communities. Some 925 plant species have been inventoried in the preserve. Of the many variables that affect plant life—drainage, light exposure, orientation, topography, soil texture—precipitation, and thus elevation, and soil composition are the most influential. The preserve's flora is this diverse to a large extent because elevations span such a large range—7,000 feet. The lower fans are dominated by plants highly adapted to heat, especially creosote bush—locally the largest biomass—bursage, desert holly, cheesebush, and Mojave yucca. The upper fans, which can reach up to 5,000 feet, are the home of Joshua trees and creosote bush, as well as lycium, grasses, and armies of cacti, chollas, and yuccas. On still higher ground, in the mountains, Joshua tree woodlands grade into conifer forests. Juniper occur first, then comes a mixed zone of juniper and pinyon pine, and finally pinyon pine alone. This community is characterized by a thicker and greener ground cover dominated by blackbrush, ephedra, cliffrose, and big sagebrush. There are also smaller niche communities. Canyon floors generally have slightly different plant associations than the surrounding slopes, including a higher representation of rabbitbrush, mesquite, catclaw, and grasses. Perennial springs often support water-loving trees such as willows and occasional cottonwoods, as well as squawbush, catclaw, and baccharis. At the other end of the spectrum are the chemical shores of Soda Lake, where the high salinity limits plant life to mixed stands of desert holly, saltbush, and salt grass.

Plants have developed a well-stocked toolbox of tricks to survive not only the desert's low precipitation and temperature extremes, but also the large diurnal temperature changes, high winds, and low soil nitrogen. Annuals avoid most of these problems by laying dormant as seeds, sometimes for years, until conditions—especially precipitation—are right and they sprout for a few weeks. To handle the heat, plants minimize evaporation by having small leaves, wax coatings, hair and thorns, curling leaves or shrinking stems (like cacti), thick epidermis, or tissues with high water-storage capacity. To increase water capture some plants have developed widespread root systems (like creosote bush) or deep roots to tap underground water (like catclaw). These clever strategies, many of them noticeable with casual observation, are a poignant celebration of evolution and of the desert environment it has created.

Wildflowers. Wildflowers are a common denominator that permeates all plant communities. The blooming season usually starts on the lower fans between mid-March and early April. If the winter rains have been evenly spaced and temperatures not too severe, annuals can be so abundant that entire fans are carpeted with millions of flowers—pale yellow desert dandelion and tackstem, blue phacelia, bright-yellow desertgold, evening primrose, and many others. Terrains normally dull brown turn tender green for a few weeks under a veneer of young shoots. The flower show gradually migrates to higher elevations, eventually reaching the highest summits in summer. Common flowers include globemallow, Indian paintbrush, Mojave aster, penstemon, and Goodding's verbena. Fall brings another wave of flowers, albeit smaller in magnitude. It is difficult not to spot at least a few flowers any time of year. If you need to become familiar with the desert's bewildering array of flowering plants, start with Adrienne Knute's *Plants of the East Mojave*. Its close-up photographs make identification easy.

There are classic beauties not to be missed, flowers so attractive they will stop you dead in your tracks: the masses of rose-purple blossoms of giant four o'clock, the deep-purple indigo bush, the arresting snow-white desert lily, the delicate pink globes of desert five spot, and the huge white trumpets of sacred datura. But the most phenomenal displays go unquestionably to cacti. Every single species puts forth unbelievably bright flowers in shades of pink, vermillion, red, magenta, yellow, and orange so vibrant they seem out of place in the desert.

Cacti, yuccas, and agaves. The east Mojave Desert is one of North America's archetypical cactus empires. Some 23 species of cactus,

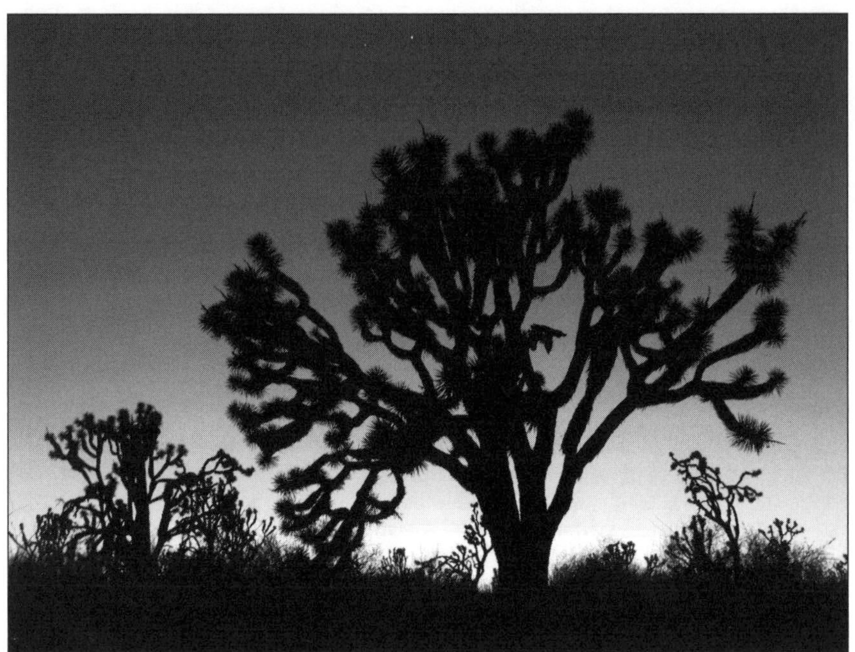

Joshua trees at sunset, Cedar Canyon

yucca, and agave share hundreds of square miles of the preserve, often in dense arrangements. Our sense of familiarity with the desert is greatly enhanced by a little knowledge of these intriguing plants. So it helps to learn to identify them, which is fortunately not too difficult. Stephen Ingram's *Cacti, Agaves, and Yuccas of California and Nevada* is the greatest popular resource on the subject. Concise yet filled with essential facts and dramatic photographs, this elegant volume turns a scholarly topic into a delightful read.

No plant better symbolizes the Mojave Desert than the Joshua tree. This enigmatic multi-branched yucca stoically standing under the wilting sun is a common sight in the preserve. Until it was destroyed by a major wildfire in 2020, Cima Dome, approximately in the middle of this vast domain, was home to the world's largest Joshua tree forest. There are still in all likelihood more Joshua trees in the preserve than in Joshua Tree National Park itself.

The Joshua tree is known as an indicator plant: in its natural state, it occurs almost exclusively in the Mojave Desert. It does not grow everywhere in the Mojave, but if you see one you are probably in the Mojave. The Joshua trees found in California's Red Rock Canyon, in Nevada's Valley of Fire, above the Virgin River Gorge in southwestern

Utah, and in Detrital Valley in Arizona, are all denizens of the Mojave Desert. In spite of this broad distribution, Joshua trees are particular about their habitat. They need well-drained loamy soil, at least 3 but no more than 12 inches of rain a year, and temperatures neither too high (they find it too hot in summer below about 3,500 feet) nor too low (winters are too cold above about 6,000 feet). When conditions are just right, they can grow up to record heights of 40 feet. The Joshua tree's former predilection for Cima Dome stemmed in part from the dome's fine-gravel slopes and mean elevation. Selective grazing also favors Joshua trees and other plants that cattle do not care for.

There are two varieties of Joshua trees. The one found in the preserve, *jaegeriana,* is slightly shorter and has a denser crown, which gives it a more compact and symmetrical appearance. The *brevifolia* variety, which has a taller trunk and larger leaves, lives in the southern and western Mojave, in particular in Joshua Tree National Park. The overlap between the two species is limited to a small area in southern Nevada, which suggests they have not coexisted long. They might have diversified in the Pleistocene, when the Mojave was a region of rivers and lakes and they became separated by the Salton trough.

Two other species of yucca live in the preserve. The blue (or banana) yucca has a rosette that is slightly rounded and made of long blue-green spikes. It is found in association with juniper at higher elevations. The Mojave yucca has spears that are yellower, and mature plants often develop an erect, spine-covered trunk up to 15 feet tall. Much more common, Mojave yucca often grow in colonies that rise well above the ground cover. In both yuccas the spikes have curly fibers along their edges, and they are much wider (typically one inch or more) and longer (several feet) than in a Joshua tree.

Agaves have a similar general look as yuccas, but among several obvious differences the edges of the leaves are lined with sharp teeth. Most agaves flower once and die. The rosette then sprouts a tall stalk crowned by profuse clusters of showy yellow flowers. Long after the flowers have withered the protruding stalks remain the best indicators of agaves. Only two species of agave occur in the preserve. The simple desert agave is confined to limited areas in the Ivanpah, Granite, and Providence mountains. The pygmy agave occurs in the Clark Mountain Range and the New York and Ivanpah mountains. It is much smaller, and its leaves curve inward, so the rosette looks like a sphere. Each leaf is terminated by a long, wispy, pale thread.

Cacti are represented by several species, including chollas (see table). The chollas have multiple branches composed of jointed cylindrical segments. The largest is the staghorn cholla; its long disheveled arms often stand high above the ground. The silver cholla is the most widespread, and the staghorn cholla a close second. The silver cholla grows as a compact bush with a thick crown of shorter stem-joints. In the spring, it is adorned with greenish yellow blossoms; in contrast, the staghorn cholla's flowers are bright yellowish orange. The diamond cholla is easy to recognize by its thin, pencil-like stem-joints armed with very long spines. The teddy-bear cholla is limited to the southeastern edge of the preserve, which coincides with the northern end of its range. Its bright and plump stem-joints densely covered with spines make it unmistakable.

Seven species of prickly-pears occur in the preserve. The beavertail cactus is easiest to single out because of its blue-green pads with small clumps of bristles in lieu of spines. The pancake prickly-pear is distinguishable by its flatter and more rounded pads, and the straight trunk of mature specimens. One of the most common prickly-pears at middle to upper elevations is the grizzly bear cactus, also known as old man cactus. It has smaller pads and shows great variation in the density and length of its long spines, which can blend into a whitish mass resembling tousled hair. Identifying the other three prickly-pears—the brown-spined, curve-spined, and Engelmann—takes a little more practice. They can be differentiated by the number of areoles across a pad, the number of spines per areole, and the length of the spines.

Desert oaks. Most desert ranges are sky islands, tracks of high country surrounded by low desert valleys and biologically cut off from the rest of the world. Being higher, they are cooler and receive more precipitation, conditions that create a local climate hospitable to a much greater variety of plants and animals. Unable to make the journey across the much hotter and drier surrounding valleys, much of this richer life is stranded, both guest and prisoner of this nurturing microclimate. This isolation can be so extreme and long-lasting that sky islands are often home to species not found for tens of miles around—or anywhere else on Earth.

In the Mojave, the most blatant of these residents are oak trees. Oaks cannot tolerate extended droughts, so they do not typically hang around deserts. But a few do, congregating strictly in cooler and wetter mountains, and in rocky terrains where water can percolate to their roots. Only two related species, scrub oak and canyon live oak, exist in and around the preserve. Scrub oak is a deciduous shrub or small tree that does not get much taller than 10 feet. It resembles the live oaks of California's coastal and inland regions, with curled leaves no more than an inch long protected by spiny margins. The only other plants

Cacti, Yuccas, and Agaves		
Common name	**Species**	**Range**
Barrel cactus	*Ferocactus cylindraceus*	Widespread, up to 5,200′
Beavertail cactus	*Opuntia basilaris* var. *basilaris*	Widespread, up to ~6,000′
Beehive cactus	*Coryphantha vivipara*	Eastern preserve, > 3,500′
Blue yucca	*Yucca baccata* var. *baccata*	Northern half of preserve, 4,000′–6,000′
Calico cactus	*Echinocereus engelmannii*	Widespread, up to ~7,000′
Common fishhook cactus	*Mammillaria tetrancistra*	Widespread, up to ~5,400′
Cottontop cactus	*Echinocactus polycephalus* var. *polycephalus*	Widespread, up to 4,800′
Desert pincushion cactus	*Coryphantha chlorantha*	~1,600′–5,600′
Diamond cholla	*Cylindropuntia ramosissima*	Widespread, up to 4,000′
Joshua tree	*Yucca brevifolia* var. *jaegeriana*	Widespread, ~3,500′–6,000′
Mojave yucca	*Yucca schidigera*	Widespread, up to lower woodlands
Mound cactus	*Echinocereus triglochidiatus*	Widespread, above ~3,000′
Parish club-cholla	*Grusonia parishii*	Widespread, 3,000′–5,000′
Pigmy agave	*Agave utahensis* var. *nevadensis*	Clark, Ivanpah, and New York mountains
Prickly-pear	*Opuntia*	
Brown-spined	*O. phaeacantha*	Widespread
Curve-spined	*O. Xcurvispina*	East side of New York Mountains
Engelmann	*O. engelmannii*	Widespread, above ~2,200′
Grizzly bear cactus	*O. polyacantha* var. *erinacea*	Middle & upper elevations
Pancake	*O. chlorotica*	Widespread, above ~2,000′
Silver cholla	*Cylindropuntia echinocarpa*	Widespread, up to ~6,000′
Simple desert agave	*Agave deserti* var. *simplex*	Granite, Ivanpah and Providence mountains
Staghorn cholla	*Cylindropuntia acanthocarpa* var. *coloradensis*	Widespread, ~1,000′–4,000′
Teddy-bear cholla	*Cylindropuntia bigelovii*	Extreme southeastern corner of the preserve

that look a little like it are barberry and hollyleaf redberry, but as their names suggest they bear berries, not acorn. In contrast, canyon live oaks grow to be real trees, up to 30 feet tall. In the preserve only three ranges support oaks: the Providence and Granite mountains, where a few isolated individuals and small groves survive, and the New York Mountains, where they occur in greater concentrations.

Conifers. A more common manifestation of range insularity is conifer forests. Deep pockets of greenery that provide shade, coolness, and higher humidity, these woodlands are the antithesis of the desert. Paradoxically, we seek them to escape the very environment we came here to enjoy, as they provide a temporary antidote to the desert's harshness. Desert conifers include two species of juniper, the only member of the cypress family sufficiently drought-tolerant to live in the desert. By far the most common is the Utah juniper. It is a sturdy tree, usually under 30 feet high, often with a twisted trunk and peeling bark. It often relinquishes some of its branches to concentrate its limited moisture resources to the remaining branches. Every one of the preserve's five main mountain ranges has extensive forests of Utah juniper. Smaller mountains, like Kessler Peak, support dispersed groves. Others, like Hackberry Mountain, have just a handful of isolated trees. The California juniper, on the other hand, is a shrubby tree that does not have a single main trunk. It is more common on the inner coast ranges. It grows in the Granite Mountains near Granite Pass.

The single-leaved pinyon pine is an aromatic tree with a profuse crown of short needles arranged, unlike all other pine trees, in single needles. Slow-growing, they can reach a height of 40 feet and live to be about 200 years old. Another stranded resident of the highest sky islands is the two-needle pinyon pine. Unlike the single-leaved pinyon pine, its needles occur in bundles of two. It is rare—it occurs in a few areas in the New York Mountains, hiding among single-leaved pines.

Even more extraordinary is the presence of relict groves of white fir, a beautiful conifer shaped like a classic Christmas tree, with handsome steely blue needles. Its range has shriveled from a much wider former distribution to small stands in the New York Mountains and Clark Mountain, huddled on cooler north-facing slopes. The closest white-fir groves are miles away in the Kingston Range.

Wildlife

The Mojave Desert's extremes turn away not only humans but animals as well. On a typical day you will see birds and lizards, perhaps a rabbit, but likely no larger animals. You will have to settle for less—

Kit fox

tracks, droppings, bones, or a hollow in the gravel where a bighorn sheep curls up to sleep—to know that others are sharing this place with you. But in spite of appearances, the preserve's fauna is relatively diverse and abundant—much of it is just shy and elusive. The eastern Mojave Desert is habitat for dozens of species of mammals, at least 33 species of reptiles, and more than 160 species of birds. You may never see most of these critters, yet the simple knowledge of their presence and admirable adaptation to the desert's environment adds richness to the land. It makes an encounter even more precious.

Mammals. Bighorn sheep are arguably the preserve's most majestic mammals. They live in small groups generally confined to remote mountainous areas. They will come down to lower elevations to get to watering holes, often in the early morning. Every major mountain range has bighorn sheep, with estimated populations varying greatly, from about 40 in the Granite Mountains to 30 in the New York Mountains and a handful on Hackberry Mountain. An encounter is a rare thrill, and usually regretfully brief, as bighorn sheep tend to dash off at great speed even over the rockiest terrain.

Another exciting encounter is with mule deer, residents most visitors do not expect in the desert. The preserve is one of their prime strongholds in the Mojave Desert. One reason may be the release in 1948 of nine bucks and 31 does in the New York and Providence mountains. The mule deer is the largest native animal, and the most commonly seen of the large mammals. They live mostly in sagebrush and forested habitats. When faced with adversity they can exhibit admirable perseverance. I have often seen deer wandering through the burn in the Mid Hills, patiently looking for tender browse.

The top predators are mountain lions and coyotes. Mountain lions live in mountainous areas, including the Providence, Granite, and New York mountains, and the Clark Mountain Range. They probably number less than 20, and are very rarely seen. In contrast, coyotes favor mostly open bajadas, although they also range into the high country. Signs of their passage are plentiful in the backcountry, but they tend to be leery of humans and are keen-eyed, so they are often spotted trotting away in the distance. They like hanging around the exposed shores of Soda Lake. Their chilling howls can often be heard in the wee hours of morning in Lanfair Valley and Kelso Basin.

Many smaller mammals live at all elevations. Black-tailed hare (jackrabbit) and desert cottontail are fairly common. When out on a hike it is not uncommon to spook one out of hiding. In the lower desert you might be lucky and spot a kit fox, badger, ringtail cat, or bobcat. Higher elevations support some of the same species as well as gray and red fox (often in brushy and wooded terrain), skunks, squirrels, and occasional chipmunks. There are also several species of mice, rats, gophers, and bats, and the desert shrew. The burrows common in sand are dwellings dug by rodents, often kangaroo rats. Rodents are collectively fairly numerous and often seen, which is unfortunately less than a thrill for most visitors.

Reptiles. Many reptiles inhabit the preserve. The Granite Mountains alone host 18 species of snakes and 15 species of lizards. The list includes three kinds of rattlesnake, the Mojave rattlesnake, the sidewinder, and the speckled rattlesnake. Highly venomous, they are the most dangerous locals. To make matters worse, they are fairly common and well camouflaged, and they live at all elevations (the sidewinder only up to about 5,000 feet). Some snakes have patterns that somewhat resemble a rattler's. The slim, cat-eyed lyre snake does, and it is mildly venomous. The common kingsnake does too, but it is harmless, although when cornered it might try to pass for a rattler by vibrating its upright tail. Snakes exert on us a conflicting mixture of apprehension and fascination. Learning to identify the dangerous ones enables us to enjoy looking at the harmless ones without fearing for our lives. If you see a suspicious snake with red, yellow, and black crossbands, it is a long-nosed, a western shovel-nosed, or a ground snake, all harmless. There are other impressive snakes, such as the lithe and speedy coachwhip, which can exceed 8 feet in length; the albino, worm-looking western blind snake; and even a boa misleadingly named rosy, who kills the small animals it preys on by constriction.

Lizards are abundant and easy to spot. The creosote bush and scrub jungles of the lower fans are the hangouts of zebra-tailed lizards (especially sandy washes), western whiptails, side-blotched lizards, desert iguanas, and long-tailed brush lizards (especially shrubby washes). The upper fans are home to desert horned, desert spiny, and desert night lizards. Higher up, isolated in the rocky canyons and woodlands of sky islands, live Gilbert's skinks and western fence

Chuckwalla

lizards. Chuckwallas have a predilection for rocky outcrops; they like to wedge themselves in cracks and inflate their bodies when threatened. Collared lizards favor granitic boulders at mid-elevations. Several reptiles even live in the Kelso Dunes and are rare elsewhere. The Mojave fringe-toed lizard is a good example. Superbly adapted to life in sand, it has developed fringes of pointed scales on the edge of its toes to prevent it from sinking in the sand. The fringes help it run impressively fast across loose sand—one specimen was clocked at 23 miles per hour. It also uses them to "swim" into sand, to escape either a prey or extreme weather. It even has special valves, lids, and flaps engineered to keep sand out of its nose, eyes, and ears.

The Gila monster, the largest lizard in the U.S., is quite possibly the rarest in California: it has been sighted only 26 times, 7 of them in the preserve, on Clark Mountain, in the Providence Mountains, and at Piute Spring. It is the only venomous lizard in the country. Its neurotoxic venom has effects comparable to the rattlesnake's, but fortunately the Gila monster is normally docile, and it would take teasing, handling, or stepping bare footed on one to get bitten.

Many lizards are remarkable for their colors and shape. The Gila monster has a spectacular black and coral beaded skin. The Western banded gecko, a species you would think belongs to some hotel room wall in the Yucatan, has a sinuous yellow body decorated with brown crossbands. The male collared lizard is particularly attractive. Like the long-nose leopard lizard, gravid females display flaming orange spots on their sides. The desert horned lizard has the armored body of an antediluvian beast. If you approach lizards slowly and quietly, many will let you take a close look. But not always... After following a collared lizard too long to photograph it, it let me get close, then abruptly spun around in mid-air and hissed at me like a Jurassic Park T-rex.

Another local reptile is the desert tortoise, a threatened species that inhabits gravelly or sandy washes and fans with creosote, thorny shrubs, and cacti. About half of the preserve is a federally protected critical tortoise habitat—essentially all land east of Kelbaker Road except the main chain of mountains and Lanfair Valley. Desert tortoises live in burrows that they dig with their flattened front legs, often in the bank of a wash. In the spring and fall they feed on grasses, cacti, and broad-leaved plants to build up their fat and water reserves. They hibernate from October to March, and estivate in very hot weather. Because they spend so much time underground, desert tortoises are seldom seen. But in the spring or fall, especially early morning and after a rainstorm, you might come face to ugly face with this typical denizen of the desert. If you see one, approach it slowly (or it might get scared and pee, thus losing precious water), and enjoy it from a distance. Do not touch it, as you may pass on fatal diseases.

Birds. It is likely that a few hundred species of birds live in the preserve. A small fraction, perhaps under 25%, are permanent residents, and the rest migratory birds that use the area part of the year. This diversity comes from the wide range of elevations and flora. The species count is highest during the two main pulses of migration, March through May and August through October. In the summer, bird activity is very low except during the cooler hours of dawn and dusk. Springs with water are usually an exception; birds can be active there much of the day. Winter is the quietest time, although you might still be surprised by a solitary raven flying low on some secret mission.

There is generally a gradient of bird life with elevation. The drier creosote bush habitats of the lower fans typically have limited breeding species. These include several species of sparrows, in particular the black-throated sparrow, the northern mockingbird, and thrashers. As the elevation increases and the vegetation diversifies, the species list grows rapidly. Among conspicuous species are ravens, turkey vulture, cactus wren, sparrows, hummingbirds, and Gambel's quails. One fall day in Globe Canyon I counted well over 100 of these pretty quails in a few hours. Doves are commonly seen resting on roads at dusk and night. Several bird species are so strikingly colorful you might think they are fugitives from more tropical climes. Wilson's warbler is one, with its yellow head grading into a light-green back, and so is the western tanager (yellow body and vermillion head). In Joshua tree forests you might spot the lemon-yellow and black flash of the Scott's oriole plumage. At even higher elevations, expect jays, mountain chickadee, and mountain quail. Birds of prey are also well represented, and fun to watch. They include golden eagle, American kestrel, northern harrier, prairie falcon, osprey, and several species of hawk. If you tie something red to your tent, you will be surprised how often hummingbirds come pay you a visit in the morning before you get up.

■

— 3 —

CULTURAL HISTORY

Native American History

Indigenous people have inhabited the eastern Mojave Desert for a very long time. Countless panels of rock art are scattered throughout the land. In the cinder cones area their ages are regularly distributed between 700 and 11,700 years. In the Granite Mountains the collection of rock art, including more than 1,000 pictographs, is the largest in the Mojave Desert. On a beach stranded 30 feet above Soda Lake, archaeologists have uncovered artifacts left behind by people who enjoyed the shore of Lake Mohave 9,500 years ago. In rock and cave shelters in the Providence and Woods mountains, they have found fragments of vessels and pottery sherds, awls and hammerstones, twined basketry, and fire drill hearth, many of considerable antiquity. These remains were used to reconstruct the prehistory of the eastern Mojave Desert, but data is too scanty to do much more than formulate a basic chronology and postulate migrations. But we know that these people had a good command of lithic work, hunted and practiced shamanism, knew how to make pottery and fire, and that they heroically managed to survive in this hostile land since the Pleistocene.

Around Turquoise Mountain, east of Silver Lake, are the remnants of prehistoric mines where they recovered turquoise as early as 400 AD. It is one of the earliest mining industries in North America, and it existed off and on for centuries. Some miners might have lived in nearby caves, whose roofs are covered with soot from untold years of campfires. The caves were guarded against animals and weather by walls of unmortared stone. The turquoise was pried out by chipping at the rock with stone hammers made of basalt or quartz. Some tools

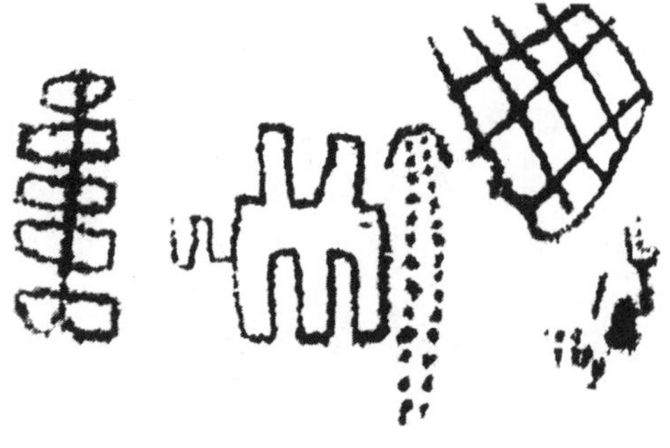

Petroglyphs,
Halloran Spring area

show signs of prolonged use. The miners protected their diggings against intruders with booby traps. It means they weren't alone. The mined turquoise was traded over a considerable area that stretched into Nevada, southern Arizona, and maybe Mexico.

A legend told around the 1890s by the son of famous Southern Piute chief Tecopa recounts how, centuries ago, strangers with paler skin came to the area from the south and west, made friends with the Desert Mohave, and co-exploited the turquoise with them. They taught the Mohave some of their skills, including rock carving. The Piute, afraid of the changes brought by the outsiders, slayed them and the Mohave. The mines have been idle ever since. This slice of oral history suggests that perhaps the Mohave Indians inhabited this land centuries ago. It also reminds us that in spite of limited mobility, natives were highly cognizant of their natural environment and were eager to expand their horizon. They knew the existence and intrinsic rarity of gems and metals. They knew how to improve their living conditions by trading what they had aplenty for what they had little of.

In more recent times the inhabitants of the eastern Mojave Desert were not the Mohave but the Chemehuevi Indians. The Chemehuevi were originally Southern Piute who migrated into eastern California fairly recently, likely in the 17th century. Some historians believe they split off from an indigenous tribe that lived in Las Vegas Valley, others that they came from further north in Nevada. Their territory is generally believed to have covered almost the entire eastern Mojave Desert, roughly land east of a wiggly line that starts near the Kingston Range south of Death Valley and passes through the Avawatz Mountains, Silver Lake, Cave Mountain, Bristol Lake, the Coxcomb Mountains, and ends on the Colorado River near the Palo Verde Mountains. They also ranged into the Tehachapi Mountains and as far as the Panamint Range, which they held sacred. The only portion of this huge territory that was not theirs was a strip 15 to 40 miles wide along the Colorado

River, which belonged to the Mohave, to the Halchidhoma south of them, and to the Yuma still further south. The Chemehuevi homeland encompassed some 9,000 square miles, nearly four times the preserve's area. It was the largest geographic distribution in California of any indigenous people of homogeneous dialect. This territory ranked among the poorest in the state, and it was accordingly very thinly populated. The Chemehuevi numbered between a few hundred and 1,000—on average, only one inhabitant per 10 or 20 square miles.

To find the food and medicine they needed in this country of sparse resources, the Chemehuevi were on the move a good part of the time. For greater efficiency, they lived and traveled in small groups, probably centered around a family nucleus, and covered great distances to harvest wild plants and hunt game. Chemehuevi men had the caricatural profile of weightlifters, with broad shoulders and slender waists. Early observers mentioned that they walked very fast and carried a hook to pull small animals like gophers and rabbits out of their holes. They also hunted large game like deer and bighorn sheep with bows and arrows made of willow tipped with a stone point. They had mastered the fine art of weaving baskets, vessels much lighter and more shock-resistant than pottery, and better adapted to a migratory life. Their settlements ranged from temporary campsites to permanent villages established near springs. They also occasionally farmed on small lots at well-watered springs, although with limited success. Being constantly on the quest for sustenance, it is doubtful that they had time to develop a new tribal identity, perhaps not even a band structure. Culturally and linguistically, they remained indistinguishable from Southern Piute tribes, with whom they might have had periodic contacts.

Chemehuevi basket

From the standpoint of cultural affiliations and environments, eastern California tribes were more closely related to inland regions than to California. The Quechan, Mohave, and Halchidhoma had close cultural ties with the American Southwest. The Kawaiisu, Western Shoshone, and Southern Piute, including the Chemehuevi, were rooted in the Great Basin. These indigenous groups formed complex relationships, not always aligned with their cultural background or lifestyle.

The Chemehuevi had long-standing friends, like the Mohave and the Yuma. It is a source of constant wonder that in spite of the great distances separating them, they managed to stay in touch. They did so by cumulating marathons. The Mohave routinely crossed the desert on foot to the coast to trade with local groups. The Chemehuevi, too, were famous for "visiting"—which meant constantly being away. Their trans-desert jaunts command admiration. They could walk 20 miles a day for days without a break. They completed these arduous journeys without the benefits of sturdy shoes, lightweight packs, power bars, and water filters. Most humans today do not have the stamina for a fraction of such epics, and could not find the ocean without a GPS.

One can only imagine that to isolated bands constantly moving, a more sedentary life along the Colorado River must have been a tempting alternative. The river provided reliable water, safety, food, arable land, shade, and greater comfort. It was no doubt a coveted resource, and competition for it must have been fierce at times. Territorial war occasionally broke out between the tribes that lived along the river. Being a small and widely dispersed people, the Chemehuevi were more inclined to staying out of trouble than more aggressive tribes like the Apache and the Mohave. That they tried farming under adverse conditions at desert springs rather than along the river suggests that their difficult nomadic life was dictated in part by geopolitics.

Eventually, however, some Chemehuevi did move to the Colorado River. The exact date is not known. In 1540 Alarcón, the first Spanish explorer who traveled up the Colorado River, did not encounter Chemehuevi. Neither did the Oñate expedition of 1604-1605, which entered the Colorado along Bill Williams Fork and met Mohave Indians, especially in Parker Valley where they lived in large numbers. The first explorer known to have encountered Chemehuevi was Francisco Garcés, a Franciscan father who visited Mohave country in 1776. While traveling inland with a Mohave guide, Garcés met a group of about 40 Chemehuevi out in the desert. He later reported his impressions of the Chemehuevi in complimentary terms. "Six Indians of this nation that were on a hill came down as soon as we called them, with the speed of deer, and regaled me with very good mezcal. The garb of these Indians is Apache moccasins, shirt of antelope skin, white headdress like a cap with a bunch of those very curious feathers which certain birds of this country have in their crest. These Indians gave me the impression of being the most swift-footed of any I have seen. [...] They conducted themselves with me most beautifully; by no means were they thievish or troublesome, but rather quite considerate." On his way back, Garcés saw several Chemehuevi settlements in the vicinity of Soda Lake and in the Providence Mountains, but none along the river. In subsequent decades, the rare parties that ventured to the Colorado River—explorers, fur trappers, army troops, and surveyors—encountered Mohave or Yuma, but no Chemehuevi. All this time the Chemehuevi were still a nomadic people roaming the desert.

Between 1827 and 1829, after years of fighting against a Mohave-Yuma alliance, the Halchidhoma lost and evacuated the Colorado River valley where they had been living. Some Mohave moved into the valley, and, because they did not live there all the time, they either invited or tolerated small bands of Chemehuevi to live there with them. The Chemehuevi adopted Mohave practices and began floodwater farming. During his historic visit to the area in 1854, Lieutenant A. W. Whipple met with some 50 Chemehuevi in Chemehuevi Valley, where they were growing maize, wheat, beans, and squash. They were eager to trade their grain and vegetables with him, but they were cautious to stay away from the Mohave, who lived a short distance up the river.

Chemehuevi Indian basket weaver making splints (Reproduced by permission of The Huntington Library, San Marino, California)

In 1865, the year the Colorado River Indian Reservation was created, this precarious co-habitation was interrupted when hostilities broke out between the Mohave, Yuma, and Yavapai in one camp, and the Chemehuevi and Piute in the other. As emigrant settlements along the river displaced Chemehuevi families, the Chemehuevi responded by stealing and acts of violence, and the Mojave and Yuma often took the blame for it. The Chemehuevi were forced to abandon their fields and villages and retreat to the desert. When peace returned two years later, many of the Chemehuevi were allowed to return to the river corridor and live in Parker Valley, Chemehuevi Valley, and on Cottonwood Island. In 1874 the reservation was expanded and the Chemehuevi were convinced by government officials to permanently settle down on the west side of the river. By then the eastern Mojave Desert had largely been abandoned by its indigenous population.

Mining History

Monetary gain is a powerful attractor. For 130 years, countless people braved the eastern Mojave Desert to reap whatever mineral treasures it might hold. At last count, 19,500 claims were filed over hundreds of thousands of acres, and thousands of workings were developed. They yielded gold and silver, the most sought-after commodities, but also copper, lead, zinc, tin, iron, tungsten, vanadium, cinder, and evaporites. There is not a mountain that was not poked by the picks and shovels of prospectors. Most claims were never exploited. Many of the ones that were did not produce much. But a few were rich enough to fare well. At times, mining these privileged places took nothing short of epic proportions. It involved full-fledged companies, millions of dollars in investment, rowdy towns, and the sweat and blood of hundreds of hard-working people. In retrospect, it was the greatest human adventure this desert ever saw.

Mining came early to the eastern Mojave Desert. The first valuable metal discovery was silver, in Macedonia Canyon, probably in 1863. It was a little over a decade after the start of California's gold rush. The first major discovery took place a few years later, in 1868, when copper was reported on the southern slope of Clark Mountain. This deposit would not be exploited for three decades, but it drew attention to the area, which sparked a second major strike—rich silver deposits on the other side of Clark Mountain. By 1870, a town of 300 called Ivanpah had sprung up in the foothills, the region's first mining district. Those were the most euphoric years. The region was largely unexplored, and minds were brimming with grand expectations. Clark Mountain did deliver. It had enough ore to spawn great mines and keep the Clark Mining District busy for a decade, and it continued to produce after that, albeit at a slower pace, for several years. By 1890 it had grossed $3.8 million, a rare achievement in the California Desert.

The third major discovery was the Bonanza King property in 1880. Located in the Providence Mountains, this exceptional silver mine benefited from unusually cooperative geology. Much of the ore was confined to long veins, some as wide as 20 feet. In some tunnels, a blast of dynamite yielded mostly pay dirt. It was indeed a bonanza. The mine's output occasionally exceeded 60,000 ounces of silver a month. Between 1882 and 1885, it operated nearly continuously and churned out around $1.8 million, 95% in silver.

Desert mines being isolated, transporting the ore to a refinery was a substantial fraction of operating costs. Around 1870, the freighting cost was as high as $70 a ton. After including the cost of labor and equipment, only ore worth around $100 or more a ton might have been

Main Historic Mines of the Mojave National Preserve			
Discovery date/Name	Main commodities	Main periods of activity	Approximate production
1860s? Giant Ledge Mine	Copper	1902–1912	Unknown
1868 Copper World Mine	Copper	1898–1918	$1,380,000
1870- Eugene Mine	Silver	1870–1871	~$20,000
1870 Beatrice/Monitor M.	Silver	1870–1882	$2,500,000
1870 Sagamore Mine	Lead/Silver/Gold	1907–1917	$24,000
	Lead/Copper/Zinc	1942–1951	$14,000
1871 Lizzie Bullock Mine	Silver	1871–1882	$1,200,000
1879- Bullion Mine	Silver	1879–1917	>$10,000
1870s? California Mine	Copper/Gold	1906–1945	$72,000
1880 Colosseum Mine	Gold/Silver	1929–1939	$18,000
~1880 Alley Mine	Silver	1880–1886	$100,000
1880 Bonanza King Mine	Silver	1880–1925	$1,870,000
1882 Hidden Hill Mine	Gold	1895–1916	>$64,000
1885- Perseverance Mine	Silver	1885–1891	~$250,000
1891 Vanderbilt mines	Gold/Silver	1891–1942	>$200,000
~1892 Trio Mine	Copper/Lead	1916–1917	$18,000
1894 Big Horn Mine	Gold	1898–1943	>$130,000
1890s Oro Fino Mine	Silver	1902	$10,000
	Gold	1937–1948	~$14,000
1900- Mohawk Mine	Lead/Zinc/Silver	1917–1952	$606,000
~1900 Carbonate King Mine	Zinc/Silver/Lead	1941–1951	$640,000
~1900 Paymaster Mine	Gold	1910–1914	>$50,000
	Gold	1932-1944	$10,600
1900? Evening Star Mine	Tin/Tungsten	1939–1944	$31,000
1902 Vulcan Mine	Iron	1942–1947	~$7,500,000
1902- Standard No. 1 Mine	Copper/Silver	1906–1919	>$137,000
1905 Brannigan Mine	Gold	1930–1940	>$68,000
1906 Death Valley Mine	Silver	1906–1931	<$130,000
~1907 Mojave Mine	Tungsten	1916–1918	$14,000
1916- Francis Copper Mine	Copper/Silver	1916–1949	>$47,000
1916- Revenue Copper M.	Copper	1917–1919	$12,000
1917? New Trail Mine	Copper	1917–1950	>$139,000
1930 Telegraph Mine	Gold/Silver	1932-1948	$100,000

Only the main, pre-1955, periods of operation are listed. A year followed by a minus sign indicates that the discovery may have occurred earlier than that year.

worth shipping. Lower grade ore—most of the mined rock—had to be stockpiled. This ore had cost money to extract, so if this situation persisted, the mine could not turn a profit and had to shut down. The common solution was on-site milling. The role of a mill was to crush the ore and extract from it the precious metal. The end product was a metal-rich concentrate much lighter and typically 4 to 6 times cheaper to freight than the original ore. The delivery of a mill in a district was always an exciting time. The stockpile could now be processed and shipped. It meant more jobs for miners and mill workers, and sometimes, for smaller mines that could not afford their own mill, a place to process their ore. It meant a greater output, greater visibility, and easier fundraising. But mostly, it meant survival.

Numerous mills were brought into the region. The first documented mill was hauled into Sagamore Canyon in 1873. Two years later, after it was found too inefficient for the local rock, it was moved piece by piece to Ivanpah, where it was put to good use for at least 15 years. In 1876, a second mill was brought into Ivanpah for the Lizzie Bullock Mine. It, too, ran long shifts until at least 1890. The rich Bonanza King Mine had a 10-stamp mill, purchased and hauled from San Francisco for $50,000 in 1882. It was so vital to the mine's welfare that when it burnt down in 1885, the company could no longer operate profitably and shut down. Other "communal" mills worked hard at crushing everybody's ores, especially at Valley Wells and in Needles.

Even back in the 1880s, prospectors were impressively knowledgeable about their trade. They could identify from afar the major groups of rocks, knew to focus on plutonic terranes, especially near faults and boundaries with sedimentary formations. They knew how to read the local geology to estimate the size of a deposit. By about 1890, most of the richest deposits had been identified. In the ensuing decades, however, mining actually intensified. Several factors stood behind this apparent paradox. First, the deployment of several railroads into the region, especially the Salt Lake Route in 1905, made mining more attractive by lowering the cost of transportation. This was vital for smaller mines, which meant most properties. Second, the market price of mineral commodities generally increased over time. The price of gold, which had been pegged around $20.65 per ounce for decades, was increased to above $34 by the U.S. government in 1934. It provided new incentives to look for gold again in little-explored areas, and to rework mines and tailings abandoned when the price of gold was too low. Finally, the advent of automobiles in the 1910s, together with the road infrastructure that gradually came along with it, revolutionized desert mining by providing much easier access.

Other events affected mining trends. The overall decline in the price of silver, from $1.06 per ounce in 1890 to 25¢ per ounce in 1932, stimulated renewed interest in gold. In 1942 a war order prohibited gold mining for a few years to move the mining labor force toward strategic metals such as iron. During the Great Depression, unemployed men came to the desert looking for work at the mines. This influx of inexpensive labor gave a boost to the extraction industry.

For these various reasons, many mines were in operation in the first few decades of the 20th century. Vanderbilt, in the New York Mountains, generated some of the most publicity. Between 1900 and 1942, at least one of its many properties always managed to ship ore every few years. The Ivanpah Mountains made a name for themselves for their copper properties, especially the Standard No. 1 Mine (mostly from ~1900 to 1919) and the New Trail Mine (1918–1950). In the same range the Evening Star Mine gained notoriety for producing tin in the 1940s. The Providence Mountains witnessed a flurry of activity. In Macedonia Canyon, gold came out of the Columbia Mine and copper out of the Francis Copper Mine shafts. Gold was also produced at the Big Horn and Hidden Hill mines south of the Bonanza King. On Old Dad Mountain, the Paymaster, Oro Fino, and Brannigan mines yielded gold and a little silver sporadically until the 1940s. In the Halloran Springs Mining District, the Telegraph Mine shipped gold almost every year from 1932 to 1948. The Sagamore Mine produced lead, copper, and zinc in the 1900s, 1910s, and 1940s. Several of these mines had a lively camp for a while, and even a mill. But although they were often praised in county newspapers, most of them brought in less than $10,000. Only a handful reached the six-digit figure in their lifetime.

This period had, nevertheless, a few winners. When the Copper World Mine was finally developed in the early 1900s, it quickly rose to stardom. In three distinct periods of two or three years each between 1898 and 1918, it generated around $1.4 million in copper and became one of California's leading copper producers. The Mohawk Mine, at the southern tip of the Clark Mountain Range, shipped ore every year between 1944 and 1952 and yielded about $530,000 worth of lead, zinc, and silver. From 1941 to 1951 the Carbonate King Mine, high on the flank of Kokoweef Peak, output nearly $650,000 in zinc, more than the total prior zinc production in the region.

The last star was the Vulcan Mine, in the Providence Mountains. It broke all records, and it did so with a much more prosaic metal—iron. The Vulcan deposit had been known since 1902, but for lack of need it was left alone until World War II. The grand master behind its exploitation was shipbuilding tycoon Henry John Kaiser. In 1942 he opened the Vulcan Mine to supply his plants with the millions of tons of iron ore required to manufacture his fleets of steel naval vessels. Between December that year and July 1947, his task force extracted a staggering 2.64 million tons of iron ore, almost all the iron that came out of this desert. The raw ore was valued at $7.5 million, three times the output of the next most prolific historic mine. It nearly doubled the value of all the ores extracted from the region.

The history of these mines was weaved by remarkable characters. Many properties, including the larger ones, were managed during their most productive years by a single man. All too aware of the highly unpredictable nature of their business, these astute operators were often involved with several properties simultaneously. In the 1870s and 1880s the rich Lizzie Bullock Mine up in Ivanpah gave out most of its silver under the supervision of an industrious mine operator named J. A. Bidwell. In the 1890s, a man from Salt Lake City, Allen G. Campbell, ran the Boomerang Mine and a few other Vanderbilt properties for many years. Dr. L. D. Godshall was in charge of the Copper World Mine during its glory days in the 1900s and 1910s. When it played out, he continued to specialize in copper ventures. In the 1920s he was busy with the Francis Copper Mine, where a shaft was named after him, then at the Sagamore Mine in the 1940s. J. Lee Strawn and his wife worked the Death Valley Mine for four decades starting in 1915. The Big Horn Mine was associated for most of its life with Thomas Gannon. The notorious exception is the Beatrice and Monitor mines at Ivanpah. They were run by the famous McFarlane brothers, all four of whom were experts in one aspect of mining or another.

The mining industry had its share of lost lodes and frauds. In the 1870s an old German named Erick Vontrigger reportedly found a rich gold deposit in the southeastern section of the preserve, from which he periodically brought back rich samples. After he died accidentally in 1880, his undisclosed mine became a legend. Years later the area was still occasionally searched by treasure hunters. Even after a new mining district was founded, promoters continued to use Vontrigger's lost lode to lure investors. Expectedly, even the area's largest venture, the California Mine, was not particularly impressive. Vontrigger's gold, if it ever existed, may still be buried near the hills that now bear his name. There was also Colorado con artist B. X. Dawson, who started the rumor in 1905 that he had discovered a prodigiously rich deposit of pure gold under Death Valley. He incorporated a company and launched a big advertising campaign to sell company shares. Perhaps to play the part, he purchased a mine in the east Mojave and called it Death Valley. Two years later he had vanished with some $250,000 in

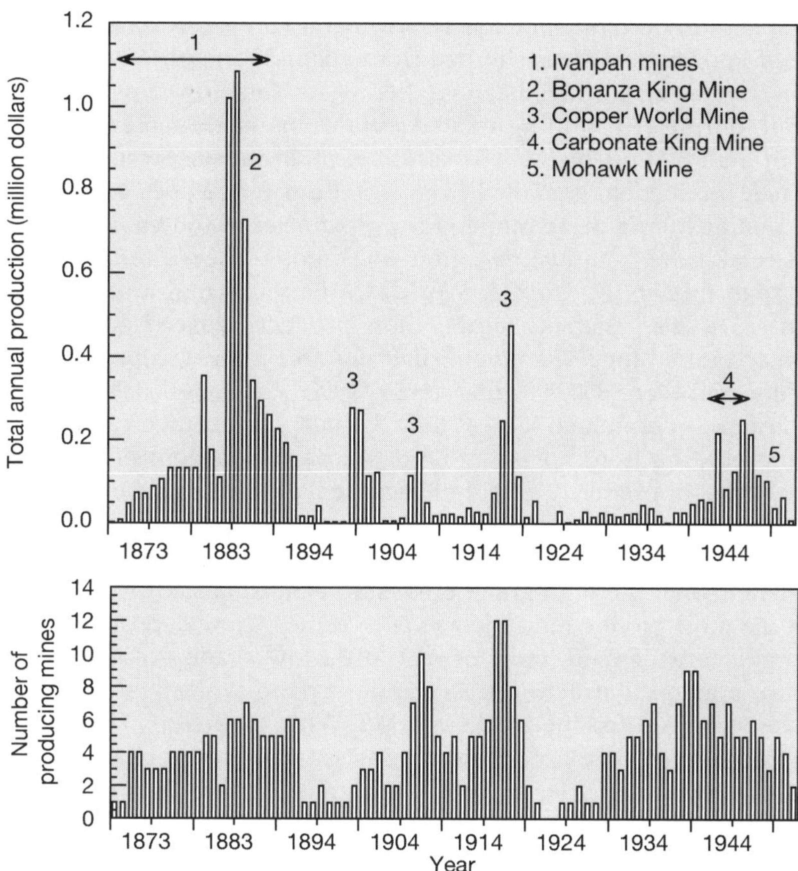

stock sale money. As ludicrous as this scheme may seem, it was outdone in 1940 by Earl Dorr, a late-coming prospector who claimed to have found a river of gold underneath the Ivanpah Mountains. He went as far as publishing an affidavit describing in imaginative details the grand system of underground caves that led him to his fabulous find. Dorr never made money on his farcical tale, but since then the whole mountain has been scrutinized by numerous parties. Its exclusion from the preserve may in part be attributed to this alleged lode. At the time of this writing, a privately funded company continues to bring in the latest technology to look for Dorr's river of gold...

Some measure of clarity came decades later, long after the last ore car was wheeled out of the last tunnel, pieced together by pouring over volumes of data and painstakingly separating reality from fantasy on silicon-based machines. Between 1863 and 1953, in Mojave

National Preserve plus the adjacent Mineral Hill and Kokoweef areas, ore of known value was shipped from about 53 mines. About half as many mines again have been credited with some unknown, usually small, output. All mining-related operations likely never occupied more than 300 people at a given time, often much fewer. The total known production, compiled from U.S. Bureau of Mines records and the mining literature, amounted to approximately $17.6 million. 79% of this total came from just five groups of mines—the Vulcan Mine, the Ivanpah mines, the Copper World, Carbonate King, and Mohawk mines. These are the only mines whose production exceeded $500,000. Iron accounted for $7.5 million, silver for $6.2 million, copper for $1.7 million, gold for $860,000, zinc for $670,000, lead for $560,000, and tin and tungsten combined for less than $50,000. The average value of this ore, excluding iron, hovers around $62 per ton. About one in three mines sought primarily gold, but because high-grade gold ore suitable for underground mining was scarce, gold made up for less than 5% of the total output. All of the historic gold would fit in a wheelbarrow.

Almost all the high-grade ores had been exhausted by the 1960s, but the most prolific mines were yet to come. A few deposits still had literally tons of gold, most of it in ultra-low grade—less than 0.05 ounce per ton. Extracting it via underground workings would not have even paid for the workers' food. What took care of these vast dilute reserves was large-scale mining, stimulated by cheap energy, the steadily rising price of gold—and greed. Rather than burrowing puny tunnels, a whole chunk of mountain is blasted away, the worthless rock discarded, then everything else is crushed and its gold content squeezed out chemically. By processing enormous volumes of rock, a few gold mines extracted unprecedented amounts of gold. The historic Colosseum Mine in Clark Mountain was re-opened in 1987 and produced until 1993 at the tune of 7,000 ounces per *month*. The old Oro Belle and Big Chief mines in the Castle Mountains suffered the same fate. After gold was discovered there in 1907, the lively town of Hart, named after one of the discoverers, came to life on a carefully laid-out grid of numbered streets and avenues, only to die just a few years later for lack of high-grade ore. In the early 1990s a Canadian company reworked the deposit and chewed off the tail of the mountains to extract the low-concentration gold the old timers had left behind—more than 500,000 ounces. The same went on at the Morning Star Mine in the Ivanpah Mountains, and at Mountain Pass to recover rare-earth elements. Collectively, these three mines produced hundreds of millions of dollars. They put out more gold in a single year than all of the historic mines combined did in 80 years.

Railroad History

Throughout the early decades of the settling of the West, the Mojave Desert was a major impediment to transportation between southern California and the east. The scarcity of water, high summer temperatures, rough terrain, and angry native populations made overland travel dangerous. The paucity of arable land was also a disincentive for settlers. Railroads were the first transportation system that effectively penetrated this isolated region and opened the Pacific Coast to the heartland. The first line, completed in 1883, was the Atchison, Topeka and Santa Fe Railway, which skirts the southern border of the preserve. By connecting the eastern Mojave Desert to the national rail system, it jump-started the region's economy. Local miners, ranchers, and homesteaders alike all benefited from it. The railway also brought a bit of civilization to the desert. In 1889, to appeal to its clientele, the Santa Fe railway launched a stylish line of Harvey House train stations, founded by the same Fred Harvey whose empire feeds visitors in our national parks. The crown jewel was the now famous El Garces Hotel in Needles, built in 1908. The upscale stations served fine food in luxurious settings, a welcome improvement from the bad coffee and tasteless sandwiches that were traditionally offered at train depots.

The rail line that passes through the preserve, originally known as the San Pedro, Los Angeles & Salt Lake Railroad, was completed 22 years later. The Union Pacific, one of the two companies that completed the first transcontinental railroad in 1869, was a major proponent of this route. The company had laid tracks out of Salt Lake City southwest to Milford, Utah—towards California—as far back as 1880. Low earnings, a weak economy, scarce manpower, and the multiplicity of routes being pursued slowed down further work to a crawl. The next segment out of Milford was still being worked on in 1893. Even then, extending the line to Los Angeles was not much more than a project on paper. The landscape changed considerably with the arrival on the scene of Senator William A. Clark, a wealthy copper magnate from Montana with an unstoppable determination. In August, 1900, Clark purchased the Los Angeles Terminal Railway and started planning his own independent railroad to Salt Lake City. The following years witnessed ruthless competition between Clark and the Union Pacific. The two parties fought bitterly to gain control over key segments of the route, especially in Nevada, which led to political disputes and lawsuits. In 1902, an agreement was finally signed by which the Union Pacific relinquished some of its right-of-ways, while Clark sold 50% of his stock in his railroad. Track-laying resumed at both ends in July 1903, the Union Pacific expanding southwest across Nevada, and

Clark's work force pushing across the Mojave Desert. From the coastal port of San Pedro near Los Angeles, Clark's line crossed the western Mojave Desert to Barstow, continued east through Afton Canyon and today's preserve, then angled northeast across Ivanpah Valley into Nevada. It is there that the two tracks met, on January 30, 1905, 22 miles past the California stateline. Senator Clark was of course aboard the historic train that made the first trip from Salt Lake City to Los Angeles, on February 9, 1905.

The Salt Lake Route was a major contributor to the development of the West. It gave the Union Pacific access to southern California's huge developing markets. For many communities, the proximity of the railroad was a powerful economic catalyst. The most spectacular instance was a spring-fed ranch lost in an empty desert valley in southern Nevada, which was transformed overnight by the railroad into a full-fledged town that eventually became Las Vegas.

The Salt Lake Route had sidings every 10 to 15 miles, stops where a train could be pulled off the main track for repair or to make room for a passing train. Some sidings had water tanks for locomotives, and a section house for a maintenance crew. Along the east-Mojave portion of the line, siding No. 16 was the most critical one. It was located near the foot of the 19-mile, 2,000-foot grade up Cima Dome, which was too steep to climb with a single engine. Siding No. 16 was a helper station: it was the base for helper engines that were coupled to the front of eastbound trains to help them climb the grade, then returned "light" to the siding. The siding also provided water for the locomotive's boiler before the grueling ascent. Railroad engineers selected the perfect location: they put siding No. 16 near the foot of the grade and closest to Cornfield Spring, a reliable source of water in the Providence Mountains. To deliver the spring water to the siding, railroad workers laid down an aqueduct made of more than 3,000 six-inch-diameter steel pipes across 5.5 miles of rocky desert. The story goes that to name this siding, two warehouse workers put their names into a hat along with that of a third worker, who had left the area. The name that was pulled out was that of the absentee, John H. Kelso, and siding No. 16 became known as Kelso.

Another key station was Nippeno Camp, a small, isolated mining settlement on the eastern edge of Ivanpah Valley. Here too, the new railroad stimulated the local economy. Nippeno Camp became a convenient loading station for livestock and freight headed either north to Nevada and Utah or west to the coast. A hotel was constructed to accommodate visitors. A depot opened in Kelso in 1905 as well. Because of its special role, it was not only a depot; it also had a boarding and rooming house for employees, and an "eating house" for passengers and railroad workers. A post office was later added to Kelso, and an engine house to maintain the trains.

The existence of transcontinental rails made it attractive for mining interests to develop local railroads that would branch off these main lines and haul their ores at a lower cost. The first of these short-lived rails was the Nevada Southern Railway, the brainchild of a mining expert from Denver named Isaac Blake. Blake's vision was to tap the business of the many promising mines scattered in California and Nevada north of Needles. His railway would start from the Santa Fe line, head north across Lanfair Valley, cross the New York Mountains, then cut through Ivanpah Valley and continue into Nevada and points beyond. Blake was hoping that the mines in the New York Mountains, especially in Sagamore Canyon and at Vanderbilt, would be major suppliers to his railroad. Grading of the first segment of the Nevada Southern, from Goffs to Manvel on the southern fringe of the New York Mountains, began in January 1893. It was completed six months later, and regular services began soon after. A stage coach brought passengers the remaining few miles from Manvel to Vanderbilt.

Financing this first segment was not easy. Blake had to mortgage each completed section to pay for the next one. The mines were not providing much business. Construction past Manvel was halted while Blake unsuccessfully tried to raise the next round of funding. In February 1894, shortly after its first anniversary, the railroad was turned over to the sheriff for auction. Blake never managed to get out of the financial hole he had dug himself into. In December his railway went into receivership. The Nevada Southern never reached Nevada.

The following year, a former manager of the defunct railway and a partner gave it a second life as the California Eastern Railway. Expectedly, the new venture did not fare better. The opening of the Copper World Mine in Clark Mountain in 1898 instilled new hopes for increased business. To create a shorter route between the mine and the smelter being built in Needles, the California Eastern was extended from Manvel over the mountains to Vanderbilt and Ivanpah Valley. The new segment was graded with Santa Fe capital in 1901–1902, mostly by Mohave Indians' labor. Upon its completion, the Santa Fe purchased the remaining interest in the California Eastern and operated it from then on. The line managed to scrape by for a few years, supported largely by the mines at Vanderbilt, Ivanpah, and Goodsprings, as Blake had predicted. However, the opening of the Salt Lake Route in 1905, which generally followed the projected northern extension of the California Eastern, stole all the traffic from the north. There was just

Train 7419 on the Union Pacific line along Cima grade

not enough business for everyone. The California Eastern somehow survived on limited traffic, offering a weekly train for the longest time, then only trains on demand, until it was finally abandoned in 1923.

The second local rail, the Barnwell & Searchlight Railway, was not much of a success either. Its intended purpose was to connect the booming mining town of Searchlight in southern Nevada to Manvel (renamed Barnwell in 1907), which was already linked to the Salt Lake Route via the California Eastern. Once again it was the Santa Fe that put out the money for this venture, in part to offset the traffic it was losing to the Salt Lake Route. Construction turned out to be painstakingly slow, impeded by unusually high labor turnover. Started in early 1906, the 23-mile track was not completed until March 1907. As luck had it, Searchlight started declining just about then, although the area continued to produce modest amounts of ore every year until around 1940. It was, however, not enough for the Barnwell & Searchlight to turn a profit. It offered fewer rides as time went on, until it was finally abandoned in 1924 after storms washed it out in several places.

The last rail that was grafted to a mainline was the Tonopah & Tidewater Railroad. Its mastermind was Francis Marion "Borax" Smith, the rich investor heading the Pacific Coast Borax Company's vast empire. Smith's motivation was to facilitate ore transportation out of his famous borax holdings up in Death Valley. The name of the line hints of a more ambitious route linking the gold fields of Tonopah to the southern California coast. Impeded by rebellious geography and weather, rivalry and high costs, Smith was forced to settle for less. Completed in the fall of 1907, the T&T started from Ludlow on the Santa Fe line, traveled north to Baker, pushed on to Death Valley Junction, then through the Amargosa Valley to Beatty, Nevada. Regular service started right away between Beatty and Los Angeles. Smith's borax operations, then concentrated on the Lila C. Mine, produced refined colemanite that was railed to the company's refinery near San Francisco. When the mine played out in 1914, Smith shifted his operations to the nearby Biddy McCarthy Mine. After 1908, the T&T was operated jointly with the Las Vegas & Tonopah Railroad developed by Senator Clark. The LV&T provided the missing link between Beatty and Goldfield, only 30 miles shy of Tonopah, thus nearly completing Smith's vision. Although it had its ups and downs, the T&T did comparatively well. For years it was the lifeline of the small communities scattered along its 250-mile course. It picked up business where it could, in marble quarries, clay pits, passengers, and special events. It even had its own version of a Harvey House station, a small restaurant at the scheduled stop in Shoshone. Until its last run in June 1940, the T&T carried on average one train a day, a minor feat considering the sparseness of its territory.

For three decades following its opening in 1905, traffic on the Salt Lake Route steadily increased as Los Angeles emerged as a major business center. In 1921 Clark sold the rest of his shares to the Union Pacific, which reaped most of this enormous market. To remain competitive with the Harvey stations, it established its own glamorous station hotels at a few of its sidings. The facilities offered restaurants and employee quarters in elegant buildings unified by the same Spanish-mission architecture. The Kelso Depot was built along these guidelines in 1923 and opened the following year. The spacious two-story building housed a waiting room, a ticket office, a telegraph office, a baggage room, dormitory rooms for staff, boarding rooms with a central bath for railroad employees, and even a billiard room and a library. A 24-hour restaurant called "The Beanery" was added later. The large basement was used as a community center. The depot also served local mine workers, whose mining towns were by then either dying or dead, ranchers and farmers, and passengers who stopped for a quick look at the desert from the depot's tree-shaded lawn.

Nippeno followed suit. For many years its hotel faithfully served the railroad and its users. After the Union Pacific became full owner of the line in 1921, to avoid confusion with an existing station named

Nippomo, the town's name was changed to Nipton. Much of Nipton's subsequent expansion was the work of Harry Trehearne, a miner from England who immigrated in 1906 at the age of 20. In 1922 he moved to Nipton and leased the railroad station from the Union Pacific. Two years later he had built a store, which operated as the Nipton Mercantile Company. He repaired and re-opened the Hotel Nipton for business. He brought in electricity, helped build a school on land he eventually deeded to the Cima School District, and was for a time the school district's clerk. In the late 1930s he had a 550-foot well sunk by hand for the town. In August 1935 he filed a homestead claim on the 120-acre site of Nipton, which was granted a few years later. After an ill-fated trip back home in 1940 (his ship was torpedoed), Trehearne returned to Nipton and continued expanding the station. In 1945 he built the Nippeno House, a two-bedroom home for himself, his wife Ella, and his stepson, then added a new store and town hall.

Kelso's activity reached an all-time record around 1942. The first impetus was the Second World War, which required moving troops and supplies by train to the Pacific Coast. The second one was the opening of the Vulcan Mine a few miles south of Kelso. Between Kelso's regular business, the few dozen mine workers and their families living in trailers, the extra rail employees who loaded the mine's daily 2,500-ton production of iron ore into Union Pacific cars for shipment to southern California, and the merchants and employees needed to support this crowd, Kelso's population grew to nearly 2,000. This was Kelso's apogee. In 1947, the Vulcan Mine ran out of good ore, and the boom was over. By then diesel engines had replaced steamers, trains no longer needed to make water stops, and Kelso slowly declined. In 1962, the role of Kelso as a depot was discontinued, although the restaurant and boarding rooms remained open.

Nipton suffered similar struggles. After Trehearne died in 1949, and Ella four years later, the Union Pacific abandoned the station at Nipton. The school was moved to Mountain Pass, and Nipton started to spiral down. Over the next three decades, the townsite went through no less than six owners, who all had difficulty keeping it alive.

In the 1970s, Kelso still had about 75 residents. The area was already feeling the wind of change. It was starting to attract nature lovers, a new breed of enthusiasts who came here to enjoy the remoteness and seclusion. In 1985, the Kelso Depot had become such a financial drain on the Union Pacific ledgers that the company closed it for good. Worse still, plans were made to demolish it to avoid liability issues. To attempt preserving the historic building, concerned citizens rallied under the banner of the non-profit Kelso Depot Fund. With the

Manvel, ca. 1900 (Larry Vredenburgh collection)

help of Congressman Jerry Lewis and managers of the newly created East Mojave National Scenic Area, they convinced the Union Pacific to spare the structure. After a lengthy political battle, in 1992 the BLM acquired title to the depot and an adjacent lot for the symbolic sum of one dollar. With the passage of the California Desert Protection Act in 1994, the scenic area, including the depot, became Mojave National Preserve and was transferred to the National Park Service. After two years of renovation by its new owner, the refurbished building reopened as the preserve's main visitor center in October 2005.

Nipton again coincidentally followed a similar fate. What saved it from decay and vandalism was Gerald Freeman and his family, who purchased the town in 1984. The Freemans renovated the hotel and opened it as a Bed and Breakfast, converted the store into a trading post, and opened a trailer park for workers at nearby large-scale gold mines, especially the Morning Star and Colosseum mines. Today, with all the mines closed, like Kelso the small settlement is supported almost entirely by tourism.

Thanks to these visionary parallel efforts, the Kelso Depot and the Hotel Nipton have survived into the 21st century, one as an elegant train station, the other as a funky outpost. The T&T, the California Eastern, and the Barnwell & Searchlight were dismantled long ago for scrap metal. But the two giants, the Union Pacific and the Santa Fe (now the Burlington Northern/Santa Fe) are still very busy today. Together with Kelso and Nipton, they are vivid reminders of a not-so-distant past when the railroad was the main system of transportation in the developing American West.

Ranching and Homesteading History

Ranching is one of the eastern Mojave Desert's most enduring human adventures. Although the high desert is not exactly lush, it hosts a surprising density of grasses and tender shrubs that cattle love to munch on. By 1890 several ranches had been established throughout what is now the preserve, especially in the higher east-side valleys, which receive more rain and are more temperate. In 1894 they were consolidated into a single concern, the Rock Springs Land & Cattle Company. It was eventually headquartered in Barnwell, a pivotal stop on the railway, and a convenient place from which to ship livestock to markets. The main ranch house at Barnwell, thought to have been built in 1910 and still in existence, was the company's headquarters. Until it was dissolved in 1929, the Rock Springs company was the largest ranching operation in the east Mojave. It was running thousands of heads of cattle over more than one million acres, one of the last large open ranges in the state.

Large-scale homesteading came later, in the 1910s. The catalyst was the Enlarged Homestead Act of 1909. The government had identified large tracts of land throughout the country, including in the eastern Mojave Desert, where anyone who qualified could apply for a homestead on a parcel increased to 320 acres from earlier laws. The homesteader was required to live on his claim at least seven months a year for three years, to build a house at least 10 feet on the side, and to clear and cultivate 10 acres the first year, 20 the second year, and 40 the third. The homesteader then became owner of the land.

This legislation (and earlier versions of it) was intended to stimulate the development of arid lands in the country, and it worked well. Starting in April 1910, and for many years, it enticed many people to gather their worldly possessions, a few pieces of furniture, tools, and kitchen utensils, and relocate to the eastern Mojave's cooler high-desert valleys. They came here with a dream, a chance to try something new, to move away from the city, to live off the land on a large secluded property, to seek a more adventurous life, and eventually own land of their own. The more fortunate ones moved into a claim relinquished by a discouraged homesteader, and they inherited cleared land and an existing house. Others had to start from scratch.

By 1917 a few dozen families had settled on a checkerboard pattern across the valleys east of the Providence Mountains. Claims were clustered mainly in four areas: around Lanfair in Lanfair Valley, around Ledge, renamed Maruba in 1915, which was 5 miles north of Lanfair, in Pinto Valley, and in Round Valley. The population was soon large enough that Maruba and Lanfair each had a school, a post office,

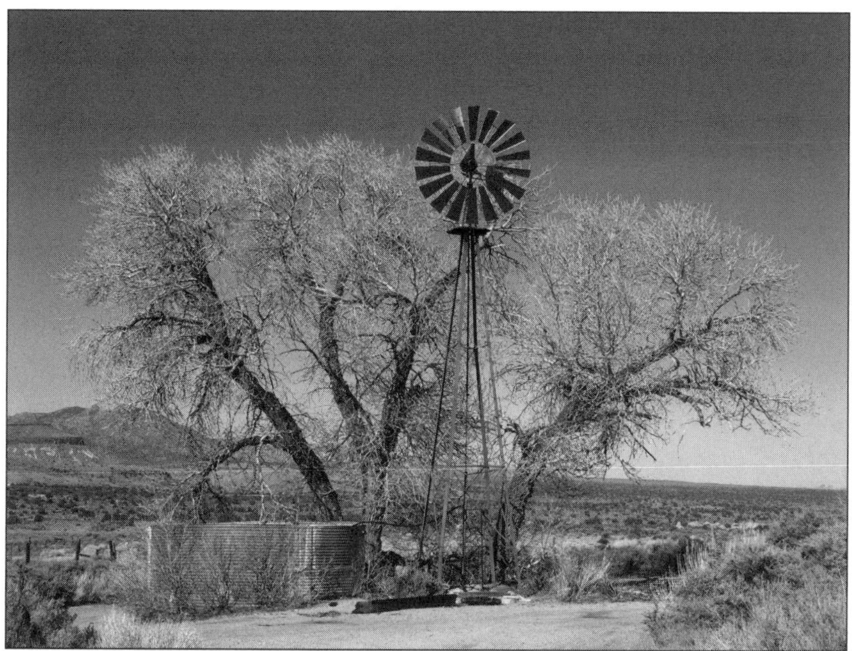

Government Holes in early spring (2012)

and a grocery store. One of the stores was kept by Ernest L. Lanfair and his wife Olive, early settlers after whom the valley and town were named. There was also a school near Rock Spring, and one in Pinto Valley. Attendance ranged from half a dozen to as many as 25 children. The large living room of an abandoned dwelling housed the Yucca Social Club, an outfit that organized dances and potlucks. It was also used for religious services. The California Eastern Railway passed through Lanfair and Maruba on its way to Barnwell, and it was for years the area's lifeline. Some stations, like Vontrigger and Barnwell, had a store and a restaurant. The train brought in mail and supplies, as well as perishables in a refrigerated car twice a week. It shuttled people across Lanfair Valley, and provided a convenient connection to southern California and Arizona via the Santa Fe Railway.

As elsewhere in the West, there was tension between ranchers and homesteaders, the age-old conflict between interests tapping the same finite resources—here land and water. Because this was open range, it was the homesteaders responsibility to protect their cultivations from cattle by erecting a fence around their fields. For the homesteaders, this meant a substantial additional cost and labor. For cattlemen, it meant that fences were cutting off livestock from choice grazing areas.

Cattle would still occasionally break through fences and ruin sometimes a year's worth of planting, and the cattle company was not liable for the damage. Understandably, few settlers were on good terms with cattlemen. The conflict was never resolved; each side only protected its own interest. The cattle company refused to sell beef to homesteaders. The underdogs repaid themselves for their trouble by catching a cow now and then to put meat on their table.

In spite of this substantial influx, the very foundation of the homesteaders' subsistence, desert farming, was a perilous enterprise. Water was the single biggest problem. Few farmers could afford to drill a well, and most wells were controlled by ranchers. Some well owners, in particular the Lanfairs, sold water for 15 to 25¢ a barrel, which was too expensive for irrigation purposes. Dry farming was often the norm. Crops were therefore at the mercy of the scant and undependable desert rains. They were also threatened by livestock, rabbits, insects, and the occasional hailstorm and coyote. The soil was often too sandy and poor in loam. Even when planting crops fairly tolerant of these harsh conditions—wheat, barley, watermelon, and beans—the land generally gave poor returns.

One person did manage to make a living with farming in Lanfair Valley; his name was Millard Elliott, and he was by trade a farmer. He fenced his 10-acre lot with heavy-duty netting to keep rabbits out, and spent a great deal of time plowing, tilling, weeding, and hauling water. Intensive care enabled him to grow all kinds of vegetables, grapes, and an orchard of peach and apricot trees. Another success story is that of Julius and Gertie Alexander and their children. They lived in Pinto Valley, which is slightly higher, wetter, and greener. The water table there is higher and thus cheaper to tap, and they had a well. Out of the hardscrabble land they produced everything needed for the table, from chicken to vegetables, fruits, butter, and even peanuts. The Alexanders belonged to the exclusive group who lived here without extra income. They hung on nearly 30 years, longer than almost anyone else.

Those were exceptions. To make ends meet, generally the man of the house had to take a part-time job. Some worked for the railroad, which might require going all the way to Needles. A few were hired by the cattle company, in particular to maintain watering holes. Others worked at local mines, like the Sagamore and the Giant Ledge, to perform assessment work, repair buildings, or guard the property. The mines being far away, the whole family sometimes camped near the mine for extended periods. Others worked in the community as postmaster, mechanic, cook, or storekeeper, or took odd jobs like fur trapping. Enterprising people accumulated functions, sometimes in uncon-

Barnwell (2008)

ventional combinations. Elliott was postmaster and kept a store and a gas station. Sunday services were conducted by the Sagamore Mine superintendent. In 1929, the justice of the peace delivered the mail.

Homesteaders were a disparate demography. There were ranchers, farmers, a mine operator, carpenter, mule skinner, tinsmith, and a small army of housewives. They were united by the same love for seclusion, yet they sought each other's company fervently and formed a tightly knit community. They helped each other, lent heavy equipment such as plows in exchange for manual labor, paid social visits, shared meals, and generally looked out for each other. The demographic diversity provided a greater range of skills to solve everyday problems, a saving grace for everyone. Their life was centered on work, family, and a few friends, with little outside entertainment, so they created their own. The community's social schedule was busy with picnics, gatherings, dances, and annual celebrations that drew people from all over the area. The small populations of Barnwell, Goffs, and local mines often participated in the festivities.

For many, over time it became clear that eking a living in this refractory land was not as sweet as in the dreams they had fashioned for themselves. The hardships clawed at their mind until they became too intense to bear. Many left soon after they obtained legal title to their land. They returned episodically to give it another try, which usually turned out just as unsuccessful. The long drought of the 1920s broke the resolve of the most adventurous spirits. To make matters worse, the railway shut down in 1923. Had there been no better alternatives, more homesteaders would have likely stayed on indefinitely. But there was one—returning to the urban setting they had come from, which, after years of scraping by, no longer sounded so bad. One by one the settlers left, and fewer moved in to replace them. By 1929 most of the early homesteaders had departed. The Lanfair School closed its doors in 1931. Only a few homesteads remained until the 1940s.

It is easy to romanticize life in the desert, but the record sets us straight: a small percentage of homesteaders stayed longer than 15 years. Very few managed to make the eastern Mojave Desert their permanent home. No town emerged from this wave of homesteading. Yet despite the hard times, some homesteaders remembered this chapter of their lives with fondness. Margaret Sharp Moore, who was born and raised as a child in Maruba, recalled decades later, "For all four of us, Maruba was always a kind of personal Promised Land."

Today, the OX Cattle Company, the successor of the Rock Springs company, no longer exists, and its grazing allotment in Lanfair Valley is retired. The former owner of the Kessler Springs Ranch, rancher Clay Overson, sold his property in the late 1990s to a land trust, which donated it to the NPS. Only three areas is the preserve are now still being grazed. The largest one stretches across Clipper Valley and Fenner Valley, from the eastern Providence Mountains to Fenner and from Hole-in-the-Wall to Interstate 40. The Blair 7IL Ranch, headquartered near the mouth of Barber Canyon, is still active in this area; it uses allotments in the Colton Hills and in Gold Valley. The second largest area occupies the northeast side of Clark Mountain. It is operated by a ranch headquartered outside of the preserve. There is also a small cattle operation in Round Valley, just south of Pinto Mountain.

In contrast, most of the homesteaders' homes and improvements have gone. What is left are the miles of dirt roads homesteaders plowed to travel across the valleys. After a century of neglect, the fields they cleared are still plainly visible from these roads, shaved lots still largely devoid of the native cover of shrubs and Joshua trees that delineate their geometric perimeters. Occasionally you will run across a small house standing by itself in the middle of nowhere. Do not assume it is abandoned. It may well belong to the descendants of homesteaders. They still occasionally come to visit the place of their ancestors' dream and youth, perhaps envisioning that some day they might settle here too, as their forefathers did.

■

— 4 —

SAFETY TIPS AND REGULATIONS

The Mojave National Preserve is ours to enjoy. It is also our responsibility to keep it in its natural state, so that others can enjoy it after us. Some regulations are self-evident to people with good wilderness ethics. Other regulations are not. The desert can also be unforgiving, especially in summer. An emergency situation that would be taken care of with a simple phone call elsewhere can become life-threatening, and help may not arrive for days. This section provides a brief summary of what to do and not do to minimize both your impact on the desert and your chances of running into trouble. This is *not* a survival guide. Refer to one if you need substantial advice, for example survival techniques you might need should you become stranded.

Safety Tips

Driving. The preserve's paved roads were not designed for high speed. They only have two lanes, do not have a paved shoulder, and the tarmac is not in its prime. Respect posted speed limits (55 mph at most). The graded roads are generally wide and straight, and they invite a higher speed than is safe to travel, mostly because their gravelly surface makes braking distances dangerously long. Do not exceed the safe common-sense speed limit of 35 mph, even if it is not posted.

The most common breakdown on unpaved roads is flat tires. A flat tire is often caused by nothing bigger than a tiny sharp pebble that gets rammed into the treads. The incidence of flat tires gets rapidly worse with increasing speed—a higher speed means a higher force thrusting pebbles into treads. To minimize the risk of a flat tire, never drive faster than 15 mph on dirt roads (unless graded), with any vehicle.

SUV drivers are particularly at risk. They are generally unaware that SUVs are often equipped with city tires too wimpy for primitive roads, thus they have a false sense of safety, drive faster, and get more flats. Take a flat tire kit with you; it may fix your tire long enough to get you back to town. A second spare tire is also a good idea.

There are no gas stations in the preserve, and the closest ones are fairly far from the heart of the preserve. Monitor your gas gauge frequently, and drive out to a service station well before it is too late.

If you get stuck or if your vehicle breaks down and you can't fix the problem, stay with your vehicle and wait for help to come to you. It is much easier for rescuers to spot a stranded vehicle than a wandering person. If it is summer, open all doors to make your vehicle more visible and provide shade. Use the horn and headlights for signals. Leave your vehicle only if you are certain you can walk to help safely.

Be prepared for such emergencies. Always let someone know your itinerary and schedule, at least approximately, and stick to them. Keep in your vehicle plenty of water and food, a flashlight, matches, a rope, jumper cables, a tool box, and flares. Inspect your spare tire before each trip. Sleeping gear is also a must, especially in winter: you must be able to survive overnight in the wild if it comes to that.

Tips for summer hiking. Much of the preserve lies at elevations high enough that summer temperatures are noticeably lower than in the low desert. Above about 4,500 feet, summer days are actually quite comfortable. Up in the mid-elevations of the New York Mountains in mid-July, on a day Baker's thermometer is about to explode, the temperature is likely to be in the 90s only, and it will dip as low as the 70s at night. So hiking in July and August is not as crazy as it may sound, and there is a wide choice of comfortable places to go for a hike.

Hiking in 100-degree heat is, however, not free of dangers. My own experience tells me that statistically, of the few perils that await a hiker in the desert, only three are far more likely to occur than others: physical exhaustion, dehydration, and heat exhaustion. This statistic is of course not applicable if you happen to be prone to twisting ankles, tripping in your own bathroom, or taking risks that far exceed your abilities; these issues may well get you in trouble first. But barring such unusual dispositions, you should be concerned first and foremost about these three potential problems.

When hiking in challenging terrain in a physically stressful environment such as the desert in the summer, physical exhaustion, dehydration, and heat exhaustion tend to occur in unison, and it helps to think of them as one combined issue. The first manifestation of dehydration is thirst, a signal from your body that it has lost too much water (between 0.5 to 1 quart, depending on your weight) and needs to be hydrated. A subsequent sign is dark urine. Prolonged exposure to heat without sufficient drinking produces further water loss and may lead to heat exhaustion. Blood is then directed away from the brain to irrigate and cool the skin, resulting in excessive sweating, dizziness, tiredness, and vomiting. If water loss and exertion persist, a heat stroke may occur. Blood becomes too thick to be pumped fast enough through the body and glands stop producing sweat. The body's main cooling mechanisms essentially shut down. The symptoms are red, dry skin, headache, fever, dizziness, delirium, and nausea.

These various stages of warnings foreshadow trouble. Learn to recognize them, to take them seriously, and to take timely measures. First, make a habit of drinking often. Don't save your water for later. Thirst lags behind your body's need for water, so don't wait until you are thirsty to drink. In hot weather, drink every 15 minutes, even if you think you don't need it. At the first signs of dehydration, start drinking more right away. If you feel you are getting into the second stage of dehydration, rest in a place sheltered from the sun and wind. Drink plenty of mineralized water, at least a couple of quarts. Often this will restore sufficient strength to hike again, at which point you should return to your vehicle. The third stage is a serious condition that requires prompt medical attention. In the meantime, keep the body cool in the shade, covered with wet clothes, if possible.

Other simple preventative measures help deal with the heat. Wear a wide-brimmed hat to reduce evaporation through your head and exposure to harmful ultraviolet radiation. Dress lightly, but do wear a light-colored long-sleeve shirt and long pants. It will reduce water loss by insulating your body from the sun and wind. Use high-strength sunblock and chapstick, liberally and often. Avoid hiking around midday. Relax in the shade instead, and resume hiking in the late afternoon when there is more shade and the temperature is lower. When it is windy, your rate of dehydration can be significantly higher. Drink more, and stay out of the wind during the hottest hours. To replace the minerals and salts lost through perspiration, take multi-vitamin/mineral tablets, or drink a mineralized drink in addition to water. The salts and minerals prevent your muscles from cramping, in particular your stomach, which is important to keep the water down.

The corollary is: *always take plenty of water with you*. Do not wander into the desert without water, even for an intended short walk. In 100°F weather on easy terrain, allow at least one quart per hour. You'll need less while resting, about one or two cups per hour, and more when going up steep terrain, as much as two quarts per hour. To complete a 10-hour hike you may therefore need to haul 10 to 20 pounds of water on your back, which will affect how far you can hike. But do not short-change yourself. A common mistake is to think you can personally get by with drinking less and realize too late this is not the case.

If you run out of water, and you are too far from potable water to reach it without getting in more trouble, check your map for springs, creeks, wells, guzzlers, and windmills. Make sure to treat the water before drinking it, either by boiling, filtering, or chemical treatment, as it is likely to be contaminated by wildlife, in particular with giardia. Carry a vial of iodine pills for such emergency. Remember that this treatment does not get rid of minerals: if the water is heavily mineralized, it may upset your stomach. Otherwise, use the water to soak your clothes and a headband to cool you down. If there is no water around, rest in the shade and do not resume walking until the temperature has dropped. Always keep at least a couple of gallons of water in your car, for both human and machine emergency needs.

If you are new to desert hiking in the summer, start with short, easy walks to put all this to the test safely. Keep track of your water needs on an hourly or per mile basis. Slowly work up to more substantial hikes, increasing the amount of water you take with you accordingly. It might take a few dozen outings to graduate to a challenging full-day hike, but by then you will be better prepared for what you are up against. It will also give you a chance to calibrate your tolerance to sun and heat and your hiking speed. This last point is important because desert hiking is mostly cross-country, which is slower and more strenuous than trail hiking in cooler climates.

Tips for winter hiking. In the winter the mercury often climbs no higher than the low 30s or even 20s (see *The Preserve at a Glance*). The wind chill can drop the apparent temperature well below freezing. An overcast, windy day can be miserable enough to make you wonder why you are out here in the first place. In the morning, it is not uncommon to find frost and your bottle of water frozen. There can be snow up in the mountains. So if you are planning to enjoy your hike, come as well prepared as for any winter hiking in temperate climates. To avoid hypothermia, bring and wear lots of layers, including a toasty jacket, gloves, and a warm hat. Avoid elevations above 5,000 feet; reserve them for the summer. Concentrate on the westernmost portion of the preserve, around Soda Lake, which is lower and noticeably warmer. Winter days are deceptively short. In December sunset occurs around 4:50 p.m. If you are planning a long hike, get an early start (sunrise in December is around 7 a.m.). Bring a flashlight, just in case you finish your hike in the dark, which is easy given the short days. For camping, you will need a warm sleeping bag and a good tent, as the nights are often frigid.

Tips for year-round hiking. Much of the cross-country hiking in the preserve's mountains is over rough rocky terrain. Use lightweight hiking boots, especially if you are prone to twisting your ankles. I prefer running shoes padded with air or a gel. Though not as sturdy, they are lighter, more comfortable, and on long hikes the padding greatly reduces wear and tear on knees, ankles, and hips. Be sure to stay clear of cacti and other spiny plants, which are abundant in many areas and will easily find a way to your foot. If possible, hike along old roads rather than cross-country; even if it means a slightly longer route, it will likely be easier and in the end faster. On any serious hike, take a topographic map with you, and a copy of the maps supplied in this book. For your own safety, hike with a friend, at least until you have become proficient at dealing with the desert's multiple pitfalls—a skill that may require hundreds of miles of walking to master. When the wind is blowing hard, protect your eyes against dust.

Hazards. The desert has in store several natural and human-made hazards that are largely out of your control. A few of them, like falling rocks or lightning, are extremely unlikely. But a few others should not be discounted. Of these, an encounter with a venomous snake is the most probable. Only three of the preserve's many species of snake are venomous. The first two, the desert night snake and Sonoran lyre snake, are mildly toxic and not considered dangerous to humans. Mojave rattlesnakes are more aggressive than the speckled rattlesnake and the sidewinder, and their bites are more serious, because they inject both hemotoxins and neurotoxins. Neurotoxins affect the nervous system and may result in breathing difficulties or heart failure. Hemotoxins attack muscles and the circulatory system, and may cause loss of motor skills. A rattlesnake bite often, though not always, requires prompt medical attention. It can be painful, harmful, sometimes fatal, often temporarily disabling, and you may not be able to walk very far to get help. Learn to recognize rattlesnakes, especially by their triangular heads, the narrowing of their necks, skin patterns, and rattles. Be familiar with the physiological effects of a bite, and learn what you should do to take care of it. To minimize the chance of getting bitten, stay alert. Unless molested or cornered, a rattler is much more likely to warn you or escape than fight. If you hear one rattling (they sound like some kitchen buzzers or a loud cricket) but do not see it, do not run off in a random direction, which could bring you closer to it. Instead, stop, identify its location by sound or sight, then move away from it. If you cannot determine its location, take one step in one direction and listen. If you are getting closer to it, the snake will detect it and crank up the rattling noticeably. If you are moving away, it will soon reduce the rattling intensity. When the temperature exceeds 90°F rattlers do not survive long in full sun, and they hole up. So in hot weather it is relatively safe to walk in the full sun. But do not jump onto a shaded area or an area you can't see. Be particularly careful when climbing up. This being said, snakes are not numerous in the desert. They are largely nocturnal, and daytime encounters are rare—I see on average only about one rattler a year.

Mojave rattlesnake

Another hazard—this one entirely under your control—is mining areas, which abound in the preserve. Many mine tunnels are old, unsupported, and dangerous. Sometimes a tunnel will lead into a hidden shaft. Tunnel roofs are often badly fractured and waiting for a disturbance to collapse. Rats and mice like to live in tunnels, and they may infect the air inside it with hantavirus. So it is safest to consider all mine workings as hazardous and stay away from them. The chance of getting in trouble is slight, but it could lead to a catastrophe. Sadly for geology-minded visitors, to reduce its liability the NPS has been closing off shafts and tunnels with stainless-steel caps and bars. So this hazard should be lessened in the future.

The preserve is open to hunting year-round and 24 hours a day, although most of the hunting is done in the fall and in the daytime (see details under *Hunting* in the next section). Game being relatively scarce, and humans generally lazy, hunters do not exactly abound. In all the years I have visited the preserve, I have run into hunters only twice. But while hiking be aware of their possible presence. If you see a hunter, make your presence known; sneaking up on people wearing strange clothes is a bad idea. Shout if they cannot see you. It may save your life (and that of another hapless critter).

Mountain lions generally avoid contact with humans, but elsewhere they have occasionally attacked and sometimes killed humans, so be watchful. Should you encounter a lion displaying hostility, do not approach it. Don't run away either, which might trigger a chase. Do all you can to appear as large as possible, for example by spreading out your arms or opening your jacket. Do not crouch or bend over. Speak firmly in a low voice. If attacked, fight back. On occasions, throwing stones has been known to work. But mountain lions are rare in the preserve, so don't let them be in the way of your enjoyment.

Flashfloods are less frequent and tend to be less dangerous than in some other desert areas, primarily because mountains here are comparatively low and collect less storm water. But flashfloods do occur, especially in summertime. Consult the weather forecast before heading into a narrow drainage. If a major storm is expected, postpone your trip or be particularly careful. Periodically inspect the sky up canyon, and stay alert for advance warnings such as rumbling sounds. If a storm is brewing, walk on higher ground. In narrower passages, keep an eye open for escape routes to places at least 10 feet above the wash. Always camp at least 20 feet above the wash, and never in narrows.

Persistent winds can cause irritability, anxiety, insomnia, and allergic reactions. If you are susceptible to these symptoms and windy conditions are forecast, you might want to postpone your trip. If the wind is keeping you awake, try to escape to higher elevations. On many stormy nights I have had to fold my tent and drive quite far to try to find a less windy area—and often ended up sleeping in my vehicle.

Reliance on a GPS can also become a hazard. Continual use of a GPS to get around in the wild is creating a new breed of hikers who have difficulty getting oriented without electronic guidance. If their GPS dies at a time of emergency, because of poor reception, dead battery, or system failure, they may not find their way back quickly enough. It is wise to kick the habit, at least once in a while, to keep your native orienteering skills toned.

Regulations

Off-road driving and bicycling. Driving off roads is prohibited. Stay on established roadways to spare the land and wildlife. Bicycles are allowed on all paved and open dirt roads. They are not allowed off roads, on trails, or in the wilderness areas of the preserve.

Developed campgrounds. Campgrounds are available in the Mid Hills and at Hole-in-the-Wall. Each site has a fire ring and a picnic table. There are no hookups. A dump station is available at the Hole-in-the-Wall Campground. Reservations are not accepted. The campsite limit is eight people and two vehicles. The Black Canyon Equestrian and Group Campground near Hole-in-the-Wall does require a reservation (call (760) 928-2572 or (760) 252-6104). Limit your stay to a maximum of 14 consecutive days and a total of 30 days per year. Quiet hours are 7 p.m. to 7 a.m.

Backcountry camping. There is no permit or registration system for backcountry camping in the preserve. To minimize impact, select a site that has been previously used for camping, as indicated by a fire ring. Do not camp in day-use areas; within 1/4 mile of a paved road or developed area; within 1/4 mile of water sources (so wildlife has free access to them and to protect them from overuse); within 1/4 mile of any cultural site; within 1/2 mile of Fort Piute or Kelso Depot; and within 1 mile north or 1/4 mile south of the Kelso Dunes Road. Avoid camping near mines, for your personal safety and to protect these resources, and in washes, to avoid possible flashfloods. Store all food and garbage in a manner that will prevent access by wildlife.

Campfires. To prevent wildfires and preserve the backcountry's wild character, campfires are allowed only in existing fire rings or in a portable fire pan. Building new fire rings is prohibited. If there is no fire ring and you must have a campfire, move on to one of the many camp sites that has one. Keep your fire small and use a fire pan, which makes it easy to pack out ashes (even though it is not required). Do not leave fires smoldering or unattended. To conserve the scant supply of desert wood, the gathering of native wood, dead or alive, including kindling, is unlawful. Do not burn lumber from historical structures. Bring all wood from outside the preserve, or a camp stove with fuel for cooking.

Garbage. Carry plastic bags and pack out all garbage; do not bury any of it, biodegradable or not. Bury human waste in holes six to eight inches deep, at least 300 feet from water, camp, and trails. Pack out all toilet paper and hygiene products.

Hunting. Hunting in the preserve is regulated by the California Department of Fish and Game. All California hunting regulations apply. A California State hunting license is necessary, as well as special permits for some game animals. No shooting or hunting is permitted within 1/2 mile of campgrounds, dwellings, trails, visitor centers, and public gathering areas. Fort Piute, the preserve's three campgrounds, and the Sweeney Granite Mountains Desert Research Center are closed to hunting and the discharge of all weapons. All wilderness areas are open to hunting, but access is by foot or pack animals only. Spotlighting is illegal. Hunting at water sources is limited to a 30-minute period every hour. Special hunting regulations are in effect at the Providence Mountains SRA. Hunting seasons run throughout the year, although for many game animals the season is open only a few weeks or months.

Weapons. Other than while legally hunting, the possession and discharge of weapons, in particular for target shooting, are strictly prohibited. This applies to firearms, air guns, bows and arrows, slingshots, and similar weapons. All firearms transported within the preserve must be unloaded, broken down, and cased, except during lawful hunting activities.

Wildlife. Do not pester or harm wildlife, including rattlesnakes. Feeding all wildlife is also prohibited. Wild animals fed by humans tend to become dependent on this easy food source. They lose their ability to be self-sufficient and function properly in the wild, which puts their very survival at risk. Some visitors have difficulty understanding this simple concept. If you are one of them, please read up on it, or just trust these statements blindly. Some wild animals also carry communicable diseases, like rabies.

Cultural resources. All cultural resources in the preserve, including historical structures (mines, mining camps, ghost towns, and railways) and archaeological sites are protected by federal law. At historical sites, do not disturb, damage, burn, or remove anything, even the seemingly worthless bits of metal and wood lying around. They all have historical value, and one of the higher purposes of the preserve is to protect them. If every visitor was to take away even just one piece, there would soon be nothing left, and an irreplaceable component of the Mojave Desert would be forever lost. The sea of broken artifacts littering many historic sites as a result of years of vandalism is a sad reminder of the high cost of ignorance. Leave everything where you find it so others have the pleasure of discovering it too. Sanctions for breaking this law include jail time and/or hefty fines.

It is equally illegal and punishable by law to disturb, damage, or remove anything from archaeological sites. This applies to rock art (which tarnishes and wears under repeated contact and should never be touched), rock alignments (which lose their significance when disturbed), artifacts, and camps. These sites are part of the heritage of contemporary Native American tribes. They are important to their traditions, and many of them are sacred. Treat them with respect.

Horseback riding. Horses, llamas, and mules are allowed on all trails, backcountry roads, and in the open country, including wilderness areas. A special use permit is required for groups of more than seven animals. Free-trailing and loose-herding are prohibited. So is ranging/grazing: bring your own feed. All manure must be raked over a large area. Horse camps should be at least 200 yards from a water source. Developed camping facilities are available at the Black Canyon Equestrian and Group Campground.

Natural environment. The removal of rocks, plants, or animals is strictly prohibited, and so is the possession of metal detectors.

Pets. Pets are welcome in the preserve. They must be leashed and never left unattended. Pet excrements must be collected and disposed of in garbage cans. Pets are not allowed inside information centers.

Private properties. Respect all private properties, including mining claims and ranches.

Wilderness Ethics

- When other hikers are nearby, be as quiet as possible.
- Avoid hiking in large groups. It violates the wilderness spirit, and it has a negative impact on the desert environment. Large groups are also more noisy and visible, which is unfair to other visitors.
- Minimize the traces you leave behind: walk softly, on gravel rather than on the plants, on rocks rather than gravel.
- Most perennial desert plants are slow growers. Avoid stepping near them when possible, as they heal very slowly.
- Pack out what you pack in.
- Do not discard organic matter, which may take months to decompose in the dry climate.
- Practice low-impact camping.
- Build cairns only when absolutely necessary for your own benefit, and destroy them on your way back. They may otherwise mislead other hikers, and will often be resented as an intrusion.
- Avoid beeping your vehicle when closing or opening it (use the key instead of the remote), especially in campgrounds. When arriving late, be quiet, and do your best to open and close all doors only once.

■

— 5 —

KELSO BASIN

BOUNDED TO THE EAST by the long alignment of high mountains that slices through the core of the preserve, the preserve's western section comprises Kelso Basin and a small portion of Shadow Valley, a region of interior basins sprinkled with isolated mountains. This wide-open land framed by far-away ranges vividly typifies both the low desert—it is home to the Mojave River sink—and the high desert surrounding it. Many of the preserve's iconic attractions are concentrated here—the majestic Kelso Dunes, the Devils Playground's immense eolian fields, the cinder cones and lava beds region, Cima Dome, salt-coated Soda Lake, and part of the historic Mojave Road. Host to the most diverse collage of environments in the eastern Mojave Desert, this area is also one of its greatest sources of recreation.

Access and Backcountry Roads

The main paved arteries in the western part of the preserve are the Kelbaker Road and the Kelso-Cima Road in Kelso Basin, and the Cima Road along Shadow Valley. These roads provide easy general access, but they are fairly far from most major attractions. The valley floors and fans are crisscrossed by many primitive roads that get closer to the action. Several of them are quite long and provide the opportunity for extensive explorations. Try, for example, the Mojave Road, the Aiken Mine Road through the Cima volcanic field, the largely forgotten Kelso Road along the west side of Old Dad Mountain, or the scenic byway up through Piute Valley. Shorter primitive roads are plentiful. This part of the preserve has been parceled off into large adjacent wilderness areas separated by narrow corridors where driving is permitted.

Suggested Backcountry Drives in Kelso Basin					
Route/Destination	Dist. (mi)	Lowest elev.	Highest elev.	Road type	Pages
Aiken Mine Road	23.6	3,100'	4,370'	H	109-114
Big Horn Mine	6.7	1,655'	2,330'	H	102
Cima Cinder Mine	11.7	3,735'	4,130'	H	114-115
Death Valley Mine Road	7.3	4,176'	4,510'	P	138-139
Green Rock Mill	7.9	940'	1,010'	H	94
Jackass Canyon	8.8	~1,900'	3,133'	H	125
Kelso Dunes Road	4.0	2,535'	2,815'	G	119
Mojave Road	107	930'	5,165'	F	433-440
Oro Fino Mine	4.6	1,655'	2,096'	H	101-102
Paymaster Mine	4.3	1,655'	2,096'	H	101-102
Key: G=Graded H=Primitive (HC)	P=Primitive (2WD) F=Primitive (4WD)				

Consult the National Geographic *Trails Illustrated Map* to find out which roads are open.

Be prepared for a wide spectrum of difficulties when driving these roads. Many of them are fairly smooth, compact sandy loam and passable with a standard-clearance vehicle. Deep sand or a rocky stretch may ultimately stop you; but not always, so give it a try. Just be careful, and stay tuned to your vehicle's limits. On the other hand, a few roads are particularly challenging because of persistent sand. The road to the Rainy Day Mine in the lava bed area is a good example, and so is the power-line road west from Jackass Canyon (a long byway to Ludlow). The toughest is the Mojave Road. For several miles along Willow Wash it swims through soft sand, then out in the middle of Soda Lake it turns into a nightmare of fluid mud. No other unit of the National Park Service lets us have such serious driving fun...

Geology

The western and northeastern portions of the preserve belong to the Great Basin: all drainages collect into one of three inland lakes—Soda Lake in Kelso Basin (also referred to as Soda Lake Valley), Silurian Lake in Silurian Valley (via Shadow Valley), and Ivanpah Lake in Ivanpah Valley—which have no outlet to the sea. This physiography was created in the Early to Middle Miocene, by the same intense extensional faulting responsible for the Basin and Range Province. Whereas elsewhere the ranges are aligned predominantly a little east of north, here they have been significantly altered by subsequent movements on normal and thrust faults. The topography is a more haphazard collection of isolated mountains of irregular shape, a characteristic feature of the eastern Mojave Desert. Soda Lake Valley and Shadow Valley are not separated by a mountain but by an upland sometimes referred to as the Ivanpah upland, while true mountains—Cowhole Mountain, Old Dad Mountain, the Kelso Mountains, the Marl Mountains—protrude unexpectedly in the middle of Kelso Basin. The three basins are distorted enough that they share a common divide, crowned by celebrated Cima Dome. Only the Ivanpah Mountains, between Shadow Valley and Ivanpah Valley, constitute a well-defined division.

Since these basins started opening up, erosion has been steadily filling them with debris. By about 10 million years ago, it had seriously ground down much of the former mountains, and it kept going. This widespread weathering has produced the extensive fans and bulging uplands that dominate the landscape. Ivanpah Valley is flanked by some of the largest alluvial fans in the eastern Mojave Desert, and they are still actively growing. Kelso Basin is equally impressive: the pile of unconsolidated sediments beneath it is at least 2,000 feet thick. This period of erosion is also responsible for several uncommon dome-shaped mountains, the largest of which is Cima Dome.

The region is underlain mostly by Teutonia Adamellite, a quartz monzonite pluton that crystallized during the Cretaceous. This is the preserve's most widely exposed formation: it outcrops over much of the Kelso Mountains, Cima Dome, and the Ivanpah upland. The coarse sand that permeates the local soil comes largely from erosion of this large-grained quartz monzonite. The other hard rocks exposed in the area's mountains consist mostly of gneiss and granitoids (Early Proterozoic and Jurassic), incomplete sequences of limestone and dolomite formations (Cambrian, Permian, and Devonian), and volcanic and sedimentary rocks (Mesozoic).

The region's most striking geological attractions are fairly recent additions. The large field of cinder cones and lava flows that straddles the Ivanpah upland was formed from 7.6 million years to roughly 10,000 years ago as a result of numerous eruptions that spilled first into Shadow Valley, then toward Soda Lake. The Devils Playground and the Kelso Dunes were built up over the past 25,000 years with sand worn off the San Bernardino Mountains and ferried down the Mojave River. Twice, about 18,000 and 13,700 years ago, the bottom of Kelso Basin was flooded under a pluvial lake, each time for more than

Suggested Hikes in the Kelso Basin					
Route/Destination	Dist. (mi)	Elev. gain	Mean elev.	Access road	Pages
Short hikes (under 5 miles round trip)					
Aiken Cinder Mine	0.3	100'	4,080'	H/7.2 mi	111-114
Brannigan Mine*	4.6	770'	1,990'	H/4.0 mi	105-108
Cima Cinder Mine	0.4	80'	4,130'	P/11.7 mi	114-115
Cowhole Mountain	1.9	1,280'	1,250'	H/8.1 mi	98-100
Death Valley Mine*	1.0	60'	4,410'	P/2.5 mi	139-140
Kelso*	2.0	80'	2,130'	Paved	14-15
Kelso Dunes summit	1.65	600'	2,720'	Graded	121-122
Lava tube	0.25	160'	3,570'	P/4.7 mi	115
Little Cowhole Mtn (north)	1.1	590'	1,360'	H/7.0 mi	94
Little Cowhole Mtn (south)	1.25	690'	1,190'	H/8.8 mi	94-96
Paymaster Mine*	4.3	1,100'	1,960'	H/3.4 mi	104-108
South Teutonia Peak	2.3	970'	5,320'	Paved	132-134
Teutonia Peak	2.0	900'	5,300'	Paved	132-134
Teutonia Peak Trail	1.9	720'	5,300'	Paved	131-132
Twin Cone*	2.6	500'	2,930'	P/0.3 mi	116
Zzyzx (Soda Springs Trail)*	0.9	10'	935'	Paved	90
Intermediate hikes (5-12 miles round trip)					
Devils Plygrd's north dune	3.3	720'	1,620'	H/8.8 mi	128-130
Kelso Dunes–Cottonwd W.*	9.7	1,510'	2,500'	Graded	124
Marl Mtns (Old Gov't Rd)*	7.2	950'	3,930'	H/8.3 mi	440
Mount Hephestus	3.6	1,030'	3,140'	P/0.3 mi	116-118
Old Dad Mtn (both loops)*	8.9	1,870'	1,970'	H/3.4 mi	103-108
Soda Lake crossing	3.0	~20'	935'	Paved	92
Soda Lake loop*	9.3	30'	935'	Paved	92
The Granites	2.6	40'	940'	Paved	92
Long hikes (over 12 miles round trip)					
Devils Playground					
Kelso Dunes–Mojave Rd	27.5	3,450'	1,690'	Graded	126-130
Northern field loop	12.6	2,700'	1,490'	H/8.8 mi	128-130

Key: P = Primitive (2WD); H = Primitive (HC); F = Primitive (4WD)
Distance: one way, except for loops (round-trip, marked with *)
Elev. gain: sum of all elevation gains on a round-trip basis & on loops

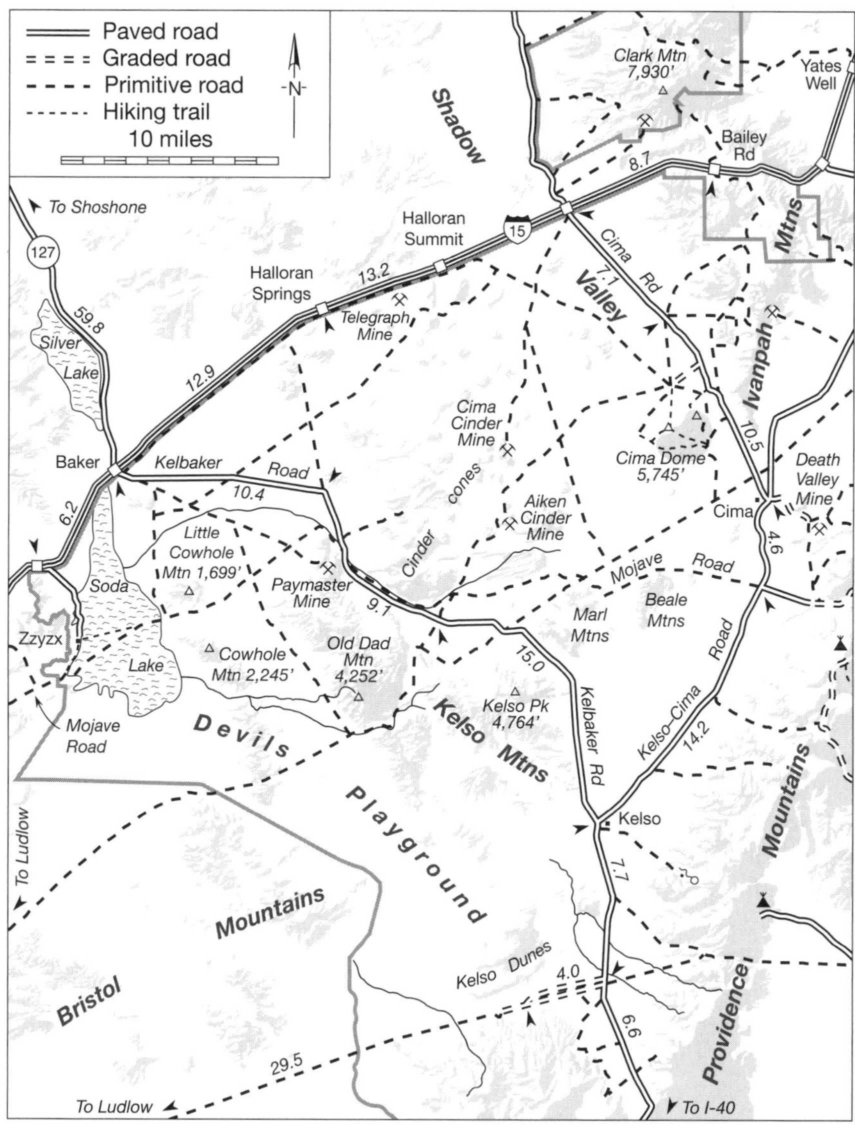

2,000 years. Soda Lake's alkali flat is the accumulation of salts leached from the basin's rocks by rainwater, as well as salts brought in by the Mojave River. Ivanpah Valley is the recipient of a smaller watershed, and it only acquired a mud playa. Shadow Valley also had a playa in the Miocene, but sedimentary and tectonic deposits have filled it up since then. Rainwater now drains into Silurian Valley, farther north and west toward Death Valley.

Mining history

This area witnessed relatively few historic mining ventures, none of which enjoyed great success. Around the turn of the century several gold mines sprang up in the foothills of Old Dad Mountain. The richest properties remained active until the 1950s. Originally the stage of a successful scam, the Death Valley Mine at the very upper rim of Kelso Basin ended up producing about $130,000 in silver between 1906 and the 1950s. From 1907 until the 1910s two foolhardy outfits attempted to extract and process Soda Lake's deposits of sodium salts, going as far as deploying two short railways to harvest the evaporites. The Telegraph Mine near Halloran Springs produced modest amounts of gold and silver from 1932 to 1948. From 1954 until the 1980s–1990s, the huge reserve of cinder on the lava beds was tapped by two commercial outfits at the Aiken and Cima cinder mines. They each tallied substantial productions. From historic and technological perspectives, these few mines happen to be fairly different from most, and they make up in interest what they lack in number.

Hiking

This region is blessed with the preserve's greatest diversity of landforms, including most of the desert's quintessential classics, and as such it is a haven for visitors willing to walk. You can trudge over quasi-endless dune fields, enjoy spectacular views from the summit of isolated mountains, frolic through cactus groves, slog across a salt pan, or poke around abandoned mines and camps. A ubiquitous local attraction is Joshua trees, whose spiny profiles grace large portions of the landscape, from the lava beds east to Ivanpah Valley. The region also holds a number of geological features found in few other desert parks. Where else can you climb so many cinder cones, explore recent lava flows, and view a mountain as symmetrical as Cima Dome? There are many springs and rock climbing sites to check out, and stunning scenery to stumble upon. Rock art is plentiful, although thankfully most sites are undisclosed.

This region has the lowest elevations in the preserve. In the summer, there is no better place to experience the desert's blazing madness. In the spring, this is where the wildflowers come out first and in the greatest numbers. This is the best area to witness the magical transformation these vibrant displays bring to the land. In the late fall and winter, this is also the warmest area to seek refuge from the high desert's biting cold. You might end up spending more time here than anywhere else in the preserve.

▪

ZZYZX

Nestled on the sear edge of Soda Lake, Soda Springs is the only well-watered oasis in hundreds of square miles of parched desert. As such, it played a vital historic role as a military outpost, a resting place for emigrants, and a siding along the famous T & T Railroad, before a radio evangelist transformed it into a health spa called Zzyzx in the 1940s. Walk along the old spa's palm-shaded streets and an artificial lake alive with frogs and coots. A short path leads to derelict salt evaporators and a tiny pond in which survives a rare species of desert fish from the Ice Age. This is a perfect starting point for longer hikes across Soda Lake's dazzling expanses of salt.

General Information

Road status: Hiking on old roads and trails; paved access road
Zzyzx: 0.9 mi, 10 ft up loop / very easy
The Granites: 2.6 mi, 30 ft up, 10 ft down one way / easy
Soda Lake: 9.3 mi, ~30 ft up loop / moderate–difficult
Main attractions: A historic lush oasis, desert fish, salt lake, salt mines
USGS 7.5' topo maps: Soda Lake North*, Soda Lake South
Maps: pp. 91*, *83*

Location and Access

Zzyzx (pronounced "zeye-zix") is on the western edge of Soda Lake, near the preserve's western boundary. It can be accessed by car only from the north. Take the Zzyzx Road exit 6 miles west of Baker on Interstate 15. The Zzyzx Road descends on an alluvial fan to Soda Lake, then snakes lazily along its shore, a fusion of vast alkaline playa and verdant pockets of vegetation. After 4.7 miles the road reaches the Desert Studies Center at Zzyzx. Visitors are welcome but must park in the lot to the right of the gate and proceed on foot. Respect the privacy of the residents, and of the students when in session.

History: From Padre to Radio Evangelist

Because of its rare abundant water and strategic location on the edge of Soda Lake's playa, Soda Springs has long played a key role in human history. The Chemehuevi Indians depended on it on their far-ranging hunting-and-gathering journeys. Here they filled up on water, harvested plants, hunted, cooked, chipped stone tools, and engaged in social and ritualistic activities. The Mohave Indians also used the springs on their trading expeditions to the coast. Fear of the desert kept isolated Soda Springs virtually unnoticed well into the 19th century. Only a few intrepid explorers came by, every few decades. The first known development was Hancock's Redoubt, a wood-and-adobe building the U. S. Army built in 1860 to protect travelers on the Mojave Road against the natives. It was abandoned a few months later, and replaced by a blockhouse and a corral in 1867 when Indian ambushes escalated following increased traffic of gold miners to the new territory of Arizona. After the mail and military routes were moved further south in May 1868, the troops pulled out of Soda Springs for good.

Until around 1882, a succession of keepers occupied what was then known as Soda Lake Station and offered accommodation to the increasing number of ranchers, homesteaders, miners, and emigrants. In 1885 a group of prospectors moved in and renamed it Shenandoah Camp. In October 1887, the station was occupied by Frank and Sarah Riggs, who owned silver claims near Silver Lake. Two years later, they filed a claim on the Hetzel Mill Site, which covered the station and five acres of springs. The Briggs likely did not stay long, nor did they do much milling. By 1900 they had moved closer to their mine. The completion of the Santa Fe Railway in 1883 had drained much of the traffic from the Mojave Road, and Soda Springs was deserted again.

Soda Springs' peace was short-lived. In 1905, Francis Marion Smith, the capitalist who owned the famous borax mines over in Death Valley, was building a railroad to replace his twenty-mule teams. His railroad, the Tonopah and Tidewater, connected Ludlow to Goldfield, Nevada, and it went right by Soda Springs. From 1907 until its last day of operation in June 1940, on average one train puffed through Soda Springs every day. In 1907, two companies with oddly similar names—the Pacific Salt and Soda Company and the Pacific Coast Soda Company—took advantage of the new railroad and set out facilities to extract and refine sodium salts from the lake bed. Each party installed evaporation ponds, driers, cabins, and a narrow-gauge railway to access the playa's fields of evaporites. But neither was successful. The Pacific Salt and Soda Company may have operated for less than two years. The Pacific Coast Soda Company reported a small production in 1908. By 1918, and likely earlier, both had vacated the area.

The man who had the most profound impact on Soda Springs was Curtis Howe Springer. A Methodist minister, self-proclaimed medical doctor and salesman of health products, Springer had been a radio evangelist since 1928, advertising his products on the air, as well as in public lectures in Los Angeles. Kind, charismatic, and an accomplished public speaker, he was remarkably successful. In September 1944, he

Lake Tuendae at Zzyzx

and his wife Helen moved to Soda Springs with plans to turn the site into a health resort. The extreme temperatures and lack of infrastructure did not make it ideal for a resort, but it had ample mineralized water, and its isolated desert location added appealing mystery.

Springer was a visionary man, resourceful and driven by a strong motivation to dispense happiness. To build his resort, he used war-surplus materials and recruited men on unemployment or from missions in Los Angeles, to give them another chance in life. Over the next 10 years, his crews erected a cozy compound that housed a kitchen, a dining hall, offices, a church, and a 10-room motel known as Sunrise. An existing pond was reshaped into a scenic lake decorated with a stone fountain. Dr. Springer called his resort Zzyzx, an enigmatic name he coined so that it would become the last word in the English language.

Zzyzx Mineral Springs and Health Resort was a triumph. It could accommodate about 100 guests, and it was often full. Guests enjoyed rest and relaxation, fresh air, sunshine, health-food diets, alternative health treatments, and mud and mineral baths. Years ahead of modern spas, Springer provided holistic healing rather than only body repair, and his approach worked for many. The Springers made comfortable benefits. They were also generous, and admitted those in financial need free of charge. From Zzyzx, Springer continued to broadcast throughout the U. S. and many countries, spreading the word about his oasis and delivering messages of hope. His business boosted the local economy. Guests frequently stayed in Baker while waiting their turn to get into the resort. The small town even had to acquire a large post office to handle Springer's volumes of health-food mail orders.

Every paradise has its serpents. Springer's was the government. In the late 1960s, more than 60 charges were gradually brought against him by multiple agencies. He was accused of tax evasion, false advertising, and selling health products of questionable value. Most of these charges were technicalities, and they were all dropped, even tax evasion. But the Springers most ruthless adversary, the BLM, did not let go. The agency built a case that the Springers were misusing mining claims and trespassing, even though all these years the Springers had frequently appraised the BLM of developments at Zzyzx. In 1968 the BLM took legal action, and won. On April 11, 1974, the Springers were bodily evicted from their residence of 30 years. Dr. Springer was 77.

Curtis Springer lived in a bubble, and he did make a few mistakes, as he admitted. But they stemmed from ignorance and inattention, not malice. It would have been honorable to let the Springers continue their business until they passed on. Dr. Springer died in Las Vegas 11 years later, without seeing Zzyzx again.

Not that the BLM had urgent plans for Zzyzx, which fell prey to vandals. While the agency was rooting for demolition, special-interest groups endeavored to convert Zzyzx into a hub for recreational activities or a youth hostel. In 1976, its custody was given to the California State University, which established a teaching and research facility. The Desert Studies Center is still today Zzyzx's much-needed guardian. Every year, a few thousand students come here on field trips to learn about the desert and enjoy the rustic accommodations. Unlike guests of the past, they are no longer greeted by Dr. Springer waving from his Cadillac convertible. But Zzyzx lives on, in the spirit of Springer's dream, as a provider of self-improvement.

Route Description

Zzyzx. Just past the gate, turn left on Boulevard of Dreams, and go 125 yards to Lake Tuendae—the 1.4-acre reservoir created by Springer to embellish his oasis, and Zzyzx's crown jewel. The contrast between the lake's lush environment and the harsh surrounding desert is stunning. Cattail line its shores, and an elegant row of California fan palms tower around it, reflected with perfect symmetry in its smooth surface. The stone fountain still parades in the middle of the lake. A whole fauna lives literally rooted to Lake Tuendae, a tiny life capsule stranded in an inhospitable world. The colorful dragonflies darting about are locals, born from larvae that inhabit the lake. So are the American

Evaporation ponds of the Pacific Coast Soda Company on Soda Lake

coots that drift across the lake and dive to feed on pondweed; the Pacific tree frogs that breed in the lake; and the marsh wren that nest in the vegetation. The lake is also vital for bobcat, bighorn sheep, coyote, and gray fox, which visit to quench their thirst. Migratory birds like the great blue heron also stop here to rest.

The open area just north of Lake Tuendae was the site of the Pacific Salt and Soda Company operations. In 1908 there was a wooden cabin and a canvas tent, a water tank, and scattered equipment. Today all that has survived is the evaporation ponds, salt-saturated railroad ties, low foundations, and remnants of the sluice gates that regulated flooding of the ponds. The compartmented ponds extend 350 yards onto the playa. Their straight ridges of salt-covered mud are surprisingly well preserved, as are the traces of the company's short, 36-inch-gauge rail.

The quaint buildings at the foot of the limestone hill south of Lake Tuendae were the inner sanctum of Dr. Springer's empire. Painted a pale beige highlighted by brown trims, decorated with stone walls and shady arcades, they are reminiscent of southern California's architectural style of the 1940s. The Castle and Zycott are the buildings where guests were fed, housed, and entertained. The Pool House is at the end of the Boulevard of Dreams. The long building just south of it, facing Soda Lake, was Sunrise. Shaded by large palms, sprinkled with benches and picnic tables, this timeless hamlet is an idyllic spot to soak in the peacefulness of a desert oasis.

Soda Springs Trail. At the south end of the Sunrise Building the road turns into a trail. Only 0.25 mile long, it wanders along the strip of flat land between the limestone hill and Soda Lake, right along the lake's open shoreline. The ground is covered with halophytes, plants that thrive in salt-saturated soils. A prime example is salt grass, the ubiquitous cover of short forked blades: its relatives live in similar soils all over the world, from the Galapagos Islands to East Africa. The compact, scraggly trees laden with mistletoe are honey mesquite.

The highlight of this trail is the small artesian spring it passes by near its midpoint. Called Mojave Chub Spring, it consists of two tiny pools rimmed with cattail. It hosts the rare and endangered Mojave tui chub, a fish that lived in large numbers in Lake Mohave during the Ice Age. The lake was then surrounded by extensive marshlands inhabited by birds and mammals such as camels and mastodons. As the Ice Age drew to a close, the lake slowly dried up, forcing the last survivors to seek refuge in isolated water holes. Related to Death Valley's famous below-sea-level pupfish, the Mojave tui chub was originally found only in the Mojave River, where it had hybridized with the coastal chub. The pure breed was thought to be extinct until the 1950s, when the ultimate remaining population was discovered in this very spring. To reduce its risk of extinction, it has been introduced in new habitats, including Lake Tuendae. Approach the pool slowly, and you will see the chubs floating below the surface. The larger individuals, as long as four inches, may dash into hiding, but they don't take long to reappear. They are hanging on for dear life; do not pester them.

After 0.2 mile, the trail reaches the south end of the hill. On the playa just east of it are the remains of the Pacific Coast Soda Company's evaporative ponds. The narrow-gauge track that the company constructed in 1907 was the region's shortest: it extended onto the playa less than a mile! The long ramp of salt just south of the ponds was the rail's dock. The railroad grade is still visible, aligned beyond it. With binoculars one can make out the first ties a few hundred yards out. They were no more than skinny logs plopped on the playa. If you walk out there to check them out, stay clear of the rail and the ponds' ridges to avoid damaging these historic structures.

At the south end of the hill the trail angles right and reaches a few concrete foundations and pads supported by retaining walls. We do not know whether this was the Riggs' 1889 Hetzel Mill Site, or part of the Pacific Coast Soda Company's plant. Perhaps it was used by both.

Soda Springs Trail ends 400 feet west of the mill ruins, at a wide north-south road. This is the abandoned bed of the T & T Railroad. Turn right (north) to return to Zzyzx.

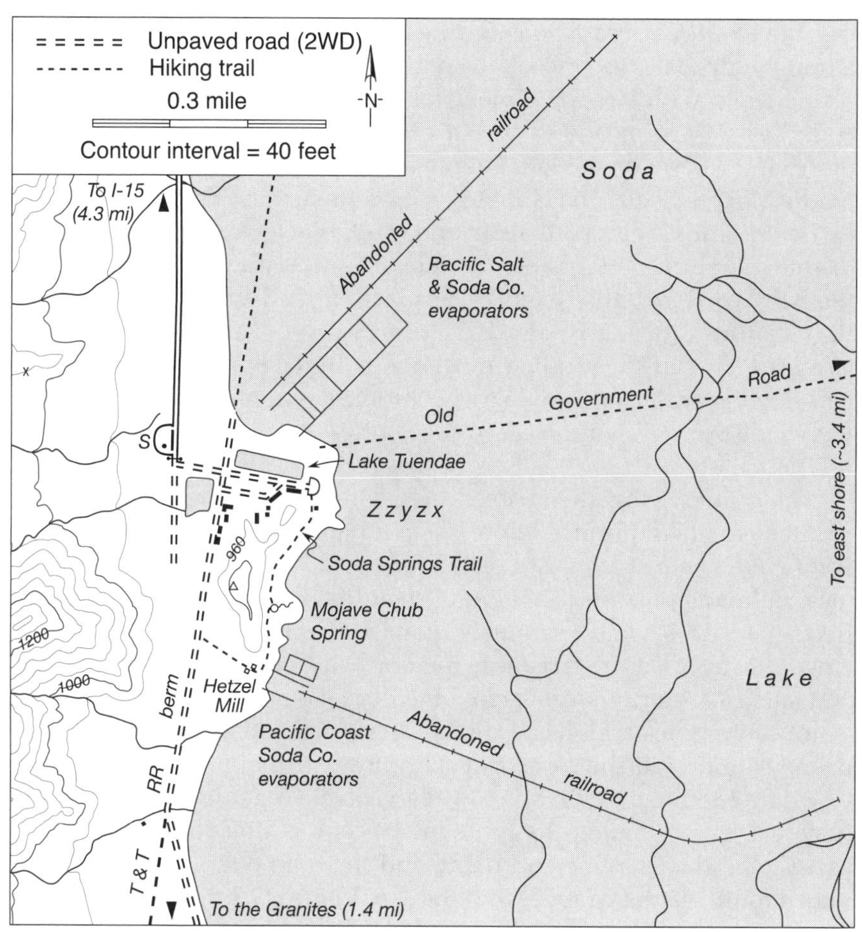

Zzyzx		
	Dist.(mi)	Elev.(ft)
Parking area	0.0	940
Lake Tuendae	0.1	935
Pacific Salt & Soda Co. ponds	(0.1)	932
Lake's east side (Old Gov't Rd)	(2.9)	~940
Pool House	0.25	935
Soda Springs Trail	0.3	935
Mojave Chub Spring	0.4	935
Pacific Coast Soda Co. ponds	0.45	932
End of Soda Spr. Trail/Road	0.6	940
The Granites (Bitter Spring)	(1.9)	945

The Granites. From Soda Springs Trail, the T & T berm cuts south along the dry lake to a desolate spot known as the Granites. This is a scenic walk, with sweeping views of the barren Soda Mountains and Soda Lake's vast meadows of salt grass. After 0.25 mile a road splits off from the berm on the left. Follow it 1.3 miles to a split, and turn left on the Mojave Road. The Granites is 0.4 mile further. Frequently swept by fierce winds laden with alkali and sand, this low granitic outcrop is disintegrating into misshapen boulders. Lost at the stark terminus of the Mojave River, this is an eerie place, in full view of the Devils Playground's ocean of sand. Two mesquite clumps grow at the Granites. The larger, southernmost one is Bitter Spring. In the past it had flowing water, and some early chroniclers might have confused it with Soda Springs, which casts uncertainties on the local history.

Soda Lake. Together with dunes, salt flats are the desert's most quintessential landforms. Zzyzx is a good jumping-off place to explore Soda Lake's purest expanses of salt. Please do not use the salt companies' railroads as paths. These important historic remains are extremely fragile, and it would seriously damage them. Instead, hike the Old Government Road. It starts near the northeast corner of Lake Tuendae and cuts 14.5° north of east across the dry lake near its widest point. It is not continuous, and illegal tracks can be distracting. Where it disappears, continue in the same direction, toward the wide gap north of Cowhole Mountain. Zyzzx is always visible, so getting lost is not an easy feat. After 3 miles, the route intersects the Mojave Road near the east shore. This is a fine end point, and the road offers a well-defined return route via the Granites and the T & T berm (9.3-mile loop).

Crossing the lake is muddy, slushy, tedious business. It is so messy you may not even make it through. But this hike throws you instantly into a different world, alien and raw yet strangely attractive. The landscape vibrates with the surreal light reflected by the salt pan. Across the lake rise the jagged ridges of Cowhole and Little Cowhole mountains, set off against the imposing Providence Mountains beyond. The land is extraordinarily flat, covered with crystals and geometric stress patterns, and crisscrossed by meandering rivers—all of it made of salt. Miles out you might see coyote tracks or driftwood that rafted on floodwaters and was slowly shredded by the corrosive power of salt. Specular reflections off the playa will often trick your brain into thinking there is water out there, when most of the time the surface is bone dry. The trick is reversed in the winter, and you will doubt your sight when you spot a blue pond in the middle of this extreme desolation.

■

LITTLE COWHOLE MOUNTAIN

Little Cowhole Mountain is an unusual mountain to climb—most of its short ascent takes place on a sand dune. This fun mountain will appeal to hikers new to desert mountaineering, who may find it less inhibiting and easier testing ground than full-size mountains, and to anyone looking for one last quick climb before the long drive back home. Made of Paleozoic dolomite deeply corrugated by sandblasting, the windy summit offers good views of the Mojave River Sink and its ring of distant mountains.

General Information
Road status: Hiking on old road and cross-country; HC access road
Little Cowhole Mtn (north): 1.1 mi, 590 ft up, 0 ft down one way / easy
Little Cowhole Mtn (south): 1.25 mi, 690 ft, up 0 ft down one way / easy
Main attractions: A scenic climb on a dune, views of Mojave River Sink
USGS 7.5' topo maps: Soda Lake North*, Seventeenmile Point
Maps: pp. 95*, *83*

Location and Access

Little Cowhole Mountain is about 7 miles as the crow flies south-southeast of Baker. From Interstate 15's northbound exit at Kelbaker Road in Baker, drive the paved Kelbaker Road 0.9 mile east-southeast to a left bend. Two primitive roads branch off on the right. Take the first one (south-southwest). After 1.5 miles, turn left at a Y junction between two small hills. In 0.1 mile the road reaches the northwest corner of the former Baker dump (fenced). Turn left, follow the enclosure 0.2 mile to its northeast corner, and make a right. After 0.25 mile, at the southeast corner, turn left (east-southeast). In 1.15 miles the road veers right (south) and merges with a smaller road coming in from the left. Continue south 1.9 miles to a road on the left. To climb the mountain from the north, take this road and park after approximately 1.9 miles. Little Cowhole Mountain's summit is the narrow dome 1 mile south.

To climb the mountain from the south, at the last junction continue straight (south) instead of turning left. This portion of the drive is shown on the accompanying map. The road passes between Soda Lake and Little Cowhole Mountain, then crosses a short, normally dry stretch of Soda Lake (do not attempt crossing it when wet). Stay on the tracks closest to the mountain; a metal post indicates where the road resumes on normal ground. After 2.6 miles the road angles left at the southwest corner of the mountain and reaches a wide road crossing. The road on the left (northeast) goes to the large concrete foundations of the Green Rock Mill visible up ahead. Take the second road from the left (east-northeast) instead. After 1 mile it merges with the Mojave Road. Continue east 125 yards to a three-way split, and park. The high point of Little Cowhole Mountain is visible to the north. The smaller, leftmost road can get you a little closer, but it is a bit rough, and walking it is just as easy. The roads to either starting point are level and generally smooth, but a few short lopsided sections will stop some standard-clearance vehicles. A high-clearance vehicle makes it easier.

If you are coming from the direction of Kelso, follow the directions to Cowhole Mountain. After driving the Mojave Road 6.9 miles to the fainter road on the left where you would turn left to climb Cowhole Mountain, continue straight 1.1 miles to the three-way split and park. This itinerary has some deep sand and requires high clearance.

Route Description

On the north side the climb starts on the smooth fan that smothers the mountain. The fan is usually dominated by a monoculture of scattered creosote, as preened as a manmade garden. After the first heavy rains in the fall and winter, the sandy ground becomes for a short time a green lawn of young shoots. At the top of the fan it is easy to navigate among the low open hills to the saddle north of the summit. From there it is a short scramble over a rocky slope to the summit. The local rocks are all light-grey dolomite from the Cambrian–Ordovician era. Sand and salt particles blown in by the often strong local winds have blasted and chemically etched into them intricate markings of rills and points, as sharp as steel needles. Every single exposed surface has a unique texture and pattern, as beautiful as it is dangerously abrasive.

The climb from the south side is more interesting, and it offers better views on the way up. From the three-way split, walk up the leftmost road (north-northeast) toward the deep bay that cuts into the mountain. Most of the tall dune that covers the steep slope up ahead has been colonized by a tight cover of blond grasses. To avoid damaging this fragile vegetation working hard at stabilizing the dune, do not climb on that part of the dune. Instead, go 0.65 mile up the road, then leave it and head northwest across a shallow wash to the closest (southernmost) end of the dune, which has no grass. Climb east to the top of the dune—the only steep part of the climb. From there head north across the grass-free top of the dune to just below the shallow saddle south of the summit. The dune is covered with an interesting assortment of plants, from isolated cholla to beavertail cactus and

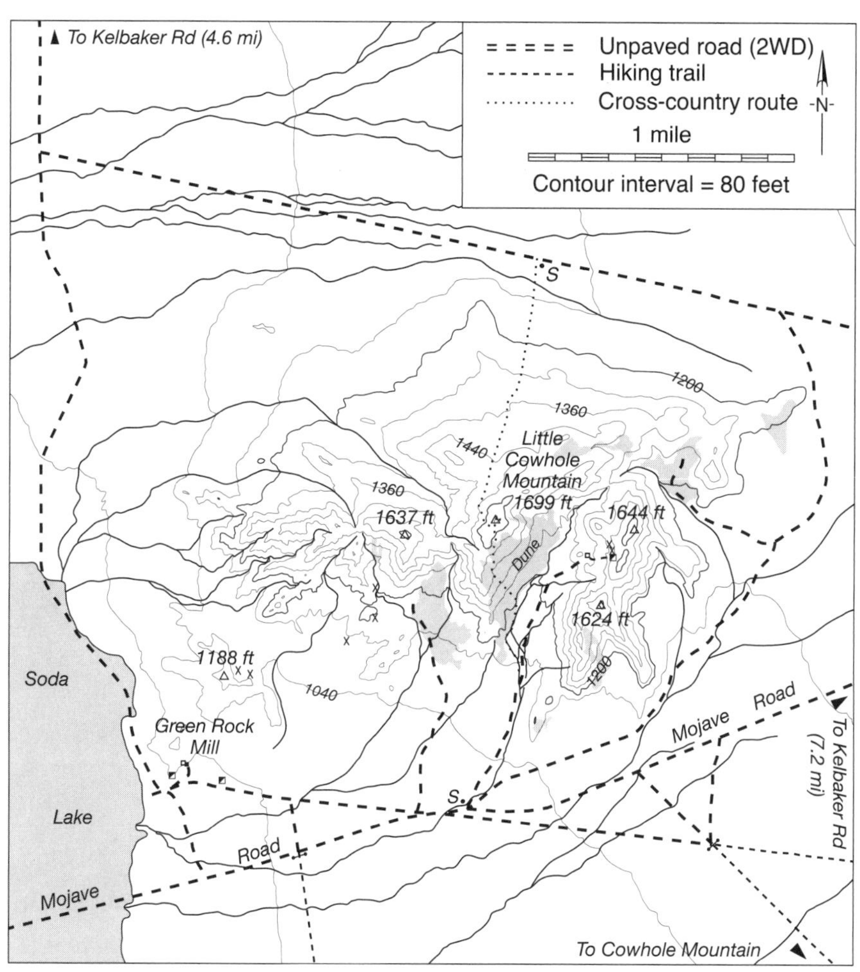

Little Cowhole Mountain		
	Dist.(mi)	Elev.(ft)
North-side climb		
Road	0.0	1,105
Little Cowhole Mountain	1.1	1,699
South-side climb		
Mojave Road	0.0	1,015
Leave mining road	0.65	1,100
Upper end of sand dune	1.15	1,575
Little Cowhole Mountain	1.25	1,699

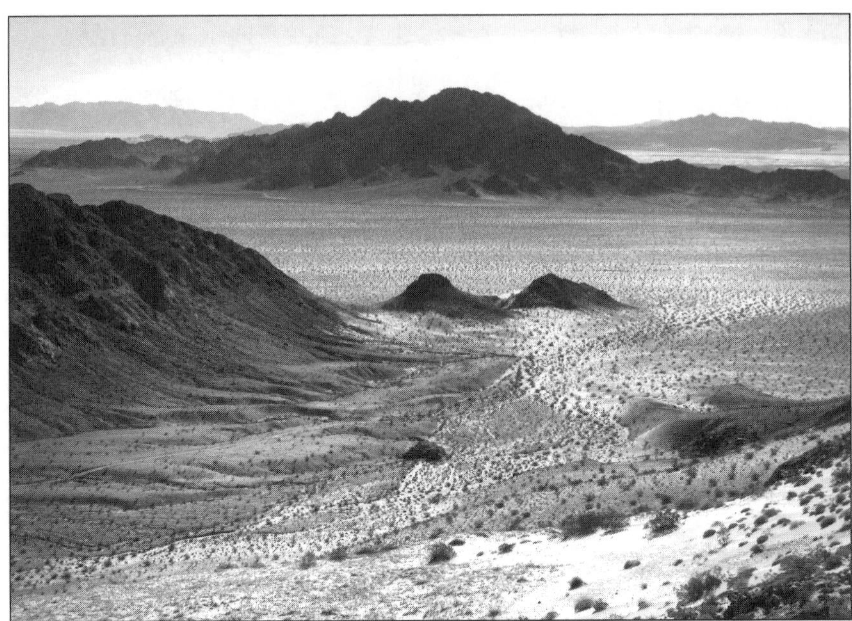

View south down the sandy slope below the top of Little Cowhole Mountain

birdcage evening primrose. In the colder season, the primrose's barren crown of white stems curl inward like an arthritic hand. In the spring, they transform themselves beyond recognition and decorate the parched sand with thousands of oversized white flowers. The last 0.1 mile from the top of the dune to the saddle, then from there to the summit, is over broken bedrock. The summit is easiest reached by contouring it on the east side.

Thanks to its central location, the small rocky summit of Little Cowhole Mountain commands sweeping vistas of the vast Mojave River Sink, encompassing the briny salt flats of Soda Lake, the austere Soda Mountains, Turquoise Mountain, the rough scarp of Old Dad Mountain, and the sprawling sawtooth crest of the Bristol Mountains. If you cannot make Cowhole Mountain, this is a worthy second prize.

Being circumvented by primitive roads, Little Cowhole Mountain can be readily climbed from many other directions, and a variety of loop hikes can be conceived to climb it one way and return another. The summit west of the high point, for example, has even better, unobstructed views of Soda Lake. The summit east of the high point is more rugged and challenging.

■

COWHOLE MOUNTAIN

Isolated on the far-flung eastern shore of Soda Lake, Cowhole Mountain is a beautiful accretion of desolate desert peaks. Climbing its abrupt summit is hard work, along an insanely steep gully, but I cannot praise this breathtaking ascent enough. The physical effort is exhilarating, the variety of rocks and fossils impressive, and the views from the summit rank among the most otherworldly in the preserve. On a clear day, this is a perfect place for a wild winter workout.

General Information
Road status: Roadless; sandy high-clearance access road
Cowhole Mountain: 1.9 mi, 1,230 ft up, 50 ft down one way / difficult
Main attractions: A scenic peak climb, awesome views, geology
USGS 7.5' topo maps: Seventeenmile Point*, Cowhole Mountain
Maps: pp. 99*, *83*

Location and Access

Cowhole Mountain is the isolated pointed eminence that rises from Soda Lake's low eastern floodplain. It can be reached by a short hike from a side road along the Mojave Road. Take the Kelbaker Road east 12.1 miles from the northbound exit on Interstate 15 (or 10.9 miles from the Edison Company power line) to a primitive road on the west side. Drive this road 0.8 mile until it merges with the Mojave Road. Follow the latter 4.2 miles to a four-way junction (this stretch is sandy and requires good clearance), then straight 2.7 miles to a fainter road on the left. The rugged mountain to the south is Cowhole Mountain. The lower, sand-covered hill to the north is Little Cowhole Mountain. Turn left and park after 0.4 mile at a five-road junction (the road straight ahead is blocked off by a wilderness boundary sign).

If you are coming from Baker, there is an alternative route that is shorter and also less sandy and less troublesome for standard-clearance vehicles (although it should still be undertaken with care). From the interstate's northbound exit, drive the Kelbaker Road 3.9 miles to a primitive road on the right (look for it carefully). Follow it 1.3 miles to a crossroad and make a left. Go 2.4 miles to a Y junction and make a right. After 2.9 miles, you will reach the Mojave Road at the four-way junction mentioned earlier. Make a right, and the rest of the route is the same.

The lunar landscape looking southeast from Cowhole Mountain

Route Description

Of the many possible routes up Cowhole Mountain, the one suggested here is the shortest and most straightforward. From the wilderness boundary head cross-country due south down the gently sloped creosote plain, aiming for the deep cove at the base of the mountain directly below the summit. After 0.9 mile you will cross a large wash coming down from the east, then start climbing into the cove. Just inside the cove the wash splits; take the wash on the right. About 0.1 mile further, it forks again; take the left fork, toward a dark dike transverse to the wash 0.2 mile away. (Better yet, follow the low bench that parallels the main wash on its east side (see map); it offers easier footing and ends at the dike). Just after the wash crosses the dike, it splits again. Keep left and stay in this steep and fairly straight rock-strewn gully until it emerges on the crest at a V notch just east of the summit block. The rest of the way (~0.1 mile) is along a course just south of the crest, mostly across limestone slickrock.

Considering its modest size, Cowhole Mountain certainly holds its own. The total elevation gain is only about 1,200 feet, but most of it occurs in 0.4 mile up the gully, over terrain progressively steeper and rougher. Starting as a narrow field of sturdy boulders, the gully soon runs into a few falls, then the slope becomes so steep that gravity has

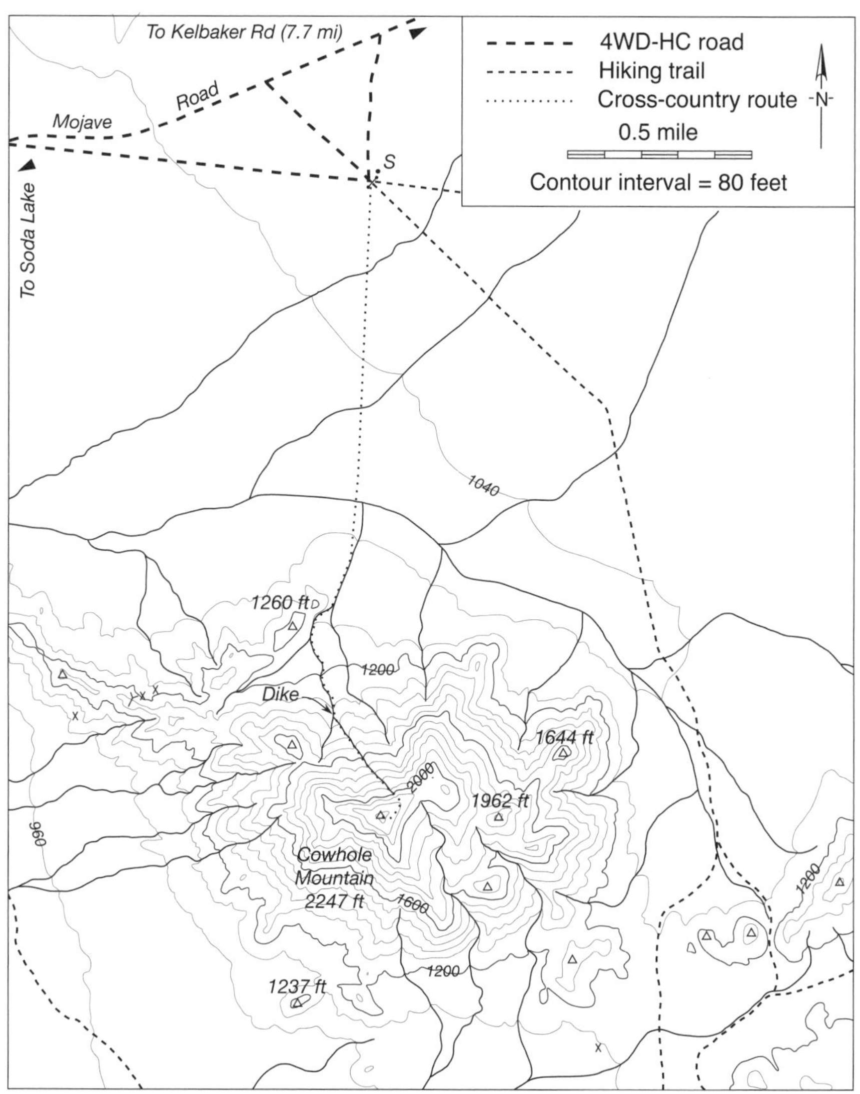

Cowhole Mountain

	Dist.(mi)	Elev.(ft)
End of road / wilderness bdry	0.0	1,066
Major wash crossing	0.9	1,020
Dike crossing	1.5	1,300
Ridge	1.8	2,150
Cowhole Mountain	1.9	2,247

stripped off all large boulders, leaving behind a slippery river of loose cobbles tipped at a reckless 50° angle. It is a grind, but at least it is short and plants are scarce. Even climbing part way has its rewards: the abrupt slope commands sweeping views of Soda Lake and Little Cowhole Mountain, draped in long skirts of virgin sand.

One of the perks of this hike is the remarkable variety of rocks. The wind-swept sandy plain leading to the mountain is sprinkled with beautifully gnarled ventifacts, as well as black and red chunks of vesiculated lava flushed all the way down here from the cinder cones area. In the spring, the open spaces between them can be filled with dandelions in bloom. Up on the mountain, at least seven formations outcrop on the north face alone. The dikes at lower elevations are beige-gray felsite thickly coated with auburn desert varnish. The profusion of crags on the lower half are pinkish quartz monzonite (Granitoid Rocks of Cowhole Mountain). They are topped by thin-bedded shale, siltstone, and limestone (Carrara Formation), and above this by mostly dark dolomites (Bonanza King and Nopah formations to possibly Ely Springs Dolomite). The thick tilted limestone beds forming the summit block belong to yet another one, the Bird Spring Formation. Most of the boulders in the gully are made of this distinctive light-gray limestone. Wind-blasted to a skin-shredding finish, they provide good anchors to hang on for dear life as you scramble up. They are covered with fossils, especially corals and primitive amebas called fusulinids. The several species of fusulinids found here are particularly important: they have helped geologists reconstruct the evolution of the inland sea that sliced across the Americas in the Permian, at a time the equator passed close to Cowhole Mountain. There is an excellent exposure at the crest about 10 yards west of the gully's upper end—dark-gray grains of rice swimming across a tilted face of limestone.

The geology, the workout, and the setting all add up to a great climb, but it is the views that make it exceptional. When I crested the ridge and first stared down at the southern portion of Cowhole Mountain, my jaw dropped. Down below, clinging to the foreground like a nightmarish vision, a stark range of jagged peaks and ridges jutted sharply above a desert floor swirling with bleak shades of browns, grays, and reds. Beyond it, the Devils Playground stretched for tens of empty miles, past the deeply furrowed slopes of Old Dad Mountain to the ghostly Kelso Dunes outlined against the Granite Mountains. I gazed a long time at this forsaken moonscape, mesmerized by its primordial attraction. Even after I left and headed back down, the summit's edges were so precipitous that I was still floating above it.

■

OLD DAD MOUNTAIN

Early in the 20th century, before asphalt highways and fast-food joints, many gold mines boomed in the remote northern reaches of Old Dad Mountain. They have been mostly idle ever since, their access roads have slowly disintegrated, and it has been decades since they could be reached by car. But desert rats will enjoy searching the timeless desert hills, up and down twisted canyons and vanishing segments of mining trails, for these once proud properties, and for the convoluted loop that connects them all.

General Information
Road status: Mostly roadless; high-clearance access roads
Paymaster Mine: 4.3 mi, 1,110 ft up loop / easy–moderate
Brannigan Mine: 4.6 mi, 770 ft up loop / easy
Main attractions: Historic gold mines and camps, scenic desert hills
USGS 7.5′ topo map: Seventeenmile Point
Maps: pp. 107*, *83*

Location and Access

Old Dad Mountain's historic gold properties are widely disseminated up and down the mountain, but the three main mines—the Paymaster, Oro Fino, and Brannigan—are clustered in a small area near the mountain's northern tip. All three are misplaced on the USGS 7.5′ map, so refer to this section's map for their actual locations. To get to this general area, drive the Kelbaker Road 12.1 miles east from the northbound exit on Interstate 15 (or 10.9 miles west from the Edison Company power line) to a primitive road on the west side. Drive this road 0.8 mile until it merges with the Mojave Road coming in from the left. Continue 1.8 miles southwest to a crossroad and turn left on the Brannigan Mine Road. From this junction, it is 0.8 mile to a first junction (the road on the left is the Paymaster Mine Road), and 1.4 miles to a second junction. The main road, straight, is the Oro Fino Mine Road. The fainter road on the right has been cherry-stemmed out of a wilderness area, so make sure to keep your vehicle on it. After 0.55 mile it reaches the edge of a wide floodplain and continues left up a wash as a rougher track, skirting the base of a low ridge. In another 0.65 mile it passes by the mouth of a broad canyon on the left. A road once climbed into it to the Brannigan Mine, but there is no longer a trace of this junction. The canyon is inside the wilderness area, so park here to hike to this mine. The road continues 1.5 miles south across the floodplain and ends at the Big Horn Mine.

To hike to the Paymaster Mine, make a left at the first junction. The Paymaster Mine Road drops into a wash, climbs into a narrow canyon, and after 0.9 mile angles sharply right and climbs out of the wash. It is washed out soon after, so park just before the bend and continue on foot. To hike to the Oro Fino Mine, at the second junction go straight on the Oro Fino Mine Road, and park after 0.6 mile at a gate. To hike the Paymaster Mine loop or both loops, start from the first junction. To hike the Brannigan Mine loop, start from the second junction.

If you are driving a standard-clearance vehicle, you may have difficulty on the Mojave Road, which has deep sand. If you make it, you should have no problem to the second junction. You will be able to drive some distance on the side roads, but maybe not all the way.

History: Gold-Mining Spree

Most of the Old Dad Mountain's gold occurred in veins that pinched and swelled along widely spaced fractures: there was gold all over, but nowhere very much of it. Over time, no fewer than 18 gold mines were developed over an area of only 2.5 square miles, one of the highest concentrations in the eastern Mojave Desert. Gold was first discovered in the 1890s at the Oro Fino Mine, around 1900 at the Paymaster Mine, then in 1905 at the Brannigan Mine. Jointly, these mines might have made a few hundred thousand dollars, but the gold was so dispersed that none was a frank success. This situation might have been recognized early on, because mining was slow to start. The earliest recorded production at the Oro Fino Mine, 20,500 ounces of silver worth close to $10,000, was not until 1902. At the Paymaster Mine, most of the work was done between 1910 and 1914, when an adit with 1,700 feet of galleries was blasted and between $50,000 and $100,000 was said to have been produced. The gold was recovered by amalgamation at a 10-stamp mill, perhaps the mill that was operating in 1911, using water piped from Indian Spring, at nearby Seventeenmile Point. In 1909, the Brannigan Mine was being developed in conjunction with other local claims by the Precious Metals Development Company of Los Angeles—the combined claims were later known as the Whitney Mine—but it shut down in the 1920s before producing much.

Everything changed in March 1930, when two miners, M. A. Sisley and John Herrod, relocated the Brannigan claims and uncovered high-grade ore. Their initial shipment brought back a meager $2,000 after milling, but their discovery touched off a lasting revival. The old mines were re-opened and new claims were staked. The Oro Fino Mine

Camp at the La Paloma Mine

shipped off and on until 1948, reportedly producing about $50,000 in gold. From 1932 to 1944, the Paymaster Mine was operated by several owners but it produced almost every year, yielding around $11,000. Sisley and Herrod continued running the Brannigan Mine until 1935. They shipped several thousand tons, sometimes as rich as $110 per ton.

These figures illustrate once again the hardships of most historic desert gold mines. The veins were neither large nor rich enough for viable sustained production using small-scale techniques. In their waning years, each property brought in no more than $2,000 annually. The hard work, high cost of labor, low gold prices, and isolation eventually broke the spirit of the most resolute miners. By the 1950s, most activities had ceased. In the end the Old Dad Mountain was not nearly as lucky as the Old Woman Mountains, which yielded a 6,070-pound iron meteorite worth far more than all of Old Dad's gold…

Route Description

Visiting this collection of mines can be done one area at a time, by driving to the end of a road and taking short hikes from there. The most satisfying approach is to hike one of the two loops suggested below—or better still, both. The Paymaster Mine loop (4.3 miles, 1,100 feet up) winds through the Helenback, Paymaster, and Oro Fino mines. The Brannigan Mine loop (4.6 miles, 770 feet up) explores the Brannigan Mine and the canyon north of it. The following description of these loops will help inspire shorter circuits as well.

The Paymaster Mine loop. From the first junction, keep a course about 20° east of north for 250 yards, and you should run across an old road. If you miss it, try catching it by making a wide curve to the east and north. The road gradually curves east, then southeast into a short canyon. The two tunnels, large ore bin, and tramway ruins of the Helenback Mine are just inside it. Beyond, the road deteriorates as it climbs alongside the steepening canyon wash to a high road, in much better shape, that circles across the head of the canyon.

At the high road, hike cross-country over the ridge straight ahead and down its far side to a mining road, high on the slope of a larger canyon. The two large tailings visible across the canyon mark the Paymaster Mine's main adit. To the left, this road ends at prospects that also belonged to the Helenback Mine. To the right, it drops to the Paymaster Mine Road, in the canyon wash. Follow this road up canyon 0.1 mile to where it curves sharply right and climbs out of the wash. It ends in 0.2 mile at a wide apron on top of the tailings. The portal there is the Paymaster No. 3, the adit from the 1910–1914 era.

To continue, look for the trail that takes off from the apron, on the north side of the adit. It is a couple of feet wide, lined with rocks, and partially concealed by creosote bush. It climbs steeply to a ridge, crosses it, goes on to a saddle, crosses it, then passes by another tunnel as it slices southeast across the head of a drainage up to a plateau (~0.25 mile). Except for one steep section, this trail is in decent shape and hard to lose. At the plateau it runs into a road, which passes by several shafts, all part of the Paymaster Mine.

The Oro Fino Mine is located in the drainage to the south. Work your way on the network of roads that crisscross the plateau to the sharp elbow in the southeasternmost road. The northern roads are more interesting, especially around the Gold Cycle Mine and Sunrise Mine. From the elbow, cut cross-country southwest into two shallow drainages, then over a low ridge into a larger canyon. It is then a short hike down a steep, rock-strewn ravine to the Oro Fino Mine's main shafts. The upper end of the Oro Fino Mine Road starts just below the uppermost shaft. It leads in 0.3 mile down to the fairly recent camp of the La Paloma Mine. To complete the loop, follow the road 0.9 mile down to the Brannigan Mine Road at the second junction. It is then 0.6 mile northeast on this road back to your starting point.

Soda Lake Valley from the trail to the Brannigan Mine

The Brannigan Mine loop. Although wilder, this route is much more straightforward. From the second junction take the fainter left fork 1.2 miles to the mouth of the canyon where the Brannigan Mine is located (see earlier description). Hike into the canyon, which is wide open at this point. Stay left where the wash forks 0.1 mile in. Soon after, you will pick up the mine's old road up on the right bank, then you will come to a large dugout. The road is washed out shortly after. About 300 yards up canyon, the wash scoots by a short cliff. The road resumes in the steep, straight, and narrow ravine that climbs at an angle on the right past the cliff. At the ravine's upper end the road tops a ledge, then continues along the side of the canyon to a junction. The left fork drops to a series of shafts dug one above the other in a steep hillside, all part of the Brannigan Mine. The main fork climbs on to a pass, then winds down the far side to end at the Brannigan Mine's lowest tunnel.

To complete the loop, drop into the wash below the lowest tunnel, and follow it downhill along a little canyon. The stony braided wash winds past tall hills sprinkled with chocolate outcrops. This is not the most exciting canyon, but it does have a variety of pretty rocks, including mica schists, and a narrow passage punctuated with easy falls scooped out of white marble. The long vines of coyote melon like to hang around the cooler plunge pools below the falls. In the spring brittlebush bloom all over. After 1.2 miles you will reach the wide mouth of the canyon. You may pick up, shortly after on the open fan, an abandoned track that connects to the Brannigan Mine Road (0.4 mile). Otherwise aim toward Baker's white water tower in the far distance until you reach this road. It is then 0.2 mile north on the Brannigan Mine Road back to your starting point.

The mines. Although it was the mines that first drew me here, the area's many natural attractions quickly competed for my interest. This rarely-visited little mountain is a beautiful region of twisted gulches and canyons separated by crinkled slopes and rocky ridges, all of it bathed in perennial silence. The vegetation is particularly desert-like, a veneer of solitary creosote bush and low shrubs growing out of rocky

The gold mines of Old Dad Mountain

	Dist.(mi)	Elev.(ft)
The Paymaster Mine loop		
First jct (Brannigan Mine Rd)	0.0	1,660
Helenback Mine	0.7	1,910
Top of mining trail/high road	0.9	2,020
Paymaster Mine Road	1.0	1,875
Paymaster Mine (No. 3)	1.2	2,010
Paymaster Mine (last shaft)	1.6	2,330
Elbow in road	2.25	2,380
Oro Fino Mine (upper shaft)	2.5	2,135
La Paloma Mine (camp)	2.8	1,935
Second jct (Brannigan Mine Rd)	3.65	1,736
Back to first junction	4.3	1,660
The Brannigan Mine loop		
Second jct (Brannigan Mine Rd)	0.0	1,736
Canyon mouth	1.2	1,895
Dugout	1.4	1,960
Trail junction	2.0	2,275
Brannigan Mine (shafts)	(0.15)	~2,300
Brannigan Mine/end of trail	2.45	2,295
Brannigan Mine Rd via canyon	4.1	~1,750
Back to second junction	4.3	1,736

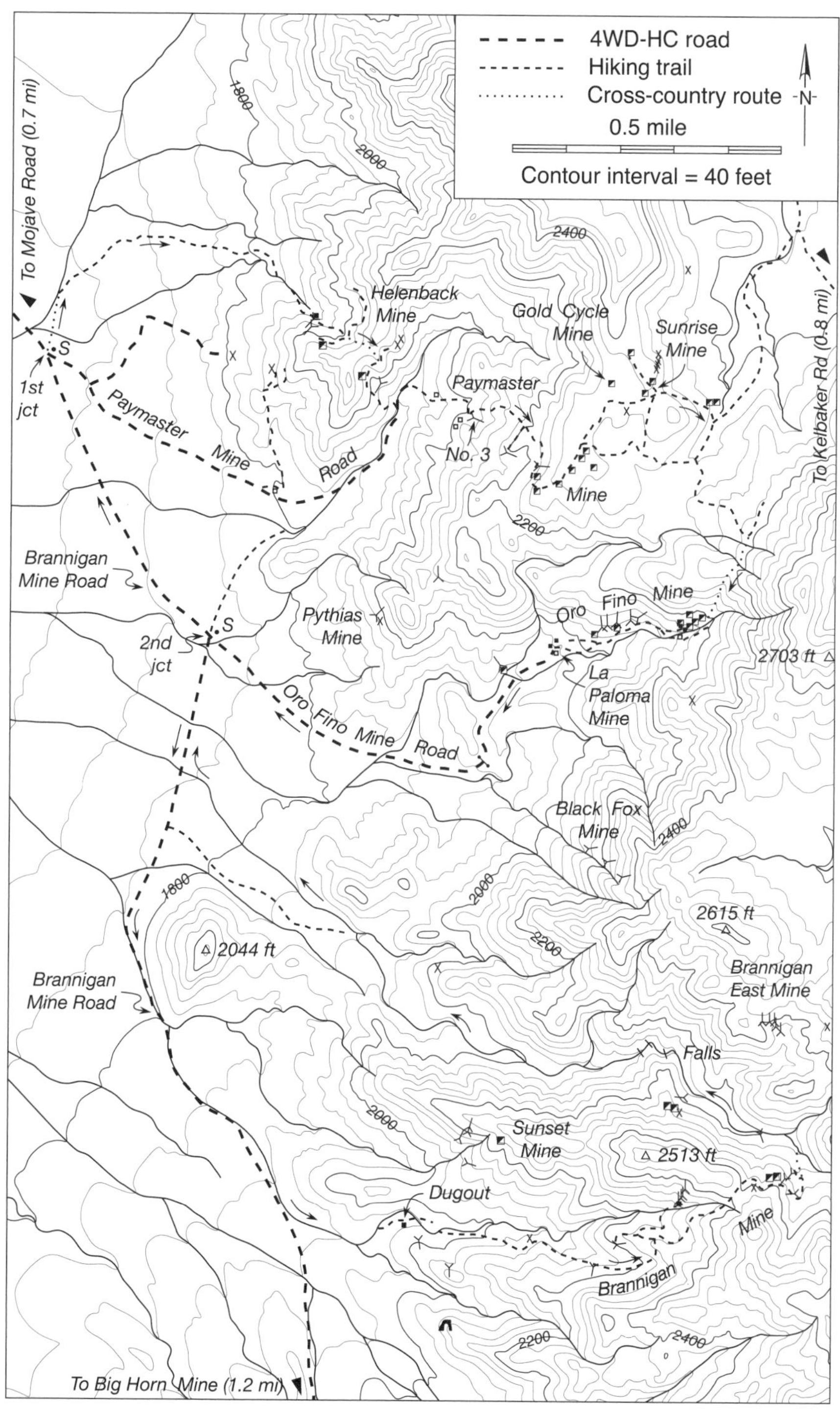

4WD-HC road
Hiking trail
Cross-country route
N
0.5 mile
Contour interval = 40 feet
To Mojave Road (0.7 mi)
To Kelbaker Rd (0.8 mi)
1800
2000
2400
2200
Helenback Mine
Gold Cycle Mine
Sunrise Mine
Paymaster
No. 3
Mine
S
1st jct
Paymaster Mine Road
Brannigan Mine Road
2nd jct
Pythias Mine
Oro Fino Mine
La Paloma Mine
2703 ft
Oro Fino Mine Road
Black Fox Mine
2615 ft
2044 ft
Brannigan East Mine
Brannigan Mine Road
Falls
Sunset Mine
2513 ft
Dugout
Brannigan Mine
To Big Horn Mine (1.2 mi)

soil, looking lifeless most of the year. This drab monopoly is occasionally broken by arresting groves of barrel cactus or silver cholla. Every ridge, plateau, and high point commands good low-angle views of Soda Lake Valley and the Mojave River drainage, from the white slash of its sink past many desert ranges all the way to its headwaters high up in the San Bernardino Mountains.

Most of the rocks here date back to the Early Proterozoic; they are at least 1.6 billion years old. Expectedly, they have had ample time to be metamorphosed. Quartzite, gneiss, paragneiss, and shists abound in uncommon variants. At the Paymaster Mine, brecciated gneiss intensely veined with white quartz—the extension of the gold-silver quartz-pyrite zones mined in the past—can be traced more than 100 feet outside the portal. The Brannigan Mine has gray-green bladed crystals of pyroxene and pretty green and purple quartzite. The mosaics exposed on the plateau are Paleozoic limestone and dolomite breccias. Along a wash I spotted a lone rock as black as an iron meteorite.

Somehow, here more than at most places, a greater part of the fun is to stumble upon mining remains. In an area with at least 70 shafts and tunnels, there are many more manmade structures than the few I mentioned, and many more mines to explore. One of the brightest stars is the scenic camp at the La Paloma Mine. Its two sizable cabins pose peacefully against the backdrop of a massive pointed cliff. You might run across a slender headframe, a water pipe ingeniously fashioned into a ladder, ore chutes and rails, a vaulted tunnel slashed with vermillion veins, and the exploded body of a vintage car. Collectively, these remains are a rare eyewitness to life at desert mines in the early to mid 20th century. An astute mind can coerce from them a surprising number of everyday-life details—how the ore was moved out of a tunnel, where it was loaded into trucks, where the miners welded, slept, smelted their ore, and barbecued on hot summer nights. The funky dugout below the Brannigan Mine may be the most eloquent. With its canted smokestack and sturdy back wall of carefully selected mortared stones, it was obviously built by someone with the intention to stay. Hopefully, in spite of the hardships, he did.

■

CINDER CONES AND LAVA BEDS

The scenic wilderness of extinct volcanoes in the preserve's northwestern section is one of only a few recent volcanic fields in the American deserts. Studded with Joshua trees and well-formed cinder cones, this is a great place for a fun day of four-wheeling. It also offers miles of foot trails and a host of hiking destinations, anything from derelict cinder mines and lava flows to intriguing formations, spectacular cones to climb, arches, rock art, and isolated springs.

General Information

Road status: Roadless; standard- and high-clearance access roads
Twin Cone: 2.6 mi, 500 ft up loop/easy
Mount Hephestus: 3.6 mi, 980 ft up, 50 ft down one way/moderate
Main attractions: Scenic drives and hikes among volcanoes, geology, cinder mines, lava tube, Joshua tree forest
USGS 7.5' topo maps: Valley Wells, Cow Cove*, Marl Mtns, Indian Spr.*
Maps: pp. 113*, 117*, *83*

Location and Access

Known among geologists as the Cima volcanic field, the preserve's cinder cones and lava beds region covers 60 square miles straddling the Ivanpah upland, west of Cima Dome. Its outstanding geologic significance was acknowledged in 1973 with its designation as a National Natural Landmark. More recently, it has been further protected in two adjacent wilderness areas. The only access to the heart of this region is the Aiken Mine Road, which cuts between the two wilderness areas. It starts off Cima Road 0.25 mile from the northbound exit on Interstate 15, on the west side. It ends after 23.6 miles at the Kelbaker Road, 19.5 miles from the northbound exit at Baker on Interstate 15 (or 15.0 miles north of the junction at Kelso).

Geology: From Bubbles to Rubble

Cinder is a light, chunky volcanic rock filled with interconnected vesicles. It is thought to originate from lower viscosity magma, which facilitates the formation of gas bubbles. When the magma enters the atmosphere, the internal pressure of the hot gases splatters it into small lumps that cool rapidly and trap the bubbles. It typically takes a single eruption lasting a few weeks or months to form a cinder cone, a steep conical hill capped by a bowl-shaped crater. Steam often wafts through the cinder for months, even years, after the eruption. The steam oxidizes the iron in the cinder and gives it its characteristic color. At a later stage, a cone may emit lava. The lava often flows not from the crater, which is structurally too weak to support it, but at the base or on the side, and it usually carries away a portion of the cone.

The Cima volcanic field is composed of about 40 cinder cones, ranging in height from less than 100 feet to 560 feet. Most of them have erupted lava. It has resulted in a mosaic of more than 60 lava beds of different ages, compositions, and morphologies. By measuring the traces of potassium and argon isotopes in the lava, geologists have identified three periods of volcanism. The earliest one started 7.6 million years ago and lasted, off and on, 1.1 million years. The only exposures from that time are a few highly degraded cones and flows at the eastern edge of the field, especially around Whitney Peak. The second period, 4.5 to 3.6 million years ago, occurred in the northern half of the field. It was by far the most intense. Thick molten rock flowed mostly eastward down an old dome toward Shadow Valley, eventually building sheets of basalt up to 400 feet thick. The third period began about one million years ago. This time the lava drained westward, toward Soda Lake. These younger vents and flows dominate the field's southern half. The most recent episodes are only about 15,000 years old.

Because these flows span a fairly recent window of time, they teach us a great deal about the erosion of volcanic landforms in arid climates. The first erosional agent is not water, but wind. Fresh lava is porous; rain water penetrates it rather than eroding it. On the other hand, the rough surface of fresh lava efficiently traps wind-borne sand, silt, and salt. Through cycles of wetting and drying, these particles wear the lava surface. In a second phase, soil forms on the lava, and erosion slows down. But long-term exposure to soil enriches the lava surface in clay and carbonates, and it loses its permeability. This paves the way for the third phase: erosion from storm runoffs. The first phase took around 250,000 years, the second one twice as long, and the last one is still going after 7 million years. Erosion takes twice as long to turn a cinder cone to rubble as tectonism took to create Death Valley.

Route Description

The Aiken Mine Road. This is a long and fun road, across a scenic open landscape visited by few, and explored in depth by even fewer. The best direction to drive it is southbound: it is downhill through the cinder cones, and the views are more spectacular. The scenery evolves from the creosote-covered floor of Shadow Valley to an extensive forest of Joshua trees at higher elevations, then back down to the low desert.

View of cinder cones from the Aiken Cinder Mine

The first cinder cones appear after about 10 miles. The cap rocks projecting above the western skyline, including Club Peak, are the degraded cones from the second wave of volcanism. From here on, the cones generally get younger. A few miles further, the prominent twin cone that shows up 1.5 miles to the west is Button Mountain. Like the main cones at the cinder mines, it was active sometime between 750,000 and 250,000 years ago. South of the Aiken Mine, the low cone that the road neatly circumvents last erupted less than 200,000 years ago. The last three cones are younger still. The aging process in volcanoes is as striking as in humans. Around the pass the lava is old and broken, inconspicuous under a thicker plant cover. In contrast, the youngest flow by the Kelbaker Road is solid, naked, black pahoehoe and a'a lava, reminiscent of the bleak landscapes of Hawaii.

Only a few junctions require a decision: the Y junction after 5.8 miles (make a left), the T junction after 11.3 miles (right across the small power line), and at the Aiken Mine (west across the playa between the two cones). South from the Cima Road, the Aiken Mine Road is mostly hard-packed coarse sand, locally a little soft, and gently sloped. North from the Kelbaker Road, it is mostly graded. If you are driving a standard-clearance car, exercise caution in sandy areas. Also, the grades on either side of the Aiken Mine are steep and rocky; you might have to walk the remaining distance (~0.7 mile) to the mine.

Aiken Cinder Mine. In the 1940s, as access to the eastern Mojave Desert improved, the Cima field's enormous cinder reserve—in excess of 50 million tons—became a coveted construction material. Many parties bulldozed roads and pits all over the area. They found that on most cones the cinder either had been stripped by erosion or was too weathered for commercial use. The Aiken and the Cima cinder mines are the only ones that were fully developed. Their original claims were filed in 1947–1948, and production started in 1954. For several decades, they were substantial suppliers for markets in Las Vegas and southern California. By 1983 the total production of the Aiken Cinder Mine had reached 1.28 million tons—the volume of a tall skyscraper—and an estimated $2 million. Some of it went into building the sidewalks of the Las Vegas Strip. In the late 1980s, the mine had nearly 8 million tons of stockpiled cinder, but sales had slowed down, perhaps from increased competition. When it could no longer pay rent in 1990, the mine was abandoned almost overnight, and with it all its equipment.

For many visitors this unusual mine is the highlight of the cinder cones area. The camp's main structure is the pale-blue 50-foot trailer home that housed the mine office. Next to it stands a tall water tank and a cinder-block house with two tiny bedrooms. Battered pieces of equipment lie around. Most of them require a fertile imagination to work out their purpose. Since the mine closure, the camp has deteriorated markedly. But it remains a valuable witness to life at a remote desert mine in the second half of the 20th century.

Once known as Red Beauty, the rust-colored cone behind the camp produced most of the cinder. From the camp a road zigzags past the three terraces that were carved into it. The cinder was harvested by blasting the cliff backing the upper terrace, an immense, perfectly level playa of cinder gravel. This is a stark mineral wasteland, oddly appealing because it is so different. Hundreds of thousands of tons of crushed scoria are stockpiled all around, still untouched by erosion. Only a few plants manage to grow, in nearly pure stands, widely spaced, their crowns shining like ghosts against ground as dark as wet earth.

Aiken Mine Road

	Dist.(mi)	Elev.(ft)
Cima Road	0.0	3,735
Rock Tank crossroad (straight)	4.0	3,905
Cima Mine Road jct (left)	5.8	4,020
Cima Cinder Mine (gate)	(5.9)	4,130
Cross power line at jct (right)	11.3	4,230
Aiken Cinder Mine	16.4	4,035
Mine's upper terrace	(0.3)	~4,135
Lava Tube Road jct (left)	19.2	3,560
Mojave Rd crossing (straight)	22.9	3,125
Y junction (left)	23.1	3,100
Kelbaker Road	23.6	3,133

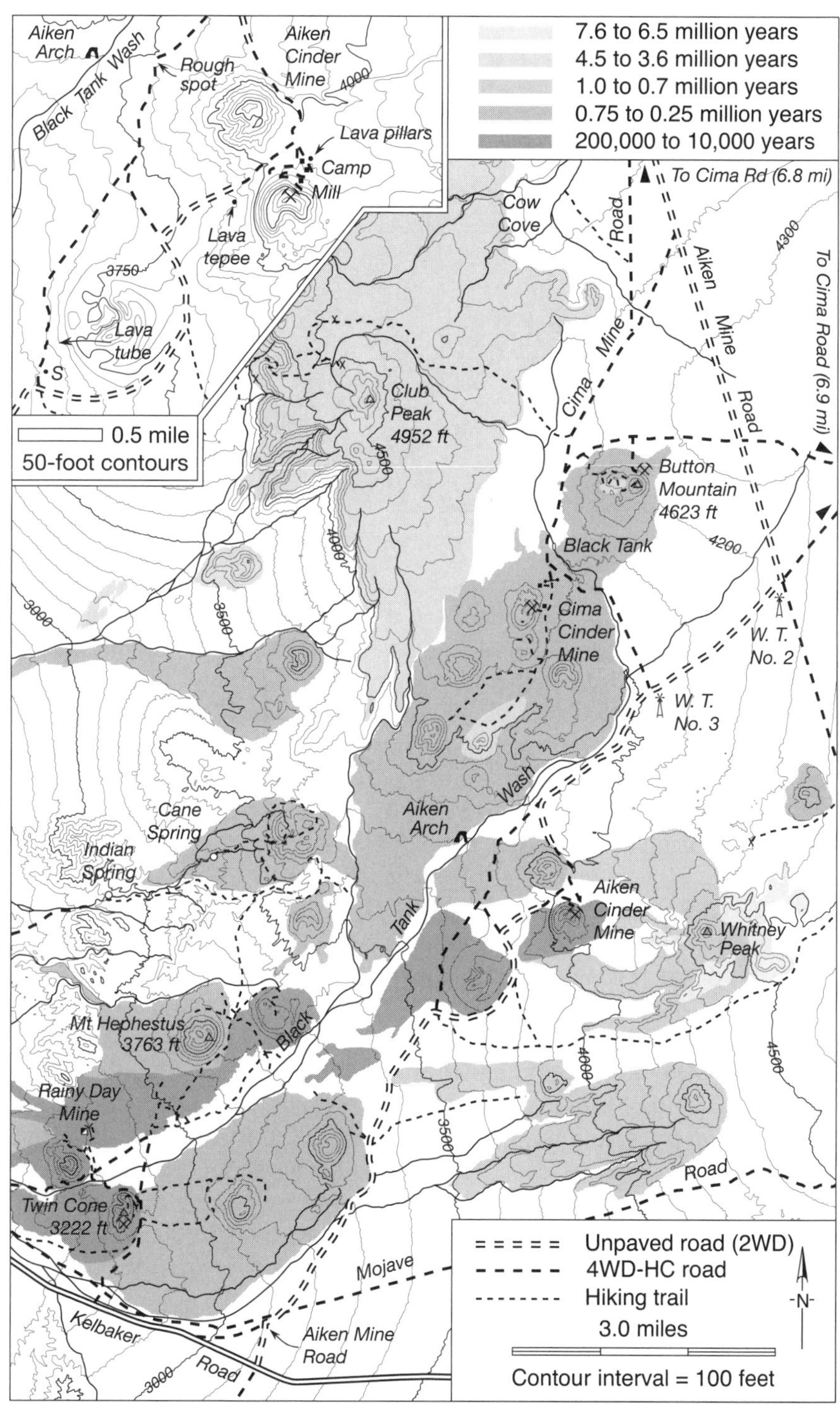
7.6 to 6.5 million years
4.5 to 3.6 million years
1.0 to 0.7 million years
0.75 to 0.25 million years
200,000 to 10,000 years
Aiken Arch
Black Tank Wash
Rough spot
Aiken Cinder Mine
Lava pillars
Camp
Mill
Lava tepee
Lava tube
0.5 mile
50-foot contours
To Cima Rd (6.8 mi)
To Cima Road (6.9 mi)
Cow Cove
Club Peak 4952 ft
Aiken Mine Road
Cima Mine Road
Button Mountain 4623 ft
Black Tank
Cima Cinder Mine
W. T. No. 2
W. T. No. 3
Aiken Arch
Cane Spring
Indian Spring
Aiken Cinder Mine
Whitney Peak
Black Tank Wash
Mt Hephestus 3763 ft
Rainy Day Mine
Twin Cone 3222 ft
Road
Mojave
Kelbaker Road
Aiken Mine Road
Unpaved road (2WD)
4WD-HC road
Hiking trail
3.0 miles
N
Contour interval = 100 feet

Crusher and conveyors at the Aiken Cinder Mine

The middle terrace is where the rock was crushed, screened, and sorted. The hulking metal contraption a bit larger than a townhouse is the crusher. Behind it are the diesel generator that powered it and the cinder-block shed that housed the electrical controls. Everything here is *big*, from the generator's 5-foot fan to the ominous conveyors that tossed the crushed rock into underground chutes. The rock resurfaced below, at the lower terrace, on aerial beltways that dropped it into trucks. In this alien landscape, the alignment of belts conjures disquieting images of a way station on a distant planet animated by silent robots. At the bottom of the road, the concrete road flanked by a narrow metal cabin is the weigh station. The old Fairbanks-Morse scale is still tucked under it, waiting for a next shipment that will never come.

Cima Cinder Mine. To reach this mine, from the Cima Road drive the Aiken Mine Road 5.8 miles to the Y junction and make a right on the graded Cima Mine Road. Follow it 5.9 miles, through a pretty forest of Joshua trees, to the mine's gate, and park. It is a short walk to the mill and pit (0.4 mile, 80 feet up). The mine is on park land and open to visitors, but its equipment and improvements are private property.

Located in 1948 by Emerson and Fay Ray, the Cima Cinder Mine was a successful family-owned operation. Its only known production of 130,000 tons between 1954 and 1961 likely reflects a mere fraction of its total output. Yet it ended on a very sad note. It was still running in 1994 when this area became a national preserve. Soon after, a coalition of environmental groups threatened to file a lawsuit against the NPS unless the mine was shut down. A main concern was the endangered desert tortoise, which the coalition claimed was threatened by mining activities. To forestall the lawsuit, in August 1999 the NPS evicted the owners, after 50 years of operation—for trespassing...

In spite of being contemporary, the Cima and the Aiken mines are quite different. They used similar equipment, but the Cima Cinder Mine is neater, more compact, better kept. The centerpiece, the towering crushing and screening plant perched on huge steel legs, is a mining gem. The impressive open pit above it commands great views of Cima Dome. Its cliff of coarsely stratified deep-red cinder stands 100 feet tall, draped with nearly vertical taluses. The cone's interior structure, exposed by mining operations, reveals large volcanic fragments entombed in the cinder, some of them beautifully honeycombed. This is as close as it gets to standing inside a volcano.

Lava tube. When lava flows down a slope, its surface cools and forms a solid crust. Thermally insulated by this crust, the lava stays molten and continues to flow beneath it. If the lava drains properly after it becomes exhausted, a hollow bore known as a lava tube is left behind. Later eruptions will often send new lava down the same tube.

The Cima field's most popular lava tube is easily accessible from the Aiken Mine Road. Take this road 2.8 miles south from the Aiken Mine's weigh station (4.4 miles from the Kelbaker Road) to a spur road on the north side. Drive it 0.3 mile to a turnout and park. A sign identifies the continuation of the road as the Lava Tube Trail. The trail is 275 yards up the road on the right, marked by posts. It goes 100 yards to the lava tube's main entrance, accessed by a sturdy ladder.

Caves and tunnels often exert an unspoken attraction. It might be the hope of discovering, in their dark confines, something everyone else has missed. It rarely happens. But you might well find something few people ever see. Just take your time. Try not to kick up too much of the fine dust that covers the ground; it might be infected with hantavirus. If the sky is partly cloudy, wait for the sun to come out. Sunlight entering the tube through the skylights is scattered by the dust injected into the air by your walking and solidifies into brilliant beams of light—a rare sight that occurs commonly here.

Twin Cone. If you are looking for an easy and scenic cone to climb, try Twin Cone, the area's youngest. Drive the Kelbaker Road 2 miles west from the Aiken Mine Road (or 17.5 miles from the northbound exit at Baker) to a primitive road on the north side. Twin Cone is the closest one, due north. This road goes right by it, but the crossing of Willow Wash after 0.3 mile is rough. Park at the wide pullout before the road drops into the wash and walk from there.

This hike actually gives access to two cones, the main one and the smaller satellitic cone attached to it. After 0.5 mile the road crests a low swell at the southeastern foot of the satellite, then crosses a small wash. A fainter road branches off at 10 o'clock 20 yards further. It climbs the satellite's lower flank to an open pit, crosses a few shallow trenches, then reaches a junction. The road on the left winds up to the crease between the cones, climbs the main cone to its rim, circles half way around the rim, then descends steeply on the north slope. At its lower end, which is gone, just slide down to the road 20 feet below, then take this road right (up) 250 yards back to the last junction.

This little volcano is a treat. Its rim overlooks the steep edge of the cone's gutted core. Down below, the great tongue of lava responsible for this giant wound spreads out for a mile from the base of the cone. As the lava spilled out from under the cone, it rafted a chunk of the cone with it. The lava is so young that it is still neatly scalloped. From the horseshoe rim—the signature of a breached crater—several well-formed cones are visible in the middle ground. Beautiful outcrops of cinnamon-red, clinkery scoria are exposed at the rim. This is arguably the most convoluted rock on Earth. Its surface is a labyrinth of depressions, rills, and razor-sharp asperities of all sizes, as wild as a fractal.

Only a few tenacious plants cling to this chemical desert—except for the spring wildflowers, which can thrive in unbelievable numbers. I saw here uncommon plants such as spotted langloisia (and a mushroom called desert puffball), but what made my day was the profusion of desert five spots. One can go years without seeing a single one of these arresting beauties. Here there were hundreds, their globe-like shocking-pink corollas floating above the dark cinder.

Mount Hephestus. For a more substantial hike, push on to Mount Hephestus, the next cone north and the field's tallest. From the junction at the southeastern foot of Twin Cone, continue north on the main road across the wide braided floodplain of Black Tank Wash. In 1.25 miles it reaches a wilderness boundary, where a road comes in from the left, in full view of Mount Hephestus to the north-northeast. Several roads crisscross the area up ahead. For the shortest route, take the road that heads north, to the cone's western base. After just over 1 mile, at the base, it runs into a road that climbs clockwise around the flank of the cone. Turn left on it. After 0.2 mile, shortly before this road ends, a fainter road on the right climbs straight up the spine of the

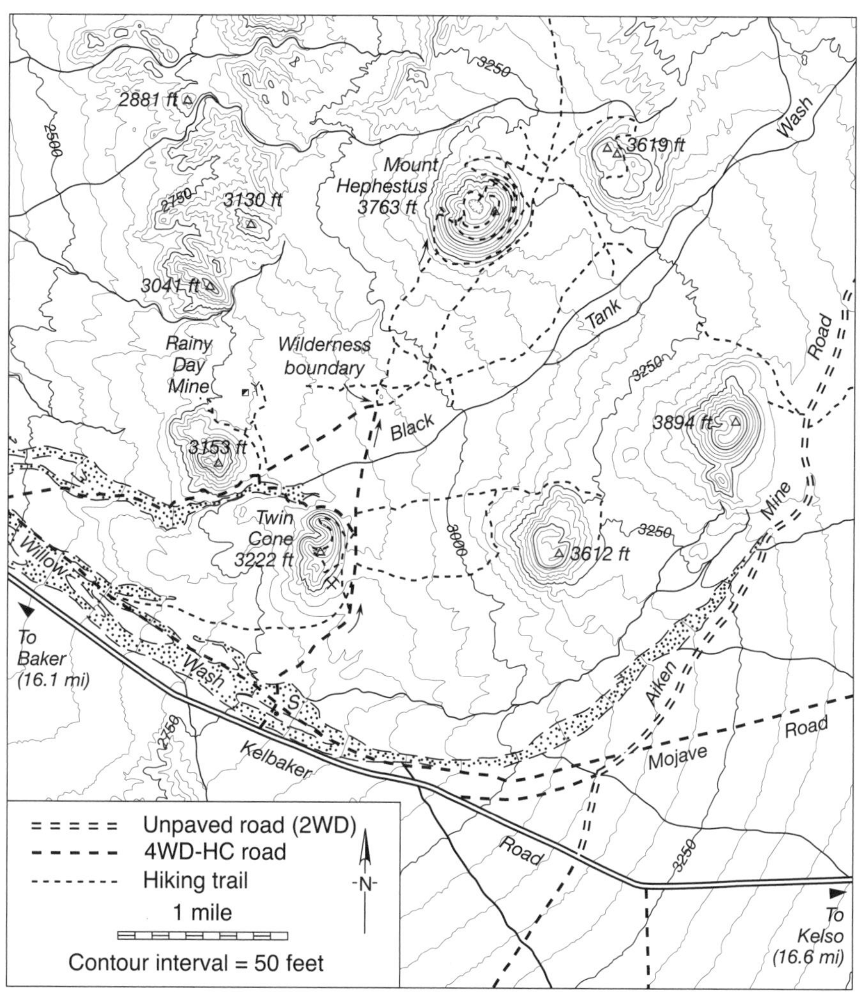

Twin Cone and Mount Hephestus

	Dist.(mi)	Elev.(ft)
Willow Wash crossing	0.0	~2,780
Y junction (left to Twin Cone)	0.65	~2,880
Spiral road to Twin Cone	(0.3)	2,975
Twin Cone	(0.6)	3,222
Back to Y junction via rim	(1.25)	~2,880
End of road / wilderness bdry	1.9	2,930
T jct at base of Mt Hephestus	2.9	3,200
Mount Hephestus	3.6	3,763

Cinder cone and lava flow from rim of Twin Cone

cone to yet another junction (0.1 mile). The road on the left (northeast) climbs 125 yards to the crater's rim. Finally, turn right on the rim road. The summit is 0.3 mile up and down this road, on the eastern rim.

All along this approach the terrain is a newborn volcanic wilderness. You will cross a vast plain of cinder pebbles, bypass dark young lava flows, and enjoy increasingly fine views of this imposing, highly symmetric cone. The desolation is barely tempered by a scatter of Mojave yucca. The road cuts on the cone reveal attractive sections of cinder. In the spring, large spreads of sand verbena and showy mimulus often decorate the ground, and the entire cone bristles with tiny white flowers. Climbing the road, with its plunging views down the cone's unobstructed 45% slope, is an aerial thrill.

This is one of the few cones that is not breached. Circumnavigating its neat oval crater along the faint rim road is an unusual experience. In its shallow cup the crater holds a miniature dry playa, the fine sediments collected by this tiny suspended basin since it cooled down 22,000 years ago. Cinder cones rise all around. Even after so long, the flows that weld them together seem to still be pouring down Cima Dome's curvature. This is a desolate land, miles of slowly recovering destruction, animated only by the wind singing over the volcanic jags.

■

KELSO DUNES

Rising 500 feet above their surrounding, the spectacular Kelso Dunes are the second tallest in the California Desert, exceeded only by Eureka Valley's mighty dunes. Climbing their highest summit is understandably the preserve's most popular hiking destination. Yet the Kelso Dunes are so vast that they offer endless possibilities for enjoying the magic world of sand in seclusion—the immense barren playas, the rippled slopes, the sensual hollows and finely sculpted crests. With a little luck you might even hear them boom...

General Information

Road status: Roadless; graded access road
Kelso Dunes (highest dune): 1.65 mi, 550 ft up, 50 ft down one way/easy
Northern dune field: 9.7 mi, 1,510 ft up loop/difficult
Main attractions: Majestic high dunes, geology
USGS 7.5' topo map: Kelso Dunes
Maps: pp. 123*, *83*

Location and Access

The Kelso Dunes are at the northern foot of the Granite Mountains. From the stop sign at Kelso, drive 7.7 miles south on the Kelbaker Road to the signed Kelso Dunes Road, a wide graded road on the west side, 600 yards before a transmission line. Coming from the south, look for it 6.6 miles north of Granite Pass. Drive the Kelso Dunes Road west 2.9 miles to the interpretive sign by the main trailhead and park. For a more secluded access, drive another 0.65 mile to the second trailhead.

Geology: How Do Dunes Boom?

Covering about 45 square miles, the Kelso Dunes are the culmination of the Devils Playground, an enormous eolian deposit that extends 25 miles from Soda Lake to the foot of the Granite Mountains. The sand is composed primarily of light-colored quartz and feldspar, with traces of magnetite and amphibole, darker minerals that often accumulate on higher slopes. The composition and shape of the sand grains suggest that most of it probably came from granitic rocks in the San Bernardino Mountains. The sand was first transported some 120 miles north and east along the Mojave River, then the prevailing winds gradually herded it southeastward. When sand-laden air masses run into the Granite and Providence mountains, they are forced upward,

Kelso Dunes in approaching winter storm

lose their velocity, and drop their sand cargo at the foot of the Granite Mountains—the location of the Kelso Dunes. Unlike many dunes in eastern California, the Kelso Dunes were deposited in steps. During a period of dry climate, the plant cover that normally stabilizes the desert ground shrinks and the ground dries up. These two effects increase the supply of sand particles exposed to the wind. The Kelso Dunes are the result of five major dry episodes that occurred over the last 25,000 years, which makes them one of the oldest in the West. Most of the dunes' eastern field was formed during the latest period of drying, when Soda Lake and Silver Lake evaporated, which availed the lakes' sediments to wind transport. Sand continues to accumulate at the west end of the Devils Playground. But no new sand has been deposited on the Kelso Dunes for a few thousand years now, and plants have been progressively colonizing and stabilizing them.

The Kelso Dunes are famous for their eerie ability to boom. Sometimes they emit a low-frequency rumble resembling a bass note on a cello or a low-flying propeller aircraft. It can last for up to a minute and be strong enough for ground vibrations to be felt. This phenomenon is rare: at last count, it has been observed at only about 30 dunes around the world. When Marco Polo witnessed it in the Gobi Desert around 1295, he attributed it to evil desert spirits. Centuries later superstition is still embarrassingly prevalent, but we know now that booming is the natural result of avalanches. Within a flowing sheet of sand, grains rubbing against each other are sheared mechanically and vibrate somewhat in unison. This vibration is transferred to the air, thus generating the booming sound. What causes an avalanche? When wind blows sand over a dune, sand accumulates just below the crest on the leeward side. When the slope exceeds the angle of stability, the unstable sand is dragged down by gravity. Few dunes boom because many conditions must be met simultaneously—the dune must be very large, the sand very dry, and the grains well rounded and smooth, among others.

But several mysteries remain unresolved, in particular the boom's complex frequency spectrum. Several fundamental frequencies are often present, always between about 65 and 105 Hz, simultaneous or sequential, pulsed or continuous, as well as higher harmonics and very low rumbling notes below 10 Hz. From California to Morocco, scientists have lugged expensive geophones and microphones up and down countless dunes to record detailed acoustic and seismic maps of booming events. Some researchers believe the boom frequency is imposed by grain size. Others think it is set by an acoustic waveguide formed by the flowing sand sandwiched between harder underlying sand and air. Sand behaves in strange ways, sometimes capricious and counterintuitive. It flows between our fingers yet we can walk on it. A few extra grains of sand at the wrong place can cause a massive landslide. It will be decades before all the secrets of booming dunes are unlocked.

Route Description

Kelso Dunes summit. From the trailhead a wide trail hemmed in by creosote bush crosses the first 0.2 mile to the open sand. Hikers' tracks usually point the rest of the way: up to the saddle on the crest northeast of the summit, then up along the crest to the summit. Most of the approach is gradual, across a tilted sea of sand hummocks. Only the last 0.5-mile stretch is steep. Remember the hiking etiquette in dunes: do not step on plants, and in heavy-traffic areas follow the path made by previous hikers. Do not climb, up or down, the dune's steep and highly unstable south face, to preserve its fragile vegetation.

The Kelso Dunes are covered with one of the most diverse dune plant communities in the California Desert. North from the trailhead, the creosote-bush community gives way to a sparser cover of mostly perennial herbs, shrubs, and even small trees. You might recognize cheesebush, sandpaper plant, or even species that do not typically grow in dunes, like fagonia and wild rhubarb. The larger, darker clumps widely dispersed on the slopes are catclaw. Out in the open sand, grasses are the uncontested rulers, mostly big galleta grass but also Indian ricegrass and dune panic grass. Some grow right up to the crest. The slender blades of these hardy plants add much charm to the dunes. If the winter rains have been generous, many wildflowers come out in the spring. Local beauties include woolly marigold, Borrego locoweed, and desert lily. The prize goes to sand verbena. On a good year, their clusters of bright-pink flowers flood large swaths of sand.

I have explored the Kelso Dunes on many occasions. The experience was always delightful, for reasons that varied with the season—the flowers in spring, the intoxicating heat in summer, the longer shadows in winter, and, now and then, the rare union of sand and rain. But no visit was as memorable as when my cousin and I climbed the highest dune in a winter storm. A particularly wet cold snap had dumped much snow on the mountains. The large temperature gradients between the sunlit basin and the frigid summits were driving hurricane-force winds. Even in the relatively sheltered lower dunes, the wind was strong enough to erase footprints in less than a minute. At the saddle, the wind was rushing over the crest at nearly 100 miles per hour. Long plumes of sand were hurtled high in the air, as bright as powder snow whisked off a mountain. Visibility was reduced to a few yards. Simply staying upright was a challenge. On the final ascent, sand infiltrated everything—our noses, eyes, ears, and mouths. When breathing away from the wind to avoid the sand, it literally sucked the air out of our lungs. We walked holding our hoods down over our faces. The gusts knocked me down several times, and nearly threw me over the edge. I tried crawling, but at ground level the sand-laden wind was so fierce I could not keep my eyes open. When we finally reached the summit, there was no way to stand. We plopped down, our backs against the wind, rocking under its ceaseless assaults. The din was deafening. During the brief moments I dared take a peek, I caught visions of apocalypse. Far beyond the blinding whirls of sand, the Kelso Mountains were glowing in supernatural light. The Providence Mountains had gone under, swallowed by ominous clouds the color of lead. We were sitting in a well of light, surrounded by fury, acutely aware we were living rare moments.

Kelso Dunes

	Dist.(mi)	Elev.(ft)
Kelso Dunes trailhead	0.0	2,610
Saddle on ridge	1.4	2,850
Highest dune	1.65	3,113
2,800-foot dune	3.3	~2,800
2,565-foot dune	5.5	~2,565
Trailhead via Cottonwood W.	9.7	2,610

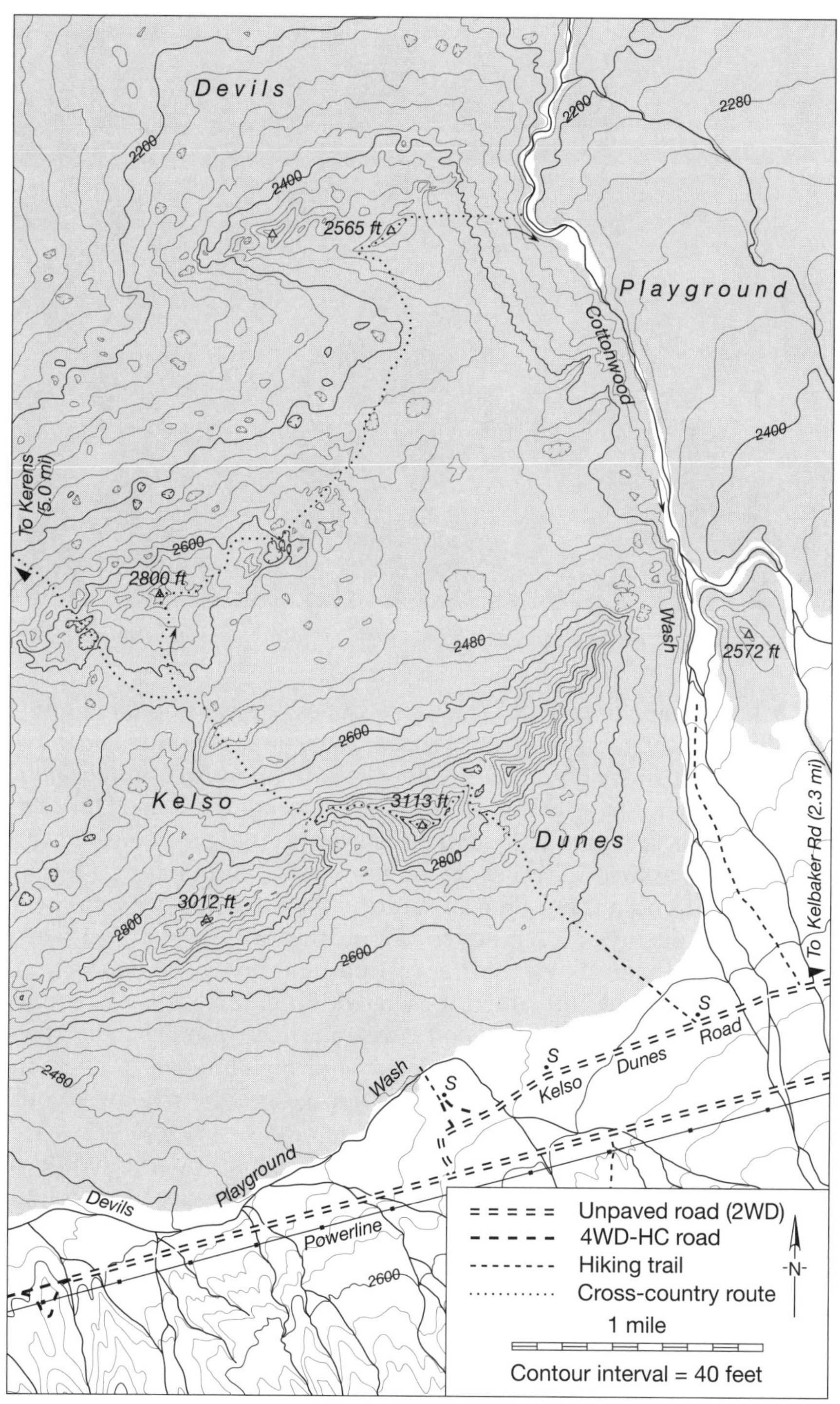
Devils
Playground
Cottonwood
Wash
2200
2280
2400
2565 ft
To Kerens (5.0 mi)
2600
2800 ft
2480
2572 ft
Kelso
Dunes
3113 ft
2800
3012 ft
To Kelbaker Rd (2.3 mi)
S
Road
Dunes
Kelso
Wash
Playground
Devils
Powerline
Unpaved road (2WD)
4WD-HC road
Hiking trail
Cross-country route
1 mile
N
Contour interval = 40 feet

Hikers on Kelso Dunes in a sand storm (Photo Nike Weintraub)

The northern dune field. The Kelso Dunes' vastness becomes obvious the moment you peer over the crest—on a day the wind is not having a fit, that is—and you stare down at row upon row of delicately chiseled dunes. The greatest pleasure of exploring the Kelso Dunes is sampling this exceptional landscape. If you need a goal, consider the next highest dunes 1.7 miles to the northwest, culminating around 2,800 feet. If you are not tired of sand by then, trudge on to the next highest set of dunes 2.2 miles to the north-northeast (~2,565 feet). Looming 300 feet above their surroundings, these clusters of star dunes are beautiful and superbly isolated. From there it is faster and easier to return along Cottonwood Wash, a rare canyon of sand. If you prefer a less structured approach, make your own itinerary instead; in a land free of obstacles, your whim is your best guide. Wherever your steps will take you, you will cross pristine ridges, curvaceous swales, deep sinks, and flat aprons of naked sand, much of it decorated with fine ripples and the dainty signatures of wildlife. The views are grand. The number of combinations is infinite. As North American sand dunes go, it does not get much better.

■

THE DEVILS PLAYGROUND

Embedded deep in the preserve's lonesome southwestern quadrant, the Devils Playground is the third largest dune complex in the country. The best way to discover this immense icon is to indulge in a multiple-day trek across its entire length. If you find the distance daunting, take the long drive down through Jackass Canyon to the playground's northern reaches and explore its stunning system of eerie dunes and rocky knolls. There are not too many places on this continent to hike in dunes this extensive, pristine, and uncrowded.

General Information

Road status: Mostly roadless; graded or primitive access road
Isolated dune: 3.3 mi, 150 ft up, 570 ft down one way / easy
Devils Playground: 27.5 mi, 1,000 ft up, 2,450 ft down one way / moder.
Main attraction: One of North America's largest dune fields
USGS 7.5' topo maps: Kelso Dunes, Glasgow, Old Dad Mountain, Cowhole Mountain, Seventeenmile Point, Soda Lake South, Soda Lake North
Maps: pp. 123*, 129*, *83*

Location and Access

The Devils Playground stretches some 25 miles from the south shore of Soda Lake all the way to the Kelso Dunes. There are three ways to get close to it by car. The first one is the Kelso Dunes trailhead (see *Kelso Dunes* for directions). The second one is the Mojave Road around Cowhole Mountain (see *Cowhole Mountain*). The third one is the Edison Company's power-line road, which crosses the playground and provides the closest foot access. To get to it, drive the Kelbaker Road 19.5 miles from the northbound exit at Baker (or 15.0 miles north of the junction at Kelso) to a graded road on the south side, across from the Aiken Mine Road. Go 1.7 miles on the graded road to a T junction and turn right. After 2.2 miles the road angles right and starts following the power line. Continue 3.9 miles, down through the wide gorge of Jackass Canyon, to the canyon mouth on the edge of the Devils Playground. A high-clearance vehicle is required to get through the soft gravel in the canyon. After 1 more mile the road is usually buried in deep sand. With a four-wheel-drive vehicle and the right skills, you can drive another 4 miles and hike north into the dunes from there. Otherwise, start hiking where the road becomes too sandy.

Route Description

Backpacking the playground. This hike is not for everyone. It takes about three days to cover the playground from end to end. Walking on soft ground for this long is tiring. There is virtually no shade, and no water. In hot weather, your pack will be heavy with water. Sand storms are common, often unpredictable, and they can strand you or cause injuries. The extended isolation may fray your resolve. Add the fact that help is far away, and you are left with little margin for error. So I am suggesting this trek only for desert afficionados who have done this sort of thing before. If you are not one of them but would still like to do it, first take day hikes of increasing length in dunes, then hike a small portion of the route with a backpack. Irrespective of your level of expertise, apply all basic precautionary measures: let someone know your itinerary and schedule; have a rescue plan; do not hike it alone, or in summer; and carry enough water.

If you are pondering which direction of travel is best, here are the decisive factors. Getting lost is hardly an issue: from the Kelso Dunes one can clearly see Cowhole Mountain, and vice versa. The northbound direction offers finer views because you are looking down at the scenery the whole way. Except for the short Kelso Dunes climb, most of your walking is also downhill and facing away from the sun, and thus easier. The only downside is that southeast is the prevalent wind direction. So if there is a sand storm, you will likely be headed into it, and this one disadvantage may well wipe out the benefits. If light winds are forecast, select the direction so that you will be hiking with the wind. If strong winds are in store, postpone your trip.

If you do get caught in a sand storm, sit down with your back to the wind, preferably in a hollow. Unless the storm is moderate, do not pitch a tent, or it might get blown away, even with you inside it. Cover your eyes and mouth with a cloth. Drink often to offset the dehydrating power of the wind. Make sure to bring a map of the entire playground and its vicinity should you need a quick escape.

In spite of these cheerful warnings, I have to stress that this is the most unusual hike described in this book. Only a couple of other places in North America offer this invaluable opportunity to wander across such an ocean of sand. The experience is liberating, like navigating in open sea. There is no barrier, no imposed route, only boundless space that makes the mind reel.

Kelso Dunes to the power-line road. From the high crest of the Kelso Dunes, the land drops into a stunning field of sculpted dunes framed by the high-rising Kelso Mountains. To the northwest, as far as

Devils Playground's lava and dunes against the Bristol Mountains

the eye can see, the Devils Playground flows out to the distant shores of Soda Lake like an immense river of sand. The first several miles, across the dunes, are the most exciting. You'll slog up, down, and around countless hollows and delicately ruffled slopes. The sharp contrast between the luminous smooth sand and the dark-brown rugged mountains rearing up all around is a constant source of visual delight. The isolation is raw ecstasy.

The dunes gradually morph into small hummocks, the hummocks into long undulating swells, and the swells into a nearly featureless valley of sand. In this immensity, the only sign of civilization you will run across before Jackass Canyon is the Union Pacific Railroad and the service road that parallels it. This incongruous sight can be spotted long before reaching it, a black cut slicing across the sands like a mortal burn. You will likely cross it around Kerens, a siding distinguishable by its double tracks. It was named after Richard C. Kerens, an ambassador who made a fortune in railroad construction and co-founded this line with Senator William A. Clark and others. This place ranks high on the desolation scale, a futuristic scene right out of Ray Bradbury's beloved Red Planet.

Beyond the tracks, the Devils Playground turns into a gently sloping valley funneled between the Kelso Mountains and Old Dad

Mountain on one side and the Bristol Mountains on the other. The bases of the mountains are festooned with virgin sweeps of eolian fines. The only close points of reference are these mountains, and ultimately the metallic towers of the power line. The scenery evolves only imperceptibly. Lulled by this static surrounding and your repetitive steps, your mind slips into a meditative state for long minutes at a time. And every time you wake up, you could swear that the view is the same as it was ten minutes ago, or one hour ago.

The vegetation evolves just as gradually. Grasses dominate almost everywhere, but as you proceed northward other plants make an appearance, such as the greener bushes of California croton and sandpaper plant. As you approach Jackass Canyon you will start seeing a curious perennial herb called birdcage evening primrose. In the colder season its crown of thick, white, barren stems curved inward resembles a small bird cage. In the spring, its large white flowers are easily the most striking living things around.

The playground's northern field. The northern portion of the playground spills out across a broad valley that descends gently towards Soda Lake. This is one of the two or three most beautiful and secluded areas in the preserve. If you only want to sample the playground, this

The Devils Playground

	Dist.(mi)	Elev.(ft)
Backpacking route		
Kelso Dunes trailhead	0.0	2,610
Highest dune	1.65	3,113
Kerens (U. P. Railroad)	8.6	1,620
Edison Co. Road	17.4	~1,490
Isolated sand dune (summit)	19.4	1,480
Road by Cowhole Mtn	23.0	~1,230
Mojave Rd (Cowhole Mtn jct)	27.5	1,080
Northern playground loop		
Edison Co. Road (edge of sand)	0.0	~1,900
Isolated sand dune (summit)	3.3	1,480
Back of dune field (low point)	5.5	1,110
Bottom of sink	8.2	1,270
Edison Co. Road	9.4	1,380
Back to road at edge of sand	12.6	~1,900

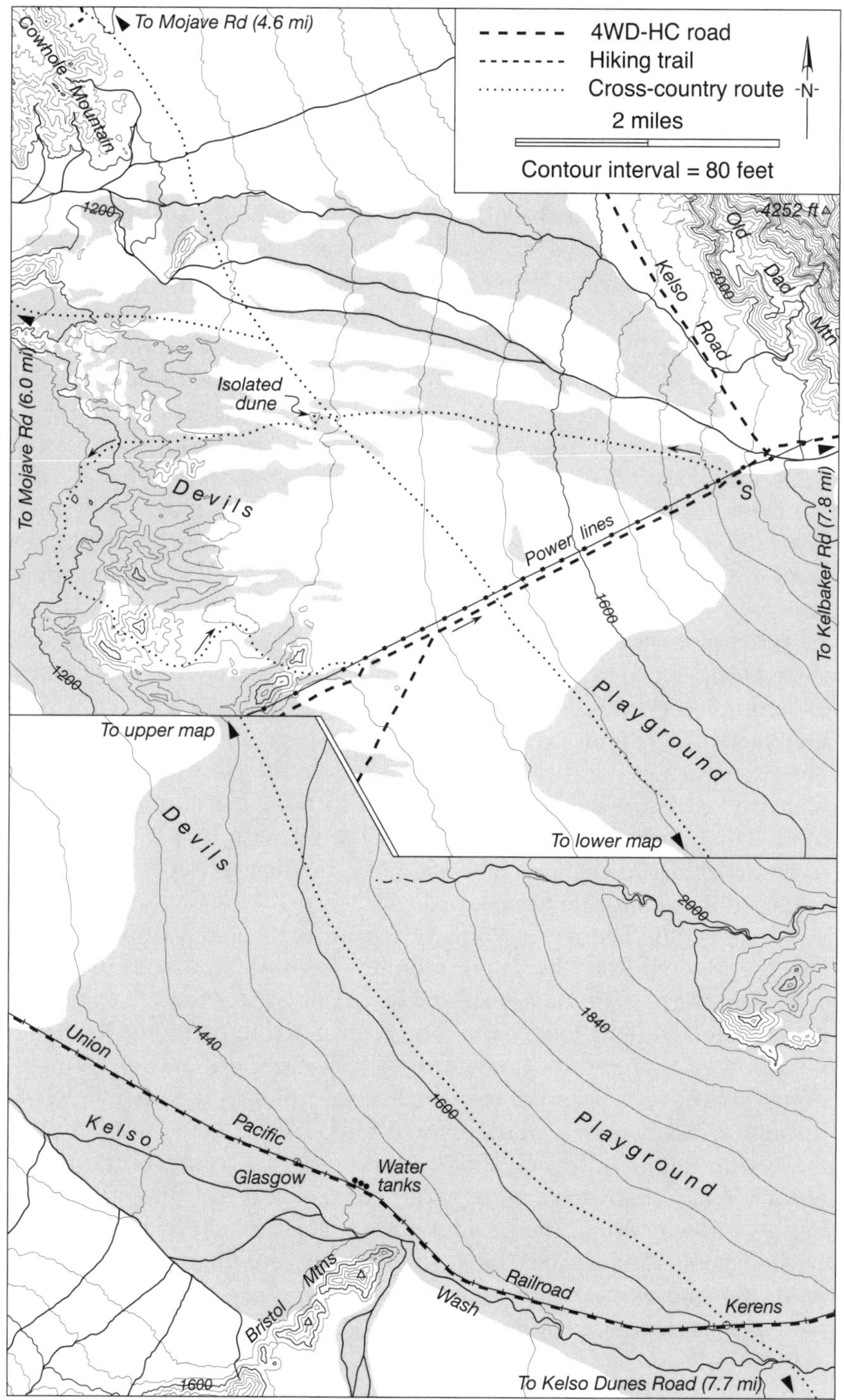

4WD-HC road
Hiking trail
Cross-country route
N
2 miles
Contour interval = 80 feet
To Mojave Rd (4.6 mi)
Cowhole Mountain
1200
4252 ft
Old Dad Mtn
Kelso Road
2000
To Mojave Rd (6.0 mi)
Isolated dune
Devils
S
Power lines
To Kelbaker Rd (7.8 mi)
1600
1200
Playground
To upper map
To lower map
Devils
2000
1840
1440
1600
Union
Pacific
Railroad
Kelso
Glasgow
Water tanks
Playground
Bristol Mtns
Wash
Kerens
1600
To Kelso Dunes Road (7.7 mi)

is the place to visit. Start where the power-line road is covered in sand and head west on the open sand. The valley is cocooned from the rest of the world by mountains. The west side is framed by a 4-mile row of free-standing hills encroached by well-formed dunes. On the east side rises Old Dad Mountain, a sheer slab of dark-brown Mesozoic limestones and dolomites. Up ahead, the dissected peaks of Cowhole Mountain soar against the glistening white slash of the salt pan. Far beyond, the sawtoothed skylines of great mountains pierce the horizon. Along this ultimate stretch, the playground gradually breaks up into long waves of sand, hardly ever higher than 10 feet, then into a subdued plain. Everywhere the ground is sprinkled with tall bunches of yellow grass, scattered shrubs, and the ubiquitous birdcage primrose. In the sand hollows, multicolored pebbles donated by the mountains have found their resting place. I saw large anthills and wasp nests, indigenous beetles, burrows, and curious ventifacts.

In this generous landscape, it is hard to single out a best destination for a day hike. Cowhole Mountain is a natural initial goal; perhaps head towards it and let inspiration do the rest. The isolated dune about 3 miles southeast of it makes just as fine a destination. Its base is surrounded by exquisite ripples and elegant gardens of big galleta grass. Deep scoops have been gouged out along its crest by wind turbulence. Its summit is crowned with black cobbles of vesiculated lava 170 million years old. If you have the stamina, push on another mile or so to the extensive field of rocky hills and dunes to the west. Cross it southward to return to the power line, then to your car along the utility road. This maze of sand valleys punctuated with bright dunes and dark mounds of congealed lava is one of the most extraordinary landscapes in the California Desert.

If this is the last leg of your trek, from the isolated dune you can join the Mojave Road by going around Cowhole Mountain on either side (see map). The east-side route crosses the broad flat tucked against the southern foot of the mountain, often tinged with rust from a million eriogonum. Not far north of it is the south end of an abandoned road that will guide you the last 4.5 miles to the Mojave Road, through a moonscape of stark pointed hills. The lake-side route is even more stunning. For several miles a lonesome track crosses the bright no man's land between the rugged mountain and the alkali flat, passing by a green spring, then a sprawling golden marsh fringed by salt-crusted pools. This is wild land. In all of my amblings, the only large wildlife I saw was a solitary raven flying overhead, as much at home here as everywhere. I felt like no one had been here before me.

■

TEUTONIA PEAK

Short and moderately sloped, the Teutonia Peak Trail was once a popular trail that wandered through beautiful cactus gardens. Largely destroyed by the 2020 Dome Fire, it is now a sad reminder of mankind's folly. The hike is still worth taking, as the trail leads up a scenic ridge overlooking vast tracts of desert. The crowning jewel is the summit block just beyond the trail, a miniature maze of textured granite formations guarding a hidden route to the summit.

General Information

Road status: Roadless; paved access road
Teutonia Peak Trail: 1.9 mi, 700 ft up, 20 ft down one way / very easy
South Teutonia Peak: 2.3 mi, 830 ft up, 140 ft down one way / moderate
Main attractions: Short peak climb, rock formations, botany, views
USGS 7.5' topo map: Cima Dome
Maps: pp. 133*, *185**, *83*

Location and Access

Teutonia Peak is an isolated mountain known as an inselberg ("rock island") that protrudes prominently from the northeastern slope of Cima Dome. To get to the Teutonia Peak Trail, drive the Cima Road 6.4 miles north of Cima (or 11.3 miles south of the gas station on Interstate 15) to the signed trailhead on the west side.

Route Description

Teutonia Peak Trail. From the trailhead, the serrated ridge of Teutonia Peak is in plain view less than 1.5 miles away, rising from the smooth swell of Cima Dome like a medieval fortress. The trail ambles gently to the foot of the inselberg, across a plain once studded with Joshua trees. Before it was destroyed by the 2020 Dome Fire, the area was famous for its abundant flora. Now only a short stretch of trail has been left untouched, juxtaposing on one side the full glory of the original vegetation, and on the other a grey cemetery of dead Joshua trees.

After 0.5 mile, the trail crosses the Cut Spring Road, then continues 0.45 mile to an old mining road. This area was the site of a small-time silver mine called Teutonia. First worked in 1896, it was soon idle, then it was picked up again 10 years later by a man named Charles Toegel. In spite of the property's modest showings, Toegel managed to raise a little capital to develop it. He built a camp consisting of a few cabins, a blacksmith, and a general store, which he grandly named Toegel City. His hopes were short-lived. Over the next few years, he shipped all of 100 tons of ore bearing at most 150 ounces of silver per ton, and a little lead. A decade later the mine and the camp were gathering dust. The main shafts are to the right along the road, the camp to the left. Dug in friable soil, many of the shafts have caved in, their former collars now splintered lumber. The only visible ore is yellowish coatings of limonite and smearings of copper ore. What was left of the camp, mostly the large wooden floor and collapsed walls of what may have been the store, was consumed by the 2020 Dome Fire.

Make a right on the old mining road; the trail resumes 75 yards further on the left. In 150 yards, it crosses a third road, and switchbacks 0.25 mile up to a low saddle on the inselberg's ridge. To the northwest, across a ravine, the ridge continues as a dramatic alignment of turrets and fins. The trail veers south and closely follows the ridge line, along displays of sculpted granite. Unlike the bulk of Cima Dome, these exposures as well as Teutonia Peak are not made of Teutonia Adamellite but of Jurassic Ivanpah Granite. Being harder than the adamellite, the granite has resisted erosion and now stands prominently above the dome's worn surface. The trail ends in 0.4 mile at a tall gap between sheer cliffs, at the edge of the mountain block.

I cannot think of many climbs that offer such high-caliber vistas for so little effort. To the east rise Kessler Peak, the Ivanpah Mountains, and the rugged New York Mountains. To the northwest, Shadow Valley's immense creosote plain stretches out for miles, bounded in the far distance by Clark Mountain and the lofty Kingston Range. The highest summit visible to the northwest is no other than Telescope Peak itself, the roof of Death Valley, more than 100 miles away...

Teutonia Peak. The best part is yet to come—climbing the summit. It is only 200 yards from the end of the trail, but unscalable from this vicinity. The first challenge is finding the route to it; the second one is climbing the crux. To take stock of the setting, from the end of the trail go back about 100 steps to an opening on the right (east). Turn right and work your way down the slope just far enough to get a good view down the north flank of the mountain block. About 400 yards to the southeast, at the same elevation, a saddle connects the south end of the mountain block to a 60-foot outcrop east of it. The summit is on the central part of the block, which is roughly a cube separated from the crest line by two narrow, sheer-walled trenches 40 to 80 feet deep, one on each side of the summit. To get to the summit, continue toward the saddle, paralleling the crest, 100 yards down a first declivity, then up

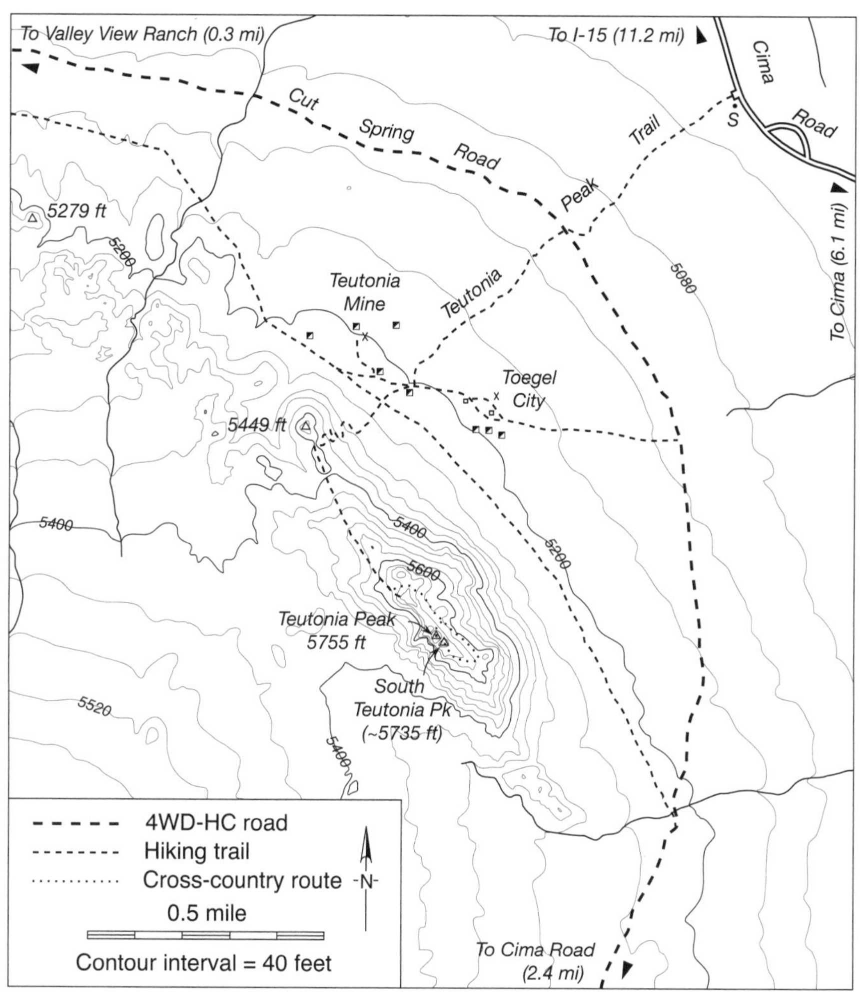

Teutonia Peak		
	Dist.(mi)	Elev.(ft)
Trailhead	0.0	5,025
Junction at Teutonia Mine	0.95	5,200
Toegel City	(0.2)	5,180
Road crossing	1.05	5,225
Saddle on ridge	1.3	5,400
End of Teutonia Peak Trail	~1.7	5,700
Teutonia Peak	(0.2)	5,755
South Teutonia Peak	(0.35)	~5,735

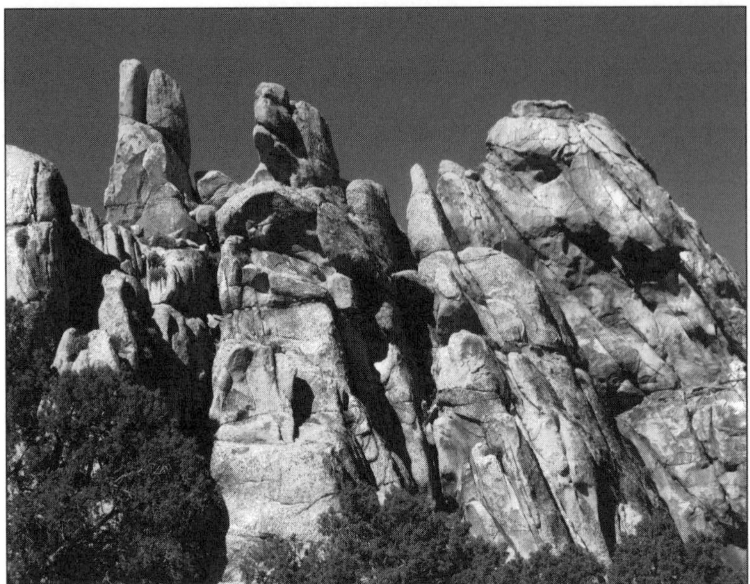

Juniper and granite formations in the trench north of Teutonia Peak

its far side 100 yards to a local high point. About 20 yards past it, look up to the right for a break in the cliff. Scrambling up to it will take you into the northern trench. The summit can be reached via a circuitous route near the trench entrance, at the northern corner of the central block. It is not an easy climb, it is exposed, and if you peel you may fall a long way. Apply extreme caution, and do not attempt this ascent alone.

If you cannot make it, there is fortunately a fine consolation prize. South Teutonia Peak, a stone's throw to the south, is only a few feet lower than the summit yet easy to reach, without even a scramble. From the local high point continue in the same direction 200 yards or so, down and out of another declivity, to the saddle. Climb the short slope west of the saddle to the crest, then follow the slickrock northwest to the summit near the rim of the southern trench.

Exploring this area is exhilarating for multiple reasons. The views from the summits are of course even better than from the trail, especially of the sweeping curve of Cima Dome spreading right under your feet. But the views are eclipsed by the sheer delight of wandering through the imposing underworld of slots, high cliffs, and hoodoos that make up Teutonia Peak's chaotic ridge. The quest for the summit becomes its own reward, more enticing than the summit itself.

■

THE DEATH VALLEY MINE

If you are in the mood for a leisurely ride, try this seldom-visited backcountry road at the foot of the Mid Hills' panoramic granitic peaks. Narrow most of the way, it traverses a healthy Joshua tree forest to historic Death Valley Mine, the site of a 1907 swindle with an unlikely connection to Death Valley. Then take a stroll through the well-preserved mining camp. With its two large residences, hoisting equipment, and mid 20th century mill, it ranks amongst the largest and most interesting mines in the preserve.

General Information

Road status: Hiking on old roads; standard-clearance access road
Death Valley Mine: 1.0 mi, 60 ft up loop / very easy
Main attractions: A scenic backcountry road, a historic mining camp
USGS 7.5' topo map: Mid Hills
Maps: pp. 139*, *185**, *83*

Location and Access

The Death Valley Mine is at the upper rim of Kelso Basin, near the foot of the Mid Hills. The best direction to drive the primitive road that leads to and away from it is northbound: it is generally more scenic when heading away from the sun. To get to the south end of the road, drive the Cedar Canyon Road 3.0 miles east from the Kelso-Cima Road, or 2.9 miles west from the Black Canyon Road, to the Death Valley Mine Road, on the north side. From here the Death Valley Mine Road goes 4.4 miles to a T junction. This stretch has a couple of rough spots, but with a little care they are passable with a standard-clearance vehicle. To go to the Death Valley Mine, make a right, then park after 0.2 mile at the mine's gate.

To continue, drive back to the T junction and go west on the second leg of the Death Valley Mine Road to the Morning Star Mine Road at Cima, a distance of 2.45 miles. This stretch is graded and wide, and passable with a standard-clearance vehicle.

To drive the Death Valley Mine Road in the other direction, from Cima drive the Morning Star Mine Road 0.1 mile to a left bend. The graded road on the east side is the Death Valley Mine Road. Cross the tracks and take the middle fork.

History: The Dawson Brothers' Scam

Throughout the West, gold rushes often attracted colorful con men who attempted to make it rich without the hard work, usually by peddling mining claims that were as fabulously rich as they were imaginary. The eastern Mojave Desert did not have too many crooks, but it did have B. X. Dawson—and his crime made up in magnitude what was lacking in numbers.

In 1905, major gold strikes were made all over Death Valley. Places like the Bullfrog Hills and the Keane Wonder Mine had just been discovered and were poised to make history, and the great Skidoo would soon follow. Walter Scott, soon to be known as Death Valley Scotty and Death Valley's premier con artist, had just gained national fame, purportedly striking it rich with a gold mine of his own. No one had seen it, which was hardly a surprise since it didn't exist, but he had sweet-talked investors into bankrolling him, money that he spent, of course, not exploiting his mine but supporting a lavish lifestyle.

Over in Colorado, someone was watching Scott's success and scheming his own plan to cash in on the general boom-time euphoria. His name was B. X. Dawson. A 32-year-old mining promoter, Dawson was a calculating man, full of himself, self-serving, and blessed with a wild imagination. If Scotty could do it, he knew he could do it too. In November 1905, Dawson started the rumor that he had just returned from a grueling trip to Death Valley, where he had discovered an incredibly rich prehistoric mine on Furnace Creek that he called Hidden Hell. He published a grand theory that explained its formation, proclaiming that Death Valley was once a "lake of fire" that purified his gold. His find was nothing other than the lost mine of the Aztec, an immense lode that had "enriched many men for many centuries and eventually led them all to their death!" But he, B. X. Dawson, had overcome the great perils of the dreaded valley to reclaim it, and he was determined to harvest its prodigious wealth. With his brother, he incorporated the property as the Death Valley Gold Mining and Milling Company, and launched an ambitious campaign to sell its three million shares. He ran ads across the country in mining journals, financial newspapers, and investment magazines, generously portraying himself as "one of Death Valley's most successful mine owners" and promising fabulous profits.

Dawson's story was absurd. But we are dealing with humans, a remarkably gullible species. In all ages, people aware of this little flaw have milked it for everything it was worth. B. X. Dawson was one of them—and he accomplished wonders. Within a month, his stock was selling like hot cakes for 3 cents a share. A year later, it was up to one

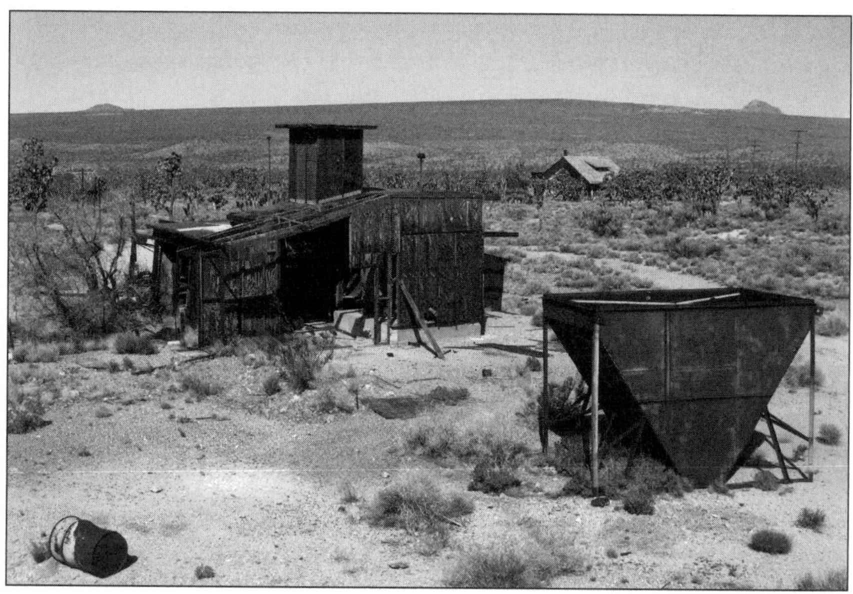

Mill building at the Death Valley Mine; Cima Dome in the background

dollar and sales were still going strong. The Dawson brothers were getting rich fast selling a mine that did not exist.

Or did it?... In July 1906, Dawson did purchase a mine. It is not clear why. Perhaps he wanted something to show should anyone investigate his company's assets. Perhaps he wanted his company to generate a little cash so he could keep its share value up. The mine Dawson bought was not a gold mine, nor was it located in Death Valley, but it was close enough. It had just been discovered that year by a man named J. L. Bright of Kelso. Yes, the mine Dawson bought was out in the eastern Mojave Desert, and he called it Death Valley. The man had a sense of humor.

No mine could possibly meet the wild expectations Dawson had set for his Hidden Hell. But the Death Valley Mine did have a few pockets of high-grade silver ore, with a little gold for good measure, so it wasn't a total loss. Under the management of the brothers' company, a shaft was sunk and it started producing fair returns. A small settlement called Dawson Camp sprung into existence near the mine. The first shipment was made in September 1907, using old and new technology: the ore was hauled to Cima in 12-horse-team wagons, then shipped by rail to the Needles smelter. Later shipments went to Salt Lake City. The Death Valley Mine had a neighbor, the Arcalvada Mine, which was also actively extracting rich silver-lead ore from its own shaft. In September 1907, the two companies merged and formed the Death Valley Arcalvada Mining Company. Two months later, a crew of 75 was busily working the two shafts, and the year's total production reached a respectable 74,600 ounces of silver.

This was the Death Valley Mine's only great year. In September 1907, the Dawson brothers had sold nearly two million shares, and they decided to quit while they were ahead. They disappeared from the scene, taking with them around $250,000 from the sale of stock. A few months later, the mine became involved in litigation. It continued producing, but by the time the litigation was resolved in 1915 it had not managed to even double its 1907 production.

In 1915, the Death Valley Mine had a second chance. It became the property of J. Lee Strawn, who kept it for more than 40 years. Strawn had already been working the mine with his wife's help for several years. His wife ran the hoist and dumped the buckets while he mined. They kept at it for many years, processing their ore at the on-site 30-ton mill. By 1921 they had pulled out $38,000 worth of silver, and they closed shop. Hopeful that one day the shafts would be reactivated, Strawn kept the pumps running for years so the timber in the shafts would not get flooded and rot. But it was in vain: in June 1927, the main shaft's timber and parts of the plant were destroyed by fire.

For many years, the installations remained dormant—the 100-resident camp, the mill, and a six-room residence. To make a little money, in 1946 the mill was moved to the Owl Spring Mine in southern Death Valley. In 1951, Strawn leased his claims to the Rose Marie Mining Company of Los Angeles. The lessee began to clean up and re-timber the charred shaft, with the intention to install a 50-ton mill. But the mine had already been gutted, and not much more came out of it. After nearly 50 years, it had put out about $130,000 worth of silver.

B. X. Dawson never achieved a fraction of Scotty's notoriety, but the old Aztec curse didn't kill him after all. He stayed in the mining business much of his life, though he never learned. In the mid-1930s he was still trying to squeeze gold out of second-rate tunnels in Idaho.

Route Description

The Death Valley Mine Road. This is a beautiful road. Close to nature, it cuts through a forest of fairly large Joshua trees that spreads out all the way to the conspicuous bulge of Cima Dome to the west. The scenic Mid Hills rise to the east, their slopes streaked by a dark band of conifers, their crest festooned with sharp peaks. Thanks to the relatively smooth ground, the driving is pleasant and easy, and you can devote more attention to your surroundings. Stop occasionally—

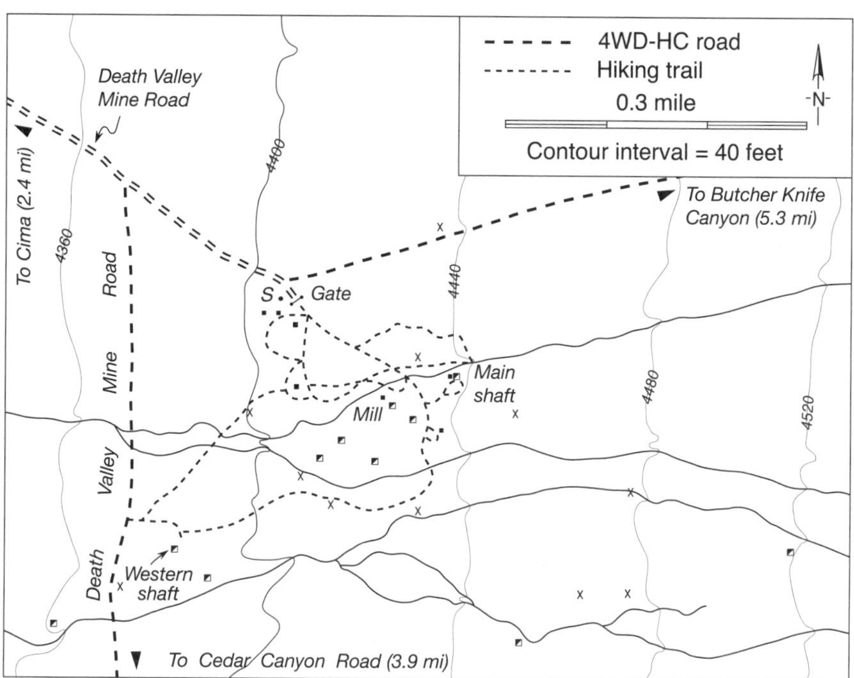

The Death Valley Mine		
	Dist.(mi)	Elev.(ft)
Death Valley Mine gate	0.0	4,410
Main shaft	0.2	4,438
Cabin	0.25	4,438
Western shaft	0.6	4,380
Back to gate	0.95	4,410

there is no room to pull over, so anywhere will be fine—and get out to examine the flora. It is composed of literally dozens of species of cactus, yucca, and shrub, as well as many wildflowers in the spring.

The Death Valley Mine. Other than its intriguing connection with a shrewd con man, what makes this mine so interesting is its well-preserved structures. The residence just past the gate is one of the preserve's largest historic dwellings. Built around 1910, it was the manager's quarters. Unlike most mine cabins, it is a full-sized two-story house with electricity and a bathroom, spacious and comfortable, so uncharacteristic that at the time it was compared to an emperor's palace. A couple lived here as caretakers in the 1970s. Someone took great care to liven up its surroundings with flower beds, vines on trellises, oleander, and a hedge of Joshua trees to shield its wide veranda. The curious small shed partly buried on the house's northwest side was the cellar. The rickety plywood shed to the west was used for storage, mechanical repairs, and to raise small animals, perhaps hens or rabbits. Shelves and drawers still held an assortment of spare parts, jars of pickled vegetables, and other homestead essentials, until the NPS cleaned it all out in 2008. The smaller dwelling further south was probably the bunk house. Since the camp was vacated, the two houses have been boarded up to keep people, animals, and weather out of them.

The main mining ruins are along the short road that loops behind the houses. The most interesting site is the mill housed in the large plywood structure crowned by a square turret. Ore was dumped into it through the feeder near its top, mixed with water from the tank on the roof, then spun around and crushed to a fine powder by steel balls or rods inside the mill. The nearby mill tailing is small, so this mill likely did not work very hard. Quite a bit of mining paraphernalia is scattered around, including a large steel hopper and a concrete trough perhaps used for cyanide processing. The low gravel tailing to the east is historic. The inclined shaft at its north end has a one-of-a-kind conveyor belt that brought ore out to the surface in a series of small metal scoops.

The elaborate shaft along the side road at the east end of the loop is likely the main producer from Dawson's era. The small cabin next to it houses two generations of gas-powered hoists. The complex arrangement of cogs, spools, and cables outside the cabin is another hoist, much older. The shaft's steel headframe, gated platform, and custom ladder were installed after the 1927 fire. Although this is desert land, water isn't far—the shaft is flooded less than 30 feet below the surface. The picturesque cabin just down the road, with its gaping boards, creaking floors, and obligatory junkyard, may have been part of the original Dawson Camp.

Even if mine ruins don't do it for you, come here for a scenic stroll along the many abandoned trails that crisscross Dawson's old claims. The most obvious one is the longer loop to the western shaft. From the cabin, continue south on the road until it turns to a trail. It is only 0.35 mile across open desert to the shaft, then the same distance back along a different trail to the gate (see map). This is a beautiful secluded area, crowded with sizable Joshua trees.

■

— 6 —

Clark Mountain Range

The Clark Mountain Range is a 15-mile-long, northeast-trending range that stretches from Mountain Pass, its boundary with the Mescal Range to the south, to the Nevada border at Stateline Pass. Bounded to the west by Shadow Valley, to the north by Mesquite Valley, and to the east by Ivanpah Valley, it has the typical topographic expression of the Basin and Range Province. Its south end, including the rugged main mountain block, is protected as a separate preserve unit of 37,743 acres. At its core lies a spellbinding 13,560-acre wilderness crowned by the impressive rimrock of 7,930-foot Clark Mountain, the highest point in the eastern Mojave Desert. People come here to tackle the steep routes up to this commanding summit, to hike or four-wheel drive its rolling foothills, to climb some of the best limestone cliffs in the country, to enjoy the area's unique flora, explore its numerous historic sites, or simply spend a night away from it all in a cool desert forest.

Access and Backcountry Roads

The Clark Mountain unit is generally easily accessible from paved roads on its west side (the Excelsior Mine Road, which eventually connects with Tecopa and Shoshone) and south side (Interstate 15). Access can be gained from the north with sturdy vehicles on the graded power-line road that follows the unit's northern boundary. The Yates Well Road, which can be picked up on Interstate 15, slices diagonally across the eastern portion of the unit and provides high-clearance access to some of the area's most interesting sites. In 2011, it was temporarily re-routed while solar plants were being installed in the area, but it should be re-opened afterward. Access from the Bailey Road exit

Suggested Backcountry Drives in the Clark Mountain Range					
Route/Destination	Dist. (mi)	Lowest elev.	Highest elev.	Road type	Pages
Alaska Hill	8.1	3,256'	4,590'	H	147
Clark Mountain picnic area	9.5	3,678'	6,140'	H	163
Colosseum Lake	10.8	2,645'	~5,620'	F	155-158
Copper World Mine	6.1	3,670'	5,350'	H	167
Curtis Canyon Road (loop)	3.4	5,160'	5,660'	F	160-161
Ivanpah at Willow Spring	7.3	2,645'	4,300'	H	155, 157
Pachalka Spr./Valley Wells	5.7	3,668'	4,970'	F	167, 175
Key:	H=Primitive (HC)		F=Primitive (4WD)		

requires bypassing the sprawling MP Materials (formerly Molycorp) Mine complex at Mountain Pass. Its complicated network of roads has changed several times in recent years, and it is not clear what portion of it, if any, is open to the public. To get to Clark Mountain this way, it is safest to ask permission and directions at the mine's entrance gate.

Although the stony heart of Clark Mountain is roadless, the broad apron of hills that wraps around it is crisscrossed by old mining roads. A high-clearance vehicle is often required to navigate these aged byways, and at places four-wheel drive as well. They offer a wide range of experiences, the most prevalent being dusty rides to rarely visited historic mines and camps. Try the Benson Mine and its odd little red cabin, or the lonesome cutoff between the Yates Well and Excelsior Mine roads west of Alaska Hill. To get further off the beaten track, drive the lonesome track north of the preserve to Mesquite Pass and down its far side to Mesquite Valley. This one is *wild*.

Geology

Clark Mountain is the preserve's best representative of sedimentary and meta-sedimentary rocks. It is a shattered mosaic of sandstones, siltstones, dolomites, limestones, shales, and quartzites that only the central Providence Mountains come close to in total footprint. The majority of it is made of the Late Proterozoic and Cambrian units between the Kingston Peak Formation and the Nopah Formation, generally getting older toward the base of the mountain. The rest—Sultan Limestone, Monte Cristo Limestone, and Bird Spring Formation—is exposed in an arcuate band that wraps around the summit's east-side scarp. These geological units are responsible for the majestic cliffs framing that most vertical flank of the mountain.

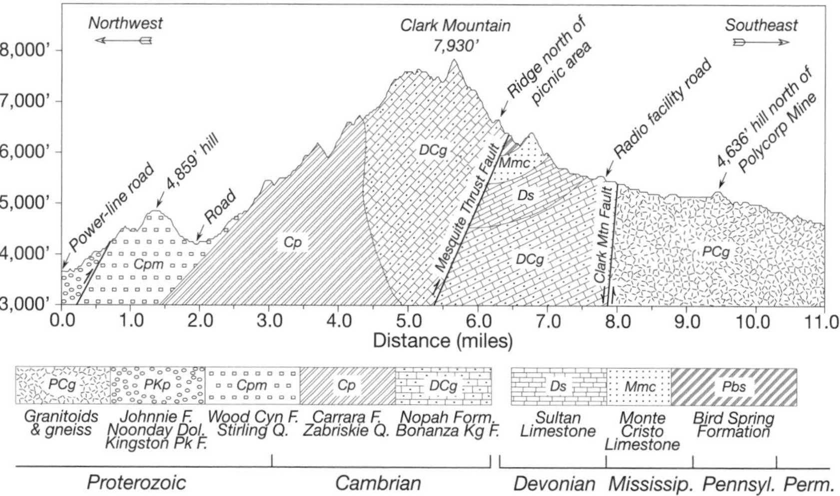

Some formations contain abundant fossils. For example, the Monte Cristo Limestone and the Bird Spring Formation host numerous species of mollusk shells, bryozoans, horn and tabulate corals, and crinoids. Fusulinids, complex single-celled organisms that look like a grain of wheat, are also common. Widespread and diversified, they are extremely useful to correlate the age of rocks from different parts of the world. Most routes to the summit cross fossiliferous ground.

The original stratigraphy has been majorly altered by movements along two northwest-trending faults, the Mesquite Thrust Fault just east of the summit, and the Clark Mountain Fault about 1.5 miles east of it. Sequences west of the Mesquite fault have been shoved over the block sandwiched between the faults. They have thus eroded faster and been stripped of their younger top formations, which now survive only on the middle block. On the east side of the Clark Mountain Fault, the damage is far greater: all the sedimentary strata were removed. What is left is the continent's crystalline basement, a block of Early Proterozoic gneisses and pegmatites exposed down to the eastern Ivanpah Mountains. You can check out this abrupt change when driving the Yates Well Road from Ivanpah Valley. You will be in 1.7-billion-year-old terrain all the way to 0.3 mile before Curtis Canyon, then you will cross the Clark Mountain Fault and enter the Cambrian.

Just north of Mountain Pass the crystalline basement contains a 1.4-billion-year-old intrusion of carbonatite. This rock is geochemically unique: it is based on carbonates instead of silicates, and it is stuffed with rare-earth minerals—indeed a rare occurrence on the planet. This is the commodity that has been exploited for decades at Mountain

Suggested Hikes in the Clark Mountain Range					
Route/Destination	Dist. (mi)	Elev. gain	Mean elev.	Access road	Pages
Short hikes (under 5 miles round trip)					
Alaska Hill mines*	3.7	1,540'	5,000'	H/8.1 mi	150-154
Alaska Hill summit	1.5	1,610'	5,240'	H/8.1 mi	150-152
Clark Mountain	1.8	1,970'	7,170'	H/9.5 mi	163-166
Colosseum Lake*	0.3	~0'	~5,400'	F/10.8 mi	159
Colosseum Mine loop*	1.4	390'	5,770'	F/10.5 mi	158-160
Copper Commander Mine	1.0	740'	5,430'	F/6.1 mi	170-171
Copper World Mine	0.3	190'	5,420'	F/6.1 mi	169
Curtis Canyon	1.0	500'	~5,400'	H/10.7 mi	160-161
Dewey Mine*	0.5	220'	5,240'	H/5.8 mi	174
Ivanpah at Willow Spring	0.1	70'	4,310'	P/7.3 mi	157
Pachalka Spring*	0.3	220'	4,870'	F/5.7 mi	167
The Knife Edge	1.4	1,590'	6,990'	H/9.5 mi	163-166
Valley Wells*	1.35	50'	3,710'	P/0.35 mi	177-180
Intermediate hikes (5-12 miles round trip)					
Pachalka Spr. from mine	2.8	1,970'	5,360'	F/6.1 mi	171-172
Pachalka Spring-CW Mine*	7.8	1,990'	5,010'	F/6.1 mi	169-174
Key: P=Primitive (2WD) H=Primitive (HC) F=Primitive (4WD) Distance: one way, except for loops (round-trip, marked with *) Elev. gain: sum of all elevation gains on a round-trip basis & on loops					

Pass. Our technological world uses rare earths in tiny quantities but in billions of devices, so what little it needs is vital. Without erbium for example, there would be no high-speed Internet.

Mining History

Clark Mountain is the eastern Mojave Desert's mining champion. In 1868 it was the site of the earliest major base-metal strike in the region. Up until around 1891, several rich silver properties were extensively developed on Alaska Hill. In the foothills on the other side of Clark Mountain, a mining town called Ivanpah was buzzing. The three richest mines alone—the Monitor, Beatrice, and Lizzie Bullock—took out a whopping 3.7 million dollars in silver. In 1898, after the best ore had run out, the Copper World Mine took over on the southwest side of the mountain. Twenty years later it was the largest copper producer in southern California, with more than $1,300,000 in revenue. Several

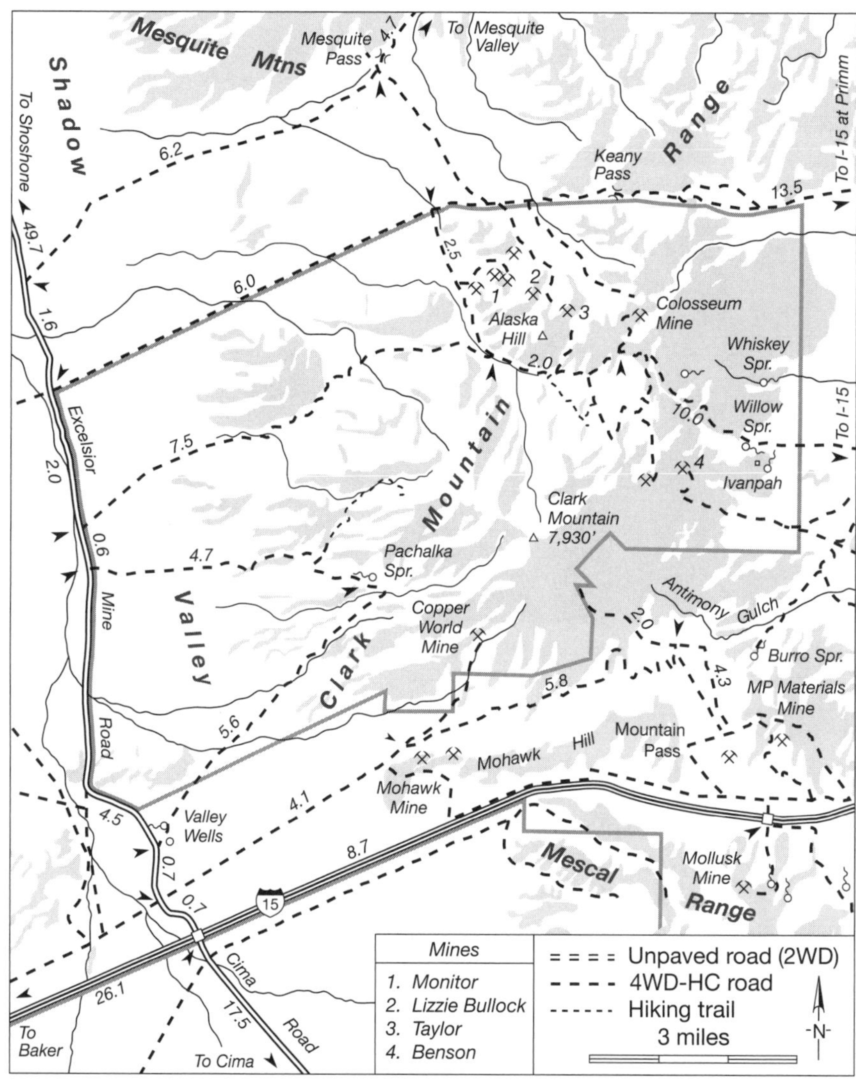

of these mines underwent repeated revivals until at least the 1940s. The Mohawk Mine, south of Clark Mountain, was yet another success story. Probably first developed in conjunction with the Copper World Mine, it was active in the 1910s and from 1944 to 1952. Its total output exceeded $600,000, two thirds in lead, the rest in zinc, silver, and copper. It was a landslide: excluding iron production, the district inherited three of the region's four richest historic properties. The grand finale was yet to come. Between 1987 and 1993, the Colosseum Mine ripped up from the range's ancient crystalline core more than 10 tons of gold!

Storm over the Mesquite Mountains seen from Clark Mountain

Hiking

The Clark Mountain unit is definitely not as remote as the majority of the preserve. But most places of interest are fairly far from asphalt, and the sense of isolation is still prevalent. A few special perks also make up for it. The forest is a major pole of attraction; it is thicker, cooler, more forest-like than anywhere else. It is home to less common plants like desert pincushion cactus, and rare ones such as limber pine and agaves; at places these strange plants are actually dominant. A sizable population of bighorn sheep roam the impregnable high country, and feral burro thrive in the immense Joshua-tree and cactus flats of Shadow Valley. If you are lucky you might run into a desert tortoise or a gila monster. The high country can be explored on mining roads now closed to motor vehicles, especially around Pachalka Spring and Curtis Canyon. In fact, most roads open to vehicles are seldom used, and they can be put to good use for hiking. Except on Clark Mountain, you are never further than a mile from an open road, so there are plenty of short cross-country hikes to choose from. Clark Mountain is, of course, the prized destination, with several distinctive climbing routes. From late fall to early spring, come prepared for snow and ice. In summer, anticipate very large diurnal temperature variations.

■

ALASKA HILL

During the famous silver boom of the 1870s, Clark Mountain's richest mines were concentrated on a little mountain then known as Alaska Hill. If you have a penchant for history and grand vistas, you will enjoy hiking the scenic loop up and down and around this mountain in search of the many mining gems from that distant era. Set against a backdrop of tall hills peppered with Joshua trees, agave, and pine, overlooking seldom-seen ranges, Alaska Hill is a befitting celebration of the eastern Mojave Desert's earliest mining days.

General Information

Road status: Hiking cross-country and on roads; HC access road
Alaska Hill summit: 1.5 mi, 1,450 ft up, 160 ft down one way / difficult
Alaska Hill mines: 3.7 mi, 1,540 ft up loop / moderate
Main attractions: Historic silver mines, ruins, botany, views, peak climb
USGS 7.5' topo maps: Pachalka Spring, Clark Mountain*
Maps: pp. 153*, *145*

Location and Access

Alaska Hill is 3 miles north of Clark Mountain. The main mines are clustered in two adjacent canyons on its north slope. They can be reached by driving local roads and taking short walks, or better yet, by hiking the loop described below. From the southbound Cima Road exit on Interstate 15, drive the paved Excelsior Mine Road 8.5 miles north to the graded power-line road that cuts east-west across the Clark Mountain Range. Turn right and drive it 6 miles to the Yates Well Road on the right. Go 1.2 miles to a crossing and turn left on a primitive road. At the five-road junction 0.1 mile further, take the second road from the left, which heads northeast. Continue 0.8 mile (ignore the left fork half way through) as the road curves right to an open area with large stone ruins on the right, and park. The power-line road is fairly good, but along the last 3 miles a dozen long steep grades will stop low-power vehicles. The rest of this itinerary requires high clearance.

History: The Saga of the McFarlane Brothers

Silver mining on Alaska Hill was sparked by the discovery of copper in 1868 in a then nameless range near the Nevada stateline. It was made by a Native American, who showed his find to his friend John Moss, an experienced pioneer with a flair for lucrative lodes. Moss

The Ivanpah Con Mill, ca. 1878 (Larry Vredenburgh collection)

rode with his native friend to the desert to assess the site; he found there the expected copper, and silver as well. His reputed skill for mining investors' wallets served him well. In April 1869, after returning to San Francisco with rich samples, he had secured financial backing, formed the Piute Company, and outfitted a party of prospectors. Between the discovery site and Nevada, they located some 130 claims and created a new district, which they named in honor of William H. Clarke, a Visalia saloon keeper and member of the party. The mountain became known as Clark Mountain (the "e" was eventually dropped).

Late in 1869 the Piute Company laid out the 160-acre townsite of Ivanpah around small springs in the eastern foothills of Clark Mountain. Moss hired Piute Indians to work at one of the company's main properties, the Eugene Mine, just west of Ivanpah. He had a road surveyed to San Bernardino, along the mail route to Camp Cady. Fueled by Nevada's recent silver rush, the new strike drew instant attention. By the following summer, 300 miners, prospectors, merchants, and adventurers had converged on the area, a mix of Anglos, Piutes, and Mexicans. Teamsters brought in supplies from San Bernardino, and returned loaded with raw ore worth as much as $800 a ton, which was shipped to the new Selby Smelter near San Francisco.

Ivanpah's uncontested rulers were the McFarlane brothers. They were four: Tom and Andrew arrived in February 1870, John soon after, and William joined them in 1875. They all had extensive mining experience. In 1859, they had made headlines at the Kern River gold mines, where Andrew discovered the famous Long Tom Mine. Tom and

Andrew repeated this feat on Alaska Hill, where they made the area's richest silver strikes and set out to develop their mines, the Monitor and the Beatrice. For some reason the Piute Company died early on, in 1871. By then the district had more than enough good mines to move on without missing a beat. The other mine central to Ivanpah's economy was the Lizzie Bullock. Discovered by two prospectors in 1871, it was run after 1876 by a seasoned miner named Julius Bidwell.

In early years mining and milling equipment was primitive. The second-grade rock was crushed in arrastres near town, then smelted and amalgamated. Ore worth less than the high cost of labor ($125 a ton) was stockpiled in hope for better days. The McFarlanes were the first to take steps toward solving this processing bottleneck. In the spring of 1873, they put up a furnace near their mines. Two years later they brought in the district's first mill, a modest five-stamp mill relocated from the New York Mine that they erected right in Ivanpah. In 1876, Bidwell followed suit and installed a 10-stamp mill. He also subsequently filed numerous claims in the area, including on the future Colosseum and Copper World properties. The McFarlanes incorporated their assets under the banner of the Ivanpah Consolidated Mill and Mining Company. Together with the Lizzie Bullock Mine, the Ivanpah Consolidated employed a sizable fraction of the local labor. Business did not always go smoothly. The company changed hands twice. But each time the shrewd McFarlanes landed back on their feet and at least one of them remained in a position of control at the mines.

Year after year, between the local mines, more distant mines, and chloriders bringing in ore for custom milling, there was enough work for Ivanpah to sustain a critical population. In the spring of 1880 rich ore was uncovered at the Alps Mine and the Alley Mine, the latter by Tom McFarlane and J. B. Alley. The Ivanpah Con was flushed with milling ore—in April alone it shipped $10,000 worth of bullion. At its peak around 1879, Ivanpah boasted hotels, saloons, stores, blacksmiths, shoemakers, a post office, and a butcher shop. Like other frontier towns, it had its share of drunks, gambling disputes, and gun fights. One of the victims was John McFarlane himself. In 1881, when the financially strapped Ivanpah Con refused to pay taxes (all of $1,480), a collector was sent to put a lien on the company's assets. John, who had a temper, confronted the man in charge of guarding his company's mill. Tension rose, guns were drawn, and John was shot dead.

Through the 1880s and 1890s, as the price of silver was falling and the richest ore running out, Alaska Hill gradually declined. In 1885 most mines had either shut down or greatly reduced their workload. Five years later Ivanpah had only 11 residents, although the mills were still in use, fed in part by the Lizzie Bullock and the Alps mines. In December 1892 the business district had shrunk to a store, a boardinghouse, and the post office, managed by Bidwell and his wife. Even the opening of the rich Copper World Mine across the mountain in 1898 did not revive Ivanpah. By 1900 the town was all but deserted. Tom and William McFarlane moved to San Bernardino in the mid-1880s, although William and Andrew were involved at Vanderbilt for a while. Bidwell passed away around 1893, and Andrew in 1905. But these businessmen had fulfilled their passion: Bidwell brought in $1,200,000, the McFarlanes $2,500,000, and their enterprises supported a whole town for nearly 20 years. No historic mine surpassed these figures.

Route Description

The Beatrice Mine. Much larger than most and fairly well preserved, the stone ruins at the end of the road may have historic significance. The south group has two houses with thick stone walls standing up to 6 feet tall. The north group is a cluster of four rooms with a back enclosure and front patio. Pieces of refractory bricks and metal straps used to hold bricks together to make a portable furnace, as well as glassy slag, suggest that the north group had an assay office or a small smelter—perhaps the one ran by the McFarlanes in 1873.

From the trailhead, first follow the continuation of the access road into the canyon to the southeast toward the Beatrice Mine—its cabin is visible high on the canyon's west ridge. The road does not last long. It soon enters a canyon so steep erosion had a field day ripping it apart. Joshua trees and yucca, blackbrush, staghorn cholla, and platoons of pygmy agave share the hillsides. Higher elevations are pinpricked with outcrops of blue-gray limestone and the quiet green of Mormon tea, juniper, and pinyon pine. The tall tailings flowing down the slopes up ahead testify that this faulted Paleozoic block carried in its fractures considerable silver. The rubbled homes of forgotten miners line the wash. You are approaching the region's richest historic properties.

After 0.3 mile the main canyon angles left at a fork. To reach the cabin and the Beatrice Mine, climb the canyon's western ridge starting at the left end of the long benchcut at the fork. A trail winds up to not far below the cabin, but it is so far gone that it is just as easy to pick your own route up the ridge line. Made of a patchwork of sheet metal nailed to a wooden frame, the cabin is a funky construction, with empty shelves, a rickety table, and an attached stone cellar. It would be hard to find a shorter commute: the main tunnel and shafts are mere steps away; the furthest tunnel is 50 yards to the south, at the end of a tall and narrow tailing. Trapped on the narrow space between a rock

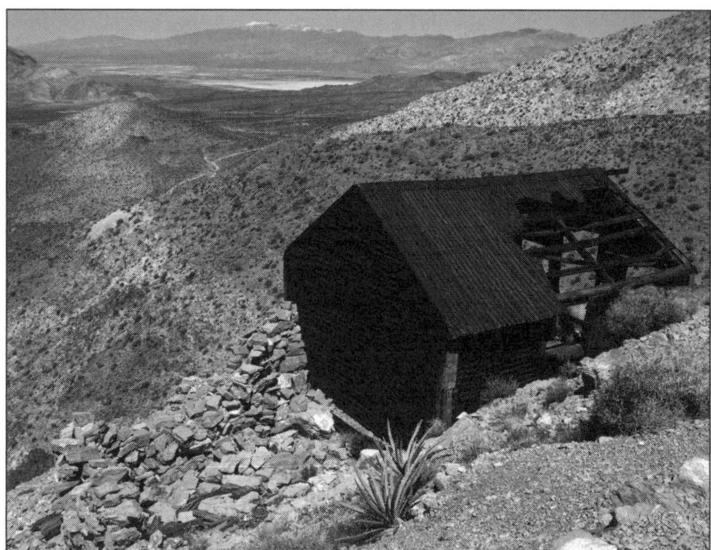

Cabin at the Beatrice Mine; snow-covered Charleston Peak in the distance

wall and the sheer edge of a tailing, this humble home commands eye-filling views across pristine Shadow Valley to the Mesquite Mountains, the Kingston Range, and the high Panamints. To the north sprawl Mesquite Valley and its pale dry lake shining beneath the lofty Spring Mountains. It is well worth trekking up this lopsided piece of real estate just to check out this breathtaking panorama.

The Monitor Mine. To continue, drop back down to the wash. From here on up, it is largely taken up by the overlapping tailings of the Monitor Mine. The fun part is looking for a path around these massive slants of pulverized rock. There is something powerful about this place, a persistent haunting stimulated by a sea of mementos from the past, anything from bits of trails to mittens, stone ruins, and a spectacular collection of tunnels. Many of them have interesting remains—strap rails, inclined railways, rough-hewn ties, and stopes shored with trellises of pine logs. The views get increasingly finer. The last major working is the largest, a long trench ending at three dank tunnels. From there, cut a beeline northeastward to the last three smaller tailings. The divide with the next canyon east is just above them, in the shadow of Alaska Hill's summit. At the divide there is a shaft. Just past it, a mostly level trail cuts south-southeast across the slope, overlooking a scenic area bristling with limestone outcrops. It passes above the last Monitor Mine tunnel, then after 800 feet it reaches a saddle.

Alaska Hill. From this saddle the summit of Alaska Hill is just 0.5 mile and 500 feet up. It overlooks a beautiful province of roomy valleys and prominent mountains that makes the short climb well worth it. Proceed roughly south up the rounded ridge. There is a stony false summit to bypass on the right, then a low hill, and finally the summit's pine-covered north slope. The panorama is overwhelmed by pristine Shadow Valley and the rugged wilderness of the Kingston Range. To the north the view opens up onto Mesquite Valley, its small town of Sandy and oval dry lake dwarfed by the lofty Spring Mountains. To the south Clark Mountain's forested north face rises impressively in deeply chiseled limestone buttresses. On a clear winter day there might be half a dozen summits in sight competing for snow.

The Alley and the Lizzie Bullock mines. After returning to the saddle, descend the ravine northeast cross-country to the upper end of the canyon road visible below. Go far enough to your right to bypass (and avoid falling into) the two large workings below, at the end of the road. One of them is a high-vaulted tunnel capped with giant unstable limestone slabs. The other one is a gaping shaft held open by a tree trunk harvested more than a century ago. They belonged to the original Lizzie Bullock Mine, one of the three brightest local stars.

The rough road drops in steep steps, past pale waves of overburden, into a broad canyon. After it veers north and levels off a little, it enters the Alley Mine claim, which includes the workings on the hillside to the east. After 0.4 mile there is a road junction at a fork in the wash. Turn right and follow the side road 0.25 mile up to its end at a long ore chute, Alaska Hill's most impressive structure. This sinuous

Alaska Hill

	Dist.(mi)	Elev.(ft)
Stone ruins at end of road	0.0	4,590
Beatrice Mine (cabin)	0.5	~5,080
Divide/trail	0.8	5,400
Saddle	0.95	5,450
Alaska Hill	(0.5)	5,875
Upper end of road	1.0	5,350
Canyon fork	1.4	5,000
Lizzie Bullock No. 2 cabin	(0.4)	~5,420
Cutoff road	2.4	4,630
Back to starting point	2.9	4,590

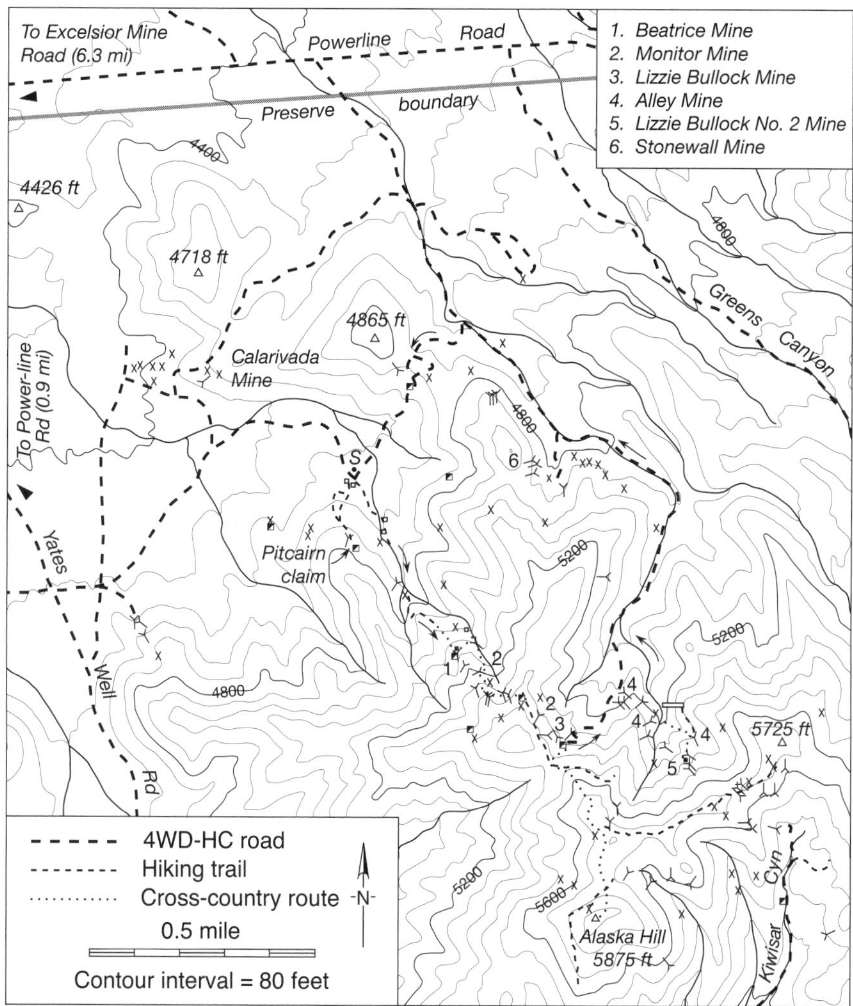

contraption of boards and corrugated iron dropped ore 180 abrupt feet from the mine's high workings down the rocky mountain side. This area likely belonged to the Alley Mine. To climb to the top of the ore chute, walk a short distance up the wash to the mine's long tailing on the left, and ascend its right side. At the north end of the mine's apron, a raised, level trail meanders to the collapsed loading dock at the top of the ore chute.

Alaska Hill is a touching repository of antiques spanning multiple generations since the 1870s. This apron is a good example. The yellow bricks lying around were manufactured by Joseph Cowen and Company, a British outfit that operated between about 1823 and 1904.

Ore chute at the Alley Mine

Many of the cans rusting on domestic dumps are of the hole-and-cap type; the cap was soldered over the hole, a process discontinued after 1904. A stump and scrap metal suggest that there was a blacksmith shop—an anvil was secured to the stump. It also had an assay office, as evidenced by fragments of slag and crucibles. The stripped engine of an endangered species of motor vehicle is entombed in the nearby tunnel. Enjoy discovering these tokens from yesteryear, but leave them for others to enjoy after you.

At the south end of the apron, climb the low rise south to the stone cabin and extensive workings of the Lizzie Bullock No. 2 Mine. Reminiscent of the architectural style of Providence, the once elegant cabin probably dates from the 1890s. Its back wall cleverly incorporated a short adit for cold storage. After a hard day's work blowing up rocks, this would have been a restful place to soak in the beautiful views of the canyon and Mesquite Valley.

The return. After poking around on unstable ground all day, the return down the well-behaved canyon road is a walk in the park. The canyon is carpeted with blond grasses, russet patches of prickly-pear, and a scattering of Joshua trees and full-grown pine trees. Along the way you will pass by a side road on the left, which leads into a deeply cut draw and the hanging tunnels of what may have been the Stonewall Mine. One mile from the fork, another side road takes off on the left. Follow it 0.6 mile over the low ridge bordering the canyon back to your starting point. This is a short loop, but if you let curiosity distract you, it might well be sunset by the time you return.

■

THE COLOSSEUM MINE

If you are looking for a relaxing day of exploration by car and short walks, take the scenic drive up Colosseum Gorge to the Colosseum Mine, a gold property that was active in the 1980s and 1990s. The highlights are the hike around the mine's two colorful pits, and the short walk around the azure lake at the bottom of the larger south pit. In the high country beyond, a rough road climbs up thickly forested Curtis Canyon to a great viewpoint of the mine.

General Information

Road status: Hiking on old roads; HC and 4WD roads throughout site
Ivanpah: 0.1 mi, 40 ft up, 30 ft down one way / very easy
Colosseum Lake: 0.3 mi, ~0 ft up loop / very easy
Colosseum Mine: 1.4 mi, 390 ft up loop (or more) / easy
Main attractions: A scenic gorge, modern gold mine, forested canyon
USGS 7.5' topo maps: Ivanpah Lake, Clark Mountain*
Maps: pp. 161*, 159, *145*

Location and Access

The Colosseum Mine is in the eastern foothills of Clark Mountain, near the head of an east-draining canyon called Colosseum Gorge. Start from the Yates Well Road exit on Interstate 15. From the southbound exit's stop sign, drive 0.4 mile west to a T junction and turn right. After 0.3 mile, angle left at a fork. After 0.3 mile, at the four-way junction at the corner of the Primm Valley Golf Club, continue straight. From there, go 1.8 miles, first northwest, then west, under a power line, then south, to a T junction at the edge of the Ivanpah Solar Electric Generating System—a 3,500-acre devastation that testifies to the colossal environmental cost of industrial solar plants. Turn right and go west along one of the three installations. After 0.8 mile, turn left on the unpaved Yates Well Road. Drive it 2.7 miles to a side road on the left at 11 o'clock, just past the preserve entrance sign. This is the turnoff to Ivanpah. Up to this point high clearance is preferable.

History: The Last Goldfield

Gold mineralization at the site of the Colosseum Mine was first observed as early as 1880. Most of the gold occurred in extremely weak concentrations—less than 0.05 ounce per ton—which made traditional mining unprofitable. Except for the production of $18,000 between

1929 and 1939, the area remained mostly idle for more than a century. The only path to profitability was large-scale mining, which involves processing enormous volumes of rock. Such operations are investment intensive and risky, but the deposit's colossal size was too tempting. Starting in the 1970s, various outfits conducted extensive exploratory drilling and feasibility studies. By 1984, the wealth of the property had been clearly established. After an environmental impact statement was approved in July 1985, Australian company Dallhold Resources, Inc. purchased the property in September 1986. Mining began in late 1987. The mine changed ownership in November 1989 when Lac Minerals, Ltd. of Canada acquired it and put its subsidiary Colosseum, Inc., in charge. Mining continued until July 10, 1992, at which point operations were no longer economical. The mine closed down on May 31, 1993, after the last of the stockpiled ore had been milled.

Like other large-scale extraction industries, the Colosseum Mine is a vivid portrayal of the politics of excess. During its comparatively brief existence, it produced on average 7,000 ounces of gold per month—a cube 8.5 inches on the side. The facilities were spread over half a square mile and averaged 110 employees. The ore bodies were blasted in two huge pits up to four times a week. A 13-cubic-yard front-end loader excavated the broken rock and dumped it into 50-ton and 85-ton trucks, which hauled it to the waste-rock piles, the low-grade stockpile, or the mill. Every week day, between 15,000 and 30,000 tons of rock were removed. By 1993, tens of millions of tons of waste rock had been stored in four piles 300 to 600 feet tall. At the mill, the ore was ground by half a dozen giant crushers. The resulting slurry was leached in a 33,000-ton carbon-in-pulp plant comprising seven 130,000-gallon steel tanks. The metals were stripped from the carbon in a 3.8-ton cyanide tank, separated from the solution with electrowinning and electrorefining, and smelted in a furnace. The final product, a doré containing 70% gold and 30% silver, was sent to off-site refiners. The plant could handle up to 3,400 tons a *day*, and it often ran near capacity, 24/7. The total production was valued at over $100 million, many times the combined outputs of all the preserve's historic mines.

When the mine first opened, it was located in the Clark Mountain Area of Critical Environmental Concern, and mine operators had to obey strict state and federal laws. Many parameters had to be monitored to check whether the mine met regulatory limits, from the proximity to ground water to chemicals discharges and safety features on impoundment dams. Government representatives regularly visited the site to verify compliance. After mining ceased, Colosseum, Inc. had to apply numerous mitigation measures to offset the damage it had inflicted to the land. It graded and recontoured the waste-rock piles and stockpiles, revegetated certain areas, covered the tailings dam with waste rock to minimize erosion, and treated fresh rock surfaces to give them the appearance of desert varnish. Site reclamation cost Lac Minerals more than $30 million—a good fraction of its gains.

Route Description

Ivanpah. Ivanpah is the oldest mining camp in the eastern Mojave Desert: it was a bustling outpost in 1870, when San Bernardino was just a village (see *Alaska Hill*). Check it out on your way to the Colosseum Mine. Time and cattle have taken their toll on the town, and the most important area, the Ivanpah Con Mill, is on private land. But if you resonate with the local mining history, you will enjoy searching the hills for its ghosts.

There are several areas worth exploring. Consult the map and make your own itinerary. Make sure to respect the no-trespassing signs. Of the areas open to the public, Willow Spring is the most interesting. From the turnoff to Ivanpah, turn left on the smaller high-clearance road that parallels the main graded road. After nearly 1 mile you will reach a road on the left, next to a stone ruin and across from Willow Spring's stately lone tree to the south. Park here and walk this road to the spring (0.1 mile). The area west of the road has many stone ruins, the homes of Ivanpah's miners and merchants. Some houses had adobe walls and shake roofs. Most were made of pretty igneous and meta-igneous rocks. Willow Spring hosts a variety of green shrubs, including squawbush, catclaw, and honey mesquite. It also has a well and the ruins of a mill. Quails, peregrine falcons, Steller's jays, and ravens often visit the spring's green strip of water-soaked grass. In the spring, the hills are lavishly sprinkled with brilliant bouquets of sand-wash groundsel and the dainty flowers of purple sage.

The Colosseum Gorge. From the turnoff to Ivanpah, the Yates Well Road (graded) starts climbing into the Colosseum Gorge. "Gorge" is a bit of an exaggeration. It more closely resembles a glacier-carved valley than a chasm. Ignore the desert shrub and barrel cacti, and you could be in a heather-cloaked glacial glen in the Hebrides. But it does exude a certain majesty. From its start near Ivanpah to the crest of the range, the road gains 1,300 feet in just 2 air miles. Look back occasionally to enjoy the dramatic views, down the long U-shaped gorge, of forested Clark Mountain, Ivanpah Lake's pale playa, and the unbroken wall of the New York Mountains and McCullough Range. The final grades are steep and require engine power.

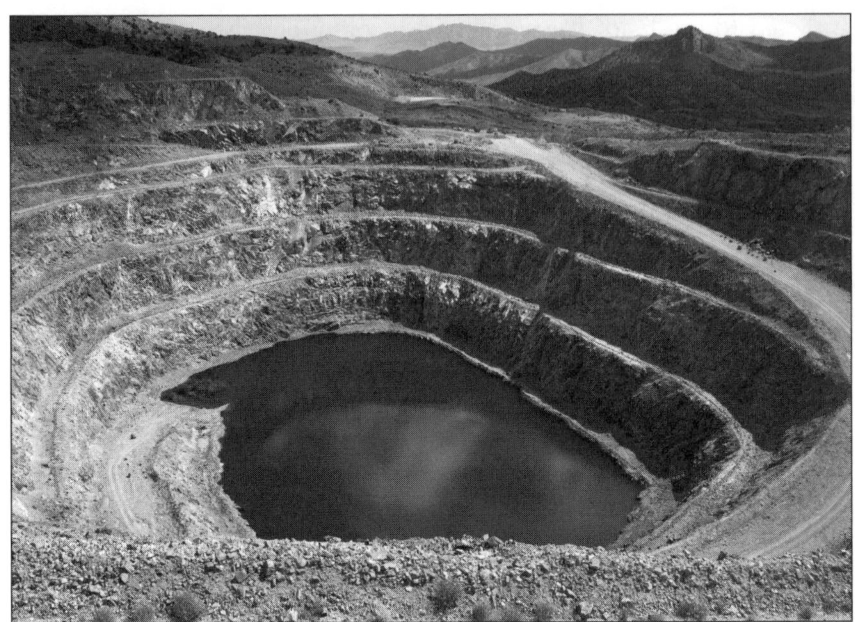

South pit and Colosseum Lake

About 3.4 miles from the Ivanpah turnoff the road crests the top of the gorge and skirts the beautiful area of rolling sagebrush meadows that straddles the range. This is crisp high country, cooler and brighter, sheltered beneath the tall cliffs of Clark Mountain. In 0.4 mile you will reach a junction. The road on the right climbs over a rough section 0.4 mile to a gate in the fence that encircles the Colosseum Mine pits. Although both pits are on private property, the owners leave the gate open for visitors to drive down into the south pit. If this right of entry is revoked in the future, please comply with posted signs.

The Colosseum Mine. The Colosseum Mine gold had a complicated genesis. It was found in two breccia pipes, dikes of rhyolitic magma less than 250 yards in diameter that intruded the gneiss basement 100 million years ago. Subsequently, brecciation broke and mixed the rhyolite with surrounding rock units down to a depth of 3,000 feet. A second rhyolitic intrusion was later added to the mix. Each intrusion injected pyrite in the breccias, where it replaced chunks of carbonates. Gold occurred as free particles and grains within the pyrite. The same process also produced silver, galena, chalcopyrite, and sphalerite. The dark 8-foot boulder with a side coating of yellow limonite just outside the gate is a fine example of the original mineral-rich breccia.

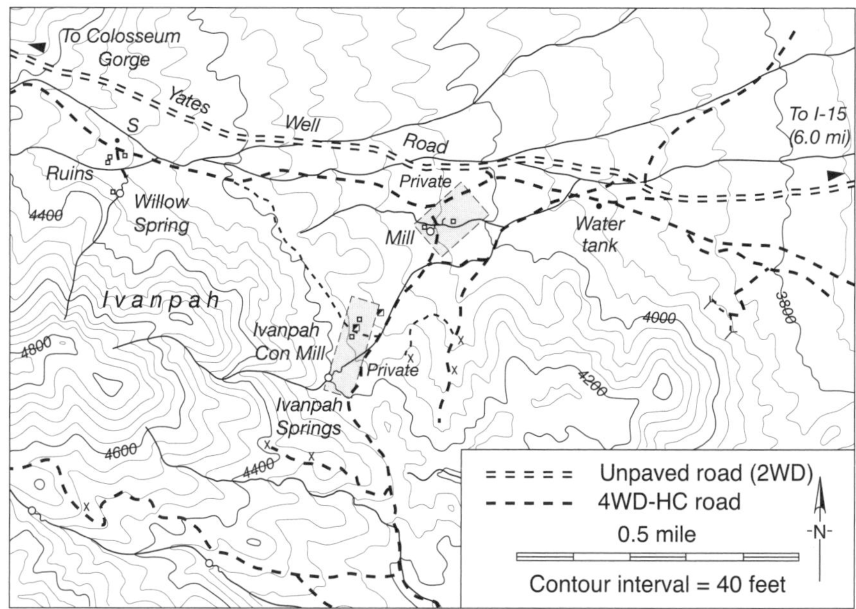

Whoever named this mine had his wish: the larger south pit is nothing short of colossal. Where the road first crests the pit's angular rim, the land falls off at a 55% angle into a cliff-bound hole 220 feet deep and a third of a mile across. The access road spirals down into this raw slice of Earth, cutting through several 60-foot benches before reaching the shore of the sparkling lake that fills the pit. The cliffs bare long streaks of colors, from bright gray to black and rust to yellow. Driving down this grand staircase is a unique experience, as close to subterranean exploration as it gets without going underground.

At the bottom of the road, take the very easy walk around Colosseum Lake (0.3 mile). The lakeside cliffs are locally loaded with shiny clusters of little cubic crystals of pyrite. Fallen blocks of limonite are incrusted with masses of pyrite, chalcopyrite glance, and white calcite crystals. On a sunny day the lake holds the luminous turquoise of Moorea's lagoon; you might be compelled to dive in and check for trigger fish. In stormy weather it morphs into a moody Scottish loch.

Smaller and not as rich, the north pit was mined mostly when the south pit was not producing, up until 1991 when it was also heavily blasted. Its half a dozen towering benches can be viewed by walking the outer perimeter of the fence that encloses the pits (1.4-mile loop). A road of sorts follows most of the fence. From the gate, proceed clockwise up around the south pit, then down to the foot of the north pit, and return, up then down, around the pits' east sides. The fence lowers the wilderness quality of this hike, but novices will appreciate that it makes it tough to get lost. It is also interesting to witness how plants, including ephedra and platoons of scented penstemon, are recolonizing the highly disturbed ground. The high points command good views of Shadow Valley and the Mesquite Mountains.

Curtis Canyon. From the turnoff to the Colosseum Mine, continue on the Yates Well Road down the west side of the range 0.6 mile to a junction. Take the second road on the left, up Curtis Canyon. The preserve does not have many densely forested canyons. This is one of the few that have an open road. The wash *is* the road, an inclined battlefield of bedrock and rubble where a vehicle can only crawl its way up slowly. The forest is impressive for a desert. Tall juniper and pinyon pine thrive in tight ranks right up to the edges of the wash. Plants here are bigger, thicker, greener. Cliffrose, normally a large bush, grows to 12-foot trees with crooked trunks and tousled crowns. The understory hosts a motley crew of blackbrush, blue yucca, ephedra, and brown-spined prickly-pear, their purple-tinged pads cozy against the rocky ground. In the upper canyon there is a small camp. Built in 1958, the camp's one-room, metal-clad cabin is nicely shaded by large pine trees. Frank Curtis, a man we know little about, lived here for 27 years. The

The Colosseum Mine

	Dist.(mi)	Elev.(ft)
Road access (driving)		
Yates Well Road exit on I-15	0.0	2,645
Turnoff to Ivanpah	6.3	3,950
Top of Colosseum Gorge	9.7	5,545
East end of Curtis Cyn loop	9.75	5,530
Turnoff to Colosseum Mine	10.1	5,420
Colosseum Mine (gate)	(0.4)	~5,620
Colosseum Lake	(0.75)	~5,400
West end of Curtis Cyn loop	10.7	5,160
Viewpoint	(1.0)	5,660
East end of Curtis Cyn loop	(2.8)	5,530
The pits loop (hiking)		
Colosseum Mine (gate)	0.0	~5,620
Foot of north pit	0.75	~5,760
Divide between pits	0.9	~5,960
Back to gate	1.4	~5,620

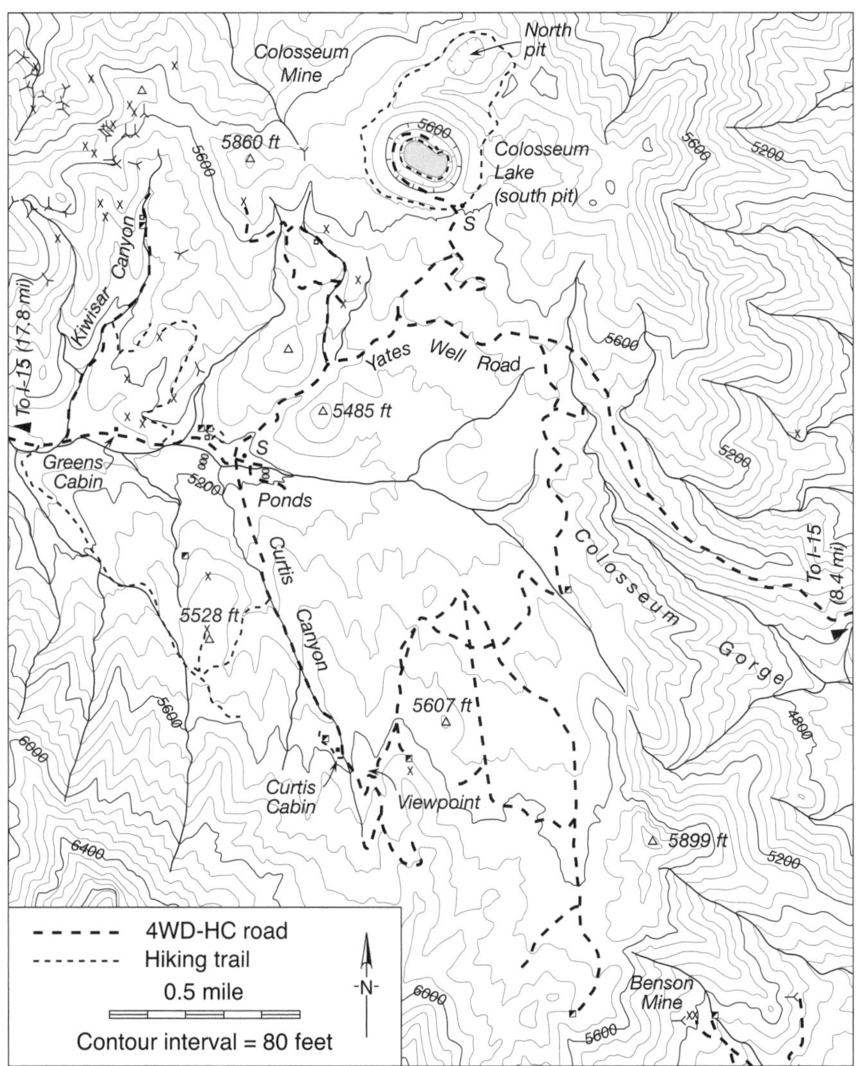

Spartan amenities packed inside—a stove, tiny bed, and shelves—were his sole life support. A couple of curves beyond the camp, the road crests a ridge overlooking the Colosseum Mine's remodeled landscape. It then drops along an open ridge with plunging views of the meadows to return to the Yates Well Road 1 mile from the start of this loop. If your vehicle can't make the grind up the canyon, hike it. It is so pretty and seldom visited that the road does not take away from it. And it is all of 1 mile to the viewpoint.

■

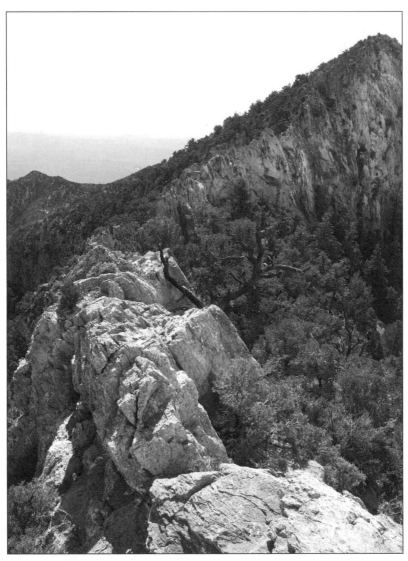

The Knife Edge and the final ridge to Clark Mountain

CLARK MOUNTAIN

At nearly 8,000 feet, Clark Mountain is the highest summit in the preserve. This thrilling ascent calls for mandatory rock climbing to negotiate a long wall tipped with jagged outcrops called the Knife Edge. You will be rewarded with shaded pinyon-pine forests, extensive stands of a rare agave, spectacular cliffs, and the eastern Mojave Desert's largest grove of white fir. If all goes well, you will still remember the views when you knock on heaven's door.

General Information

Road status: Roadless; high-clearance access road
The Knife Edge: 1.4 mi, 1,540 ft up, 50 ft down one way / difficult
Clark Mtn: 1.8 mi, 1,880 ft up, 90 ft down one way / strenuous (Class 3)
Main attractions: A great climb on forested slopes, spectacular views
USGS 7.5' topo maps: Mescal Range, Clark Mountain*
Maps: pp. 165*, *145*

Location and Access

Clark Mountain is the prominent massif north of Interstate 15 near Mountain Pass. Of the several possible routes to climb it, the one described here is the shortest. The starting point is a small picnic area in a secluded valley in the mountain's forested foothills, about 1 air mile southeast of the summit. From the stop sign at the Cima Road southbound exit on Interstate 15, drive the Excelsior Mine Road north 0.7 mile and turn right on the power-line road (signed NN 388). Drive this road 4.1 miles to where it merges with a better road coming in from the right. Go 0.1 mile to a fork and make a right, leaving the better road. In 0.2 mile go left at another fork, staying with the power line. Proceed 2.7 miles to a junction and turn left, now leaving the power line. After 1.3 miles, the road ends at a larger road. Bear left. This last road soon drops into a wash and follows it uphill. There is yet another split after 0.65 mile (make a hard left), then a last fork 0.45 mile further. Continue straight; the picnic area is 0.1 mile up ahead. It is easy to get lost: a topographic map definitely helps. High clearance is required.

Route Description

The ridge. As you drive the last stretch of road, you will not fail to notice up ahead the long cliff band that slashes sideways from base to crest across the face of Clark Mountain. The summit is the first prominence left of where the cliff joins the crest. As much as 180 feet thick, this cliff is the sheer edge of an immense dolomite plate, and the main impediment to reaching the summit from the south side. On the north side of the crest, even taller cliffs cut off access to the summit. Whether you approach the summit from the picnic area or up Fir Canyon on the north side, you will need to tackle the difficult challenge of climbing this cliff band up a Class-3 wall on the south side, at the juncture between the crest and the cliff.

The most gradual of the several hiking routes to the Class-3 wall is along the ridge directly north of the picnic area. Start along the wash in the ravine a few yards east of the picnic area. After 100 or 200 yards, climb onto the ridge to the right. Then follow the ridge line about 1 mile to the crest east of Clark Mountain. Besides the constant tug of gravity, this climb presents no particular obstacle. It is a fairly even grind up a slope averaging 30%, sprinkled in the middle with more level stretches to catch your breath, and near the top with pitches exceeding 40% to raise the ante. Circling around the vegetation and occasional outcrops lengthens the distance by about 25%. Hiking is a little easier 50 to 100 feet west of the ridge line, where the ground is more open and faint segments of trail are emerging.

There is a pervasive correlation between effort and reward, and this ascent does not break the rule. As you climb, the land opens up to the south and the Mescal Range comes into view, then all of Cima Dome, and ultimately the preserve's entire central chain of mountains. The ridge is a rich botanical garden boasting dozens of high-desert plants—blue yucca, blackbrush, prickly-pear, and cliffrose—thriving in an open woodland of juniper and pine. In warm weather the air is pregnant with the aroma of resin basking in sunlight. This is one of the strongholds of the pygmy agave—also known as Clark Mountain agave. Their neatly spherical rosettes thrive here in huge numbers. Many plants blossom in the late spring, including the striking scented penstemon and giant four o'clock, flax, woolly daisies, longleaf phlox, and mound cactus. Along the ridge the limestone (Monte Cristo Limestone, then Bird Spring Formation) has sheared off into a fluid litter of rubble, unstable underfoot but locally crawling with fossils. The most common are tangles of short, light-gray segments on darker limestone plates, probably the imprints of invertebrate burrows.

The Knife Edge. The views from the crest are awesome. The mountain's north face has been cleaved into high silvery cliffs streaked with long draperies of orange lichen. The base of the cliffs is plated with grand prismatic pinnacles. Nestled below this abrupt rim is a relict for-

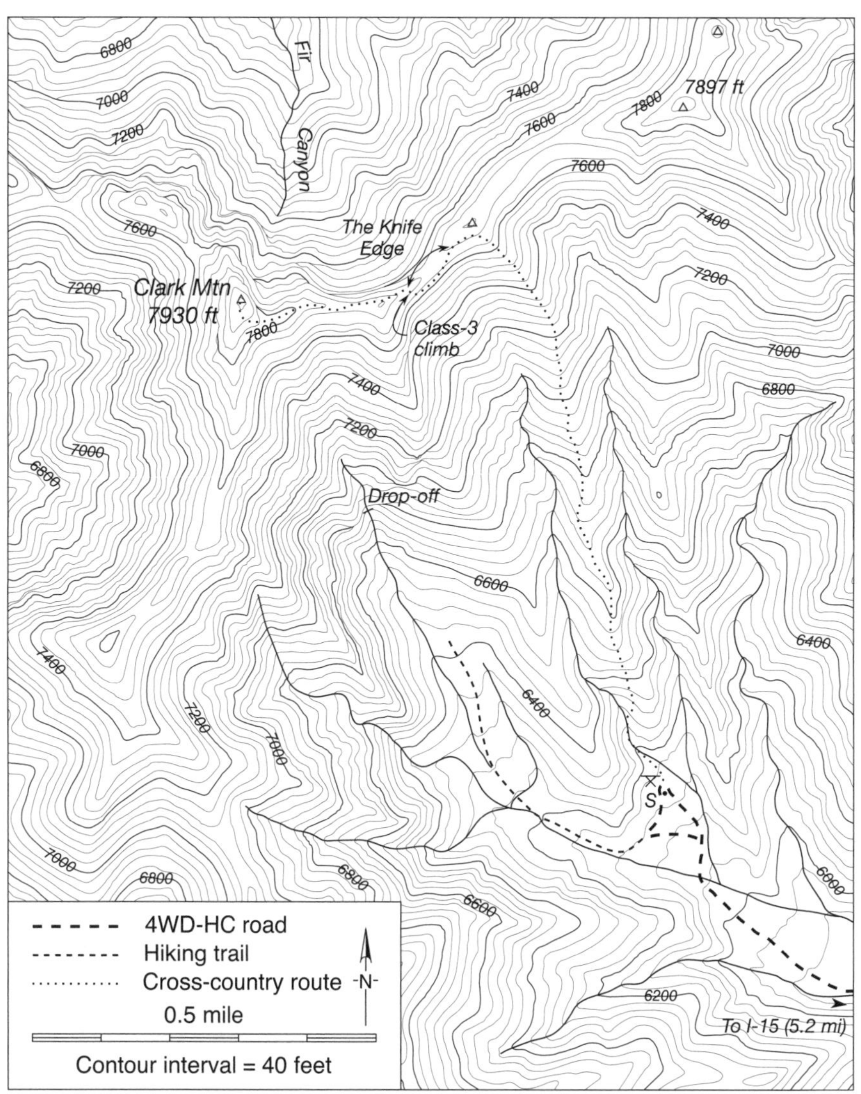

Clark Mountain		
	Dist.(mi)	Elev.(ft)
Picnic area	0.0	6,140
East end of Knife Edge	1.3	7,680
White-fir forest	(0.1)	~7,640
Class-3 climb (via talus)	~1.45	~7,740
Clark Mountain	1.8	7,930

est of white fir, one of the rarest trees in the California desert. About 1,000 strong, it spills down into Fir Canyon in a long emerald sweep of alpine aberration.

The summit is only 0.4 mile away and less than 300 feet up, but between you and it the crest pinches down to a high arcuate wall of upturned dolomite, about 150 yards long and barely four feet wide at its widest. The Knife Edge, as it has been aptly named, resembles a gargantuan jaw bone holding an irregular set of teeth. If you cross it along its top, you will be precariously balanced on narrow pinnacles high above the tree tops on both sides. Where a tooth is missing you will have to climb down and up again to the top of the next one. The rock is pitted by erosion, friction is excellent, and the holds tend to be generous. But this is an aerial experience, exposed and dangerous.

The easier, yet not easy, alternative is to bypass the Knife Edge. From the Knife Edge's east end, walk down the steep talus on the south side of the crest and follow the base of the Knife Edge to where it meets the cliff band. To the right, a steep wall, about 20 feet high and topped with two large trees, climbs to the top of the Knife Edge. It is a Class-3 ascent up this wall, with good foot and hand holds, but it is exposed too. A rope and harness may come in handy. Like tight-roping the Knife Edge, it will stop most hikers disinclined to rock climbing.

Even if you have no intention to go further than the Knife Edge, it is well worth climbing up to it to check out this unusual geological formation and the views, which are nearly as good as from the summit. Hang around and explore. From the east end of the Knife Edge it is easy to scramble down to its north side as well. There you can take a closer look at the white-fir forest and its interesting plant community, which includes currant, single-leaf ash, and mountain maple, all quite uncommon in the eastern Mojave Desert.

The summit. Once the Knife Edge is behind you, the rest of the climb is very steep but short and straightforward. Other than the satisfaction of conquering a mountain, the greatest reward is the stupendous panorama from the summit. To the south it encompasses all of the western preserve and several ranges beyond. To the northeast Clark Mountain drops off abruptly toward Mesquite Valley, one of the least visited corners of California. In this monochromatic landscape of neutral browns, Mesquite Lake's white evaporites stand out like an anomaly. To the northwest rise the Kingston Range, the Nopah Range, and Death Valley country. On a clear day one can scan across 130 miles of desert bliss between Wildrose Peak and the Granite Mountains.

■

THE COPPER WORLD MINE AND PACHALKA SPRING

Exploited between 1898 and 1918, the famous Copper World Mine was the east Mojave Desert's richest copper property. Starting from its colorful tailings, this scenic hike will take you up and down the canyon-incised foothills of Clark Mountain to Pachalka Spring's large grove of willow and mesquite, and bring you back on local tracks along the edge of Shadow Valley. Expect great views, rugged canyons, rock art, bright minerals, and a bevy of mining relics.

General Information
Road status: Partly roadless; HC and 4WD roads throughout the site
Copper World Mine: 0.3 mi, 120 ft up, 70 ft down one way / very easy
Copper Commander Mine: 1.0 mi, 540 ft up, 200 ft down one way / easy
Pachalka Spring: 2.8 mi, 760 ft up, 1,210 ft down one way / difficult
Main attractions: Historic copper mines and ruins, lush spring, botany
USGS 7.5' topo maps: Valley W., Mescal R., Clark Mtn*, Pachalka Spr.*
Maps: pp. 173*, *145*

Location and Access

The Copper World Mine is in the southwestern foothills of Clark Mountain. Pachalka Spring is 1.8 air miles northwest of the mine. Both sites can be reached on roads and explored on short hikes. The more eventful hike suggested here connects these two sites cross-country, with a possible return along local roads. To get to the Copper World Mine, from the southbound Cima Road exit on Interstate 15, drive the Excelsior Mine Road 1.4 miles north to the Pachalka Spring Road on the right, signed NN 628. Turn right and go 0.35 mile (either fork will get you there) to a fork by the large cottonwoods just west of the Valley Wells slags. Turn right on the Copper World Mine Road (NN 395). It crosses Valley Wells and goes 3.8 miles northeast to the junction with a larger road. Turn left and proceed 1.2 miles to the NPS boundary sign, just inside the foothills of Clark Mountain. Continue 0.7 mile to the end of the road and park. High clearance is required, and four-wheel drive to negotiate the deep-gravel wash along the last 300 yards.

To drive to Pachalka Spring, at Valley Wells take the left fork (Pachalka Spring Road). Keep right at the fork after 0.9 mile. Continue 4.1 miles to a steep, rough ramp climbing over black shale (four-wheel drive is imperative). Another 0.2 mile past it a side road on the right overlooks Pachalka Spring. It ends in 0.1 mile at the spring.

History: Copper Cornucopia

Although it pales in comparison to modern copper mines, in the early 1900s the Copper World Mine was one of the largest copper properties in operation in the country. The deposit was first spotted in 1868, a discovery that led to a major silver rush at nearby Ivanpah (see *Alaska Hill*) but little immediate action on the Copper World claims. A small quantity of very rich ore was shipped in 1869. Nine years later, then-owner James Boyd built a furnace in San Bernardino to treat some ore, but he could not turn a profit. The reason was likely simple economics. Even though the Copper World ore averaged a decent 4% in copper, it was worth only around $10 a ton, far less than the going rate for shipping ore to San Francisco—around $70 per ton. The Copper World lode would not be opened for 30 years.

The first outfit that worked the mine in earnest was the Ivanpah Smelting Company. In 1898, in part because of a hike in the price of copper, the company sank two wells and had a 50-ton smelter installed at Valley Wells, in Shadow Valley a few miles below the mine. The mine and smelter employed 85 men and 140 beasts of burden. Twenty-mule teams hauled the ore from the mine down to the smelter to the tune of 35 tons per trip. The copper concentrate, or matte, from the smelter was then transported 30 miles to Manvel, on the California Eastern Railway. Every four or five days the mule teams hauled up to 20 tons, worth around $7,000, and returned with coal and supplies for the smelter and the mine. Operations ran smoothly for about a year, with a remarkable production of about $530,000. But too much copper was wasted, and the company was losing money. In November 1899 the smelter's general manager, W. Robinson, filed a lawsuit against the company for unpaid income and refusal to issue his shares in the company. The litigation forced operations to be suspended in July 1900.

To lower their costs, the mine owners endeavored to shorten the long haul to Manvel by convincing the California Eastern to extend its line closer to the mine. The ailing railway company saw in the rich mine a much needed opportunity to expand its business, and it agreed. When the new 15.5-mile segment into Ivanpah Valley was completed in April 1902, a station called Ivanpah, consisting of a few stores, was established at the new railhead. Mining resumed, and a steady stream of ore arrived daily at Valley Wells. But the smelter was still too inefficient, and extending the rail did not save the day. Operations stopped again after less than two years and an additional output of $220,000.

The Copper World Mine came back to life a second time, in 1906. Dr. L. D. Godshall, a seasoned mining expert who eventually owned or managed other mines in the area, in particular the Mohawk and the

Sagamore, acquired title to the property and formed the Cocopah Mining Company. The ore was then hauled by mule teams directly to the Ivanpah station and by rail to the company-run smelter in Needles. In 1906 and 1907 the price of copper was at an all-time high, and the company did well. It produced around 230 tons of copper and a little silver worth around $110,000, most of it in 1907. When operations shut down in late 1908, likely because of a 34% drop in the price of copper, the California Eastern abandoned its station at Ivanpah.

The Copper World had a third life during World War I, when the price of metals soared again. The Cocopah Mining Company was reorganized as the Ivanpah Copper Company, and operations resumed in 1916. In November 1917, a new 100-ton blast furnace was installed at Valley Wells. Mules were replaced by tractors to haul 100 tons of ore every day to the smelter, and to take the matte to Cima, where it was shipped to a Utah smelter for further refining. Some 13,000 tons of copper-rich slag from earlier years were also gradually treated. All this activity employed a work force of about 60 through 1918. Metal prices dropped sharply at the end of the war, and the Copper World Mine shut down again.

Other than smaller efforts to clean up the old tailings and slags in 1943 and 1949, and to mine a rare mineral called royal gem azurite from 1977 into the 1980s, these were the Copper World's final throes. It had put out 60,800 ounces of silver and 3,300 tons of copper worth about $1,400,000, the greatest copper output in the east Mojave Desert.

Route Description

The Copper World Mine. The massive tailings straddling the low ridge at the end of the road mark the site of the Copper World Mine. A beat-up ramp climbs onto the tailings, then sprouts several short branches. The main haulage way winds by the historic workings, first a trench on the left, followed by a deep shaft, then more than half a dozen tunnels. Near the top of the tailings the road ends at the base of a rock wall, perpendicular to a straight 40-foot-wide corridor blasted into the ridge top. This channel cuts clear across to the northwest side of the ridge, where the tailings spill into the next canyon.

Although an eye-sore to many visitors, this misshapen rock cemetery churned by decades of mining is nevertheless a rich outdoor museum. Desert mines are not often so brightly colored. The trenches, rock faces, boulders, and adits are awash with the pastel blues and greens of copper ores. Chrysocolla, malachite, azurite, tenorite, limonite, and other minerals stain the rubble, both a visual pleasure and a witness to the Copper World Mine's exceptional wealth.

Ore chute and inclined tram at the Dewey Mine

The Copper Commander Mine. From the crest of the tailing a cabin is visible 300 yards down the canyon wash. To get to it, work your way down to the broad bench at the western foot of the tailing. Just a few steps down canyon is the upper end of the canyon road, faint at first but well-defined further down. Where it crosses the wash after 0.25 mile, walk back up the wash a little to the cabin. The front room, with its makeshift stove and tiny table, was the living area. The back room, closed off from the smoky front room, might have been the bedroom. In spite of having lost its back wall, this picturesque dwelling still hangs on for dear life, its dark iron cladding straining in the wind.

This area was part of the Copper Commander Mine. The mine was split into four levels strung up and down the steep ravine high behind the cabin. From the cabin a faded road goes up canyon to the mine's dying ore chute. A little further, it makes a sharp U bend left, passes above the ore chute, then shoots straight up the east side of the ravine. Even in its prime this rough grade was too steep for anything but mules. It ends at the third mining level, which has two tunnels and the ruins of a stone dwelling. The fourth level, reached by a short climb, has a long gaping stope that collapsed into enormous blocks of blinding-white marble.

Pachalka Spring. Getting to this lush spring from the Copper Commander Mine is the most satisfying part of this hike. The route crosses a variety of terrains, and it is challenging enough for a good adrenaline fix. From the mine's fourth level, climb the short remaining distance to the top of the ridge, then follow it west 0.4 mile, mostly downhill, to a local summit. Just past it the ridge splits. Take the right fork, which descends 0.4 mile to the windy canyon below. Follow this canyon downhill 0.25 mile until it runs into the wash of the larger canyon to the north, which has a road. In 0.15 mile this road joins the Pachalka Spring Road 150 yards south of the black-shale grade. The turn-off to the spring is 0.2 mile past the grade.

This little hike deserves a lot of praise. The ridge is dominated by immense shelves of blue-gray limestone, their surfaces inscribed with the random doodling of wind-blown particles. Yucca, ephedra, bitterbrush, blackbrush, and several species of cactus cling on to these barren inclines. Pygmy agave thrive to the point where their erect stalks are locally as dense as saplings in a second-growth forest. Juniper and pinyon pine grow a little everywhere. All along the ridge the views reach out one way to the Avawatz and Panamint mountains, and the other to Cima Dome, the cinder cones, and the Granite Mountains. There are impressive cliff-bound canyons along the way, their wide washes covered with shiny drifts of prickly-pear. The canyon walls are stamped with striking tapestries of alternating light and dark limestone strata.

Pachalka Spring's beautiful grove is set on a wide-open slope that curves steeply uphill and morphs into a towering bank of colorful banded cliffs. The side road to the spring ends at a small clearing framed by furrowed willows and dense growths of rabbitbrush. A field of green grass spills down the slope under tall trees and shaggy mesquite. In June, it is sprinkled with the intricate white blossoms of yerba mansa, and the catalpa introduced by homesteaders display

Cabin at the Copper Commander Mine

their large convoluted flowers. Somewhere, cold water flows out of a pipe into an old-fashioned galvanized tub. Leafless and forlorn in winter, in the hot season this spring is a calming enclave of shaded softness lost in a harsh wilderness.

A rutted track slices down through the spring to the ruins of an abandoned homestead. It may have been associated with the millsite located here in December 1875 under the name of Pochokki Spring, then relocated two years later by Julius Bidwell, of Ivanpah fame, as Pahchalka Spring. All three names are believed to be a phonetic version of Pachoca, a Piute chief of the time. The area has caves, water, and bighorn sheep. I can see how a shaman high on sacred datura would want to draw petroglyphs on the local canyon walls.

The return. From the spring return on the Pachalka Spring Road to the black-shale grade, then continue on this road about 1.6 miles. At this point the ridge on the south side is low enough to be easily crossed (0.2 mile). Once over the ridge, hike 0.6 mile east to join the

The Copper World Mine and Pachalka Spring

	Dist.(mi)	Elev.(ft)
Copper World Mine Rd (end)	0.0	5,345
Copper World Mine (top)	0.25	~5,470
Cabin	0.6	5,305
Copper Commander Mine	1.0	5,690
Ridge	1.15	~5,870
Start descent	1.6	~5,810
Foot of ridge at canyon wash	2.0	~5,100
Pachalka Spring Road	2.4	4,930
Pachalka Spring	(0.4)	~4,890
Leave Pachalka Spring Road	3.9	~4,375
Join road to Copper Com. Mine	4.7	4,560
Copper World Mine Rd (end)	7.0	5,345
Turn-out to Dewey Mine	(0.3)	5,175
Dewey Mine tram (top)	(0.6)	5,365

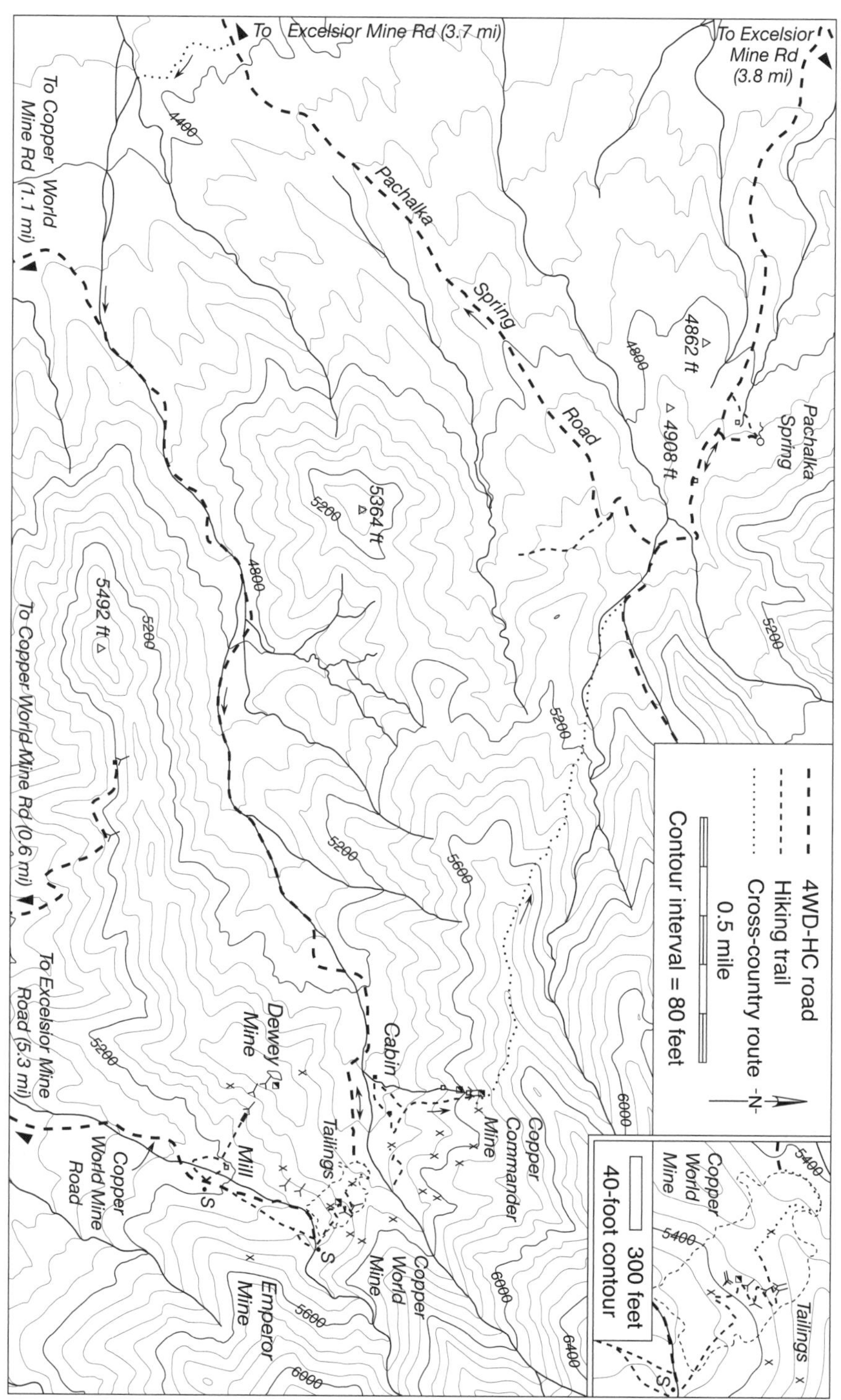
To Excelsior Mine Rd (3.7 mi)
To Excelsior Mine Rd (3.8 mi)
To Copper World Mine Rd (1.1 mi)
Pachalka Spring Road
Pachalka Spring
4862 ft
4908 ft
5364 ft
5492 ft
To Copper World Mine Rd (0.6 mi)
To Excelsior Mine Road (5.3 mi)
Copper World Mine Road
Dewey Mine
Mill
Tailings
Cabin
Copper Commander Mine
Copper World Mine
Emperor Mine
S
4WD-HC road
Hiking trail
Cross-country route
N
0.5 mile
Contour interval = 80 feet
Copper World Mine
Tailings
300 feet
40-foot contour

road to the Copper Commander Mine, just inside a prominent canyon. Follow it up through this forested canyon to the Copper World Mine tailing, and retrace your steps over the tailings to your vehicle. This part of the hike offers good low-angle views of Shadow Valley and Turquoise Mountain, often incorporeal in the afternoon haze. With a little luck, you will run into descendants of the burros who slaved at the mines more than a century ago.

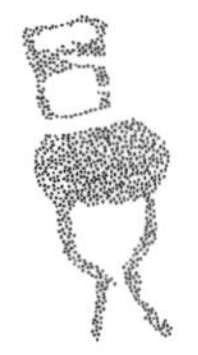    

The Dewey Mine. To end on a high note, from the end of the road drive back 0.3 mile to a small turn-out on the west side, facing a long outcrop parallel to the road, and park. The tailings up the hillside behind the outcrop belong to the Dewey Mine. It was operated in 1906–1908 by Dr. Godshall, and its small output was combined with the Copper World Mine's. Its uniqueness resides in the inclined tram that lowered the ore from its main tunnel 530 feet down to a loading platform. The tram's steep grade and ore chute are visible from the road. They can be reached by hiking one of two overgrown roads. The lower one starts behind gravel heaps just downhill from the turn-out, at about 45° from the road. It heads down across a wash to the south end of the outcrop, then angles right and climbs behind the outcrop to the foot of the grade (250 yards). The upper road heads uphill to the concrete foundations of a small mill. Left of the mill, a very short spur climbs and joins the lower road at the foot of the grade (125 yards).

At the top of the tram's rocky grade is the Dewey Mine's long ore chute, still connected to the upper end of the inclined tram—a local gem, and a fun piece of engineering to study. The tunnel behind it is one of the most complex in the preserve. Whatever copper the mountain had was thoroughly scooped out of its cathedral ceilings. As elsewhere in the area, the ore occurred near the boundary between limestone and an intrusive stock—here diorite, the salt-and-pepper rock stained with green ore on the tailing. The affinity of the pygmy agave for limestone is nowhere as striking as near this tunnel, which was sunk at the boundary. On the limestone side this agave is so profuse that it is the dominant plant; on the diorite side, not a single one grows.

■

VALLEY WELLS

Valley Wells is an important historic site where for several years around 1900 over one million dollars worth of copper ore was smelted for the nearby Copper World Mine. With its wealth of physical remains, including a mill, slag heaps, chemical treatment plants, and a troglodytic ghost town, as well as its large mesquite spring and badlands with interesting geology, it is a delightful place for an educational stroll in the desert.

General Information
Road status: Partly roadless; standard-clearance primitive access road
Valley Wells: 1.35 mi, 50 ft up loop / very easy
Main attractions: Ruins of historic copper smelter, spring, geology
USGS 7.5' topo map: Valley Wells
Maps: pp. 179*, *145*

Location and Access

Valley Wells is in the flats of Shadow Valley just north of Interstate 15. From the stop sign at the southbound Cima Road exit, drive the Excelsior Mine Road 1.4 miles north to the Pachalka Spring Road (NN 628) on the right. Follow it 0.15 mile to a fork, and take the right fork. Park 0.2 mile further at a junction, between Valley Wells' black slag heaps on the right and a cluster of cottonwoods on the left.

History: Trial and Error in Early Metallurgy

The smelter at Valley Wells was constructed in 1898 to process ore from the rich Copper World Mine, located about 5 miles away at the foot of Clark Mountain. The two operations had a symbiotic relationship. Smelters were vital to copper mines because they separated the metal from the host rock and greatly reduced shipping costs. The mine supplied the ore that the smelter needed to run, the smelter processed it, and the sale of the copper brought cash to both.

In the simplest implementation of smelting, a carbon-rich fuel like coal is covered with ore and fired up. The combustion is hot enough to melt the ore. When the ore is an oxide, the carbon removes oxygen from it to form carbon dioxide and reduces the oxide to metal. The denser liquid metal sinks to the bottom, while the unwanted fraction, the slag, rises to the surface. After cooling, the vitreous slag is broken off and discarded, leaving behind concentrated copper. When the ore

Dugouts at Valley Wells

is a sulfide, such as chalcopyrite, smelting produces a matte, a poorer mixture of copper sulfides. For proper chemistry, a flux was often added to the mix—limestone, sand, or pyrite, depending on the ore and host. It was more efficient to smelt oxides than sulfides, but unfortunately oxides tended to be confined near the surface of a deposit and were less common. There were, and still are, many variants of smelting. At Valley Wells the ore was first crushed, then ground in a ball mill. Sulfur oxide obtained by roasting pyrite was passed through the ground ore. The ore was washed to get a solution of copper and iron sulfates, which was reduced with iron cans in concrete tanks to precipitate the metal. The resulting copper-iron cake was finally smelted.

Valley Wells operated during the Copper World Mine's first and third periods of activity, from about January 1899 to early 1904 (with a hiatus between July 1900 and April 1902) and November 1917 through 1918. The coal came from New Mexico, and pyrite from the Francis Copper Mine (also ran by the Ivanpah Copper Company) in the Providence Mountains and mines near Jerome, Arizona. Valley Wells had a bit of a town too. Its small population of smelter operators and mule skinners was easily exceeded by the mules that did all the hauling. The town even had a post office, which was moved from dying Ivanpah in April 1899, but it closed shortly after, in July 1900.

Years later, a Federal Bureau of Mines investigation concluded that most small-scale smelters in the country had been unsuccessful. Although the science of smelting was well known by 1900, it still had enough black magic that the chemistry was often not optimized and too much copper ended up in the slags. In the 1900s Valley Wells shipped some rich copper bullion, which suggests that it was treating copper oxides. Later on, the workings were deeper and yielded sulfides. The smelter then shipped mostly matte, and profits were likely lower. The installation of a larger blast furnace in 1917 might have been dictated in part by the need to process greater volumes of sulfides. It was also used to treat 13,000 tons of older slags, which contained 2 to 10% copper—they were richer than the ore! Earlier smelting runs had indeed been inefficient, but not unsuccessful in this case. Valley Wells certainly did well enough; without it, the copper might still be in the ground.

Route Description

Valley Wells has four main attractions: the historic smelting center, the spring, the cemetery, and the nearby badlands. Roads lead to all these sites, but walking a loop from site to site provides a fuller experience. If you know a little about Valley Wells' rich history and let your curiosity take charge, the visit will take a couple of hours.

The smelter, mill, and ghost town. First follow the road east up to the top of the slag, on the south side of the road. This 15-foot-tall black bench is Valley Wells' iconic centerpiece. It is one of the very few slag heaps left today in the desert, and it is in fairly good condition. A mixture of iron, copper, and calcium silicates that was poured and cooled rapidly, a slag has the interesting properties of metal-rich glass. It has a nearly black luster and smooth conchoidal fractures. The original top surfaces of the two main slag heaps are coated with purple iridescence, and still encrypted with fine parallel flow lines, as crisp as on fresh lava. After more than a century, still nothing grows on it. The heart of the smelter, on the south edge of the slag, is an alchemist's den of concrete vats topped by a curious octagonal funnel.

The most interesting ruins are in the shallow ravine north of the road. Remnants of a wooden ore chute and trapezoidal concrete footings capped with bolts mark the site of a fairly large mill. This is possibly where the copper ore was ground prior to treatment. Below it, several tall concrete tanks occupy a good portion of the wash. These and other nearby structures provide enough clues to reconstruct where the various ore-processing stages—the pyrite roasting, the sulfur-oxide treatment, washing, and reduction—were taking place.

The Valley Wells community lived in wood cabins and in dugouts built into the sides of the ravine. Miners were a resourceful bunch. There is a thin horizontal strata of hard caliche just below the ravine's rims. They excavated their one-room dugouts in the soft clay that lies underneath the caliche, and used the caliche as the roof. In some

Smelter at Valley Wells, ca. 1900 (Larry Vredenburgh collection)

dugouts, they carved shelves or a fireplace and a chimney right into the clay walls. These unique troglodytic dwellings are still in place next to the treatment plant. It is easily the largest and most interesting collection of dugouts in the eastern Mojave Desert.

The spring and the cemetery. The pale formations exposed between Valley Wells and Cima Road are not a dry lake but wetland deposits. They are composed of crudely layered cream-colored silt, pale-green clay, and tufa. The wetlands were thriving between the Late Miocene and Early Holocene, when increased precipitation replenished the aquifer and water breached the surface. Ice-age mammoths, camels, and horses visited this providential oasis. The spring that surrounds the smelter today, irrigated by groundwater that no longer surfaces, is the final stage of these once extensive wetlands. It is still fairly big: its open grove of mesquite covers several acres. The soil encourages plants that prefer higher alkalinity, like salt grass and saltbush.

Disheveled in winter, surprisingly green in summer, this spring is a pleasant area to discover on foot. From the cottonwoods, walk west on the abandoned road that runs through it. In 125 yards, at the edge of the spring, it merges with another road that cuts west toward the paved road. Soon after, leave the road and aim northwest across the open desert toward the Valley Wells cemetery. Surrounded by a tall fence of stocky wooden posts, it is easy to spot in the distance. Larger than most, it has a few headstones, including graves of the Yates family (Valley Wells was the headquarters of the Yates Ranch Cattle Company from 1894 until around 1950). Most of the graves are unmarked heaps of gravel, adorned only by a few forlorn Joshua trees.

The well and the badlands. From the cemetery, aim back toward the south side of the spring's mesquite grove. It should take you to the

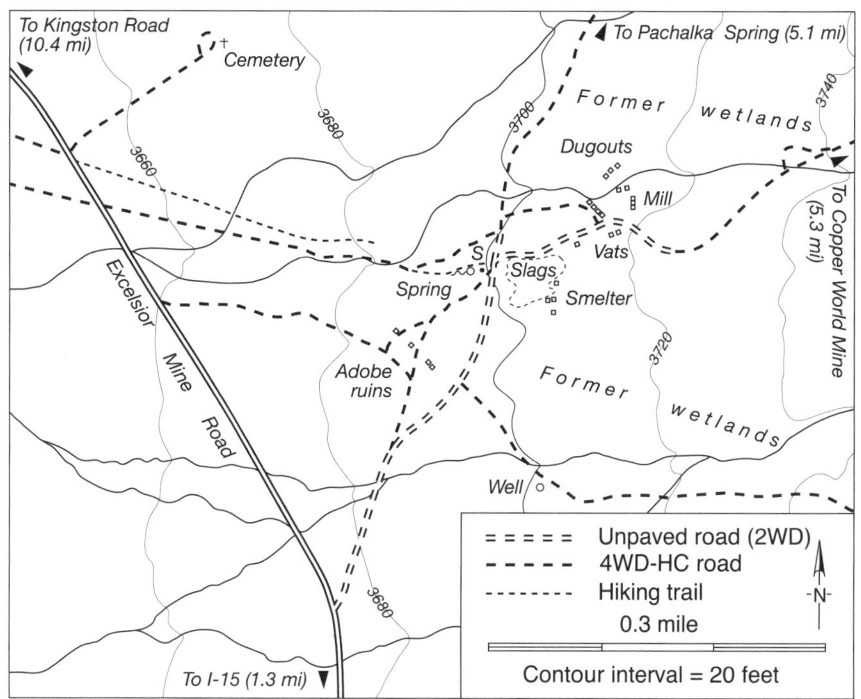

Valley Wells	Dist.(mi)	Elev.(ft)
Spring (road junction)	0.0	3,700
Smelter and mill ruins	0.1	~3,720
Dugouts	0.25	3,715
Cemetery	0.7	3,670
Adobe dwellings	1.0	3,690
Well	1.15	3,700
Back to spring	1.35	3,700

ruins of a few buildings, now reduced to crumbling adobe walls and foundations, perhaps the remains of the post office and of the Yates Ranch. Just past them you will get to the access road you drove on, at its junction with a side road running perpendicular to it. This road leads 200 yards southeast to one of Valley Wells original wells, a gaping square hole partly occluded by a collapsed wooden structure. Interestingly, the location of this well, and of the smelter itself, was dictated by the same natural underground plumbing that created the wetlands. Around 1898, a hundred centuries after the wetlands dried up,

Valley Wells mill foundations, vats, and dugouts

the plumbing was still in place, the mesquite betrayed the proximity of groundwater, and someone chose this site to dig the well.

The well is at the western edge of the wetlands, a bright region of hummocks carved out of adobe-colored clay. Their steep slopes and round summits are peppered with mesquite. Make a wide loop through this dissected landscape (stay along drainages to preserve the fragile crests). Half a mile south, it loses much of its plant cover and turns into miniature badlands, quite scenic around sunset. With a little effort you might spot, locked in the friable soil, the dainty shells of the gastropods and bivalves that lived here in the Pleistocene.

A few words of advice. Valley Wells gives us the rare opportunity to examine a historic smelting facility. Being easily accessible and fairly well known, it receives a good number of visitors. On almost every visit I noticed that something had changed, not always the work of entropy. This place deserves our respect. *Do not step on the slag surfaces;* they are very brittle. Stay away from the dugouts; they are on their last leg. Walk gently wherever you go, so that in another century this little treasure may still be around for our great-grand children.

■

— 7 —

IVANPAH MOUNTAINS

COVERING ONLY ABOUT 30 SQUARE MILES, the Ivanpah Mountains are the smallest of the preserve's main ranges. Long and skinny, they are more like an aggregate of massive hills than a main mountain block. Their largest elevation differential, on the east face of 6,163-feet Kessler Peak, is only about 1,800 feet. But they make up for this unfortunate oversight of nature with a passion. Their rugged look, scenic granite outcrops, and colorful limestone formations put them in a class of their own. Extensively mined in the past, they are also home to some of the best preserved camps and mining-related ruins in the region. Much of all this is easily accessible by car and on hikes short enough to qualify as walks. For a change, we can rough it the easy way!

Access and Backcountry Roads

The Ivanpah Mountains are the most accessible of the preserve's major ranges. Three roads in particular give the opportunity to take a close look at most of the main local attractions. The Morning Star Mine Cutoff closely hugs for several miles the southeastern side of the mountains. Several secondary roads climb from it to historic mines, in particular the Billy Boy, Kewanee, Allured, and New Trail mines. The Kessler Peak Road follows most of the mountains' west side, from near Kessler Peak to the southern base of Kokoweef Peak. It also passes by several historic properties—the Copper King, Evening Star, and Standard mines—and several summits, including eye-catching Striped Mountain. The area's most scenic byway is the Zinc Mine Road. From the Cima Road it climbs leisurely to and through Piute Valley, the serene high-desert valley that separates the Ivanpah Mountains from

Suggested Backcountry Drives in the Ivanpah Mountains					
Route/Destination	Dist. (mi)	Lowest elev.	Highest elev.	Road type	Pages
Copper Cove loop	7.5	4,400'	5,340'	H	195-200
Evening Star Mine	3.4	4,400'	4,928'	G	201
Kessler Peak Road	8.7	4,810'	5,330'	H	181, 213
New Trail Camp	4.3	3,136'	4,425'	H	207
Zinc Mine Road/Kokoweef	11.5	4,400'	5,245'	H	181, 187
Key: G=Graded (2WD) H=Primitive (HC)					

the Mescal Range, and ends after many miles at Mountain Pass. Little-traveled Piute Valley is covered with one of the densest, most extensive, and most beautiful Joshua-tree forests in the preserve. To avoid confusion at the many forks along the road, take the 7.5' USGS maps with you.

Geology

A major regional fault called the Clark Mountain Fault slices diagonally across the Ivanpah Mountains, from just east of Kokoweef Peak to the mouth of Oro Wash. North of this fault are the oldest rocks in the east Mojave Desert—gneiss, migmatite, and granitoids ranging in age mostly from 1.66 to 1.71 billion years. This swath of ancient rocks extends continuously from the northern Ivanpah Mountains up to the east side of the Clark Mountain Range. The presence of migmatite is the signature of the Ivanpah Orogeny, a major mountain-building event that deformed and metamorphosed pre-existing granitoids around 1.71 billion years ago. The younger granitoids were emplaced over a vast region during the subsequent 50 million years. Only a few enlightened geologists are likely to recognize these peculiar rocks—metagabbro, pelitic gneiss, meta-quartz diorite, and many more—yet their variety will impress anyone with a keen sense of observation.

Directly south of the fault the geology is radically different. Here Paleozoic formations are exposed in a mile-wide band that abuts the Clark Mountain Fault from New Trail Canyon to Kokoweef Peak. Similar carbonate formations crop out at the western tips of Copper Cove and on Striped Mountain. On Kokoweef Peak these formations hold caves that have yielded a wealth of fossils. In the 1970s paleontologists recovered nearly 100 Late-Pleistocene species, including fishes, fossilized in the sediments of Kokoweef Cave. The Quién Sabe Cave yielded the bones of 21 small vertebrate species.

Granite formations in the Ivanpah Mountains above Riley's Camp

The rest of the range—all of the southern half—is made of 145-million-year-old Ivanpah Granite. This unit of coarse-grained syenogranite and monzogranite makes up the Ivanpah Mountains' handsome signature of dark-pink, weather-worn formations.

Mining History

Precious and base metals have been extracted from the Ivanpah Mountains since at least 1879, when the Bullion Mine in New Trail Canyon was rumored to have shipped rich silver ore all the way to Wales for refining. This might have been a good omen, because in the course of its long subsequent history this little range made headlines on a remarkable number of occasions. Fewer than 20 mines were in operation at one time or another, but several of them broke records. In 1906 the district gained notoriety when the Standard No. 1 Mine shipped a large tonnage of very rich copper ore. By 1919 it had yielded $140,000. Over the next 30 years this record was matched by the New Trail Mine. In the 1930s another strike rocked the Ivanpah Mountains when tin ore was discovered at the Evening Star Mine. The mine had a modest output—about $30,000—but it became famous for being the sole tin producer in the eastern Mojave Desert.

Suggested Hikes in the Ivanpah Mountains					
Route/Destination	Dist. (mi)	Elev. gain	Mean elev.	Access road	Pages
Short hikes (under 5 miles round trip)					
Bullion Mine	1.1	420'	4,530'	P/4.3 mi	212
Evening Star Mine*	1.3	260'	4,900'	Graded	202-204
Kessler Peak	1.9	1,175'	5,350'	P/1.3 mi	213-216
Kessler Peak loop*	4.2	1,280'	5,370'	P/1.3 mi	213-216
Kokoweef Peak	1.2	880'	5,440'	P/3.8 mi	187-190
Kokoweef/Kokoweef Peak*	2.4	880'	5,440'	P/3.8 mi	187-190
New Era Mine	0.5	250'	5,440'	H/4.5 mi	200
New Trail Canyon to crest	2.0	1,320'	4,830'	P/4.3 mi	210-212
New Trail Magnesite Mine*	0.9	220'	4,510'	P/4.3 mi	209
New Trail Mine (headframe)	1.0	510'	4,570'	P/4.3 mi	212
Revenue Copper Mine*	3.1	780'	4,690'	P/4.3 mi	210-212
Riley's Camp & viewpoint	0.7	180'	5,420'	H/4.2 mi	200
Riley's Camp loop	1.1	200'	5,400'	H/4.2 mi	198-200
Silverado Mine	0.4	140'	5,290'	P/4.7 mi	191-192
Standard No. 1 Mine*	0.6	90'	5,210'	P/4.3 mi	197-198
Standard No. 2 Mine*	1.0	120'	5,080'	P/3.1 mi	200
Striped Mountain	1.1	1,080'	5,480'	P/4.7 mi	191-194
Intermediate hikes (5-12 miles round trip)					
Copper Cove loop*	9.1	~1,200'	5,240'	P/2.9 mi	197-200
Key: P=Primitive (2WD) H=Primitive (HC) Distance: one way, except for loops (round-trip, marked with *) Elev. gain: sum of all elevation gains on a round-trip basis & on loops					

The area was in the limelight again just a little later, this time for gold. In 1934, a farmer named Earl L. Dorr signed an affidavit that described in flamboyant details how he and a civil engineer named Morton had discovered, in an undisclosed location now believed to be Kokoweef Peak, an underground river lined with gold. Somehow he failed to find it again, and he spent much of the rest of his life looking for it. As expected, since then many treasure hunters have tried to locate Dorr's lost lode—but the search is still on.

Kokoweef Peak did ultimately have a strike of its own, but it was not gold. In 1940 the Carbonate King Mine opened a zinc deposit on the west slope of the summit that had been left untouched since its discovery in 1900. Until 1951, it exhumed nearly 10,000 tons of concentrat-

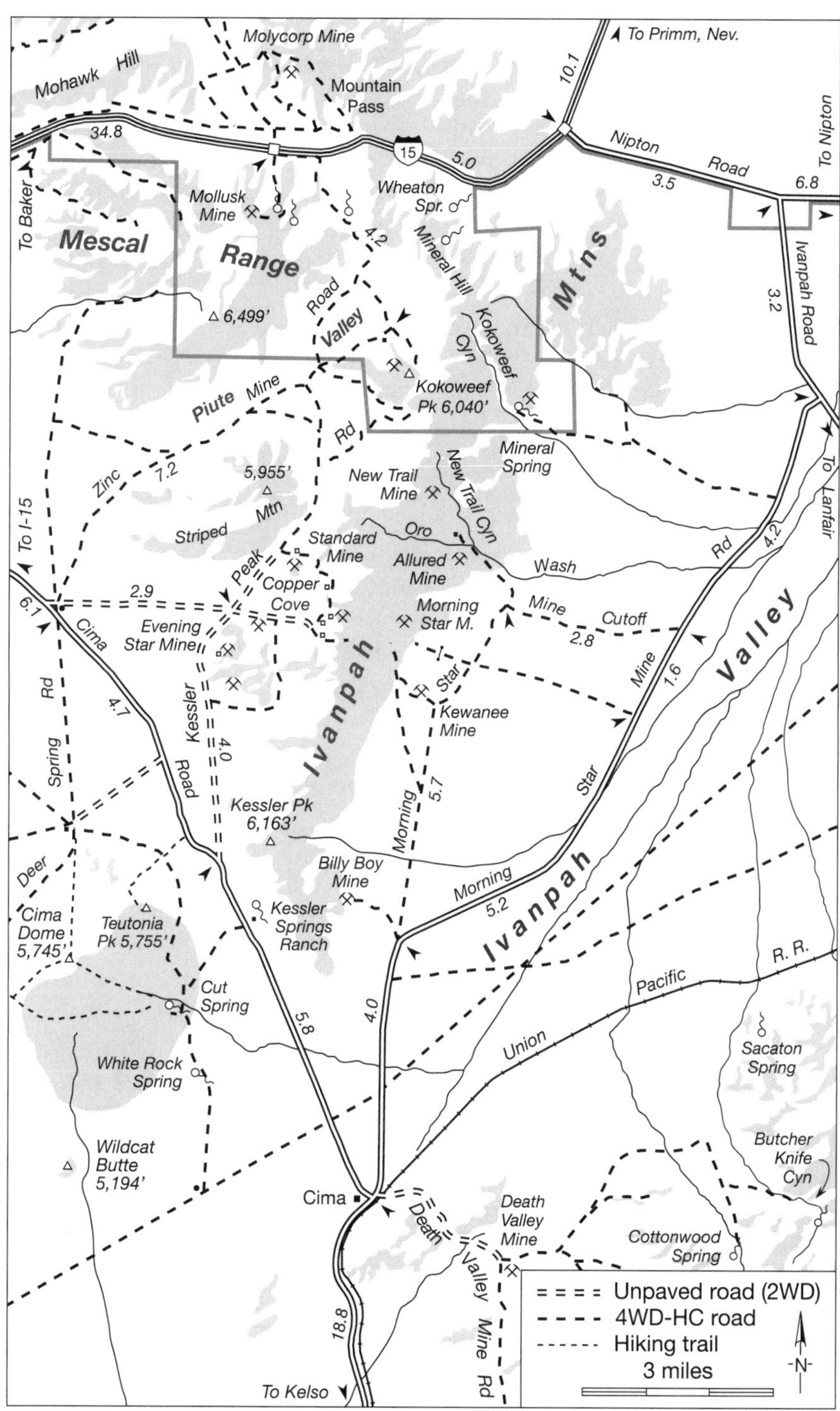

Molycorp Mine
To Primm, Nev.
Mohawk Hill
Mountain Pass
10.1
To Nipton
34.8
15
5.0
Nipton Road
3.5
6.8
To Baker
Mollusk Mine
Wheaton Spr.
Mescal
Range
4.2
Mineral Hill
Mtns
Ivanpah Road
3.2
Road
Valley
6,499'
Kokoweef Cyn
Kokoweef Pk 6,040'
Piute Mine Rd
Mineral Spring
Zinc
7.2
5,955'
New Trail Mine
New Trail Cyn
To Lanfair
To I-15
Striped Mtn
Standard Mine
Oro Wash
Rd
4.2
Peak
Allured Mine
Copper Cove
2.9
Mine Cutoff
Morning Star M.
6.1
Evening Star Mine
Cima
2.8
Star
Mine
Valley
Kewanee Mine
1.6
Rd
4.7
Kessler
4.0
Ivanpah
Spring
Road
5.7
Star
Kessler Pk 6,163'
Morning
Deer
Billy Boy Mine
Morning
Cima Dome 5,745'
Teutonia Pk 5,755'
Kessler Springs Ranch
5.2
Ivanpah
Cut Spring
R. R.
Pacific
4.0
5.8
Union
White Rock Spring
Sacaton Spring
Wildcat Butte 5,194'
Butcher Knife Cyn
Cima
Death
Death Valley Mine
Cottonwood Spring
Valley Mine Rd
18.8
To Kelso
Unpaved road (2WD)
4WD-HC road
Hiking trail
3 miles
N

ed zinc-silver-lead ore. It was the second largest production of zinc (nearly six million pounds) in this part of the Mojave, and it brought in more cash—about $640,000—than any other mine in the district.

This record did not last. From the 1980s to 1993 the Morning Star Mine strip-mined the southeastern tip of Ivanpah Mountains to leach out more than $10 million worth of gold. So it was that this little range would generate more excitement than many ranges ten times its size.

The Dome Fire

One of the preserve's most unique and iconic geological features, Cima Dome attracts many first-time visitors. Located at the southern tip of the Ivanpah Mountains and about 10 miles across and 1,200 feet tall, it holds the record for being the most symmetrical dome in the US. Over a radius of nearly 1 mile centered on its summit, its contour lines are almost perfectly concentric ovals. Until 2020, Cima Dome was host to the world's largest Joshua-tree forest, a particularly dense and green botanical garden of Joshua trees, juniper, cacti, yucca, and shrubs. In August that year, all of it was completely destroyed by fire in just a few days. Ignited by a lightning strike, the Dome Fire consumed 43,300 acres and killed 1.3 million Joshua trees. Firefighting assistance was denied because major fires were raging throughout California. A state with an annual revenue of $160 billion lost a world-class treasure for lack of one small dedicated aircraft and a large water tank that would have quickly extinguished the brush fire before it got out of control…

Hiking

Each range has something different to offer to hikers. Because of their smaller dimensions and the abundance of access roads, in the Ivanpah Mountains you are never more than a couple of miles from a road. Most places can be reached on short hikes. Even the summits are comparatively easy to climb. Canyons are few and neither very long nor deep, but they can be quite colorful. In the southern range, much of the scenery is composed of beautiful displays of carved granite, often enhanced by Joshua trees and juniper. The Ivanpah Mountains are also home to locally sizable populations of uncommon pygmy agave. Other appeals include the many well-preserved homesteads, camps, and workings left behind by decades of mining. Some historic sites rank among the most impressive in the preserve. If you run out of places to explore on foot, expand your horizon to the northern Ivanpah Mountains just outside of the preserve. More isolated, that area has a few springs and interesting mines, in particular on Mineral Hill.

▪

KOKOWEEF

Kokoweef Peak is an isolated limestone mountain 1,000 feet high in the northern Ivanpah Mountains with a strange claim to fame. Local lore claims that it rests on top of a vast underground canyon flushed by a river of gold. Spawned in the 1930s by a prospector with a vivid imagination, this legend has drawn legions of fortune seekers. Climbing Kokoweef Peak, which is still actively explored, is a rare opportunity to share the excitement of a modern tale.

General Information
Jurisdiction: Private property
Road status: Roadless; standard-clearance primitive access road
Kokoweef Peak: 1.2 mi, 880 ft up, 0 ft down one way / moderate
Main attractions: Legend of Dorr's lost river of gold, peak climb, botany
USGS 7.5' topo maps: Cima Dome, Mescal Range, Mineral Hill*
Maps: pp. 189*, *185*

Location and Access

On Interstate 15, take the Bailey Road exit. At the bottom of the northbound exit ramp, turn right, go 70 yards, and turn left on the frontage road (Zinc Mine Road). After 0.75 mile, it veers right and turns to dirt. At the fork 0.45 mile further, make a left. Continue 1.8 miles to a fork just beyond the pass into Piute Valley. The Zinc Mine Road continues straight; turn left (southeast) instead. After 1.1 miles, turn right at the fork just below Kokoweef Peak, then go 0.1 mile to a road coming in from the left. Turn right. Park at the camp of Kokoweef 0.3 mile down the road. This route can usually be driven with a standard vehicle. *The area is actively mined. Do not walk around or climb the summit without obtaining permission from someone in charge at Kokoweef.*

Route Description

Kokoweef Peak was immortalized by Earl L. Dorr, a blue-eyed, gun-toting gentleman farmer who came to this area in the 1920s, hoping to strike it rich. In 1934, he reported in a mindless affidavit how he and a partner had explored, somewhere in San Bernardino County, eight miles of underground passages that led 5,000 feet down to a river of gold. The largest chamber "was encrusted with crystals fashioned into festoons of innumerable stalactites." They ultimately reached a canyon that rivaled in depth with the Grand Canyon. A stalactite hung

The Ivanpah Mountains' crest south from Kokoweef Peak

1,510 feet down into it, "perpetually washed by water flowing down over it and falling into the dark canyon depths." At the bottom, a 300-foot-wide river flowed past 100-foot banks of black sand thick with placer gold. The sand Dorr allegedly brought back was immensely rich, assaying over $2,000 per cubic yard. After his return, Dorr blasted the cavern shut to protect it from looters—and lost track of its entrance. In 1940, he published another affidavit in the *California Mining Journal*, but it failed to interest investors in financing his search. When the Carbonate King Mine opened up that year on the mountain's west flank, it scoffed the river of gold and made a mint producing zinc instead. The rest of his life, Dorr was consumed by the search for his lost lode. He died in 1957, still holding on to his secret.

Dorr's story is a fabulous tale, instilled with the same sense of wonder as Jules Verne's fantastic *Voyage au Centre de la Terre*, an unbelievable epic rooted in excess, yet so magical that it makes us want to believe in it. Kokoweef Peak does have sizable caves called Quién Sabe, Crystal, and Kokoweef, and it became the prime contender. Since the late 1940s, numerous cavers and mining outfits have diligently explored them in search of Dorr's alleged river of gold, all moved by the staunch obstinacy that can only be fueled by passions, riches, or insanity. Kokoweef (pop. 3) is the mining camp of the latest venture.

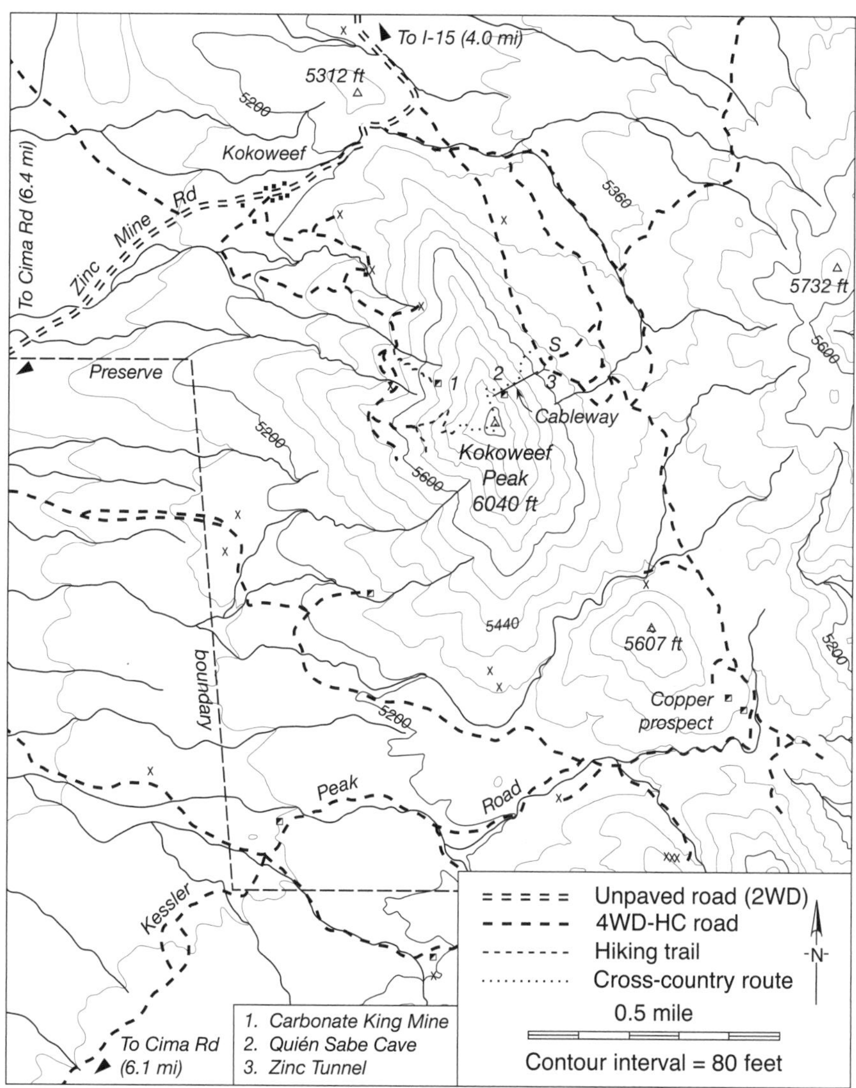

Kokoweef	Dist.(mi)	Elev.(ft)
Kokoweef	0.0	5,160
Zinc Tunnel	0.85	5,545
Kokoweef Peak	1.2	6,040
Upper end of mining road	1.35	5,795
Kokoweef	2.4	5,160

The residential end, stretched thin on both sides of the road, is a time-warp of cabins and trailers in a forest of Joshua trees. The business end is an avalanche of high-testosterone cranes, graders, flatbeds, trucks, and drilling rigs. On weekends a motley crew of believers—store keepers, waitresses, and construction workers from Las Vegas and Los Angeles—come over and tirelessly search for a giant void that reason tells us must be imaginary.

Kokoweef Peak is a relatively subdued prominence that can be climbed from almost any direction—the roads that encircle it offer a few loops to go up one way and return another. The only route that is a bit of a workout—and the most fun—is the bank of cliffs on the east side. From Kokoweef, walk east up the main road to the steep grade on the east flank, and the Zinc Tunnel at its end. The grade closely follows the Clark Mountain Fault. Movements along it have made strange bedfellows: the carbonates on the mountain side abut on the downhill side a city-size block of Proterozoic gneiss and pegmatite—a time gap of 1.5 billion years. Starting 20 yards north of the tunnel, hike up the talus to a downed cableway directly uphill from the tunnel. Follow it to the blocked entrance of the Quién Sabe Cave. This ascent is short but tedious, over outcrops, loose slides, and thorny plants. From the cave, climb at 45° to the right (when facing uphill) to the only break in the cliffs, a rocky couloir lined with juniper and shrubs, just north of where the cableway is tethered to the crest. A little scrambling leads to the crest. The summit is 250 yards south up the open crest.

From a distance, Kokoweef Peak is not the most remarkable mountain, but closeness reveals hidden riches. The slopes are covered with Joshua trees, juniper, cliffrose, and pygmy agave. Clumps of uncommon mat rock spiraea cling to the naked rock. The bulk of the mountain is a thick sequence of sedimentary formations spanning most of the Paleozoic, from the Permian around Kokoweef to the Cambrian south of the peak. The Ordovician–Cambrian middle of the stack crops out all along the crest's scenic hogbacks in beautiful upturned smoky limestone. Between the summit's rocky spine and the horizon, a hard-scrabble piece of real estate spreads in all directions and laps in the distance with a ring of intriguing mountain backbones. Presiding over this unruly landscape is the crenulated crest of the Ivanpahs, the hump of Cima Dome, and the eastern Mojave Desert's 70-mile chain unfolding from Nevada's McCullough Range to the Granite Mountains. Yet perhaps the most powerful inspiration is not the mountain itself but the pull of the legend, the constant awareness that you might be walking on top of a river of gold... We would be fools not to dream.

■

STRIPED MOUNTAIN

This is a fun little mountain to climb, easy and obstacle free, across the contrasted sequence of Paleozoic limestone strata that gave it its striking appearance and name. The area was the home of a famous miner who collected local mines and left his mark all over, including at the silver-tungsten mine on the way to the summit. This is a luminous place, peppered with Joshua trees, blue yucca, and rare agave, with an openness and a quality of light that invite lingering.

General Information
Road status: Mostly roadless; standard-clearance access road
Silverado Mine: 0.4, 110 ft up, 30 ft down one way / very easy
Striped Mtn: 1.1 mi, 910 ft up, 170 ft down one way / easy–moderate
Main attractions: Geology, mines, history, botany, long views
USGS 7.5' topo map: Mescal Range
Maps: pp. 193*, *185*

Location and Access

Striped Mountain is a crescent-shaped ridge joined to the western flank of the Ivanpah Mountains by a low isthmus. The starting point is the decrepit road to the Silverado Mine, on the mountain's east side. From the gas station at the Cima Road exit on Interstate 15, drive the Cima Road 7.1 miles south to two large water tanks on the left. From the other direction, this is 10.5 miles north of Cima. A hard-packed dirt road starts on the left side of the tanks. Follow it east 2.9 miles, past Striped Mountain's striated slope to the left, to a four-way junction. Turn left (northeast) on the Kessler Peak Road. At the fork after 1.1 miles, turn left again. In 0.6 mile, just past a right bend in a ravine, the rough road to the Silverado Mine splits off at 10 o'clock. Park 100 yards up this road, at a cutoff on the right. This route is rock-free and suitable for most vehicles, with care at the few ruts if clearance is low.

Route Description

From the starting point, walk up the old road toward the Silverado Mine, located on the low ridge up to the left. This mine dates back to the late 1880s. The ruins of a stone house stand by the roadside a short distance in on the right; two more are along a faint track that loops up on the hillside to the left. One was an assay office, the other a little cabin with a chimney and three walls enclosing bedrock. The road climbs a little, hooks a sharp left, then ends in 0.25 mile on a low ridge in full view of Striped Mountain's twin peaks. The mine's main 60-foot shaft and several shallower shafts are aligned down the ridge to the south, neatly tracing the skarn that they explored. The skarn was formed in the Jurassic, when the hornblende-diorite pluton exposed just east of the mine intruded the Cambrian carbonates west of it. Notwithstanding its glamorous name, the Silverado Mine was not the richest. Its only known production was a few tons of silver ore in the 1880s and 1890s. Its main claim to fame is its connection with John "Riley" Bembry, a World War I medic who came here in 1928 and became a local legend by amassing an impressive portfolio of abandoned mines (see *Copper Cove*). Many had played out, so he reigned over a gutted empire. He acquired the Silverado Mine in 1938, perhaps hoping for tungsten, which had just been discovered at the nearby Evening Star Mine. By 1950, the mine had indeed been expanded to include tungsten claims and renamed Silverado Tungstite. But the tungsten ore—scheelite—was too sparse to have commercial value. Bembry supplemented his meager miner's income with a stable job at the Molycorp Mine at Mountain Pass.

From the end of the mining road, follow the rougher, overgrown road that heads north along the ridge, past the small pits of the Silverado Tungstite Mine. After 0.25 mile, the road ends. Cut a beeline across the hillside, aiming for the white tailings on the low ridge to the northwest. Up there you will join a quarry at the upper end of another road. This was one of many claims held by the Georgia Marble Company since 1980–1981, most of which were never developed.

From the quarry the route is in plain view, generally west down to a shallow saddle and up the mountain's shoulder to the first summit, then northwest across a short saddle to the summit. From saddle to summit it is a steepish ascent, 550 feet up and down in less than 0.5 mile. You travel from the Middle Devonian to the Late Mississippian, 48 million years of rocks built on the lives and deaths of a quadrillion hard-shelled sea creatures. They stacked up on the sea floor in strata shaped by the vagaries of climate and tectonic plates. The strata now carve across the ridge parallel bands of limestones and dolomites, an alternation of cream, blue gray, and smoky white. The thickest striations bulge out in short strips of bumpy slickrock spaced by splintered rubble. Each strip holds a few hundred thousand years of ocean memory. The thinnest are fine parallel striations within the striations, as thin as a nail, less than a century's worth of sedimentation.

The 2020 Dome Fire destroyed the lush botanical gardens that once lined the access roads, but Striped Mountain was fortunately spared.

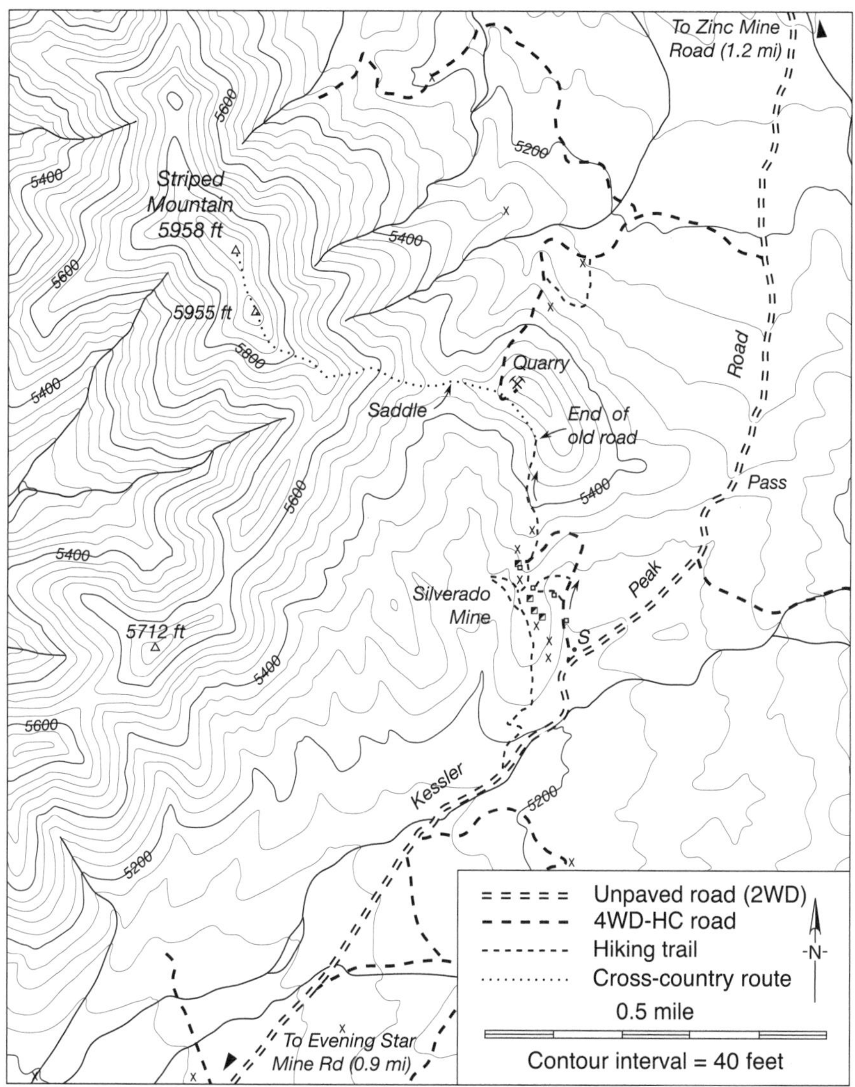

Striped Mountain	Dist.(mi)	Elev.(ft)
Kessler Peak Road	0.0	5,220
Silverado Mine (ridge)	0.25	5,330
North end of road	0.45	5,480
Quarry road	0.5	5,520
Striped Mountain	1.1	5,955

Striped Mountain lit up against the Mescal Range

The open ridge is freckled with Joshua trees and blue yucca, blackbrush, green ephedra, and bitterbrush, and occasional juniper and big sagebrush higher up. Just about every cactaceae live up here, content with mere cracks in the bone-dry bedrock. There are battalions of pygmy agave, clusters of overgrown artichokes with spiky leaves and three-inch nails; startlingly big mound cactus gathering well over 100 individual plants; and small bulbous heads of pincushion cactus poking out of rock debris. In this open land barely shielded by plants, reflection ratchets up the sun's glare to the brilliance of driven snow.

From the summit the panorama extends for tens of miles to a horizon lined with giant ranges—the San Bernardino Mountains east of LA, the Spring Mountains west of Las Vegas, and the Avawatz Mountains north of nowhere. The Mescal Range looms close by, a colorful tapestry of upturned beddings. At least two dozen mountains dot the landscape, from Cima Dome's bulge to the Castle Mountains' spires and the Bristol Mountains' sprawling crest. Down to the southeast is Copper Cove, the lifelong haunt of Riley Bembry, whose story is so intimately linked to this mountain. They are all there, spread across his sleepy hollow—the mines where he toiled, the scenic granite knolls where he lived, and the tiny cemetery where he now rests.

■

COPPER COVE

On the western edge of the Ivanpah Mountains, a primitive road loops around Copper Cove, a high-desert valley that witnessed a copper rush around 1906. Beautifully situated in a serene landscape of Joshua trees, juniper, and reddish granitic outcrops, the area's many historic mines and camps are fun to leisurely explore by car and on foot. Look forward to great scenery, colorful homesteads from the 1930s, hidden springs, and wonderfully antiquated equipment.

General Information
Road status: Standard-clearance access road; HC loop road through site
Riley's Camp / viewpoint: 0.7 mi, 180 ft up, 0 ft down one way / very easy
Copper Cove camps: 9.1 mi, ~1,200 ft up loop (or more) / moderate
Main attractions: Copper mines, well-preserved camps, woodlands
USGS 7.5' topo maps: Cima Dome, Mescal Range
Maps: pp. 199*, *185*

Location and Access

This section focuses on what I refer to as Copper Cove, a small valley tucked between Striped Mountain and the western foot of the Ivanpah Mountains. To get to it, drive the Cima Road 10.5 miles north of Cima (or 7.1 miles south of the gas station at Interstate 15) to a wide graded road on the east side, just north of a corral with two water tanks. Follow it east 2.9 miles (ignore the spur roads at the start) to the second four-way junction, at the west end of Copper Cove. Make a left on the Kessler Peak Road, then a right 1.1 miles further. The Standard No. 1 Mine is 0.3 mile ahead. From there the road loops by other historic mines and camps before returning in 3.2 miles to the four-way junction. With a standard-clearance vehicle and a little care this loop is usually passable up to the Standard No. 1 Mine, and up to near Geer Camp coming the other way. The rest requires high clearance.

History: A Little Copper Field

The presence of copper southeast of Striped Mountain was known as early as 1882. William A. McFarlane himself staked the very first claim here, the Little Gem, in November that year. Actual mining did not start until much later, when two prospectors from Manvel, A. E. Moore and Joseph Nelson, filed the Excelsior claims, in June 1898 and the following spring. Prior to 1902, the Excelsior Mine had a small camp named Copper, and it might have produced some ore. The rumor mill worked well: before the end of 1905, some 80 claims had been filed all over the valley. But none was as rich as the Excelsior.

In the summer of 1905, Nelson leased his mine for 10 years to the Standard Mines Company of Los Angeles. Development work started in November on what became known as the Standard No. 1 and No. 2 mines. Over the next few months, $25,000 was spent sinking a two-compartment shaft on the Standard No. 1 Mine and building a boarding house and a bunkhouse for 100 people. The ambitious camp had a store, an assay office, and a telephone. The first 18 months of operation were the most prolific. The shaft was pushed down several hundred feet, and long lateral workings were drilled along the copper veins. The ore was hauled first the old-fashioned way, in wagons pulled by 16-horse teams to Cima, then on the newly completed railroad to Salt Lake City for smelting. By the end of 1906, around 210 tons of copper and 9,400 ounces of silver had been shipped.

In August 1907 the *American Mining Review* reported that the Standard No. 1 Mine "has been stripped of practically all ore that was developed, and is now closed down owing to exceptionally bad management." 1907 had indeed been a lean year. But it was likely because the mine was tied up in litigation, not because it had played out. In spite of trouble, it remained active until 1910, yielding nearly as much silver and a third as much copper as in 1906. It re-opened in 1917, perhaps in response to the spike in the price of copper coincident with World War II. But by then the good ore had indeed been exhausted, and only about $7,000 worth of copper and silver was scraped out.

The Standard No. 2 Mine did not fare as well. It produced copper around 1906 and in 1917–1919, then lead-copper ore in 1934–1935. It was most active during the last two periods. In its early years, its main working was an inclined shaft that eventually reached around 250 feet in depth. Later on, the mine totaled more than 1,000 feet of tunnels and shafts along a 1-mile belt. It shipped about four cars of 22% copper ore around 1906, and a little after that, but this may have been it.

This mine had a brief revival in 1940, when it was leased by W. W. Hartman and exploited for tungsten. The ore was extracted from small trenches and cuts across the same mineralized zone that had yielded the copper ore. Hartman was already busy digging up tungsten at the nearby Evening Star Mine, which was much richer. The Standard No. 2 Mine only added a small tonnage to his shipments, which were refined at the Valley View mill. In 1951, the California Tungsten Corporation dug a few shallow shafts and adits in search of additional tungsten, but did not succeed. Despite this unglamorous ending, the Standard

Cabin below the crest of the Ivanpah Mountains

Mine did have a decent output—700,000 pounds of copper and 20,000 ounces of silver worth around $140,000, nearly two thirds of it in 1906.

Route Description

With a high-clearance vehicle one can drive to many of this loop's points of interest, but stopping and going gets tedious. Parking at each side road and exploring it on foot is more pleasant, and it requires little walking. A few short hikes are outlined on the map. If your vehicle has insufficient clearance, drive as far as practicable and walk the loop's more scenic eastern half. Hiking the whole loop, including all main side roads, is about 9 miles for 1,200 feet of elevation gain.

Standard No. 1 Mine. The old copper workings of the Standard No. 1 Mine are the most extensive and interesting. The mining camp scattered along the road consists of ruins from several generations, from a historic dugout and tin shed to a more recent trailer and gutted school bus, a rusted caterpillar tractor, and dismantled appliances. The shaft with a wooden ladder near the east end of the long tailing across from the dugout was the mine's bread and butter. Reportedly 356 feet deep, it had the most underground workings. Sadly, the NPS covered it with yet another uglifying metal cap to avoid an improbable lawsuit. It also fenced off the area's best mining feature—an intriguing maze of trenches, drifts, connecting tunnels, and buried shafts.

The side road south from the school bus leads to two other shafts. Like most other mines here, they explored mineral-rich altered dolomite at the contact zone between Teutonia Adamellite and Paleozoic limestone; the latter is widely exposed on the Ivanpah Mountains' west slopes. Some of the tailings are still coated with sky-blue chrysocolla and a bit of olivine, garnet, malachite, and azurite.

The camps. From the Standard No. 1 Mine the road winds up and down through the Ivanpah Mountains' beautifully forested foothills. The high elevation, just above 5,000 feet, supports a rich transition zone between the high desert and the mountains. Large Joshua trees mingle with juniper, Mormon tea with yucca and grizzly bear cactus.

Would-be prospectors and miners often scoured old districts in search of overlooked ore. Mining was not always part of their long-term plans. Sometimes their claims were a legal means of enjoying free rent on government land, a quiet piece of real estate to build a cabin and settle down for a while. Copper Cove was such a place. In the wake of the Standard Mine's earlier success, hundreds of claims were recorded within its small boundary—the last one in 1991—and a few people made this area their home.

Copper Cove

	Dist.(mi)	Elev.(ft)
Four-way junction	0.0	5,015
Junction (right)	1.1	5,090
Side rd to Standard No. 1 Mine	1.45	5,200
Standard No. 1 Mine shafts	(0.2)	~5,225
Side road to camp No. 1	2.25	~5,325
Side road to camp No. 2	3.0	5,330
Side road to Geer Camp	3.2	5,330
Side road to Riley's Camp	3.3	5,325
Riley's Camp	(0.25)	~5,410
Viewpoint	(0.65)	5,500
Side road to Johnny Tunnel	3.85	5,170
Side road to Standard No. 2	4.35	5,030
Standard No. 2 upper shaft	(0.5)	5,150
Four-way junction	4.6	5,015

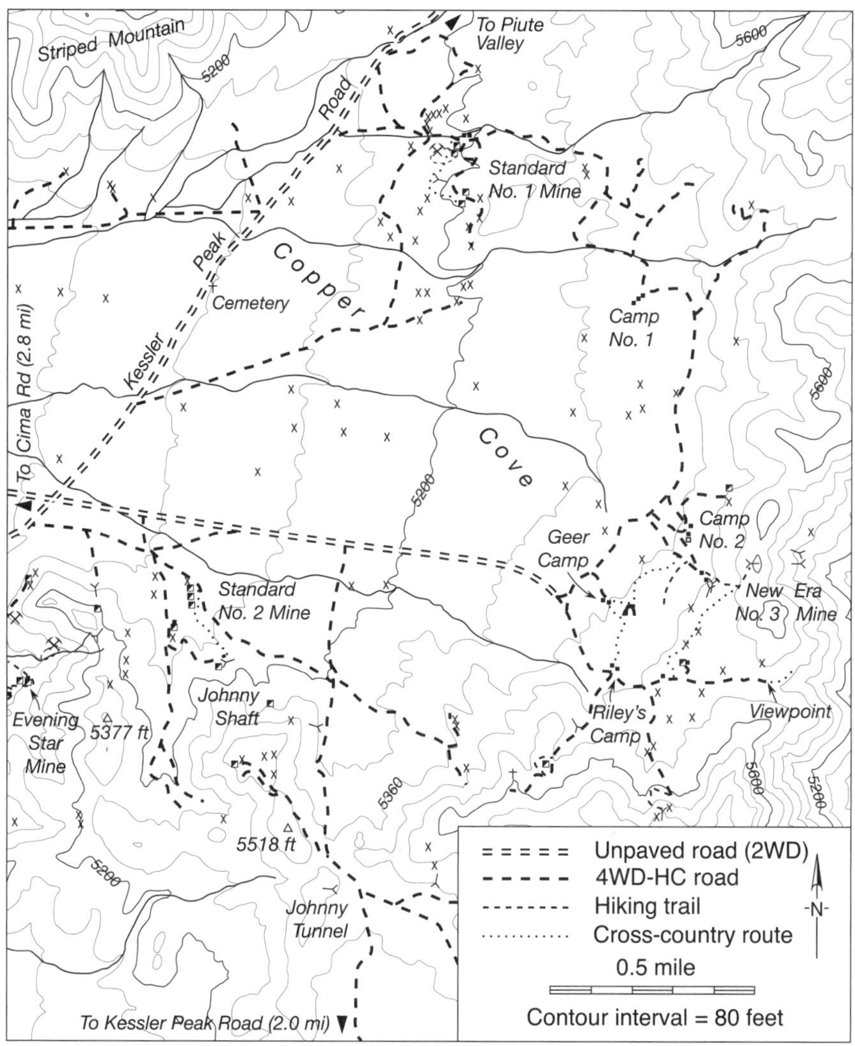

The loop road bypasses four of these old-timers' camps, giving us the rare opportunity to visit the humble homes of modern desert hermits. The first one is a cluster of cabins and trailers, the second one a spread-out compound sheltered in a secluded cove. Geer Camp, a little further, has a well-kept red wooden cabin. It was the residence of Robert R. Geer, who staked his first claims here in July 1928. He was still poking around the old Standard No. 2 Mine 20 years later. The last one, Riley's Camp, is posed on a low ridge with commanding views of Copper Cove. Its long cabin was built by Geer's friend John "Riley" Bembry. A medic in the Army during World War I, Bembry arrived in

1928 too. Over his extended stay, he acquired several mines and filed over 60 mining claims, including the New Era Mine near his camp. In 1953 he owned the Standard No. 1 Mine and had renamed it Riley. He filed his last claim in 1981, three years before his death. Bembry was buried in the tiny cemetery along the eastern portion of the loop road.

What makes visiting these three camps particularly rewarding is that they are nested in a spectacular setting of polished monzonite formations. These complex displays of pinkish fins, knolls, and hoodoos protruding from the green woodland create a brightly colored landscape unique in the preserve. To make the most of this exceptional scenery, take a slow hike through it. Start from Riley's Camp and pick your own path over the slickrock undulating below it. Aim for Geer Camp, then for the second camp. Each camp is visible from the previous one, and there are plenty of easy routes to get through. You are likely to stumble across a wealth of visual treasures. Flamingo Arch is a shapely opening in a low fin near Geer Camp. The old trail to the New Era Mine meanders through fragrant juniper to the mountains' crest. The camps themselves have enough buildings, old vehicles, and obsolete equipment to entertain a curious mind for hours. For variety, return a different way, perhaps across the rugged hill further east.

The area generally south of Riley's Camp also has many scenic enclaves, tucked along intricately eroded walls. While poking around, letting myself be drawn by natural paths between handsome boulders, I uncovered a deep pool of dark cool water under a granite overhang, a nicely preserved headframe, and the decorated grave of a fondly remembered local legend. A short walk from the end of the road east of Riley's Camp took me to a breezy overlook of the open pits and tailings of the Morning Star Mine.

Standard No. 2 Mine. The last mining area, south of the loop road about 1 mile west of Riley's Camp, is the Standard No. 2 Mine. The well-preserved collared shaft with a headframe and short trestle bridge is probably the main inclined shaft from around 1906. The large trench and 60-foot tunnel about 600 feet southwest of it were worked for tungsten in the early 1940s. The workings all along the irregular ridge to the southeast, including Johnny Shaft and Johnny Tunnel, are also from that era. Like all other high ground along the loop, this ridge commands good views of Copper Cove, especially of Striped Mountain's fine tilted striations. At the end of a long day of wandering, this is a befitting place to enjoy the sunset, when the mountains' shadows spill blues and purples across the earth.

■

THE EVENING STAR MINE

Sheltered within high hills dotted with Joshua trees and Mojave yucca, the Evening Star Mine ranks among the most scenic in the preserve. Exploited mostly in the 1940s, it produced tin, tungsten, and a little copper. The short loop road that goes around it can be either driven or hiked to visit its small camp, numerous workings, and massive headframe, one of the largest and most impressive mining structures extant in the preserve.

General Information
Road status: Hiking on old roads; standard-clearance access road
Evening Star Mine: 1.3 mi, 260 ft up loop / very easy
Main attractions: A historic tin mine, headframe, camp, Joshua trees
USGS 7.5′ topo map: Cima Dome
Maps: pp. 205*, *185*

Location and Access

The Evening Star Mine is on the western slope of the Ivanpah Mountains. For the most direct approach, drive the Cima Road 7.1 miles south of the gas station at Interstate 15 (or 10.5 miles north of Cima) to a corral and two large water tanks on the east side. A wide graded road starts just north of the tank. Follow it 2.7 miles east to a four-way junction near the foot of the mountains. The tall headframe of the Evening Star Mine is visible up ahead much of the way. Make a right and continue 0.2 mile to the Kessler Peak Road. Turn right and drive 0.45 mile to the second primitive road on the left. Park at this junction, which is the southwestern corner of the Evening Star Mine's loop road.

If you are coming from the south on the Cima Road, it is a little shorter to come up on the Kessler Peak Road. Look for the south end of this road on the right, 5.8 miles north of Cima, at the start of a left bend. It is 3.3 miles north to the starting point of the loop. Both routes are suitable for most vehicles.

History: The Tin King

The Evening Star Mine had slow beginnings. Its four claims covered a mineralized skarn near the contact between limestone and Jurassic granitic rocks (possibly Striped Mountain Pluton). The skarn had a host of metals, but few in sufficient quantities, and it eluded two generations of miners. Sometime between 1900 and 1910 a 740-foot exploratory shaft was sunk on the Rex claim in search of copper. Chalcopyrite was encountered, but showings were poor and no ore was produced. The Evening Star Mine was not revived until years later when tin was discovered, allegedly by John "Riley" Bembry in 1936. A war veteran then in his mid thirties, Bembry had just moved to the Mojave Desert (see *Copper Cove*) and bought the Evening Star Mine in 1935. Following his tin strike, Bembry sold the mine, and the new owners started tin mining in 1938. Operations were again unsuccessful, and over the next two years the Evening Star Mine changed ownership and operator several times. But there was a lucky one, an Angelino named W. W. Hartman who worked the Bernice claim not for tin but for tungsten. In 1939 and 1940, he shipped 1,000 tons of tungsten ore from a single tunnel—which was not bad for a little mine.

In August 1940 new explorations uncovered an area rich in cassiterite (tin oxide) and instilled new hopes. The Steel Service and Sales Company of Chicago leased the mine and finally made it work. The ore was initially mined from an open cut and a shaft, then from a second shaft in 1943. Crushers installed on the main shaft's 60-foot headframe ground the ore, then the tin and copper ore were separated from waste rock by screening. In 1942 the company shipped 25 tons containing 6% tin by truck to Cima, then by rail to a Texas smelter. To process its ore locally, company owner Carl Wendrick put up a 30-ton mill at Windmill Station, at the north end of Cima Road. From then on the classified ore was trucked to his mill, where it was cleaned and further concentrated. It was a modest operation—eight people worked at the mine and four at the mill—but it did honorably well. Until 1944, 400 tons of tin ore were processed at the mill.

In 1944 long-hole drilling at the bottom of shaft No. 2 failed to encounter new ore, and tin mining stopped. A vertical shaft was sunk on a nearby copper vein in 1949, and Hartman's tungsten tunnel was extended to 340 feet in 1951–1952, but no ore was shipped. In the end, the Evening Star Mine did have one good claim to fame—it was the only tin producer in the east Mojave Desert.

Route Description

The tungsten workings. The area has several points of interest, all either right along or close to the road that loops around the site. The first one is the historic tungsten workings. They are reached by the road that branches off to the right 0.2 mile east of the southwest corner of the loop road. The tunnel guarded by a wooden door at the end of this side road (150 yards) is where Hartman mined tungsten ore in

1939–1940. With 570 feet of galleries and drifts, it is one of the area's most extensive tunnels. The tungsten ore was scheelite. The road that winds around the hill to the south passes by more tunnels and many parallel trenches, and eventually ends at a shaft, all of which were explored for tungsten.

The Evening Star Mine. The first of the Evening Star Mine's copper shafts is 250 yards past the junction to the tungsten workings, by the north side of the road. It is the 67-foot inclined shaft sunk in 1949. It still has its original lumber collar and long wooden ladder. The colorful ore near the tip of its short tailing is about all that remains at the surface of the Evening Star Mine's mineral-rich skarn. It is mottled with dark-green malachite, mustard-colored jasper, dark-red garnet-like crystals, and gray spots of chalcocite (copper sulfide).

The road winds its way, as a vague trace towards the end, to the heart of the tin mine—a small stone building, which was the powder house and erected a safe distance from the mines, a sheet-metal cabin, and the spectacular wooden headframe, all nestled in a ring of hills. Shaft No. 1, next to the headframe, was the main producer. It drops nearly vertically for 35 feet, where it opens onto a trench, then continues as a 45° shaft for 70 feet. Shaft No. 2 is the collared square opening west of shaft No. 1. The trench that connects them was dug to determine whether the tin-bearing vein was continuous between the shafts, which it was. At the bottom of shaft No. 2, 100 feet down, a 75-foot tunnel was sunk towards shaft No. 1 to mine the vein between them.

About 60-feet tall and made of a series of superposed levels, the headframe is one of the largest mining structures in the preserve. The reason for its size is that it was not just a hoist but also a mill. This was one of the few headframes in the California desert that had a crusher at its top, which makes it all the more interesting. Ore from the shaft was hoisted by cable to the top of the structure. It was fed by gravity through a jaw crusher, then a cone crusher, mounted on the slanted side of the headframe. The crushed ore was stockpiled in the 100-ton bin at the bottom of the headframe. Powered by a gasoline four-cylinder engine, this mill had the capacity to process 10 to 15 tons per hour—but it probably never worked this hard. Ore from shaft No. 1 had about 2% tin. The ore body contained a lexicon of minerals—tremolite, serpentine, forsterite, garnet, epidote, wollastonite, pyrite, chalcopyrite, scheelite, cassiterite, and magnetite. Only a little remains today on the dumps.

The loop road continues north of the headframe and swings east to the prominent two-level quarry on the hillside. On its way there, it

Headframe of the tin workings at the Evening Star Mine

crosses a junkyard of vintage space heaters and refrigerators. The quarry was also part of the tin mine. Its white rock is dolomite crystallized to coarse marble by the intrusion that mineralized this deposit.

To complete this loop, from the quarry head west on the loop road to the Kessler Peak Road, then 0.3 mile south to your starting point. Along the way, about 400 yards from the quarry, you will come across the shaft of the Suzanne R Mine. It has a spindly wooden headframe and a small whitish tailing. An aging ladder, now too rickety to hold even a fool, drops 35 nearly vertical feet to a dark tunnel. The pretty sky-blue ore on the dump is chrysocolla, a copper silicate. It is mixed with calcite crystals and sparkles of peacock ore and chalcopyrite.

The return. The area has several other workings. The ones to the north might have been part of the Standard No. 2 Mine, while to the south they belonged to the Copper King Mine. The best deal around may well be climbing to higher ground along the old roads that lead up to them. The surrounding hills command sweeping vistas of the desert floor all the way to Cima Dome and beyond.

■

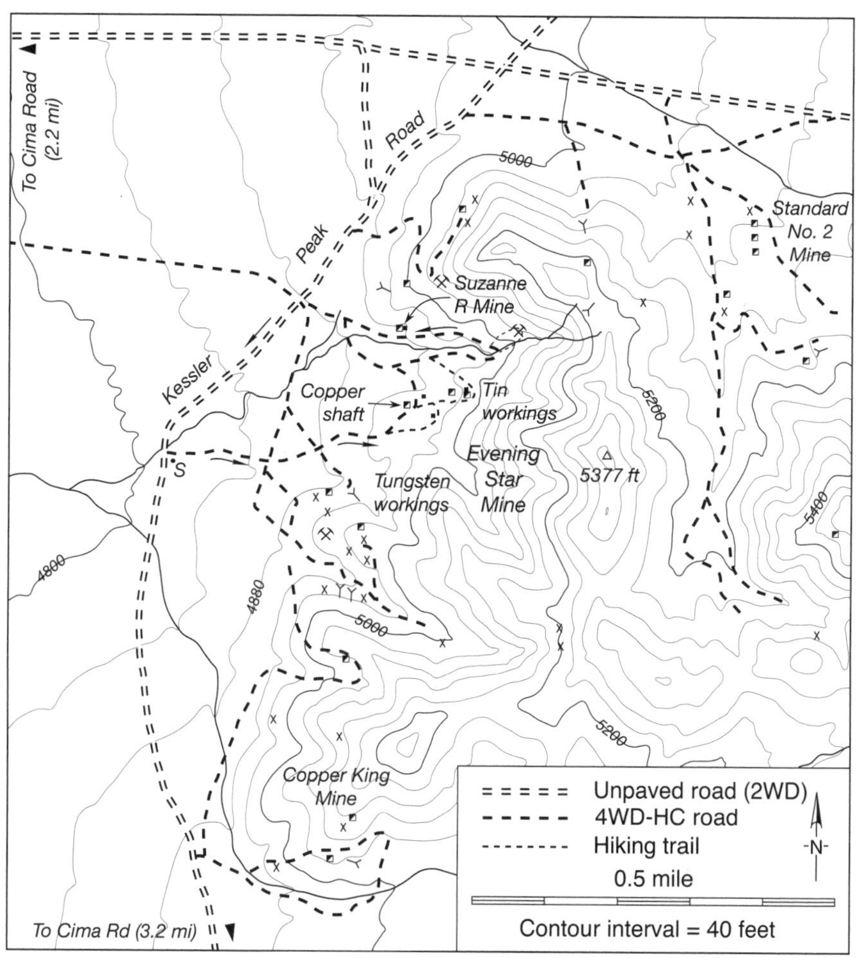

The Evening Star Mine	Dist.(mi)	Elev.(ft)
Southwest corner of mine loop	0.0	4,810
Junction to tungsten workings	0.2	4,880
Tungsten tunnel	(0.05)	4,890
1949 copper shaft	0.35	4,930
Headframe	0.45	~4,965
Open cut	0.65	5,000
Copper shaft	0.75	4,920
Junction with access road	0.9	4,875
Back to starting point	1.2	4,810

Headframe at the New Trail Mine

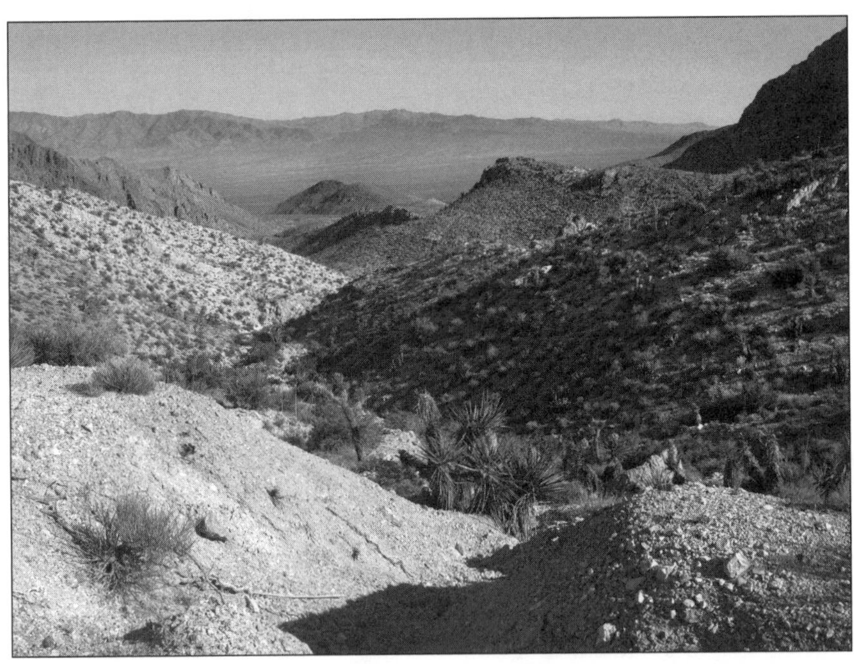

New Trail Canyon from the upper end of the mining road

NEW TRAIL CANYON

> *Some places get more than their fair share. New Trail Canyon is brimming with geological wonders, from fossil sea ripples and corals to a plethora of minerals. Some sites can be reached on short hikes near the mouth of the canyon. The centerpiece is the canyon itself, a colorful kaleidoscope of granite, limestone, and dolomite. It leads to the historic ruins of the Bullion Mine and New Trail Mine, and eventually to the spectacular crest of the Ivanpah Mountains.*

General Information

Road status: Roadless upper canyon; high-clearance access road
New Trail Mine: 1.0 mi, 490 ft up, 20 ft down one way / easy
Bullion Mine: 1.1 mi, 400 ft up, 20 ft down one way / easy
New Trail Cyn (crest): 2.0 mi, 1,300 ft up, 20 ft down one way / moder.
Main attractions: Historic mines in a scenic canyon, geology
USGS 7.5' topo maps: Joshua, Mineral Hill*
Maps: pp. 211*, *185*

Location and Access

From the crest of the Ivanpah Mountains south of Kokoweef Peak, New Trail Canyon drains southeast into Oro Wash, which continues east into Ivanpah Valley. The old road to the mines can still be driven into the lower canyon. To get to it, drive the Morning Star Mine Road 10.8 miles from Cima (or 4.2 miles from the Ivanpah Road) to a dirt road on the west side, by a large shed and tank. This road first climbs a long alluvial fan 2.8 miles to a T junction. Turn right. The road soon veers left, climbs along Oro Wash, passes by mill ruins, then reaches the New Trail Camp after 1.5 miles. Parts of it are steep and have a small crown. High clearance is recommended, although perhaps not essential. Beyond the camp all roads are very poor or washed out.

History

New Trail Canyon is not even 2 miles long, yet it inherited enough minerals to cover most of the alphabet—from azurite to bornite, chrysocolla, diopside, epidote, flint, garnet, hemimorphite, all the way to sphalerite. Over the years, half a dozen mines sprung up to tap this treasure chest. The earliest one was the fabled Bullion Mine, on the canyon's east side. In the 1860s and 1870s, it was said to have produced high-grade silver-lead ore so valuable that it was shipped for refining half-way around the world to Wales via the Sea of Cortez. It might have been confused with another rich mine by the same name south of Ludlow. But the confusion was never cleared, and its past remains shrouded in mystery. What we do know is that in March 1879, owner James Boyd, who also owned the rich Copper World Mine, located here a silver ledge that assayed a nice $350 per ton. He set up a camp, hired a Native American to drive a burro and pack water, and set out to work his ledge. In May, his shaft ran into an equally rich vein of milling ore, and for a while he had a team hauling five tons of ore every few days, some of it to Ivanpah for milling. This activity was likely short-lived; by 1890 little additional work had been done. The Bullion Mine was worked again, by different parties, in 1905, 1909–1913, and 1916–1917, when it shipped 250 tons of lead-copper-silver ore. It has probably been mostly idle since.

The New Trail Mine, across the canyon, was more extensive. All over that side, fractures in granite dikes were hydrothermally filled with skarns stuffed with an unusual concentration of copper, as well as silver, gold, iron, and lead. The steep fractures had to be accessed by shafts, from which crosscut tunnels were dug when a skarn was encountered. The New Trail Mine was most prolific between 1917 and 1919, when it shipped about 2,000 tons of sorted ore valued at over $100,000. By 1929 the main shaft was 180 feet deep and sprouted half a mile of galleries. By then other workings had been developed on magnesite and mica deposits down canyon. From at least 1930 until the mid-1940s, the New Trail Mining Company of Riverside operated the property, which included 28 claims and most of the west-side deposits. The main shaft was extended to 280 feet and a tunnel sunk at the bottom, but it returned only about $10,000 over a total of five years. The last known production took place from 1947 to 1950, when a private party cleaned out nearly $30,000 of copper ore. In 1950 and 1951, the Alloy Mining Company explored the area with 2,300 feet of drill holes and tunnels. Other than later milling efforts, these were likely the mine's final days. In its life the New Trail Mine generated over $140,000, a noble achievement in a land where failure was the norm.

Route Description

The New Trail Camp area. The camp's two handsome cabins of richly patinaed wood and corrugated-iron outbuilding are clustered on a flat overlooking the canyon. Behind them rise the Ivanpah Mountains, a rainbow of rust knobs and pale-gray ridges studded with dark-green Joshua trees. On the rare winter days when the cabins are covered in snow, they look as cozy as Swiss chalets in a storm. Things

Cabins at the New Trail Camp

have not always been this idyllic. In 2001, park rangers intercepted four men leaving the camp and discovered that the cabins were being used as a methamphetamine lab. More than $50,000 worth of meth oil was waiting to be processed into crystal meth. The men were ultimately linked to the operation. One of them served a 13-year jail sentence.

The camp is peaceful again. Dead bramble laced on old trellises hint of the vines that decorated the cabins. A gust whistling through gaps in the walls scares a rabbit from behind a discarded pump. The sole furniture in the outbuilding is a rustic stove kludged from an oil drum and recycled pipes. Every spring it has new ashes. Outside in the sun, a pink lounge chair invites relaxation. It moves around. People do come up here once in a great while. Not all are ill-intentioned.

If you like mineralogy, you may need most of a day to explore the camp area alone. The loop trail northeast of the cabins is a good example. It leads to a quarry of bright copper minerals, then a framed shaft, before circling back via the New Trail Magnesite Mine. The white porcelain-like magnesite there forms thin parallel veins and exhibits striking blooming patterns, like cauliflower. Another interesting area is the mill along the access road. Its water tank is big enough to support a small town. Its misshapen metal chute, battery of cinder-block vats, and giant screen, all custom made, may have been used to process historic tailings. The workings on the low hill to the southeast expose phlogopite, a brownish mica known for imaging a light into a six-point star. In the wash south of it, a slate-like rock called phyllite is covered with fossilized ripple marks nearly half a billion years old.

New Trail Canyon. From the camp, walk the road that descends to the northeast. After 250 yards, its washed-out ramp drops into the wash of New Trail Canyon. At first it is an easy walk up the open wash. Bordered with willow, cliffrose, and squawbush, it winds lazily between long colorful slopes soaring up to craggy summits. Buff Cambrian dolomite crops out in the lower canyon, blue-gray Devonian to Permian limestones in the upper canyon, and dark pink Ivanpah Granite all along the western margin. The slopes are bristling with equally colorful gardens of Joshua trees, Mojave yucca, beavertail cactus, and other cacti. In the spring, the local flowers love to go wild, especially the astounding giant four o'clock and the Mojave aster. Even the empty wash sprouts tall pink bouquets of scented penstemon. The best treat is the pygmy agave, a pretty mescal with toothed leaves, each tipped with a long spine. Although endemic to only a few ranges, it occurs here in such numbers that its tall stalks protrude all over.

Pygmy agave

The canyon changes character, often suddenly, as it reaches deeper into the Ivanpah Mountains. Small round boulders appear in the wash. The ground gets greener with blackbrush and ephedra. Then the first juniper make an appearance. Past the Bullion Mine, the wash squeezes through narrower passages lined with white marble slickrock. In its uppermost reaches, around the 1899 Red Copper claim, the wash becomes a boulder-filled trench as it ascends the steepening funnel-

New Trail Canyon

	Dist.(mi)	Elev.(ft)
New Trail Camp	0.0	4,425
New Trail Canyon (wash)	0.15	4,420
New Trail Mine Road	0.5	4,500
New Trail Mine (main shaft)	(0.5)	4,895
Revenue Copper Mine	(1.1)	~5,080
Side canyon to Bullion Mine	0.75	4,585
Bullion Mine (upper shaft)	(0.3)	~4,810
Upper end of mining road	1.5	~5,030
Viewpoint at crest	~2.0	5,710

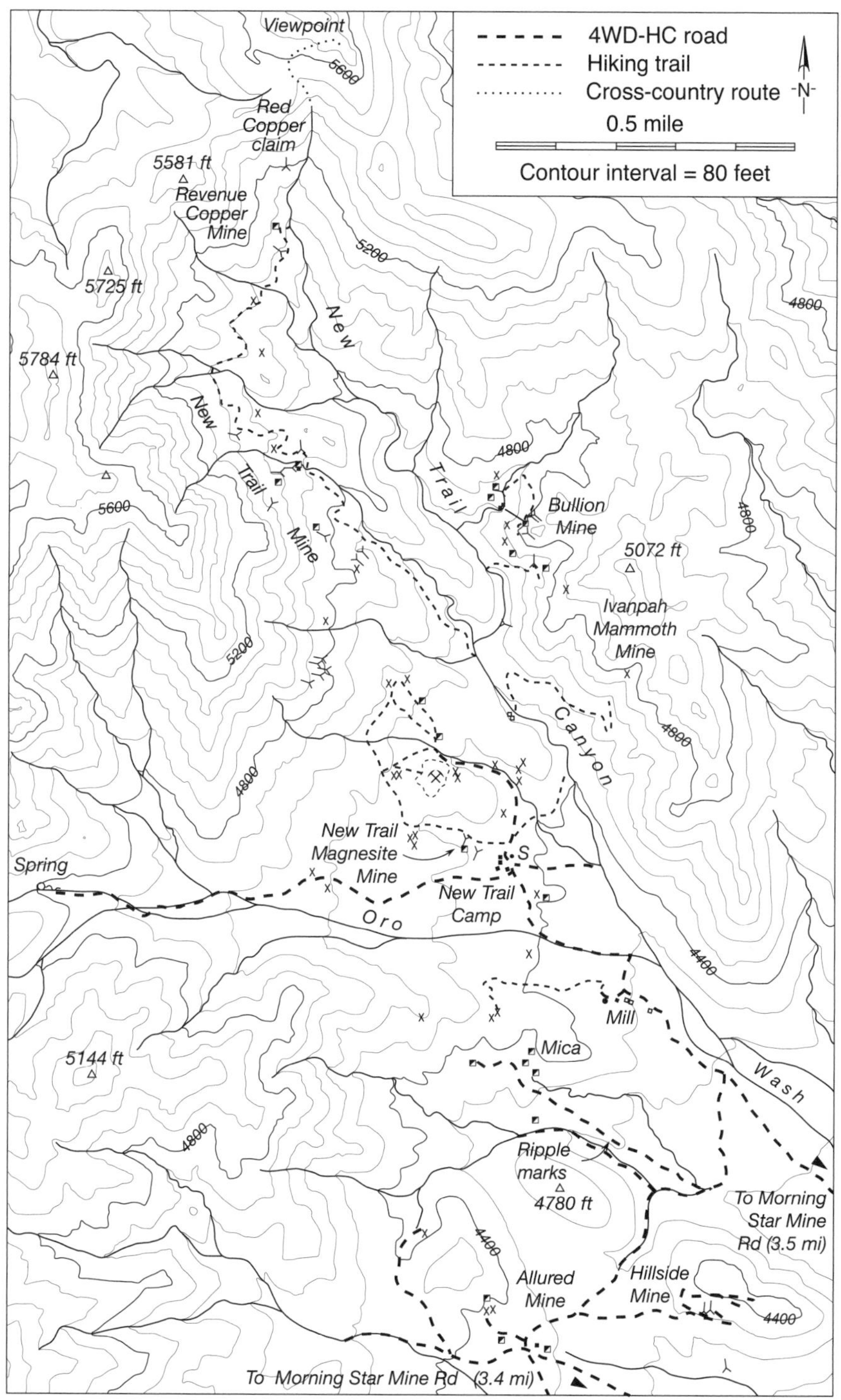
4WD-HC road
Hiking trail
Cross-country route
N
0.5 mile
Contour interval = 80 feet
Viewpoint
Red Copper claim
5581 ft
Revenue Copper Mine
5725 ft
5784 ft
New Trail Mine
New Trail Canyon
Bullion Mine
5072 ft
Ivanpah Mammoth Mine
New Trail Magnesite Mine
Spring
New Trail Camp
Oro Wash
Mill
Mica
5144 ft
Ripple marks
4780 ft
To Morning Star Mine Rd (3.5 mi)
Allured Mine
Hillside Mine
To Morning Star Mine Rd (3.4 mi)

shaped head of the canyon. It takes some scrambling to reach the crest, over rocks with a nasty skin-shredding ability. But the cardiovascular workout is good, the scenery is beautiful, and the summit offers good views of the Mescal Range and the wrinkled Ivanpah Mountains.

The Bullion Mine. About 0.7 mile from the ramp a beat-up grade on the right climbs steeply to a tunnel. The side canyon on the right 150 yards further is the way to the Bullion Mine—the area's most exciting mine. Just inside the twisted side canyon lie concrete foundations and a large metallic tipple, the remains of a loading dock and perhaps of a mill. The tall tailing and skinny cableway south of the wash point to retaining walls more than 100 feet higher. The Bullion Mine's main shaft is up there. To climb to it, walk up the wash 70 yards to a tunnel on the left. The short foot trail to the shaft starts across the wash about 20 steps further. It is so faint that you will have to believe it is there to find it. The inclined shaft at the top of the trail was dug at the foot of a slick stope timbered with tree trunks more than a century old. The area commands impressive views of the canyon, and of the awesome ridge of vertical carbonate strata exposed to the south. The dolomite hosts vugs of small quartz crystals and large masses of Devonian corals.

The New Trail Mine. The road to the New Trail Mine branches off on the left 0.4 mile from the ramp. It climbs along a parallel side canyon and returns to the canyon after 1.2 miles. It is the quickest way to the mine. But if you can, hike up the canyon and return down the road. The views from the road are better when heading downhill, and the road is shaded earlier in the day. To find the upper end of the road from the wash, look for the overgrown grade that drops down from it.

If you hike the road downhill, you will first come across the dissected tailings and 70-foot shaft of the Revenue Copper Mine, which produced a little copper in 1917–1919. From there the weathered road drops along the flank of the canyon and passes by the New Trail Mine's numerous workings and associated ruins. Scattered along a 0.6-mile stretch, they are reached by anything from short strolls to cross-country walks, sometimes assisted by trail segments. The most interesting area is the main, two-compartment inclined shaft, about half way down. Its awkward headframe is one of the best preserved in the preserve. Rising 20 feet above the mine's large tailing, it stands as an enduring symbol of a bygone era. Although almost all the visible ore is copper—and there is a lot of it—tailings still hold nearly 2 ounces of gold per ton, the highest known concentration in the preserve.

■

KESSLER PEAK

The highest point in the Ivanpah Mountains, Kessler Peak is a delightful summit to climb. Although not as exciting now that its once abundant plant life was exterminated by a wildfire, the route is only moderately difficult and decorated with dark-pink granite outcrops. The views from the top extend over much of the western preserve and reach well into the northern Mojave Desert.

General Information

Road status: Roadless; standard- and high-clearance access roads
Kessler Peak: 1.9 mi, 1,150 ft up, 25 ft down one way / moderate
Kessler Peak loop: 4.2 mi, 1,280 ft up loop / moderate
Main attractions: A short cross-country climb, scenic views
USGS 7.5' topo map: Cima Dome
Maps: pp. 215*, *185*

Location and Access

Kessler Peak is the isolated summit near the south end of the Ivanpah Mountains. As you drive on the Cima Road to get to it, its sharp profile stands out up ahead for miles. From the stop sign at Cima, count 5.8 miles and look for a primitive road at a shallow angle on the right side, just before a left bend. This is the Kessler Peak Road. It is harder to spot coming from the other direction; look for it 0.6 mile past the signed Teutonia Peak Trail. Drive the Kessler Peak Road 1 mile north to a junction. Turn right and go 0.3 mile to where this rougher road angles left and another road continues straight along a sandy wash. Park near this junction. Kessler Peak is the dome-shaped mountain to the southeast. A standard-clearance vehicle can usually make it to the first junction. High clearance is helpful beyond.

Route Description

The climb. There are many ways to climb Kessler Peak. Several steep routes up the peak's west slope are possible starting from around the south end of the Kessler Peak Road. They are the most direct, but Kessler Springs Ranch spoils the views. The route suggested here, up a more gradual wash on the northwest face, is much wilder. From the suggested starting point, follow the road east as it winds along a nearly level sandy wash. After 0.45 mile, past the tip of a low ridge pointing north, leave the road and head up the broad floodplain that opens

Shadow Valley and Mescal Range from the crest north of Kessler Peak

up to the south. It is crisscrossed by narrow braided gullies at first, but a well-defined wash soon emerges. Follow it to about 0.5 mile from the road, where it reaches a tall bank of granite outcrops at the foot of Kessler Peak. The wash angles right along the outcrops, then veers left and starts climbing. Keep right at the two forks. This route is nowhere very steep, and the wash is a little rocky but never too brushy. After half a mile of climbing you will reach the prominent east-west shoulder of Kessler Peak. The summit is 0.2 mile east up this ridge.

Before the Dome Fire of August 2020, which blew east right over the peak, one of the best attributes of this climb was the vegetation. All along the base of the mountain Joshua trees thrived in a vast belt intermixed with mature Utah juniper. Both trees grew right up to the summit, albeit stunted by high winds. Staghorn cholla, pancake pricklypear, grizzly bear cactus, calico cactus, and mound cactus were plentiful at lower elevations, and ephedra, squawbush, and cliffrose higher up. Now all of this is gone. Over the next few years, the standing skeletons of the burnt trees will continue to create a strange, otherworldly mood, until they will all have collapsed. A few lucky juniper and shrubs, sheltered from the flames by rocky outcrops, have fortunately survived, giving us both a flavor of the former landscape and hope for swifter recolonization.

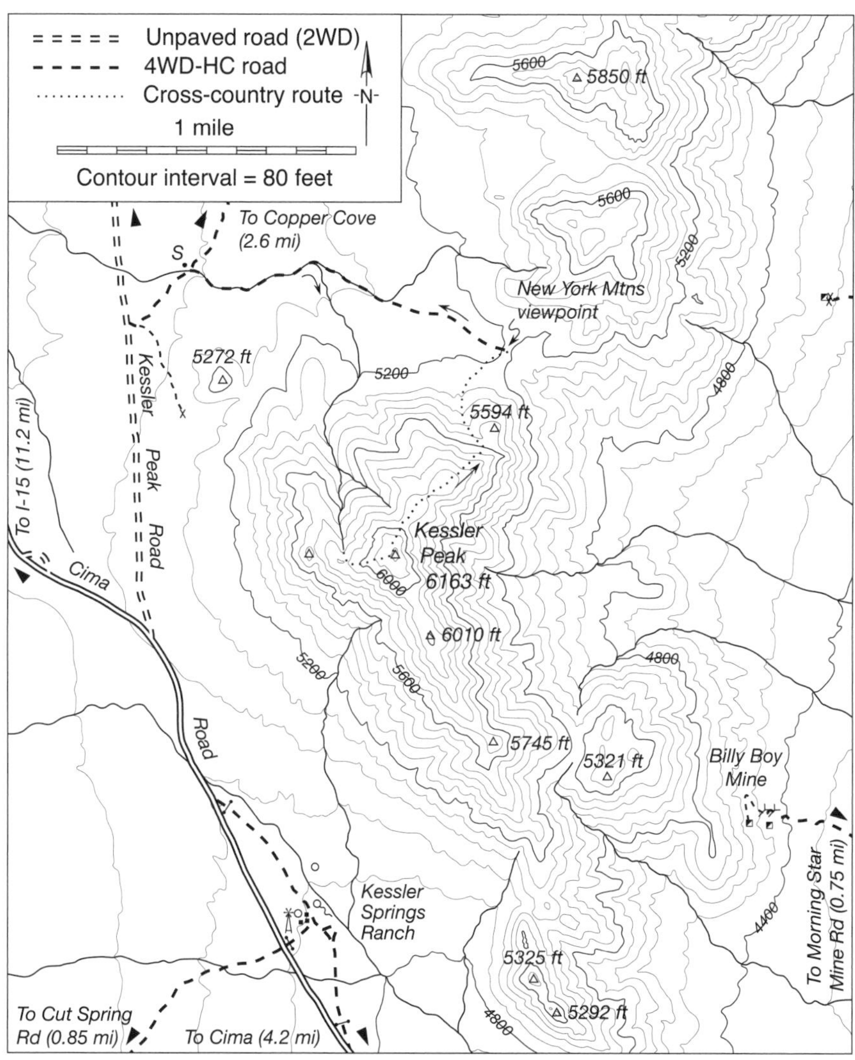

Kessler Peak

	Dist.(mi)	Elev.(ft)
Access road (junction)	0.0	5,033
Leave road up broad wash	0.45	5,085
Ridge	1.7	5,770
Kessler Peak	1.9	6,163
New York Mtns viewpoint	3.0	5,200
Back to starting point	4.2	5,033

In spite of the sad, naked ground, this is still a good out-of-the-way climb. Much of Kessler Peak's north face is covered with interesting granite outcrops chiseled into pinnacles and stacks of vertical fins. From its central position, Kessler Peak commands a sweeping perspective of the western half of the preserve. Striped Mountain, the Mescal Range, and Clark Mountain profiled against each other to the north are particularly scenic. The preserve's magnificent mountainous core fills up all of the eastern and southern horizons. To the southwest Cima Dome's symmetric curvature is sharply delineated against the Kelso Mountains and the pointed humps of the cinder cones. I was here once in Indian summer, and several localized storms were adding drama to this grand scenery. Entire mountain ranges were obscured by ominous clouds and black curtains of slanted rain. Yet here and there vast tracks of land remained inundated with sunlight, from the Kelso Dunes all the way to Death Valley's Black Mountains.

Kessler Peak's crest. If you feel as I did that it would be a waste to interrupt these views too soon, consider prolonging them by returning along the crest. One option is to follow it south, then to drop along the drainage of your choice and loop back along the foot of the Ivanpah Mountains. Kessler Springs Ranch is NPS residential property; to avoid it, do not return any farther south than the 5,745-foot peak.

I much preferred the other direction, northeast along the crest to the deep gap in the mountains, then back along the access road. All along the billowing ridge, granitic outcrops compose a lively foreground floating high above the surrounding valleys. Here as all over Kessler Peak, the rock is Jurassic Ivanpah Granite, a variety that contains very little dark minerals, mostly biotite, hence its light appearance; some fresh cuts are nearly pure white feldspar. The views alternate between the New York Mountains and the Mescal Range, depending on which side of the ridge the rocks and the path of least resistance take you. The descent to the gap is very steep, strewn with boulders at lower elevations; it is the hardest part of this hike, but it is fairly short. Aim for the east end of the access road visible down below. Like many ranges, the Ivanpah Mountains are not symmetric, and nowhere is this asymmetry as impressive as from this descent. On the west side, just below you, the mountains are buried right up to their crest under a long alluvial fan that sweeps down gently into Shadow Valley. On the east side they drop 700 abrupt feet into Ivanpah Valley. The access road ends on the cusp of this prominent discontinuity, overlooking the New York Mountains on one side and nothing much on the other.

■

— 8 —

NEW YORK MOUNTAINS

THE NEW YORK MOUNTAINS FORM a long and rugged range that slashes 25 miles across the northeast corner of the preserve to end just inside Nevada. Reaching 7,532 feet above sea level, they are the second highest in the preserve. They receive more moisture than most places in the eastern Mojave Desert, and a good portion is covered with evergreens. Combined with cooler weather, an abundance of scenic canyons, spectacular geology, and a rich mining history, this attribute makes the New York Mountains one of the most attractive in the preserve. Because much of this range is protected as wilderness, it holds a great potential for hiking, backpacking, and mountaineering. Four-wheelers are not left out, as several of the forested canyons remain partly open to motor vehicles. The preserve's recreational wealth would just not be the same without this refreshing sky island.

Access and Backcountry Roads

The New York Mountains can be accessed on several backcountry roads, especially in the four main canyons—Fourth of July, Carruthers, Sagamore, and Keystone—on the range's south side. These roads are among the very few in the preserve that give vehicular access to evergreen forests. The New York Mountains Road and the Ivanpah Road also pass relatively close to the mountains' green belt. The first one skirts the southern edge of the range, a mixed zone of Joshua trees, juniper, and pinyon pine in a beautiful mountain setting. If I had to name one road with the highest scenic value in the preserve, I may well pick this one. The Ivanpah Road cuts across the range at a low pass just east of the main mountain mass. Several primitive byways

Suggested Backcountry Drives in the New York Mountains					
Route/Destination	Dist. (mi)	Lowest elev.	Highest elev.	Road type	Pages
Carruthers Canyon Road	9.0	4,411'	5,620'	H	253-254
Castle Peaks	3.8	4,606'	4,965'	H	223
California Eastern Railway	3.5	4,000'	4,470'	H	229, 233
Keystone Canyon Road	2.8	4,895'	5,535'	F	239-241
New York Mountains Road	12.8	4,350'	5,425'	H	217
Sagamore Canyon Cutoff	2.3	4,997'	5,460'	F	245-246
Sagamore Canyon Road	3.6	4,530'	5,415'	F	245, 248
Vanderbilt Road	2.2	4,150'	4,500'	H	235-238
Vanderbilt Rd-Railway loop	6.3	4,000'	4,500'	H	233-238
Key: H=Primitive (HC) F=Primitive (4WD)					

branch off these two roads and gain access to more remote sections of the mountains. In the northeastern area, the sawtoothed crest known as Castle Peaks is also well worth exploring. Although it lies at the heart of a wilderness area, it is relatively easy to reach by road.

Geology

In addition to everything else going for them, the New York Mountains feature an unusually diverse geology. The southwest part of the range is composed of Mid Hills Adamellite, the northeastern extension of the Cretaceous granitic rock underlying much of the Mid Hills. It is responsible for the sensuous landscapes prevailing in Cliff, Fourth of July, and Carruthers canyons. Directly against this pluton, near the east end of the range's main mountain block, lies a discontinuous band of sedimentary rocks, oriented roughly north-south and 1 to 3 miles wide, stretching from Carruthers Canyon to the mouth of Willow Wash. It is the remnant of a sequence of Paleozoic and Triassic carbonate formations, mostly Bird Spring Formation, Monte Cristo Limestone, and Sultan Limestone. Sagamore and Keystone canyons cut right across these fossil-bearing formations. The northeast section of the range is different still. Its southern slope, in particular the Castle Peaks area, is composed mostly of Miocene andesite and basalt. In contrast, the northern slope is a faulted patchwork of gneiss, granites, and migmatite around 1.7 billion years old—some of the preserve's oldest formations. Not too many other desert ranges will put you in contact with such a cross-section of rocks, and the enhanced variety of landforms and weathering patterns that comes with it.

Botany: Oaks and Fir in the Desert

With more than 5 miles of crestline above 6,000 feet, the New York Mountains are a prime sky island that hosts a remarkable botanical diversity. Aside from the usual associations of Cactaceae grading into Joshua trees and conifers as the elevation increases, several unexpected species occur here. Two species of oak, scrub oak and canyon live oak, are found in the New York Mountains' four main canyons. Scrub oak shrublands are rare in California, while in the Mojave Desert canyon live oaks are only known to occur in the eastern Mojave Desert. In Carruthers Canyon the larger canyon live oaks are found in nearly pure stands covering a good fraction of an acre. In Live Oak Canyon they form a thick green corridor, with specimens standing as tall as 30 feet. Much larger areas, locally intermingled with oaks, are occupied by chaparral plants, including manzanita and desert mountain lilac, more commonly indigenous to the California coast. Higher elevations are home to the two-needle pinyon pine, also rare in the Mojave Desert. It grows mixed with single-leaf pinyon pines at several places, in particular in Carruthers Canyon and up on the highest ridges. The rarest resident of all is the white fir. This handsome conifer occurs at a single location, on about 2.5 sheltered acres on a steep ridge north of the highest summit. This tiny stand of about 30 trees, most of them under 25 feet tall, is the last remnant of a once extensive boreal forest. Searching for these dispersed ecosystems is one of the rare pleasures of exploring the New York Mountains.

Mining History

Among the first in the preserve to yield valuable minerals, the New York Mountains were a major catalyst in the history of the eastern Mojave Desert. Copper was discovered in Carruthers Canyon possibly as early as the 1860s, and silver in Sagamore Canyon in 1870. Early reports suggest that silver ore might have been mined and even milled in the early 1860s, perhaps by Spanish operators. If milling did take place, it was one of the earliest attempts at reducing ore in the history of the region. When the New York Mining District was organized in April 1870, it missed being the region's first by only a few months.

In subsequent years, mining centered mostly in two areas. From 1870 until the 1920s, the mines in Sagamore Canyon produced off and on a little silver and lead, then copper and zinc in the early 1940s. The Vanderbilt gold mines, active from 1891 to around 1942, were among the most diligently worked in the area. For about a decade Vanderbilt was a busy town supported by several mills and numerous properties, as boisterous as any of the famous mining camps in the California

Suggested Hikes in the New York Mountains					
Route/Destination	Dist. (mi)	Elev. gain	Mean elev.	Access road	Pages
Short hikes (under 5 miles round trip)					
California Eastern Railway				Graded	
eastern segment	1.6	~380'	4,590'		234-235
Carruthers Canyon				P/7.7 mi	
to Keystone Cyn divide	2.0	1,380'	6,060'		255-260
to wonderland of rocks*	0.6	110'	5,660'		255
Castle Peaks viewpoint	1.5	380'	5,100'	H/3.8 mi	224
Giant Ledge Mine (east)	1.1	930'	5,910'	P/7.7 mi	255-258
Giant Ledge Mine (west)	1.2	580'	5,820'	P/7.7 mi	255-257
Keystone Canyon				P/2.0 mi	
to Carruthers Cyn divide	2.3	1,480'	5,750'		239-244
to Keystone Spring	1.6	580'	5,520'		239-244
to quarries	1.5	780'	5,630'		239-241
Live Oak Canyon	1.9	750'	5,580'	P/2.0 mi	239-244
Sagamore Canyon				F/3.6 mi	
Alpha Lode loop*	1.75	400'	5,570'		249-250
to Tin Camp	0.4	110'	5,420'		249
to triple-divide viewpoint	1.8	1,200'	5,920'		249-252
Vanderbilt and mines	1.2	380'	4,310'	H/1.1 mi	235-238
Vanderbilt Road–Rail loop*	4.2	1,030'	4,340'	Graded	233-238
Intermediate hikes (5-12 miles round trip)					
California Eastern Railway				Graded	
both segments	4.8	910'	4,350'		233-235
western segment	3.5	~610'	4,250'		233-234
Castle Peaks loop*	7.1	1,300'	5,170'	H/3.8 mi	224-226
Dove Spring	4.3	1,430'	4,920'	H/3.8 mi	224-228
Keystone–Carruthers Cyns	4.3	2,860'	5,890'	P/2.0 mi	239-244
New York Peak					
via Carruthers Canyon	2.6	2,430'	6,620'	P/7.7 mi	255-260
via Keystone Canyon	3.0	2,540'	6,110'	P/2.0 mi	239-244
North New York Peak					
via Carruthers Canyon	2.5	2,160'	6,290'	P/7.7 mi	255-260
via Keystone Canyon	2.8	2,270'	6,020'	P/2.0 mi	239-244

Key: P=Primitive (2WD) H=Primitive (HC) F=Primitive (4WD)
Distance: one way, except for loops (round-trip, marked with *)
Elev. gain: sum of all elevation gains on a round-trip basis & on loops

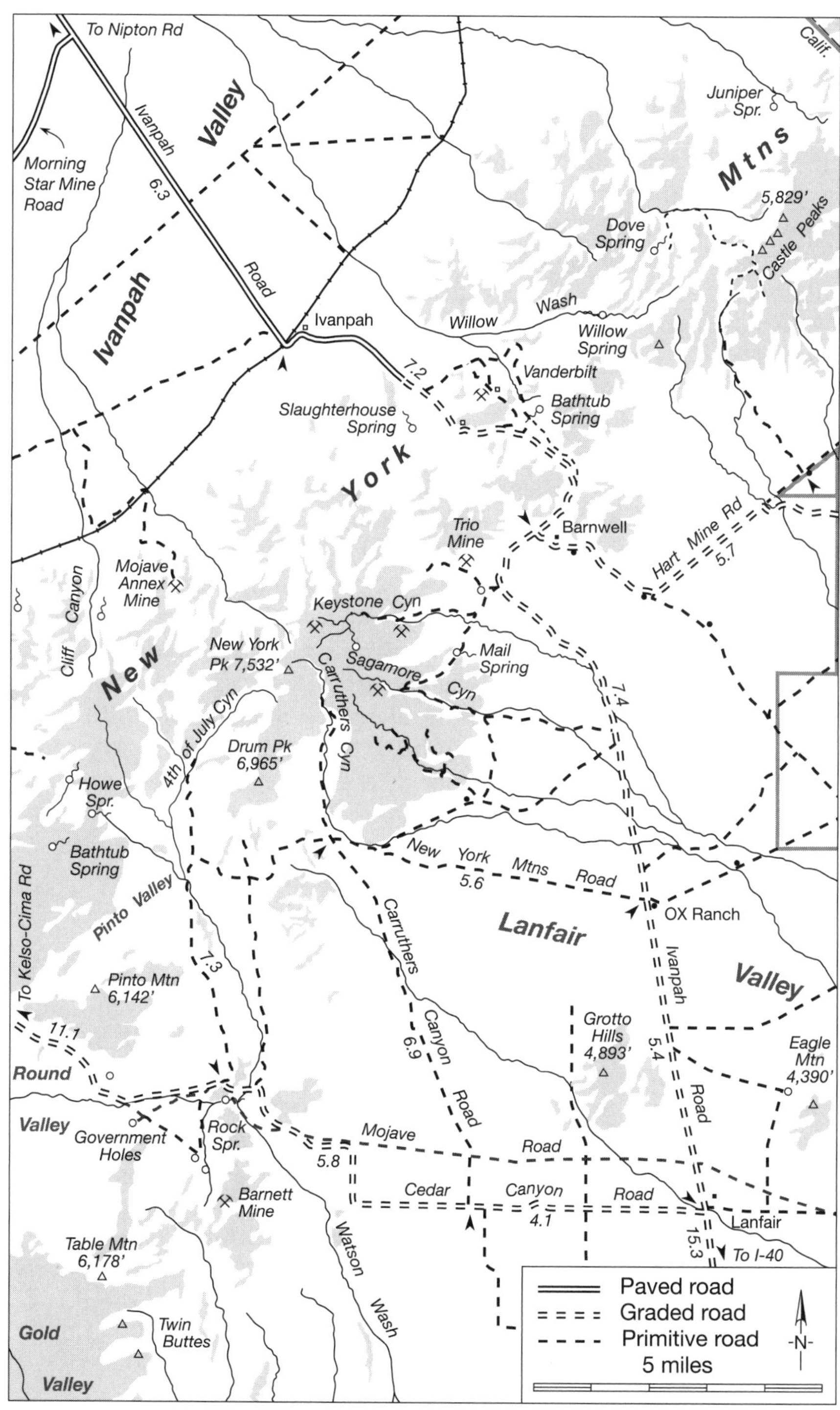
To Nipton Rd
Calif.
Juniper Spr.
Ivanpah Valley
Ivanpah Road
6.3
Morning Star Mine Road
Mtns
5,829'
Castle Peaks
Dove Spring
Willow Wash
Willow Spring
Ivanpah
7.2
Vanderbilt
Bathtub Spring
Slaughterhouse Spring
New York
Barnwell
Hart Mine Rd
5.7
Trio Mine
Mojave Annex Mine
Cliff Canyon
Keystone Cyn
Mail Spring
New York Pk 7,532'
Sagamore Cyn
Carruthers Cyn
7.4
4th of July Cyn
Drum Pk 6,965'
Howe Spr.
Bathtub Spring
New York Mtns Road
5.6
OX Ranch
Pinto Valley
Lanfair
Valley
To Kelso-Cima Rd
Pinto Mtn 6,142'
7.3
Carruthers Canyon Road
6.9
Ivanpah Road
5.4
Grotto Hills 4,893'
Eagle Mtn 4,390'
11.1
Round Valley
Government Holes
Rock Spr.
Mojave Road
5.8
Cedar Canyon Road
4.1
Barnett Mine
Lanfair
15.3
To I-40
Watson Wash
Table Mtn 6,178'
Twin Buttes
Gold Valley
Paved road
Graded road
Primitive road
5 miles
N

desert. All other mines were far less productive. The Giant Ledge Mine in Carruthers Canyon, mostly active between 1902 and 1912, produced only a little copper and gold, and the Live Oak Mine in Keystone Canyon a bit of silver and lead. Several properties had tungsten, an uncommon commodity in the region, but not much of it. The Mojave Annex Mine, the Tungsten King Mine, and the Garvanza Mine in Cliff Canyon shipped a few tons of high-grade tungsten ore around World War I, although the Sagamore Mine may have done better. In 1969, decades after its peak, Vanderbilt was reactivated when the Goldome Mine installed a large mill and chemical complex to recover the gold and silver the historic mines had missed. When it shut down in the early 1990s, it was one of the last mines in operation in the preserve.

The combined output of all the historic mines in the New York Mountains probably did not exceed a few hundred thousand dollars, yet mining there had a significant impact on the local history and economy. By establishing early on the presence of mineral assets in the eastern Mojave Desert, it sparked further prospecting and additional strikes. To service the New York Mountains and other districts further north, in 1881 a reduction plant was installed in Needles, even before the town was founded. A railway, known first as the Nevada Southern, then as the California Eastern, was constructed across Lanfair Valley to connect the mines to the mill. The Barnwell & Searchlight Railway, later grafted onto it, brought in business from Nevada. Although short-lived, these rails helped open Lanfair Valley to homesteaders and supported Vanderbilt and other mines as far north as Death Valley. Ironically, this beneficial infrastructure stemmed from a mistake—a gross overestimation of the New York Mountains' mineral worth.

Hiking

The New York Mountains rank among the best places in the preserve for hiking forested canyons and high mountains. The terrain is generally not as steep and rugged as in the Providence Mountains, although the high crest offers challenging mountaineering. The four main canyons are the most natural places to visit first. Three of them are described in the following sections. For more remote destinations, try the main canyons on the northern slope. Generally, they lie far from roads and take much longer to reach on foot. Most of the main canyons on the southeastern slope have seasonal streams and/or springs. Fed by snow melt and rain, they are at their prime in the winter and early spring. Their flows vary greatly from year to year, so they should not be relied upon as a source of drinking water.

■

CASTLE PEAKS

Visible from as far away as Interstate 15 in Nevada or the heart of Lanfair Valley, the massive volcanic monuments known as Castle Peaks that project above the crest of the New York Mountains constitute one of the most distinct landmarks in the eastern Mojave Desert. Everything seems to have conspired to make this area special—its intriguing pinnacles, the cover of scattered juniper, the variety of wildflowers, the dense cactus gardens, the views, and the slow-winding canyons that will eventually take you back.

General Information
Road status: Roadless; high-clearance access road
Castle Peaks viewpoint: 1.5 mi, 350 ft up, 30 ft down one way / easy
Dove Spring: 4.3 mi, 640 ft up, 790 ft down one way / difficult
Castle Peaks loop: 7.1 mi, 1,300 ft up loop / moderate–difficult
Main attractions: Volcanic monuments, mountain hiking on old roads
USGS 7.5′ topo maps: Castle Peaks*, Crescent Peak
Maps: pp. 227*, 221

Location and Access

Castle Peaks are the tall volcanic spires that crown the northern New York Mountains. They are part of a wilderness area and can only be reached on foot. To get to the trailhead, drive the Ivanpah Road to its signed junction with the graded Hart Mine Road. Follow this road 4.8 miles to a sharp right bend. The Hart Mine Road continues to the right. At the start of the bend, a primitive road goes straight, in the original direction of the Hart Mine Road. Drive this road 0.9 mile to a four-way junction. This road, and the portion of the Hart Mine Road you drove on, are the berm of the old Barnwell & Searchlight Railway, a 23-mile track that operated, albeit mostly at a loss and at a slow pace, between 1907 and 1924. The many dry ponds that have pooled against the north side of the berm are the result of a century of runoffs from the New York Mountains. At the four-way junction, turn left. Go 2.3 miles to the steep and rocky grade that climbs the side of an earth dam, then 0.6 mile to the wilderness boundary, marked by green metal posts. If you are driving a standard-clearance vehicle, the couple of rougher spots along this last road may stop you. Even if they don't, park at the foot of the grade, which requires good clearance, and walk from there.

Route Description

The approach. The first part of this hike is along a shallow canyon that climbs leisurely to the crest of the New York Mountains. Its slopes are nicely forested with a green spread of Joshua trees, juniper, and shrubs. The walk is easy, either along the narrow sandy wash or the few surviving segments of road that parallel it. Many wildflowers grace this area, even in drier years. Depending on the season, you may see the vermillion splashes of Indian paintbrush, the light-purple clusters of Goodding's verbena, apricot globemallow, and the usual gang of high-elevation cacti in bloom. The most industrious of them, the mound cactus, is hard to miss. When it blooms, which is earlier than most, its numerous stems can hold dozens of large flaming-red flowers.

After 1.3 miles the road crests a first summit, descends a little to a fork (stay left, with the obvious main road), then climbs to the true pass over the New York Mountains. This area of subdued relief is a vast and beautiful desert garden, and a good place to witness segregation in the plant kingdom. Over small areas, sometimes only an acre, one plant is often dominant, favored by the combination of soil chemistry, drainage, and sun exposure. The ground cover is a patchwork of prickly-pear here, blue yucca over there, and staghorn cholla a little further. Barrel cactus, as is often the case, almost exclusively congregate on steep south-facing slopes.

Early in the hike, Castle Peaks occasionally poke their heads above the horizon. The pass is the first place where you will get your first eye-filling view of these majestic spires. They stand proudly astride the mountain's crest like invincible sails riding colossal waves. Even on a cloudless day they seem defiant. A good viewpoint to enjoy them is the knoll 50 yards northwest of the left fork in the road at the pass; a short spur road climbs up to it.

Castle Peaks, like the area's multiple smaller pinnacles, are made largely of andesite breccia. Named after the Andes, this volcanic rock has the same composition as diorite: it consists mainly of feldspars and dark minerals like biotite (a mica), but unlike granite, it contains no quartz. Andesite usually erupts from explosive volcanoes, often above subduction zones, and this andesite may not be an exception. It was dated back to around 25 million years ago, a time when the Farallon Plate was subducting beneath the North American continent.

The peaks loop. From the pass only four of Castle Peaks' six spires are visible. The closest one I call Blade. The second one (to its left) is Castle Peak. The third and fourth ones are concealed behind it. The

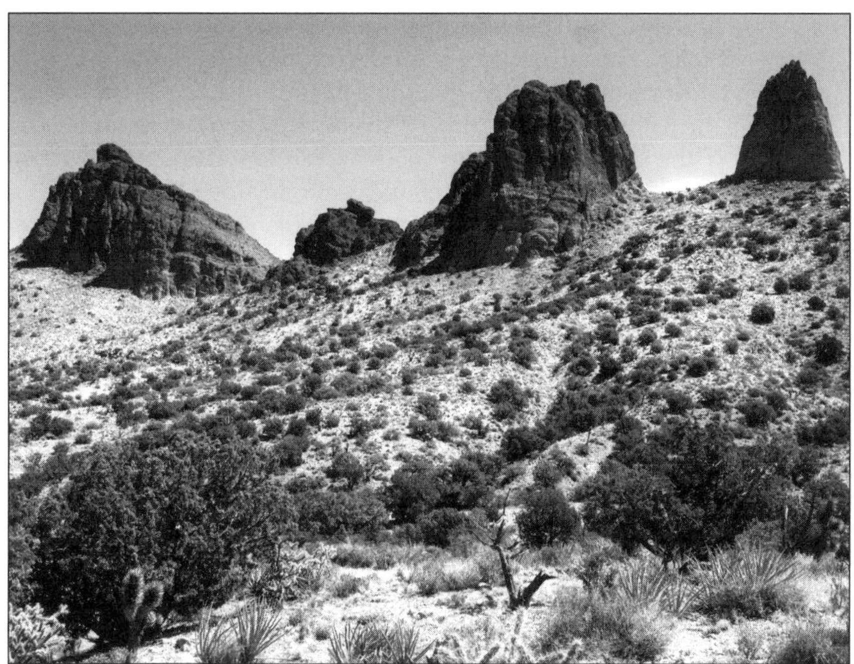

Castle Peaks from the west slope below the main pass

fifth is labeled "Dove" on USGS topographic maps. The sixth one, capped by a rectangular block, is North Castle Butte, the furthest north and the highest (5,896'). Scaling any of them requires technical climbing, and few people tackle these serious challenges. But ambling among these giants is within the reach of any reasonably fit hiker, and as exhilarating—minus the adrenaline rush.

From where the two forks in the road meet again north of the pass, hike northeast across the wavering talus slope below the spires, following a course parallel to them. Then aim for the pass of your choice between any two spires (only one pass requires a little scrambling), drop down the far side, and make a loop back through a different pass. If in doubt as to which loop to choose, consider the longest one, through the sixth pass. As you cross the talus the views of the spires change continuously. A diversity of rocks litter the ground—sparkling gray mica schists, milky quartz, pinkish monzonite, and nearly black hornblende. Much of the year, wildflowers are everywhere—desert-gold, phacelia, phlox, desert mariposa, and many more. Small grasslands thrive near the wind-swept passes. Walk up to the base of the pointed fifth spire. Its andesite is beautiful, fine-grained and reddish brown, with gray and black volcanic inclusions, some many feet across—pieces of mosaic straight from the center of the Earth.

The best is yet to come. At the sixth pass, you gaze down the far side at an impressive gulch framed by dark pinnacles, against the backdrop of the Castle Mountains' notched skyline. The most striking one is a slim isolated slab at least 60 feet tall that resembles a foot, if a foot had three toes. As you descend along this windy little canyon, over granite and volcanic boulders, more crags, fins, and cliffs come into view. Sheer walled and sharp, striated with vertical crevasses, they ride high above scenic displays of blue yucca, Joshua trees, chollas, and cool juniper. By the time the wash reaches more open and level terrain, Castle Peaks are in plain view again, looking very different from this side.

About 1.3 miles below the pass, past a barbed-wire fence, the wash joins a main wash coming down from the west. Following this wash uphill will get you through another pretty canyon back up to the crest at the first pass, just below Blade. Quite a few monuments line this canyon, including a long buttressed wall. In spite of the constant conspiracy from spiny plants, trees, and rocks, the canyon's brave little sandy wash manages to remain uninterrupted most of the way up.

From the pass it is a short walk down the hill back to the northern fork in the road. Stop under one of the large shady juniper first to enjoy the view from half a mile above Ivanpah Lake. One can see as far as Charleston Peak, nearly 70 miles away, covered in snow often as late as May.

Castle Peaks

	Dist.(mi)	Elev.(ft)
Road's end (wilderness bdry)	0.0	4,965
Road junction	1.3	5,165
Southern fork/Main pass	1.5	5,250
Castle Peaks viewpoint	(0.05)	5,285
Northern fork/Leave trail	1.55	5,250
Dove Spring	(~2.7)	~4,800
Sixth pass	2.8	5,470
Wash Junction	4.1	4,865
First pass	5.3	5,300
Back to northern fork	5.55	5,250
Back to road's end	7.1	4,965

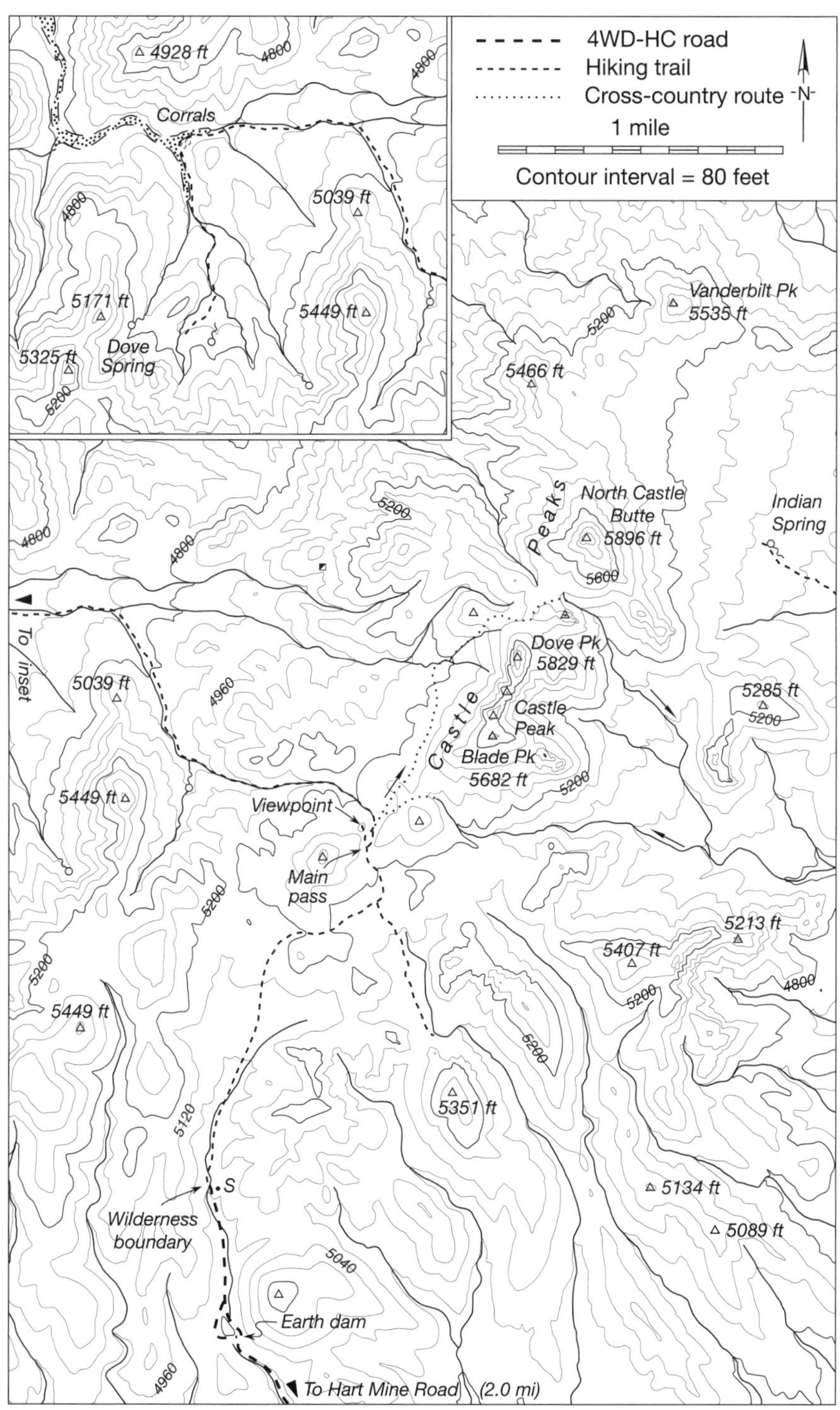
4WD-HC road
Hiking trail
Cross-country route
N
1 mile
Contour interval = 80 feet
4928 ft
4800
Corrals
5039 ft
4800
5171 ft
5449 ft
5325 ft
Dove Spring
5200
Vanderbilt Pk
5535 ft
5200
5466 ft
North Castle Butte
5896 ft
Peaks
Indian Spring
5200
4800
4800
5600
To inset
Dove Pk
5829 ft
5039 ft
4960
Castle Peak
Castle
5285 ft
5200
Blade Pk
5682 ft
5200
5449 ft
Viewpoint
Main pass
5200
5213 ft
5407 ft
5200
4800
5200
5449 ft
5200
5351 ft
5120
S
Wilderness boundary
5134 ft
5089 ft
5040
Earth dam
4960
To Hart Mine Road (2.0 mi)

Head of the gulch at the sixth pass; Castle Mountains in the distance

Dove Spring. From the northern fork, the road continues 2 miles, mostly down a widening wash, to a couple of old circular corrals, then it hooks a sharp left and climbs south into a draw. After 0.3 mile, at the first fork in the canyon, a fainter road branches off on the right. The USGS topographic maps show Dove Spring at the end of the side canyon that this road follows, but if there is a spring in this fork it is certainly not the largest of the springs in this drainage. The left fork continues up the wash 0.1 mile, and the wash splits off again. There are two springs in the right fork (about 0.6 mile), and another one, the largest, in the left fork (0.7 mile).

This is a great place for a longer outing or a one-night backpacking trip, into a desolate and seldom-visited area. The hills on the way down are capped with spikes and slanted outcrops of the same reddish andesite as Castle Peaks. I am still not sure which spring is Dove, but looking for these relict oases hidden in this contorted volcanic landscape was a lot of fun, like some larger-than-life treasure hunt.

■

VANDERBILT

Once acclaimed as the richest gold property in the eastern Mojave, Vanderbilt was worked off and on for more than a century. For a while it supported a lively town and several mines and mills; a railroad was even constructed in part to haul out its riches. Today, the area holds an extensive collection of headframes, shafts, tunnels, mills, stone ruins, and dugouts. They can be discovered by driving, or better still walking, the network of dirt roads that crisscrosses this hilly region, or the old railway that neatly circles around the mines.

General Information

Road status: Hiking on HC roads and trails; graded access road;
Vanderbilt and mines: 1.2 mi, 350 ft up, 30 ft down one way / easy
Vanderbilt Road/Railway loop: 4.2 mi, 1,030 ft up loop / easy–moderate
Cal. Eastern Railway: 4.8 mi, 810 ft up, 100 ft down one way / moderate
Main attractions: Historic gold-mining ruins, abandoned railway
USGS 7.5′ topo maps: Ivanpah, Castle Peaks
Maps: pp. 237*, 221

Location and Access

Vanderbilt's mining area is about 10 miles south of Nipton, on the northern slopes of the New York Mountains. It can be accessed at several points from the Ivanpah Road. The easiest one is the west end of the abandoned grade of the California Eastern Railway, much of which has been used as a road for decades. It branches off the Ivanpah Road on the north side, 9.05 miles south of the Morning Star Mine Road (or 4.4 miles north of the Hart Mine Road). This is 0.4 mile south of the end of the pavement on the Ivanpah Road, in sight of the large buildings and green tanks of the Goldome Mine. To reach the railway's east end, which is closed to motor vehicles, drive the Ivanpah Road 3.4 miles further south. It is marked by carsonite wilderness signs.

History

Although mining claims were likely filed much earlier, the discovery of gold that started Vanderbilt took place in January 1891. The discovery was made by a Piute Indian from near Death Valley named Robert Black. Black convinced Montillion Beatty, whose wife belonged to Black's Piute family group, to help him secure his find. Beatty did, and filed claims of his own, which he modestly named the great Beatty lode. Ore samples taken to Providence proved to be loaded with gold. Upon hearing about the strike, two miners from Providence, Richard Hall and Samuel King, located claims too. Before long, the whole side of a mountain had been claimed.

Three properties quickly emerged as the most promising: the Boomerang Mine, the site of the original discovery; the Gold Bronze Mine, on Hall and King's claims; and the Gold Bar Mine. By June, Hall and King had enrolled two Providence miners to sink shafts and take out a few tons of high-grade ore. Beatty was joined by Allen Green Campbell, an experienced mine operator from Salt Lake City who purchased shares of the great Beatty lode from him and renamed it the Boomerang Mine. Beatty soon moved on to grander things—his ranch east of Death Valley eventually became the town that now bears his name. Left in charge, Campbell became the most prominent figure in Vanderbilt's early history. The area looked so hot toward the end of 1892 that it attracted the interest of several capitalists, including some famous Comstock mine owners.

Drawn by the new business potential, people flocked to the camp of Vanderbilt that had sprung up near the mines. By the spring of 1892 it had grown into a town of a few dozen souls with a small business district, housed mostly in tents. Vanderbilt gained notoriety from a couple of its residents. The two-story saloon, which doubled up as a hotel, was run by Virgil Earp, the one-armed brother of Wyatt Earp, who took part in the famous gunfight at the OK Corral. The general store was owned by William McFarlane, a key figure at both Ivanpah and the Bonanza King Mine. In the fall, a rich strike at the Gold Bronze Mine triggered another influx of residents. In January 1893, the population exceeded 150, and business had expanded. Residents could play billiards, gamble, choose from three restaurants, consult a doctor, get medication at the Vanderbilt Drug Store, ride a stage to Goffs, or shop for fresh fruit and meat. The upstairs room in Earp's saloon served also as a church and polling place. The birth rate of saloons outpaced that of all other businesses—seven liquor licenses were ultimately granted. A township was established, with a justice of the peace, a post office, a school district, and two weekly newspapers, the *Vanderbilt Shaft* and the *Nugget*, although the latter died after just a few issues.

In the summer of 1893, civilization came a notch closer to Vanderbilt when the Nevada Southern Railway, spearheaded by mining entrepreneur Isaac Blake, reached the town of Manvel, just a few miles from Vanderbilt. Vanderbilt's residents could now take a stagecoach, the Pioneer Stage, to Manvel, then ride the brand new train to connect with the Santa Fe line at Goffs. Blake had planned to continue

Boomerang Mill, Vanderbilt (2008)

his line to Vanderbilt, Ivanpah Valley, and into Nevada, siphoning along the way business from the New York Mountains' mines to support his rail. So Vanderbilt's welfare was critical to his success.

Vanderbilt entered a new era in 1894, when two 10-stamp mills were delivered, one to the Boomerang Mine, the other to the Gold Bronze Mine. Campbell's mill was first fired up in March, producing a 25-ounce bar of gold on day one. The Gold Bronze mill became operational soon after. To increase its business, in June the mill started treating ore from some of the many local independent miners as well. Unfortunately, both mills were designed for the rebellious ore of the Rockies, and they crushed much too slowly. To make matters worse, the shafts at the three main mines had reached the water table. The water was not the problem. Vanderbilt, after all, was a dry camp, and water was badly needed. The problem was that below the water, the ore contained sulfides and did not amalgamate well. So not only were the mills slow; now they were also wasteful. Some miners tried off-site mills, but their ore was not rich enough to cover shipping costs.

Vanderbilt probably peaked in 1894. Its population was about 400. The Gold Bronze Mine had 25 men taking out ore worth $10 to $100 per ton. The Boomerang shaft was around 500 feet deep and kept 50 men busy on three eight-hour shifts. The Gold Bar Mine employed 14 miners. But production was insufficient to support this many people. In June, the Gold Bronze went into receivership. Most owners began leasing their properties. By August more than half the residents had left, and the *Shaft* was suspended. In December, Virgil Earp sold his saloon, and a second store closed down. The Nevada Southern was also in trouble. To build his line to Manvel, Blake had to mortgage each completed 10-mile section to pay for the next one. The Sagamore Mine was not giving him as much business as he had hoped for, and his New York group of mines were unproductive. Construction was stopped while Blake tried to raise additional funding. He never succeeded. In December 1894, his railway went into receivership too.

Although its fortune fluctuated, Vanderbilt did survive into the 20th century. The school still had 45 students in early 1896, and it did not close until 1898. In spite of the post office closure in March 1900, the census reported a population of 329, about 30% miners. The residents enjoyed a good social life, with periodic dances, masked balls, and banquets. Free of competition, Campbell tried a bit of everything. He developed the Brick Mine. He leased, then purchased, the Gold Bar Mine, hired a team to lay a pipeline from it to the Boomerang mill and haul its ore down to the mill. For a while 20 tons of rich ore were produced every day. In 1896 he had grand plans to drill the Boomerang shaft down to 1,000 feet. A few independent ventures kept him company while they tried their luck. Campbell did not give up until shortly before his death in 1902—and even afterwards his spirit still hung on as his estate continued to manage his mines.

The Nevada Southern died in 1894, but it came back to life the following year. Rebranded the California Eastern, the new railway was organized by two of Blake's former managers and sponsored by the Santa Fe line. Its next segment, from Manvel to Ivanpah, was graded by hand by a team of about 150 Mohave Indians starting in April 1901. The line was completed in 1902, and for a number of years Vanderbilt finally had a train of its own.

Over the next 40 years, Vanderbilt went through multiple revivals fueled by businesses recovering the gold and silver lost by the earlier mills. Around 1900 two men from Manvel, Karns and Eckins, erected a small cyanide facility to treat the Boomerang mill's old tailings, supposedly worth $60,000. In 1911, someone else was cleaning up what they had missed. In 1909, lessees revamped the Gold Bronze mill and worked the Gold Bar and Gold Bronze mines. In 1910 a large cyanide plant installed by another party was extracting gold, to the tune of $5 a ton, from the Boomerang Mine's tailings. By 1924, new buildings had been erected at Vanderbilt, and a ball mill was waiting to be installed. From 1934 to 1935, a lessee used a 25-ton flotation plant to produce rich gold and silver concentrates that were shipped to a Utah smelter.

By 1942 Vanderbilt's high-grade pockets were mostly gone. But there was plenty of low-concentration gold left in the ground to mine profitably with new techniques. In 1965 the Heavy Metals Corporation drilled the area to assess the ore reserves, then installed a 500-ton mill and treated some 100,000 tons from 1969 to 1970 and again from 1974 to 1975. Operations shifted to the Transcorp Corporation in 1978. The Goldome Mine and its huge industrial complex, in operation until the mid-1990s, was by far the largest operation Vanderbilt ever saw.

In spite of its longevity, Vanderbilt has little to show. From 1929 through 1940, the main mine produced around 2,000 ounces of gold, 8,000 ounces of silver, and a little copper and lead, all worth $70,000. The three best years—1934, 1935, and 1938—yielded about two thirds of it. The total historic production might have reached a few hundred thousand dollars, a far cry from the millions so many had dreamed of.

Dugout at Vanderbilt

Route Description

Vanderbilt has many sites of interest, and many roads and trails to get to them. The two main access roads are the California Eastern Railway grade, which makes a half-loop around the mines, and the Vanderbilt Road, which cuts across it and passes by most of the ruins. Both roads require a high-clearance vehicle. They are seldom visited, so hiking them is a good alternative. The railway grade is deteriorating, so eventually it will be accessible only on foot. To maximize your payoff, hike up the railway and return on the Vanderbilt Road. In the lower foothills the scenery is a little bland, but higher up the views improve with the addition of Joshua trees and the banded summits of the New York Mountains. If possible, pick a partly cloudy day. The clouds' moving shadows sharply set off the hills against each other and create a rapidly changing landscape with dramatic depth.

The California Eastern Railway. To accommodate the intolerance of the iron horse for steep climbs and to squeeze the California Eastern through this hilly region, railroad surveyors had to carve a circuitous route and seriously rearrange the topography. Whenever they encountered a hill, they cut through it. Whenever they encountered a wash, they filled it with rocks. So this railway is a series of trenches blasted into the hills, interspaced by steeply sloped berms. This gives it a different rhythm than an ordinary road. One minute you are balanced on a narrow lane high above the land; the next you are trapped within rocky walls often only 30 feet apart.

From the Ivanpah Road, along the first 1.3 miles four roads branch off on the right. The first one is the gated road to the Goldome Mine's large industrial facility. This site is private property and closed to the public. The next three roads, which include the Vanderbilt Road, lead through the mining area and return to the Ivanpah Road. Along the remaining 1.9 miles there is no side road. The western segment ends at an overgrown berm blocked off with rocks; an exit road on the right joins the Ivanpah Road in 0.3 mile.

Driving this railway grade can be challenging. The trenches are slowly filling up with fallen rocks. The berms are narrow, and their edges deeply eroded. Much of the grade has a serious crown and is hemmed in by large armed shrubs—blackbrush, cholla, and catclaw. If you cannot drive through, you may have to back up some distance to turn around. If you are fussy about your paint job, or if you are in the mood for a relaxing ride, perhaps consider going somewhere else...

In spite of its antiquity, this railway is a remarkable piece of engineering. A culvert was cut at the base of the berms that cross large washes to evacuate storm waters. The engineer in charge knew to pay attention to details. He had these tunnels built with neatly quarried slabs of local andesite. Some culverts are adorned with pointed pillars and retaining walls, which betrays both a sense of aesthetics and a concern for durability. And they did last—13 decades, and counting. Where the wash was too large to be drained by a tunnel, a bridge was erected across it. The bridges have been long gone, so now the grade ends abruptly, high above a wash, only to resume on the opposite bank. The traffic now goes around these gaps on bypass roads. At some crossings, the rock walls that once supported the bridge trestles are still in place.

The eastern segment of the California Eastern is in a wilderness area and closed to vehicles. But do hike it. It passes by more missing bridges, and offers some of the same features as the western segment. It is, however, much more scenic, skirting under a steep slope spiked with imposing volcanic fins. After 125 yards, a side road on the left

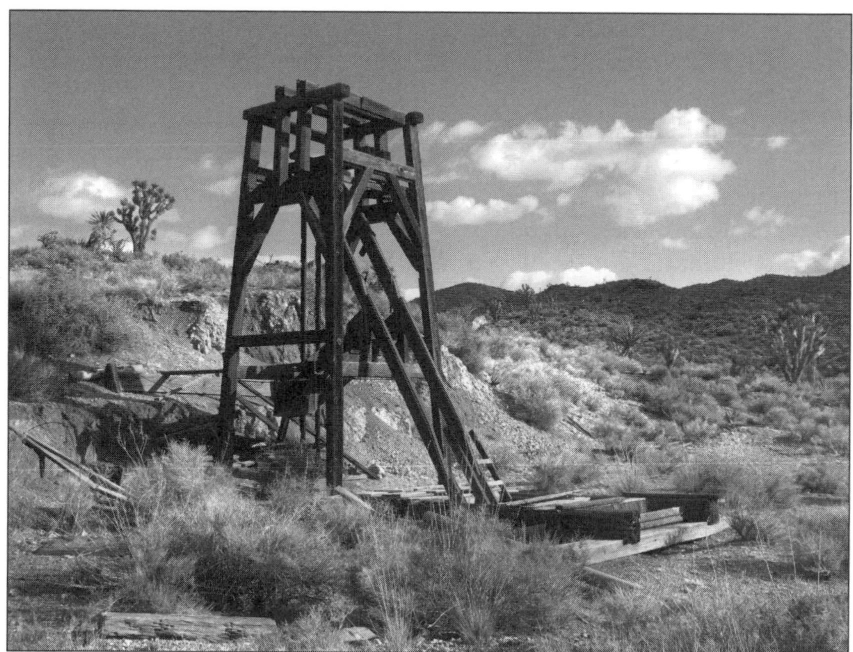

Headframe at the Darling Mine

climbs to Bathtub Spring (0.25 mile). The spring itself is of limited interest, but it commands sweeping views of Ivanpah Valley.

The Vanderbilt Road. From the railway grade this road first climbs leisurely across open hills to a level area, then descends a little into a gulch, follows it up to a pass, and finally drops to the Ivanpah Road (see map). The interesting ruins are all before the pass. Some are right along the road, others are reached by short side roads or require a little walking. If you are driving, getting in and out of your car to look for them is going to get tiring. Hiking this road instead is more relaxing and satisfying. Many of the remains are hidden, and your search will push you deeper into the creases of this expansive landscape.

The Darling Mine. The first side road on the left leads shortly to the claims of the Darling Mine. Its main shaft, at least 300 feet deep, was worked off and on for decades, and as recently as the 1950s. It has the best preserved headframe in Vanderbilt, a tall wooden construction that straddles the inclined shaft. The custom steel rail at the top of the incline displays the scratches made by the buckets as they slid repeatedly over it. The collared shaft has both its ladder and galvanized pipe.

The leveled areas near the shaft mark the sites of the large residence and other structures that stood here until at least the late 1950s.

Vanderbilt. The town was concentrated along the road, starting roughly at the level area lined with low stone walls. The main buildings, including Earp's saloon and the stores, probably stood around here. A couple of nice dugouts remain nearby. A handful of stone ruins are also standing a little further, along the gulch. The largest one is a one-room structure about 20 feet on the side with rough walls over 6 feet high. One had a fireplace; another was just large enough for a bed. There is a lot more—after all this town hosted, at one point, some 400 people...

The historic mines. The mess of wood and steel by the east side of the road where the Vanderbilt Road reaches the gulch is the site of the Gold Bar Mine. The lumber is what remains of a headframe; the opening next to it is the Gold Bar Shaft. The huge crushed shell was a water

Vanderbilt		
	Dist.(mi)	Elev.(ft)
California Eastern Railway		
West end at Ivanpah Road	0.0	4,000
Goldome Road (off limits)	0.45	4,040
Gold Bar Portal Road	0.9	4,115
Vanderbilt Road	1.1	4,150
Exit road (hiking only beyond)	3.2	4,470
Ivanpah Road	(0.3)	4,395
East end at Ivanpah Road	4.8	4,715
Vanderbilt Road		
California Eastern Railway	0.0	4,150
Road to Darling Mine	0.3	4,265
Darling Mine	(0.15)	4,250
Vanderbilt (dugout)	0.4	4,315
Gold Bar Shaft	0.55	4,335
Road to Gold Bronze Mine	0.75	4,410
Gold Bronze Mine	(0.25)	4,490
Pass	1.05	4,500
T junction by wash	1.4	4,337
Ivanpah Road	1.8	4,395

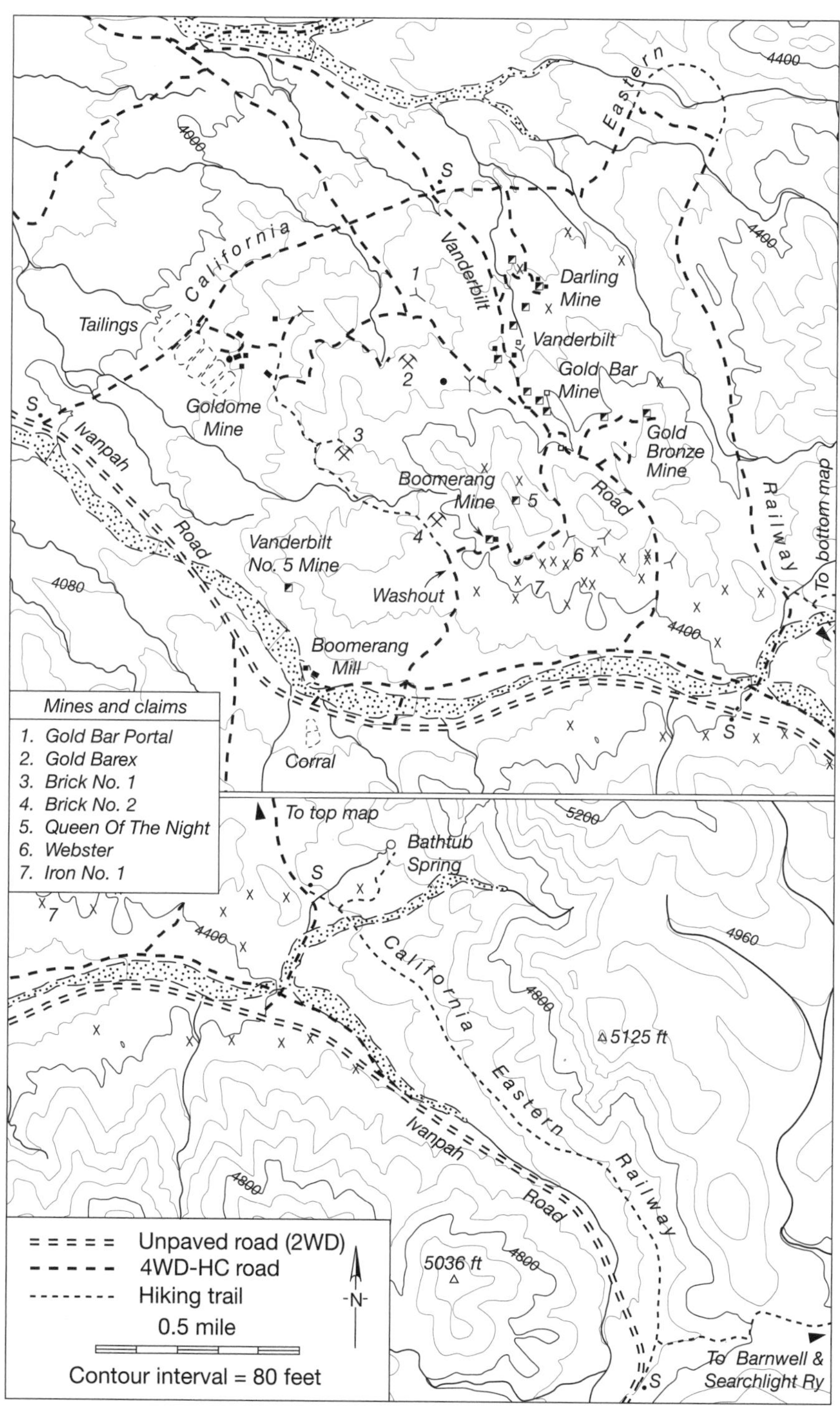

California Eastern Railway
Vanderbilt Road
Ivanpah Road
Tailings
Goldome Mine
Darling Mine
Vanderbilt Gold Bar Mine
Gold Bronze Mine
Boomerang Mine
Vanderbilt No. 5 Mine
Washout
Boomerang Mill
Corral
To bottom map
To top map
Bathtub Spring
5125 ft
5036 ft
To Barnwell & Searchlight Ry
Mines and claims
1. Gold Bar Portal
2. Gold Barex
3. Brick No. 1
4. Brick No. 2
5. Queen Of The Night
6. Webster
7. Iron No. 1
Unpaved road (2WD)
4WD-HC road
Hiking trail
0.5 mile
Contour interval = 80 feet

tank; its construction of welded metal is rather unusual. Until 2010, the Ed Shaft's lopsided headframe stood vigil on the flat above it. It finally collapsed of old age soon after, and a safe closure was installed over the shaft by the NPS. To check it out, continue up the road 150 yards to a faint road that makes a hard left, and walk up to it. The first collared shaft is the Baldwin Shaft, the second one the Ed Shaft, and the third one the Gold Bar Shaft. The three shafts are connected by several levels of drifts. In the 1890s, their headframes used either a steam-powered hoist or horse-drawn whims. There is a very old tub-shaped settling tank at the end of the road.

Just past the Gold Bar Mine a road takes off on the right, in a narrow gully. It climbs to a ridge, then winds down the far side to the Boomerang Mine. It once continued down to the Ivanpah Road, but a very steep section just below the mine is now washed out. It is only 0.5 mile to the mine, and the road is rough, so it is just as easy to walk it. Located on the site of Vanderbilt's original discovery, the Boomerang Mine was likely the area's richest. Its main ruin is a nicely framed historic shaft and its simple stainless steel headframe. The shaft is impressively deep: a stone dropped into it triggers diminishing echoes that never seem to end. Many prospects are scattered over the surrounding hills. This is a scenic place, overlooking acres upon acres of deeply dissected slopes, and distant mountains beyond.

The last main mine is reached by an overgrown and circuitous track that starts on the left side, about 75 yards past the stone house. It leads to the Gold Bronze Mine's two shafts and collapsed lumber. The main shaft at the end of the trail (0.3 mile) had a steam hoist and a 100-foot air shaft. By generating a few rich strikes, this mine played a key role in Vanderbilt's history. It caused the most excitement in January 1893 when a lucky blast opened a large cave lined with crystal quartz speckled with free gold valued at $1,200 per ton...

To end on a high note, swing by the Boomerang millsite. It is visible just across the wash from the Ivanpah Road, and a short walk from this road. It is the area's largest and most interesting ruin. Built at the height of Vanderbilt, this proud edifice processed ore for only a few years. The centerpiece is its long and tall retaining wall, a colorful mosaic of local stones precisely fitted together. Several of the original water pipes remain, as well as two primitive arrastres. The mill tailings sprawl below the wall in long billowing banks of golden sand. The two wooden structures on top of them might be the cyaniding tanks used by Karns and Eckins around 1900. The tailings are so toxic that after more than a century, not a single plant has yet colonized them.

■

KEYSTONE CANYON

When I think of the most enjoyable places I have visited in the preserve, Keystone Canyon often comes to mind first. Much of its appeal lies in its shaded cover of pinyon pine and canyon live oak. Combined with the old road that runs nearly the length of the canyon, it makes hiking particularly pleasant. Several points of interest are tucked along the way—a spectacular quarry, small springs, the colorful camp and tunnels of a small-time mine, and ultimately superb views from the head of the canyon.

General Information

Road status: Roadless upper canyon; 4WD roads in lower canyon
Keystone Spring: 1.6 mi, 560 ft up, 20 ft down one way / easy
Live Oak Mine: 1.9 mi, 710 ft up, 40 ft down one way / easy–moderate
To Carruthers Cyn: 4.3 mi, 1,590 ft up, 1,270 feet down one way / moder.
Main attractions: A forested canyon, mining camp, springs
USGS 7.5' topo map: Ivanpah
Maps: pp. 243*, 221

Location and Access

Keystone Canyon is the easternmost major canyon in the central New York Mountains. The Keystone Canyon Road begins at the Ivanpah Road 6.2 miles north of the New York Mountains Road (or 1.2 miles south of the Hart Mine Road), on the west side. At the first fork 70 yards in, keep left. At the fork about 0.6 mile further, turn right. In 1.4 miles, the road reaches the first wash crossing, just below the mouth of Keystone Canyon. Up to this point the road is fairly smooth and accessible to most vehicles. It is also very scenic and fun to drive. It crosses elevated open terrain and commands beautiful views of the surrounding hills. The Joshua trees and juniper give the countryside a surprisingly green look, as bucolic as it gets. There is a nice campsite just before the first wash crossing, and many more in the canyon.

Driving is allowed up to the posts across the road 0.8 mile inside the canyon, but the first crossing has rough dips that require very good clearance. If you are not sure you can make it, park before the crossing.

Route Description

Keystone Canyon. Keystone Canyon is different from the other canyons of the New York Mountains. It cuts through high-rising desert hills that get higher as you penetrate deeper into the mountains. The scenery is dominated by the impressive tetons of Mid Hills Adamellite that crown the ridge to the west, a prominent landmark of this range. The vegetation is noticeably greener, and the trees are larger and closer together. Along the edges of the wash and on the lower slopes, the groves of canyon live oak, pinyon pine, and manzanita are extensive enough to support a rare understory of acorn and pine needles spotted with fragrant resin. From mid-spring through summer, many wildflowers grace the area. The most common are the profuse pale-pink blossoms of scented penstemon, balanced at the tip of stalks up to 5 feet tall. The bright scarlet flowers of firecracker penstemon are smaller but even more showy. Several species of high-elevation cacti dot the landscape, expecially grizzly bear cactus and its large yellow flowers. In the fall, rabbitbrush blankets the open wash with gold.

This exceptionally dense woodland stranded in the desert makes a walk through Keystone Canyon one of the most unusual experiences in the eastern Mojave Desert. The road also makes the walking easy, and the grades are quite modest. Even on a hot summer day, deep shade is plentiful. And the next point of interest is never far away.

The canyon road is often hardly discernible from its surroundings, and many of the wash crossings are badly damaged. If you manage to

Mining ruins in Live Oak Canyon

drive through here, park 0.8 mile past the first wash crossing, just before the first side canyon (Elev. 5,545'). The rest of this drainage is inside a wilderness area, and driving further is prohibited by law.

The quarry road. At the complicated junction 0.5 mile into the canyon, a steep grade climbs on the south side to a quarry. This road is hidden by a screen of trees, and easiest to spot from up canyon looking back. It is open to motorized traffic but very rough, and most drivers will not make it. Instead, walk up its tight switchbacks. The quarries are nothing special, and I would not suggest going up there if it weren't for the good cardiovascular exercise up 600 feet of mountainous terrain, and the views. As the road swings back and forth across a sharp ridge, it offers alternatively plunging views into Keystone Canyon and sweeping vistas of desolate Lanfair Valley, the sawtoothed Castle Mountains, and further ranges into Nevada.

Live Oak Canyon. The short road to this rarely visited canyon is on the right side, just before two large facing groves framing the wash. The metal post cemented to a pile of rocks at the Y junction marks the gate that once guarded access to the Live Oak Mine. The road bypasses the brushy lower section of Live Oak Canyon over a low ridge overlooking the long sweeping slopes of Keystone Canyon. A nice outcrop of blueish limestone is exposed on the ridge. As the road descends from the ridge into Live Oak Canyon, the limestone grades into white crystallized marble metamorphosed during the intrusion of the granite that crops out in the upper canyon.

Gutted truck at Live Oak Mine

The small camp at the end of the road was part of the Live Oak Mine. With its wooden cabin and well-preserved ore bin complex, it paints a vivid picture of what it was like to operate a small-scale mine in such a remote desert location in the mid 20th century. To survive, self-sufficiency was imperative. The camp still has many of the vital components that made life here possible. There is the obligatory homemade stove in the cabin, a high-clearance bug-eyed truck to get around, a grader to periodically fix the road, small cleared terraces to grow vegetables, a junkyard for spare parts, and a reliable spring.

The Live Oak Mine was not exactly a glowing image of success: its only recorded output is one ton of ore containing 10% lead and a smidgeon of silver. Its main tunnel and utility tin shack are just above the camp. About 350 feet long, the tunnel was sunk to an 8-foot vein of fluorite near the contact between Teutonia Adamellite and Paleozoic carbonates. The white pebbles speckled with pyrite, chalcopyrite, and copper oxides on the tunnel's wide tailing are pieces of dolomite bleached by the intrusive rock. The tunnel has collapsed, but its narrow-gauge rail still emerges from under the rubble. The rail winds across open ground to a graceful trestled bridge that curves in mid-air to a massive ore bin. Constructed with century-old wooden beams patinaed to a rich orange grading into browns and black, this loading complex is a wonderful paraphernalia to study.

This canyon is one of the Mojave Desert's last strongholds for desert oaks. With the exception of Carruthers Canyon, canyon live oak occur in higher concentrations here than anywhere else in and around the preserve. The wiry thickets that have taken over the camp are almost all scrub oak. Many healthy canyon live oak grow as individuals and in small groves throughout this canyon. Some of the older specimens are majestic giants nearly 30 feet high. Both species of oak have curved spiny leaves that stay green year round. They bear acorn, a fruit that is relished by many animals and was a prized source of food for Native Americans.

Wander on up the canyon a little, along the overgrown vestige of the final stretch of road. The spring, just past a beautiful large oak, is

Keystone Canyon

	Dist.(mi)	Elev.(ft)
First wash crossing	0.0	5,300
Side road to quarry	0.5	5,435
Second quarry	(1.0)	~6,080
Wilderness boundary	0.8	~5,545
Live Oak Canyon Road	1.2	5,615
Live Oak Mine camp	(0.55)	5,880
Spring/Pyrite tunnel	(0.65)	5,960
Keystone Spring Road	1.3	5,665
Keystone Spring	(0.3)	5,845
Queen Mine (lower tunnel)	2.0	6,235
Divide with Carruthers Cyn	2.3	6,775
Carruthers Cyn (forested camp)	4.3	5,620

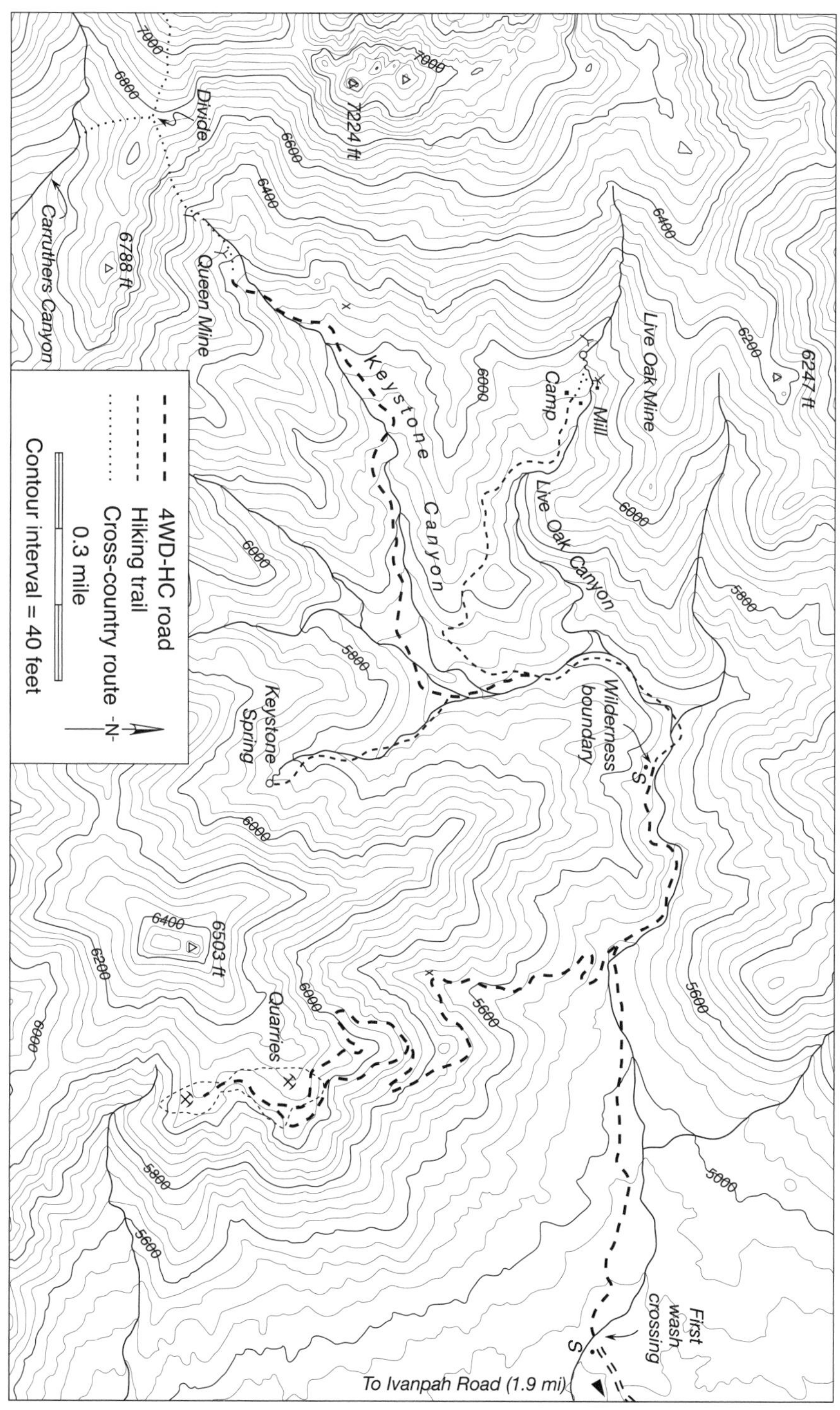
Divide
7224 ft
6788 ft
Caruthers Canyon
Queen Mine
Keystone Canyon
Camp
Mill
Live Oak Mine
6247 ft
Live Oak Canyon
Wilderness boundary
Keystone Spring
6503 ft
Quarries
First wash crossing
To Ivanpah Road (1.9 mi)
4WD-HC road
Hiking trail
Cross-country route
N
0.3 mile
Contour interval = 40 feet

unusual. Instead of flowing out into the open, water seeps and collects in the dark confines of a manmade tunnel. Year-round there is standing water just inside the low wooden door that protects the tunnel entrance. The second tunnel is a hundred yards further. It explored a small copper-bearing vein rich in iron. The tailing below the partly collapsed tunnel is loaded with coarse crystals of pyrite imbedded in milky quartz. The tailing is slowly staining with rust as the iron sulfide is being oxidized by rain and snow.

Upper Keystone Canyon. The road continues 0.8 mile up canyon. As it gains elevation, eventually reaching above 6,200 feet, the pines get more majestic. Along the way, take the side road on the south side to Keystone Spring. Located in a slight widening in a shallow canyon, this spring has minimal surface water but a nice meadow surrounded by trees. This area and the forested upper canyon are great for birding. You might see cliff swallows swooping in graceful arcs along the escarpments overlooking Live Oak Canyon, where they feed and sometimes nest. Along the washes, encounters with coveys of Gambel's quails are common. If you sit quietly in the shade and wait, you might get the visit of a blue-gray gnatcatcher, a wren, a warbling vireo, or a pinyon jay. Deer, bighorn sheep, and coyotes also frequently pass through here and leave their prints in the soft stretches of wash. The shallow scoops in the wash are places where ungulates have pawed sand or gravel to bed more comfortably.

The road ends as a steep grade near the Queen Mine's tall tailings, a pale chute sprinkled with light-green copper oxides and iron-ore stains. Above it a short rail leads into the mine's lower adit. Miners often appeared to dig for ores at random spots, and this mine might seem like a good case in point. But there was usually a reason for their madness. These tunnels were dug to reach the contact zone between the carbonates on their southeast side and the adamellite on their northwest side. Such contacts are often rich in heavy metals. Their reasoning was sound: after a few hundred feet, the miners struck a quartz vein containing fluorite, chalcopyrite, and pyrite. There was just not enough of it to sustain production.

If this short hike on unobstructed roads leaves you hungry for more exercise, climb the very steep slope above the workings to the saddle at the head of Keystone Canyon, if only for the views. Then continue either downhill to explore Carruthers Canyon (both canyons can be hiked in a long day), or uphill along the crest to New York Peak, the beehive-shaped summit to the southwest (see *Carruthers Canyon*).

■

SAGAMORE CANYON

Although seldom visited, Sagamore Canyon ranks among the most scenic and interesting canyons in the preserve. Mined for silver off and on for decades, it holds many mining ruins and the well-kept buildings of Tin Camp. The access road is a bit challenging, so you might have to walk a little to get to it. The canyon itself, gently sloped and shaded by mature pines and oaks, is a delightful place for a leisure hike, livened by an intermittent creek. The upper canyon leads to a high ridge commanding spectacular views of the region.

General Information

Road status: Roadless upper canyon; HC-4WD road into lower canyon
Tin Camp: 0.4 mi, 90 ft up, 20 ft down one way / easy
Alpha Lode loop: 1.75 mi, 400 ft up loop / easy
Sagamore Cyn divide: 1.8 mi, 1,180 ft up, 20 ft down one way / moderate
Main attractions: A forested canyon with numerous mining ruins
USGS 7.5' topo maps: Grotto Hills, Pinto Valley, Ivanpah*
Maps: pp. 251*, 221

Location and Access

Sagamore Canyon is on the south side of the New York Mountains, between Keystone and Carruthers canyons. To get to it, drive the Ivanpah Road 2.9 miles north of the signed New York Mountains Road (or 4.5 miles south of the signed Hart Mine Road) to a rocky road on the left. This is the Sagamore Canyon Road. Pay close attention to your mileage, as there is another road on the left 0.25 mile south.

The Sagamore Canyon Road traverses open desert to the canyon. It crosses the Sagamore Canyon wash several times, first after 0.75 mile, then 2 miles further, just inside the canyon. Most crossings require four-wheel drive and high clearance. They gradually worsen; you might have to start walking before the end. After 3.6 miles, the road crests a steep slope with a wide graded area on the right, then it drops 0.1 mile to the wash and ends. From here on up, the canyon is closed to vehicular traffic. For convenience, park at the graded area.

Alternatively, this canyon can be reached via the Sagamore Canyon Cutoff, a road that drops in from the next drainage north and joins the Sagamore Canyon Road just before its upper end (see map). To get to it, drive the Ivanpah Road 3.3 miles north of the Sagamore Canyon Road and turn left on the Keystone Canyon Road. At the first fork 70 yards in, go left. At the second fork 0.6 mile further, make a left on the Sagamore Canyon Cutoff. After 0.6 mile there will be a road on the right. Keep left, then pass by the green grassy patch of Mail Spring 0.2 mile further. Standard-clearance vehicles will have to stop at the steep wash crossing 0.3 mile past the spring. Beyond it, the road ascends a long steep grade. Most high-clearance vehicles will have to give up 0.5 mile past the wash crossing, where a deep erosional trench bisects the grade. At that point the road is too narrow to turn around, so park in the pronounced bend at the bottom of the grade (see map). From here it is a short walk (0.9 mile) to the upper end of the Sagamore Canyon Road, with great views of the Castle Mountains.

History: Blake's Gamble

Originally known as the New York Mine, the small mine in Sagamore Canyon has a long and bumpy history of modest production. It would not stand above the rest if it weren't for its venerable age—it was one of the very first mines to be opened in San Bernardino County—and for its connection with the ill-fated Nevada Southern Railway. It was not as rich as early strikes led people to believe, but it still lived through multiple revivals spanning seven decades.

Silver was first discovered here in 1870 by Mormon pioneers who spotted narrow quartz veins laced with cerargyrite and extracted an unknown amount of high-grade ore. The ore looked good at several locations in the mountains, and the next few years witnessed feverish activity. In August 1873, the Elgin Mining Company of Elgin, Illinois hauled a mill from Los Angeles to the district, including a 40-horsepower steam engine and boiler to power a 15-stamp crusher. The mill was running in December, and the first silver bullion was brought into San Bernardino in mid-February 1874. Unfortunately, the mill proved to be ineffective. It was shut down in May that year and moved later to Ivanpah, but it was nevertheless one of the two or three earliest milling works in the region. Although production records are missing, the general enthusiasm surrounding the New York Mine that persisted until the 1890s suggests that it produced valuable ore.

As was often the case, this early success paved the way for future attempts. Over the next 20 years, other metal deposits were discovered and exploited in the New York Mountains. Isaac C. Blake, a mining magnate from Denver, saw in this intense activity an opportunity to service the many mining centers scattered in the east Mojave and southern Nevada. After building a mill at Needles, in January 1893 he started grading the Nevada Southern Railway, a route that would reach north from the Santa Fe line at Goffs to the promising gold fields of Vanderbilt in the New York Mountains, then continue into Nevada all the way to Pioche. Blake was so confident that well before the completion of his railway, he purchased the New York Mine and interest in nearby mines to secure ore for his mill and train. Soon he had 80 men on his payroll extracting lead, silver, and copper ore. In July 1893, the Nevada Southern reached Manvel, past the New York Mine and a few miles shy of Vanderbilt. It was an ambitious endeavor, but Blake's business plans unfortunately never took off. The New York Mine and the Vanderbilt mines were both failing expectations, and his railway had trouble finding sufficient traffic. By early 1894 Blake was bankrupt and dispossessed of his mill, railroad, and mines (see *Vanderbilt*).

Strong attractions, however unjustified, die hard. The New York Mine gathered dust for years while the litigation surrounding Blake's ownership was cleared. It was then acquired in 1907 by N. P. and H. T. Sloan, who organized the Philadelphia-based Sagamore Mining Company. It then consisted of eight claims, located on both sides of the canyon. A 50-ton mill was brought to the site in 1908, but for some reason it did not last either, and it shut down after six weeks. The company nevertheless produced silver, copper, and lead until 1910.

When tungsten was discovered a few years later, the Sagamore Mine re-opened its doors and witnessed considerable activity. In spite of earlier milling failures, a small concentration mill was erected to recover the tungsten ore by magnetic separation. Other than a small production in 1915, not much tungsten was found, but the search did uncover rich streaks of other metals. Excluding the unknown production of the 1870s, 1917 was the mine's most productive year: it yielded nearly 110,000 pounds of lead and 5,200 ounces of silver, more than all other years combined. Mining continued until the early 1920s.

For many years starting around 1930, the Sagamore Mine was owned by the Ivanpah Copper Company, which had worked the rich Copper World Mine on Clark Mountain in the 1910s. It remained largely idle until 1942, when a sub-lessee cleaned up the old tunnels and exposed a wide shoot containing up to 50% lead and 25% zinc. This and other areas were exploited until 1945, but production was modest. Other than intermittent small-scale efforts in the 1950s under yet another ownership, these were the Sagamore Mine's last hurrahs. Between 1907 and 1951, the great mine once believed to be rich enough to feed a whole railroad yielded only 1,100 tons of ore.

Geology: Ore galore

Sagamore Canyon's ore bodies were contained in four roughly parallel quartz veins that cut through Early Cambrian quartzite.

Sheet-metal buildings and rock walls at Tin Camp

Although their ores were similar, the veins held different combinations of numerous minerals. The southernmost vein (No. 1), south of the wash, ran high in silver, with some copper and a little gold. Vein No. 2 carried cerargyrite. The third vein, the most extensively exploited, is nearly a mile long and can be traced first on the north side, then on the south side near the upper end of the mine. It contained mostly lead, zinc, copper, and manganese. Vein No. 4, further north, was similar. The ore is quite diverse and can be loaded with metals. The main minerals were galena, sphalerite, chalcopyrite, and huebnerite. The nuggets were wolframite, rhodochrosite, and antimony sulfide.

Route Description

The Sagamore Canyon Road. This is one of a few roads in the preserve that reaches into a high-altitude conifer forest. At lower elevations, Joshua trees and a scenic undergrowth of cacti and yucca dominate the land. The first juniper, canyon live oak, then pinyon pine appear in the foothills. They grow healthier and denser along the way, until they eventually supplant their spiny rivals. If you end up walking part of the road, there are plenty of shady trees where you can rest.

The wide graded area at the crest of the Sagamore Canyon Road is the top of a sprawling tailing from relatively recent mining efforts. The tunnel at the edge of it has impressive proportions. Guarded by a huge metal door, it punches a gaping square hole over 12 feet wide into the hill. The tunnels and shafts, now largely caved or flooded, scattered in the hills to the east and north are considerably older. Some of them are the original workings sunk by Mormon miners as early as 1870, while others were exploited for copper, lead, and zinc in the 1890s.

Lower Sagamore Canyon. Sagamore Canyon is a rare treat. Past the end of the road, its wash winds up through a heavily forested canyon, never very deep but confined between angular rock walls and steep hillsides. Short falls occasionally interrupt the wash, some of them nicely sculpted by the creek that ran through here long ago. The creek is no longer perennial, but water still flows under the gravel. Each fall locally dams up this underground water and forces it to resurface as a miniature cascade that spills over the fall. The cascade gives rise to a short-lived creek, often no more than an algae-clogged trickle that sinks into the gravel after a few yards. In spite of the water, nothing much grows in the wash. Flashfloods rip through it with some regularity and wipe it clean. In just a few decades, they have deepened the wash by two feet. Only the few road segments that bypass the falls on higher ground remain, neatly clipped where they meet the wash.

One of the appeals of this canyon is its abundance of mining ruins. Over the first 0.6 mile, more than a dozen sites line the wash. The main one is the mining camp 300 yards up canyon. Known as Stone Camp in the 1860s and Tin Camp in the 1930s, it was probably last occupied in the 1950s during the mine's final throes. It is one of the preserve's largest remaining historic mining camps. The long bunkhouse was the miners' residence. It is still in good shape and relatively free of rodents. It has a working cast iron stove and firewood, a table and shelves, mattresses, and a veranda. In the winter, hikers occasionally sleep in it to keep warm. The large rust-red shed across the wash is a curious hybrid construction of rock walls and an artful patchwork of welded sheet metal. The concrete stairs that climb down from it now fall short of reaching the wash—also the handiwork of floods. There is a well nearby, and a funky outhouse.

As you walk on up canyon, points of interest are so closely spaced that you do not even have time to develop a sweat walking from one to the next. There are many ruins of stone cabins, the tall chimney of a departed house standing incongruously by itself, a large two-chute ore bin, a long retaining wall snaking high above the wash, pipelines, and tailings. Poke around long enough and you might come across a pair of very old arrastres made of neatly cut flagstones.

The last mining area, 0.6 mile past the camp on the south side, is the one that was worked the most over time. Befittingly, it was called the Alpha Lode. The inconspicuous side road that leads up to it is 140 yards past the side canyon lined with tailings. It climbs shortly to a level area with a shaft, a collapsed 700-foot tunnel, and the stone buttresses of a small mill. The shaft connected with a long tunnel, now inaccessible, located about 60 feet underfoot. These workings exploited vein No. 3, and they crossed mineralized streaks as much as 12 feet wide. The adit's external wall is a fine example: it is copiously stained with green copper minerals. The large heap of lumber covering the shaft is the collapsed 20-foot headframe. From this high ventage point, you can trace vein No. 3 as it continues across the opposite side of the canyon as a long band that protrudes 15 to 25 feet from the surface.

If you are not continuing further, for a different perspective of this canyon return via the upper trail that serviced the north-side claims. It starts 300 yards down canyon from the side canyon lined with tailings, a few yards before the 15-foot-long retaining wall of a massive platform on the north side. This well-defined mining road follows a course roughly parallel to and about 100 feet above the wash, and it gives access to other ruins. Here as elsewhere on the canyon's north side, the shafts have slippery, unprotected rims; stay a respectable distance from them. The upper trail ends at the Sagamore Canyon Cutoff, 250 yards from the main tunnel at your starting point.

Upper Sagamore Canyon. From the Alpha Lode area it is a short distance to the end of the canyon, up an uncluttered river of pebbles. Narrow most of the way, the canyon twists and turns over and over, hemmed in here and there by cleaved outcrops stained with desert varnish and colorful lichen. The scenery is surprisingly green, and

Sagamore Canyon

	Dist.(mi)	Elev.(ft)
Sagamore Mine's main tunnel	0.0	5,415
End of road at wash	0.2	5,395
Tin Camp	0.4	5,480
Jct with upper trail	0.60	5,540
Back to tunnel via upper trail	(0.5)	5,415
Side road to Alpha Lode	0.85	5,665
Alpha Lode	(0.05)	5,700
Triple-divide viewpoint	1.8	~6,570

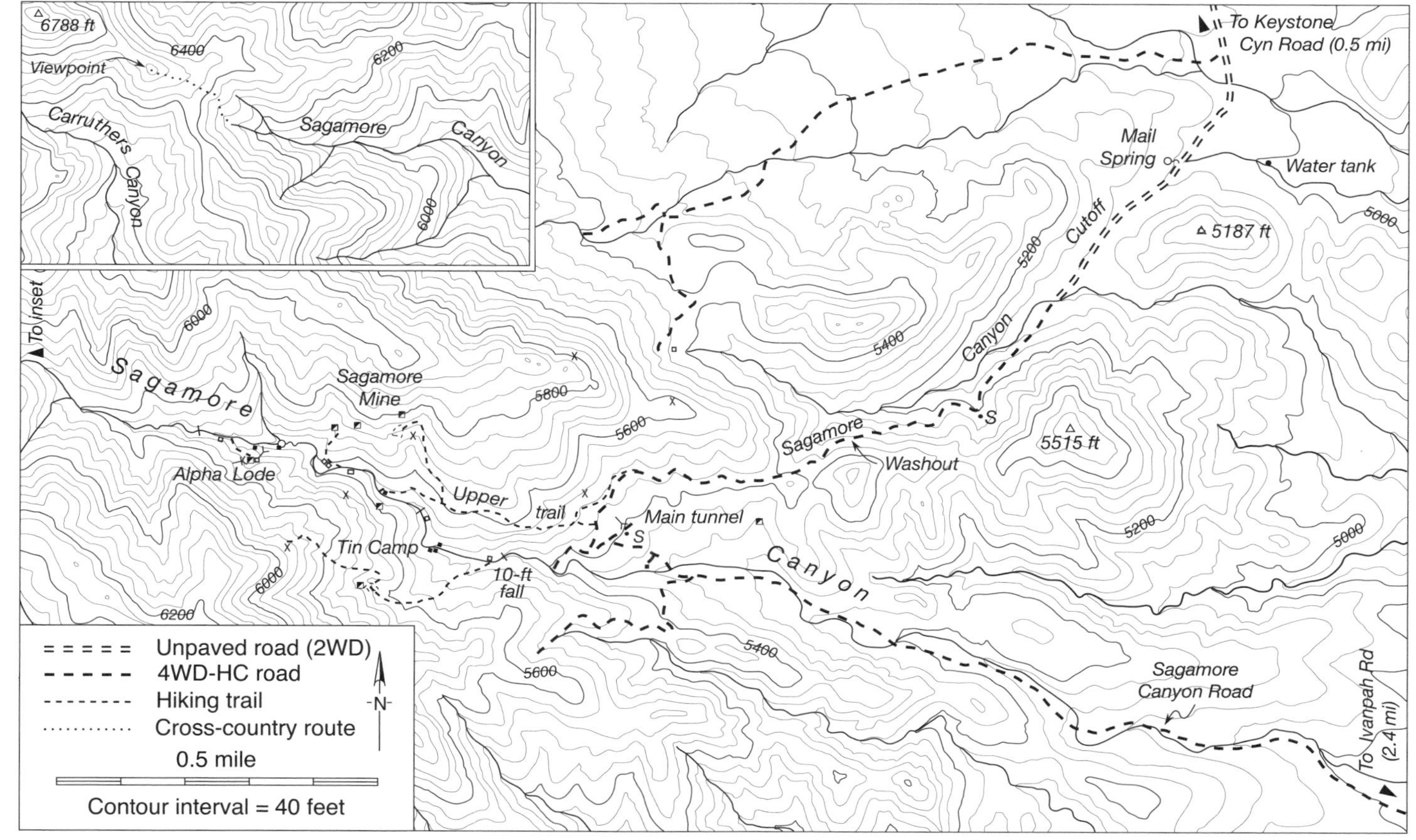
6788 ft
6400
6200
Viewpoint
Carruthers
Canyon
Sagamore
Canyon
6000
To inset
6000
Sagamore
Sagamore
Mine
5800
5600
Alpha Lode
Upper
trail
Main tunnel
S
Tin Camp
10-ft
fall
6000
6200
Canyon
5400
5600
To Keystone
Cyn Road (0.5 mi)
Mail
Spring
Water tank
5000
5187 ft
Cutoff
5200
Canyon
5400
Sagamore
S
Washout
5515 ft
5200
5000
Sagamore
Canyon Road
To Ivanpah Rd
(2.4 mi)
Unpaved road (2WD)
4WD-HC road
Hiking trail
Cross-country route
N
0.5 mile
Contour interval = 40 feet

stately pines grow right down to the edge of the wash. This is a peaceful retreat, fragrant and mercifully shaded, yet hardly ever visited.

After 0.7 mile from the Alpha Lode, bear right at the fork. At the next fork a little further, work your way up the left fork to the head of the canyon, a 250-foot ascent. Then climb on 150 yards west to the rocky summit (see map). This viewpoint marks the divide between three canyons—Sagamore, Keystone, and Carruthers—and it commands spectacular vistas all around. To the west it faces the long serrated crest of the New York Mountains. To the east and southeast it overlooks Ivanpah Lake and Nevada's McCullough Range, the Piute Range, and the Whipple Mountains along the Colorado River. Turn south and you will be staring, past the crisp granitic gorge of Carruthers Canyon, at the chocolate volcanic crags of Hackberry Mountain and the Clipper Mountains beyond.

■

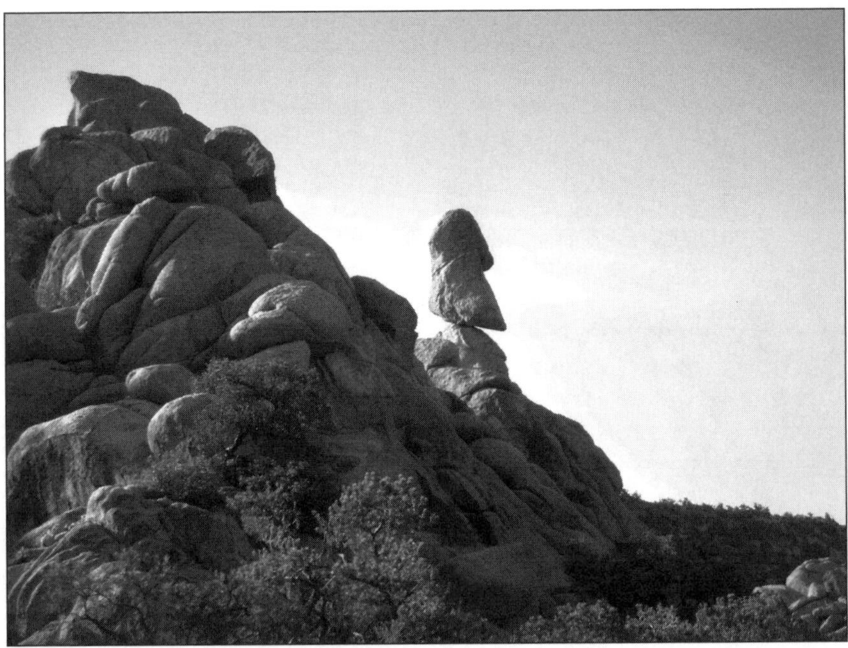

Easter Island Rock, Carruthers Canyon

CARRUTHERS CANYON

This is perhaps the most beautiful canyon in the preserve. Most of it is an enchanting landscape of boulders, knobs, cliffs, overhangs, and pinnacles artfully sculpted in granite and parading before an audience of oak, juniper, and pinyon pine. A beat-up road conveniently climbs through this wonderland to a little mine sprinkled with colorful minerals. The roadless upper canyon wanders through a handsome conifer forest to high ridges and eventually New York Peak, which overlooks some of the most awesome views in the eastern Mojave Desert. For under 3 miles of walking, this is a steal.

General Information

Road status: Roadless upper canyon; 4WD road in lower canyon
Giant Ledge Mine (west): 1.2 mi, 530 ft up, 50 ft down one way/easy
Giant Ledge Mine (east): 1.1 mi, 750 ft up, 180 ft down one way/moder.
New York Peak: 2.6 mi, 2,170 ft up, 260 ft down one way/difficult
Main attractions: Forested canyon, spectacular formations, peak climb
USGS 7.5′ topo maps: Pinto Valley, Ivanpah
Maps: pp. 259*, *221*, 265*

Location and Access

Starting just below the soaring heights of New York Peak, Carruthers Canyon cuts a deep swath south through the New York Mountains. It can be accessed via the Carruthers Canyon Road, which goes more than half way up the canyon. This primitive road starts off the Cedar Canyon Road 10.9 miles east of the Black Canyon Road (or 4.15 miles west of Lanfair). It heads north 6.9 miles to the New York Mountains Road, crosses it, and enters Carruthers Canyon 0.4 mile further. The lower canyon is very wide. Ignore the side roads, which are all on the left and dead-end at campsites. In 1.6 miles, the road starts crossing the overgrown canyon wash. On the far side, 200 yards further, it curves left and passes by the first of a few forested campsites on the right side. The road then deteriorates rapidly. Unless you have the right vehicle and skills, park around here and continue on foot.

The portion of the Carruthers Canyon Road north of the New York Mountains Road is passable with most vehicles up to the first forested campsite. However, the stretch south of it is a little rough at places. With a standard-clearance vehicle, it is easier to bypass it on the New

York Mountains Road. Look for this signed road on the Ivanpah Road 5.4 miles north of Lanfair (or 7.4 miles south of the Hart Mine Road). Drive it 5.6 miles west and turn right on the Carruthers Canyon Road.

The Carruthers Canyon Road is one of the preserve's most scenic byways. For the first several miles it crosses an open fan dotted with Joshua trees and staghorn cholla, with fine views of the serrated New York Mountains. The lower canyon is an open meadow a good fraction of a mile wide, funneled between steep monzonite slopes peppered with conifers. This is a pleasant area, blessed with cooler weather and great views of the mountains. The campsites, shaded under large oaks and pines, rank amongst the most delightful in the preserve.

History: Slow Agony

The Giant Ledge Mine was likely discovered in the early mining years of the New York Mountains, perhaps as early as the 1860s. Unfortunately, not much is known about its history. It might be because it produced copper, a resource that does not raise as much excitement as more noble metals—unless it occurs in phenomenal amounts, which was not the case here. In the summer of 1902, the known ore reserve included the Giant Ledge vein, which was said to be 1,000 feet long, and a gold-bearing quartz vein 600 feet long and four feet thick. A team was working day and night, and as much as 500 feet of workings had been developed. The owners of the California Eastern Railway were so impressed that they contracted for the construction of an extension along the west side of the New York and Providence mountains. This extension did not happen, but the Giant Ledge did make the short list of copper mines that State Mineralogist Lewis Aubury compiled in 1908 in *The Copper Resources of California*, one of the earliest government reports of this kind. The mine then belonged to the Giant Ledge Gold and Silver Company of Los Angeles. The company had completed a 700-foot tunnel intended to cut through a massive quartz ledge as much as 60 feet wide filled with copper. The proximity of the railway and the abundance of wood in the canyon made the future look promising. But if the Giant Ledge was prosperous, it was not for long. Four years later, it was idle—and it seems to have been mostly dormant ever since. Every time someone checked up on it—in 1931, 1943, 1956—it was still idle. In 1943 the main tunnel was not any longer than it was in 1908. By 1956, a second, shorter tunnel had been sunk, but no production was reported. Chances are that it did not produce much of anything, copper or gold.

The canyon in which the Giant Ledge Mine is located is named after George F. Carruthers, a settler who homesteaded in 1915 at the mouth of the canyon. He was then a middle-aged man, likable in spite of his rumored background as a remittance man from England (his homestead application form claims he was born in Nevada). His was one of the most beautiful homesteads around. Surrounded by striking granitic slopes, its expansive meadow was both visually inviting and blessed with plenty of fresh water. Located at higher elevation, it was also greener and cooler in summer, and its scattering of juniper provided pleasant shade. Carruthers alternatively worked his homestead and as a watchman at the Giant Ledge Mine. He briefly mined tungsten with a couple of partners in the 1910s at the Carbonate Mine in Cliff Canyon, on the other side of the mountains. Although he lived mostly alone, he was an integral part of the local community, lending a helping hand, sharing his water when wells broke down, and looking after his distant neighbors. He hung on to this arduous lifestyle for about two decades. After the mid-1930s, he moved to Newberry Springs, where he bought and ran a motel and restaurant.

Carruthers' name is often spelled Caruthers, as on the USGS quadrangle maps. This is a mistake. Out of respect for this unsung pioneer, I am using the correct spelling of his name.

Route Description

The lower canyon. The reason Carruthers Canyon is so special is its giant field of Cretaceous quartz monzonite, which erosion has fashioned into countless hoodoos. The start of the rough road passes by fine samples. The most striking one is Easter Island Rock, a slender monolith that towers over the road's east side. It rests on a contact point so narrow that it seems to violate the laws of gravity. About 150 yards past it, just before the first rough spot in the road, an opening on the west side provides easy foot access down into a particularly scenic wonderland of rocks. You can walk and scramble to your heart's content among fantastic formations resembling erect beetles and gargantuan molars. In another 100 yards an unusual formation known as Foot Rock stands by the road—it looks remarkably like a bare foot seen from the bottom, toes wiggling in the air.

After 0.4 mile, the road splits. The right branch, easy to miss, climbs into the east fork. The main road continues up the narrower canyon, closely hugging the wash. The stone walls the miners carefully erected over abrupt ledges have kept the road from collapsing, but time is still slowly winning. The road is now an impressive mess of rocks and gouged bedrock. Over time, I have seen a few jeeps grind their way up here, but none made it very far. The hard limit is the 10-ton fallen slab that blocks the road 0.5 mile from the fork. Once again

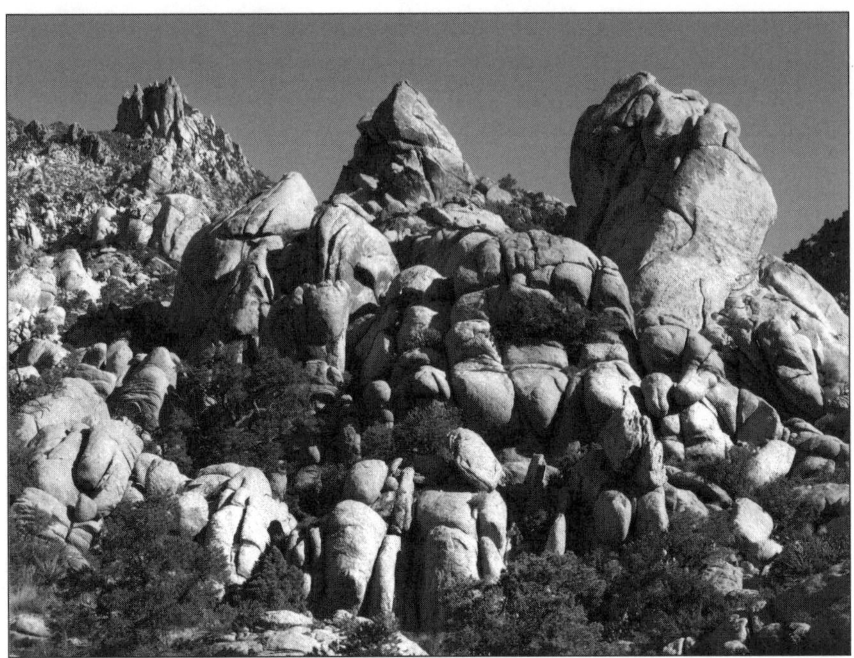

Sculpted quartz-monzonite monoliths along Carruthers Canyon

we can be thankful to miners for such a path. On both sides of it, great inclines of reddish monzonite rise hundreds of feet. All of it has been diced into bewildering gardens of jointed fins, bulging boulders, and fat pinnacles. Up on the high rims loom even more formidable monuments. The most distinctive one is the pointed mountain that towers on the east side of the canyon. Crowned with a tilted spire of barren rock and shaped like a Chinese hat, this landmark is visible for miles. The Giant Ledge Mine is on the far side of it, at the end of this bumpy little road.

One of Carruthers Canyon's other delights is its vegetation diversity, encouraged by its higher moisture. Species that are more at home in the Pacific Coast chaparral live among the boulders—hollyleaf redberry, manzanita, desert mountain lilac, silktassel, and scrub oak. Rock spiraea coats shaded nooks. In late spring, the blooms of mound and grizzly bear cacti, globemallow, penstemon, and many annuals brighten the slopes. Year-round the air is saturated with the smell of sap.

The Giant Ledge Mine (west group). The road ends at the top of the long and slender tailing of the Giant Ledge Mine. This area was exploited via two tunnels, one of which has collapsed. In spite of its unimpressive past, this small mine has a profusion of minerals, from galena to chalcopyrite, scheelite, huebnerite, pyrite, and bornite. Between two shallow shafts, a rock face is coated with a dazzling palette of azurite and malachite. Colorful ore sparkles on the tailing. Blue and green minerals outcrop in small veins along the candelabra-shaped corridors of the tunnel, which is still partly timbered and coursed by a narrow-gauge rail. The wooden dock where the ore was unloaded from the mine car still teeters lopsided on the tailing's edge.

There is another tunnel about 60 feet up the slope. To get to it, from the azurite wall climb the short loose talus to the flat area where the shaft emerges from the tunnel below (be careful not to fall into it!). To your left, away from the shaft, a narrow trail circles around steeply 100 yards up to the upper tunnel near the top of the hill. This very short tunnel also has a shaft. Its entrance is decorated with smears of sky-blue chrysocolla and a stockpile of greenish ore.

East Fork of Carruthers Canyon. To visit the east fork, you will probably need to walk. Few vehicles are powerful enough to negotiate the steep stretch of rutted, slanted bedrock at the start of the road. The road is less than 300 yards long anyway. The open area at the end of the road was the Giant Ledge Mine's camp. Surrounded by green scrub oaks, conifers, and scenic outcrops, it was once a fine little camp. But time has hit it hard too. The cabin is now a pile of lumber, concrete floors are disintegrating, and not much else is left. The centerpiece is the rusted body of a classic car, a harmonious design marrying sleek flow and sensuous volumes, sadly damaged by senseless bullets. The date "Aug. 1, 1906" is etched in old-fashioned lettering on a concrete pillar.

The Giant Ledge Mine's east group is scattered up canyon on the west-facing slope. The lower tunnel, whose white tailing is visible from several miles back, was the main working. Searching for these old workings gives us another incentive, if we needed one, to get deeper into this handsome canyon. In front of the car body is the canyon's narrow entrenched wash. About 40 steps up this wash, there is a trail on the opposite bank. It parallels the wash, then switchbacks up to the lower tunnel (0.3 mile). This is a fine trail, rocky and irregular, lined with colorful arrangements of blue yucca, oak, manzanita, pinyon pine, and frazzled snags.

At one time 700 feet long, the lower tunnel explored several quartz veins up to 9 feet wide, probably for gold. Caving closed off its far end years ago; now its entrance is partly obstructed by gravel, and much of it is flooded. Like the trail, it overlooks panoramic views of Carruthers

Canyon, from the steep slopes of the Chinese hat to the green lower canyon and Table Mountain beyond.

The upper tunnel is 200 feet higher, almost directly up the slope. There is no longer a trail to it; find by trial and error the route you dislike the least. The upper tunnel is dug in solid milky quartz. There is a caved inclined shaft above it just below the ridge, then twin tunnels and a deep prospect down the far side of the ridge. I saw beautiful samples of chrysocolla and azurite, traces of galena and fluorite, black botryoidal coatings of sphalerite, and plenty of milky quartz everywhere. The ridge is pleasantly forested and decorated with cacti, including desert pincushion, and it embraces great views of Carruthers Canyon's granitic exposures.

Upper Carruthers Canyon. The upper canyon offers an altogether different experience. Whereas most of the Mojave Desert's canyons are hopelessly barren, Carruthers Canyon abounds in the opposite excess—it is filled with trees. Progress is slow, and slower deeper into the canyon—dodging pines, circling around fallen boulders, and bushwhacking when all else fails. It makes us better appreciate the convenience of old mining roads. The highlight is the slickrock wall, a massive nose of polished monzonite that looms over the canyon's west side shortly past the mine. The wash describes a long arc around its base, for the only purpose, it seems, to give us better views of this work of art. In the summertime, hawks often circle overhead;

Carruthers Canyon

	Dist.(mi)	Elev.(ft)
Forested campsite	0.0	5,620
East fork road	0.4	5,700
Giant Ledge Mine camp	(0.15)	5,765
East group (lower tunnel)	(0.4)	6,000
East group (lower shaft)	(0.65)	6,190
Slab across road	0.9	5,905
Giant Ledge Mine (west group)	1.15	6,100
Slickrock wall (start)	1.35	~6,160
Leave wash	1.8	6,580
Divide with Keystone Canyon	1.9	6,775
Keystone Cyn Rd (1st crossing)	(2.3)	5,300
North New York Peak	2.4	7,463
New York Peak	~2.6	7,532

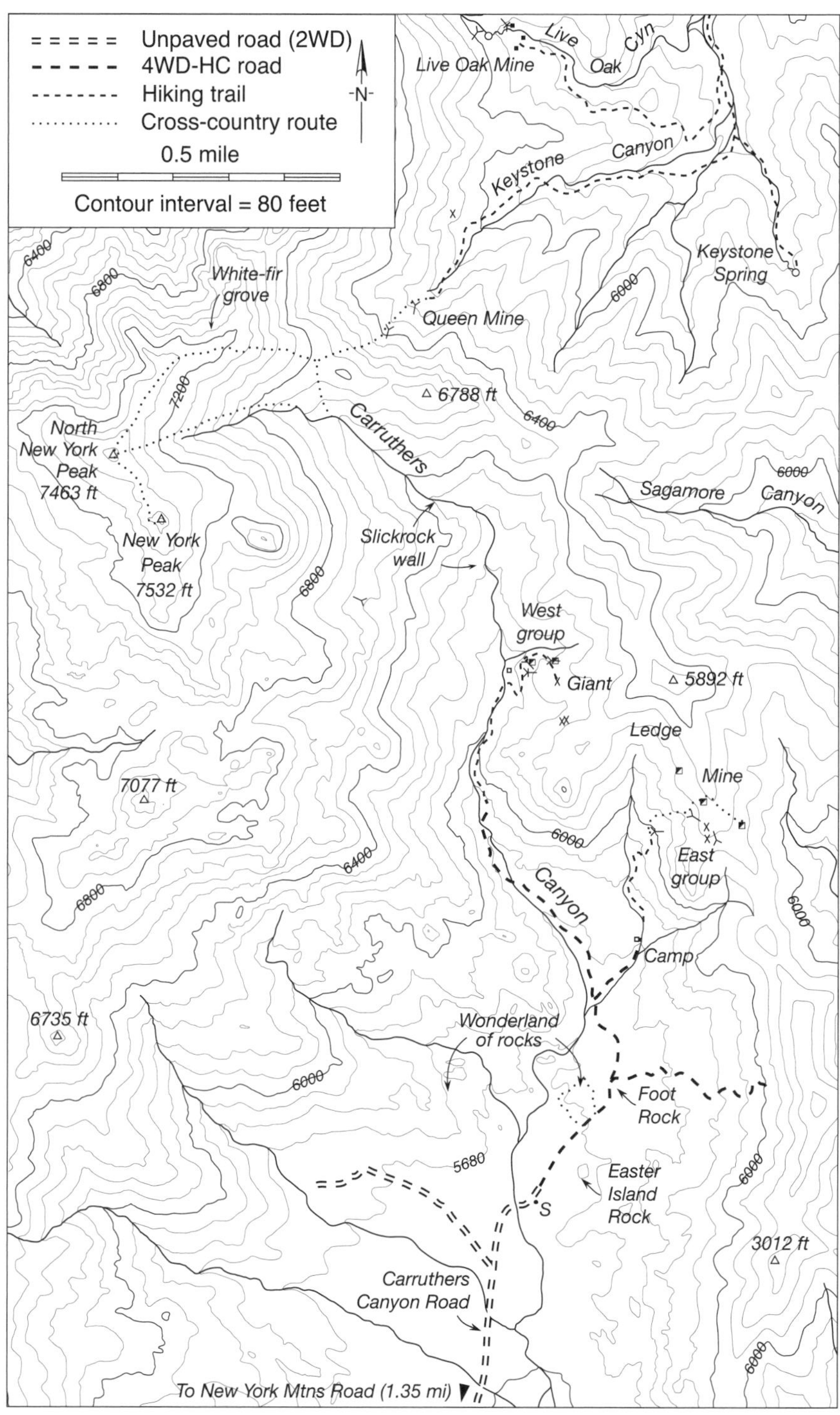

Unpaved road (2WD)
4WD-HC road
Hiking trail
Cross-country route
0.5 mile
Contour interval = 80 feet
N
Live Oak Mine
Live Oak Cyn
Keystone Canyon
Keystone Spring
White-fir grove
Queen Mine
6788 ft
North New York Peak 7463 ft
New York Peak 7532 ft
Carruthers Canyon
Sagamore Canyon
Slickrock wall
West group
Giant
5892 ft
Ledge
Mine
East group
7077 ft
Camp
6735 ft
Wonderland of rocks
Foot Rock
Easter Island Rock
S
3012 ft
Carruthers Canyon Road
To New York Mtns Road (1.35 mi)
6400
6800
7200
6000
5680

hummingbirds buzz by, drawn by the Indian paintbrush. In early spring or after a storm, a little water sometimes flows over the wash's bedrock. For a great view of the upper canyon from above, 0.25 mile past the end of the slickrock wall scramble up the canyon's steep northern slope to the divide with Keystone Canyon (this is also the route to hike on into this canyon).

New York Peak. This action-packed canyon does not quit... The chiseled sugarloaf that looms above its head is New York Peak, the highest point in this range, and climbing it is this canyon's crowning glory. From the slickrock wall it is only about half a mile away as the crow flies, but nearly 1,400 feet higher, hard work across the canyon's thickly forested upper drainage. Follow the wash as far as practicable. When the bushwhacking gets too tedious, climb up the canyon's north slope a little and continue on a course roughly parallel to the wash. This very steep, lopsided tract ends at North New York Peak (labeled "New York" on the USGS 7.5' map). The rest of the route is across a gentle saddle to the foot of New York Peak (labeled "New York Two").

For a more aerial route, from the divide with Keystone Canyon continue up the even steeper ridge west-northwest to the main crest, and follow it as it circles around the head of Carruthers Canyon to the two peaks. Both routes have sharp grades and require a lot of zigzagging around obstacles. The canyon route has fewer outcrops but more trees and brush. The high route is about 0.25 mile longer, but it commands awesome views and passes right over the small grove of white fir that graces the New York Mountains' abrupt north slope.

The summit block is an impressive pointed pyramid of tightly packed fins and spires rising above the heads of pine. Several routes zigzag up to its small summit, all at least a Class-3 scramble, with some exposure; choose carefully. The easiest access is from the west, but the north side is a go too—it is a matter of taste. Even if you don't make the very top, the panoramas and the arresting sight of the stony peak are fine rewards in themselves.

It is a demanding ascent, but the views from the summit rank among the most breathtaking in the eastern Mojave Desert. The southern slope is a fantastic landscape worthy of a science-fiction master, buckled and distorted, bristling with hundreds of pinnacles. Beyond it, a rolling sea of pine and juniper washes down to the bright edge of Lanfair Valley. On a clear day you will gaze across thousands of square miles of largely empty desert, from the San Bernardino Mountains to western Arizona and Death Valley country.

■

— 9 —

MID HILLS

FROM BUTCHER KNIFE CANYON at their north end to just north of Columbia Mountain at their south end, the Mid Hills are all of about 10 miles long and 6,430 feet high. More the whim of a forgotten cartographer than a well-defined range, they are a squat aggregate of hills that bridges the gap between the New York and Providence mountains. But this diminutive range has merits of its own. Made almost exclusively of granitic rocks, it is a scenery-charged collage of iconic monoliths. Obliterated by a major fire in 2005, much of the range's woodlands have been turned into an eerie world of bleached trunks and naked boulders, a combination that will remain a source of surreal photography for years to come. The comparatively subdued topography makes the Mid Hills a good place to indulge in easy hikes and to seek these uncommon landscapes, as well as scenic boulder formations, springs, and hidden vestiges of the original forest.

Access and Backcountry Roads

A well-developed network of roads makes the Mid Hills easily accessible. About in their middle, the Mid Hills are severed by Cedar Canyon and the wide graded road that runs along it, which connects the eastern and western poles of the preserve. The graded Black Canyon Road branches off the Cedar Canyon Road and heads south several miles along the high plateau that flanks the Mid Hills' east side. The Wild Horse Canyon Road, also graded, makes a loop from the Black Canyon Road and closely follows the southern crest of the range. South of Cedar Canyon, a long nameless road leads south to a series of remote springs. North of Cedar Canyon, the Death Valley

Storm over the Mid Hills from Macedonia Canyon

Mine Road skirts the west side of the Mid Hills, and several spurs branch off to springs and short canyons. A few roads in Pinto Valley provide more distant access to the northeast side of the range. The Mid Hills Campground, just off the Wild Horse Canyon Road, still has much of its original tree cover, and it is a refreshing place to camp in warm weather. Spaces are limited, so get there early.

Geology

The Mid Hills are made largely of weathered 93-million-year-old Mid Hills Adamellite. It is by far the largest of the seven plutons that make up the Teutonia batholith: it extends nearly continuously from near Slaughterhouse Spring in the New York Mountains to Macedonia Canyon in the Providence Mountains, and smaller exposures occur south to Globe Canyon. Much of this formation is monzogranite and fairly uniform—light-colored, with medium grains of comparable sizes. Some outcrops contain very large feldspar crystals, dark gray hornblende, and olivine. Although this pluton exhibits intense mineralization elsewhere, especially molybdenum in the New York Mountains, much of it is bare in the Mid Hills, and mining here was very limited. Some of the region's most ancient rocks—gneiss and granitoids between 1.66 and 1.7 billion years of age—extend in a narrow north-south band generally slightly east of the crest, from Live

Suggested Backcountry Drives in the Mid Hills					
Route/Destination	Dist. (mi)	Lowest elev.	Highest elev.	Road type	Pages
Butcher Knife Canyon	8.3	4,176'	5,005'	H	267
Death Valley Mine Road	7.3	4,176'	4,510'	P	138-139
Wild Horse Canyon Road	11.4	4,150'	5,550'	P	261
Key:	P=Primitive (2WD)		H=Primitive (HC)		

Oak Spring to the Mid Hills Campground and beyond. The only non-intrusive rocks are the Peach Springs Tuff and Wild Horse Mesa Tuff in the tablelands at the eastern and southern edges of the Mid Hills, in particular Pinto Mountain, Table Mountain, and Wild Horse Mesa.

Botany: The Hackberry Fire Complex

In June 2005 almost all of the Mid Hills were destroyed by a devastating fire. It was a complex of fires ignited on Hackberry Mountain by hundreds of dry lightning strikes. An unfortunate conjunction of factors made it particularly damaging. The previous winter and spring had brought 20 inches of rainfall, more than twice the normal amount, which had given rise to exceptionally thick vegetation. By June, all this biomass was dry and poised as a huge reservoir of fuel. On the day the fire started, winds up to 40 miles per hour raged over the high desert. It was a perfect storm. Firefighters could not contain the blaze, which died out when the wind subsided three days later. By then almost 71,000 acres had been consumed, much of it to the ground, including extensive woodlands of evergreens and Joshua trees, from the northern Providence Mountains north to the southern New York Mountains, and from Cedar Canyon east to Hackberry Mountain. It was the greatest natural make-over to hit the preserve in human history.

Almost everywhere you go in the Mid Hills, you will be confronted with charcoaled ground and decimated vegetation. It is easy to think of this aftermath as a heart-breaking finality. It is harder to see it as a new beginning. For eons entire landscapes have been destroyed and reborn; Earth is a recovering mosaic of past catastrophes. The Mid Hills happen to be going through the rebirth phase of one of these endless cycles. Habitats are changing. Plants that had taken decades to grow, like juniper, are largely gone. Plants that did not have enough space, light, or water to flourish before the burn are now thriving. Springtime floods the newly created open spaces with more annuals than might have grown here in centuries. By 2010 much ground had

Route/Destination	Dist. (mi)	Elev. gain	Mean elev.	Access road	Pages
Suggested Hikes in the Mid Hills					
Short hikes (under 5 miles round trip)					
Banshee Canyon	0.2	60'	4,260'	Graded	289-290
Barber Peak					
summit	0.9	950'	5,020'	P/0.8 mi	295-296
Wild Horse Mesa viewpt	1.0	970'	5,060'	P/0.8 mi	295-296
Butcher Knife Canyon				H/8.0 mi	
East fork	1.8	830'	5,250'		267-270
Gorge	1.3	500'	5,120'		267-268
Ivanpah Mtns viewpoint	2.4	1,160'	5,370'		267-270
Eagle Rocks	0.8	370'	5,550'	P/0.3 mi	275-276
Eagle Rocks loop*	2.1	1,070'	5,570'	P/0.3 mi	275-278
Pinto Mountain	2.3	1,170'	5,480'	Graded	272-274
Rings Loop Trail*	1.4	110'	4,230'	Graded	290-291
Table Mountain	2.0	1,050'	5,540'	P/1.2 mi	279-282
Intermediate hikes (5-12 miles round trip)					
Barber Peak Loop Trail*	5.1	1,520′	4,460'	Graded	291-294
Butcher Knife Canyon loop*	5.4	1,310'	5,410'	H/8.0 mi	267-270
Table Mountain loop*	5.3	1,300'	5,710'	P/1.2 mi	279-282
Long hikes (over 12 miles round trip)					
Mid Hills to HITW Trail	7.9	3,060'	5,000'	Graded	283-286

Key: P = Primitive (2WD); H = Primitive (HC)
Distance: one way, except for loops (total), marked with an asterisk
Elev. gain: sum of all elevation gains on a round-trip basis & on loops

been partially reclaimed, albeit by different combinations of species. It will take years for shrubs to mature and for diversity to build up, 20 to 30 years for trees to become established, and 100 to 150 years for old growth to rule again. As transient visitors, we are witnessing in slow motion a snapshot of a long dynamic process. It gives us a chance to observe how plants and animals cope with this extreme change in environment, and what brand new worlds rise from the ashes.

Hiking

The Mid Hills are small but packed with interesting features. Besides more than a dozen springs (Live Oak is one of the best), there

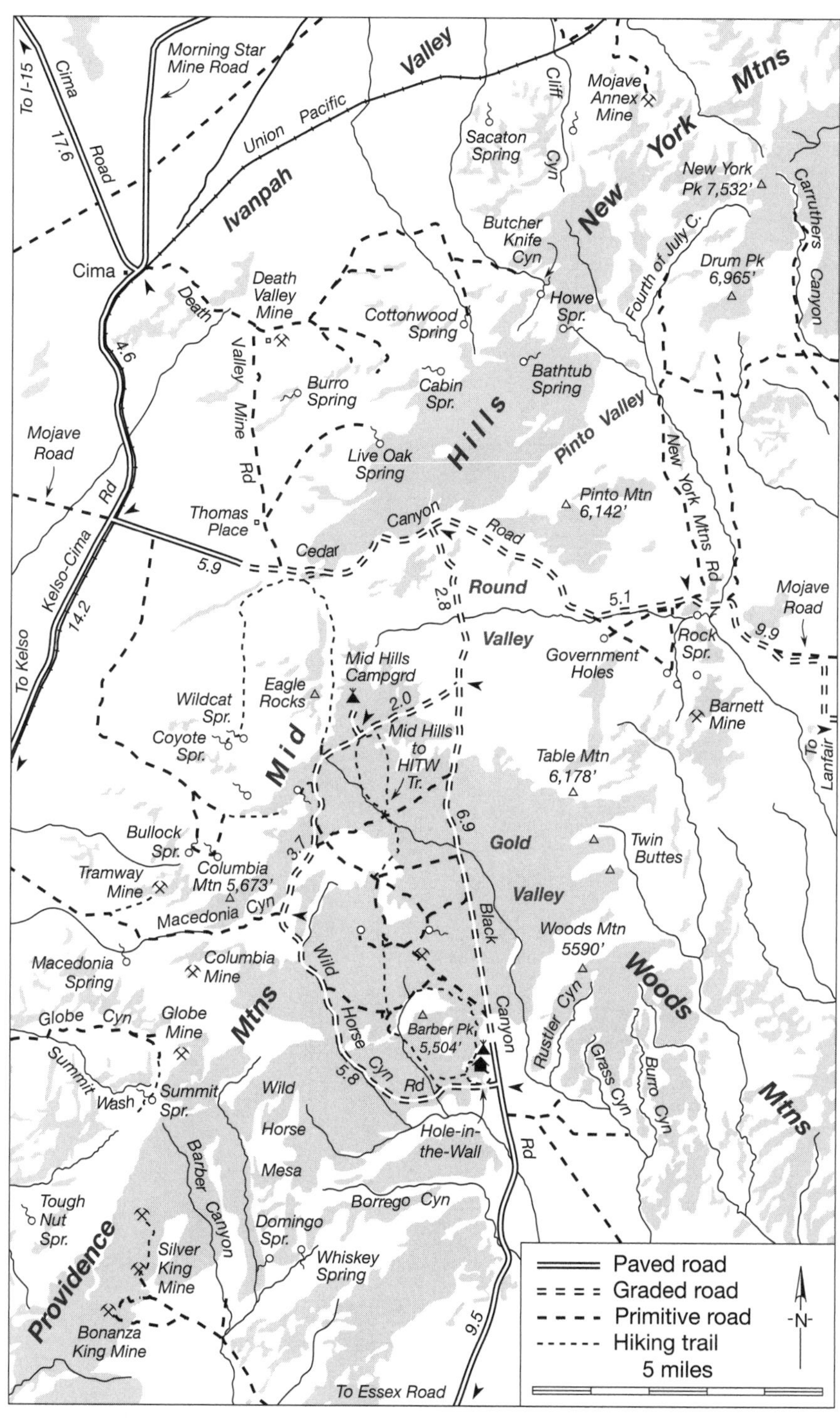
To I-15
Cima Road
17.6
Morning Star Mine Road
Union Pacific
Ivanpah Valley
Cliff Cyn
Sacaton Spring
Mojave Annex Mine
New York Mtns
New York Pk 7,532'
Carruthers Canyon
Butcher Knife Cyn
Fourth of July C.
Drum Pk 6,965'
Cima
Death Valley Mine
Death Valley Mine Rd
Cottonwood Spring
Howe Spr.
Bathtub Spring
4.6
Burro Spring
Cabin Spr.
Mid Hills
Pinto Valley
Mojave Road
Live Oak Spring
New York Mtns Rd
Pinto Mtn 6,142'
Thomas Place
Kelso-Cima Rd
Cedar Canyon Road
5.9
2.8
Round Valley
5.1
Mojave Road
14.2
Rock Spr.
9.9
To Kelso
Government Holes
Mid Hills Campgrd
Eagle Rocks
Wildcat Spr.
2.0
Barnett Mine
Coyote Spr.
Mid Hills to HITW Tr.
Table Mtn 6,178'
To Lanfair
6.9
Gold Valley
Twin Buttes
Bullock Spr.
3.7
Tramway Mine
Columbia Mtn 5,673'
Macedonia Cyn
Black Canyon Rd
Woods Mtn 5590'
Macedonia Spring
Columbia Mine
Wild Horse Cyn Rd
Woods Mtns
Globe Cyn
Globe Mine
Mtns
Barber Pk 5,504'
Rustler Cyn
Grass Cyn
Burro Cyn
Summit Wash
Summit Spr.
5.8
Wild Horse Mesa
Hole-in-the-Wall
Barber Canyon
Tough Nut Spr.
Borrego Cyn
Providence
Domingo Spr.
Whiskey Spring
Silver King Mine
9.5
Bonanza King Mine
To Essex Road
Paved road
Graded road
Primitive road
Hiking trail
5 miles
N

are countless areas for scrambling and bouldering, several short canyons, beautiful exposures of boulders and weather-worn outcrops, a few old roads turned to trails, and good views from the range's low crest. The furthest you can be from an open road is only about 2 miles, and the terrain is generally gentle, so this can be experienced with little effort. If one of the motivations of hiking is the quest for exceptional landscapes, surely the post-apocalypse world of the Mid Hills' seared ecosystem should rank high on any destinations list. Moving through this otherworldly desolation takes on a dreamy quality. If you are attracted to unusual scenery, this is a journey to seek, not to shun.

■

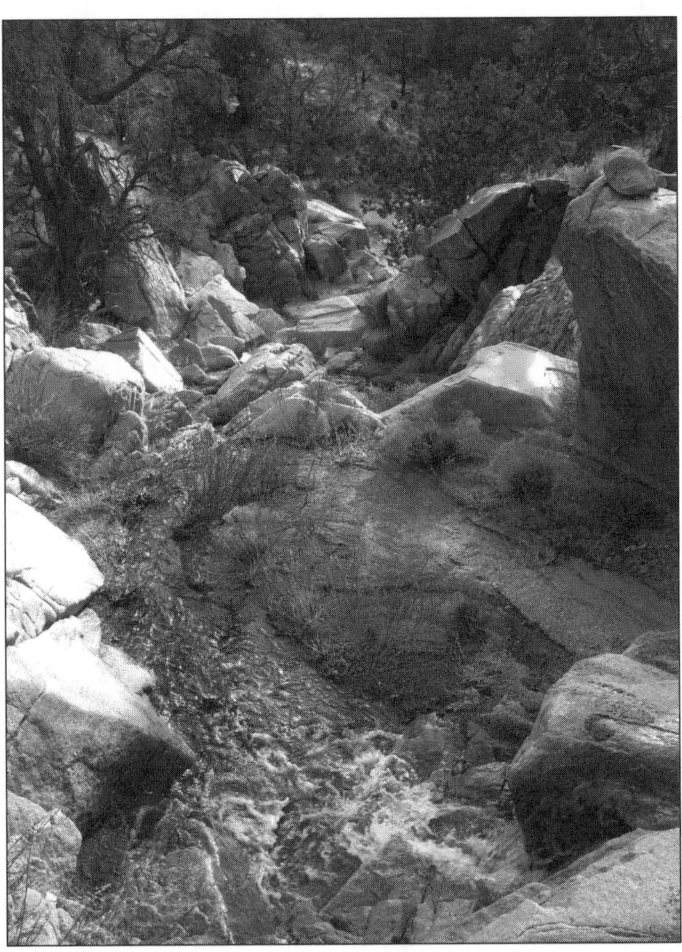

Waterfall and boulders in Butcher Knife Canyon

BUTCHER KNIFE CANYON

In spite of extensive fire damage, Butcher Knife Canyon is still a delightful place thanks to its boulder-strewn rocky gorge, which preserves a strip of its original woodland. The best time to visit is early spring, when the Butcher Knife Creek is at its peak and courses through the entire length of the gorge. Even in summer there is usually water, the pine trees provide pleasant shade, and the scrambling is fun. The upper canyon and its main side canyon offer several climbs through surreal fields of boulders and charred forests to remote vista points.

General Information

Road status: Roadless; high-clearance access road
The gorge: 1.3 mi, 500 ft up, 0 ft down one way / easy, with scrambling
Butcher Knife Canyon viewpoints: 5.4 mi, 1,310 ft up loop / moderate
Main attractions: A short scenic canyon, creek, boulders and pine trees
USGS 7.5' topo maps: Mid Hills*, Pinto Valley
Maps: pp. 269*, 265

Location and Access

Butcher Knife Canyon is the northernmost canyon in the Mid Hills, at the suture with the New York Mountains. Although it is fairly remote, a convoluted road goes all the way to it. From the stop at Cima drive the Morning Star Mine Road 0.1 mile to a left bend. The graded road on the right is the Death Valley Mine Road. Across the tracks it splits three ways; take the middle fork 2.6 miles to the gated entrance to the Death Valley Mine. Turn left and proceed 0.8 mile to a junction. Turn left again at a junction 0.8 mile further. After 2.3 miles there will be a corral. Make a right in front of it, and drive 0.65 mile to a fork. The left fork goes 0.8 mile to the edge of Butcher Knife Canyon's wash. One can drive 0.3 mile up the wash to the wilderness boundary, but the ramp down into the wash is steep, the wash has deep sand, and driving back up the ramp can be tricky. It is safer to park above the ramp. A standard-clearance vehicle can make it up to the mine, and possibly as far as the corral. High clearance is required beyond.

Route Description

Much of Butcher Knife Canyon was ravaged by the Hackberry Fire Complex. The first part of this hike, up the lower canyon's wide sandy wash, vividly illustrates the extent of the damage. Once covered with a hardy forest, the canyon banks and slopes are now grim stages for the skeletons of seared trees. In stark contrast to the green frenzy of Joshua trees and yucca the access road threads its way through, this is a forlorn desolation. But do not let it stop you. Butcher Knife Canyon's little gorge, which was largely spared by the blaze, is not far away. It is announced by a gradual tightening in the hills, the first pinyon pine, and a portal of two massive granitic pillars. If it is early spring you might be treated to a rare desert sight before getting there—a rivulet of limpid water crawling across the bare sand. This is the terminus of Butcher Knife Creek, one of the largest seasonal streams in the preserve. When recharged by snow melt and winter rains, the swollen creek ventures far down the open wash. It is vigorous enough to have incised in it a long zigzagging trench more than 3 feet deep. Even this far below the canyon it can be astonishingly loud.

The gorge is a twisted cleavage worn into the Mid Hills' plutonic underbelly. Although neither very deep nor tight, for a good fraction of a mile it is a rocky passage confined between steep hillsides of monzogranite boulders. Not all the pines have survived, but the lucky ones are elegant old timers, their luscious crowns dark against the pale rocks. This is a scenic canyon, not yet overgrown, and fun to scramble where boulders take over. But it would not be half as exciting if it weren't for its playful creek. When in full force, Butcher Knife Creek is a boisterous stream with contagious exuberance. Not far inside the gorge it breaks into a string of singing cascades as it tumbles down a tall scree of boulders. A little further, it surrenders to gravity with careless abandon and leaps over an abrupt ledge to spawn a 9-foot waterfall. It sluices over slickrock, splashes over stones, and feeds small ponds of emerald watercress. Most of the time it wanders peacefully beneath low amber walls, along soft channels it has carved for itself in the narrow sand wash, hemmed by tufts of grass and hairy clumps of baccharis. I remember catching trout in Irish brooks that weren't much wider than this...

The canyon splits 0.6 mile up from the portal, just below the end of the gorge. The 15′ and 7.5′ USGS maps disagree as to which fork is the main canyon. The west fork is the longest and widest, and it has the only perennial spring, so it is the most logical choice. Both forks merit exploration.

The east fork. From the split the east fork goes through a short narrow gulch filled with evergreens. Then it opens up and enters the burn, and the mood changes dramatically. A tight forest of charred

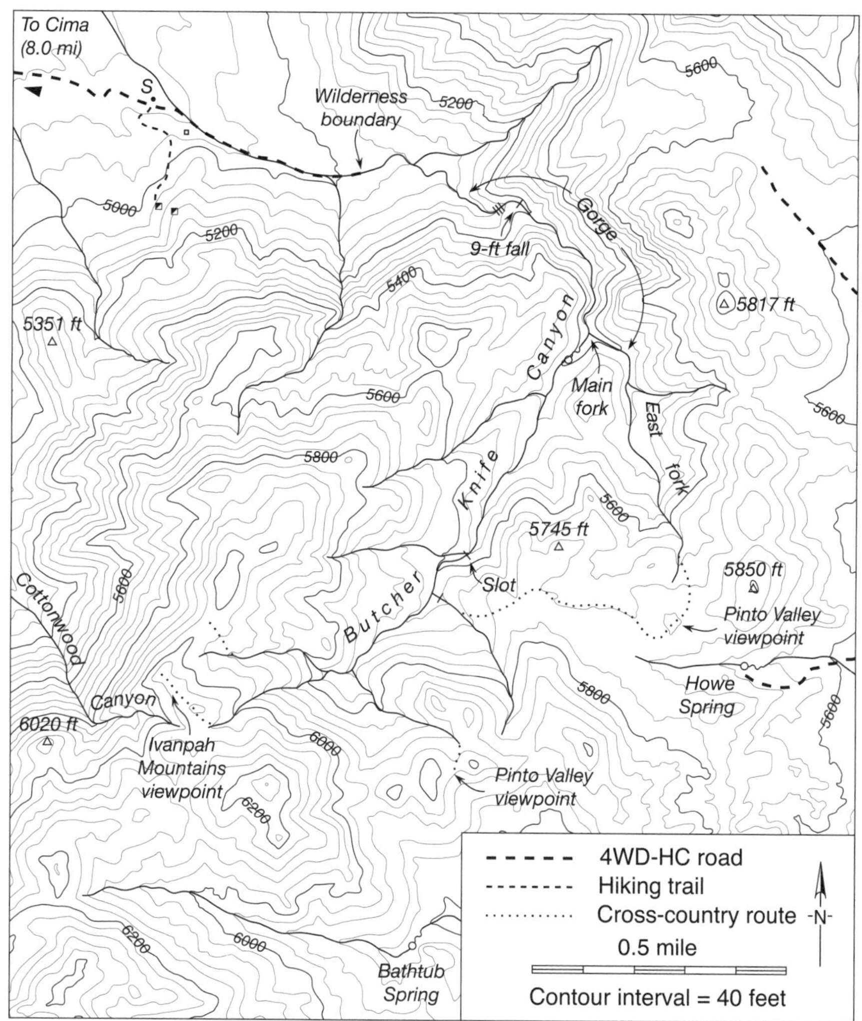

Butcher Knife Canyon		
	Dist.(mi)	Elev.(ft)
End of road at ramp	0.0	4,915
Wilderness boundary	0.4	5,005
Lower end of gorge/portal	0.6	5,035
Main fork	1.2	5,365
End of east fork (viewpoint)	(0.6)	5,750
Upper fork	2.05	5,425
Head/Ivanpah Mtns viewpoint	2.4	6,080

pinyon pine stretches as far as the eye can see, their black and white trunks outlined sharply against the stripped-down earth. As disturbing as the landscape is, it holds a definite aesthetic appeal. Like surreal art it distorts reality just enough to prompt disbelief. In the cooler months, the creek persists stubbornly, and it is compelling to hike on just to see what becomes of it. It disappears and reappears several times, at the mercy of the sand's thirst. Along the steep final climb to the head of the canyon it bounces between boulders and slithers down a long crack in a broken outcrop. The level bench at the top is a jungle of rounded boulders and dead trees guarded by a few sheer monuments. Walk to the divide for good low-angle views of secluded Pinto Valley and Pinto Mountain behind it.

To rejoin Butcher Knife Canyon without backtracking, follow the gentle bench among large boulders 0.35 mile west to the divide with the main canyon. Then cross into the next ravine 150 yards to the southwest, and descend along it to the main canyon's wash. This should put you 0.6 mile up canyon from the main fork.

Upper Butcher Knife Canyon. The main canyon shares the same severity, on a larger scale. About 500 feet up from the main fork is the canyon's main spring, a swamp of aquatic plants that floods the wash. Above it the canyon widens and turns into a burnt wasteland. The broad, unobstructed wash is lined with the static sculptures of torched trees and gray clumps of mesquite and catclaw. Large green clumps of barberry, cliffrose, yucca, globemallow, and prince's plume are slowly growing out of the ashes. The wash is interrupted only once, by a short 8-foot slot. Sometimes crystal-clear water percolates from under it into a foot-wide pool in the sand. Like the 9-foot waterfall in the gorge, it can be bypassed with little effort.

Nearly 1 mile above the main fork the canyon splits again, at the foot of a steep hill capped with slanted outcrops. The left fork climbs to the east rim, which also has good views of Pinto Valley. The right fork splits after 100 yards. Heading left will take you up a steep slope of boulders to the divide with Cottonwood Canyon to the west. The right fork climbs more moderately to the same divide. Both end points offer fine overlooks of Cima Dome and the Ivanpah Mountains.

To preserve these rare desert streams, throughout this canyon system do not step in water, on wet sand, or on the brittle edges of sand banks. Walk on the rocks instead. They have survived 93 million years so far; they can take the pressure.

■

PINTO MOUNTAIN

Of the few remaining exposures of the colossal lake of molten lava and ash that flooded the Lanfair Valley area in the Miocene, Pinto Mountain is the most colorful. Its south face is a striking mesa capped by a mile-long cliff balanced high on sheer taluses. The valley below it is a luminous grassland dotted with conifers that sweep up the graceful arc of the mountain's flank. In contrast, the north side has a subdued topography softened by erosion and stripped bare by the 2005 wildfire. When you climb Pinto Mountain, you swing from one side of it to the other and sample both worlds—the arboreal pre-fire desert, and the slowly healing post-fire holocaust.

General Information
Road status: Roadless; good graded access road
Pinto Mountain: 2.3 mi, 1,100 ft up, 70 ft down one way/moderate
Main attractions: Forested canyon, easy climb, views of the preserve
USGS 7.5' topo maps: Mid Hills, Pinto Valley
Maps: pp. 273*, *265*

Location and Access

Pinto Mountain is in the northeastern Mid Hills, overlooking the New York Mountains to the north and the spacious plains of Lanfair Valley to the east. If you drive long and scenic Cedar Canyon Road across the preserve east toward the remote ghost town of Lanfair, it is the first unmistakable landmark you will come upon as you reach the top of Cedar Canyon and enter Lanfair Valley. To get there, from the service station at the Cima Road exit on Interstate 15, drive the Cima Road 17.5 miles south to its end at Cima's railroad yard. At the stop sign just before the railroad, turn right on the Kelso-Cima Road, toward Kelso. Go south 4.6 miles to the signed Cedar Canyon Road on the left (coming from the south, this junction is 14.2 miles north of Kelso). Drive the Cedar Canyon Road east 6.0 miles to the Wild Horse Canyon Road on the right, then 0.9 mile past it to where Cedar Canyon opens up. Pinto Mountain will be the cliff-bounded mesa rearing up half a mile to the northeast. Look for a small dirt road on the left (the way to the summit), facing a dirt road on the right, and park near this intersection. The Cedar Canyon Road is paved for the first 2.3 miles, then it is a good, broad, graded road.

Route Description

The beginning is leisurely, up along the easy grade of the dirt road on the north side of the Cedar Canyon Road. In 100 yards it reaches a wilderness boundary and angles right, along the boundary. Go straight instead, into the wilderness, up an abandoned track that aims toward the obvious canyon at the west end of Pinto Mountain. This area is particularly scenic. It is a grassy flood plain sprinkled with evergreens, Joshua trees, and occasional cactuses, right under the mountain's colorful cliffs. The mountain's west face records two major regional volcanic eruptions. The top cliffs are made of locally famous Wild Horse Mesa Tuff, the same formation that makes up the wildly pitted escarpments at Hole-in-the-Wall. The lower layer is a bulging drop of fluted tuff as gray as ash, the top layer a crew cut of columnar basalt in warm earth tones. Smaller cliffs protrude from the abrupt taluses well below them, which are the remaining ledges of the older Peach Springs Tuff.

After 0.5 mile, where the track comes down to the sandy wash just inside the canyon, leave it and continue up the wash. In 0.4 mile, and 50 yards before the first sharp right bend, a side canyon opens up on the right, pointing northeast. It is walled in on its left by a low ridge with vertical outcrops and stately pine. A 35-foot rock fall is visible blocking the way 0.1 mile up the side canyon's narrow wash. Walk up to the fall, which is easy to climb, a few Class-2 moves over large boulders and bedrock. Here as in the canyon, the country rock is Rock Spring Monzodiorite, nearly white monzonite grading into black hornblende diorite. This small pluton from 97 million years ago was named after a nearby spring with perennial pools deep enough to drown.

From the sandy patch at the top of the fall, count 130 steps and you will come to a fork. Both forks will get you to the summit, but take the right fork, where route finding is a bit easier. Above the fall the original forest is intact, and you find yourself instantly immersed in totally different terrain. You walk in a narrow, dimly lit wash that meanders in a tight ravine thickly forested with juniper, barberry, pinyon pine, and squawbush. Many trees seem too large for a desert, easily centennial, with deeply carved trunks and roots clutching at boulders. You have to duck under low branches, climb over fallen trees, and brush against juniper garlanded with strips of peeling barks.

A tenth of a mile past the fork the forest ends at the edge of the burn, and the scenery changes again. The rest of the way, the land has been torched by the blaze. Everywhere the grey ghosts of juniper claw at the air. Another 0.1 mile up the ravine, a naked gully opens up on the left. Climb it to the top of a ridge, where Pinto Mountain's squat summit first becomes visible, less than a mile due east. Descend 70 feet

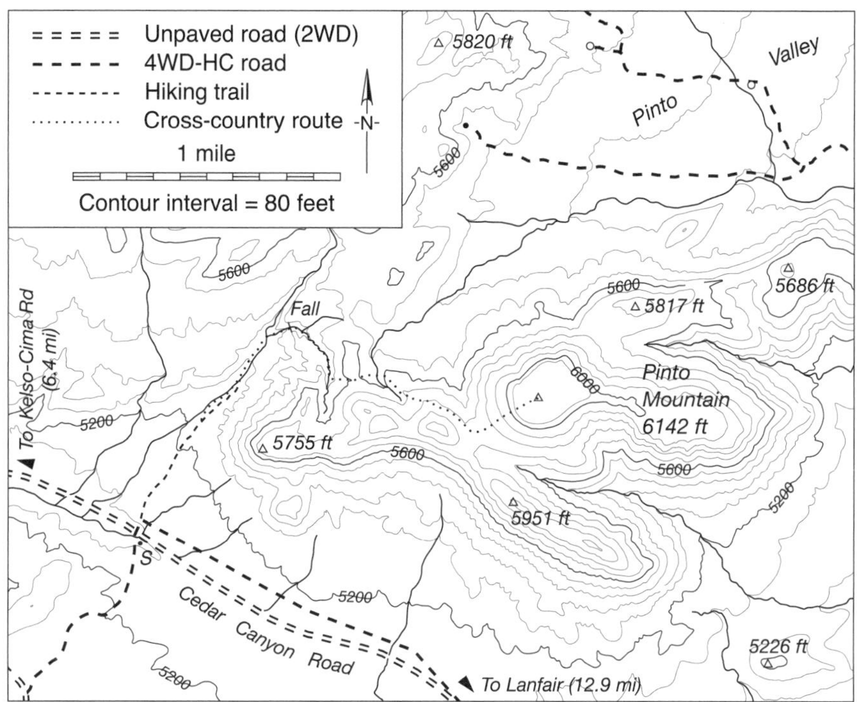

Pinto Mountain		
	Dist.(mi)	Elev.(ft)
Cedar Canyon Road	0.0	5,115
Side canyon (right)	0.9	5,305
Fork (go right)	1.1	5,420
Gully (go left)	1.3	5,505
Top of ridge	1.45	5,615
Saddle on crest	2.0	5,785
Pinto Mountain	2.3	6,142

into the ravine directly below, cross it, and continue up the ravine's west flank to an eroded bench on the side of the hill west of the summit. Then contour the hillside to the saddle between that hill and the summit. The rest is up Pinto Mountain's broad southwest shoulder, a steep but short and unobstructed slope, and likely the only place where you might puff a little.

The summit is a desolate plateau fortified by needle grass scattered with grizzly bear cactus and blue yucca, a meager garnish that barely

Pinto Mountain from Cedar Canyon Road

keeps the soil from being blown off to bedrock. It is so broad and flat that it clips the view in most directions; the half-mile walk around the plateau is a better way to enjoy this central observatory. The views extend remarkably far and touch on all the preserve's major ranges. On the horizon, from Nevada and Arizona to the edge of southern California, more remote ranges collapsed by distance rise in single, hazy-blue ridges, too far to identify, except for the formidable hump of the San Bernardino Mountains.

This is certainly not the desert's most charismatic summit. But during certain times and seasons, it is transfigured by light. In the spring, the whole mountain comes alive with the myriad orange-red blossoms of thousands of globemallow. In late fall and winter, brittlebush flood the washes with pale-green fluorescence. In the slanting rays of late afternoons, every bush on every hillside glows gold and trails a long blue shadow across the land. In the final hours of a sunny day, the cliffs burn from within in deepening shades of apricot, as spellbinding as alpenglow.

■

EAGLE ROCKS

Eagle Rocks are the majestic twin granitic peaks that crown the Mid Hills, a prominent landmark visible from much of the preserve. A scenic trail leads through a cool conifer forest to the foot of these striking monuments. Circumventing Eagle Rocks is a little challenging, but it will take you across a steep slope crammed with huge boulders where you can scramble to your heart's content and enjoy breathtaking views of Kelso Basin.

General Information

Road status: Roadless; access on short 2WD primitive road
Eagle Rocks: 0.8 mi, 200 ft up, 170 ft down one way / easy
Eagle Rocks loop: 2.1 mi, ~1,070 ft up loop / moderate
Main attractions: Scenic granitic peaks and boulder fields, pine forest
USGS 7.5' topo maps: Columbia Mountain, Mid Hills*
Maps: pp. 277*, 265

Location and Access

To get to the Eagle Rocks trailhead, drive the graded Wild Horse Canyon Road from its north end 2.7 miles southwest to a primitive road on the right, just before a left bend. Take this road 0.15 mile to a fork. Along the way, you will see Eagle Rocks occasionally protruding over the horizon up ahead. Turn right, and park after 0.15 mile in a small pullout on the right, 20 yards before the junction with the left fork (see map). Most vehicles can make this road. The trail starts just beyond the wilderness boundary signs on the north side of the road.

Route Description

The access trail. The trail to Eagle Rocks is an aging road that climbs up a little, then descends gently along a broad canyon. The start of it traverses a refreshing forest of pinyon pine and juniper. The tree cover is exceptionally dense, with crowns almost touching. The air is filled with the smells of sap, big sagebrush, and warm desert soil. Even on the hottest day large patches of cool shade flood the sticky carpets of pine needles. The forest soon disappears on the abrupt edge of the 2005 burn. It leaves the stage to open ground studded with upright charred trees. As is often the case, the demise of one ecosystem is the boon of another. Encouraged by increased sunlight, opportunistic plants are proliferating with a vengeance. From mid-spring through

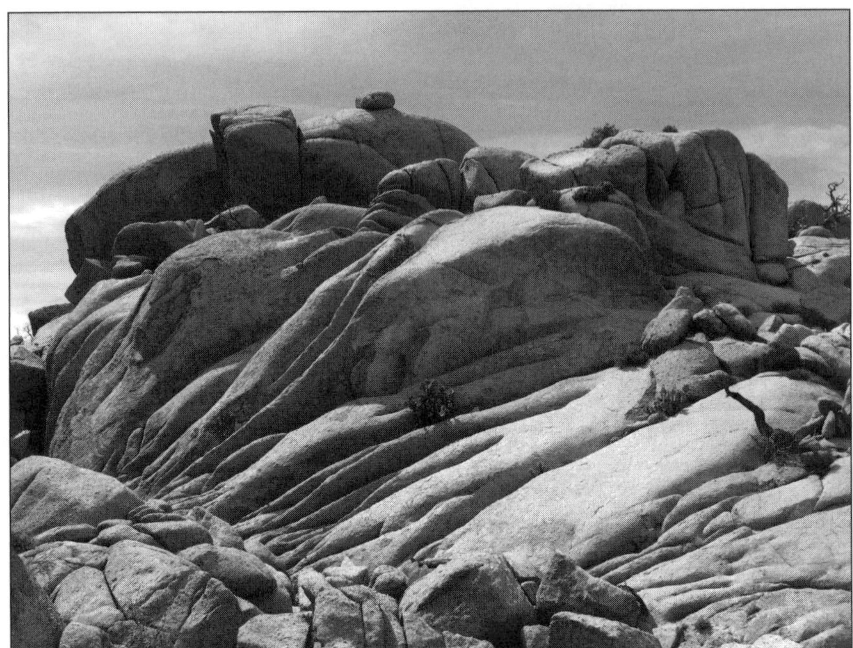

Wrinkled quartz-monzonite outcrops near Eagle Rocks

summer wildflowers often flood this area, especially globemallow, giant four o'clock, Goodding's verbena, and evening primrose.

Shortly into the burn Eagle Rocks come gradually into view, two magnificent sugarloafs of sheer naked stone towering 200 feet above the crest to the west. After about 0.5 mile the trail angles left towards them. A fainter trail marked by a wilderness sign branches off to the right, and continues down canyon several miles to Cedar Canyon. Before the burn, this shaded canyon made for a delightful hike. I would not suggest hiking it today—its empty slopes lined with dead trees are not so exciting. But if you are reading these words in the 22nd century or later—having likely found this book in an antique shop—do try it, as the pinyon will likely have established dominance again. Until then, continue on the main trail instead, up the short remaining slope to Eagle Rocks. Both monoliths are surrounded by a chaotic skirt of huge boulders. The road crests and ends just east of the northernmost and highest one. From there a vague track climbs northwest to its eastern base and ends.

Eagle Rocks loop. All these rocks belong to 93-million-year-old Mid Hills Adamellite—another name for quartz monzonite, a close

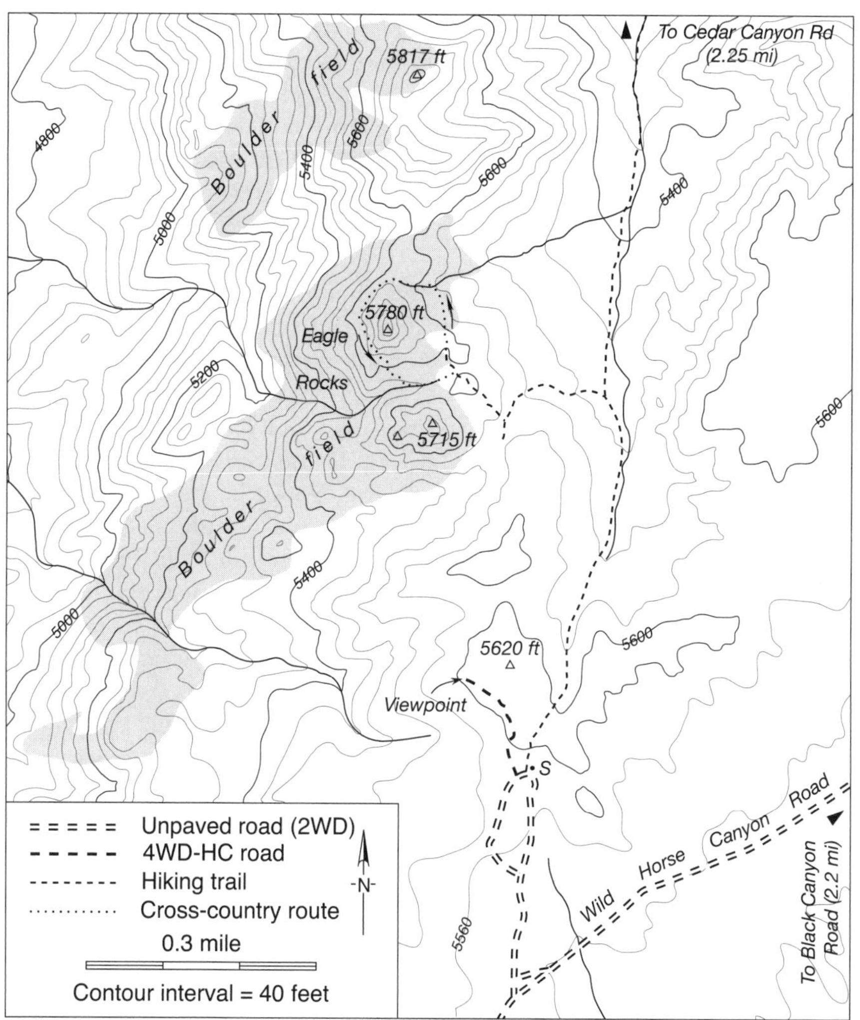

Eagle Rocks		
	Dist.(mi)	Elev.(ft)
Trailhead	0.0	5,570
Jct (trail to Cedar Cyn Rd)	0.55	5,465
Cedar Canyon Road	(2.75)	4,575
Crest at Eagle Rocks/end of rd	0.7	5,555
North end of trail	~0.8	5,600
Back to trail	1.35	5,595
Back to trailhead	2.1	5,570

cousin of granite. Its main constituent, feldspar, often forms large prismatic crystals. The best part of this hike is to explore this beautiful mineral world. Do not expect to scale Eagle Rocks: they are almost vertical and unprotected. But there are many other options. Good climbers can try some of the other nearby summits instead. They involve mostly scrambling across boulder taluses to the summit blocks, then comparatively easy technical climbs (low 5's) if you pick the right routes.

The all-around best way to sample this area is circumventing the highest peak. The route is straightforward: from the end of the faint trail proceed north into the ravine at the north end of Eagle Rocks. Clamber up this ravine west to the crest. Then find a route across the western slope beneath the peak to the ravine between the twin peaks, and finally climb this ravine west back up to the trail. This loop is very short but action-packed. The only area that is a little tough is the west side, which is steep and covered with massive boulders. Averaging some 10 feet across, they just rest on top of each other, with no soil or smaller rocks to fill the gaps between them. If you slip you might drop into a deep cave and break something vital. While I was scrambling across, a couple of turkey vultures circled over me, ever so alert for a free lunch. The easiest route I found is to stay as close as possible to the foot of the peak's wall. Further down the gaps are bigger, the jumps higher, the blocks steeper, and the fun is greater—but so is the risk.

This 300-acre playground is loaded with surprises. At the top of the north-side ravine, a small enclave of vegetation has been spared by the flames. Sacred datura, manzanita, locoweed, bitterbrush, and grasses thrive in the lifesaving shade of a few thick hollyleaf redberry and pinyon pine. Stepping through this greenery and over the crest is like going through Alice's looking glass—a whole new world bursts into view. Waves upon waves of rounded boulders spill down the range, merging seamlessly below with the vast plains of the Kelso Basin. The show is stolen in the middle ground by a cluster of eerie pointed hills slashed by long dikes. In summer, the landscape gets even more alien as the perpetual haze dissolves the surrounding mountains into an ethereal blur. There are some mighty rocks out there. Against the western base of Eagle Rocks, chiseled monuments point skyward like prehistoric temples to the stars. On the south peak, a colossal block over 3,000 tons rests in impossible equilibrium against a nearly vertical surface. The south-side ravine is obstructed by a long monolith the size of a mansion. If you like scrambling, the sky is the limit.

■

TABLE MOUNTAIN

The short but action-packed climb to the high plateau of Table Mountain is one of the eastern Mojave Desert's unavoidable classics. It calls for navigating through the mountain's surreal core of granitic boulders to reach the seemingly impregnable cliff-bound volcanic mesa that caps the mountain. The exercise is aerobic, the volcanic rocks are wild, and the desolate mesa commands far-reaching views of the Lanfair Valley area.

General Information

Road status: Roadless; high-clearance access road
Table Mountain: 2.0 mi, 970 ft up, 80 ft down one way / moderate
Table Mountain loop: 5.3 mi, 1,300 ft up loop / moderate–difficult
Main attractions: Climbing a volcanic plateau, views, granitic boulders
USGS 7.5' topo maps: Columbia Mountain, Woods Mountain
Maps: pp. 281*, *265*, 221*

Location and Access

The shortest route up to Table Mountain starts from the end of the ridge that extends west from the mountain. To get there, drive the Black Canyon Road 5.15 miles north from the turn-off to the Hole-in-the-Wall Information Center (or 1.5 miles south of the Wild Horse Canyon Road) to a primitive road on the east side, just north of a cattle guard. Drive this road 0.65 mile until it runs into another road, and make a hard left. Continue 0.6 mile to a windmill and water tanks at the southern foot of the ridge, and park. High clearance is required to handle a couple of rutted spots near the start.

Route Description

The ascent. Table Mountain is one of the many insular remnants of the huge plateau of volcanic ash and lava spewed out by the Woods Mountains' caldera around 18 million years ago (see *Rustler Canyon*). Its free-standing geometric outline protruding from the high-desert plain is an eye-catching landmark visible from many locations throughout the eastern part of the preserve. It can be ascended either from the open plain on the south side of the mountain, or along the ridge. I recommand climbing the first route, which gets you to the summit faster, and returning along the rougher ridge, which will keep your interest peaked even after the high of the climb.

The high cliffs of Table Mountain

From the windmill, head southeast along the long fence that parallels the ridge. After about 0.5 mile, cross the fence and cut a beeline east toward the cove at the base of the ridge below the western tip of the mountain. Two broad gullies converge at the east end of the cove; one drops from the northeast, the other from the east. Climb the latter, then continue in the same general direction, staying in the boulder-free areas when possible. After 0.3 mile of moderate climbing, angle left (northeast) and climb the remaining 0.1 mile to the ridge's crest. A broad, grass-covered gully framed by boulders traces the crest. Follow it east up to a local rise (~5,870 feet), then down a lopsided incline to a saddle at the foot of the long talus that shoots up to Table Mountain. The most demanding part of this hike is ascending this 40° slope of soil sprinkled with juniper, pine, and small rocks. The talus ends at the western foot of Table Mountain's circle of cliffs, layers of cream and chantilly volcanic ash capped by milk-chocolate columnar basalt. Work your way south along the base of the cliffs about 80 yards to a rock-strewn breach in the cliffs, then climb up through the breach to the rim. The summit, all of 10 feet higher, is just 50 yards north.

This is a fun climb, short and easier than it looks—scrambling is not even necessary. The volcanic rocks are remarkably diverse, the cliffs imposing, and the vegetation has healed enough since the 2005

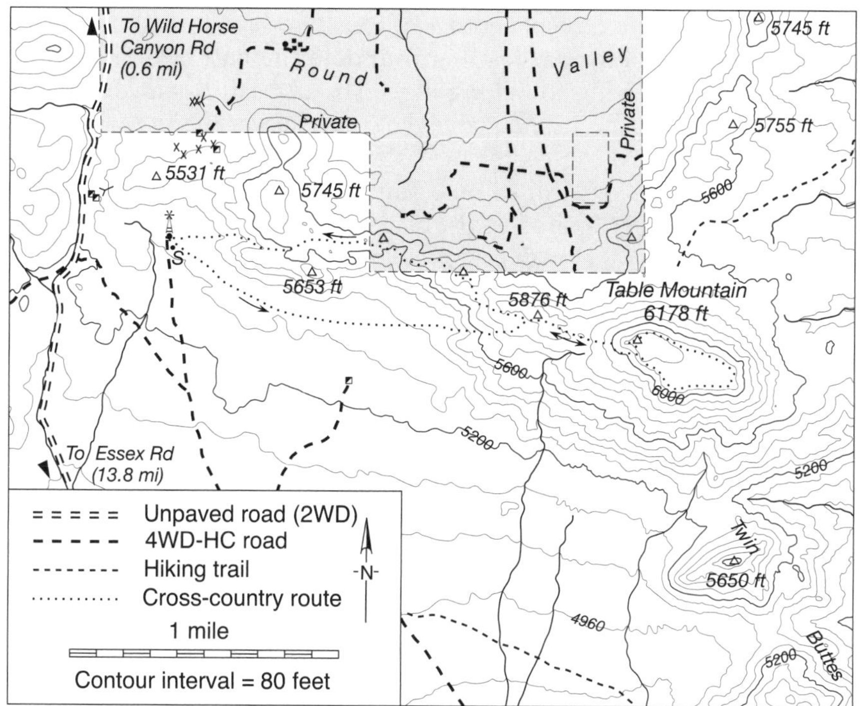

Table Mountain		
	Dist.(mi)	Elev.(ft)
Windmill	0.0	5,290
Cross fence	~0.6	~5,395
End of cove	1.1	5,410
Ridge crest	1.5	5,810
Table Mountain	2.0	6,178
Table Mountain (east end)	2.5	6,135
Return via ridge	5.3	5,290

fire to liven up the desert again. The area is home to quite a variety of wildflowers, among the most striking sacred datura, white tidy tips, Goodding's verbena, and giant four o'clock. There are also good opportunities for spotting quails, turkey vultures, ground squirrels, cottontails, and black beetles.

Table Mountain. The climax is still to come—the gentle stroll around the perimeter of the mountain top. Rimmed by sheer cliffs, the eerily flat plateau feels like a lost world, far above civilization, sprouting anemic bushes and isolated dwarf trees, most of them burnt. The vivid pools of woolly daisies that inundate the bare ground in the spring seem too lively to belong here. The plateau floats above the desert like a mountain island above the ocean, closer to sky than earth. If you walk toward the center of it and sit down, its edges become your horizon, as closed-in as on a tiny planet. On the south side, a small grove has been spared by the blaze. Inside it, the warm fragrance of juniper and big sagebrush brings back a modicum of earthiness.

As you circumvent the mesa the desert revolves slowly around you, constantly changing, superb in every direction. At the east end of the mesa, slabs of congealed lava hang over the sharp rim like diving boards over an empty pool. Hundreds of feet below, the land rebounds in great waves of pale monzodiorite that gradually fade into the emptiness of Lanfair Valley. Range after range rise on the far horizon, from the Castle Mountains out to the far-flung Old Woman Mountains. To the southeast lies ground zero, the gaping void in the Woods Mountains where the caldera blew its top and created this volcanic summit. There is no sound but the wind and the cliff swallows darting in and out of the cliffs below to perform reckless aerobics. Everyone should be so lucky to see this spectacle once in a lifetime.

The ridge. When you finally manage to tear yourself from this spacious scenery, try returning along the more challenging ridge. Getting lost is not easy; the only difficulty is occasionally applying trial and error to search for a path through the jumble of boulders that cover much of the hilly ridge. The least obstructed route is always south of the crest; the north side is often steeper and clogged with boulders. The terrain is relatively open along the first third of the way. The middle third is the roughest. There is no way to cross this wall-to-wall accumulation of close-packed boulders without getting intimate with the rocks. Some routes require minimal scrambling; others can be a welcome excuse to indulge in bouldering. Past this stretch progress is easier again, across more open, wavy terrain that will guide you to the head of a steep ravine. The last leg is down this rock-filled drainage, where you might need hands again.

Wandering across this spectacular warehouse of boulders is one of the greatest rewards of this hike. Plump and well rounded, ranging in size from basketball to blimp, the boulders compose an ever-changing landscape suspended high against thin air. The blackened crowns of the dead trees add a tangible touch of hellishness. On many occasions the scenery literally stopped me dead in my tracks.

■

MID HILLS TO HOLE-IN-THE-WALL TRAIL

Nearly 8 miles long, the Mid Hills to Hole-in-the-Wall Trail crosses a variety of high-desert terrains, from a sagebrush valley to broad hills strewn with pinyon pine, juniper, and granitic boulders, then descends amid multicolored volcanic mesas to the distorted landscapes of Hole-in-the-Wall. Ravaged by fire in 2005, this area provides a rare glimpse of how the desert heals. Hike this moderate trail one way if you can arrange a ride, as an easy backpacking escapade if you have the energy, or just sample short segments of it.

General Information

Road status: Hiking on old roads and trails; graded access road
Mid Hills to HITW Tr.: 7.9 mi, 1,060 ft up, 2,000 ft down one way/mod.
Main attractions: A longer trail in the high country, views, volcanic formations, slot canyon
USGS 7.5′ topo maps: Mid Hills, Columbia Mountain*
Maps: pp. 287*, 293*, *265*

Location and Access

Starting just off the Wild Horse Canyon Road, the Mid Hills to Hole-in-the-Wall Trail (Mid Hills Trail for short) follows a 7.9-mile north-south course that connects the southern Mid Hills to Hole-in-the-Wall. Because it is mostly downhill southbound, people will prefer starting from its north end. To get there, drive the Wild Horse Canyon Road from its north end 2 miles to the Mid Hills Campground turnoff. Park at the large parking area on the south side of the road. To hike the trail northbound, park at the picnic area just north of the Hole-in-the-Wall Information Center. Both trailheads are well signed.

Route Description

The Mid Hills Trail can be divided into four distinct segments. First, it traverses the western edge of Gold Valley toward two low hills. It then crosses the hills via the saddle between them. On the south side of the hills it descends along a long open slope to the western foot of Barber Peak. On the last segment, where it overlaps with the Barber Peak Loop Trail, it follows the base of this scenic volcanic mesa counterclockwise, then squeezes up through Banshee Canyon to emerge at Hole-in-the-Wall. This whole region is relatively subdued, the grades are moderate, and the army of carsonite posts and cairns lining the

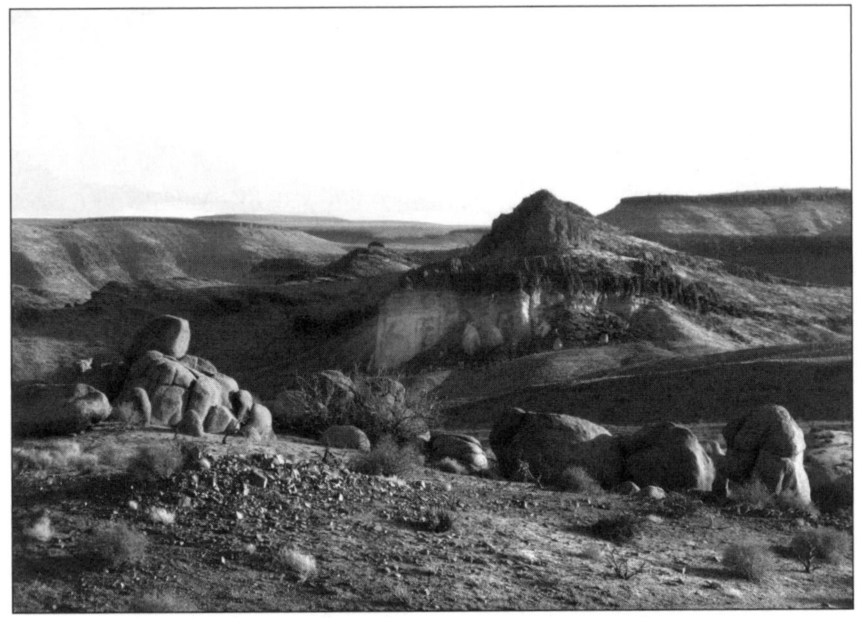

Opalite Cliffs and Wild Horse Mesa from the Mid Hills Trail

trail—one every 40 yards or so—makes it challenging to get lost. If you are fairly new to the desert and hesitant to venture out there, this is a good place to jump in.

Prior to 2005 this trail was somewhat of a local classic. It traversed what was then beautiful high country densely populated with a collage of plant communities, including a healthy big-sagebrush prairie in Gold Valley, crowded cactus gardens south of it, and fragrant conifers a bit everywhere. The Hackberry Fire Complex destroyed much of all this. The ground is now largely barren and haunted by the skeletons of scorched plants, and it will continue to be so for decades. Cattle are taking a toll on the seedlings struggling to grow back. Sadly, the proliferation of posts also put an end to the one small challenge of this otherwise even-keel hike, which was to occasionally look for where the trail was going. If you are likely to be upset by the impaired wilderness quality, skip this hike. In spite of these downsides, I included this trail here because in time it will regain its former splendor, and until then it still has several redeeming features.

At the trailhead you will have to choose between two trails that converge at the first of four road crossings. The gated road that heads south from the parking area is the shortest and easiest one. The foot trail that heads east is a little longer and more interesting because it

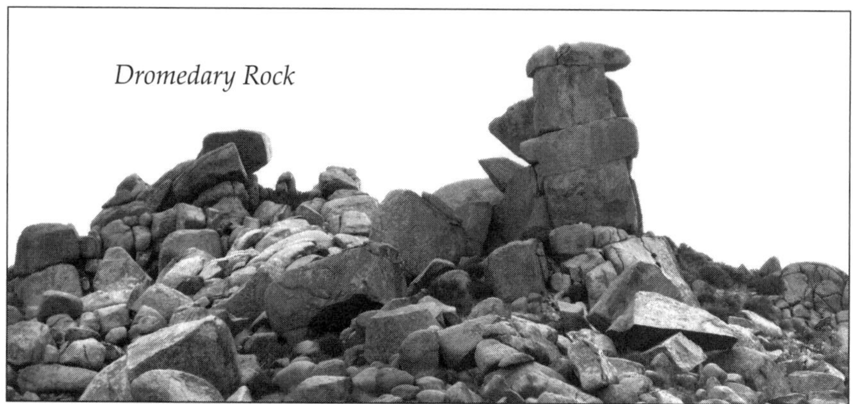
Dromedary Rock

wanders across low hills. Both trails go by small degraded pockets of original vegetation, including a few stands of big sagebrush and scattered juniper and pinyon pine. Some areas have been partly recolonized, notably by blackbrush and bitterbrush. All these tender-green pioneers started growing around the same time, so they are roughly the same size, and the land has the manicured look of newly landscaped suburban backyards. It is not uncommon to spot a deer ambling through the devastation to munch on the young plants. The open scenery fanning out in every direction to a far-off horizon of empty hills has classical desert beauty. Your eyes will often be drawn down the broad plain of Gold Valley dipping gently eastward to the conspicuous silhouette of Table Mountain. To see what this area was like before the fire, at the first road crossing leave the trail and head southwest on the road 1.15 miles to where it crosses another road, just before the Wild Horse Canyon Road; then make a left on this second road to return to the trail at the second road crossing (1.1 miles). For about 0.4 mile along both roads near their crossing, an impressive blue-green sea of 5-foot big sagebrush sprinkled with dark-green bitterbrush and juniper survived the blaze.

After 3 miles, the trail reaches a gate at the second road crossing. For the next few hundred yards it climbs to the saddle between the hills. Along this stretch the countryside is peppered with handsome Cretaceous boulders of pale monzogranite. The bare-rock ridge just past the gate is a fine example. Its northern tip is crowned by a stack of jointed blocks known as Dromedary Rock. The best direction to recognize it—if you squint just right—is from 250 yards west of the gate.

At the southern foot of the hills the trail crosses the third road, which ends a little further west at Granite Well. From this crossing onward, you will be hiking down a mile-wide plain that gradually funnels down toward colorful Barber Peak and the statuesque Opalite Cliffs about a mile south. Right after the fire this slope was a spooky plantation of burnt yuccas and chollas, their maimed stalks poking out of charcoal dust like alien life forms. But they are making a comeback too, as new shoots sprout out of the seemingly lifeless plants. The ground is smeared with a crimson dusting of eriogonum. The panorama includes several distinctive Old-West mesas to the south, including the long, straight escarpments of Wild Horse Mesa.

At the fourth and last road crossing, the Mid Hills Trail merges with the Barber Peak Loop Trail. Up ahead everything is about to change dramatically: you will soon leave the burn and enter a chaotic landscape carved out of Miocene magma. Refer to *Hole-in-the-Wall* for a description of this part of the Mid Hills Trail, which is the most exciting stretch.

The one thing to look forward to the most, just about anywhere on this trail depending on the time and conditions, is the spring wildflowers. Free of competition, a few species go absolutely wild. When the rain has been just right in its timing with the warmer season, the very same soil that is so utterly denuded most of the year is transformed into the most unbelievably colorful fields, acres upon acres of tightly packed vermillion globemallow and sky-blue Goodding's verbena. It will make you forget the burn, the cows, and the carsonite outbreak.

■

Mid Hills to Hole-in-the Wall Trail

	Dist.(mi)	Elev.(ft)
Wild Horse Canyon Road	0.0	5,522
1st road crossing via road	(1.6)	5,226
1st road crossing via trail	1.7	5,226
2nd road crossing	3.0	5,400
Pass	3.5	5,435
3rd rd crossing (to Granite Well)	4.25	5,095
4th road crossing	5.45	4,615
Opalite Cliffs	~5.8	~4,560
Trail leaves wash (bypass)	6.1	4,465
Top of narrows bypass	6.25	4,565
Jct to Hole-in-the-Wall	6.9	4,300
Wild Horse Canyon Road	(0.3)	4,215
Banshee Cyn/Rings Loop Trail	7.7	4,225
HITW picnic area	7.9	4,280

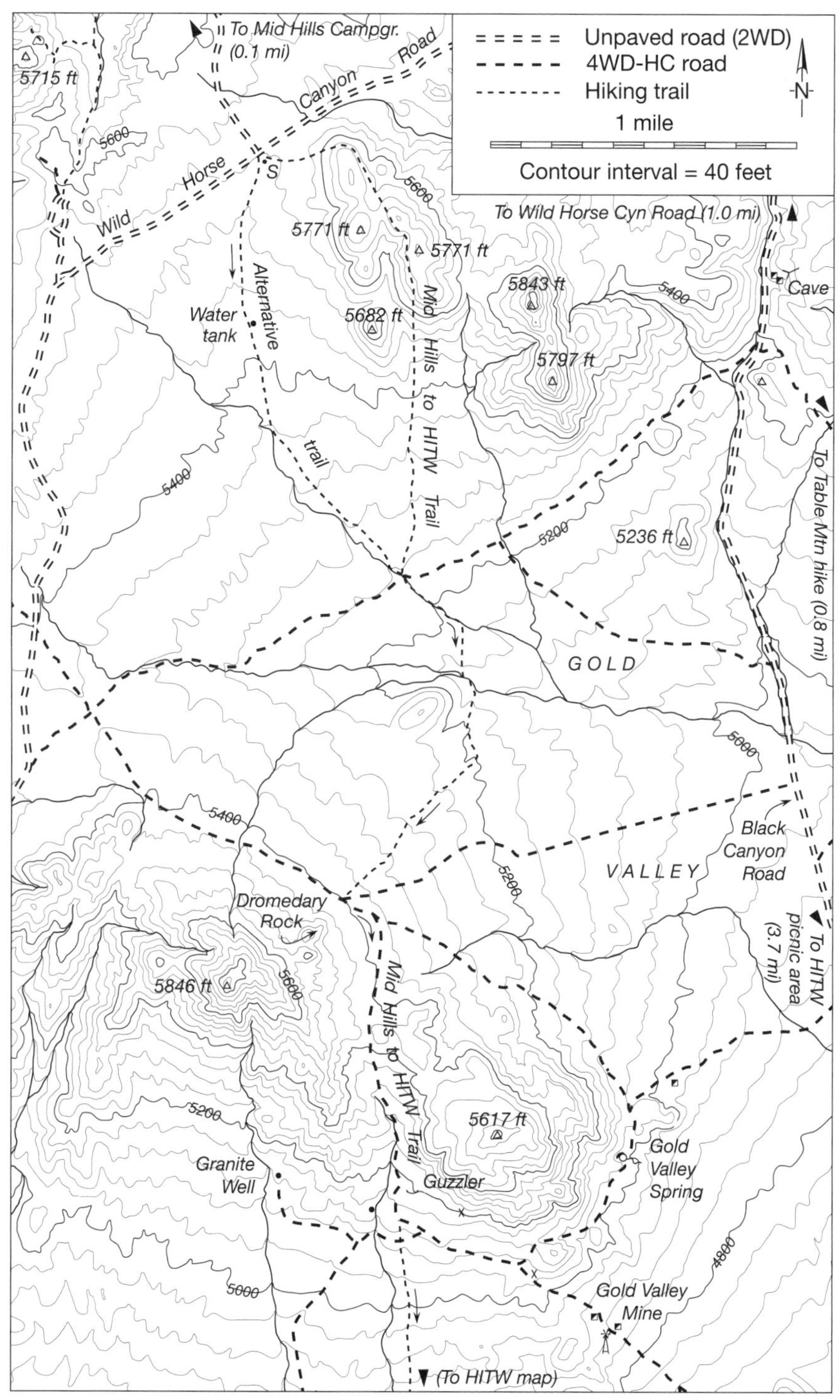
Unpaved road (2WD)
4WD-HC road
Hiking trail
1 mile
N
Contour interval = 40 feet
To Mid Hills Campgr. (0.1 mi)
Wild Horse Canyon Road
5715 ft
5600
S
5771 ft
5771 ft
5843 ft
5797 ft
5682 ft
To Wild Horse Cyn Road (1.0 mi)
Cave
5400
Water tank
Alternative trail
Mid Hills to HITW Trail
5200
5236 ft
To Table Mtn hike (0.8 mi)
GOLD
VALLEY
5000
Black Canyon Road
Dromedary Rock
5846 ft
To HITW picnic area (3.7 mi)
5617 ft
Gold Valley Spring
Granite Well
Guzzler
Gold Valley Mine
4800
(To HITW map)

Volcanic field above the narrows along Barber Peak Loop Trail

HOLE-IN-THE-WALL

Composed of a vivid hodgepodge of volcanic rocks left behind by phenomenal eruptions about 17.8 million years ago, Hole-in-the-Wall is one of the most scenic areas in the preserve. The two popular loop trails described here sample the area's most dramatic features. One is a short jaunt around a low hill bounded by pockmarked walls, the other a longer loop encircling colorful Barber Peak. Expect spectacular narrows, arches, petroglyphs, awesome cliffs, and striking desert gardens.

General Information

Road status: Hiking mostly on old roads and trails; graded access road
Rings Loop Trail: 1.4 mi, 110 ft up loop/easy, with some climbing
Barber Peak Loop Trail: 5.1 mi, 760 ft up loop/easy, with some climbing
Main attractions: Volcanic formations, loop trails, slot canyon, rock art
USGS 7.5' topo map: Columbia Mountain
Maps: pp. 293*, 265

Location and Access

Hole-in-the-Wall is part of the Providence Mountains, but it was included here for convenience, because of its connection to the Mid Hills Trail described in the previous section. The starting point of both loop hikes is the west end of the picnic area 0.2 mile north of the Hole-in-the-Wall Information Center. Both trailheads are signed.

Route Description

Banshee Canyon. The picnic area is located in a secluded cove surrounded by deeply chiseled cliffs. Banded in horizontal layers of dark gray and reddish tuffs, eroded into a tortured scape of alcoves and turrets, they compose one of the preserve's most iconic sceneries. This is all Wild Horse Mesa Tuff, the compounded outpourings of unimaginably violent eruptions that started 17.8 million years ago (see *Rustler Canyon*). Before heading out, walk to the viewpoint south of the trailhead, where a narrow platform juts out over a tight arm of Banshee Canyon lined with cavernous walls.

From the picnic area, the trail soon merges with a shallow ravine that sinks through a few tight boulder-choked bends and enters Banshee Canyon's narrows. The crux is around the corner—a sheer 8-foot chimney polished into the tuff. A set of steel rings was anchored in the fall as a climbing aid. Two bends down there is a second fall with rings, similar in height. Below the falls, the narrows open up onto a long amphitheater cocooned by towering cliffs, host to an airy garden of boulders and Mojave yucca. The cliffs are pockmarked with innumerable holes of all sizes, like so many staring eyes. This is an imposing place, powerful in a disquieting way. Its name is said to have been inspired by the howling sound of the wind blowing through the canyon. It resembles the lament of banshee, a female spirit in Gaelic lore whose wailing was believed to forecast a death in a family. For the full effect, come here on a windy evening when the shadows moan.

This is the best part of a very short canyon; take the time to poke around. The tall slot in the south wall is blocked by an 18-foot fall. Even though holes have been chipped in the fall, it takes great skill to scale it. Arches abound. One of them goes right through a pyramidal wedge of rock. Another one is a slender slit faced with a shield. When the tuff cooled, differences in the welding and crystallization conditions created areas with different mechanical strengths. The tafoni and arches were formed by preferential erosion of the weaker areas. A variety of rock fragments can be identified in the tuff. Small pieces of gas-filled, gray to jay black lava are common. Softer, they erode faster, which explains the myriad minute holes in the walls.

The Rings Loop Trail. Just outside the amphitheater, a rock-lined trail meanders out to the edge of Wild Horse Canyon. It splits right away. The right fork is the Barber Peak Loop Trail. The left fork, the Rings Loop Trail, heads along the canyon, a broad valley framed by sheer-walled mesas. Every time I come here, I find myself beguiled by the pastoral charm of this desert scene. The valley floor is an undulating meadow of golden bushes, as radiant as the east African savanna, dramatically offset by the high auburn flank of Wild Horse Mesa. In the distance, a windmill stands vigil over the low buildings of a sleepy ranch. In hot weather, cottontails hide under the bushes. There is often a covey of quails within earshot. All that is missing to complete this blissful slice of nature is a babbling brook.

The trail wanders on beneath tall honeycombed cliffs, the equally spectacular backside of Banshee Canyon. The cliffs slowly evolve into columns of congealed lava, then screes of angular rhyolitic blocks, and finally a hillside of giant tuff boulders where the valley merges seamlessly with the open desert. Long ago, the natives pecked cryptic messages on these boulders. The soft tuff was not the wisest choice of data-storage material; the weather has taken its toll on the aging writings. But the boulders' pitted surfaces still hold dozens of pale signs, wig-

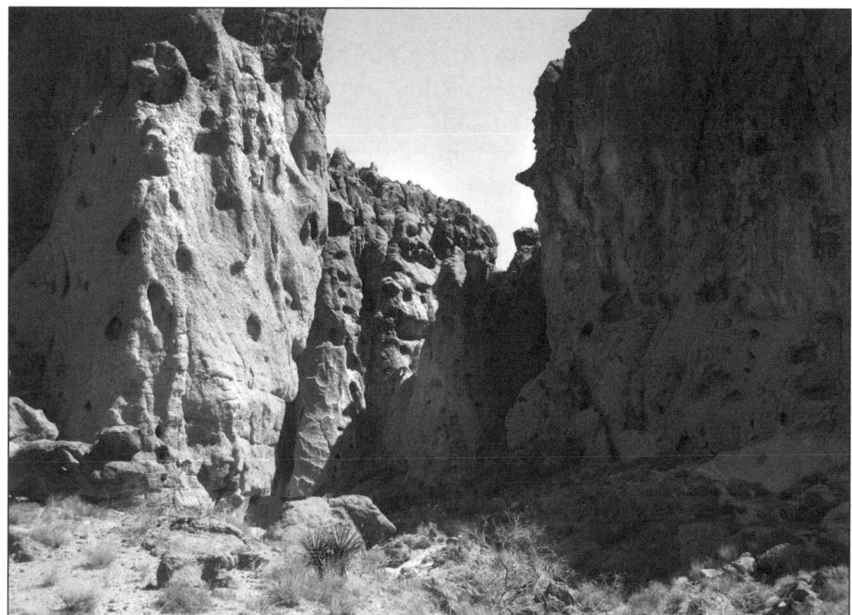

Pockmarked cliffs at the mouth of Banshee Canyon

gles, circles, and ghostly anthropomorphic figures. These entangled images remain more hermetic than the 17.8-million-year-old past of the boulders on which they are inscribed.

The rest of the trail snakes up a narrow sand wash along increasingly tall and rugged bluffs, taking you back where you started. The long mesa to the east is part of the Woods Mountains, the western rim of the awesome volcano that masterminded this volcanic apocalypse.

Barber Peak Loop Trail. This easy trail (5.1 miles for only about 760 feet of elevation gain) encircles the base of Barber Peak, the tall mesa that forms the backdrop of Hole-in-the-Wall. It has gained popularity in recent years as one of the very few longer trails advertised in the preserve. Although its northern half crosses the burn, this hike is well worth it if only to better appreciate the colorful local geology.

From the picnic area, the trail first heads north through pretty gardens of cacti, chollas, and Mojave yucca as it bypasses the campground. It then closely follows a sandy wash up around the mesa's northeastern base. This area has some of the most colorful exposures of Wild Horse Mesa Tuff, which makes up all of Barber Peak. The mesa's lower flanks rise steeply toward sculpted outcrops of gray and yellow tuffs. Higher up, a triple layer of cliffs interspaced by steep taluses caps the mesa. The cliffs are bittersweet chocolate columnar rhyolite; the taluses are peppered with green juniper. Down by the trail, long polished banks of light-beige volcanic ash protrude at several places. Filled with intriguing cavities and capped with dark rhyolitic boulders, they are great subjects for photography.

On the mesa's north side the trail reaches its highest point, then descends slowly into a broad drainage. For the next mile, the scenery up ahead is dominated by the Opalite Cliffs, an awesome buttress of pale fluted walls shooting 150 vertical feet to a spiky crown of ebony lava. Their namesake is an uncommon silicate mineral found in thick deposits of welded ash-flow tuff like this one. Shortly after merging with the Mid Hills Trail, the trail (in this area a ranching road) splits, then comes close to the cliffs. Don't pass up the short walk up to the base of the cliffs; from up close, the soaring walls command respect.

Below the cliffs, the trail continues along a broad wash, beneath a scenic rim of dark, jagged crags. The wash tapers down to a sand-filled corridor lined with catclaw as its two sides converge, then it ends abruptly at a short set of narrows that cut through a hard plug of gray welded volcanics. A small, sand-choked concrete dam blocks the head

Hole-in-the-Wall

	Dist.(mi)	Elev.(ft)
Rings Loop Trail		
Trailhead at Hole-in-the-Wall	0.0	4,280
Amphitheater	0.1	4,250
Banshee Cyn mouth/Trail jct	0.2	4,225
Information Center	1.2	4,255
Trailhead at Hole-in-the-Wall	1.4	4,280
Barber Peak Loop Trail		
Trailhead at Hole-in-the-Wall	0.0	4,280
Connecting trail to campgrd	0.65	~4,400
Campground loop (top)	(0.2)	4,355
Trail merges with road	2.0	~4,680
Fork in road	2.65	4,616
Opalite Cliffs	~3.0	~4,560
Trail leaves wash (narrows)	3.3	4,465
Jct to Hole-in-the-Wall (left)	4.1	4,300
Banshee Cyn/Rings Loop Trail	4.9	4,225
Trailhead at Hole-in-the-Wall	5.1	4,280

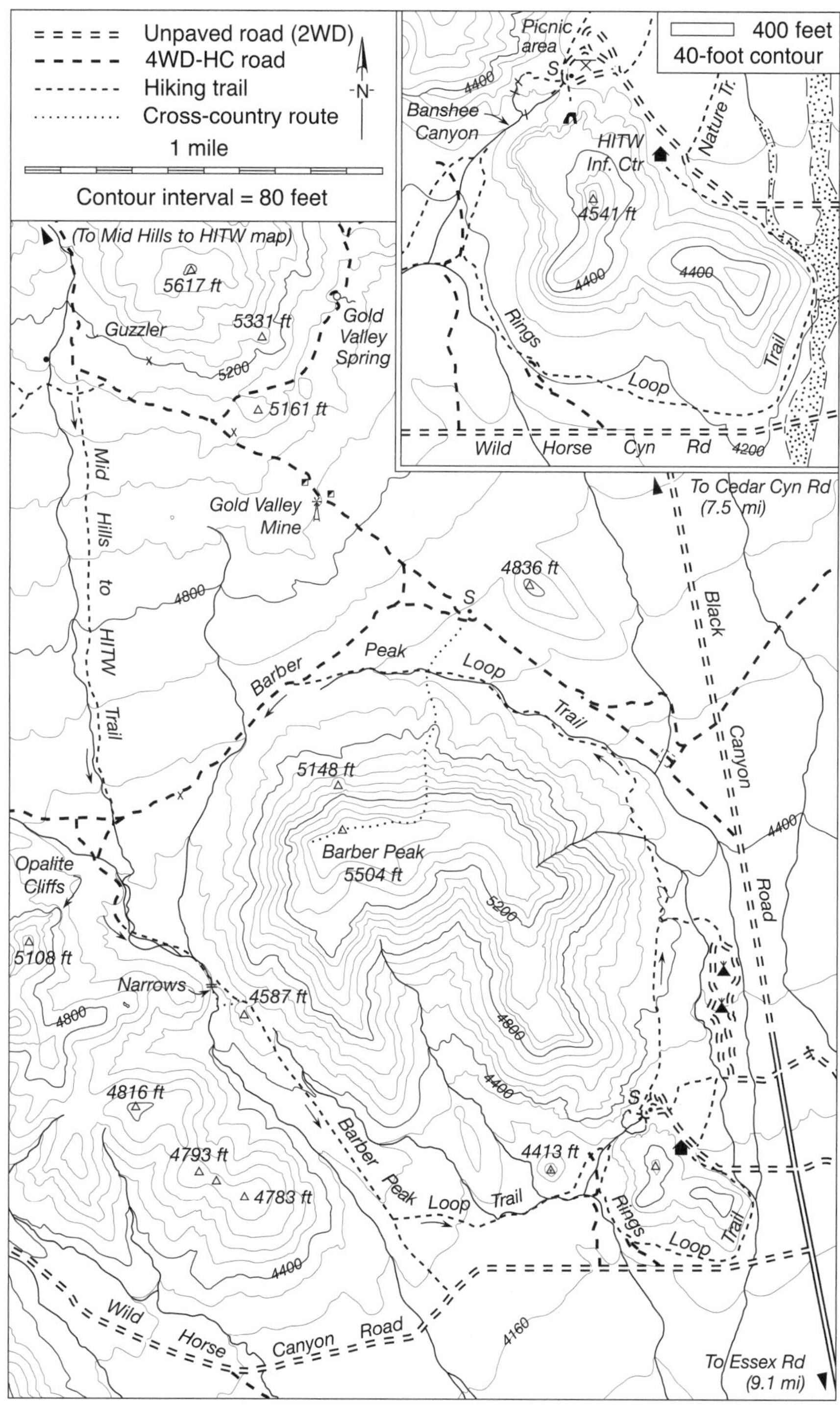
Unpaved road (2WD)
4WD-HC road
Hiking trail
Cross-country route
1 mile
N
Contour interval = 80 feet
400 feet
40-foot contour
Picnic area
Banshee Canyon
HITW Inf. Ctr
Nature Tr.
4541 ft
Rings Loop Trail
Wild Horse Cyn Rd
(To Mid Hills to HITW map)
5617 ft
Guzzler
5331 ft
Gold Valley Spring
5161 ft
Gold Valley Mine
Mid Hills to HITW Trail
To Cedar Cyn Rd (7.5 mi)
4836 ft
Black Canyon Road
Barber Peak Loop Trail
5148 ft
Barber Peak 5504 ft
Opalite Cliffs
5108 ft
Narrows
4587 ft
4816 ft
4793 ft
4783 ft
4413 ft
Wild Horse Canyon Road
To Essex Rd (9.1 mi)

of the narrows. Large chockstones are wedged between the blistered walls below it. Climbing down the dam and chockstones is risky, but there is an easy way into the narrows from below. Follow the trail as it bypasses this occlusion on higher ground on its east side. About 700 feet after the trail leaves the wash, hike down the open slope to the wash 130 feet below. The cool narrows are just up the wash.

Shortly after bypassing the narrows, the trail crests a high point, then descends into Wild Horse Canyon. The narrows effectively kept the 2005 wildfire in check: just south of them shiny cactus gardens crowd the slopes again, with such abandon compared to the burn you just left that the earth looks lush. Up ahead, Wild Horse Canyon's golden meadows unfold against great striated mesas. About 0.6 mile past the high point the trail reaches a junction. Go left to complete the loop. It is then a short walk, past a photogenic monument, to the trail junction below Banshee Canyon. The advantage of hiking this loop in this direction is that you leave the best part to the end—a stunning little canyon filled with wonders. Just be prepared to walk the extra mile on the Rings Loop Trail to get back to the picnic area, should you find that you cannot climb up the rings.

■

Wild Horse Mesa from the western rim of Barber Peak's mesa

BARBER PEAK

Barber Peak is the tall, steep-walled mesa composed of a particularly colorful stack of volcanic cliffs and taluses that parades at the heart of Hole-in-the-Wall. The climb to its flat top is very short but particularly steep, on 45% inclines studded with rocks, cactus, grasses, and photogenic charred trees, and crowned near the rim with pinyon pine and juniper. The tilted summit plateau commands awesome views of the deeply sculpted surrounding volcanic country.

General Information

Road status: Roadless; access from graded or primitive road (HC)
Barber Peak: 0.9 mi, 910 ft up, 40 feet down one way / moderate
Main attractions: Colorful volcanic rocks, views of Wild Horse Mesa
USGS 7.5′ topo map: Columbia Mountain
Maps: pp. 293*, *265*

Location and Access

From the turn-off to the Hole-in-the-Wall Information Center, drive the Black Canyon Road north 0.9 mile to a graded road at 10 o'clock. Take it 0.3 mile northwest to an old corral on the left, just past a 90° right bend. Turn left on a smaller dirt road that goes through the corral. Go 0.8 mile, along the base of Barber Peak rising to the southwest, to a faint spur on the left, near the western tip of a low hill to the right, and park. This last road has a few bumps that require decent clearance.

Route Description

The north face of Barber Peak is a grand staircase of four discontinuous bands of cliffs smothered under long screes of alluvia. The colorful Wild Horse Mesa Tuff pokes through in short banks of white vol-

Barber Peak		
	Dist.(mi)	Elev.(ft)
Road	0.0	4,629
Crossing Barber Peak Loop Tr.	0.2	4,590
Mesa's rim	0.65	~5,415
Barber Peak	0.9	5,504
Wild Horse Mesa viewpoint	1.0	~5,480

canic ash at lower elevation, and as cliffs of cavernous gray tuff and columnar rhyolite the color of cocoa higher up. South-southwest from the starting point, a long ramp of alluvia extends out from about the middle of the base of the mountain. It is the lower end of a narrow landslide that spills down from rim to base over all four cliff bands, providing a convenient passage over them. Descend toward the ramp across the open fan. After 0.2 mile, cross the Barber Peak Loop Trail, then the wash just beyond it. The ramp starts right across the wash. Its short nose climbs steeply to a long, more level bench, crisscrossed by cattle tracks, that soon meets the foot of the mesa (0.15 mile). From there it is a stiff climb up the mesa's steepening flank to the rim—an elevation gain of 600 feet in 0.3 mile. At the first two cliff crossings, the ramp pinches down to a narrow neck littered with boulders. The third crossing is almost imperceptible. The last one, just below the rim, is a jumble of angular boulders and woody shrubs (hands help). The rest is an easy walk up the gently tilted mesa top to the subdued summit.

Since the area was ravaged by the 2005 Hackberry Fire Complex, the vegetation has selectively recovered. Grasses dominate, and most types of cactaceae have grown back—barrel and calico cactus, chollas, pancake prickly-pear, and blue yucca. The whole mountain is studded with the silver and charcoal skeletons of the many pinyon pines that succumbed to the blaze. The highest slopes are still green with pygmy cedar, Mormon tea, and the full crowns of the lucky pines that survived. The broad, sloping mesa top is a scrawny tundra of small rocks and dwarf shrubs combed by the strong local winds—tuffs of blond grass, vermillion buckwheat, silvery grizzly bear cactus—and a scatter of juniper. It is a disquieting place, populated by a silent army of tree ghosts, permeated with the quiet sadness of desolation.

Barber Peak's lopsided plateau offers many good vista points, best discovered by walking its irregular perimeter. On all sides the mesa drops precipitously to grassy valleys—Gold Valley, Wild Horse Canyon, and Black Canyon Wash—each one as radiant as an African savanna. From the east rim and on the way up, there are great views of Table Mountain's iconic silhouette and of the Woods Mountains' long, prominently banded mesa. The highlight is the alien viewpoint at the mesa's west end. Sharp volcanic peaks bristling with pinnacles rise way down below, buttressed at their tip by the white fluted bluffs of the Opalite Cliffs. The terraced cliffs of Wild Horse Mesa rear up behind them, capped on the horizon by the outline of the Providence Mountains' spiky summits. It is a spellbinding landscape, tormented and primeval, carved right into the bowels of an apocalypse.

■

— 10 —

PROVIDENCE MOUNTAINS

WITH NEARLY 30 MILES of rugged crestline bisecting the high desert like an impassable barrier, the Providence Mountains rank amongst the most formidable ranges in the eastern Mojave Desert. Thanks to a particularly varied geology and elevations spanning from around 2,500 feet to over 7,000 feet, they offer one of the greatest diversities of terrains and natural features in the preserve—caves, volcanic tablelands, boulder fields, high summits, rough canyons, forested slopes, and a generous allotment of springs. Add to this cornucopia spectacular cactus and yucca gardens, an unusually high density of derelict mines, mills, and mining camps, and you are looking at more action-packed days of exploration in the wild than most people get to experience in a lifetime.

Providence Mountains State Recreation Area

Although most of this range lies within the Mojave National Preserve's boundaries, 5,900 acres on its eastern slopes are protected by the state of California as the Providence Mountains State Recreation Area (SRA). From a recreational standpoint, this enclave is particularly meaningful. It contains the famous Mitchell Caverns and the range's spectacular sawtoothed crest, including Fountain Peak (6,988') and Edgar Peak (7,162'), the highest point and one of the highest summits in the eastern Mojave Desert. The Essex Road, the potholed byway that winds up to the SRA, ends at the park's tiny visitor center, the picturesque stone cabin of Jack and Ida Mitchell, where the couple offered lodging and guided tours of the caverns until 1954. The backcountry looming behind the cabin holds a wealth of outdoor opportunities,

Suggested Backcountry Drives in the Providence Mountains					
Route/Destination	Dist. (mi)	Lowest elev.	Highest elev.	Road type	Pages
Aqueduct Road	4.1	2,110'	2,990'	H	303-305
Big Horn Mine Road	2.9	2,959'	3,830'	H	347-350
Bonanza King Mine Road*	4.4	3,517'	4,180'	F	323-324
Clipper Valley Road	8.8	2,850'	3,020'	P	347
Hidden Hill Mine	4.9	3,275'	3,835'	H	351
Macedonia Canyon Road	6.3	3,070'	4,947'	H	299
Providence Mine	~7.0	2,850'	3,730'	H	343
Vulcan Mine Rd/gas-line rd	13.6	2,380'	4,790'	F	309-310
Key: P=Primitive (2WD) H=Primitive (HC) F=Primitive (4WD)					

from deep rugged canyons to lush springs, colorful geology, multiple plant communities, and rough hiking routes to the crest. Most visitors, however, come here for the tour of the limestone caverns, located a short walk from the visitor center. The SRA also has a small campground—it has all of six sites—which is part of its charm. But it makes it up in quality. Overlooking the preserve's wide-open eastern valleys, it is charged with wild scenery, especially at sunset, and in the hot season it is a great place to sleep away from the heat.

Access and Backcountry Roads

Throughout recent history, ruggedness has been the Providence Mountains' best protection. Only one road was ever built across this range, a gas and power-line maintenance road that scoots over Foshay Pass, a low notch in the crest just south of the central mountain block. The Macedonia Canyon Road clips the very northern tip of the mountains. All other roads are cul-de-sacs that peter out in the foothills. On the steeper west side, only five roads provide access to the range—from north to south the Globe Mine Road, the Aqueduct Road to Cornfield Spring, the road to the Rex Mine, and the two short side roads that converge near Arrowweed Spring. On the east side there are a few more choices. The Wild Horse Canyon Road and the partly paved Black Canyon Road are good starting points to visit the colorful volcanic mesas in the northeastern portion of the mountains. The Ranch Road, and the Bonanza King Mine Road that branches off it, give access to the historic Bonanza King Mine. South from there the paved Essex Road climbs to timberline in the Providence Mountains

SRA. Along the southern half of the mountains, a few beat-up roads branching off the Clipper Valley Road climb east to abandoned mines, including the Big Horn Mine and the Providence Mine. At the southern tip of the mountains the Hidden Hill Road circles around to Hidden Hill, then goes on for many empty miles across Clipper Valley and Fenner Valley to Fenner. These roads span all levels of difficulty. The Macedonia Canyon Road (once a great ride through a forested gulch) can be traveled, at least downhill, with a sedan, while others are so rough most vehicles cannot make it all the way.

Geology

The Providence Mountains have the greatest diversity of formations in the preserve. Volcanic, intrusive, metamorphic, and sedimentary rocks vie for space on the mountains' convoluted geologic map, which is cut by the East Providence Fault Zone along much of the length of the mountains, the Hidden Hill Fault Zone in the southern part, and several normal faults. This complex lithology can be divided into four distinct areas of related rock units. The northern third, from around Columbia Mountain down to the large canyon east of Kelso, is composed mostly of gneiss around 1.7 billion years old. There is also a small exposure of Granite of Tough Nut Spring south of Globe Canyon, and of Mid Hills Adamellite in the foothills further west, as well as west of Columbia Mountain. The middle third, down to Foshay Pass, exposes the region's incomplete sequence of sedimentary formations, generally getting younger eastward, from Stirling Quartzite (Late Proterozoic) to the Bird Spring Formation (into the Permian). The exception is a few square miles of Fountain Peak Rhyolite (Middle Jurassic) on and around Fountain Peak and Edgar Peak, responsible for the scenic spires exposed around the high crest. The southern third, south from Foshay Pass, is almost all Middle Jurassic intrusive rocks. Much of it is Quartz Monzonite of Goldstone. The Horse Hills are made of Syenogranite of Quail Spring, Providence Peak of Quartz Syenite of Winston Basin, and the Arrowweed Spring area of Late Cretaceous garnet monzogranite. Finally, the Wild Horse Mesa area, which abuts the northeast flank of the mountains, exposes a thick stack of Miocene volcanics, mostly ash-flow tuff and lava flows.

Mining History

Between the first discovery of mineral assets in 1880 and the 1950s, close to 170 mines were opened in the Providence Mountains, by far the largest number in the preserve. The greatest concentrations were on the west slopes between Macedonia Canyon and Tough Nut Spring,

Suggested Hikes in the Providence Mountains					
Route/Destination	Dist. (mi)	Elev. gain	Mean elev.	Access road	Pages
Short hikes (under 5 miles round trip)					
Big Horn Mine (Mabel)					
from four-road junction	1.0	640'	4,040'	F/10.3 mi	349-350
Bonanza King Mine					
from Ranch Road*	4.6	1,410'	3,820'	Graded	323-330
from steep grade*	0.8	240'	4,150'	H/2.1 mi	327-330
from Y junction*	3.0	530'	3,930'	H/0.8 mi	323-330
Cornfield Spring	1.8	730'	3,260'	H/4.1 mi	305-308
Cornfield Spr. Consol. Mine	1.9	830'	3,220'	H/4.1 mi	308
Crystal Spring Trail	0.8	880'	4,600'	Paved	340
Fountain Peak (north ridge)	2.4	2,940'	5,670'	Paved	340-342
Fountain Peak (south ridge)	2.2	2,880'	5,630'	Paved	340-342
Golden Queen Mill & shaft	0.1	50'	3,350'	H/4.9 mi	354
Hidden Hill	0.9	690'	3,630'	H/4.9 mi	356
Hidden Hill Mine Trail	0.75	370'	3,510'	H/4.9 mi	354-356
Mary Beal Nature Trail*	0.4	150'	4,330'	Paved	337-338
Mitchell Caverns*	1.0	~460'	4,320'	Paved	336
Niña Mora Trail	0.3	220'	4,220'	Paved	338
Providence Mine	1.6	1,100'	4,260'	H/8.8	343-344
Providence Peak	2.4	2,810'	5,020'	H/8.8	343-346
Quail Spr. Basin viewpoint	2.1	800'	4,180'	P/0.9 mi	318-320
Silver King Mine	0.6	180'	3,930'	H/1.4 mi	326-327
Vulcan Mine				Graded	
east ore body loop*	2.4	730'	4,120'		316
pit-overlook loop*	1.8	290'	3,980'		312-314
Vulcan Lake	0.4	140'	3,860'		314
Intermediate hikes (5-12 miles round trip)					
Big Horn Mine (Mabel)				H/8.7 mi	
from washout	2.6	1,180'	3,720'		348-350
Quail Spring Basin Trail				P/0.9 mi	
loop*	5.7	970'	4,220'		318-320
to Golden Queen Mill	5.4	2,000'	4,000'		318-322

Key: P=Primitive (2WD) H=Primitive (HC) F=Primitive (4WD)
Distance: one way, except for loops (round-trip, marked with *)
Elev. gain: sum of all elevation gains on a round-trip basis & on loops

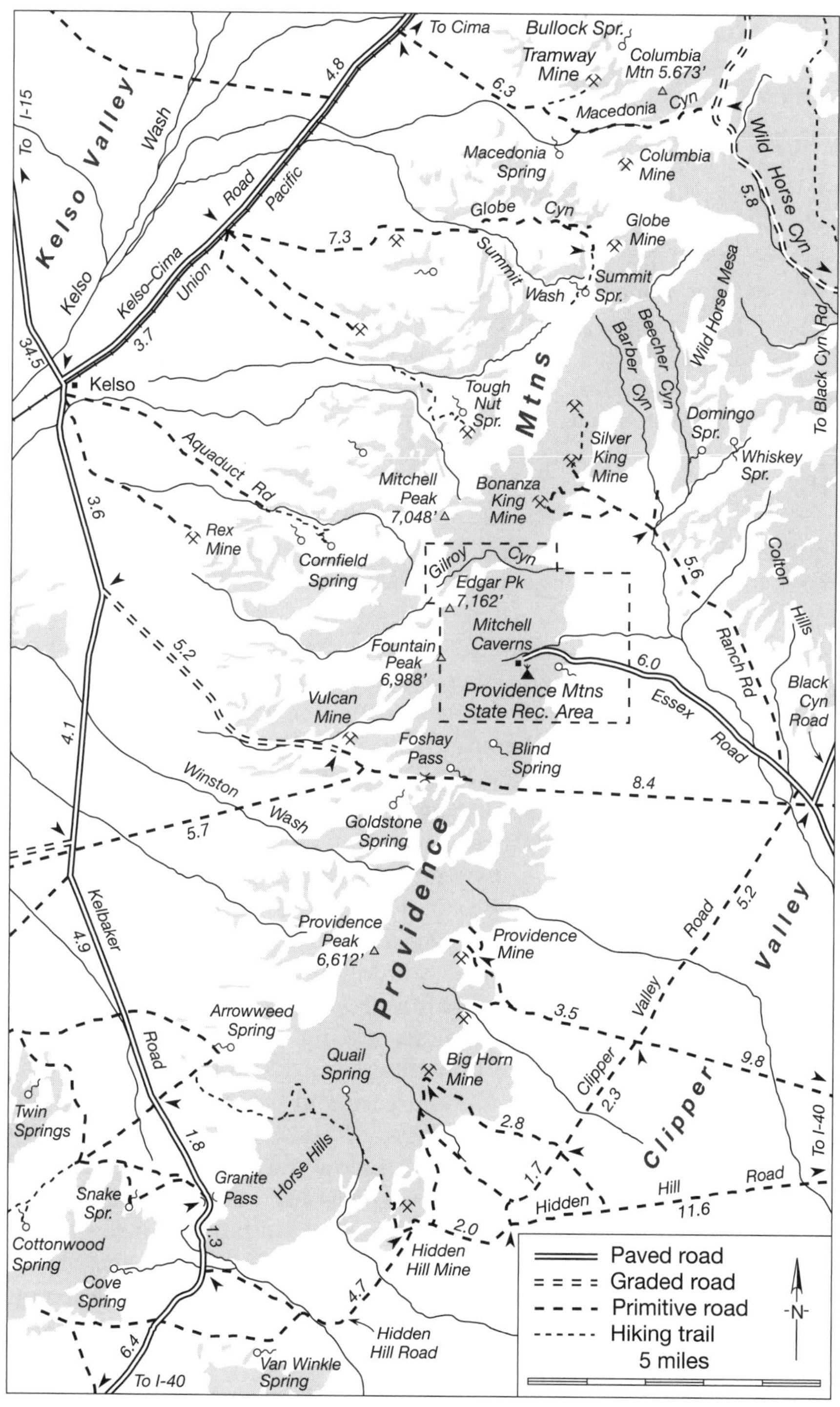
To Cima
Bullock Spr.
Tramway Mine
Columbia Mtn 5,673'
Macedonia Cyn
Macedonia Spring
Columbia Mine
Wild Horse Cyn
Kelso Valley
Wash
To I-15
Kelso-Cima Road
Union Pacific
Kelso
Globe Cyn
Globe Mine
Summit Wash
Summit Spr.
Wild Horse Mesa
Beecher Cyn
Barber Cyn
To Black Cyn Rd
Tough Nut Spr.
Mtns
Domingo Spr.
Whiskey Spr.
Silver King Mine
Kelso
Aquaduct Rd
Mitchell Peak 7,048'
Bonanza King Mine
Rex Mine
Cornfield Spring
Gilroy Cyn
Edgar Pk 7,162'
Colton Hills
Mitchell Caverns
Fountain Peak 6,988'
Providence Mtns State Rec. Area
Essex Road
Ranch Rd
Black Cyn Road
Vulcan Mine
Foshay Pass
Blind Spring
Winston Wash
Goldstone Spring
Providence
Providence Peak 6,612'
Providence Mine
Valley
Clipper Valley Road
Kelbaker Road
Arrowweed Spring
Twin Springs
Quail Spring
Big Horn Mine
Clipper
To I-40
Horse Hills
Granite Pass
Snake Spr.
Cottonwood Spring
Cove Spring
Hidden Hill Road
Hidden Hill Mine
Hidden Hill Road
Van Winkle Spring
To I-40
4.8
6.3
5.8
7.3
3.7
34.5
3.6
5.6
6.0
5.2
8.4
4.1
5.7
5.2
4.9
3.5
9.8
2.3
1.8
2.8
1.7
11.6
1.3
2.0
4.7
6.4
Paved road
Graded road
Primitive road
Hiking trail
5 miles
N

in particular around Globe Canyon, the Colton Hills, and Goldstone Spring, and on the southeastern slope between Providence Peak and Hidden Hill. Most mines shipped either only a few tons of high-grade ore or nothing at all. But a handful did stand above the rest. Between 1898 and 1943 the Big Horn Mine put out at least $130,000 worth of gold. In the 1895–1914 period the Hidden Hill Mine did about half as well. The Francis Copper Mine probably reached the $50,000 mark in copper. Most impressive are the two mines that made this range famous. The Bonanza King Mine, on the east side, was this desert's second largest silver producer: between 1880 and 1924 it made close to $1.9 million. The Vulcan Mine, below Foshay Pass, was the richest historic mine in the region, bar none. In just a few years around World War II it harvested nearly $7.5 million in iron.

Hiking

Thanks to the abundance and unique combination of natural and human history, there are more good hikes to glean out of these mountains than any other range in the preserve. Some of them are bound to become classics. Most canyons in the heart of the range are roadless. The west-side canyons draining the main mountain block tend to be short but steep and rough. The east-side canyons are generally a little easier, and so are canyons further north (for example Saddle Horse and Borrego canyons). Globe Canyon, one of the longest, was nicely forested until the Hackberry Fire Complex torched most of it. In its south fork, the short trail to Summit Spring is still worth a visit, although cattle have degraded the spring. The forgotten ruins of a nice little mill still cling to a narrow stretch of canyon below the spring.

The long crest offers a broad spectrum of peak climbs, some of them covered in the following pages. Among other prominent summits, Edgar Peak can be climbed by trudging up Gilroy Canyon or traversing the obstacle-riddled crest from Fountain Peak. Mitchell Peak is typically climbed from the Bonanza King Mine up its steep and crooked west shoulder. The unnamed summit 0.3 mile south-southwest of Fountain Peak is in the preserve and can be reached without going through the SRA. From Foshay Pass, hike to nearby Foshay Spring, gain access to the crest, then follow the crest, a difficult route with some loose rocks and scrambling. This summit is less than 30 feet lower than Fountain Peak, but the views are almost as phenomenal. For an easy climb, consider Columbia Mountain. From Macedonia Canyon, an abandoned track closed to motor vehicles will guide you easily clear to the summit.

■

CORNFIELD SPRING

The second largest in the preserve, Cornfield Spring is beautifully situated beneath the towering scarp of the Providence Mountains. For years its water was piped by a long aqueduct to the town of Kelso. Today, a bouncy ride up the rough aqueduct road and a modest hike will take you to the spring's lively perennial creek and lush vegetation. This is a peaceful place, far away from everything, livened by the soothing sound of flowing water. This visit can be extended to include a nearby hematite mine, or a hike up steep-walled forested canyons to awe-inspiring retreats in the mountains.

General Information

Road status: Hiking mostly on 4WD road and trail; 4WD access road
Cornfield Spring: 1.8 mi, 640 ft up, 90 ft down one way / easy
Cornfield Sprgs Cons. Mine: 1.9 mi, 550 ft up, 280 ft down / easy–moder.
Main attractions: A spring with perennial creek, historic pipeline
USGS 7.5' topo maps: Kelso, Fountain Peak*
Maps: pp. 307*, *301*

Location and Access

Cornfield Spring is located at the western foot of the Providence Mountains, about 5 air miles southeast of Kelso. In historic days, this abundant spring was tapped by an aqueduct. The service road that followed the aqueduct, although badly beaten up today, is still the best way to reach the spring. In Kelso, drive south on the Kelbaker Road across the railroad tracks, and make a left almost immediately at a wide open space of compacted sand. Look for the dirt road that heads south, paralleling the Kelbaker Road, and drive it 0.2 mile to a narrower road that angles to the left. This is the old Aqueduct Road.

History: Water, Water, Everyone?

Being one of a very few springs with a permanent stream in an area the size of a small country, Cornfield Spring has been coveted over time by many, from native Americans from time immemorial to railroad engineers, housewives, hard-rock miners, and, more recently, researchers loaded with advanced degrees. The first modern-time interest in Cornfield Spring goes back to early 1905, when Kelso was put into service upon completion of the San Pedro, Los Angeles & Salt Lake Railroad. As the base for extra steam-powered locomotives that helped trains climb the steep grade to Kessler Summit (now known as Cima), Kelso needed lots of water. To meet this need, the railroad turned to Cornfield Spring, in the foothills of the Providence Mountains a few miles from the tracks. A 5.5-mile gravity pipeline was installed from the spring all the way down the alluvial fan to a storage tank about a mile south of town, where locomotives stopped to refill before their long climb. The water was also used in town by Kelso residents, mostly railroad workers and their families.

In 1942, it was the turn of mining engineers to set their sights on the spring's copious flow. When the Vulcan Mine, a few miles south of the spring, was opened for large-scale exploitation in December, it also needed plenty of water for its mill. By arrangement with the railroad company, the mine started trucking water from the storage tank up to the mine on a regular basis. Over the next five years, the Vulcan Mine produced 2.6 million tons of ore, an overwhelming success of which the Cornfield Spring was a vital component.

The pipeline water continued to be used at Kelso by the railroad for many years—the spring was then referred to as Union Pacific Spring—until diesel engines replaced steam engines and the spring was supplanted by well water. But Cornfield Spring continued to draw attention, this time not as a resource but as a sheer anomaly. Over the last few decades, water engineers, herpetologists, and botanists have visited the spring to research the fascinating aspects of its lush environment. They have found that it has been an isolated source of water for so long that it hosts species of plants and animals that live nowhere else for tens of miles around. Like the miners and engineers of long ago, scientists unearthed precious treasures, all borne by the power of water.

Route Description

The Aqueduct Road. For most of its length, this road is one messy field of stones, often rutted, sometimes steeply canted or hemmed in by roadside vegetation. Unless bumping your head with the ceiling a few hundred times is your idea of fun, you will have to drive very slowly, and it will take upwards of 45 minutes to cover 4.1 miles. Under duress, we can probably *walk* there faster... The scenery is uneventful at first, as the road cavorts its way up a long alluvial plain covered with creosote bush and dessicated shrubs. At several places, sections of the buried aqueduct's large rusted pipes are exposed along the road. After the road has gained a little elevation, it enters a more interesting desert garden, and the views of the approaching mountains grow increasingly impressive.

The Providence Mountains and Aqueduct Road near Cornfield Spring

After 4.1 miles, the road reaches the foothills and a small corral on the right, then it descends gently into a wide wash filled with large rocks. The wash crossing is manageable, but just past it the road climbs straight up a long and steep embankment and turns downright nasty. Erosion has stripped this stretch to bedrock and gouged in it ruts large enough for a cow to get stuck. Seasoned four-wheelers will enjoy the challenge of wiggling their way up this exquisite mess, but most drivers will prefer to park near the corral (turning around in the wash is not easy) and walk the rest of the way.

The upper road. This is an easy hike, along a well-defined road that winds over beautiful blue-limestone mosaics, up and down a broad swell sprinkled with yucca and cacti. The highlight is the stunning views of the Providence Mountains. This is one of the truly awesome mountain fronts in the preserve, and this is the best trail to see it close-up. The whole way you will be facing the range's rugged western front, a complex tapestry of deeply chiseled buttresses and abrupt walls crowned by pine-covered taluses. Rising 3,300 feet in less than a mile, and dominated by 7,162-foot Edgar Peak, this massive barrier of stone is spectacular, looming more ominously with every step you take. In the dead of winter, snow on the summits adds another striking element to the scenery.

Cornfield Spring. After two sharp bends and 1.5 miles, the road ends just as it joins the upper portion of the pipeline, within earshot of Cornfield Spring. Blessed with a year-round stream and a scenic setting, this relatively large spring is one of only a handful of its kind in the eastern Mojave Desert. Its long and narrow carpet of greenery winds lazily along a broad, shallow ravine, nestled a short distance from the Providence Mountains. For almost half a mile, clear water flows over moss-covered stones, forming a chain of tranquil pools linked by tiny cascades. Although nowhere wider than a few feet, this little creek supports a diverse botanical garden where Mormon tea and cheesebush thrive next to squawbush and baccharis. At the head of the spring, water gurgles under a tangle of catclaw and desert willow. Just a few feet away, the ground is dry and barren again, dotted with the usual gangs of yucca, cholla, and barrel cactus. In late spring and early summer, the aromatic bell-shaped flowers of desert willow grace the stream banks. Later in the year, when the thickets of rabbitbrush lining the creek are in bloom, the whole spring lights up with a golden glow. In spite of all this vegetation, the heroic creek spends most of its brief life in open terrain, precariously exposed to the full sun. In the intense heat of summer, its vulnerability is so painfully obvious that its very survival strains our comprehension.

At the end of the road, the pipeline, intact from this point on, follows a trail overlooking the spring. For the most part, the spring's dense vegetation and lack of open banks preclude access to the creek. To discover this fragile microcosm without damaging it, follow the short pipeline trail, now invaded by creosote and barrel cactus. It will give you a good bird's-eye view of the area. After a few hundred feet there is a place where you can walk down a steep slab to the creek's edge. If you can find a level spot to sit quietly, you might receive the visit of dragonflies, water skimmers, a bird sneaking in for a quick sip, perhaps a western banded gecko, a wary desert iguana, or a nervous cottontail. In the evening you will be serenaded by the red-spotted toads that live along the creek, their universe confined to this skinny acre of land irrigated by a providential spring.

After 200 yards, the aqueduct disappears under the brush near its intake, and the trail ends. If you have time, climb to higher ground and walk upstream to and around the head of the spring. Watch for snakes. At least seven species have been spotted in this area, including the beautiful but venomous speckled rattlesnake. Like the slabs by the creek and the angular rocks supporting the aqueduct along the trail, the hard ledges of cream-colored rock you will cross about 50 feet above the creek are made of a fresh-water limestone called travertine.

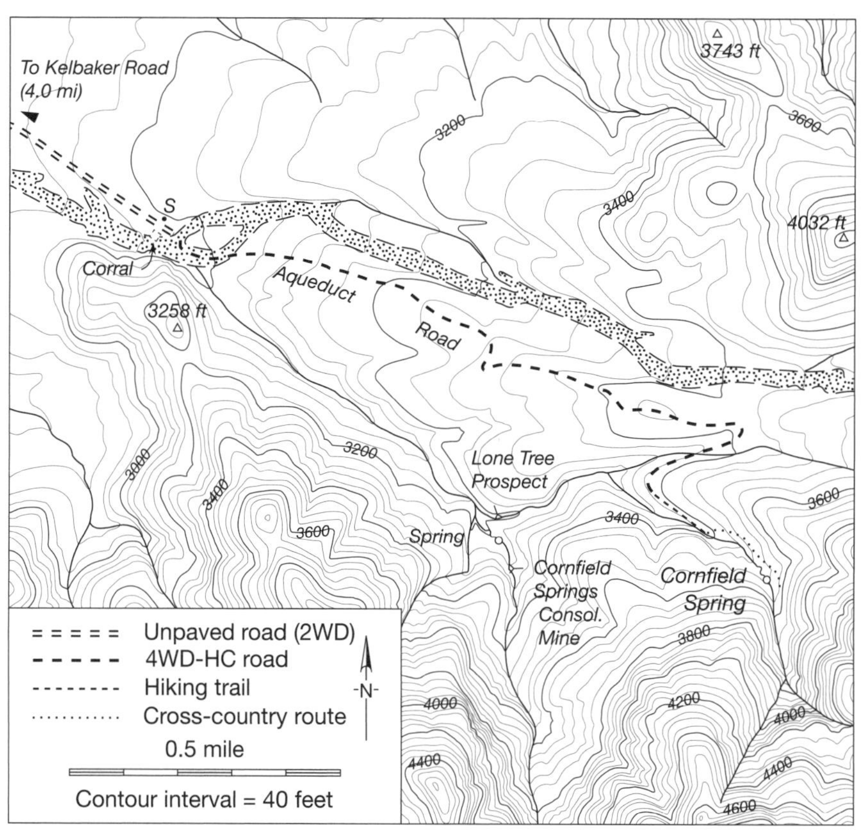

Cornfield Spring		
	Dist.(mi)	Elev.(ft)
Aqueduct Road		
Union Pacific Railroad at Kelso	0.0	2,125
Aqueduct Road	0.25	2,110
Corral before wash crossing	4.35	2,990
Upper road (hiking)		
Corral	0.0	2,990
High point in road	1.1	3,430
Wash crossing	1.3	3,360
Cornfield Sprgs. Consol. Mine	(0.6)	~3,260
End of road / foot trail	1.45	3,380
Aqueduct intake	1.6	3,395
Cornfield Spring (head)	1.8	3,540

It was deposited by the same little stream that now hugs the bottom of the ravine. Their sheer thickness bears witness to the fact that at one time, not very long ago, the climate was considerably wetter and the stream had a much stronger flow.

A jaunt into the Providence Mountains. The large canyon and its two tributaries just east of the spring rank among the most spectacular in the preserve. There is no way to get through them without serious rock climbing—this is as good as canyoneering gets around here. But take time to amble up their very steep rock-strewn washes. You do not have to go far to get exposed to the magnificence of this stunning range. Soon you will be surrounded by towering cliffs several thousand feet tall. I rested in a deep cove sprinkled with pinyon pine and juniper, gazing in awe at giant draperies of limestone shooting skyward to hidden peaks. Few places offer such imposing scenery in this part of the Mojave Desert.

Cornfield Springs Consolidated Mine. Along the aqueduct route not far below the spring there are a couple of old mines. Trace back your steps 800 feet down the road to the wash crossing before the switchback. Follow this dry wash downhill about 800 feet to its junction with the Cornfield Spring wash, then hike down this wash 0.25 mile to the short copper tunnel of the Lone Tree Prospect. The wash is irrigated underground by the spring overflow, so it is locally overgrown, but walking is fairly easy. The more interesting workings of the Cornfield Springs Consolidated Mine are located 0.1 mile up the next side canyon on the south side.

Little is known about the history of this mine. It might have been discovered around 1905 when the aqueduct was installed, around 1902 when the area was prospected for iron, or even earlier. What is known is that the main tunnel was already several hundred feet long in 1909. This early exploratory work showed that the deposit contained 110,000 tons of high-quality ore averaging 60% in iron. But in iron-mine parlance, this is pocket money, and it was never fully developed. The only known production was 200 tons during World War I. The original vein, up to 230 feet thick, is still in the ground. The site has a couple of shafts and two tunnels, most of them inaccessible, as well as three small pits. The ore that crops out is hard specular hematite, a nice variety of hematite with a blue-gray color and a bright metallic luster.

■

THE VULCAN MINE

Of the hundreds of mines in our national parks, the Vulcan Mine is one of only a few that exploited iron on a large scale. Between 1942 and 1947, it produced 2.6 million tons of iron ore, a figure that made it the eastern Mojave Desert's richest mine. Visiting this mine and its ruins gives us a chance to explore a scenic corner of the Providence Mountains. The highlight is the mine's gaping pit, an amazing window into the Earth where vertical walls of massive yellow and black iron oxides plunge straight into an emerald lake.

General Information

Road status: Hiking on old roads and cross-country; 2WD access road
Vulcan Lake: 0.4 mi, 40 ft up, 100 ft down one way / very easy
Vulcan Mine pit-overlook loop: 1.8 mi, 290 ft up loop / easy
Vulcan Mine east-ore-body loop: 2.4 mi, 730 ft up loop / easy
Main attractions: A historic iron mine, geology, scenery
USGS 7.5' topo map: Fountain Peak
Maps: pp. 315*, *301*

Location and Access

The Vulcan Mine is in an open canyon on the western slope of the Providence Mountains, south of Fountain Peak. From the stop sign at Kelso, drive the Kelbaker Road 3.6 miles south to the Vulcan Mine Road, on the east side just before a sharp right bend. From the south, this junction is 4.1 miles north of the Kelso Dunes Road. This is the road that was used in the 1940s to haul out the ore. Gently sloped and still partly paved, it is passable with a sedan. After 5.0 miles you will reach a first side road on the left, which was the western access road to the Vulcan Mine. It ends shortly at a large concrete structure below the mine's huge tailing. The second side road 0.2 mile further, lined with desert willow, was the main (eastern) access road. It is blocked off after 50 yards by a fence. Park near this junction and hike in.

The Vulcan Mine can also be reached from the east side of the mountains—but it takes more work. At the junction between the Essex Road and the Black Canyon Road, a wide and straight dirt road runs west to the Providence Mountains. It services an underground pressurized gas line. Proceed on this road 7 miles to Foshay Pass, marked by a yellow gas-line valve. West of the pass, there is a first steep downgrade for 0.3 mile. There is an even steeper and rockier downgrade up ahead.

To bypass it, take the side road on the left at the bottom of the first grade. At the junction 0.2 mile further, head right, back to the main road at the foot of the second grade. At the next junction (0.45 mile), turn right off the service road onto the upper end of the Vulcan Mine Road. The eastern access road is 0.5 mile further. High clearance is imperative for this route, as well as lots of power to drive it eastbound.

Geology: The Making of Iron

The Vulcan iron deposit was formed by a process called metasomatism. Deep below the surface, a small batholith of magma intruded limestone of the Bonanza King Formation. Near the contact zone, over a distance of at least two miles, the combination of extreme heat and pressure slowly baked the limestone to a crisp finish, wiping out its bedding and turning it into crystalline marble. The ridge east of the mine is partly made of marble from this ancient intrusion. As the limestone was pried apart, it was intensely fissured, which created pathways for mineral solutions from the magma to diffuse into it. The main mineral was iron, which oxidized to hematite and magnetite. Many other minerals also formed in smaller quantities, but no copper, which is uncommon for a metasomatic deposit. A few million years ago, this buried fortune was uplifted by tectonic forces and subsequently uncovered by erosion. After this random series of events, almost all of the iron ore still ended up concentrated in one large deposit, well exposed, and unusually soft—a perfect scenario for quarrying.

History: The Iron Man

The Vulcan Mine was a late bloomer: first discovered in 1902, its deposit remained largely untouched for four decades. But it rose to stardom with a vengeance. By 1947, it was the richest mine the eastern Mojave Desert ever had, and it remains today a rare success story in the history of desert mining in California.

The first prominent figure in the mine's history was Charles Colcock Jones, a mining engineer from Los Angeles who first visited the property in the spring of 1906 while on a professional trip in the area. Well experienced in iron deposits, Jones quickly realized the Vulcan's outstanding commercial value. Two years later, he secured rights to it with five patented claims. Rather than financing its development himself, he patiently waited for an opportunity to sell. In spite of its growing economic and demographic importance, the West Coast had no facilities for producing iron. Over the next few years, Jones repeatedly called attention to this anomaly at conferences and in mining journals. In southern California alone, he argued, some 200 million tons of high-grade iron ore were waiting to be exploited. Iron could be mined and smelted in the region where it would be used, hence reducing transportation costs. In the meantime, a few open cuts and a 100-foot tunnel were developed on his Vulcan claims through at least the 1920s to expose the formation and confirm its economic value.

Jones' strategy paid off. Around the late 1930s, he sold his claims to Henry John Kaiser, a self-taught industrialist who had achieved fame and wealth by masterminding an impressive road-building empire. It is the same Henry Kaiser who, a few years later, would co-found for his employees one of the country's first health maintenance organizations, Kaiser Permanente, the same HMO that now provides health care to tens of millions of Americans. Kaiser needed steel for the mass production of commercial and military ships at his West Coast shipyards, and for many vital industrial uses throughout the budding western states. World War II was raging, and heavy metals were also in high demand worldwide. Kaiser had already erected a huge steel smelter in Fontana, near San Bernardino, and to fuel his plant he proceeded to buy all the iron deposits he could lay his hands on. The Vulcan was up for sale, so it was the first to be exploited.

The Vulcan Mine had two major assets. First, based on bore holes and a tunnel that passed through nearly half a mile of ore, Kaiser knew he was sitting on at least six million tons of ore. Second, it was backed by a competent and financially secure organization. So, unlike most desert mines, the Vulcan Mine was developed in style. Between December 1942 and July 1947, a team of about 100 explosives experts, shovel operators, truck drivers, foremen, and engineers proceeded to excise this huge iron blister from the side of the mountain. To match the Fontana smelter capacity, about 2,500 tons of ore were shipped every day—a heap the size of a one-story house. Until 1943, the ore was removed from a wide staircase-like quarry 130 feet deep. The ore was blasted with dynamite, shoveled into trucks, then hauled to an on-site jaw crusher. The average blast ripped up 30,000 tons of ore, which took nearly two weeks to grind. Every hour of every day, trucks bounced down the long paved road to Kelso, where it was loaded into Union Pacific gondolas and sent by rail to the Fontana smelter.

After the above-ground portion of the deposit was exhausted, mining proceeded downward into an open pit that traced the oblong contour of the deposit. The pit was excavated in a succession of 50-foot benches. When a bench had cleared the ore across the whole pit, which took the good part of a year, a new bench was cut into the pit's floor.

About two thirds of the work force lived near the mine in a small camp consisting of a mess hall and several bunkhouses. The rest and their families were housed in trailers at Kelso, whose population sky-rocketed to nearly 2,000 as a result of Kaiser's operation. The large quantities of water needed for the miners and the mill were initially piped in from two nearby springs, but this proved insufficient. So Kaiser cut a deal with Union Pacific, which had plenty of water from Cornfield Spring. Water was piped from the railroad reservoir near Kelso to a tank along the mine road, then trucked to the mine. It was a nice symbiotic relationship: without the water the mine would not have functioned, and without the ore the railroad would not have had the mine's business.

By 1944, the pit was three benches deep. In July 1947, the miners had cleaned out the fifth bench. Less than 50% of the ore had been extracted, but further work would require more costly underground mining. Kaiser had also acquired a huge iron deposit in Riverside County, much closer to his Fontana smelter, called Eagle Mountain: its estimated reserve was a whopping 60 million tons. Kaiser moved its operations there, and the Vulcan Mine shut down.

In less than five years, the Vulcan Mine had produced 2.64 million tons of ore, nearly doubling California's production, and grossed over $2.5 million. Jones' old dream had come true: California was well on its way to becoming a major steel producer.

Route Description

The Vulcan Mine has multiple points of interest scattered in different directions. For convenience the following sub-sections break them up into four short hikes, all starting from the eastern access road. They can be combined into a single loop hike with minimal backtracking.

This mine's distinguishing feature is that there is ore everywhere—on the tailing, bench cuts, roads, and even in the washes. To better appreciate your visit if you are not mineral savvy, before heading in, sit by the access road and go through this short primer. The ubiquitous black ore, like the nearby boulders, is mostly magnetite, more rarely hematite. Both are iron oxides, and they are difficult to tell apart visually. If you scratch a sample on a hard white stone and it leaves a red streak, it is hematite. If the streak is black, it is magnetite. The yellow-orange layers often coating boulders is limonite, a secondary ore formed by oxidation of iron minerals. The common white to beige rocks are marble that the magma altered from limestone.

The Vulcan Mine loop. This short loop around the Vulcan Mine pit gives the most complete overview of this unique site. At the junction just past the gate, follow the road on your right. It circles along the

Vulcan Lake and the Vulcan Mine pit

chain-link fence that surrounds the open pit, then climbs to a second junction (0.3 mile). To get to the pit overlook, make a right. Just past the junction, look down the slope to the right for the large concrete foundations of an old iron mill that had a peculiar configuration. After being pulverized with a jaw crusher, the ore was dropped to a stockpile, then loaded into a truck on an inclined conveyor belt located *inside* a tunnel beneath the stockpile! This interesting installation is still in place.

Past the mill the side road switchbacks 0.3 mile to an impressive viewpoint of the pit. The land falls off into an oval excavation the size of two soccer stadiums, an awesome cavity ringed by vertical walls that drop over 100 feet into an unexpected lake. The pit's unearthly combination of colors is amazing. The lake is green, the walls ink-black with tapestries of yellow and rust. The tormented walls, the raw colors, the faint smell of sulfur, and the unsettling heights summon up a surreal tableau reminiscent of Edgar Alan Poe's chimeric landscapes.

To hike around the pit, return to the previous junction and go straight. The road soon reaches the fence at the sheer edge of the pit, then follows it along one of the bench cuts that predate the pit. You will pass by a yawning cave in black ore, pick your way between huge chunks of iron ore, and stare down into the pit's gaping void. If the fence and rock falls squeeze you out, climb to the next bench up. At the north end of the pit, the road switchbacks up to a low ridge. On the far side of it, there is a narrow wash. Follow it downhill, past blasted boulders of magnetite and limonite. After 0.25 mile, the wash dead-ends against the back side of the mine's enormous tailing. The mine's overburden was dumped right across the wash, eventually plugging it behind a 20-foot dam. A little grass grows where storm runoffs pool in this artificial sink.

To complete the loop, scramble to the top of the tailing, then follow the road that snakes across its flat top back to your starting point. If you like identifying minerals, you will want to spend time on the tailing: it is a mountain of ore. The magnetite often sparkles with copper glance—the golden specks of chalcopyrite, the iridescent blue of peacock ore. There are also light-green films of epidote, garnet crystals as dark as merlot, shiny platelets of pyrite, and dark-green serpentine.

Vulcan Lake. For a closer look at the lake, from the eastern access road walk to the fence. It was put up to prevent people from accidentally falling into the pit, but entering the fenced-in area is permitted. Go through the gate in the fence and take the haulage road that descends to the pit's edge, then spirals down into the pit. Be extremely cautious if the spiral road gets locally buried under a rock slide. Crossing the narrow space between a slide and the sheer drop into the pit is risky, and it is a long fall to the lake. The road ends at groves of tamarisk and cattail on the white-rimmed shore of Vulcan Lake.

This is one of the most unconventional walks in the California desert. You descend into the core of a massive mineralized deposit, staring up at iron-oxide cliffs vibrant with colors that hardly exist in nature, approaching a lake stolen from the Canadian Rockies. In summer, the lake's limpid water unveils a submerged garden of long waving algae as brilliant as Monet's *Nympheas*. In winter, the water turns to colloidal turquoise. This opportune exposure of groundwater is not lost on avian life. Quails congregate near the seasonal seep at the top of the road. Vultures circle overhead. I once observed for long minutes a golden eagle perched on a ledge beneath the rim. Before the NPS installed the fence in 2009, bighorn sheep and coyote regularly hotfooted down the road for their morning drink.

The mining camp. The open area up the Vulcan Mine Road starting 200 feet past the eastern access road was the mine's camp. Short roads loop through it. The low concrete foundations might have been

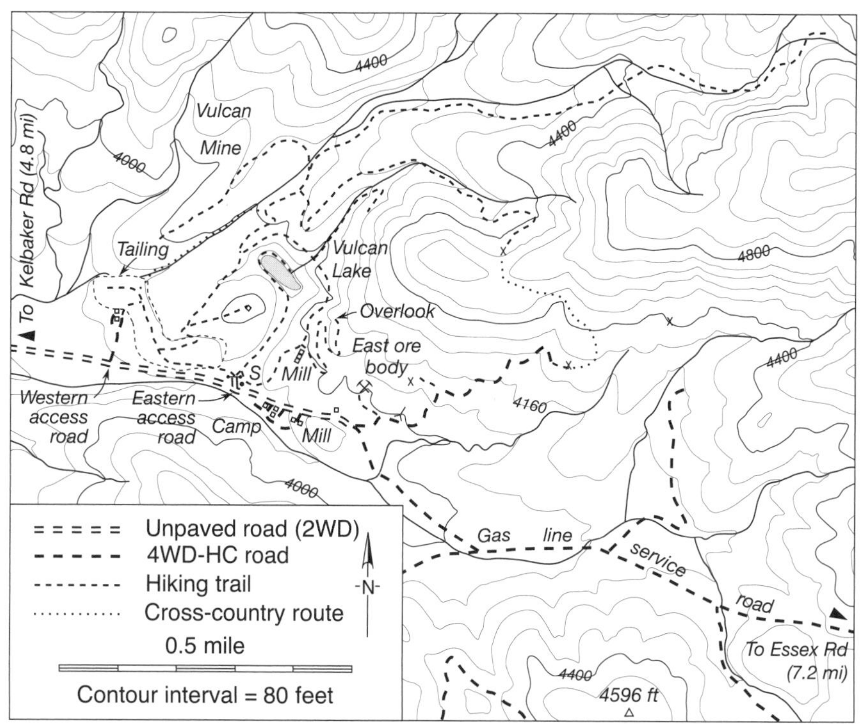

The Vulcan Mine

	Dist.(mi)	Elev.(ft)
The Vulcan Mine loop		
Eastern access road	0.0	3,870
Vulcan Lake shore	(0.3)	~3,810
Junction to viewpoint	0.3	3,990
Overlook	(0.3)	4,130
Junction at top of rim	0.5	3,950
Top of tailing	0.95	3,900
Eastern access road	1.2	3,870
The east-ore-body loop		
Eastern access road	0.0	3,870
East ore body road	0.25	3,940
End of road	0.65	4,270
Saddle at ridge crest	1.0	4,550
T junction	1.65	4,060
Eastern access road via tailing	2.3	3,870

the bunkhouses and the mess hall. The two side-by-side foundations at the east end are the ruins of a mill. The crusher, now gone, was bolted to the twin trapezoidal concrete pilings. The crushed ore was delivered to the structure next to it, and dumped from there into trucks that drove beside its six-foot wall. A little further up the road, on the north side, are the hemicircular concrete foundations of old gas tanks.

The east-ore-body loop. From the eastern access road walk the Vulcan Mine Road 0.25 mile east to a road on the left. It climbs first to a short beat-up side road on the left. The small marble quarry littered with magnetite at the end of it exposed the Vulcan Mine's east ore body. It contained a mere 300,000 tons of ore, which was too wimpy for Kaiser, and it was left alone. Just past this junction there is a framed cave-like adit, then the road degrades considerably. No one has driven the rest of it in years, and plants are zealously reclaiming it. In the spring it is inundated with pastel spills of blue Mojave aster and vermillion globemallow. The road ends after 0.4 mile, out in the middle of nowhere, as if the bulldozer operator had suddenly realized he had gone the wrong way and stopped. A short foot trail extends east to a shallow trench with a low stone wall. Continue cross-country, circling uphill until you are heading northwest toward the ridge's crest. The rounded bluffs and long stratified cliffs crowning it are made of the hard, wind-pitted bluish limestone of the Bonanza King Formation. As you approach the ridge, aim for the saddle. Below it on the north side you will catch the upper end of a road that winds down to the Vulcan Mine. From there you can complete the loop either way around the pit.

What makes this hike particularly exciting is the flora. The long, even flank of the mountain is mantled with large colonies of barrel cactus and Mojave yucca, and in smaller numbers just about every spiny plant this desert hosts. In the spring these radiant nurseries turn to a riot of colors when brittlebush, lupine, rock pea, desert gold poppy, and untold numbers of cacti decide to bloom simultaneously. Less common plants thrive here as well, including live-forever, their shocking-pink stems growing out of mere cracks in bare rock. The rarest is the simple desert agave, a mescal found at only a handful of places in the preserve. Their handsome crowns of teal-blue daggers flourish on the limey rubble. On the more sheltered north side of the ridge the cactus frenzy dies down and is replaced by a dwarf forest of scruffy juniper. Just about everywhere there are excellent views of the Kelso Dunes reaching deep into the Devils Playground, and of the sharp summit of Providence Peak.

■

QUAIL SPRING BASIN

In the southern reaches of the Providence Mountains, an abandoned road now part of a wilderness area cuts clear across the range and offers a gentle path to explore this isolated region on foot. It first climbs along beautiful outcrops of artfully weathered monzogranite boulders to the divide and a spectacular viewpoint of the Granite Mountains. It then descends along Quail Spring Basin, a desolate high-desert valley carpeted with extensive cactus and yucca gardens. It eventually ends at Hidden Hill and its historic gold mine, on the edge of Clipper Valley. If you are looking for a longer hike infused with solitude, where coyotes have outnumbered humans from time immemorial, this is the place.

General Information
Road status: Hiking on old roads; standard-clearance access road
Quail Spr. Basin viewpoint: 2.1 mi, 790 ft up, 10 ft down one way / easy
Quail Spring Basin loop: 5.7 mi, 970 ft up loop / easy–moderate
Golden Queen Mine: 5.4 mi, 770 ft up, 1,230 ft down, one way / moder.
Main attractions: A long and scenic mountain trail, boulder fields, mine
USGS 7.5′ topo map: Van Winkle Spring
Maps: pp. 321*, *301*

Location and Access

Quail Spring Basin is a broad high-desert valley near the south end of the Providence Mountains. On the west side of the mountains, an old road called the Quail Spring Basin Trail, now closed to motor vehicles, climbs to the basin and makes a wide loop around it. At the loop's east end, the road continues east and south down Quail Spring Wash to Hidden Hill, on the eastern edge of the range. To visit Quail Spring Basin you can hike the Quail Spring Basin Trail from either the trailhead or Hidden Hill and return the same way. Or you can hike it through from end to end and get picked up.

To get to the Quail Spring Basin Trail, drive the Kelbaker Road 1.8 miles north of Granite Pass (or 4.9 miles south of the Kelso Dunes Road) to the old road to Pine Tree Ranch, on the east side. Go slowly: it is easy to miss. Drive this fairly smooth road 0.9 mile up to the trailhead on the right. The trailhead is lined with white rocks, and green metal posts block vehicle access into the wilderness area beyond.

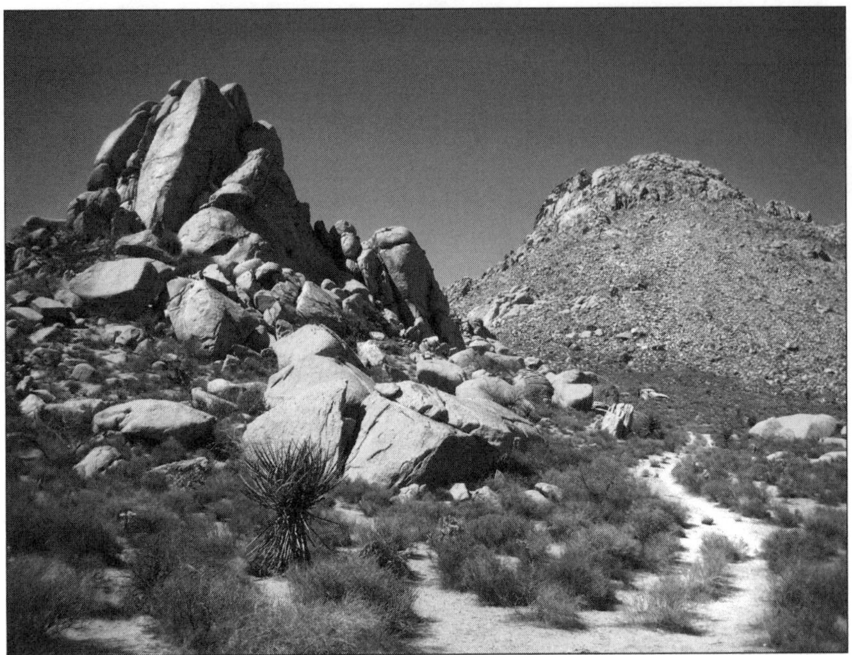

Looking north at pyramidal hill and trail at top of Quail Spring Basin

To get to the east end of the Quail Spring Basin Trail, drive to the concrete slab of an old shack on the west side of the Hidden Hill Mine (see *Hidden Hill*). Then drive or walk 0.1 mile up the wash to the trailhead, on the left in a right bend.

Route Description

Quail Spring Basin Trail to viewpoint. Almost all of this trail is still a road, gently sloped and easy to follow. For the first couple of miles it climbs steadily to the pass into Quail Spring Basin. This is the most scenic part of this hike. The trail passes the unremarkable Horse Hills to the south, but on its north side it skirts a beautiful area of sharply pointed hills peppered with wonderfully weathered boulders. This is the same late-Cretaceous biotite monzogranite responsible for the Granite Mountains' spectacular rock gardens. The most interesting boulders are a short distance north of the trail, so you might want to stray off the trail for a closer look. The hillsides are sprinkled with piles of smooth jointed rocks that hold narrow passages and cool caves, slickrock, inviting coves and occasional small arches, all of it interspaced with desert gardens. One wildly overhanging boulder is shaped like a parrot's head. Another one is precariously balanced on a

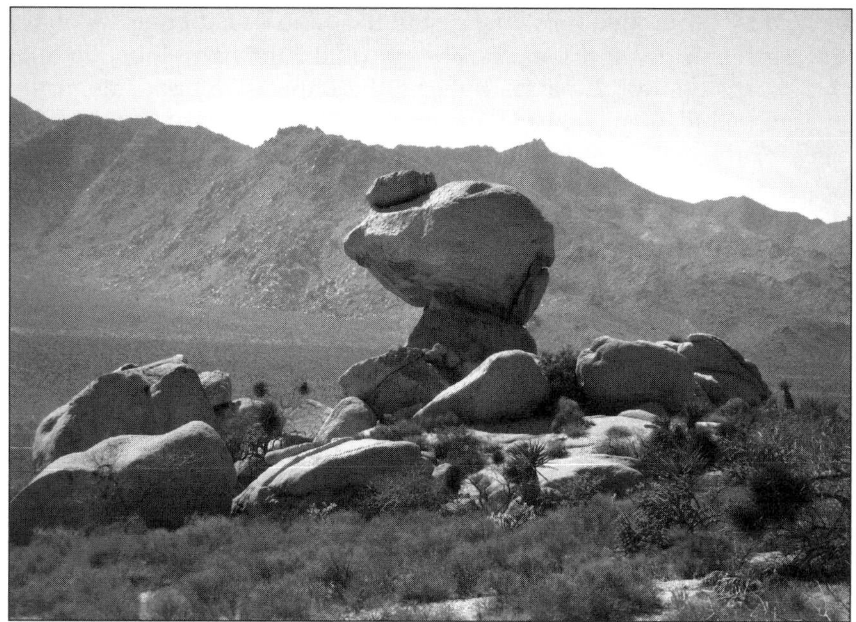

Balanced boulder along Quail Spring Basin Trail

frail pedestal. The best comes last, right at the pass—a high pyramidal hill of polished bus-size boulders crowned 100 feet up by a massive vertical slab. This is both a visual treat and a fun place to scramble up to a host of nooks and crannies. Here as elsewhere, bouldering problems are plentiful, although the rock tends to exfoliate. Bring climbing shoes, and watch your landings; they might be soft but painfully spiny... Early in this hike, turn around occasionally for sweeping views of the Kelso Dunes and the Granite Mountains.

As the elevation increases, the plant community evolves surprisingly quickly. Near the trailhead, the landscape is dominated by creosote bush. Some specimens reach unusual proportions, over 20 feet across and 10 feet tall, and probably a respectable age as well. Higher up, staghorn cholla and yucca take the lead, then silver cholla and other cacti, and finally higher elevation denizens like Mormon tea and blackbrush join in near the pass. Individual species appear and disappear quite suddenly as well, but the overall evolution is gradual, and by the time you reach the pass the ground cover has completely changed. You might spot less common plants among the boulders, such as mound and grizzly bear cactus, diamond cholla, and cliffrose.

Quail Spring Basin comes into view as soon as you crest the open pass—a broad valley sloping gently to the east, framed almost all around by tall eroded hills. Just east of the pass, a road branches off on the north side. Even if you don't want to hike the basin loop, do hike this short side trail. It passes right by the impressive back side of the pyramidal hill, then climbs to and ends at a vista point offering a great view of the boulder-strewn area you just crossed and the Granite Mountains in the background.

Quail Spring Basin loop. The loop road that circles around Quail Spring Basin starts at the upper loop junction, 0.1 mile past this first junction. It will take you by a few small granite outcrops. These are the most interesting, so again leave the trail occasionally to explore them. Because they create shade and break the wind, they attract a different assortment of plants, including solitary pinyon pine and juniper. There is a curious guzzler along the loop road. Its little concrete catchment basin collects rain water into an underground tank for the benefit of wildlife. Further on, I came upon a mushroom rock, eroded boulders in the shape of castles, and a worn-out side trail leading to a tangle of squawbush, blackbrush, and blue yucca. The loop road eventually ends at its lower junction with the Quail Spring Basin Trail, 0.5 mile east of the upper loop junction.

What I liked here was the palpable wildness, the isolation, and the soothing sense of permanence exuding from the eternal hills. A few quails startled me out of my reverie with their noisy synchronized take-off. This is also a major coyote hangout—I do not remember ever seeing so many tracks and droppings anywhere in the desert.

Quail Spring Basin

	Dist.(mi)	Elev.(ft)
Quail Spring Basin Trailhead	0.0	3,790
Pass	1.8	~4,470
Side trail to viewpoint	1.85	~4,465
Quail Spring Basin viewpoint	(0.25)	~4,565
Upper loop junction	1.95	4,442
Upper end of loop (side trail)	2.55	4,465
Lower loop junction	3.2	4,255
Back to upper loop junction	(0.5)	4,442
Trail leaves wash (east)	4.5	3,890
End of trail at wash/road	5.6	3,487
Hidden Hill Mine Tr. (east end)	6.2	3,335

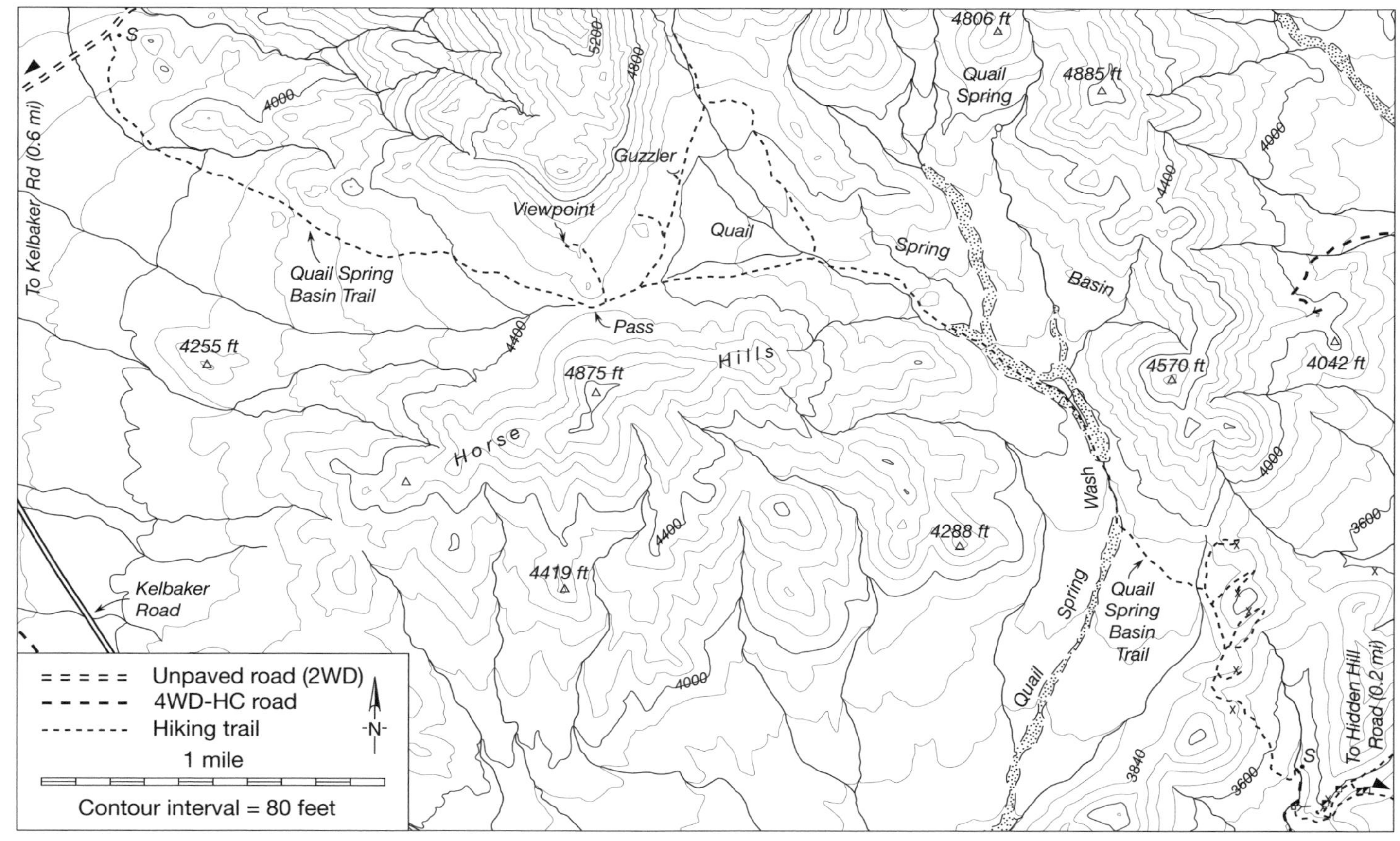
To Kelbaker Rd (0.6 mi)
S
4000
5200
4800
4806 ft
Quail Spring
4885 ft
Guzzler
Viewpoint
Quail
Spring
Basin
Quail Spring Basin Trail
Pass
4400
4255 ft
Hills
4875 ft
4570 ft
4042 ft
Horse
Wash
4000
3600
4288 ft
4400
4419 ft
Kelbaker Road
Quail Spring Basin Trail
Quail
Spring
To Hidden Hill Road (0.2 mi)
3840
3600
4000
Unpaved road (2WD)
4WD-HC road
Hiking trail
N
1 mile
Contour interval = 80 feet

Quail Spring Basin Trail to Hidden Hill. If you have the time and stamina, continue on the Quail Spring Basin Trail to the Hidden Hill area. It is only 2.5 miles, and it will take you clear across the Providence Mountains. From the lower loop junction in Quail Spring Basin, take the old mining road that heads down the basin. After 0.6 mile it meets Quail Spring Wash, a broad gravel river that drops along a colorful canyon lined with denuded hills. The scenery is typical of the eastern Mojave Desert, a serene and somewhat stark landscape studded with Mojave yucca and cacti. As the land gradually opens up, it offers increasingly finer views of the Clipper Mountains to the south.

After 0.7 mile, where the canyon widens noticeably, the road angles sharply east, out of the wash and up the canyon's left bank. It climbs over a low divide, then drops and climbs again over gentle hills. The side roads along the way lead to mining claims prospected fairly recently. Although never exploited, some of them show interesting mineralized benches. The road then descends steeply to the nameless narrow canyon along the west side of Hidden Hill. It ends abruptly at the wash, at a sharp step clipped by flashfloods.

The most satisfying way to end this hike is to continue to the nearby Hidden Hill Mine, one of the most interesting gold mines in the preserve. Walk down the winding canyon 200 yards to the concrete slab of an old shack, on the left side. Right behind and slightly above it there is a collapsed adit. The road resumes between the slab and the adit. At the four-road junction 0.2 mile further, take the low road, which circles down to the Golden Queen Mill, a stone's throw from the Hidden Hill Road. Refer to *Hidden Hill* for a description of this important historic site.

■

THE BONANZA KING MINE

The Bonanza King Mine was the eastern Mojave Desert's second richest silver property. Between 1883 and 1887, its giant shaft yielded close to $1.8 million. A visit to this iconic mine, reached by a rocky road, is a must. Its tall 10-stamp mill is one of the most complete in the region, and Providence, the town that supported the mining community, still has several stone structures. A short walk into the wilderness area to the north will take you to the camp and ruins of the Perseverance Mine, one of several historic mines that sprung up in the wake of this enviable success.

General Information

Road status: Hiking on old roads; high-clearance access road
Silver King Mine: 0.6 mi, 180 ft up, 0 ft down one way / very easy
Bonanza King Mine–Providence: 3.0 mi, 530 ft up loop / easy–moderate
Main attractions: Historic silver mines, mills, ghost town, camp
USGS 7.5' topo maps: Colton Well, Fountain Peak*, Columbia Mtn
Maps: pp. 329*, *301*

Location and Access

The Bonanza King Mine is in the eastern foothills of the Providence Mountains, north of Mitchell Caverns. To get there, drive the Essex Road 0.8 mile north from the Black Canyon Road to the signed Ranch Road on the right. Stay on this good graded road 4.8 miles to the Bonanza King Mine Road, which angles off to the left (a sign points to the mine). It heads northwest 0.8 mile to a Y junction, then makes a 2.8-mile loop to the mine and back to this junction. Take the right fork. After 0.6 mile a private road closed to the public comes in from the right. At this junction, a faint road closed to motor vehicles heads northwest into a wilderness area to the Silver King Mine. Stop here first if you want to hike to this mine. Otherwise continue 0.6 mile on the main road, past Bonanza King Well's windmill and a sharp left bend, to a split in the road. Take the left fork 250 yards to a short but very steep grade. The Bonanza King Mine is just beyond.

The Bonanza King Mine Road is rocky almost the whole way, locally high-crowned and rutted, and it requires good clearance. To climb the steep grade and the longer one beyond it, and complete the loop by car, four-wheel drive is needed as well. If you cannot make the grade, park and visit the mine on foot (~0.8 mile). If you came here to hike, park at the Y junction, hike to the Silver King Mine, then cross-country to the Bonanza King Mine, and back along the loop road via Providence. With a standard-clearance vehicle, the steeply canted spot 0.3 mile from Ranch Road will likely stop you; walk from there.

History: Silver Frenzy

In the spring of 1880, two prospectors from Ivanpah, George Goreman and Pat Dwyer, stumbled upon high-grade silver ore while poking around the Providence Mountains. Their lucky strike sparked one of the area's most prosperous mining enterprises. True to their trade, they filed claims, and the following year sold the richest one—the Bonanza King—to four businessmen from San Bernardino. One of them was Jonas B. Osborne, a mining entrepreneur with a sharp sense of business. He had spent the last four years developing rich silver-lead claims in the Resting Spring Range. Having experienced first hand the harsh realities of desert mining, he knew how hard it would be to develop this property. So he sank a few exploratory tunnels to show how good his ore was and to attract investors. In 1882, after a rich vein was exposed, Senator George Hearst, one of the world's richest men of the time and an astute mining investor, became interested. Well aware of Osborne's keen eye for mineral wealths, he acquired the Bonanza King for $200,000. The claim thus became the property of the Bonanza King Consolidated Mining and Milling Company, and with Hearst's solid backing, development began.

Through 1882, the new company hired upward of 100 miners to sink a huge shaft and access the silver veins. This small army was housed in the town of Providence, parallel rows of stone houses strung down a sloping alluvial plain next to the mine. A post office was added in June, and in the fall the booming town was large enough to become an election precinct. In July, the company put in its last major piece of equipment, a 10-stamp mill that it purchased and hauled from San Francisco for $50,000. The mill was erected at Domingo Spring, on Juan Domingo's ranch 3 miles northeast of the mine, and a second camp named Crow Town was established near the mill.

The mill went into operation on January 1, 1883. The ore came out of wide veins containing as much as $100 in silver and gold per ton, and there was plenty of it. Six months later, the mill had already churned out $573,000 in bullion. The outlook was so bright that the company started offering stock on the New York mining exchange. By then Providence boasted a population of 300. Its main street showcased a few businesses, some located in sturdy quarried-stone houses. It boasted two general stores, a saloon, two hotels, several company offices, a contractor, a blacksmith, a wagon manufacturer, a surveyor's office, and a sheriff to try to keep everyone out of trouble. For two full years, the Bonanza King Mine operated at a nice profit, spending on average $20,000 in supplies and wages and earning a minimum of $35,000 every month. It even paid its stockholders regular dividends, a rare feat for a desert mine. In early 1885, the shaft reached 800 feet below the surface, and production topped the 1.5-million-dollar mark.

As in any mining venture, the mine's welfare was at the mercy of the market. In March 1885, when the price of silver dipped from around $1.10 an ounce to near $1, profits slipped, and the mine owners suspended operations. It might have been a ploy to lower wages, because a week later they reopened the mine but hired miners for a daily pay reduced from $3.50 to $3. With a team of 40 men working the tunnels, 35 running the mill, and the ore looking as good as ever, production resumed at a whopping average of $60,000 a month. But just when everything was running smoothly again, the Bonanza King was dealt a second blow, this one fatal: in late July 1885 its mill was destroyed by fire. No longer able to process its ore, the company kept only a skeleton crew of 20 miners on the job. They did strike rich ore in early 1886, but the company folded shortly after. By then most of the businesses had drained from Providence. Nearby mines kept the town alive for many years, until the post office moved out in the spring of 1902, and the last store closed a year or so later.

In the early 1880s, in hope of a repeat performance, several small mines went into operation up and down the fault that had been so generous to the Bonanza King. There was the Mozart Group, and the Belle McGilroy below Gilroy Canyon, which later became the C & K Mine. The most prominent was the Perseverance Mine. In its earliest incarnation it was referred to as the Kerr & Patton property or the Kerr Mine, after its principals, R. P. Kerr and James Patton. It was recorded as the Perseverance Quartz Mine around 1886. It had good ore. In March 1885 a large vein of rich silver-lead ore was encountered in one of its shafts 90 feet down, and preparations were underway to scale up the work. By early summer an assayer's office had been put up and derricks brought in to sink a well to run a five-stamp mill. Ore containing more than 200 ounces of silver per ton was shipped to Kingman, Arizona. The mill was erected in 1885–1886 and fired up in January 1887. Until at least 1890 the shafts were heavily worked, the main one down to 165 feet with four levels of drifts. The Perseverance Mine did well for itself: it reportedly made $250,000 in silver. It produced again in 1918–1920, around the time when it was renamed the Silver King, but only 1,500 ounces; this time, perseverance did not pay off.

Like many mines with prior success, the Bonanza King Mine came back to life—many times. In 1906, the Trojan Mining Company reopened the shaft after installing a full-blown gasoline-powered 10-stamp mill just below it. Unfortunately, the stock market crash forced all activities to stop in September 1907. In 1914, the Hall, Rawister & Company rekindled development work. The following year, it revamped and electrified the mill, installed new gas engines, a pipeline, and the latest hoist technology, and put 30 men on the job. The mill processed rich ore that was trucked twice a day to Fenner. In July 1920, with the post-war price of silver down to 66 cents, the mine was forced to close down again. In 1923, another company gave it a go with a team of six men. It had grand plans to dewater the shaft and push downward exploration, but they never materialized. One lone car full of ore came out of the aging shaft in May 1924. Very occasional shipments were made until 1960, but they did not amount to much.

The Bonanza King Mine retired with a whimper, but it did it with pride. In its long career, it produced $1.8 million between 1883 and 1887, and at least $70,000 after 1901, most of it in silver. It was one of the richest historic mines in the eastern Mojave Desert.

Route Description

The Silver King Mine. From the loop road the Silver King Mine is a short distance up the aging mining road. It is not much of a road past the bedrock step 150 yards from its start, and it disappears in a broad wash soon after. Follow the wash the remaining 0.2 mile to the mining camp. It is a scenic walk, facing the tall grayish limestone inclines of the Providence Mountains on one side, and auburn volcanic mesas on the other. The foothills are green with creosote bush, Mojave yucca, staghorn cholla, beavertail cactus, and shiny prickly-pear. To the south, beyond the pine-covered gap of Gilroy Canyon, rises the abrupt cone of Edgar Peak. The wash contains bits of petrified wood, crushed tobacco cans, and hole-in-top cans manufactured in the 19th century.

The camp has two cabins side by side, perhaps from the late 1910s, odd-looking twins clad in corrugated sheet metal, one shiny, the other dark with rust. One has a clever sliding panel in its door to control air flow, the other a picture window framing the peaks. Up the hill a less fortunate cabin collapsed into a pile of splintered planks. Behind the cabins, a trail wanders 0.2 mile to the Silver King Mine. The workings consist of three impressively deep shafts and a shallower one along a low bench cut, and two adits dug into the bench cut. The main shaft was connected to the shaft next to it for additional air flow. In spite of its concrete pilings, the 20-foot headframe toppled against the slope.

Bonanza King Mine and Mill in May 2011

The concrete foundations of the five-stamp mill lie nearby. Be cautious around this site; the shafts are unprotected, and it takes many seconds for the echoes of a falling rock to die out.

To hike on to the Bonanza King Mine, return to the cabins and cut a beeline southwest across the low swell of land, aiming for the bend near the west end of the loop road. It is an easy walk, across mostly open ground. There are interesting limestone exposures along the way, a narrow gulch framed by vertical walls, and good views of the mine.

The Bonanza King Mill. The Bonanza King has more than 20 workings. They are all located along the East Providence Fault Zone, which is just uphill from the road and parallels the base of the mountains for several miles. On its mountain side, the country rock is Cambrian carbonates of the Nopah and Bonanza King formations—the latter was named after this very location. The ore occurred in lenses that replaced limestone in fractures along the fault. On the valley side, the rock is Early Proterozoic gneiss. The large timbered portal 100 yards up the road from the grade is the entrance to the longest tunnel. The bare wall surrounding it is stained with white calcite and red and yellow oxidized pyrite.

The mill from 1906 is just past the tunnel. Although fast falling apart, it is one of the preserve's finest examples of a stamp mill. Like most mills, it performed two functions: it crushed the ore to free the metal locked in it, and it separated the metal from the host rock. It is split into multiple levels, each one with a specific task. Early mills were often erected on a steep slope, like this mill is, to let gravity move the rocks through these levels, which saved energy and money. A mine car dumped ore into the metal contraption at its very top, which is a crusher. The crusher broke the ore into small chunks, which fell into the ore bin, the cubic wooden container resting on a stone foundation. The bin was large enough to store a few days' worth of milling. Milling could then proceed (stopping and re-starting a mill was costly) even if the mine had to shut down temporarily. The floor of the bin is slanted so that the ore could slide freely through the two chutes at the base of the bin to the stamp battery—the heart of the mill. Heavy iron stamps were dropped repeatedly by a cam wheel onto a bit of ore, until it was mashed to a fine sand. The number of stamps was a gauge of the size of the mine. Some mills had just one stamp. In the richest mines, they had as many as 100. This mill had ten—a respectable number. Stamp batteries had to be erected on sturdy foundations, or the mill would be shaken apart by the violent vibrations. The Bonanza King stamps were salvaged long ago, as was customary to generate cash after a mine closed. But its foundations' five concrete pilings are still in place. The battery rested on the two larger, trapezoidal pilings.

The ore pulp from the stamps was stored in the steel tank framed in a lumber casing below the pilings. The level below the steel tank, marked by collapsed lumber, is where the ore was concentrated. The process often involved a concentration table, a tilted table covered with parallel riffles and shaken by a motor. Ore pulp mixed with water was run over it. The denser metal particles were trapped in the riffles, while waste rock flowed over them and was discarded on the mill tailing (the white slurry spilling down below the road). The lowest level, by the road, held a wooden tank, of which only the metal hoops remain. It might have been used to amalgamate the concentrate.

Water was used throughout the recovery stages to lubricate the flow of pulp ore. So there was actually another level, above the mill and again away from vibrations, which held a water tank. It is one of the large corrugated-iron cylinders lying around the site.

The main shaft. The mine's bread and butter was the shaft located above the mill. To get to it, from the mill go 150 yards up the steep grade to a junction at a saddle. Go straight 200 feet to a T junction, and make a right. The shaft is 100 yards further, past foundations and mortared walls. With its opening 25 feet across framed by enormous

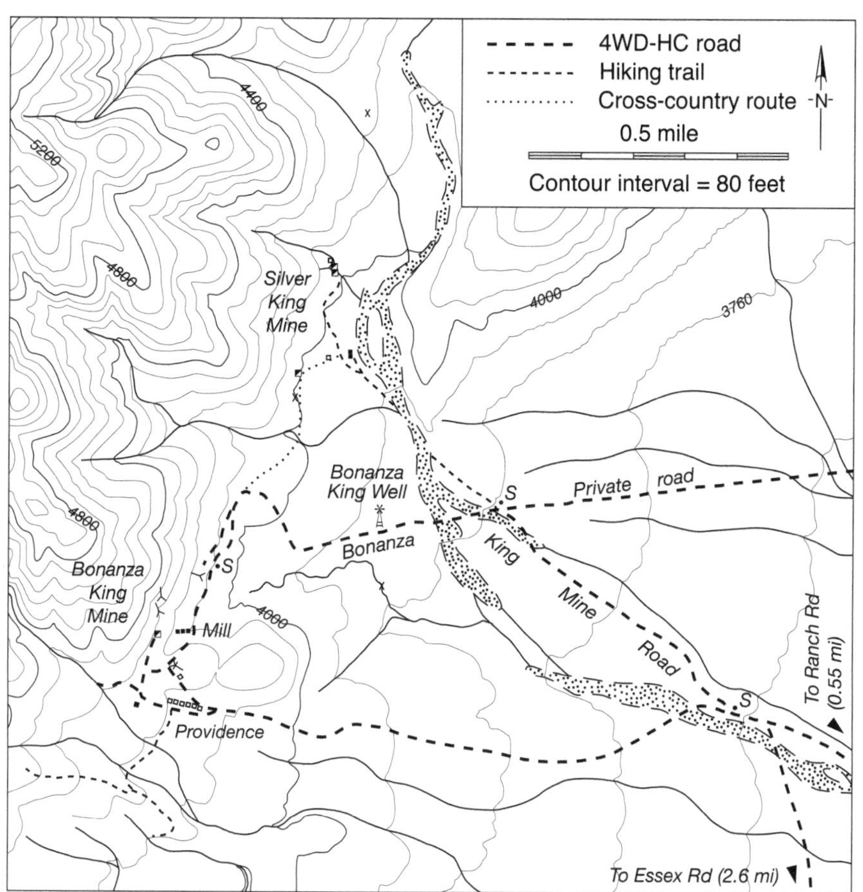

The Bonanza King Mine		
	Dist.(mi)	Elev.(ft)
Ranch Road	0.0	3,517
Y junction (start of loop)	0.8	3,690
Junction with private road	1.4	3,835
Silver King Mine (shaft)	(0.6)	4,030
Junction	2.0	4,050
Very steep grade	2.15	4,080
Bonanza King Mill	2.25	~4,130
Junction at saddle	2.35	~4,180
Main shaft	(0.1)	4,220
Providence (main house)	2.45	4,120
Y junction (end of loop)	3.6	3,690

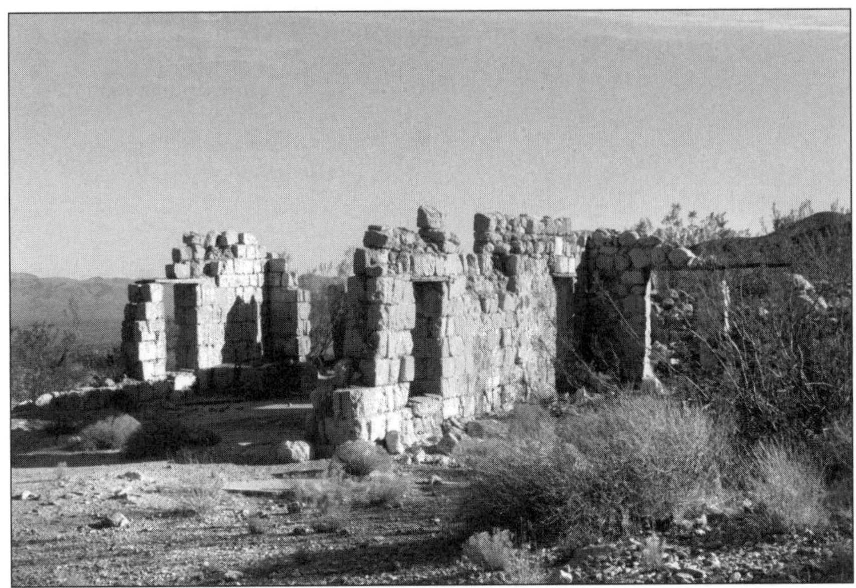

Quarried-stone house at Providence (September 2006)

lumber, this is one of the most impressive in the preserve. It plunges 600 straight feet, then continues as a winze another 200 feet. When the shaft encountered a new ore body, a drift was sank along it as far as the ore would run. This shaft eventually developed six levels and nearly four *miles* of tunnels. It produced a cornucopia of minerals: cerussite, argentite, sphalerite, bromyrite, smithsonite, cerargyrite, and galena. Its size is mirrored by the volume of the tailings—the 100-yard long pile of waste rocks around it and the conical hill looming besides the mill. The tailings still hold an estimated 2,500 *pounds* of silver.

Providence. To get to the old town, return to the saddle junction and head down the road on the right. This was Providence's main street. At the top of it is a wide dugout that served as a workshop. In 150 yards you will reach the ruins of a large house with thick walls of light-beige stones. The stones are Wild Horse Mesa Tuff quarried from nearby bluffs. This exceptional dwelling still has its concrete floor, several window and door openings, and a patio looking out over the vast expanses of Fenner Valley. Behind the house and back up the hill, the ruins of smaller rock houses, some only a few feet across, are hidden among creosote bush. A few houses had a small fireplace to ward off the cold of the high-desert winters.

■

MITCHELL CAVERNS

Only a small percentage of the world's limestone caves are easily accessible and open to the public. We are fortunate that the Mojave Desert has the Mitchell Caverns, a set of deep caves decorated with an impressive assortment of stalactites, stalagmites, columns, draperies, as well as less common cave formations. Take the fun guided tour on a hot summer day to cool off, or on an icy winter day to warm up. Three scenic short trails in the vicinity of the caves also offer unparalleled opportunities to sample the majesty and diversity of the Providence Mountains.

General Information
Road status: Roadless; paved access road
Niña Mora Trail: 0.3 mi, 80 ft up, 140 ft down one way/very easy
Mary Beal Nature Trail: 0.4 mi, 150 ft up loop/very easy
Mitchell Caverns: 1.0 mi, 460 ft up loop/easy
Main attractions: Limestone caves, history, mountain trails, botany
USGS 7.5' topo map: Fountain Peak
Maps: pp. 337*, 341, *301*

Location and Access

Located part way up the eastern slope of the central Providence Mountains, the Mitchell Caverns are protected as the Mitchell Caverns Natural Preserve, a small enclave within the Providence Mountains State Recreation Area. Coming from Interstate 40, take the Essex Road exit and drive the paved Essex Road northbound 15.6 miles to its end at the preserve's small visitor center. If you are coming from the north, drive the Black Canyon Road south to the stop sign at the Essex Road and make a right. It is 6.0 miles to the visitor center.

The caverns can be visited only on guided tours. The tour lasts around 90 minutes, including the short easy walk to the caves and back. From October through May two daily tours are given, at 11 a.m. and 2 p.m., Friday through Sunday and Mondays that are a holiday. From June through September there is only one tour, at 10 a.m. on the same days. The park is closed on Christmas Day and New Year's Day. Reservations are required. They can be made only by phone at (760) 928-2586 on Mondays between 8 a.m. and 5 p.m. (we should consider ourselves lucky: phone hours have not been restricted to leap years yet). Tours are limited to 15 persons and often sell out. If you do not have a reservation and you are in the area, check with a park ranger in case a spot has become available. Reservation holders must arrive and pay for their tours at least 15 minutes before the scheduled departure. If you miss the first tour, there is a little picnic area to wait and try your luck with the second one. The area also offers several delightful short trails to hike while you wait (see *Fountain Peak* and below).

Geology: One Drop at a Time

The stalactites and stalagmites found in some limestone caves are nowhere numerous because their formation requires a rare combination of conditions. For a phreatic cave to form, the limestone must be submerged in groundwater for hundreds of thousands to millions of years. Limestone is very poorly soluble in pure water, and caves would form even more slowly if it weren't for the precious collaboration of carbon dioxide. As rainwater percolates through the soil, it reacts with the carbon dioxide in the soil to form carbonic acid. This weak acid turns the limestone (calcium carbonate) into calcium bicarbonate, which is much more soluble in water and is carried away. With a generous allotment of time, acidic water circulating through natural cracks in the rock can widen them into huge underwater chambers. Most of this chemical etching takes place just below the water surface, which is why phreatic caves often exhibit distinct levels. Almost all the carbon dioxide involved comes from the metabolic activity of plants and organisms in the soil; little comes from the atmosphere. Without plants, there would be no caves to speak of.

Mitchell Caverns were formed in a limestone that was perfect for the job. It belongs to the Bird Spring Formation, a rock unit from the late Mississippian to early Permian made mostly of thick limestone beds with plenty of cracks. It also happens to be made of a more soluble form of limestone. But how did the limestone get to be flooded nearly a mile above sea level? When the caves were formed in the Pliocene and/or Pleistocene, the surrounding ground level was higher than it is today as a result of major lava flows in the Miocene, and the groundwater reached just above the caves.

Sometime in the Pliocene, the groundwater dropped, possibly as a result of erosion, and the caves dried up. During subsequent wetter periods through the Pleistocene, rainwater percolated down to the caves. Along the way, it dissolved a little limestone and became saturated with calcium carbonate. When the weakly acidic water reaches the roof of a cave and comes in contact with the moist air, it releases a tiny fraction of its carbon dioxide. The solution becomes supersaturated and some of its mineral load precipitates, leaving a thin ring of cal-

Entrance to Mitchell Caverns

cium carbonate on the roof. The next drop deposits another thin ring on top of it. After enough drops, a slender crystalline tube known as a soda-straw stalactite is produced. Over time, water flows through the tube's outer wall, and the soda straw thickens into the classical icicle shape of young stalactites. Where the drops hit the floor beneath a stalactite, they also deposit calcium carbonate and form another kind of dripstone known as a stalagmite. Stalagmites are wider, because water dropping on the floor splatters over a wider surface. Sometimes a stalactite will meet its stalagmite and form a floor-to-ceiling column. Dripstones grow exceedingly slowly. Depositing the volume of a dice takes anywhere from a few months to several years. The 30-foot columns that grace Mitchell Caverns took at least a few hundred thousand years to form.

Since the close of the last Ice Age, the climate around Mitchell Caverns has become much drier. For lack of water, the growth of the speleothems has slowed down considerably. But it has not fully stopped. Following a few years of heavier rains, enough water soaks the ground to bring some of the formations back to life. In the dark, out of sight, one drop at a time, water is depositing calcite again, artfully designing new structures none of us will ever see.

History: Modern-Day Cavemen

The original discoverers of the Providence Mountains caverns were the Chemehuevi people. In more recent times, caves around the world were considered evil places (the underground clearly being the domain of Lucifer) and often named after the devil, and people carefully stayed away from them. Unspoiled by this myth, the Chemehuevi lived in these caverns for many centuries. They used them on a seasonal basis, as well as for food storage. Many traces of their occupancy have been recovered, including fire pits, pottery sherds, and stone tools. The caverns were sacred to them, and they also used them for ceremonies. This belief was perhaps spawned by the cave's odd formations, or by the striking resemblance of the cave's entrance to a giant face, which they referred to as "the eyes of the mountain."

It is not known who first re-discovered the caves in modern times. Their existence was known to miners at the nearby Bonanza King Mine as early as the 1880s; they referred to them as Crystal Caves. The person who put them on the map was an Angelino by the name of Jesse Estes "Jack" Mitchell. Jack was, among many things, a small-time miner. He became aware of the caves in 1929, when visiting his friend Mark Pettit at the Domingo Ranch. When Pettit mentioned the caves, Jack was instantly mystified, and that same day the two men rode many miles to visit them. As he would recall years later, on that first visit "There was no feeling of strangeness, intrusion or trespassing in my reaction as I started to explore. [...] I was merely returning home." Jack was so taken that a year later he filed claim to the area. In June 1931 he made his first descent into the nearby Cave of the Winding Stairs. He loved to recount his grueling adventure into this 310-foot abyss, and how he remained unconscious dangling at the end of his rope for hours until a friend rescued him.

After they lost much of their savings during the Great Depression, Jack and his wife Ida turned to the desert for a second chance in life. Jack moved to the caves in March 1934, soon followed by Ida. When the couple made this radical decision, broke and disheartened, they were hoping the caves would be not only their new refuge but also their salvation. Very soon after their arrival, they started developing the caves as a tourist attraction. That first summer, Jack built a road to the small town of Essex, a foot trail to the caverns, and stairs inside the caves. For a year they lived in the caves, surviving largely on stewed rabbit, while erecting a rock cabin and a pipeline from nearby Crystal Spring. By 1935 everything was ready and they opened the caverns to the public. Occasional travelers on lonesome Route 66, then the only artery between Los Angeles and Arizona, stopped by to take a tour of the El Pakiva and Tecopa caverns, as the couple had named them, with flashlights and candles.

Over time, the caves gained popularity and the Mitchells built a few accommodations. Overnight guests came here as much for the caves and the desert peace as for the couple's hospitality and Jack's colorful tales. A few repeat visitors became life-long friends, including writers Lucile and Harold Weight and famous botanist Dr. Willis Jepson. The couple's business never grew very large, but it did give them a second chance. Thanks to it they survived in the harsh Mojave Desert more than 20 years.

The state of California had long been aware of the extraordinary geological, archaeological, and recreational values of the Mitchell's caves. When the couple offered to sell its property to the state in April 1954, officials jumped on the opportunity. Jack passed away six months later and never saw the end of the transaction. But five years later, his wish was fulfilled when his domain became the state's first and only limestone-cave recreation area. The California Department of Parks and Recreation even had a tunnel dug between the two caves, thus providing continuous access through both caves, a dream Jack had long wished for.

Route Description

Mitchell Caverns Trail. From the visitor center the caverns are reached by a well-groomed, 0.5-mile trail. Cut along the steep, rocky front of the mountains, it overlooks impressive tracks of the vast desert valleys to the east. The slopes are crowded with cacti, ephedra, yuccas, and scattered juniper. The pale rock along the trail is the same Bird Spring Formation's limestone that hosts the caverns. Look in it for fossils the shape and size of a grain of rice called fusulinids. On a smooth rock shelf at the top of the first flight of stairs, swarms of them have been brought back to light after a 290-million-year entombment. There are also crinoid stems beneath the foot bridge.

Near its end, the Mitchell Caverns Trail rounds a ridge and puts you face to face with "the eyes of the mountain"—the two dark eye sockets ensconced beneath a tall frowning forehead that form the opening of the El Pakiva Cavern. This short walk can be brutally hot in summer, and painfully cold in winter, but comfort is in sight: the caverns' constant temperature of 65°F feels blissfully cool in summer and blissfully warm in winter. Bring a sweater anyway. Year-round, after being underground an hour you might otherwise be chilled to the bone.

Mitchell Caverns. Bathed in perpetual darkness, only partially revealed by artificial light, caves are foreign worlds that exert on us a fascination like no other natural environment. Although small by cave standards, Mitchell Caverns are no exception. When you step into El Pakiva (the devil's house), your senses are instantly sharpened. You expect hidden splendors. A short distance in, the entrance tunnel opens onto a chamber of cathedral proportions. The air is cool, pungent with the earthy smell of damp stone houses. Echoes and slight air currents give away the chamber's size before the lights are turned on. Immense monochromatic walls rise to hidden ceilings. Bulging stalagmites cover the floor, and dense forests of long stalactites hang from the ceilings, like inside a giant geode.

Although stalactites and stalagmites are the most common, dripstones come in many shapes and sizes, driven by how the water flows through and out of the rock. Part of the enjoyment of this visit is identifying, with a park guide's help, curtains, pillars, and funny-shaped dripstones. Many caves contain rare forms of speleothems found in only a handful of other caves in the world. Mitchells Caverns has several such claims to fame, including shields, pyramidal crystals, and helictites—oddly contorted speleothems that grew in different directions as a result of capillary forces acting on the water drops.

There are smaller rooms deeper in, and other curious formations, such as cave mushrooms, a room with a hollow floor, and the bottomless pit where Jack loved to play tricks on his guests. Ultimately, a tight tunnel wiggles across to the Tecopa Cavern, named after a famous Southern Piute chief who occasionally used the caverns. Although it has practically no ornate dripstones, this large room with a lower exfoliating ceiling stands out for yielding an archaeological treasure, the partially articulated fossil of a ground sloth that fell into the cave to its death 11,600 years ago (it was a Monday).

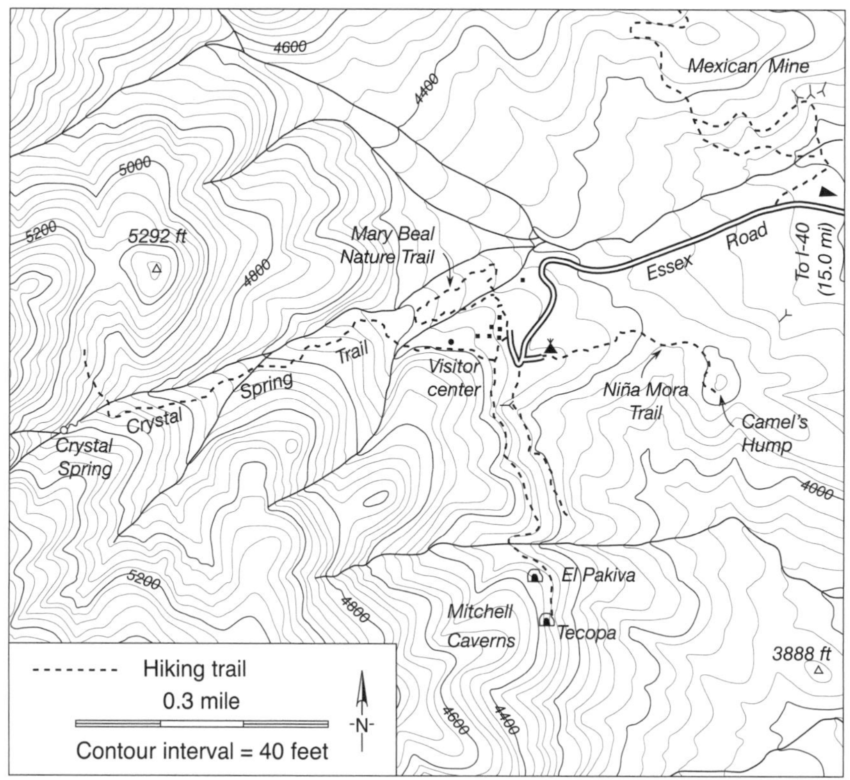

Mitchell Caverns

	Dist.(mi)	Elev.(ft)
Visitor Center	0.0	4,310
El Pakiva Cavern entrance	0.35	4,340
Tecopa Cavern exit	0.5	4,330
Visitor Center	0.95	4,310

Mary Beal Nature Trail. Like the nearby trail to Crystal Spring, this short self-guided loop trail (0.4 mile, 150 feet up) is one of the most scenic in the high desert. It is named after a good friend of the Mitchells who dedicated 50 years of her life studying the Mojave Desert flora. Around 1910, Mary Beal, then in her early thirties, moved from Riverside to the small town of Daggett to heal from a case of pneumonia. While she recovered, she developed a passion for the desert and its plants, and never left. For years Mary ranged far and wide all over the mountains surrounding Daggett to tirelessly identify, collect, and document hundreds of plants. She was occasionally accompanied by her friend Dr. Jepson, head of the Department of Botany at UC Berkeley, whose 1923 *Manual of the Flowering Plants of California* remains to this day a revered classic. When she first visited the Mitchells in the spring of 1935, she was 57 and a well-established expert. She spent days trekking the canyons of the Providence Mountains to study the local plants, which were still poorly known at the time. She came back almost every year to continue her work. She would disappear into the desert for the whole day, only to return at night for dinner and take part in the life of the homestead and entertain the guests. Mary's extensive plant collection was so vital that it was incorporated in Dr. Jepson's famous herbarium at Berkeley. A few varieties were even named after her. The nature trail was dedicated to her in June 1952 to honor this distinguished silver-haired lady and her invaluable contribution to science.

The trail starts at the north end of the parking area next to the visitor center. It drops into the wide drainage to the north, then makes a loop across a low rock-strewn bench. Many of Mary Beal's beloved plants—the disheveled chollas, the prickly-pear, the buckwheat and the New Mexico thistle—blanket the ground like a visual symphony, against the dramatic spires of the Providence Mountains. If you are unfamiliar with the desert flora, pick up a brochure at the visitor center; it identifies many of the local plants. It is a short trail. Linger for a while. Early or late in the day, you might spot a skunk, a bobcat, or a deer commuting to Crystal Spring further up the wash.

Niña Mora Trail. This very short trail (0.3 mile, 220 feet of total elevation change) starts at the east end of the campground. Near the trailhead is the grave marker of Benita Mora, who died when she was only eight days old, and after whom this trail is named. Her parents worked at the nearby Mexican Mine. The trail winds mostly down and east across open rolling terrain and ends at a rocky prominence the Mitchells named Camel's Hump, after its resemblance to the twin humps of some camels. The vegetation is less dense and drier here than along the other trails, but many of the high-desert species are still represented. The trail commands grand views of Clipper Valley on the way down, and even grander views of the rugged Providence Mountains on the way back.

■

FOUNTAIN PEAK

Loaded with loose rocks, fierce plants, and Class-3 climbs, the short but strenuous ascent of Fountain Peak is one of the most spectacular in the eastern Mojave Desert. On the mountain's precipitous slopes, nature has arranged a blind date between some of the region's most dramatic formations and the densest cactus and yucca gardens, and romance is blossoming. The lower approach alone, along a pleasant trail surrounded by towering volcanic pillars, is outstanding. The views from the pine-dotted summit are unforgettable, embracing millions of acres of mountainous desert.

General Information

Road status: Roadless; paved access road
Crystal Spring Trail: 0.8 mi, 850 ft up, 30 ft down one way / easy
Fountain Peak: 2.4 mi, 2,820 ft up, 120 ft down one way / strenuous
Main attractions: A mountain trail, cactus gardens, a hard peak climb
USGS 7.5' topo map: Fountain Peak
Maps: pp. 341*, *301*

Location and Access

Fountain Peak is the southernmost of the Providence Mountains' three highest summits. It is located in the Providence Mountains State Recreation Area. Follow the directions to Mitchell Caverns. Exploring the backcountry requires a permit, available at the visitor center.

Route Description

Crystal Spring Trail. From the visitor center, Fountain Peak is the sugarloaf summit that caps the mountain's crest; Edgar Peak is the next peak north, the highest in this range. The infrequent climbers who tackle Fountain Peak tend to take the ridge on either side of the deep open canyon behind the visitor center. The Crystal Spring Trail climbs part way into the canyon, and cuts through some of the region's most awesome sceneries. The slopes are bearded with a jungle of cacti more lush than almost anywhere in the preserve. Just about every local resident is represented, from blue yucca to prickly-pear. Boulders outcrop randomly, stained with vivid ochres and cloaked with colorful lichens. Switchbacks and short stairways constructed with local rocks make for easy navigation through the uneven terrain. Less than half a mile away, the mountains rise into a sweeping amphitheater 2,000 feet tall, bristling with ancient pinyon pine and massive spires of reddish rhyodacite—a Jurassic volcanic formation called Fountain Peak Rhyolite.

After 0.7 mile the trail crosses Crystal Spring, a rippling grove entrenched in the narrow canyon wash, most of it too thick to cross. The dominant species are willows and silktassel, an evergreen shrub native to West Coast ranges that resembles oak. Sometimes a little crystal-clear water fills small pools along the wash. The pipeline that parallels the trail was built by the Mitchells to bring water down from the spring to their homestead (see *Mitchell Caverns*).The area is often active with quails, jackrabbits, and white-tailed antelope squirrels.

On the north side of the spring the trail climbs the canyon slope and ends shortly at a pointed outcrop. If you are not climbing Fountain Peak, this is a good spot to rest before turning around. The views stretch 3,000 feet down across Fenner Valley all the way to the Piute Mountains and higher ranges beyond in western Arizona.

Fountain Peak. For the north-ridge route, from the pointed outcrop climb up to the prominent saddle on the ridge 150 yards north. Then follow the ridge southwest to the false summit at the crest. Easier said than done: you will need to gain 1,400 feet in 0.8 mile, across a terrain anything but cooperative. The main problem is the groves of rhyolite spires that outcrop all along the ridge. Some can be climbed, while others are best to bypass. The scrambling is fun, and it does not have to get technical. But all the trial and error consumes time and energy—it can take over an hour to cover this gnarly bit of ground.

For the south-ridge route, get to the south ridge up the larger wash that the trail crosses 0.5 mile in. This ridge has fewer outcrops, and it is a little easier, but it still calls for some Class-3 scrambling and a few bypasses. Near the top of the ridge, route finding can be a little tricky. Make sure not to confuse the false summit with the slightly lower 6,617-ft summit southeast of it. You will need to get off the ridge on its north side and aim between these two summits, then climb up the steep ravine below to the south side of the false summit.

Either way, it is not an easy ascent. Negotiating the rhyolite plugs and the loose rocks is demanding. There is often not enough space between cacti for a whole human foot. Chances of stumbling onto something eminently prickly are high. Gloves and trekking poles definitely come in handy.

When you reach the crest below the false summit, cairns will guide you around its south side, first down a short talus slope, then back up again. The next stretch is along a narrow, gently sloped ridgeline covered with an open pine forest. The first peak to the west is not

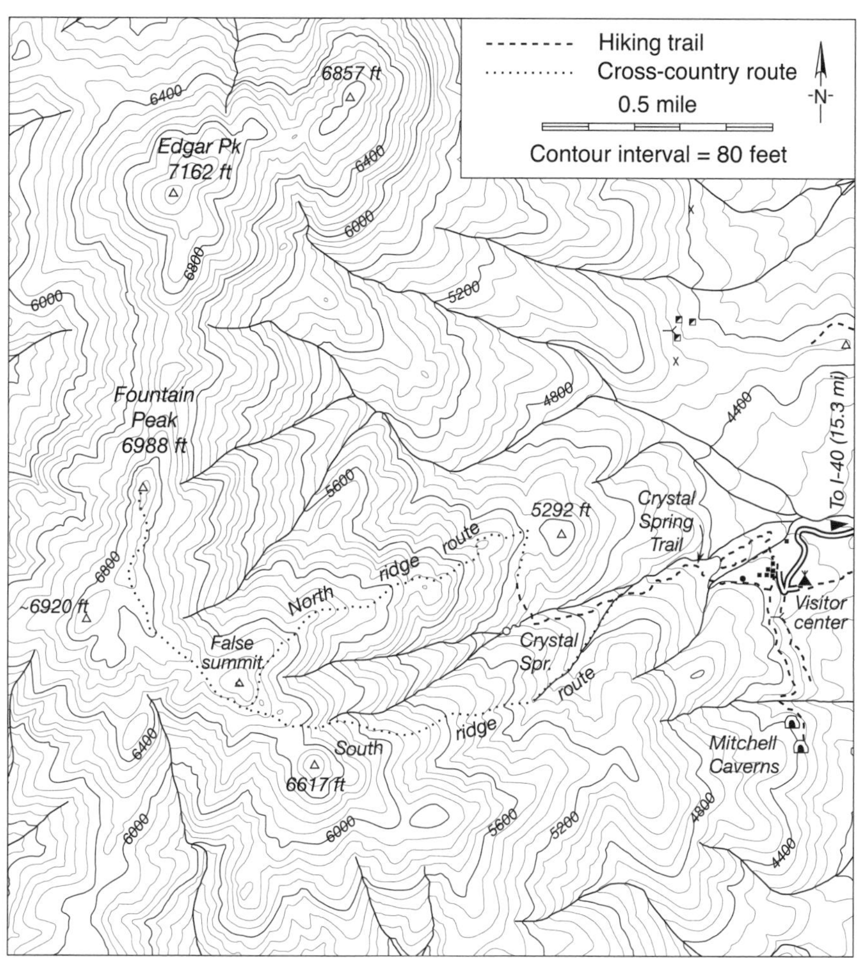

Fountain Peak	Dist.(mi)	Elev.(ft)
Crystal Spring trailhead	0.0	4,310
Wash crossing / start south route	0.5	4,630
Join north route on crest	(1.05)	6,600
Fountain Peak	(2.2)	6,988
Crystal Spring crossing	0.7	4,890
End of trail at pointed outcrop	0.8	~5,120
Saddle on north ridge	0.9	5,220
Route jct below false summit	1.75	6,600
Fountain Peak	2.4	6,988

Dead pine at sunset on the north ridge to Fountain Peak

Fountain Peak (if you wander off to it, you will run into the ruin of a rickety wooden weather station). Continue north instead, along the craggy ridge. About halfway along this final stretch, a bypass is required on the east side, just before getting to Fountain Peak.

In spite of the workout, and in fact partly thanks to it, the rewards are thrilling. Mature pines grace the slopes and provide deep shade in the hot season. The air is filled with the pleasant aroma of warm sap. In the spring, I was greeted by exuberant displays of purple phacelia and flaming-red Indian paintbrush. In the summer, desert mariposa brightened the ground with unlikely dots of vivid orange. A sizable herd of bighorn sheep inhabits this region, so chances of an encounter are comparatively high.

The narrow summit commands dizzying views down the sheer slopes of the Providence Mountains, and magnificent vistas of most of the preserve. The tree-studded pointed summit of Edgar Peak rises majestically to the north. Spin slowly clockwise and you will see one after the other the iconic volcanic mesas of Hole-in-the-Wall, the New York Mountains and Piute Range, the Clipper and the Granite mountains, the Kelso Dunes, and the sprawling mass of the San Bernardino Mountains halfway to the Pacific Ocean. Another small turn and, if the sky is clear, you might make out the distant mountains of Death Valley.

■

PROVIDENCE PEAK

Providence Peak encapsulates the most characteristic features of the Providence Mountains' high summits: the climb is comparatively short, rocky, steep, demanding, and it crosses hordes of cactus. To negotiate the tall ribs of granite near the crest, you may have to experiment and try different routes to keep it a Class-2 ascent. The summit area offers far-reaching vistas of most of the eastern Mojave Desert, millions of acres of endless valleys receding to crowns of distant ranges, including the magnificent Kelso Dunes.

General Information

Road status: Roadless, hike partly on trail; primitive access road (HC)
Providence Mine: 1.6 mi, 1,030 feet up, 70 feet down one way/moder.
Providence Peak: 2.4 mi, 2,770 ft up, 40 ft down one way/strenuous
Main attractions: Fabulous views, cactus gardens, an isolated mine
USGS 7.5' topo maps: Fountain Peak, Van Winkle Spring*
Maps: pp. 345*, *301*

Location and Access

Providence Peak is the highest summit in the southern portion of the Providence Mountains. It can be climbed from the Providence Mine, on the east side of the range. To get there, drive to the signed junction of the Essex and Black Canyon roads. A wide graded power-line road cuts east-west through this junction. Turn west on it and go 0.45 mile to the unsigned Clipper Valley Road. Turn left and drive 4.85 miles along Clipper Valley to the Providence Mine Road on the right (it is the second one of two roads within 70 yards of each other). After 2.25 miles up the Providence Mine Road, a road joins in at 7 o'clock. Continue straight 0.15 mile to a fork. Turn right, go 1.1 miles, and park on the left side, before a rocky, canted grade up. The graded Clipper Valley Road can be driven with standard clearance. The Providence Mine Road has a crown and rocks, and high clearance is imperative.

Route Description

After argentiferous lead seams were discovered below Providence Peak about a century ago, for twenty-some years miners took turns working a dozen properties. For a time the mountain echoed with the harsh sounds of hard-rock mining—drills, blasts, pumps, trucks, compressors, concentrators, generators, nearby mills, and the odd miner's snore at night. What little ore was pulled out barely paid for the dynamite, the whiskey, and the bullets that put jackrabbit on the menu. By the 1930s everyone had moved on, and the area had returned to its blissful age-old obscurity. Today's only visitors are a handful of hard-core hikers each year looking for the mine's minimal ruins, and a few skittish cows in search of food and relief from the summer heat.

The easiest route to the summit starts on the mining trail to the area's most remote diggings. If you continue on the access road 120 yards, up the grade and around a left bend, it will be there on the left. Heavily damaged, hemmed in by thorns, this narrow twin track climbs slowly across a dissected rise and enters into a deep cove in the mountain front. Providence Peak and the range's cliff-bounded crest loom steeply up ahead, a silent intimation of the hard labor to come. Here as elsewhere in this range, the desert has sprouted a remarkably verdant cactus garden. Several species have succumbed to gigantism, with staghorn cholla 5 feet high, Mojave yucca sporting multiple branches, and barrel cactus as puffy as fire hydrants. If it weren't for the trail, it would be tricky to get through without getting punctured.

After 0.6 mile, the trail angles 90° to the left as it narrows to a single track, descends a little to a small wash, and makes a right U bend across it. On the far side, it climbs gently 0.1 mile over the lower tip of Providence Peak's eastern shoulder—the way to the peak. Although it is tempting to continue on the trail to the mine, gaining access to this shoulder from the mine is an unpleasant trudge up a very steep and brushy ravine. It is easier to climb up the shoulder from this point. If you prefer to visit the mine—a considerably easier workout—stay on the trail: it is 0.8 mile further at the end of the trail. Its forgotten working does not have a lot to show, but it is fun to search for it—the trail disappears for a while, and the remains are hidden in brambles—and the cactus gardens more than make up for it.

Providence Peak

	Dist.(mi)	Elev.(ft)
Road at Providence Mine	0.0	3,890
Trailhead	0.05	3,910
Eastern shoulder	0.75	4,290
Providence Mine / end of trail	(0.8)	~4,850
Saddle on ridge	1.5	5,215
Crest	~2.1	6,330
Providence Peak	2.4	6,612

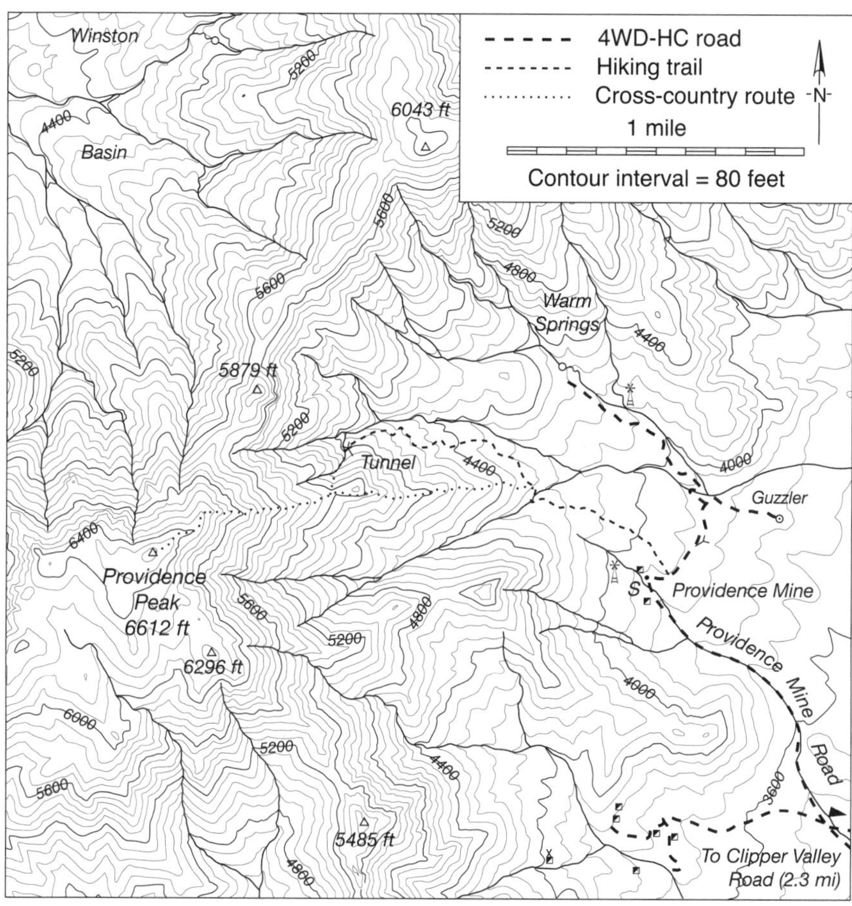

Providence Peak's eastern shoulder is fairly open and moderately steep at first. The lower elevation cactus garden extends up along it, thinner and mixed with pinyon pine. After 0.65 mile the ridge is interrupted by the first obstacle, a plug of granite artfully festooned with cactus, easily contoured on the left. Just behind it there is a shallow saddle. From there to the crest the terrain gets progressively rougher. The first part, up to about 5,600 feet, is still fairly open but much steeper, with more trees and boulders. Some of the climbing is done on the faint tracks gouged by the few temerarious cows that made it this far up. This is one of the few haunts in the Mojave for the simple desert agave, a handsome mescal with a thick blue-green rosette.

The second part is much more challenging. There the ridge is steeper still, and buried under a dorsal of tall granitic outcrops. Unless you tackle the Class 4–5 climbs on the shattered outcrops, the only

Mining trail and eastern shoulder ramping up to Providence Peak (left)

option is the steep flanks on either side of them. This stretch is ridiculously short—0.2 mile—yet so resilient that crossing it borders on laughable. You slip and slide on steep loose dirt and clamber sideways over tumbles of wobbly angular rocks. You fight prickly plants on the south flank, thick pine on the north flank, and fallen logs on both. To find your way you have to accept being occasionally redirected.

Once on the crest, the summit is a short hike south, up a much easier open woodland of juniper and pinyon accented with low rounded boulders. Up there you are suspended high between desert and sky; the vistas are astounding, encompassing most of the eastern Mojave Desert, from Nevada west to the Cady Mountains, and from the Kingston Range southwest to the edge of la-la land. On a clear day the scenery is as crisp as a diorama, each range neatly separated from its neighbors. The middle ground is bristling with individual summits—the spiky crests of the Providence Mountains and Granite Mountains, the Bristol Mountains' sprawling archipelago, the somber lava terraces of the Hackberry Mountains. Here too the Kelso Dunes hold center stage, a long graceful island of luminous sand stretched out nearly one vertical mile below. This is an exhilarating sight to be remembered.

■

THE BIG HORN MINE

The Big Horn Mine was included here mostly for the benefit of mine lovers and history buffs—it was one of the few historic gold mines in the preserve that had something to show. Driving the challenging roads that lead up to it is a good part of the fun. So is taking short hikes on abandoned roads among the yucca-studded foothills of the Providence Mountains in search of the mine's numerous ruins, which include a sizable cabin, several mills, and impressive shafts.

General Information

Road status: Hiking on roads and trails; high-clearance access road
Mabel tunnel: 1.0 mi, 590 ft up, 50 ft down one way / easy
Main attractions: An isolated historic gold mine, mills, vista points
USGS 7.5' topo maps: Colton Well, W. of Blind Hills, Van Winkle Spr.*
Maps: pp. 349*, *301*

Location and Access

The Big Horn Mine is in a nameless canyon on the eastern flank of the Providence Mountains, about 2 miles north of Hidden Hill. Work your way to the junction of the Essex Road and Black Canyon Road. A graded road cuts through it. Drive this road west 0.4 mile and turn left on the unsigned Clipper Valley Road. Stay on it 7.1 miles, southwest along Clipper Valley's sea of creosote bush, to a narrow dirt road on the right (Big Horn Mine Road). The Clipper Valley Road is a good graded road, but there is a little sand, in particular at the road crossing after 4.8 miles, and good clearance helps. It is 2.8 miles up the Big Horn Mine Road to the four-road junction below the Big Horn Mine. The first 1.2 miles are in decent shape. Then comes a washed-out stretch, followed by dips in and out of sandy washes. Along the last 0.3 mile the road straddles the wash's bank or winds along a channel too tight to turn around. Even with clearance you might have to walk.

History

The Big Horn Mine mineral deposit is hard to miss: it occurs along a dike of andesite over 100 feet wide that protrudes along the edge of the wash like a great thumb. Both buried sides of the dike were lined with quartz veins up to 12 feet wide and loaded with gold, silver, lead, and copper. Gold was first spotted here in 1894, and a dozen claims were filed. The man who first developed the mine was an Angelino by the name of Thomas Gannon. As early as 1898, he and a partner named Barker had already exposed a wide ore-bearing ledge all the way down a 200-foot shaft on the Contention claim. At the richer bottom, it assayed nearly $70 per ton, and hand-sorted samples carried over $200 in gold and 12% in copper. In April 1898, Gannon and Barker were planning to have 18 miners working around the clock by summer. Although this ambitious plan may not have come through, Gannon did keep the mine going for nearly 30 years. He sunk a shaft on the Subway claim and two on the Mabel claim, blasted hundreds of feet of drifts off the Contention shaft, and put up a small mill and concentrator near it. In the 1910s, he uncovered foot-wide streaks of gold carrying up to $500 a ton in the Mabel shaft, then ore worth $100 a ton in the Contention shaft. In June 1913, he made headlines shipping 94 sacks of high-grade ore to the Needles smelter. From late 1918 to early 1919, he cleaned out $100,000 with ore exceeding $50 per ton. Gannon was back working the Contention and Subway shafts in 1924. How much more gold he squeezed out is unknown, but it might have been substantial, because the tailings alone had 6,000 tons worth $30,000.

Gannon's era ended soon after. The mine changed hands at least twice in the early 1930s, but it laid mostly idle. Things picked up again in the late 1930s, when the Big Horn Exploration Company renamed the mine and took its development to a higher level. A new three-compartment shaft was sunk 325 feet on the Contention claim, with two levels of drifts. One level bore 400 feet through to the Subway shaft, following a foot-wide vein of pyrite, chalcopyrite, and gold. An 80-foot headframe, with ore bins and a 25-horsepower hoist, serviced the enormous shaft, and a large mill just below treated the ore. Water for the mill was pumped from the shafts and stored in two 55,000 gallon tanks. In the wash below, the camp had a large cabin and a full machine shop. In 1940 four people were still running the facilities, but by 1943 all mining had stopped, this time for good.

We may never know how rich the Big Horn was. But mining journals praised it for decades, and its veins were large enough to justify a few mills and 2,000 feet of galleries. It was certainly richer than most.

Route Description

Although not exactly spectacular, the canyon leading up to the mine is pretty, framed by low hills on the south side and higher, more rugged ridges to the north. Yucca and ephedra add touches of dark green, as do catclaw in the summer. Two miles away, the crenulated crest of the Providence Mountains rise 3,000 feet, studded with pines. The first sign of the mine is a huge metal tank stranded up ahead in

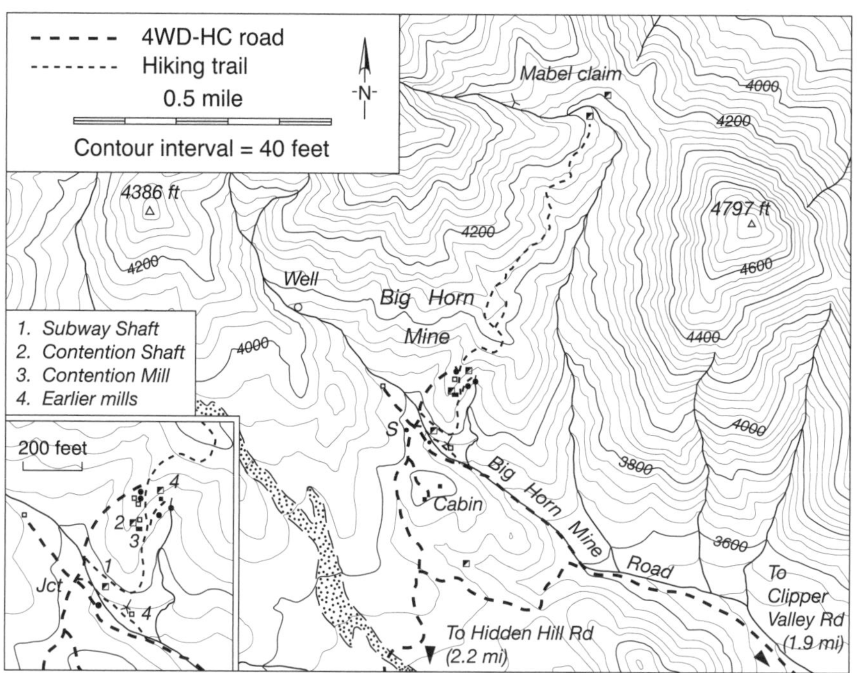

The Big Horn Mine		
	Dist.(mi)	Elev.(ft)
Four-road junction	0.0	3,775
Cabin	(0.15)	~3,810
Contention Shaft	0.2	3,895
Mabel main shaft	0.8	4,175
Mabel tunnel	1.0	4,315

the wash. The wall of brown rock that caps the canyon slope next to it, like the partly exhumed skeleton of some antediluvian mammal, is the dike that held most of the Big Horn Mine's gold.

The Big Horn Mine Road reaches the dike at a broad flat where four roads converge. The large concrete pad is the foundation of the workshop that stood here during Gannon's era and until at least the 1920s. Mining junk and custom-made contraptions with long-forgotten purposes litter the wash. The road that heads south from the junction climbs 120 yards to a fork. The left fork ends shortly at a funky house at the top of a hill. Occupied until fairly recently, it is still in decent shape. It has a main room with a brick fireplace, a bedroom, storage rooms, a toilet, and even a shower. The vintage red tow truck next to it,

Water tanks and mill foundations at the Big Horn Mine

although pumped full of lead by idiots, has tons of character. The shady veranda is an enjoyable spot to rest and admire the expansive views of Clipper Valley and the Providence Mountains.

The flooded shaft 50 yards east of the road junction, near the foot of the dike, is the Subway shaft. Its ore came mostly from a 200-foot drift 50 feet below the surface. The foundations next to it supported the three-stamp mill Gannon used in the 1910s.

Two roads climb to the old Contention claim at the top of the dike. One is the long, steep, more recent grade just west of the dike. The other one is the historic access road that ramps up above the Subway shaft. The flat area where the roads meet has one of the preserve's highest densities of mining ruins. The centerpiece is the three-compartment's Contention shaft from the 1930s revival. It is a hole of staggering proportions, 12 feet on the side and covered by the collapsed 80-foot headframe. The nearby mill is just as imposing. With its thick pilings and concrete walls cascading down the slope, it was one of the largest mills the eastern Mojave Desert ever had. The large water reservoirs are still around, including the two 55,000-gallon tanks. There is a small shaft and its own small mill 50 yards up the road.

The third extensively mined area is the Mabel claim. To get to it, follow the beat-up mining road that climbs northeast from the Contention shaft area. It winds gently above a scenic side canyon 0.6 mile to the Mabel No. 1 and No. 2 shafts, located about 750 feet apart on opposite sides of the canyon wash. This claim also had a tunnel, which is 0.2 mile up the wash to the west. The ruins are minimal, but as is often true the mining road is not just a means to an end. Much of it commands excellent views south to the Clipper Mountains and Marble Mountains, and more distant ranges beyond. In the evening they all take on dramatic shades of brown and purple.

■

HIDDEN HILL

For anyone interested in mining, Hidden Hill is well worth visiting even if it is just to inspect the historic mill of the Golden Queen Mine, which is the best preserved in the park. The short mining road that winds behind it gives access to many interesting old diggings. Even if mines do not do it for you, come here for the steep jaunt up to the top of nearby Hidden Hill, which commands superb views of the preserve's boundless southeastern valleys.

General Information

Road status: Hiking on trails and cross-country; HC access road
Hidden Hill Mine Trail: 0.75 mi, 330 ft up, 40 ft down one way / easy
Hidden Hill summit: 0.9 mi, 670 ft up, 20 ft down, one way / easy–mod.
Main attractions: A historic gold mill and mine, a short peak climb
USGS 7.5' topo map: Van Winkle Spring
Maps: pp. 355*, *301*

Location and Access

Hidden Hill is a 700-foot prominence at the southeastern edge of the Providence Mountains, facing Clipper Valley. To get to it, drive the Kelbaker Road 1.3 miles south of Granite Pass (or 6.4 miles north of Interstate 40's westbound exit) to the signed Hidden Hill Road, on the east side. This graded road descends gradually along an alluvial fan, past the desolate volcanic mesa of Van Winkle Mountain, into Clipper Valley. After about 2.4 miles, the road makes two left turns in a row, then runs parallel to the Providence Mountains. After 4.4 miles it reaches a fork. To get to the main (east) part of the Hidden Hill Mine, continue straight 0.3 mile to a windmill at a junction with a road coming in from the right. Make a left 0.1 mile past it on the Hidden Hill Mine Trail and park 250 feet further, below the mill ruins and next to large stone ruins. This route is suitable for all vehicles, with the possible exception of the short grade 3.6 miles out, which will stop some two-wheel-drive vehicles. To get to the west side of the mine, at the fork make a left instead. Follow this more primitive high-clearance road 0.65 mile to some ruins on the right, and park.

History: Hit-And-Miss in Pocket Mining

Gold was first discovered on Hidden Hill in 1882, just two years after the rich silver strike at the Bonanza King Mine a few miles north.

Golden Queen Mill at the Hidden Hill Mine

The original ore samples assayed over 50 ounces of gold per ton, and there was great hope that Hidden Hill would be another bonanza. It was not to be. But it was clear from the start that it had unusual high-grade pockets, and these nuggets kept it busy for decades.

Hidden Hill's original four claims—the Hidden Hill, Golden Queen, Bill McKinley, and Golden Queen Fraction—covered an area of 70 acres. The first two emerged early on as the most important ones. The Golden Queen, or the Queen as it was referred to, was located on the southeast slope of Hidden Hill. The Hidden Hill Claim was on the southwest side. Gold occurred in parallel quartz veins in brecciated porphyritic granite. Less than a foot wide, broken into offset segments by a swarm of small faults, these veins were a constant mining challenge. When a shaft reached the end of a vein segment, which was all too soon, it often had to be abandoned and another shaft started.

Unfortunately, production records are scant, and they focus mostly on heroic strikes. The first lucky miner was P. H. Keane. In 1895, he exposed a small fortune in just a few blasts of dynamite. Keane had so much ore at hand that he built a small arrastre to process it, and he recovered $25,000 worth of gold. Shortly after, two miners from Needles, Monoghan and Murphy, purchased the property and formed the Hidden Hill Mine. They extracted high-grade rock rich enough to be shipped without refining. To crush the lower grade ore, they erected a small two-stamp mill run by a gasoline engine. The workings were then relatively modest—the largest one was only 35 feet deep. But the mine did well, producing for a time a car load worth $9,000 every month. Other than a short hiatus during a litigation, work continued into the next century. By 1901, the Queen's shaft was 165 feet deep.

The mine underwent a major revival in early 1913. New owner T. W. Crawford hired a mining engineer from Los Angeles, A. D. Nescus, to run the property. There was enough ore in sight for two years' worth of work, and Nescus planned accordingly: first, he brought his wife. In preparation for this event, in December he had a camp erected below the Queen, including a manager's office and an apartment building. Several tons of supplies and building materials were hauled to the mine by freight and wagons. Nescus and his wife moved to the new camp in January 1914. The *Barstow Printer News* bragged that the camp was "assuming the appearance of a village." It even had the luxury of a garage to take care of the new mode of transportation that was making its first appearance at desert mines—automobiles.

Mining was moving in unison. In 1913, a pocket of 300 tons of gold-bearing ore returned $13,000. In February 1914, with eight people on its payroll, the company started digging a tunnel on the gulch side of the Golden Queen. For several months, regular ore shipments were made from the Queen dump to the railroad. A contractor was blading a road to the Santa Fe Railway. After its completion, it was said to rank among the best desert roads in the county. The labor force was soon increased to two shifts. Ore from other claims was being stockpiled for future shipment as well. Two partners from Los Angeles were also exposing good ore on the nearby Golden Spider, and new claims were being filed around Hidden Hill. The future looked bright enough that in April, Nescus, Murphy, Crawford, and a few others incorporated the Hidden Hill Mining Company for a capital stock of $100,000. Through 1915 the main shaft on the Queen was gradually opened to a depth of 240 feet, and a 350-foot crosscut tunnel was cut in it to exploit a rich vein. The shafts on the other claims were also extended as far down as 100 feet.

As Nescus had forecast, the good ore ran out the following year, and the mine closed down. Other workings were developed between 1920 and the 1950s by subsequent operators. Sometime during this period, a new mill was installed next to the 1890s' mill, but again we have no indication of how much ore it processed. The Hidden Hill Mine may have been richer than we think—we might never know.

Route Description

The mining camp. The area south of the mill was the general location of the mine camp, which hosted several generations of miners. The oldest structures are the thick walls of rough, uncemented stones below the mill. They define two adjacent rooms and the remains of a third one. The few concrete pads scattered around the windmill and 200 yards south of it are the remains of the camp built by Nescus in 1913. The raised concrete foundation inset with stone may have been his residence. If you poke around you might find the two acres of land that Mr. and Mrs. Nescus cleared in 1914 to plant—not vegetables—but spineless cactus...

The Golden Queen Mill and shaft. The mill above the road dates from the latter part of the mine's history, and it is undoubtedly the best preserved in the park. The large wooden ore bin at the top stored the raw ore from the shaft located above it. The concrete foundations below it supported a crusher, now gone. The crushed ore was gravity-fed into the funnel-shaped metal hopper underneath the crusher. It then dropped into the horizontal mill (perhaps a ball mill) on the next level. Finally, it was dumped into the partitioned concrete vat at the foot of the mill, where the gold was probably extracted with cyanide. Against the mill's east flank are the ruins of an older mill, dating probably from the earliest mining efforts of the late 1890s. What remains of it are four concrete pads cascading down the hill, a footwall decorated with mortared flat stones, and a small oven-like structure.

The hulking mass of gravel looming above the mill is the tailing of the Golden Queen's shaft—by far the mine's largest working, and its best producer. The shaft at the top of the tailing is a gaping collared hole topped with the massive lumber of its collapsed headframe. The slanted stope behind it is held open by a small army of wooden beams. The tunnel right by the road next to the stone ruins is the crosscut tunnel sunk by Nescus's team in 1915. Do not mess with it—in 50 yards it intersects the shaft way above its bottom...

Forgotten at the far corner of a forbidding desert, the old Golden Queen Mill stands over the surrounding desert like a lone sentinel, seemingly guarding the old mine that once fed it, oblivious to the flow of time. A moving testimony to the area's long and tumultuous mining past, it is a vivid reminder of a not-so-distant time when the country was a very different place. Treat it with respect.

Hidden Hill Mine Trail. From the mill the Hidden Hill Mine Trail continues, first up along a wide gulch, then up the open incline to the

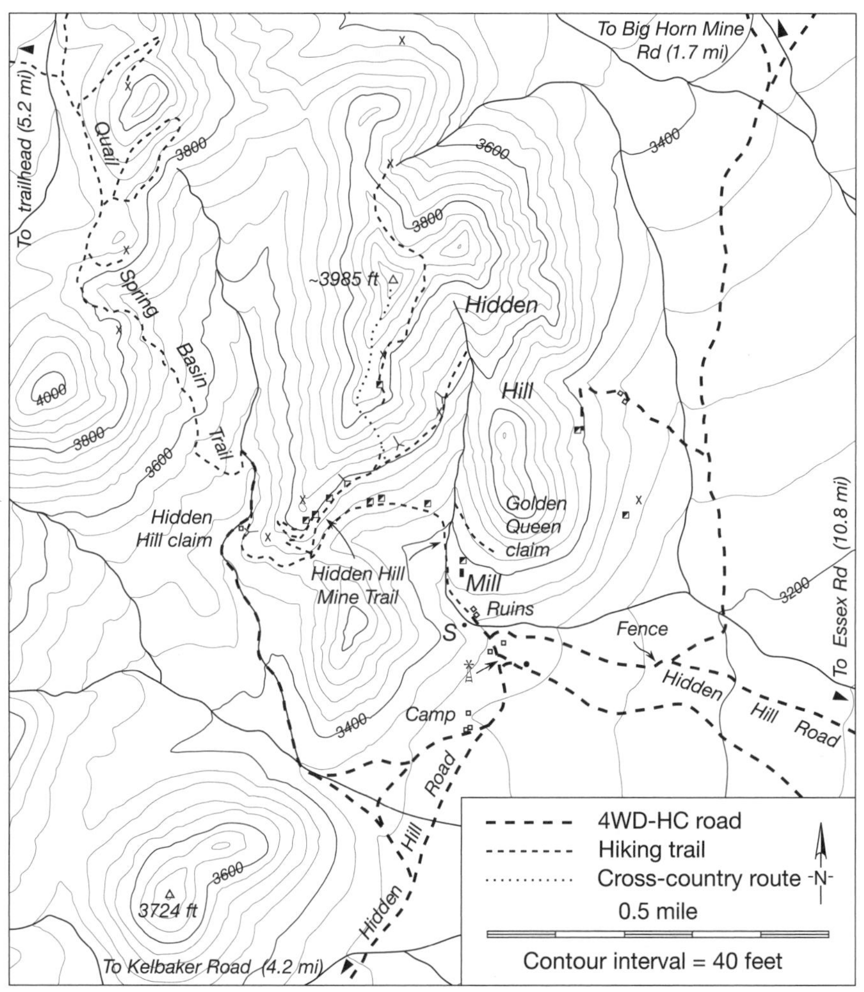

Hidden Hill

	Dist.(mi)	Elev.(ft)
Hidden Hill Mine Trail (ruins)	0.0	3,335
Golden Queen shaft	~0.1	~3,380
Four-way junction	0.4	3,515
Hidden Hill claim (road)	(0.15)	3,461
Steep gully to summit	0.55	3,610
Ridge	(0.1)	3,830
Hidden Hill summit	(0.3)	~3,985
End of Hidden Hill Mine Trail	0.75	~3,630

west to a four-road junction on the brow of Hidden Hill (0.3 mile). The leftmost road circles around the hill to the Hidden Hill claim, along the western access road. The middle road winds up a few hundred feet to a shaft. The main trail continues to the right, northeast across the slope of Hidden Hill, and ends in 0.4 mile at a rocky outcrop. This beat-up road can be driven with a high-clearance four-wheel-drive machine, but not all the way. As often, it is more edifying to walk.

Almost all of the historic workings are located either right along or close to the Hidden Hill Mine Trail. Their variety is surprising—they range from prospect holes to inclined shafts, stopes, road cuts, trenches, and tunnels. A few of them have interesting physical remains; some have been filled while others have convoluted layouts; here and there lie sprinklings of quartz, jasper, chalcopyrite, bornite, or limonite. A perk of this hike is searching for these workings, across a landscape strewn with cholla, barrel cactus, and Mojave yucca that you might be sharing with quails, lizards, or a panicked ground squirrel. I saw a healthy coyote melon growing at the bottom of a 10-foot shaft, smartly trading light for moisture. One of its gutted gourds rested on a rat's nest in a nearby tunnel. From the top of the mill and most of the trail, the panoramic vistas are surprisingly good given the relatively low elevation.

Windmill and Hidden Hill summit

Hidden Hill. The only elusive working is the upper shaft, located high up near Hidden Hill's crest. The trail that once climbed to it is partly washed out, so try the rough ravine 0.2 mile northeast of the four-way junction. It shoots straight up the 45% slope and ends a short distance southwest of the shaft. The greatest reward is the bird's-eye views from the summit of Hidden Hill, reached by a short walk north along the ridge. Hidden Hill's precipitous eastern slope sweeps down 700 feet, past the dwarfed ruins of the mine, to the bush-dotted floor of Clipper Valley. Far to the east, Fenner Valley merges seamlessly with the Piute Mountains. It is well worth the five-minute, heart-pounding climb.

■

— 11 —

GRANITE MOUNTAINS

RISING MAJESTICALLY more than 3,000 feet above the Kelso Dunes and more than 10 miles across, the Granite Mountains are the second highest in the preserve, and quite possibly the most scenic. Their namesake dominates much of the range and composes striking landscapes of weather-worn boulders, abrupt walls, slickrock, pinnacles, falls, and knobby ridges. The southern and eastern foothills are dissected into beautiful coves nestled within silvery cliffs, many graced with springs. The remote interior hosts rugged basins, the home of the preserve's most challenging canyons and beautiful conifer woodlands inhabited by a substantial herd of bighorn sheep, deer, and a few lonesome mountain lions. Unlike other local ranges, the Granite Mountains were virtually left untouched by miners; other than a couple of mining roads, they are as pristine as they ever were. Although most of the range is protected as a designated wilderness and can only be accessed on foot, several of its spectacular peripheral coves can be reached by car, and hikers and four-wheelers alike can enjoy their artful displays of igneous rocks.

Access and Backcountry Roads

To this day, almost all of the Granite Mountains remains blissfully roadless. Only two roads ever penetrated the mountains to begin with—in Cottonwood Wash and in Devils Playground Canyon. Two other roads, in Willow Spring Basin and Granite Cove, only went a short distance to the foot of the range and petered out against unsurmountable rock barriers. These roads are now either part of the wilderness that protects the Granite Mountains or on private land.

Suggested Backcountry Drives in the Granite Mountains					
Route/Destination	Dist. (mi)	Lowest elev.	Highest elev.	Road type	Pages
Budweiser Spring	7.8	3,054'	3,775'	F	383
Coyote Springs Road	10.0	2,936'	4,024'	H	358, 369
Willow Spring Road	2.7	3,068'	3,743'	H	375
Key:	H=Primitive (HC)		F=Primitive (4WD)		

The edges of the Granite Mountains, on the other hand, are relatively easy to access on three sides. The Kelbaker Road follows the east side of the range and offers excellent views of the mountains' spectacular eastern tip. Short primitive roads that branch off it get close to several secluded coves. Much of the northern foot of the mountains, including half a dozen canyons, lies within short walking distance of the graded Kelso Dunes Road and the power-line road. The south side can be accessed via a network of old ranching roads that crisscross the mountains' extensive fans between Sheep Corral and Budweiser Canyon. The west side, bordering the 70,000-acre Bristol Mountains Wilderness, is the most remote. Far from any road, it requires a couple of hours of cross-country walking to be reached.

The two longest primitive roads for exploring the periphery of the Granite Mountains are the road to Budweiser Spring (see *Budweiser Canyon*), and what I refer to as the Coyote Springs Road, a collage of sandy tracks that hugs the mountains' scalloped northeastern base. Starting just north of Granite Pass, this second road swings in and out of a few scenic granite coves, passes close to Coyote Springs and Twin Springs, and ends at the Kelbaker Road near the Kelso Dunes Road.

Geology

Rarely has a mountain range been so aptly named. At one time the area was all Paleozoic sedimentary rocks. In the Mesozoic these formations were pushed up by the intrusion of multiple plutons. The overlying Paleozoic rocks were subsequently eroded, so that today the Granite Mountains are made almost exclusively of Mesozoic plutonic rocks. Only a few roof pendants of Paleozoic rocks totaling less than one square mile remain, mostly on the eastern rim of Bighorn Basin and on Silver Peak. About 75% of the mountains are a gift from the turbulent Cretaceous. The rest, mostly on the northern and northwestern fringes of the range and along much of Bull Canyon, dates back to

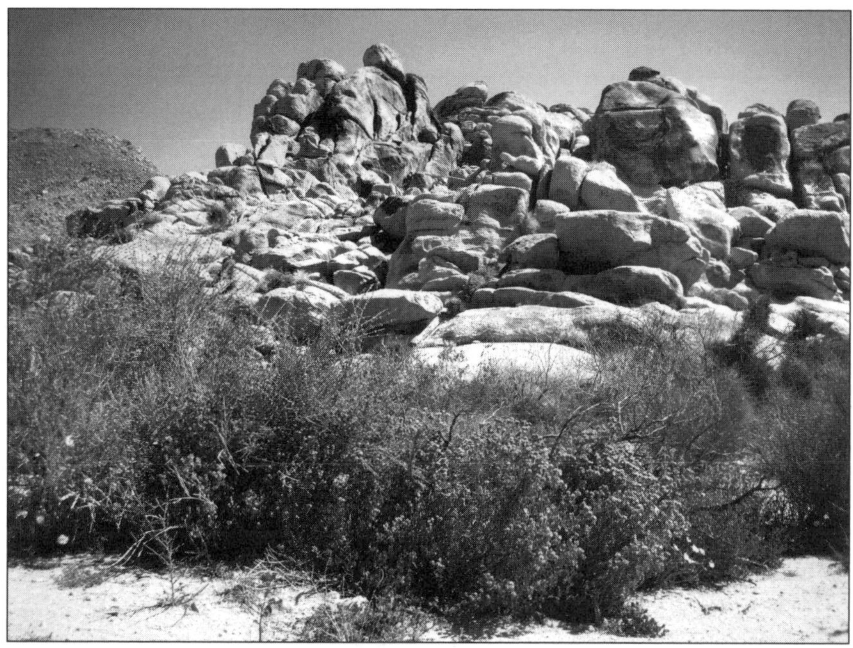

Granite knolls in Willow Spring Basin

the Jurassic. This suite of plutonic rocks covers a wide spectrum of compositions, from monzogranite (the most common) to diorite, granite, quartz monzonite, quartz monzodiorite, and syenogranite. These rocks also display a wide range of textures (fine-grained to porphyritic), structures (unaltered to gneiss), and colors (brown to dark grey and nearly white). One of the Granite Mountains greatest assets is this fortuitous agglomeration of very different formations. Very few other areas in the eastern Mojave Desert have such extensive and magnificent displays of natural features carved out of granitic rocks—cliffs, domes, turrets, narrows, arches, monoliths, slickrock, falls, and mile upon mile of boulder fields—the plutonic equivalent, on a far more modest scale, of some of southern Utah's sensuous sandstone legacy.

Natural History

The Granite Mountains are known for their exceptional biodiversity, which stems from a combination of a wide range of elevations and habitats, large variations in hydrology, and the fact that they face all cardinal points. This diversity has been accurately quantified through systematic documentation, and the numbers are impressive. The Granite Mountains are home to nearly 500 species of vascular plants,

Suggested Hikes in the Granite Mountains					
Route/Destination	Dist. (mi)	Elev. gain	Mean elev.	Access road	Pages
Short hikes (under 5 miles round trip)					
Budweiser Canyon				P/7.8 mi	
Triple Fall	0.9	410'	3,920'		385-386
6,614-ft peak	2.8	3,120'	4,750'		385-388
Budweiser Spring*	~1.5	~100'	~3,800'	P/7.8 mi	383-384
Sheep Corral loop*	3.3	480'	3,400'	P/0.7 mi	380-382
Willow Spring (lower)	1.0	460'	3,880'	H/2.7 mi	375-376
Willow Spring (upper)	1.4	810'	3,980'	H/2.7 mi	375-376
Intermediate hikes (5-12 miles round trip)					
Bighorn Basin (spring)	4.1	2,290'	3,680'	P/2.9 mi	370-374
Bull Canyon to 18-ft fall	3.9	1,080'	2,820'	H/0.7 mi	363-365
Bull Canyon's inner gorge	4.4	1,700'	2,890'	H/0.7 mi	363-366
Devils Playground Canyon				P/2.9 mi	
to lower spring	3.0	1,650'	3,450'		370-374
El Compache Trail	2.6	1,490'	3,450'	P/2.9 mi	370-371
Silver Peak	5.7	4,050'	4,130'	P/2.9 mi	370-374
Long hikes (over 12 miles round trip)					
Bull Canyon				H/0.7 mi	
to Bighorn Basin divide	8.1	3,790'	3,600'		363-368
to Granite Mountain	8.8	4,660'	3,810'		363-368
Key: P=Primitive (2WD) H=Primitive (HC) Distance: one way, except for loops (round-trip, marked with *) Elev. gain: sum of all elevation gains on a round-trip basis & on loops					

138 birds, 42 mammals, 34 reptiles, and two amphibians. It has chuckwallas and fringe-toed lizards, speckled rattlesnakes and rosy boas, mountain lions and ringtail cats, falcons and finches, foxes and feral burros, California juniper, and a whole suite of rare agaves. Several drainages have seasonal or permanent streams with abundant flows, especially Bull Canyon and Budweiser Canyon. Some 50 springs are scattered throughout the range, a few with large groves of cottonwoods and willows. Elevations above 5,000 feet support open forests of pinyon pine and Utah juniper, some as tall as 25 feet and as old as 500 years. Individual trees and small stands also grow at unusually low elevation—as low as 3,600 feet—thanks to the propitious shelter

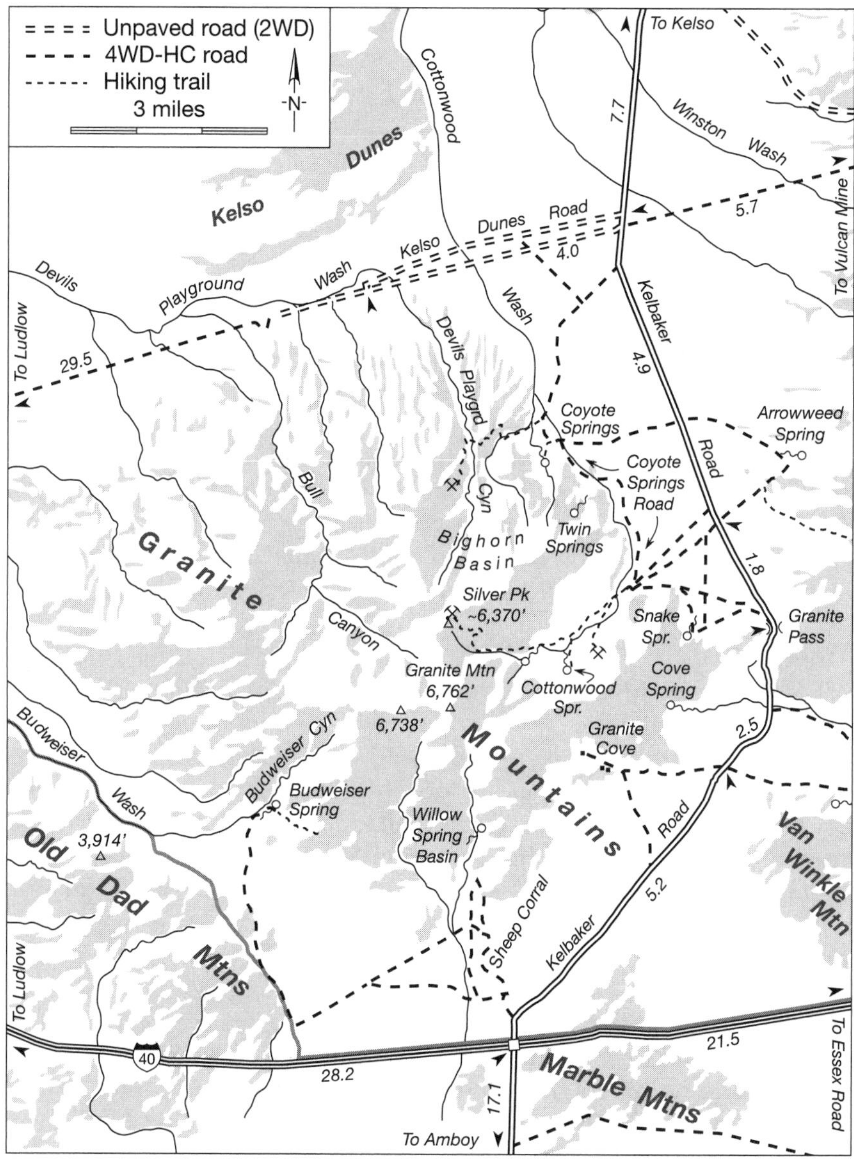

and higher humidity offered by large aggregates of boulders. Smoke trees, rare in the preserve, grow along the Kelbaker Road a few miles south of Granite Cove. In a single day you might see toads, a deer trotting among blue yucca, oaks and Joshua trees, a golden eagle and gorgeous bladderpods in bloom. This cohabitation of seemingly inconsonant species is one of the many charms of the Granite Mountains.

The Sweeney Granite Mountains Desert Research Center

About 9,000 acres of the Granite Mountains, centered on the east side, were preserved in 1978 by the University of California as the Sweeney Granite Mountains Desert Research Center. This is one of 37 protected natural areas throughout California administered by the university, and the largest such reserve system in the world. Its continuing mission is to promote academic studies of this pristine part of California, in particular to research and inventory its unusual biodiversity, to organize conferences, educate students through field trips, and support teaching and public outreach. Many of the research projects conducted in the area aim to study long-term natural processes and evolution, sometimes over decades. Many studies are very sensitive to disturbance, which necessitates prohibiting human activities on the center's lands—even walking through research plots could ruin years of critical data acquisition. Public access is strictly prohibited. The center covers the area between the upper drainage of Cottonwood Wash (including all of Cottonwood Basin) and Granite Cove, where the field station is located. Make sure not to trespass, and obey all posted signs.

Hiking

The Granite Mountains are a mecca for many outdoor activities, from hiking to climbing, photography, wildlife and plant viewing, and even, because of its remoteness from urban centers, star gazing. There is a nearly limitless selection of places for scrambling as well as technical bouldering and rock climbing on all kinds of near vertical surfaces, from low boulders to tall cliffs. The granite can be crumbly and unsafe, but at many places it is quite strong. This range has one of the greatest collections of scenic canyons in the preserve. The three main canyons are described in the following pages, but there are a dozen more, and their tributaries. Canyon hiking is generally rendered difficult and slow by the high density of outcrops and uncooperative vegetation in the washes and on the ridges. For that reason it may appeal more to seasoned desert hikers than to neophytes. The Granite Mountains are also known for their extensive displays of rock art. Dozens of panels of polychromatic pictographs, mostly abstract, some representing human or animal figures, adorn small caves and outcrops throughout the range. The quest for these ancient messages scattered across a 35,000-acre playground of igneous labyrinths can itself fuel a few years' worth of exploration on foot.

■

BULL CANYON

In every park there is one place that has it all. In the Mojave Desert, it might well be Bull Canyon. Longest in the preserve, this windy passage is blessed with narrows, slickrock, a profusion of wildly decorated granitic walls, and perennial water that supports innumerable pockets of cattail and stately willows. Count on a very long day for this rough canyoneering trek copiously sprinkled with falls, tangled vegetation, and giant boulders. With perseverance, it will take you to the highest summit in the Granite Mountains.

General Information

Road status: Roadless; mostly standard-clearance access road
Bull Canyon fall: 3.9 mi, 1,050 ft up, ~30 ft down one way / moder.–diff.
Granite Mountain: 8.8 mi, 4,400 ft up, ~260 ft down one way / strenuous
Main attractions: Remote canyon, narrows, falls, springs, a peak climb
USGS 7.5' topo maps: Kelso Dunes, Bighorn Basin
Maps: pp. *367*, 361*

Location and Access

Starting beneath the highest point in the Granite Mountains, Bull Canyon cuts a long tortuous swath clear across the mountains' northern slope. To get to the mouth of the canyon, from the Kelbaker Road drive the Kelso Dunes Road 4.0 miles to its end. Turn left on the smaller road that connects to the power-line road (0.15 mile). Turn right on this graded road and follow it 1.6 miles to a junction at the foot of a hill. The road on the left climbs the hillside to a power-line tower, then circles around this tower and descends along the far side of the hill (0.35 mile). The road straight ahead takes a steeper shortcut over the hill (0.25 mile). With a standard-clearance vehicle, you will likely not be able to drive over the hill; park at the junction and hike from there. If you are driving a high-clearance vehicle, take either road (the shortcut requires high torque). From the junction of the two roads on the far side of the hill, drive 0.3 mile to the next tower. The very wide area between this tower and the next one west is Bull Canyon's floodplain. The main wash crosses the road 0.1 mile further. Park in this vicinity.

Route Description

The floodplain. Hidden in the Granite Mountains' convoluted foothills, Bull Canyon can be hard to spot from the road. Its mouth is barely visible as a low notch in the hills a little over a mile to the south-southeast (145° magnetic bearing). A main wash leads up to it, surrounded by a braided network of narrower washes. The walking is much easier on the slightly higher ground between the washes. The burros appear to agree: this is where they have blazed the trails they use to get around. The floodplain up to the canyon is relatively sedate, but in the summer and fall it is brightened by the many light-green desert willows and catclaw that thrive in the washes. Turn around occasionally to enjoy the views of the majestic Kelso Dunes.

The lower canyon. More than any other canyon around, Bull Canyon has "water" written all over it. All along the lower canyon, sweeps of water-worn bedrock alternate with a wash of rounded cobbles caked with dried mud and algae. Almost every mineral obstacle along the wash has a water-gouged plunge pool at its base, occasionally several feet deep. One would be hard pressed to find in this desert a place with so many water-loving plants—so many groves of cattail, so many oases of tall willows, and thickets of narrowleaf willows. Even at the end of the long dry season, before the heavy rains of winter refill the canyon's underground pipes, surface water survives in rivulets and countless pools held in slickrock hollows. The stream returns every season, and when it does every boulder jam and chute gives rise to a cascade, and the plunge pools are filled to the brim again.

So much water makes for tougher hiking. Thick stands of baccharis occupy large portions of the wash. Bushwhacking is often necessary, more frequently as the elevation increases. Progress is generally not too difficult where baccharis grows alone, because there is usually enough space between plants to walk through. The harder spots are where larger woody plants—cattail, catclaw, mesquite, willow, and tamarisk—congregate. When the stream is running and the plunge pools are full, progress is even slower.

In spite of these hurdles, Bull Canyon is a joy to explore because it engages our senses on so many levels. The geology is off the chart, the flora uncommonly lush, and the scenery wild. The lower canyon cuts through dark-gray diorite and other granitoids from the Jurassic, commonly cleaved into flat surfaces coated with chocolate desert varnish. Huge white dikes draw wiggly courses across walls and bumpy slickrock. At four places the wash squeezes through short narrows trapped between these beautiful igneous rocks. The prettiest is the first one, a twisted wedge of naked stone lined with smooth chutes and shallow basins. Red-tinged colonies of barrel cactus and isolated calico cactus cling to the walls. In the fall, longstem evening primrose decorate large

Cattail and grooved chute at the second fall in Bull Canyon

areas with their papery yellow flowers balanced at the tips of 3-foot stalks. This is a rare plant, found in the preserve only at a few places in the Granite and Providence mountains. This is the home of quails, chipmunks, scorpions, black-tailed hare, bighorn sheep ossuaries, the rare simple desert agave, and burros gone wild.

The falls and the inner gorge. The lower canyon ends at the first high fall, a wavy 18-foot slant of light-gray quartz-diorite gneiss bisected by a moss-covered chute. Bull Canyon's inner gorge starts just above it. Climbing this fall is at most a 5.7. The slope is modest, the rock extremely strong, and a third of the way up a wide lip offers exceptional handholds and footholds. There is a second fall shortly above it. It is in its own right a work of art, a chimney about 14 feet high recessed at the head of a narrow passage of polished gneiss criss-crossed with white dikes. Like the first fall, it is most easily climbed on the right side, and the difficulty and exposure are comparable.

It is a pleasure to scale these two monoliths, but the climbs are exposed and many people will opt out. They can alternatively be bypassed by scrambling up the steep rock-strewn ravine on the east side 100 yards below the first fall. After gaining about 200 feet of elevation and clearing the sheer spur to the south, work your way up canyon at roughly constant elevation about 60 yards to a similar ravine, with a pine near its bottom. Then drop along this ravine back to the canyon wash, which will put you 80 yards above the second fall.

The half-mile stretch above the falls is the tightest part of Bull Canyon. It starts with a stark passage beneath towering walls. The walls exhibit again the enigmatic artistry of igneous rocks, black, gray, and white displays of convoluted gneiss slashed by wandering veins. Further on, the canyon floor pinches down to a shallow trench crowded on both sides by bulging walls of polished bedrock. Thick stands of cattail, desert willow, and tamarisk have invaded the narrow water-filled basins along the trench, leaving little space to squeeze by. Further still, slickrock and boulders take over, and bushwhacking gets a notch harder.

Upper Bull Canyon. The inner gorge ends at the junction with the first major side canyon, where Bull Canyon makes a hard right. Beyond this point, at first the canyon retains some of its earlier character. It winds between high rock walls, past slickrock benches, inundated clumps of cattail, meadows of dark-green rush, desert willow, and

Bull Canyon

	Dist.(mi)	Elev.(ft)
Power-line road	0.0	2,360
Mouth	~1.4	~2,640
Lower spring	2.5	2,910
First narrows	2.6	2,950
18-foot fall	3.9	3,410
First fork	4.4	3,600
Upper spring	7.3	4,890
Head of Bull Canyon (divide)	8.1	~5,690
Granite Mountain	8.8	6,762

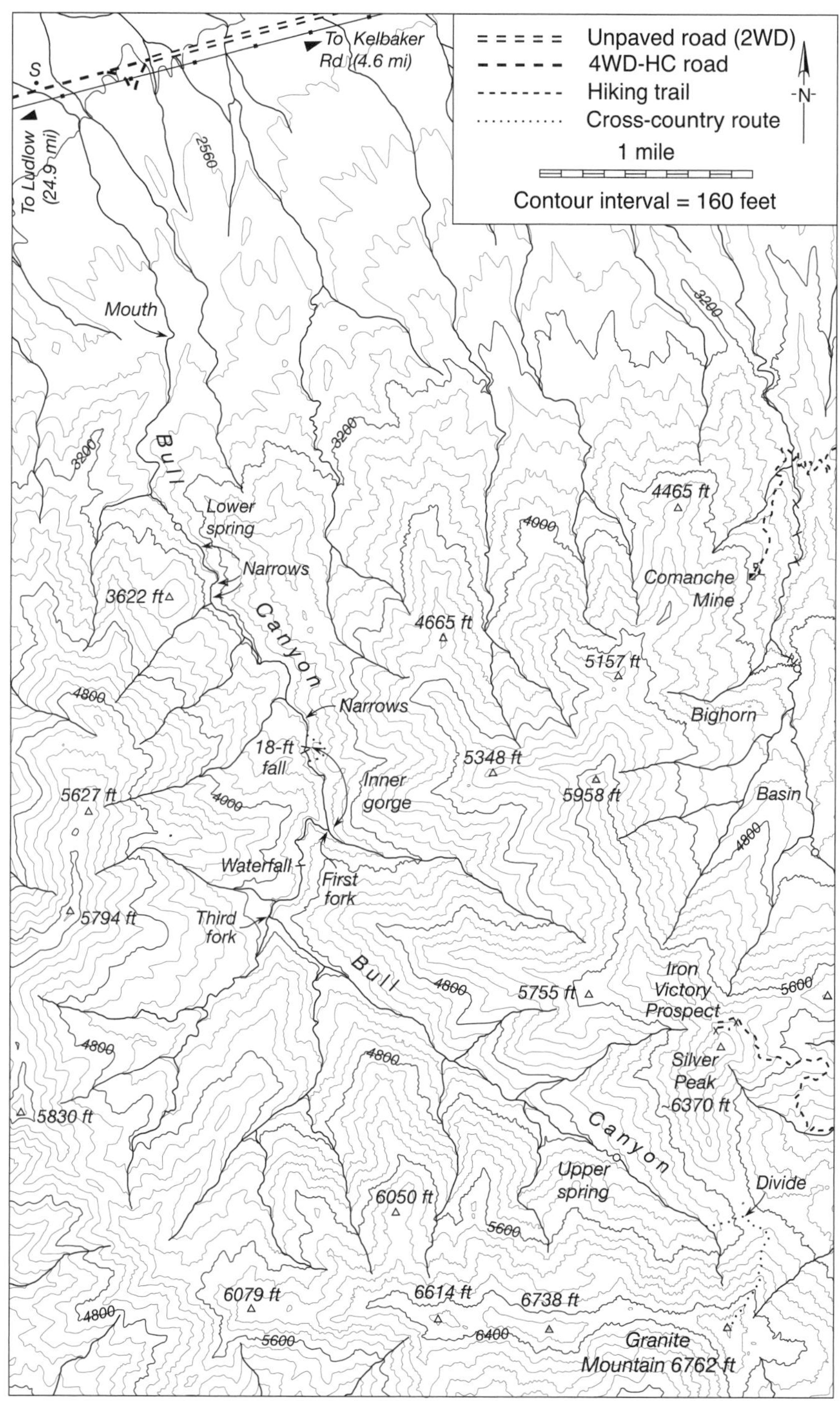
Unpaved road (2WD)
4WD-HC road
Hiking trail
Cross-country route
1 mile
N
Contour interval = 160 feet
To Kelbaker Rd (4.6 mi)
To Ludlow (24.9 mi)
Mouth
Bull
Canyon
Lower spring
Narrows
3622 ft
4665 ft
4465 ft
Comanche Mine
5157 ft
Bighorn
Basin
Narrows
18-ft fall
Inner gorge
5348 ft
5958 ft
5627 ft
Waterfall
First fork
Third fork
5794 ft
Bull
5755 ft
Iron Victory Prospect
Silver Peak 6370 ft
5830 ft
Canyon
Upper spring
Divide
6050 ft
6079 ft
6614 ft
6738 ft
Granite Mountain 6762 ft

Decorated igneous wall along Bull Canyon's inner gorge

an 8-foot waterfall concealed by exuberant vegetation. The bushwhacking intensifies gradually. Past the last major bend, the wash angles to the southeast at the second major side canyon, and it enters the Granite Mountains' extensive conifer woodland. The rest of the way to its head, the upper canyon is a beautiful V-shaped valley filled with hefty monzogranite boulders. Long monuments of this attractive Cretaceous porphyritic rock outcrop part way up the tall slopes.

This last stretch is wild and remote, but it is also the roughest. It takes nothing short of a blood-letting thrash to get through this chaos of brush, trees, fallen logs, and boulders. If you start early enough and do not get too distracted, you may have time to get to the head of the canyon at its divide overlooking Cottonwood Basin, then ascend the bouldery ridge to Granite Mountain, the highest point in this range, and make it back not too late into the night. But it is a minor epic perhaps best tackled with a backpack and at least three days. On a sunny early October day I was out there 11 hours. The last three and a half hours I walked in the dark, following the bouncy tunnel of my headlight beam. It took a month for my scratched legs to fully heal. I would go back in a second.

■

DEVILS PLAYGROUND CANYON

From the forested heights of Silver Peak to the golden edge of the Kelso Dunes, Devils Playground Canyon tumbles down some 3,300 feet in less than 6 miles. By canyoneering standards, this is the genuine product, full of high falls, boulders, brush, and fine springs. There is plenty to do here, from hiking the easy access road to the interesting remains of the Comanche Mine to exploring this scenic canyon as far as your tolerance for climbing and bushwhacking will take you. The ultimate objective is Bighorn Basin, a majestic amphitheater rimmed by 6,000-foot summits, where diehards can tackle the challenging ascent of Silver Peak.

General Information

Road status: Roadless; mostly standard-clearance access road
El Compache Trail: 2.6 mi, 1,130 ft up, 360 ft down one way / moderate
Bighorn Basin lower spr: 3.0 mi, 1,230 ft up, 420 ft down one way / diff.
Silver Peak: 5.7 mi, 3,630 ft up, 420 ft down one way / strenuous
Main attractions: A rough canyon with a seasonal creek, a trail to an iron mine, a peak climb
USGS 7.5' topo map: Bighorn Basin
Maps: pp. 373*, 367, *361*

Location and Access

Devils Playground Canyon cuts across the northeastern Granite Mountains. Upon exiting the mountains, the wash is deflected west by the Kelso Dunes and continues many languid miles across the Devils Playground to Soda Lake. The easiest route to the action-packed mid-canyon is a mining road that starts near Coyote Springs. In honor of the mine it serviced, I refer to this road as the El Compache Trail.

To get to it from the north, drive the Kelbaker Road 0.9 mile south of the Kelso Dunes Road to the Coyote Springs Road on the west side, just before a bend. Drive this dirt road 2.7 miles to a junction, and continue straight. Park 0.15 mile further at the wilderness boundary. The road that continues into the wilderness area is the El Compache Trail.

If you are coming from the south, drive the Kelbaker Road 3.4 miles north of Granite Pass and look attentively for a primitive road on the west side. Drive it 2.6 miles to the junction mentioned above, ignoring the two roads on the left along the way, and make a left. The common last stretch is a bit rocky and requires decent clearance.

Route Description

The El Compache Trail. Even if there were no mine at the end of it, this beat-up road would be well worth hiking for the scenery alone. Its gentle lower segment skirts scenic foothills so packed with granite boulders that plants have virtually no purchase on any soil. The road soon crosses a wash and ascends a ridge in one long switchback. The granite disappears, but as the road gains elevation it commands dramatic vistas of the hills you just passed, offset against the serrated southern Providence Mountains in the distance. The sawtooth rim of Bighorn Basin caps the southern horizon. After the road crests the ridge and starts descending into Devils Playground Canyon, the Kelso Dunes come into view, aberrantly bright in the dark V of the canyon walls.

The road ends after 1.65 miles in the wash of Devils Playground Canyon. To get to the mine, head down the wash 50 yards to the continuation of the road, on the left side. It climbs steeply up a ridge and follows it south to the mine. The ridge supports a thriving population of tall staghorn cholla mixed with Mojave yucca and barrel cactus. It also has good views of the Providence Mountains and of boulder-filled Devils Playground Canyon winding down below.

The Comanche Mine. Iron and a small skarn of malachite and azurite, discovered in 1902, was the sole *raison d'être* of the far-flung mine at the end of the road. It was known as the El Compache Mine in 1925, the Comanche Mine in the 1950s, and the Christopher Mine in 1965. A sizable investment was made, including the brutal access road, complete with spurs for three-point turns, ore trucks powerful enough to muscle the 20% grades, and the painstaking labor of digging hundreds of feet of gallery. Unfortunately, there was only 110 tons of iron ore in the ground. Most of it was extracted, which, at 1955 prices, brought in all of $700—not even enough to cover the *gas* to build the road...

The lower working is just before the end of the road. It is a 200-foot straight tunnel with a neat trim of white marble around its opening and an interesting custom rail. The dark-gray rock inside it and on the tailing is diorite—black granite. The upper working, located one last switchback up the road, is an inclined shaft protected by a wooden casing resting on hefty pillars. The loading platform in front of it still holds black metallic pieces of magnetite, some stained with ochre limonite and blue copper oxides. Along the road between the workings lies the exploded shell of the miners' cabin, its appliances slowly turning to rust. Perhaps the miners knew their claim was worthless. They might have found that this serene site, hung high between earth

The 20-ft fall and spring vegetation in mid Devils Playground Canyon

and sky, overlooking nothing but exuberant wildness, was just compensation for the aches and pains of hard-rock mining.

A steep foot trail, perhaps once used to access water, connects the mine to the canyon wash. It is a convenient shortcut (~0.2 mile), but it is very faint and both ends are gone. It is easiest to spot it from the El Compache Trail below the tunnel; it cuts a distinct line down across the hillside east of the tunnel. To find it from the tunnel, walk down the tailing's south side to a short trail that wanders off to an overlook. At the low point before the overlook, head left down the slope until you run into the cutoff trail. It is rocky, prickly, and locally washed out. If you lose it, clambering cross-country is not much harder work.

Devils Playground Canyon. This is one of the prettiest canyons in the preserve. Sunk deep into the mountains' igneous core, its slopes are crawling with huge monolithic outcrops and loose boulders. Most of it is a gorgeous gallery right out of the Mesozoic, square miles of chaotic light-beige monzogranite and dark-gray quartz diorite gneiss crisscrossed with massive dikes. Uphill from the mining road the wash is relatively tame at first. Many boulder jams bisect its course, but none is very high. Not for long: a third of a mile up is the first high fall. It can be climbed, but it is safer to bypass it on the east side. Above it, the frequency of obstacles increases rapidly. The second obstruction is more serious, a cove of bare granite blocked by a 20-foot fall. Lush stands of cattail and young willow thrive all around its slickrock base. I named it Fern Fall, after its thick fur of maidenhair fern—a rare plant in the eastern Mojave Desert. This fall can be circumvented over tilted slickrock on the west side, but some moves are exposed. Climbing the soft talus on the east side is safer, although the broken chute on the far side is a Class-2 down-climb. Soon after, near the lower end of the trail from the mine, another challenge shows up—a profuse cover of baccharis spiked with mesquite plugs the wash. From here on up, stretches of open wash are few and short. A choice must be made almost constantly between bushwhacking, scrambling, climbing, or taking the long way around, whichever looks least improbable.

Because of its higher elevation, Bighorn Basin receives more rain and snow than most places around. After a wet winter, all this water is funneled down to the wash and gives rise to a spirited creek. White water pours over the normally dry falls, splashes between boulders, thunders into pools, and irrigates patches of green grass. The best time to visit is when the stream is in action, even though climbing boulders is tougher when they are flushed with water. Even if you miss the stream, signs of its passage are ubiquitous months after it has retired underground. Dried mud and algae coat the wash. Masses of dead plants mark the former location of unthinkably high tides. At the foot of many cascades, the force of falling water has excavated deep

Devils Playground Canyon

	Dist.(mi)	Elev.(ft)
El Compache trailhead	0.0	3,160
Hairpin bend on ridge top	1.25	3,590
Devils Playground Canyon	1.65	3,280
Comanche Mine shaft	(0.95)	3,920
Fern Fall	2.25	3,500
Lower end of trail from mine	2.3	3,530
First fork	2.75	3,735
Lower spring	3.0	3,970
Second fork	3.25	4,115
Third fork	4.0	4,545
Upper spring	(0.1)	4,610
Silver Peak	5.7	6,368

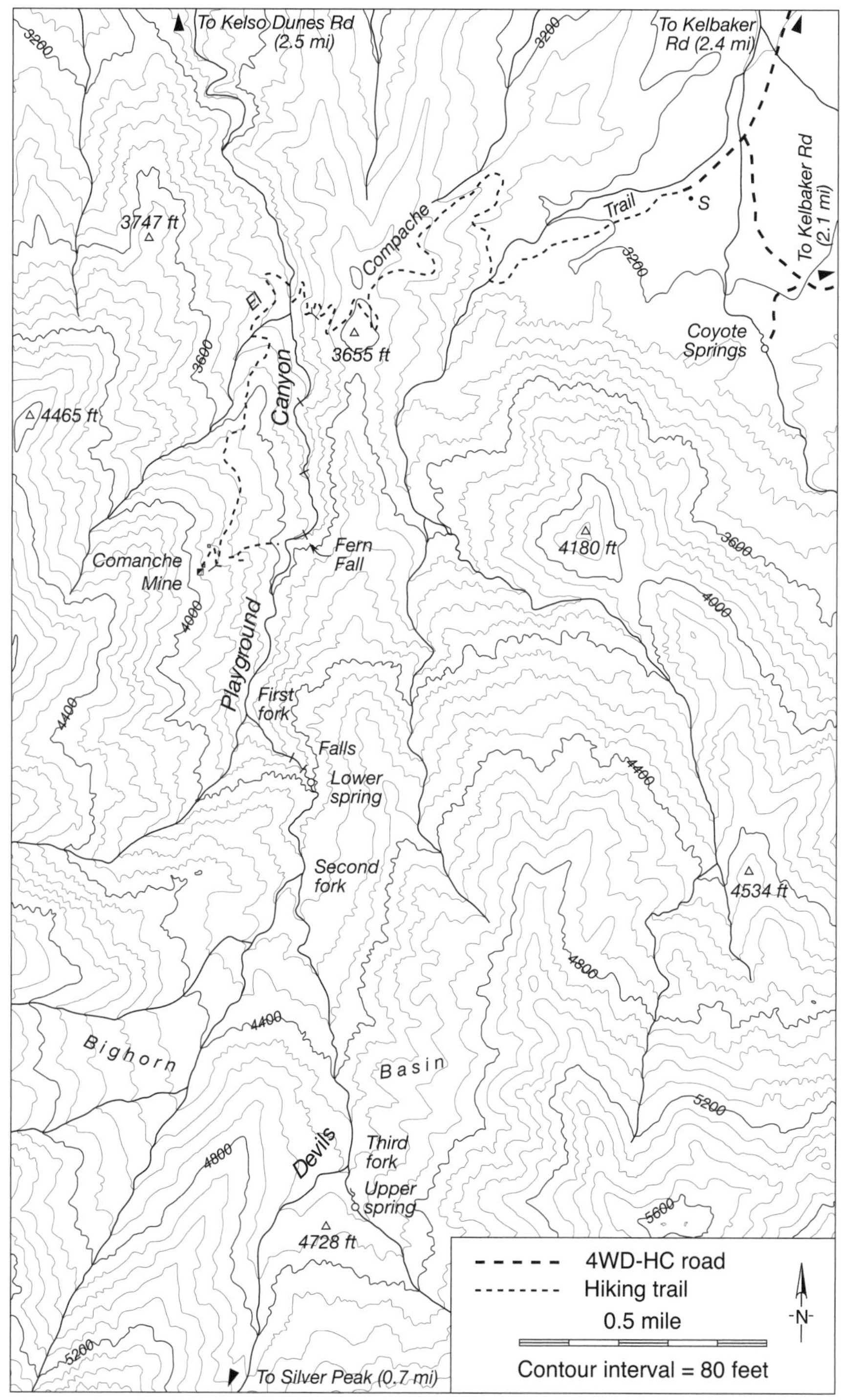
To Kelso Dunes Rd (2.5 mi)
To Kelbaker Rd (2.4 mi)
To Kelbaker Rd (2.1 mi)
3747 ft
Compache
Trail
S
3655 ft
El
Canyon
Coyote Springs
4465 ft
4180 ft
Comanche Mine
Fern Fall
Playground
First fork
Falls
Lower spring
Second fork
4534 ft
Bighorn
Basin
Devils
Third fork
Upper spring
4728 ft
To Silver Peak (0.7 mi)
4WD-HC road
Hiking trail
0.5 mile
N
Contour interval = 80 feet
3200
3600
4000
4400
4800
5200
5600

depressions in the sand. Black streaks record on rock faces the ghosts of past waterfalls. Well into the dry season the high falls usually have a pool of stagnant water, saturated with gecko-green algae. All along the canyon, cumulative stream erosion has polished neat bowls in bedrock and sleek grooves in boulders and falls.

Progress gets more difficult deeper into the canyon. Juniper and pinyon pine, which first appear shortly above Fern Fall, grow in numbers above the first fork, and the difficulty increases again. The next main challenge is about halfway to the second fork, a grand staircase of water-stained falls carved in an extensive sweep of sensual slickrock. One of this canyon's most arresting sights is the small spring just above the highest fall, a pair of shockingly bright trees in a rocky nook surrounded by stately pinyon pine.

Bighorn Basin. There are more falls and obstacles beyond, more brush, and endless variations in boulder landscapes. If you persevere long enough you will get to Bighorn Basin, an expansive ring of high summits dotted with large evergreens. The overgrown upper spring that fills the third fork is at about the center of Bighorn Basin. It takes a while just to get there, and there is plenty to see once you do, so it makes sense to bring a backpack, set up camp, and take the time to discover. Or maybe just take a well-deserved snooze on a hollow of sun-warmed slickrock. This area of sweet-scented pine and lustrous granite, shared by a small herd of bighorn sheep, is about as wild and peaceful as it gets, and it invites relaxation as much as exploration.

The crowning glory is the grind up to Silver Peak, the highest of the surrounding summits. Aim for the twin white outcrops just below the summit, which are the small marble open cut and pit at the Iron Victory Prospect. It explored a cluster of small skarns containing magnetite and hematite—the dark rocks lying around. The gold-looking specks are chalcopyrite. The claims were first located around 1912, relocated in 1942, and patented in 1956, but the deposit was not large enough to be worth exploiting. The original 100,000 tons of iron-rich ore has remained untouched. From the end of the mining road at the prospect, it is a short jaunt south up to the summit. In almost all directions the views from Silver Peak are astounding. The grand prize goes to the Kelso Basin, blanketed by the sprawling sands of the Devils Playground all the way to Soda Lake. Nearly 4,000 feet below, the Kelso Dunes rise against the barren desert in majestic defiance.

The mining road is part of the Granite Mountains research center and strictly off-limits. Make sure not to use it as a return route.

■

WILLOW SPRING BASIN

A giant alcove ringed by magnificent mountains of granitic boulders, Willow Spring Basin ranks among the most scenic in the preserve. The hike to Willow Spring provides an easy introduction to this stunning area. But the best way to discover it is scrambling. Almost anywhere in its immense chaos of boulders you will find beautiful cactus gardens, formations of startling design, and, if you climb hard enough, expansive views of the desert to the south.

General Information

Road status: Roadless; high-clearance access road
Willow Spring (lower): 1.0 mi, 410 ft up, 30 ft down one way / easy
Willow Spring (upper): 1.4 mi, 780 ft up, 30 ft down one way / easy
Main attractions: Easy hike to springs, mountains of granitic boulders
USGS 7.5' topo maps: Brown Buttes, Bighorn Basin*
Maps: pp. 377*, 361

Location and Access

Willow Spring Basin is a large cove at the southern foot of the Granite Mountains. Two parallel high-clearance roads converge to its southern edge. Beyond, the basin is in a wilderness area and closed to motor vehicles. Start from the pronounced bend in the Kelbaker Road 0.25 mile north of Interstate 40. A wide road heads north in the bend, on the west side. Drive it 0.45 mile to a road on the left, in a right bend. Make a left and go 0.45 mile to the Willow Spring Road on the right. Drive this road 1.8 miles to the wilderness boundary, where the other road joins it from the right at a sharp angle, and park.

Route Description

Willow Spring. From the wilderness boundary, walk on the old pipeline road as it cuts north across the basin's gently sloping sandy floor. The road is well defined at first. After 0.35 mile it merges with the broad sand wash coming down from the spring and shrivels to a swath only discernible by thinner vegetation. Where the wash forks, bear left. By then the road is gone. A segment survives up on the east bank, but it is short and a little hard to reach. Staying in the main wash the remaining distance is just as easy.

This short hike crosses remarkable scenery. Surrounded by a spectacular ring of pointed summits and steep granitic slopes, Willow

Spring Basin is studded with sharp hills of handsome boulders. This landscape of petrified sails stranded in a sea of rocks, which repeats itself many miles down the enormous alluvial fan to the south, is one of the most otherworldly in this desert. This visual stunt is compromised in early spring when the vegetation is festooned with cheery pale-yellow dandelion and bright-blue Canterbury bell. The combination is incongruous—the exuberant flowers bespeak loudly of Earth, in a place that seems to have so little to do with it.

Shortly after the fork, the main wash leads into the canyon where Willow Spring is located. This drainage actually has several springs. The first one is along the part of the wash bypassed by the road; in the springtime, water often trickles over polished rock and sand, just enough to keep a little algae green. Willow Spring comes next. It is easy to miss: look for greenery and an old grade up on the right side, about 100 yards away. The grade starts at the edge of the wash. It is badly eroded at first, but it still climbs to Willow Spring's narrow stand of dried cattail, inundated by a veneer of water. The spring at the next fork is the largest and most interesting. Willow, catclaw, mesquite, and bladderpod form a thorny mass irrigated some of the time by a diminutive creek. These springs are small and fragile. To minimize impact, step on rocks instead of soft ground to cross the lower seeps. At the largest spring, which is essentially impenetrable, refrain from bushwhacking. Climb to higher ground for better views.

The upper drainage. As delightful as these little springs are, they are overwhelmed by the scenery. The highlight here is exploring the extraordinary profusion of boulders that cover the basin's mountains. A good place to start is the canyon itself. To go further, bypass the spring by clambering over the boulders on its north side. Above it the wash is comparatively free of obstacles, all the way to the upper spring, in sight of the first trees. The whole side of the mountain is dominated by fantastic piles of boulders. The possibilities for climbing are endless. The local Cretaceous monzogranite has been rounded, hollowed, polished, scooped, clipped, and fractured into an infinite variety of shapes and sizes. There are gargantuan stones, pinnacles, balanced rocks, and deep caves cloaked in perpetual darkness. You can mantle, stem, slide, hop, and wiggle up and down chimneys all day—and return a different way to double the fun. Between the rocks, the spiny plants, and the steep terrain, progress is slow. But even a moderate workout almost anywhere up the canyon's slope will take you to eerie viewpoints of Willow Spring Basin, the Bristol Mountains, and the huge salt pan of Bristol Lake to the south.

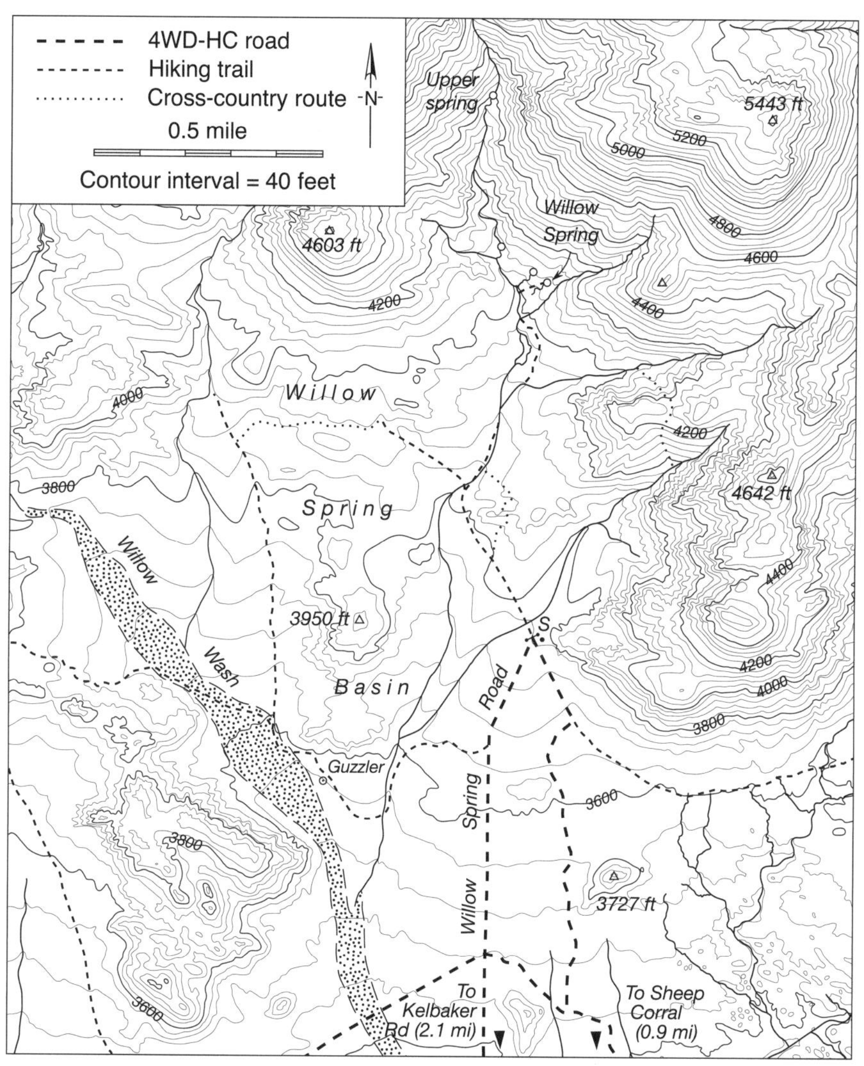

Willow Spring Basin		
	Dist.(mi)	Elev.(ft)
Trailhead	0.0	3,743
Fork	0.65	3,885
Grade to spring	0.85	4,000
Willow Spring	(0.1)	4,080
Spring in main wash	0.9	4,060
Upper spring	1.35	~4,400

Granite landscape around Willow Spring Basin

Willow Spring Basin. Many other places around the basin hold stunning fairylands of boulders (a few are outlined on the map). The low massif the road passes by 0.4 mile from the trailhead is a good example. Behind it, a narrow wash wanders between steep slopes of sensual boulders, in full view of the majestic alignment of sharp peaks that frames the basin to the east. These peaks are another fine example. The side canyon near the trailhead gives easy access to them—although scrambling quickly becomes the main mode of locomotion. Everywhere in that area, the repetitive juxtaposition of rounded shapes and individual desert plants is every bit as complex, intriguing, and aesthetically pleasing as Joshua Tree National Park's magical scenes. I found slickrock, towering cliffs, scenic gardens artfully marrying yucca and cacti with mineral sculptures, giant monoliths, and acres of nothing but handsome granite. Reaching the high peaks requires technical climbing, but some of the passes between them can be reached with "just" a lot of non-technical climbing. No matter where you go, this is a haven for photography, a superb playground to wander aimlessly, so attractive you might stay far longer than you had intended, and come back again for more.

■

SHEEP CORRAL

Nowhere in my desert wanderings have I seen anything quite like Sheep Corral—a stealth labyrinth that meanders on and on through a wonderland of sculpted boulders countersunk 100 feet beneath the surface of a fan. If you are looking for a short hike charged with scenery, this is the place. This little maze will make you wander, scramble, and climb as you ponder over and over which way to go, drawn into an intimate landscape that changes constantly.

General Information

Road status: Roadless; primitive access road, HC preferable
Sheep Corral: 3.3 mi, 480 ft up loop / easy–moderate
Main attraction: A serpentine maze through a wonderland of granite
USGS 7.5' topo maps: Brown Buttes*, Bighorn Basin
Maps: pp. 381*, *361*

Location and Access

Sheep Corral is at the southern tip of the Granite Mountains, just inside the wilderness area that protects this range. A short primitive road goes right up to it. Parts of the road are deeply gouged and require high clearance or skill. If you can't drive it, walk it. It is well worth the short extra walk. To get there, drive to the pronounced bend in the Kelbaker Road 0.25 mile north of Interstate 40. In the bend, on the west side, a road, wide and graded at the start, heads north. Drive it 0.45 mile to a road on the left, in a right bend. Continue straight 0.2 mile to a side road that drops down to the right. Park at the end of this side road (100 yards), at an open area beneath a granitic outcrop. Sheep Corral lies to the north, past the wilderness boundary signs.

Geology: Erosion's Mood Swings

Sheep Corral's maze is a bit of a geological rarity. Covering an area of about 1.3 miles long by 0.5 mile wide, it is carved into Cretaceous monzogranite sunk *beneath* the surface of a fan. Desert mountains are commonly surrounded by pediments, the smooth sloping surfaces erosion leaves behind as it etches away the foot of a mountain. Pediments are typically covered by loose fan material that protects them from further erosion: erosion brings down new rocks from the mountain as fast as it removes older rocks from the fan. So where Sheep Corral stands there should be a fan, like there is all around it. Sheep Corral exists thanks to sediment starvation. Some time ago, at least 750,000 years, the rate of erosion of the mountain front above it slowed down, perhaps because of exceptional hardness. With a weaker intake of fresh rocks, the fan was stripped off, and erosion proceeded into the exposed pediment. In the process, it widened the pediment's network of stress planes into countless joints, draws, gulches, and canyons radiating through a complex underworld of hoodoos. Upland erosion may eventually speed up again and fill it all in—it makes us wonder what other magical landscapes lie buried under desert fans.

Route Description

Discovering this sunken treasure is pure delight. The entry into Sheep Corral is a wide wash of pristine sand flanked by low cliffs of granite boulders. The wash is lined with rock sculptures and thickets of catclaw, desert willow, and blackbrush, some impressively large. Even more so than elsewhere, the mood changes dramatically with the season. On a sunny day every element in this scenery vibrates with light—every plant, every grain of sand, every crystal on every rock. In contrast, on an overcast winter day the skyline of jagged rocks and the leafless catclaw tearing at the ashen sky exude unsettling gloom. In the spring, when the edges of the wash are flushed with wildflowers, it is yet a different place.

The true nature of Sheep Corral first shows through a short distance up canyon. By then the wash has narrowed, the walls have grown taller, and the canyon forks. The main canyon seems to continue straight, but it actually angles right, even though that branch is narrower and blocked shortly by a 9-foot fall. This is a good illustration of what is in store up ahead. From here on up, the main artery that runs through Sheep Corral remains elusive as it twists and forks over and over. The side canyons have a tendency to peter out into piles of boulders, only to start again a little further. Sheep Corral's main appeal is its uncanny ability to keep the mystery constantly alive.

Describing a route through this stone labyrinth would be tedious. If you are concerned about getting lost, consider the following clockwise loop, which will take you through it downhill, the easier direction. At the first fork, go straight. This side canyon climbs gently to the top of the fan on the west rim of Sheep Corral. On the fan, narrow washes sluicing between slickrock benches will guide you north past the east side of a scenic bouldery hill (elev. 3,727'). Just north of this hill, an old road (now a foot trail) connects the Willow Spring Road to the Kelbaker Road. It is washed out at places; not to miss it, aim a little too far west. Once on the road, follow it about 0.35 mile east to where

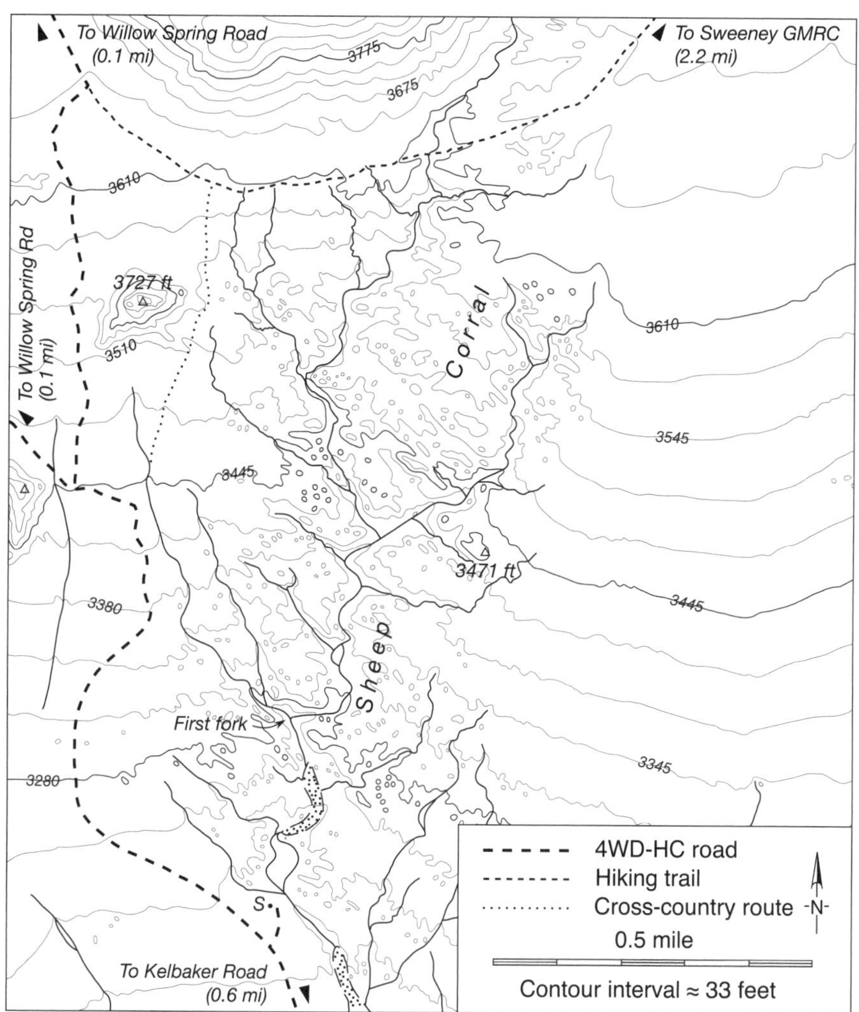

Sheep Corral		
	Dist.(mi)	Elev.(ft)
End of access road	0.0	3,155
First fork	0.35	3,240
West rim of Sheep Corral	0.65	3,380
Old road (south point)	1.4	3,600
Main wash/leave road	1.7	3,585
Back to first fork	2.95	3,240
Return via main canyon	3.3	3,155

Walls of granite boulders in Sheep Corral

it crosses the main wash that slices through Sheep Corral. Re-enter Sheep Corral either at this point, or earlier along one of the ravines that drain south into it (they may not all be passable). Once down in the maze, keep heading downhill, through many forks, to that first fork. Finding the old road the other way, uphill through the maze, is more challenging. But the pleasure is also intensified, as trial and error forces us to discover a greater portion of this wild place.

It would be difficult to overstate how delightful exploring this area is, irrespective of the route. The fan overlooks many desert ranges, including the Bristol, Marble, and Clipper mountains to the south. Many spiny beauties grace the way, often growing right out of dark cryptogamic soil. Bighorn sheep tracks are unusually abundant—not a big surprise given the area's name. Down in Sheep Corral, granite is king. It defines the entire landscape, from long jointed cliffs to slopes of house-size boulders, slits, potholes, tafoni, and sleek chutes worn by ancient water. There are short narrows to wiggle through, an enormous chockstone to scrawl under, falls to climb, and innumerable boulder jams to scramble. I walked by more friction climbs and top-rope face climbs than one could tackle in a few days of intense fun. Few short hikes in the preserve offer such diversity.

■

BUDWEISER CANYON

From its head near the highest point in the Granite Mountains to its mouth, Budweiser Canyon drops about 2,800 feet in 2.5 miles. This is two thirds as much elevation change as the Bright Angel Trail in the Grand Canyon, in only 30% the distance. Come here to indulge in a memorable trek into this remarkable world of slickrock, boulders, high falls, and cliffs irrigated by a seasonal stream, or just to browse for pictographs among the boulders surrounding the spring at the mouth of the canyon.

General Information

Road status: Roadless; high-clearance four-wheel-drive access road
Budweiser Spring: ~1.5 mi, ~100 ft up loop / easy–moderate
Triple Fall: 0.9 mi, 380 ft up, 30 ft down one way / difficult
6,614-ft peak: 2.8 mi, 2,980 ft up, 140 ft down one way / strenuous
Main attractions: A rugged granitic canyon, stream, high falls
USGS 7.5' topo maps: Brown Buttes, Budweiser Wash, Bighorn Basin*
Maps: pp. 387*, 361

Location and Access

Budweiser Canyon is a short, rugged gorge that drains the Granite Mountains southwest from their highest crest. A long two-track road crosses bumpy fans to Budweiser Spring near the mouth of the canyon. A high-clearance, four-wheel drive vehicle is required to handle the high crowns of vegetation and several rough spots. The starting point is the pronounced bend in the Kelbaker Road 0.25 mile north of Interstate 40. In the bend on the west side, take the wide road that heads north. After 0.45 mile you will reach a junction. Make a left and go 0.9 mile to a fork. Turn left and drive 1.3 miles to a crossroad. Take the road on the left and stay on it 5.1 miles to its end at Budweiser Spring. Count on a good hour for this slow jostling ride.

Route Description

Budweiser Spring. Boxed inside a corral of lumber and wire from the ranching days, Budweiser Spring is a thicket of tall baccharis and cattail. The cattail grows out of a circular concrete trough brimming with algae-saturated water. The water is piped in from a 25-foot well dug by ranchers in the hillside about 150 yards northeast of it. Around 1910, water from this area was used about 7 miles down the fan to run

Slickrock Fall in lower Budweiser Canyon

a mill at the Orange Blossom Mine in the Bristol Mountains. Remnants of the metal pipeline still protrude along the access road. It may have tapped its water from the small dam just inside Budweiser Canyon.

If you do not want to tackle the challenging canyon, exploring the fairyland of granitic hoodoos crawling all over the hills around the spring is a worthy second best. The juxtaposition of cholla, yucca, and boulders produces primeval landscapes high on the alien scale. The area has pictographs, and searching for these enigmatic figures adds excitement to a random walk through this open maze of boulders. Even if you do not find any, there is plenty to see. Near the spring an old timer left a small fireplace. Several rock faces are inlaid with handsome tafoni, spherical or ellipsoidal cavities produced in rocks by a combination of chemical and physical weathering. Some occur as a honeycomb of hollows on the side of low cliffs (sidewall tafoni), others on the underside of overhangs (basal tafoni). A few have evolved into small caves. On sunny afternoons this wilderness of stone turns into a sea of rippling amber. Camping at the spring is prohibited. But if you walk with your camping gear a few hundred feet up the road beyond the spring (it is inside a wilderness area), you will get to sleep in one of the most far-flung spots in the preserve.

The lower canyon. As soon as you enter Budweiser Canyon you know you are in for a major treat. From its mouth just below the spring the upper canyon is exposed in all its grandeur, a wide amphitheater of tall, steep slopes capped by the crest of the Granite Mountains, just over two air miles away but more than half a mile higher. The lower slopes, down to wash level, are jam-packed with rounded boulders of all sizes. Higher elevations are rimmed with huge outcrops and cliffs of naked rock. The center piece is, of course, this grand parade of sculpted Cretaceous plutons.

The sandy wash that pushes its way toward this awesome basin is fairly open at first. In the warmer months, it is a tender green woodland of catclaw and desert willow. But it is not long before the canyon shows its true nature. The reason becomes apparent after 0.25 mile, at a low dam of carefully fitted quarried stones perched on a natural rock shelf: water. A creek flows through the lower canyon, intermittently above ground some of the year, and it is creating a serious problem for hikers. The lower wash is clogged with water-loving shrubs, mostly fluffy baccharis but also less cuddly species like blackbrush and catclaw. The sides of the wash are generally no help: they are often walled in or overrun by impenetrable mesquite groves. Braving the wash's vegetation is often the easiest way to go. Progress is slow. You find yourself constantly bushwhacking or stepping right over the plants and bouncing along two feet above firm ground you cannot see. The toughest spot is a dense stand of cattail trapped between a rock wall and a tangled growth of mesquite, where the easiest passage is a dark and moist overhang invaded by willow shoots.

As rough as it may be, the lower canyon is filled with gems. On the other side of the cattail grove the wash passes by a monumental slanted sheet of slickrock, its desert varnish scarred by myriad impacts of fallen rocks. Just past it is Slickrock Fall, a beautiful incline of granodiorite that tumbles down across the breadth of the canyon in harmonious waves of polished stone. The creek cascades down along a tortuous slot etched into the side of the slickrock. At the foot of the fall, it flows in braided channels and gathers in grass-lined pools where nurseries of patient tadpoles frolic, against all odds. At the top of the fall, water oozes into a steep funnel glistening with colorful algae. Further on, the wash squeezes through a narrower passage between uneven walls, where grows the first pine. Still further, a tiny grove of four tall willows stands in the middle of the broad wash, dwarfed by boulder-filled slopes that never seem to end. The creek is the common thread that unites all of this, and the most exciting feature. In the springtime it is a nearly constant presence, gurgling over gravelly bottoms, leaping into improbable waterfalls, instilling glee in an otherwise severe landscape.

Triple Fall, the canyon's first major obstruction, is a short distance past the willow grove. It is a sumptuous stack of three lustrous sheer falls totaling at least 120 feet in height. If this is as far as you will go, climb up the west slope a little for good views of this imposing drop-off framed by massive granitic exposures.

Upper Budweiser Canyon. By the time you reach Triple Fall you have gained all of 380 feet of elevation. From here on up, Budweiser Canyon means business, and getting through takes a major workout. The least painful way to circumvent Triple Fall is up the draw on the east side 40 yards below it, guarded by a small forest of mesquite. Climb up the draw's slickrock about 100 yards, then leave the wash and scramble your way over the boulders up to the ridge on the left side. The descent back to the main wash north of the ridge is fairly short. Above the bypass, the canyon remains brushy and forks twice over the next 0.25 mile; the main wash goes left first, then right.

This last stretch is a good preview of the upper canyon: nasty brush in the washes, and a deluge of boulders a bit everywhere. The main canyon gets steeper and tougher with elevation. Many falls and boulder jams interrupt its course. Monster Fall, half way to the crest, is a towering cascade of monzogranite grooved by erosion. One of the highest in the preserve, it is a befitting gauge of the dimensions and majesty of this canyon. The ridges, especially on the northwest side of the canyon, may be easier, depending on your preference, although they offer their own set of challenges. Here the spaces between outcrops where we would love to squeeze by are often filled with plants—

Budweiser Canyon

	Dist.(mi)	Elev.(ft)
Budweiser Spring	0.0	~3,775
Slickrock Fall	0.6	4,000
Triple Fall	0.9	4,125
End of bypass	1.0	4,300
Main fork	1.25	4,435
Monster Fall	1.75	~4,730
Crest (saddle)	2.5	~6,465
6,614-ft peak	2.8	6,614

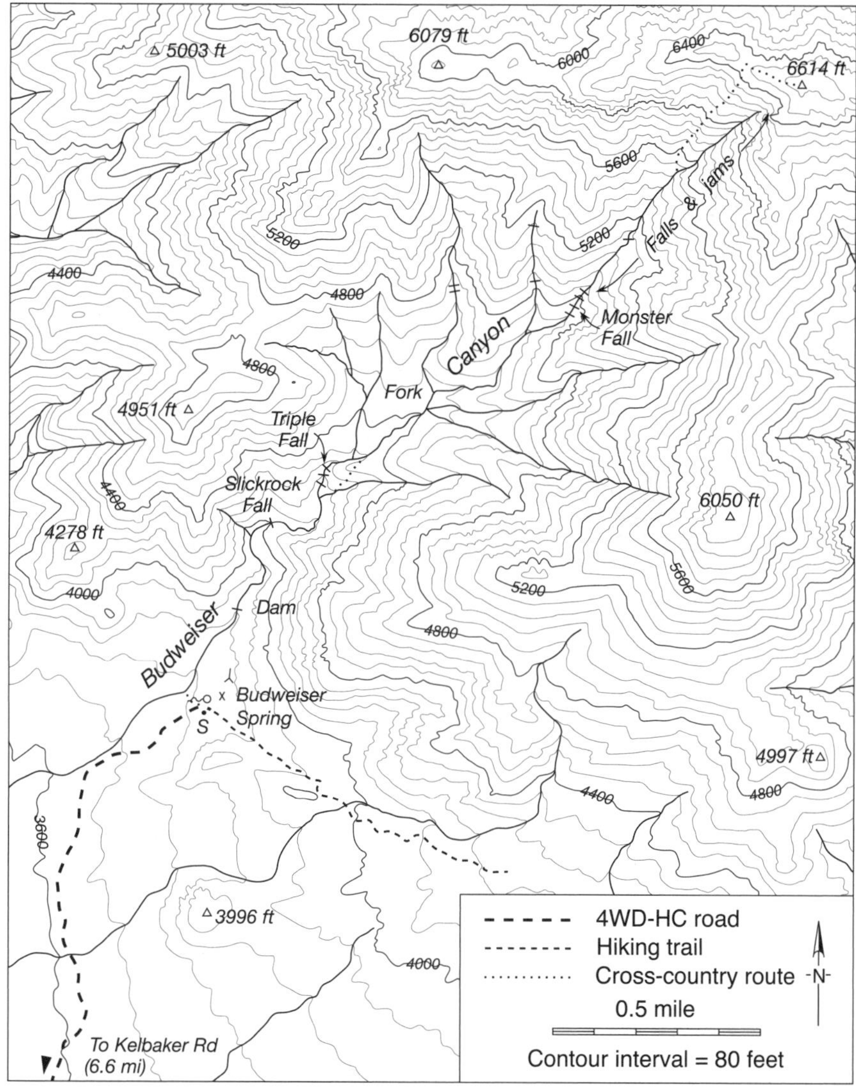

yucca, catclaw, cholla, and eventually trees. Progress is so persistently tedious that it becomes laughable—here you are, with scraped legs and arms, puffing up an intractable landscape, snagged by catclaws, poked by tree limbs, a cholla stem hitchhiking on your shoe, enjoying the healing power of nature. The rare stretches of open ground inspire ecstasy. In washes or on ridges, a great deal of time is spent scrambling and scouting. Along the last half a mile to the crest, the ground is too steep—in excess of 50%—to hold a pinyon pine upright.

Triple Fall, Budweiser Canyon

Do not let the short distance fool you into tinkering with this hellish place. Reaching the crest is a minor epic, as action-filled as an extensive journey. But if you do go, it will engage your senses so fully that years later you might still find yourself seeking other places to duplicate the experience. The scenery is outlandish. Every one of thousands of boulders is it own special art form. In the spring and early summer many plants bloom—bladderpod and rock pea, firecracker penstemon, flamboyant cacti, and exceptionally large live-forever, their striking artichoke leaves grading from pastel green to flaming vermillion. On the ridges the panorama extends far south to Bristol Lake, the Sheep Hole Mountains, and the nebulous edge of Joshua Tree National Park beyond. The crest and the 6,614-foot peak at the head of Budweiser Canyon command breathtaking views plunging into Bull Canyon, the Kelso Dunes, and all of the western preserve. Make sure to leave enough time to browse, and to get back before dark. While I was doing just that, I came across reddish painted figures that have been dancing on a granite slab for hundreds of years.

▪

— 12 —

LANFAIR VALLEY AREA

TETHERED TO THE VERY SOUTHERN TIP of the Great Basin, the eastern portion of the preserve breaks down into a vast region of gently sloping valleys and basins rimmed by distant mountains. Largest in the preserve, Lanfair Valley is bounded to the west and north by the Mid Hills and New York Mountains, and to the east by the Castle Mountains and Piute Range. It is a true valley: most of it drains southeast via Sacramento Wash to the Colorado River and the Sea of Cortez. In contrast, Fenner Valley south of it is part of the Great Basin: it drains southwest into inland Bristol Lake. The two valleys are separated by an alignment of mountainous masses diminishing in importance from west to east: the Woods Mountains, Hackberry Mountain, and the Vontrigger Hills. Four smaller valleys—Pinto, Round, Gold, and Clipper—flank Lanfair Valley and Fenner Valley to the west. This region of expansive plains pimpled with isolated hills vividly epitomizes the open desert. Its appeal lies in the sense of freedom inspired by its big sky and imposing dimensions, its endless sweep of desert shrubs, cacti, and Joshua trees, and simply because it is so different.

Access and Backcountry Roads

This region can be accessed from the north on the Ivanpah Road, from the south on the Lanfair Road, and from the west on the Cedar Canyon Road. These roads are graded (the southern part of the Lanfair Road is paved) and meet at the former town of Lanfair. From there the Cedar Canyon Road continues as a primitive road east through Lanfair Valley to the Piute Range. The area can also be reached from Highway 95 in Nevada on the Mojave Road, which crosses the valley east-west.

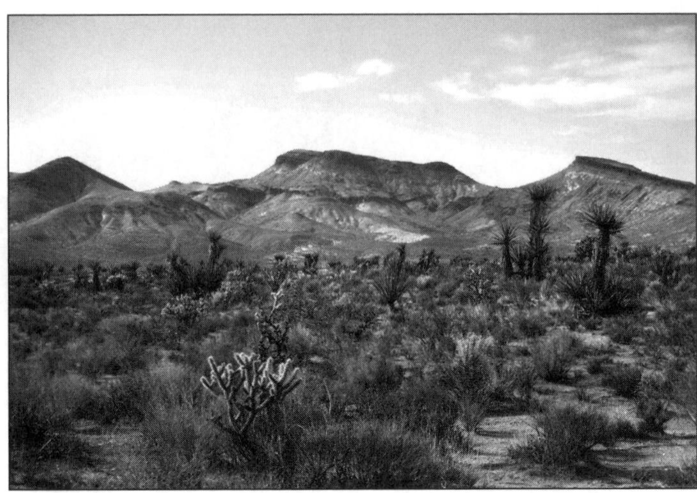

Hackberry Mountain from Lanfair Valley

For decades before the creation of the East Mojave National Scenic Area, many private interests bladed roads throughout this area. Today the valleys are lacerated with hundreds of miles of dirt roads—maintenance roads for power and gas lines, abandoned railway grades, settlement grids, mining roads, prospectors' tracks, and ranching roads. Only the Woods Mountains, Hackberry Mountain, and the Piute Range have been largely spared and are now protected as wilderness areas. This huge web represents what is possibly the largest network of primitive roads open to driving in the U.S. national parks. It also offers a smorgasbord of places to camp in the delightful middle of nowhere.

Geology

This area's distinctive geological feature is its relative lack of diversity. It is mostly a series of huge overlapping alluvial fans made of poorly sorted gravel, sand, and silt eroded from the surrounding mountains since the Pleistocene. In Lanfair Valley this material was derived dominantly from granitic rocks in the Mid Hills and New York Mountains. In Fenner Valley it came more commonly from the volcanic rocks of the Woods Mountains and Hackberry Mountain. Erosion can be seen at work in the winter when, after heavy rains, the innumerable braided channels carved into the fans fill up with a little flowing water. Large boulders stranded in washes, miles from their native mountains, bear witness to the more violent flashfloods that scour the desert plains every so often. One might better comprehend the meaning of 10 million years by considering that this is how long it took for these

Suggested Backcountry Drives in the Lanfair Valley Area					
Route/Destination	Dist. (mi)	Lowest elev.	Highest elev.	Road type	Pages
Carruthers Canyon Road	9.0	4,411'	5,620'	H	253-254
Clipper Valley Road	8.8	2,850'	3,020'	P	347
Fort Piute from Hwy 95	9.1	2,030'	2,800'	H	421
Fort Piute from Lanfair	17.0	2,410'	4,060'	H	427-428
Hackberry Spring	4.2	3,845'	4,365'	H	407-408
Hidden Hill Rd/Fenner Val.	25.6	2,000'	3,835'	H	299, 351
Lanfair to Badlands Road	20.5	3,390'	4,060'	F	417
Mojave Road	107	930'	5,165'	F	433-440
New York Mountains Road	12.8	4,350'	5,425'	H	217
Walking Box Ranch Road	12.3	4,410'	4,600'	H	413
Key: P=Primitive (2WD) H=Primitive (HC) F=Primitive (4WD)					

infrequent and modest events to erode almost all of the hundreds of feet of volcanic flows that filled these valleys in the Late Miocene.

Most of the region's mountains and numerous hills are remnants of the many eruptions that rocked the area in the Miocene. This is true of all, or almost all, of the Woods and Castle mountains, Hackberry and Eagle mountains, Piute Range, and Grotto and Blind hills. This volcanic monopoly explains the dull-brown, low-albedo rocks that prevail on these prominences. The exceptions are the Fenner Hills and the Tungsten Flat–Signal Hill area, which contain fairly large exposures of Cretaceous porphyritic granodiorite, and the Vontrigger Hills–Bobcat Hills area, which is comprised of Early Proterozoic granitoids.

Human History

The area has had a long history going back to at least the 1870s. It has involved ranching, hard-rock mining, railways, and homesteading. Homesteading started around 1910 and lasted roughly until the 1940s, with a peak of arrivals between 1912 and 1915. At one time several hundred people lived scattered in the valleys. Many homesteads were close to the California Eastern Railway, which faithfully serviced this loose-knit community. Flag stops and stations consisted simply of boxcars parked at sidings, in particular at Lanfair and Maruba. Farming was generally too unpredictable for sustainable living, and most settlers moved out soon after they obtained title to their land.

Several mines came and went over the decades. Most of them, including the Rattlesnake, Barnett, and Getchell, were unremarkable.

Suggested Hikes in the Lanfair Valley Area					
Route/Destination	Dist. (mi)	Elev. gain	Mean elev.	Access road	Pages
Short hikes (under 5 miles round trip)					
Fort Piute*	0.2	30'	2,810'	H/9.1 mi	423
Guitar Mountain	2.0	1,050'	4,360'	H/3.7 mi	412
Hackberry Mtn from fork*	3.1	1,160'	4,640'	H/3.7 mi	408-410
Hackberry Mtn from spring	1.0	1,030'	4,730'	H/4.2 mi	408-410
Hackberry Spring	0.6	190'	4,330'	P/3.7 mi	408
Hart Peak	2.0	1,180'	4,670'	P/12.2 mi	413-416
Lower Piute Spring*	1.3	190'	2,840'	H/9.1 mi	423-426
Old Government Road					
Fort Piute to Mojave Rd	2.4	1,140'	3,180'	H/9.1 mi	423-426
Piute Canyon Trail	1.1	620'	2,930'	H/9.1 mi	423, 431
Rock Spring Canyon	0.8	180'	4,850'	P/0.3 mi	396-398
Rustler Cyn (to Face Rock)	1.1	190'	4,140'	P/1.1 mi	400-402
Ute Peak (cross-country)	1.4	1,240'	3,870'	H/14.1 mi	418-420
Intermediate hikes (5-12 miles round trip)					
Hackberry Mtn–Guitar Mtn*	8.8	1,960'	4,350'	P/1.7 mi	408-412
High Table Mtn West End	4.5	920'	4,350'	F/20.5 mi	420
Marl Mountains loop*	7.2	950'	3,930'	H/8.3 mi	440
Piute Cyn badlands–Ft Piute	3.5	860'	3,130'	H/12.5 mi	429-432
Piute Cyn–Fort Piute Cyn*	8.1	1,040'	3,230'	H/12.5 mi	423-432
Piute Cyn Gorge to Ft Piute	2.5	940'	3,040'	H/11.1 mi	429-431
Piute Mesa Trail (viewpoint)	6.3	1,340'	4,470'	F/20.5 mi	420
Rustler Cyn (amphitheater)	2.7	990'	4,370'	P/1.1 mi	400-404
Ute Peak (via Piute Mesa Tr.)	7.0	1,810'	4,520'	F/20.5 mi	420
Woods Mountain	3.0	1,930'	4,610'	P/1.1 mi	405-406
Key: P = Primitive (2WD); H = Primitive (HC); F = Primitive (4WD) Distance: one way, except for loops (round-trip, marked with *) Elev. gain: sum of all elevation gains on a round-trip basis & on loops					

The California Mine did receive some publicity, in part because it was based on a scam. The most substantial efforts took place near the north end of Lanfair Valley, at the foot of the Castle Mountains. Gold was discovered there in 1907 at what became the Oro Belle and Big Chief mines. In spite of modest showings, a town named Hart sprung up and soon boasted hotels and stores, saloons, a dance hall, a newspaper, ladies of the night, and a jail. It was a prime example of a human

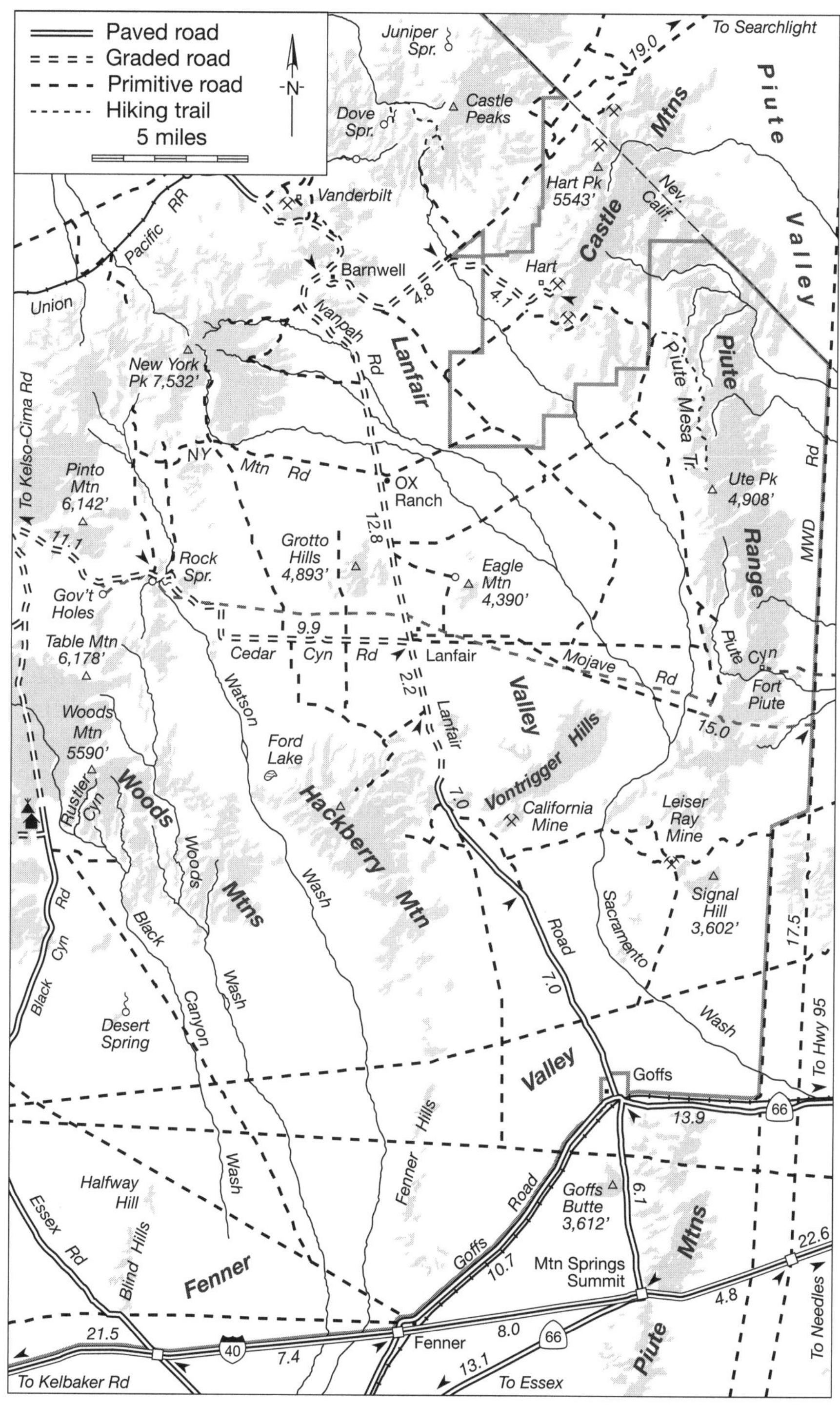
Paved road
Graded road
Primitive road
Hiking trail
5 miles
N
To Searchlight
Juniper Spr.
Castle Peaks
Dove Spr.
Piute Valley
Castle Mtns
Hart Pk 5543'
Nev. Calif.
Vanderbilt
Barnwell
Hart
Union Pacific RR
Ivanpah Rd
Lanfair
New York Pk 7,532'
Piute Mesa Tr.
Piute Range
Ute Pk 4,908'
MWD Rd
NY Mtn Rd
OX Ranch
Pinto Mtn 6,142'
To Kelso-Cima Rd
Grotto Hills 4,893'
Eagle Mtn 4,390'
Rock Spr.
Gov't Holes
Table Mtn 6,178'
Cedar Cyn Rd
Lanfair
Mojave Rd
Piute Cyn
Fort Piute
Valley
Woods Mtn 5590'
Watson Wash
Ford Lake
Vontrigger Hills
Rustler Cyn
Woods Mtns
Hackberry Mtn
California Mine
Leiser Ray Mine
Signal Hill 3,602'
Black Cyn Rd
Black Canyon
Woods Wash
Road
Sacramento Wash
Desert Spring
Valley
Goffs
To Hwy 95
66
Halfway Hill
Essex Rd
Blind Hills
Fenner
Wash
Fenner Hills
Goffs Road
Goffs Butte 3,612'
Mtn Springs Summit
Piute Mtns
To Needles
To Kelbaker Rd
40
Fenner
To Essex
19.0
4.8
4.1
12.8
11.1
9.9
2.2
15.0
7.0
7.0
17.5
13.9
6.1
10.7
22.6
4.8
21.5
7.4
8.0
13.1

microcosm fueled by ill-founded expectations. The mines were fully developed, but little high-grade ore was found. After extensive low-concentration gold deposits were discovered near old Hart in 1986, the Castle Mountain Mine ran a major heap-leach operation. From 1992 to 2001 it recovered $330 million in gold, and left behind a scar the size of 500 football fields. When the preserve was created in 1994, the Castle Mountains were excluded from it as one of the state's largest reserves of minable gold. In 2016 then-president Barack Obama created Castle Mountains National Monument. The proclamation gave the mine permission to go after the leftover 28 tons of gold. When the project is completed, the property will be incorporated in the monument.

Hiking

A very special trait of the preserve's east-side valleys is that more than a century later, one can still browse through the ruins of these departed mining communities. The buttressed concrete tank in Lanfair was on the Lanfair family's ranch. Near it, a stairway drops into the concrete basement of a long-gone house. At Maruba you might find the stone cellar of the Sharp family. Throughout the valley, isolated buildings, concrete foundations, and large fields betray abandoned homesteads. The site of Hart is marked by the fireplace and chimney of a defunct building, and a crooked headframe. The Getchell Mine had a large gold camp named Vontrigger in the late 1920s. The largest ruins are at the California Mine; the concrete foundations of its sizable mill still hang to a hillside sprinkled with copper ore.

Most of the hikes in and around Lanfair Valley are comparatively short and not overly demanding. One of the main attractions is climbing the many local volcanic peaks. Most are trailless, including the longer ascent of Tortoise Shell Mountain, a large hump of rhyolite in the midst of the Woods Mountains caldera. The Piute Range is the exception: an old road rebranded the Piute Mesa Trail winds up many miles along the crest. Twin Buttes offer a worthy challenge among awesome granitic boulders and short cliffs. Because the mountains are fairly low, good canyons are few, but some of them rank high on the scenery meter, especially Piute Canyon in the Piute Range and a few windy canyons in the Woods Mountains. There are many rock art sites, some well advertised like at Eagle Mountain, others poorly known, as in the Vontrigger Hills and Woods Mountains. The desert is filled with striking cactus gardens and extensive Joshua tree forests. No matter where you go, this part of the Mojave Desert echoes with a euphoric sense of bright open spaces stretching a long way under the sun.

■

ROCK SPRING CANYON

> *Very few of the many springs in the eastern Mojave Desert have perennial water. Rock Spring is one of a handful blessed with large ponds and a seasonal creek. The short canyon in which this scenic oasis resides provides refuge for wildlife and plants alike, and it is a wonderful place to witness how even the harshest desert can be utterly transformed by a little water.*

General Information

Road status: Roadless; two-wheel-drive access road
Rock Spring Canyon: 0.8 mi, 180 ft up, 0 ft down one way / very easy
Main attraction: A short walk in a granite canyon with a creek
USGS 7.5′ topo map: Pinto Valley
Maps: pp. *397*, 221, 265*, 393*

Location and Access

Rock Spring Canyon is a tributary of Watson Wash, a major drainage east of the Mid Hills. Most of it is a wide dry wash that does not pass the grade of canyon, except for the last half a mile just before its confluence with Watson Wash, where it forms a deep arroyo as it slices through a granitic hill. To get to the confluence, drive the Cedar Canyon Road 5.3 miles east of the Black Canyon Road. This will take you to a dirt road that angles off to the right, at the bottom of the steep down-grade into the broad flood plain of Watson Wash. This side road is the Mojave Road. From the other direction, this intersection is 9.8 miles west of the Ivanpah Road at Lanfair. Drive south on the Mojave Road 250 yards to a fork, go right, and park 250 yards further by the NPS interpretive signs. This stretch of the Mojave Road is a little sandy but manageable with a two-wheel-drive vehicle. If you do not want to take a chance, park off the Cedar Canyon Road and walk from there.

Route Description

Camp Rock Spring. Like most isolated well-watered springs in the desert, Rock Spring has long been a vital resource for travelers. For centuries, visitors periodically established camps on the low shelf where the interpretive signs are located. Look among the bushes for the scattered remains of these occupations—you will find a few foundations, rock alignments, and excavations. The Chemehuevi Indians rested here during their hunting and gathering expeditions. Emigrants, then miners, and later ranchers also used it when moving across the desert. In 1866, the U.S. Army established an outpost here, as well as at other springs along the Mojave Road, to protect the mail service (see *Fort Piute*). Camp Rock Spring consisted of primitive rock structures located on this small shelf of land. Soldiers lacked basic facilities and supplies, several of them suffered from scurvy, and desertion was epidemic. Camp Rock Spring was abandoned in May 1868.

Rock Spring Canyon. From the site of Camp Rock Spring, hike up the open sandy wash to the gray-rock gorge to the west. The large stagnant pool at the gorge's lower edge is the terminus of the canyon's valiant little creek. After giving it all its might, the creek finally dies here in the burning sand, exhausted by its half-mile-long ordeal in the merciless sun. The short canyon above the pool starts as a narrow defile trapped between short cliffs and boulder-strewn slopes. To proceed, pick your way over slickrock and large polished granite blocks. The creek spends most of its time lingering in mid-sized pools, although in early spring there is usually enough water to link the pools with trickles of water. At one place there is even a 5-foot waterfall, with just enough flow to be deserving of the name. This modest amount of water has transformed parched land into a small idyllic oasis. Green plants grow everywhere—miniature beds of grass, groves of cattail, clumps of catclaw and cliffrose, New Mexico thistle, and lush sacred datura. From mid spring into summer, dozens of species bloom, from purple phacelia and chia to California brickellia, Wright buckwheat, and the pretty woolly daisy.

Soon you reach the only mature deciduous trees that live in the canyon—a healthy cluster of willow over 18 feet tall. Just behind it there is a dark pool of clear water, deeper and larger than most, lapping the base of a tall vertical cliff. At the height of summer, it feels good to rest in the cliff's deep shadow, to enjoy the slightly higher humidity, watch dragonflies, listen to the nearby calls of quails and frogs, and the soothing sound of hidden water gurgling, somewhere. It would be hard to turn down the silent invitation for a dip if it weren't for the unappealing algae that usually cloak the pool's surface.

Further on, the canyon opens up. Shade gets scarce and the creek soon dries up, but up ahead it comes back to life, twice. The first time is at the next granite outcrop. In a cool cave under a large chockstone, I once saw a couple of frogs resting on wet sand. There is another dry stretch above the chockstone, lined with the tracks of coyotes and deer moving to and from water. Where the canyon forks at the large juniper in the middle of the wash, head up the left fork. In about 100 yards

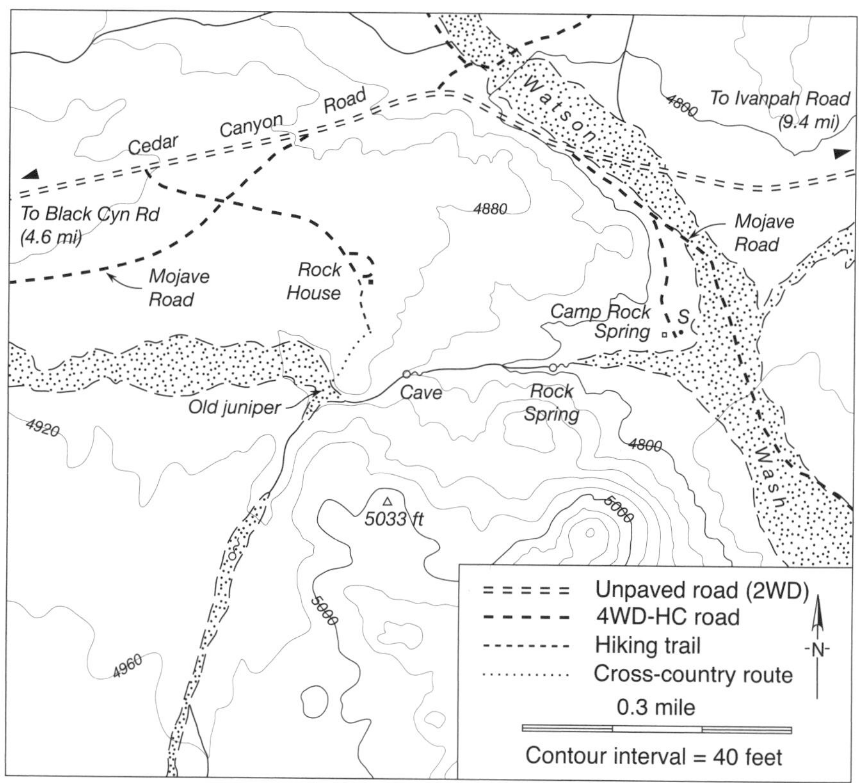

Rock Spring Canyon		
	Dist.(mi)	Elev.(ft)
Mojave Rd (interpretive signs)	0.0	4,775
Lower pool	0.1	4,790
Canyon fork/tall juniper	0.45	4,870
Rock House	(0.15)	4,895
Headwater of Rock Spring	~0.65	~4,930

there is sometimes flowing water again. By then the canyon walls have shriveled to low boulders, but this is often where both the creek and vegetation are most exuberant. The headwater of Rock Spring is a little further, in open sand churned by cattle.

Tread lightly while visiting Rock Spring Canyon. Places with running water are fragile and vital for wildlife. We all need to be careful to keep them unspoiled. It's easy. Walk on rock rather than soft ground. Make it an absolute rule not to step on any plant, however small.

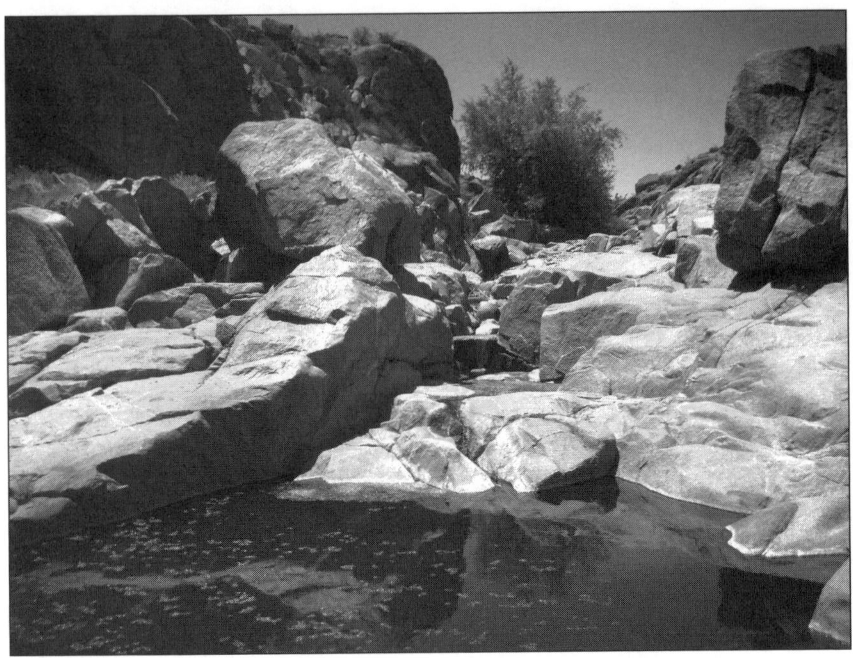

Lower pool at Rock Spring

The Rock House. In 1929, war veteran Bert Smith moved to a plot of land just above this canyon. Smith's life expectancy had been seriously shortened during World War I, and the Bureau of Veterans Affairs had sent him here hoping that the climate would extend his life a little. It did, beyond all expectations: Smith homesteaded here until the mid-1950s and lived until 1967! He built a small wood cabin, and improved it to a sturdier rock house in the 1930s. The bits of pipeline and small concrete basins you might have spotted along the canyon were his attempts at securing water for himself.

The stone cabin visible from the fork area, 250 yards away on the canyon's low north rim, is Smith's house. To take a closer look at it, from the old juniper head north up the gentle slope, first cross-country, then on an old trail. Known as the Rock House and owned by the NPS, it is a well-preserved construction, with thick walls and glass windows. In pre-freeway days, it must have been a treat to live on this open shelf commanding grand views of the desert, far away from a Los Angeles that still had fewer than one million people...

■

RUSTLER CANYON

Around 18 million years ago, a large volcano erupted with exceptional violence in the eastern Mojave Desert. What is left of its caldera is the Woods Mountains, a pile of volcanic rocks up to 1,000 feet thick. Rustler Canyon is one of the short canyons that slices through this colorful volcanic formation. I cannot say enough good things about this canyon. It is a masterpiece of variety, a fiesta of volcanic rocks, a celebration of grand open spaces decorated by wild desert gardens. I was in there for hours, not because the going was slow but because I was constantly distracted.

General Information

Road status: Roadless; standard-clearance primitive access road
Face Rock: 1.1 mi, 190 ft up, 0 ft down one way / very easy
Rustler Canyon: 2.7 mi, 970 ft up, 20 ft down one way / moderate
Main attractions: A scenic box canyon, volcanic rocks, geology
USGS 7.5' topo maps: Columbia Mountain, Woods Mountain*
Maps: pp. 403*, *265*, 393*

Location and Access

Rustler Canyon is the westernmost of five main canyons that drain the Woods Mountains' south slopes. If you want a preview of its geological setting, as you drive the Black Canyon Road in the vicinity of Hole-in-the-Wall take a look at the striking face of the Woods Mountains rising abruptly about a mile east of the road. Rustler Canyon is just on the other side of it, and it cuts through the same contrasted formations of horizontally banded volcanics.

Rustler Canyon is in a designated wilderness, but there is a road that gets close to its mouth. From the Hole-in-the-Wall area, drive the Black Canyon Road 0.5 mile south of the Wild Horse Canyon Road and turn left on a primitive road. Go 1.1 miles, staying left at the two forks. Park at the end of the road, which is at the wilderness boundary. Rustler Canyon is the wide opening in the mountain to the northwest. This road has a small crown but it is passable for most vehicles.

Geology: Catastrophism

Most geological processes—erosion, mountain building, oceanfront erosion, plate motion—occur at extremely slow rates, an inch per century, or per millenium, or slower. A time traveler with a lot of time on her hands could come back to Earth century after century and find everything essentially unchanged (recent human tinkerings excepted). Rare are the geological processes that fail this rule. A perfect exception is volcanism—and it breaks the rule with a passion.

The Woods Mountains constitute a prime example of the devastation that volcanism can inflict essentially overnight. The mountains' colorful formations were produced mostly by three major eruptions that took place between 17.7 and 17.8 million years ago. These outpourings were analogous to Mount St. Helens' in 1980—except that they were considerably more powerful. They came out of what is called a trap-door volcano. Its opening was defined by a circular fault hinged at one end, like a hinged lid on a mug. As magma approached the surface, superheated gases built up under the trap door until the phenomenal pressure blew it off. Clouds of volcanic ash were blasted across the countryside at near-supersonic speed. The sheer force of rising magma tore off chunks of basement rock up to the size of suburban houses, which were hurtled along with the ash. The wetter landscape of lakes, marshes, and rivers that prevailed then was instantly wiped out. Below the ash, geologists have recovered the fossils of many animals and plants entombed alive by the cataclysm.

Within less than 100,000 years, two similar ash eruptions took place, followed by a series of comparatively more tame lava flows over the next 100,000 years. The total volume of ejected material was equivalent to a cube 3 miles on the side—at least 30 times Mount St. Helens' ejecta. The total released thermal energy was probably upward of *1,000* megatons. The blasts left behind a caldera roughly centered on Tortoise Shell Mountain, 6 miles across and 2.5 miles deep. Its weakened gravity can still be detected nearly 18 million years later. The combined deposits formed a plateau of welded ash some 230 square miles and 1,050 feet thick at its thickest—enough to bury the Eiffel Tower. This formation is known as the Wild Horse Mesa Tuff, after its prominent exposures on Wild Horse Mesa about 8 miles west of the caldera's center. Dug hundreds of feet down into this enormous deposit, Rustler Canyon offers a perfect window into the aftermath of this mighty volcano—and a prime illustration of catastrophism.

Route Description

The lower canyon. From the end of the road walk 0.2 mile to the prominent cliffs to the north. You will cross the sandy bed of Black Canyon Wash just before reaching them. Walk west along the base of the cliffs, then north around the tip of the cliffs into Rustler Canyon.

Drop-off and giant boulders in Rustler Canyon's amphitheater

This is a box canyon, with only two main side canyons, both short and steep, so from here on up it is hard to wander astray.

Rustler Canyon starts as a broad bench bounded by steeply sloped mesas. The wash is a shallow trench that meanders lazily beneath the bench. This is cattle country. Cows being as lazy as humans, they have designed optimum paths on the bench to shortcut bends and bypass rougher areas in the wash. So if you get impatient, you can always make faster progress on these trails. Although fairly short, this drainage changes character numerous times, and it is only a matter of minutes before something new sparks your interest. The slopes are populated with a scenic mix of Mojave yucca and barrel cactus. Pretty volcanic rocks litter the canyon bottom. A nice pygmy forest of desert willow and catclaw thrives in the wash. From late spring through fall, when they both bear leaves, they lend the area an unexpected freshness, especially when the willows bear their beautiful trumpet-like flowers. Up canyon, the tree cover gets thick enough to qualify as an oasis—minus a creek.

Attracted by the greater shade and humidity in the wash, wildlife is comparatively plentiful. It is not uncommon to see jackrabbits, ground squirrels, turkey vultures, finches, and other birds. On a few occasions, while I was cooling in the shade, hummingbirds parked 6 feet away and checked me out for 10 or 15 seconds—practically eternity for a hyperactive earthling. Later on I cut off a covey of chukars crossing the bench, and as they tried to regroup their loud calls echoed against the canyon walls.

All along Rustler Canyon long horizontal bands of light-tan welded tuff outcrop across the slopes. Erosion and freezing-heating cycles have fashioned these vertical surfaces into complex arrangements of caverns, fractures, overhangs, pinnacles, and cleaved walls coated with rich desert varnish. A tall cliff on the west side has been carved into an eerie caricature of a face with giant hollowed eyes. A little further, on the opposite side, a disquieting array of gaping grottoes overlooks the wash. One of the pleasures of this hike is to climb up to higher exposures for a closer look. The diversity is quite entertaining.

Face Rock

The upper canyon. Little by little the benches get narrower, the rims grow taller, and the slopes creep in on the wash. By the time you reach the first side canyon, a steep ravine cascading down pink slickrock, the canyon has closed in on you. From here on up everything changes rapidly—the land, the plants, even the rocks. The wash, mild-mannered in the lower canyon, now alternates between obstacle courses of boulders and bare bedrock as wide open as a paved path. Falls pop up at the most unexpected places. All of them have at least one

Rustler Canyon

	Dist.(mi)	Elev.(ft)
End of road	0.0	4,040
Canyon mouth	~0.3	4,090
Face Rock	1.1	4,230
First side canyon (east side)	1.9	4,445
11-foot fall	1.95	~4,460
Second side canyon (west side)	2.05	4,495
16-foot fall	2.4	~4,700
Drop-off in amphitheater	2.7	~4,990

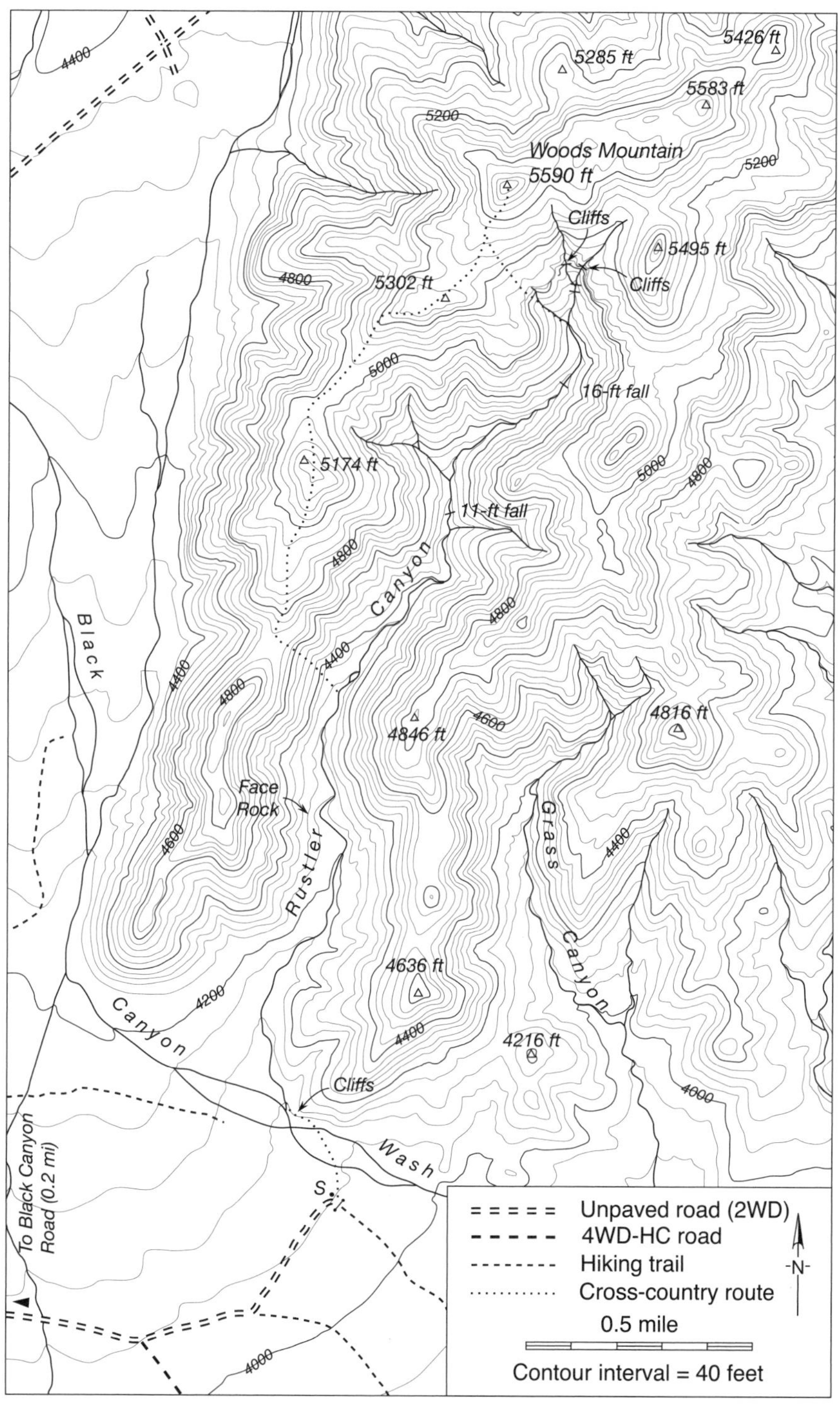

5426 ft
5285 ft
5583 ft
4400
5200
Woods Mountain
5590 ft
5200
Cliffs
5495 ft
Cliffs
4800
5302 ft
5000
16-ft fall
5174 ft
5000
4800
11-ft fall
4800
Canyon
4800
Black
4400
4400
4800
4400
4846 ft
4600
4816 ft
Face Rock
Grass
4600
Rustler
4400
Canyon
4636 ft
Canyon
4200
4400
4216 ft
Cliffs
4000
Wash
To Black Canyon Road (0.2 mi)
S
4000
Unpaved road (2WD)
4WD-HC road
Hiking trail
Cross-country route
0.5 mile
N
Contour interval = 40 feet

easy climbing route (low 5's at worst) or can be bypassed without much effort. The stream that once flowed through here has left behind neat potholes, deep excavations in the gravel, polished walls, and scooped-out chutes. After a rainstorm you might find a little water pooled in potholes or dribbling in gentle cascades over the two highest falls. By some strange osmosis, the vegetation matches these abrupt mood swings. Pinyon pine appear in the wash, their gnarled roots laced around angular boulders, then healthy stands of cliffrose, Mormon tea, blackbrush, and isolated juniper. Pancake prickly-pear and blue yucca thrive on the drier slopes. At one place, an impenetrable plug of cliffrose and hollyleaf redberry forced me to look for a bypass across hillsides choked with cacti. These sudden changes play out against an increasingly rugged landscape of sculpted mesas.

Yet, the most impressive feature is the rocks. The upper canyon cuts into the northwestern rim of the Woods Mountains caldera, and the variety of extrusive rocks is mind boggling. The wash is filled with large chunks of rhyolite, welded tuff, breccia, and uncommon grades of volcanic rocks. The rhyolite is delicately veined with white and gray, tightly curved flow lines. The welded tuff outcrops in sensuous cream-colored slickrock, as smooth as polished sandstone. Some outcrops are crisp mosaics of xenoliths, foreign rocks such as granite torn from the throat of the volcano by the force of the eruption and mixed with the tuff. The most exceptional display is a five-foot boulder of yellowish tuff freckled with black obsidian. Along the last quarter mile, exposures get larger and stranger at an accelerating pace, until just below its head the canyon comes to a crescendo at a magnificent amphitheater. Ominous cliffs rise all around, slashed with long and thick volcanic flows grading from gray into black and highlighted with white streaks. This is an impressive landscape, a vibrant symphony of underworld colors celebrating this apocalyptic volcano.

There may be a way to climb or bypass the cliffs and reach the head of the canyon just beyond, and perhaps climb from there to the nearby high point of the Woods Mountains. But you might be content, as I was, to sit in the shade of the cliffs. It is a good place to admire their vaulted surfaces, the dark crags looming high above them, and the engaging landscape of pine-dotted mesas down below. Given time, life manages to convert the most devastated land into a slice of paradise.

■

WOODS MOUNTAIN

This delightful climb is a tale of two worlds, one a canyon at the core of a volcano that exploded 18 million years ago, the other the crater's sculpted shell, which has been eroding for just as long. The canyon is a tortuous corridor through a deluge of volcanic rocks, the mountain a celebration of wide open spaces, and they stand united by a luminous patchwork of desert vegetation interspersed with evergreens. The views stretch all the way to Arizona.

General Information

Road status: Roadless; standard-clearance primitive access road
Woods Mountain: 3.0 mi, 1,740 ft up, 190 ft down one way / difficult
Main attractions: A scenic climb, volcanic rocks, geology, botany
USGS 7.5' topo maps: Columbia Mountain, Woods Mountain*
Maps: pp. 403*, *265*, 393*

Location and Access

From the Hole-in-the-Wall area, the Woods Mountains are the long sculpted mesa rising abruptly 1 mile east, emblazoned with long horizontal ribs. Woods Mountain, the high point of the range, is at the extreme northwestern corner of the mesa. It can be climbed from many directions, most shorter than the Rustler Canyon route, but none as scenic. Refer to *Rustler Canyon* for directions.

Route Description

The beginning of this route is identical to the first half of the Rustler Canyon hike. The idea is to proceed up canyon until the mood strikes to climb to its western rim, then to follow the crest north to the summit. The dilemma is whether to go into the upper canyon, at the

Woods Mountain

	Dist.(mi)	Elev.(ft)
End of road	0.0	4,040
Mouth of Rustler Canyon	~0.3	4,090
Leave wash	1.45	4,310
Saddle on canyon's west rim	1.7	4,715
Woods Mountain	3.0	5,590

Woods Mountain from the north slope of Barber Peak

price of a harder climb to the crest, or to bail out earlier but miss it. Exit routes out of the upper canyon are fewer and tend to have more outcrops. A good take-off point is 1.1 miles in the canyon (elev. ~4,310′), where the wash veers north-northeast. It is a 400-foot scramble to the saddle between two mesas on the crest. The slopes are steep but open, with the exception of a series of long horizontal cliffs, broken and easily crossed or avoided. It is a scenic climb, through spiny gardens of barrel cactus, cholla, yucca, and pancake prickly-pear. The rocks are interesting, mostly light-tan or gray tuffs and white ash flows. On the crest, there are two low mesas to cross, then the final incline to the thinly wooded summit. Each mesa is encircled by low discontinuous cliffs and crowned with green bosques of pine and juniper. The going gets steep at places, but there are ways around or through the cliffs.

The steep-walled conical summit is a perfect vista to survey the legacy of a major eruption. Millions of years later, large tracks of land are still made of its thick ejecta—the intriguing bluffs of Barber Peak and the broad hump of Wild Horse Mesa to the southwest, Table and Pinto mountains to the north, and bits of Hackberry Mountain to the east. Down below, past dark crags and twisted canyons, is the gaping caldera that spawned all of this. Lanfair Valley's enormous bajada and its distant ring of mountains dramatically emphasize the sheer size of this spectacular cataclysm.

▪

HACKBERRY MOUNTAIN

Rising 1,600 feet from Lanfair Valley's vast floodplain, Hackberry Mountain is the remnant of an extensive volcanic field that smothered this area around 18 million years ago. The short, steep climbs to its barren summit and neighboring Guitar Mountain provide an opportunity to discover isolated springs and a wealth of colorful extrusive rocks, and ultimately to embrace far-reaching panoramas of this remote corner of the California desert.

General Information

Road status: Roadless; high-clearance access road
Hackberry Mountain: 1.0 mi, 1,030 ft up, 0 ft down one way / moderate
Guitar Mtn: 2.0 mi, 1,020 ft up, 30 ft down one way / easy–moderate
Hackberry Mountain–Guitar Mountain: 8.8 mi, 1,960 ft up loop / difficult
Main attractions: Climbing volcanic peaks, geology, views
USGS 7.5' topo map: Hackberry Mountain
Maps: pp. 411*, *393*

Location and Access

Hackberry Mountain is about in the middle of the preserve's southeastern quadrant. It is the small range you will see to the south as you drive the Cedar Canyon Road west of Lanfair. Its most conspicuous feature is a tilted mesa shaped like a guitar resting on a high pedestal, west of the range's summit. Long ago, Lanfair Valley homesteaders referred to it as Guitar Mountain.

Drive the Lanfair Road 2.2 miles south of the Cedar Canyon Road (or 14.0 miles north of Goffs Road) to a dirt road that heads southwest. Follow this road toward Hackberry Mountain 1.7 miles to a junction at a cluster of corrals. This road has a few ruts and a little sand at the corrals, but with care a standard-clearance vehicle can make it.

To climb to the summit of Hackberry Mountain, turn left on the Hackberry Spring Road, which has been cherry-stemmed out of the Woods Mountains–Hackberry Mountain Wilderness. This road enters Hackberry Mountain along an open valley peppered with clusters of lava pillars and knolls. Before the Hackberry Fire Complex, this valley had an exceptional forest of giant Mojave yucca up to 10 feet tall. Now only their gray trunks remain, shooting from the ground like androids on a bad-hair day. The valley slowly pinches down to a scenic canyon dwarfed by tall taluses of rust-colored lava streaked with white and mustard tuffs. For the shortest climb, proceed 2.5 miles to the end of the road just below Hackberry Spring. To hike the summit loop, park 0.5 mile earlier, at the fork in the canyon. This road is rough, with large rocks, deep gashes, and catclaw jutting into the road on both sides. A high-clearance vehicle is mandatory.

To climb Guitar Mountain, turn right at the corrals. This high-clearance road skirts the foot of Hackberry Mountain along the wilderness boundary. After 1.4 miles, make a left at a faint junction. Continue 0.6 mile to an old road on the left, closed to motor vehicles, and park.

Geology

Almost all of this range is made of Hackberry Spring Volcanics, a large volcanic field that accumulated from a series of vents starting 18.5 million years ago. The explosions of the nearby Woods Mountains caldera about 700,000 years later (see *Rustler Canyon*) capped this field with thick layers of Wild Horse Mesa Tuff, famously exposed at Hole-in-the-Wall. On Hackberry Mountain this tuff has been largely eroded since then; it survives mostly on the northern slopes, where in fact it dominates. You will come across Hackberry Spring Volcanics on the saddle between summits, around the springs west of the summit, and at the lower end of the canyon along the Hackberry Spring Road.

Route Description

Hackberry Mountain. If you start from the fork in the canyon, walk up the road to its end just below Hackberry Spring. Although this spring was also singed, its thickets of catclaw are still standing. It usually has no surface water, but at times it discharges a few gallons per minute. In the springtime, it is blanketed with green grass and the myriad blooms of storksbill and fiddleneck. The catclaw's nickname—wait-a-minute bush—will take all its meaning if you cross the spring a little hastily and get hooked on the plants' curved spines.

From afar, Hackberry Mountain's elongated crest is reminiscent of a medieval castle ringed by impregnable ramparts. The least steep route to the summit is up the draw on the right just past the spring. The wash soon runs into tight narrows occluded by high falls. When the first fall is in sight, bypass the narrows up the draw's open southern slope. After 200 feet of elevation gain, you will reach the more level shoulder that wraps around most of Hackberry Mountain. If the wind has not blown it over, there should be a lone juniper about 100 yards to the west. Walk past it into the draw's upper drainage, then climb in the drainage southwest up to the crest. The rest of the route is along the narrow, mostly level crest. The cliffs that rim the final mountain block

Bedded ash cliff on the way up to Hackberry Mountain

have plenty of breaks that are easy to climb. This hike requires little scrambling. But most of the climbing takes place on rock-strewn slopes along 30% of the distance, so this is not exactly a walk in the park.

Hackberry Mountain is a bleak desolation, dark-toned and sparsely vegetated, swept by icy winds in winter, scorched to three-digit temperatures in summer. Yet there is something captivating about this unrevered slice of desert. The massive Miocene outpourings that created it spawned a wilderness of minerals. Sheer bluffs dissected into fins of dark-brown tephra adorn the slopes. White tuff outcrops generously in long banks of scalloped cliffs. Some exposures are stuffed with large boulders propelled by the force of the eruptions. There are trachyte dikes and rhyolite plugs, attractive olivine and pyroxene, and a rare horizon of beautiful spherical silicate crystals. The isolated summit overlooks some two dozen ranges, from the Providence Mountains to the Hualapai Mountains in Arizona, and from Nevada's McCullough Range to as far south as Joshua Tree National Park. Wildlife blissfully ignores the threats of this unforgiving environment. Chukars quacked happily down by the spring. A herd of bighorn sheep effortlessly climbed the crest while I took in the scenery near the open grove of juniper below the summit. I almost stepped on the molted skin of a rattlesnake; later on it was my turn to spook a ground squirrel. The flaming flowers of rock pea brightened even the most lifeless ground. That there is so much more than meets the eye is the best lesson this little mountain teaches us.

The south fork. To return a different way, from the summit walk the crest back to the false summit you passed by on the way up, then drop into the steep ravine northeast of it. After reaching the shoulder, cross it to the prominent flat bench to the southeast, then find the route of your choice down into the drainage to the west, which is the south fork of the access canyon. This descent is steeper than the climb, but it gives an opportunity to explore the pretty south fork. The upper canyon has an abundance of tall lava monuments. The unobstructed lower canyon leads back down to the road past relict groves of and yucca, and no fewer than three springs. The upper one was once tapped by a pipeline whose dislocated segments can still be traced all along the canyon. The middle spring is pinned on a grassy knoll, above a manmade trench. The larger lower spring has a few willow and mesquite, and a small grove of cattail. On a good day you might hear, rising from under it, the joyful sound of gurgling water.

Hackberry Mountain		
	Dist.(mi)	Elev.(ft)
Via Hackberry Spring		
End of Hackberry Spring Rd	0.0	4,365
Hackberry Spring	~0.05	~4,420
Crest	~0.6	5,215
Hackberry Mountain	1.0	5,390
Wash in south fork	1.85	4,460
Main spring in south fork	2.0	~4,420
Road at canyon junction	2.6	4,230
Back to starting point	3.1	4,365
Via Guitar Mountain		
Trailhead	0.0	4,010
Leave road toward saddle	0.65	~4,060
Ridgeline at saddle	0.85	4,190
Guitar Mountain	2.0	5,003
Saddle	2.4	4,710
Hackberry Mountain	3.4	5,390

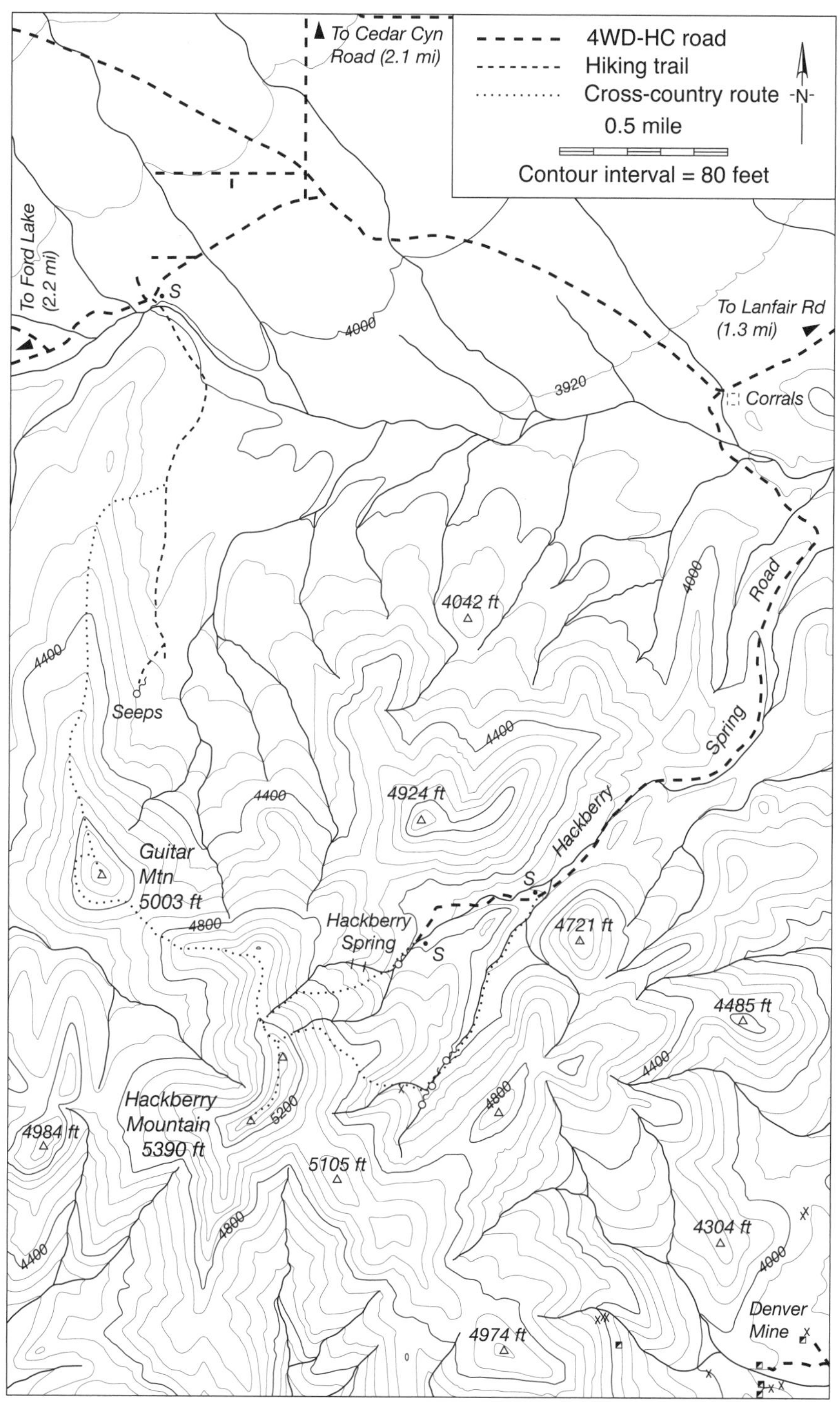

To Cedar Cyn Road (2.1 mi)
4WD-HC road
Hiking trail
Cross-country route
N
0.5 mile
Contour interval = 80 feet
To Ford Lake (2.2 mi)
S
4000
To Lanfair Rd (1.3 mi)
3920
Corrals
4000
Road
4042 ft
4400
Seeps
Spring
4400
4400
4924 ft
Hackberry
Guitar Mtn 5003 ft
S
4800
Hackberry Spring
S
4721 ft
4485 ft
4400
Hackberry Mountain 5390 ft
5200
4800
4984 ft
5105 ft
4800
4400
4304 ft
4000
Denver Mine
4974 ft

Guitar Mountain. From close up Guitar Mountain looks oddly realistic, a cliff-bound slab of dark rhyolite proudly rising skyward like a misplaced monument to rock and roll. The scenery has affinities with a Dali masterpiece; you half expect melted clocks and a caravan of slender-legged elephants. Because the terrain is open and the mountain plainly visible almost the whole way, this hike requires little orienteering skills. The hill a short distance southwest of the trailhead is the northern tip of the ridge that descends from Guitar Mountain. For the most foolproof route, climb this hill and follow the whole ridgeline to the summit. For greater diversity, hike the old road; it roughly parallels the ridge on the flat east of it. After 0.7 mile, leave the road, climb west to the saddle on the ridge, and follow the ridgeline. The road is often faint and overgrown. If you lose it, just climb to the top of the ridge from wherever you are. Both routes are about 2 miles long.

The first part of this hike, along the road or ridge, is over soft ground made mostly of small pieces of pale vesiculated lava. The wildfire left scant survivors, although as usual several opportunistic plants, including a few species of eriogonum and a host of tiny wildflowers, have reclaimed the emptiness with unbridled exuberance. The second part, up on the guitar itself, is a canted mosaic of rhyolitic slabs. The guitar was spared by the flames; the spaces between rocks are filled with grasses and green shrubs—ephedra, Wright buckwheat, and aromatic Mojave sage. The best part is the summit itself. All around, the land is sheared off into a girdle of dark cliffs plunging as much as 80 vertical feet. Here as all along the upper ridge the views are about as good as from Hackberry Mountain, encompassing Lanfair Valley and its timeless ring of sawtooth ranges.

Guitar Mountain's cliffs are largely unscalable for most humans, but a couple of breaks in the west-side cliffs make it possible to hike on to Hackberry Mountain without backtracking much. The closest break is about 150 yards down (north) from the summit. The descent requires easy scrambling on tall rock steps. If it is too steep for your liking, try the next break further down the west side. If all fails, hike to the bottom of the guitar, where the drops are short and gradual. From there, circle back up on the steep talus at the foot of the cliff to the saddle below the tip of Guitar Mountain. It is then about 1 mile up the narrow, seahorse-shaped crest to Hackberry Mountain.

If you are ambitious, make a longer loop hike by returning via Hackberry Spring and the access roads (8.8 miles, 1,960 feet up). To minimize driving and avoid the bad roads, park at the corrals.

■

HART PEAK

Once the lava-filled chimney of a small volcano, Hart Peak is a dramatic vertical wedge of craggy rhyolite. The approach to its base crosses a striking high-desert grassland festooned with cactus, juniper, and Joshua trees. Although unusually short, the ascent of the summit block is just hard enough to give a satisfying sense of accomplishment. It also provides a unique opportunity to enjoy multiple perspectives of the fantastically eroded ancient dikes, vents, and volcanoes that make up the colorful Castle Mountains.

General Information
Jurisdiction: Castle Mountains National Monument
Road status: Roadless; long standard-clearance access road
Hart Peak: 2.0 mi, 1,130 ft up, 50 ft down one way / moderate–difficult
Main attractions: Tall volcanic plugs, geology, isolation
USGS 7.5' topo map: Hart Peak
Maps: pp. 415*, *393*

Location and Access

The second highest point in the Castle Mountains, Hart Peak is near the north end of the range, less than a mile from the Nevada state line. From the Nipton Road exit on Interstate 15, drive the Nipton Road east 3.5 miles and turn right on the Ivanpah Road. Drive 16.7 miles south to the signed Hart Mine Road on the left. Follow this graded road 4.85 miles to a fork where it angles sharply right. Continue 2.3 miles east-southeast, past a white water tank on the right, to a fork, and angle left. After 0.9 mile, at a crossroad, turn left on the unmarked Walking Box Ranch Road. Drive northeast up to a low pass then down 4.2 miles to an old primitive road on the right at 5 o'clock, with Hart Peak rising to the east-northeast. With a high-clearance four-wheel-drive vehicle, this last road can be driven to the saddle at the southern base of Hart Peak (see map), but it is so short that it is not worth the effort. Park at this junction instead. These access roads are graded and in decent shape, and a standard-clearance vehicle can make it to this junction, although a little clearance helps at a couple of rougher spots.

Route Description

When you finally step out of your car you are in the middle of a postcard. On one side a blond savanna inundated with alien gardens of cactus, blue yucca, Joshua trees, and Utah juniper sweeps down to a dramatic row of spiky summits. On the other side a magnificent fin rises abruptly in jagged glory, burning in shades of apricot and cinnamon against a cerulean sky. The spiky summits are the New York Mountains' iconic Castle Peaks. The giant fin is Hart Peak, a rim of razor-edged rhyolite crags too rough and abrupt to walk. Few Mojave Desert mountains this small command this much attention.

There are routes up this well-guarded summit that do not require technical skills. One of them is the northwest nose, which is all sharp upright rocks except for a convenient break that winds up through them. Most people will prefer the east face, which still occasionally requires hands but is not as steep. From the Walking Box Ranch Road you first follow the old primitive road 0.3 mile toward Hart Peak, in and out of two small washes, to where the road crests a knoll and makes a U bend to the south. You then leave the road, descend a very short distance north to a narrow wash, and follow its tortuous channel toward the saddle south of the summit. It is easy walking, between low banks positively green with Joshua trees, juniper, plump saltbush, and an enjoyable collection of cacti. The wash crosses a cove hemmed in by colorful hills capped with pointed rhyolite plugs. In 0.2 mile it splits; the way is to the right, a lazy arroyo occasionally occupied by a tree, to a beat-up road on the left bank 0.35 mile further. The road parallels the wash for a while, so it is easy to join it at any time. It climbs 0.75 mile up the talus that skirts the base of Hart Peak and crests on the saddle.

From closer up on the saddle, Hart Peak's south face looks even more daunting, a sheer ramp crowned with a forest of tall fins and pinnacles. There is less than half a mile left to go, but this last stretch is fairly rigorous. The first half is a steep open slope that climbs to a second saddle at the base of the summit block. Part way up, it is interrupted by a stocky spur. It can be avoided either on the left (west) side across a rocky talus, or on the right side up a Class-3 cleft in a 7-foot rise. The second saddle is not far above it, a grassy hillside beneath Hart Peak's serrated arête. By then other cacti have joined the show—the red heads of barrel cactus, erect clumps of pancake prickly-pear, and occasional brown-spined prickly-pear.

Most of the difficulty is concentrated in the second half. On its hidden east side, Hart Peak breaks up into a precipitous incline covered with low angular boulders. Fortunately, most of them are well anchored, and there is minimal loose material between them. The density of boulders increases steadily, and so does the grade, climaxing at 50% near the top. The saving grace is that there is no false summit to

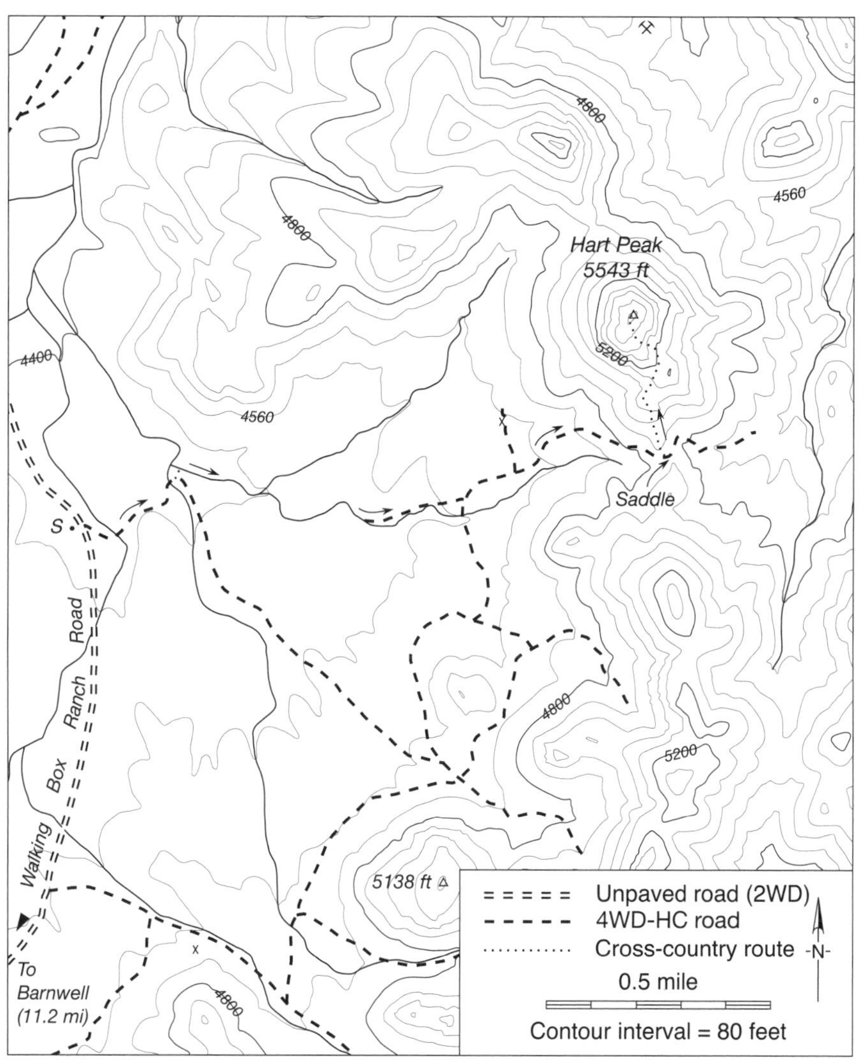

Hart Peak		
	Dist.(mi)	Elev.(ft)
Walking Box Ranch Road	0.0	4,460
Leave road at U bend	0.3	4,460
Join old road	0.85	4,510
First saddle (leave road)	1.6	~4,865
Second saddle	1.85	~5,170
Hart Peak	2.0	5,543

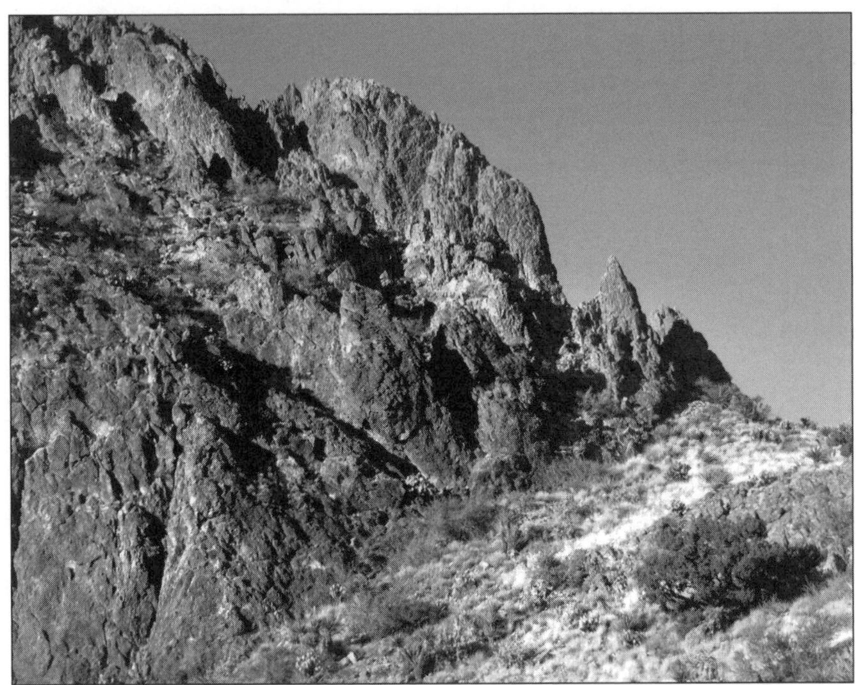

Second saddle (right) at base of Hart Peak's southern arête

fool you: when you crest the last visible outcrop and the sky suddenly opens up, you find yourself within 20 feet of the summit.

The view makes you very aware of the remoteness of this range. To the east you look across the state of Nevada's extreme southern wedge, occupied by the largely empty sweep of Piute Valley and the Newberry Mountains behind it. The valley's only buildings are those of the small communities of Searchlight and Cal-Nev-Ari. Beyond, out of sight, is the Colorado River, flooded under Lake Mohave, and on its far side the long rumpled crest line of the Black Mountains in Arizona. On Hart Peak you are practically immersed in the Castle Mountains, next to the fantastic skyline of the Castle Peaks' chiseled volcanoes. All around, the Castle Mountains show off their colorful hills of white ash flows and buff badlands pierced by sculpted dikes and vents of mahogany rhyolite. At sunset, when the shadows rise and the sunlight glows copper across its flanks, this little-known range looks richer than all the gold that it once held. Carefully picking your way through stubborn rocks and plants as you slowly return in waning light is a small price to pay for so much splendor.

■

UTE PEAK

Far off the beaten path, Ute Peak (4,908') is the highest point in the Piute Range, a stark mesa of sloped volcanic beds buttressed by weathered cliffs. It can be climbed two ways, one a short and comparatively easy cross-country route amid extravagant cactus gardens, the other up a long beat-up road that courses the yucca-dotted spine of the range. Both approaches encompass wide-open views of the California desert's desolate easternmost frontier.

General Information

Road status: Roadless; long primitive access road (HC)
Ute Peak (cross-country): 1.4 mi, 1,240 ft up, 0 ft down one way / moder.
Ute Peak (Piute Mesa Tr.): 7.0 mi, 1,380 ft up, 430 ft down one way / diff.
Main attractions: Scenic cactus gardens, view of Lanfair Valley
USGS 7.5' topo maps: East of Grotto Hills*, Hart Peak
Maps: pp. 419*, *393*

Location and Access

Ute Peak is located in the middle of the Piute Range, at the far east end of Lanfair Valley. From all directions it is a long drive to get close to it. For the shortest approach, take the Fenner exit on Interstate 40. At the bottom of the westbound exit ramp, turn right on Goffs Road and drive northeast 10.4 miles to the signed Lanfair Road, on the left at the edge of the small community of Goffs. Go north on Lanfair Road 16.2 miles (the first 10.3 miles are paved, the rest well graded) to Lanfair, at the signed junction with the Cedar Canyon Road on the left. Continue north 100 yards to the unsigned Cedar Canyon Road eastern extension on the right. Drive this dirt road due east 9.5 miles to its end at the Badlands Road, at the foot of the Piute Range. Ignore all side roads; go straight at mile 2.1, at mile 3.65, and at the triple fork (mile 5.15). Turn left on the Badlands Road, and drive 4.6 miles north to a point due west of a low swell marked 1,222 m (4,009 ft). This is 0.1 mile past a sparsely vegetated flat, and 100 feet before a split in the road. Park here for the cross-country climb.

To climb Ute Peak on the Piute Mesa Trail instead, continue 3.7 miles to a four-way junction. Turn right, drive 2.7 miles north to the next junction, and park. The poorer road to the right is the Piute Mesa Trail. High clearance is required up to the start of the cross-country route, and four-wheel drive as well beyond.

Route Description

From the start of the cross-country route, Ute Peak is the pimple about 1 mile and 1,200 feet up to the east-northeast, capped by a large cairn. To its right, the crest descends a little to a long saddle before dropping over short cliffs. Aim for the saddle across the open slopes north of the 4,009-foot swell, to a steep hillside covered with cavernous outcrops. Bypass it on the right, and climb the steep flank just south of it to the saddle. It is then an easy climb along the crest to the summit.

What makes this peak particularly enjoyable is the cactus gardens. As soon as the ground swells up to foothills, the vegetation morphs from the valley's creosote-bush forest into a thick belt of cacti. You are surrounded by bizarre plants growing right out of sunburnt rocks. Armies of red barrel cactus shoot out of the ground like an invasion of barbed fire hydrants. Staghorn cholla with shaggy crowns grow among gangs of 10-foot Mojave yucca shaped like electrocuted paint-brushes. They share the mountain with a thorny jungle of blackbrush, catclaw, and more subdued cactaceae—tufts of calico cactus, shiny sprigs of silver cholla, lone beavertail cactus, and diminutive fishhook cactus hiding between stones. Even during the chlorophyll lull of winter, this colorful cactus kingdom remains remarkably alive.

The eroded rubbles on Ute Peak's higher flanks record the vagaries of 8 million years of capricious Miocene volcanism. Pieces of basalt from runny lava are incrusted with short parallel grooves, each one a gas bubble that was stretched several times its original diameter as the lava flowed. The rhyolite is fine-grained or porphyritic, banded or chalky. Cleaved faces bear the serpentine eddies of turbulent flows. The upper slopes and the crest are littered with hunks of andesite, steel-grey cores encased in coffee-colored shells of heavy-metal oxides.

Ute Peak

	Dist.(mi)	Elev.(ft)
Badlands Road	0.0	3,670
Foot of cavernous hillside	~0.9	~4,330
Crest	1.15	~4,720
Ute Peak	1.4	4,908
Piute Mesa Trail (trailhead)	0.0	3,960
High Table Mtn West End	4.5	4,793
Upper end of trail (viewpoint)	6.3	~4,895
Ute Peak	7.0	4,908

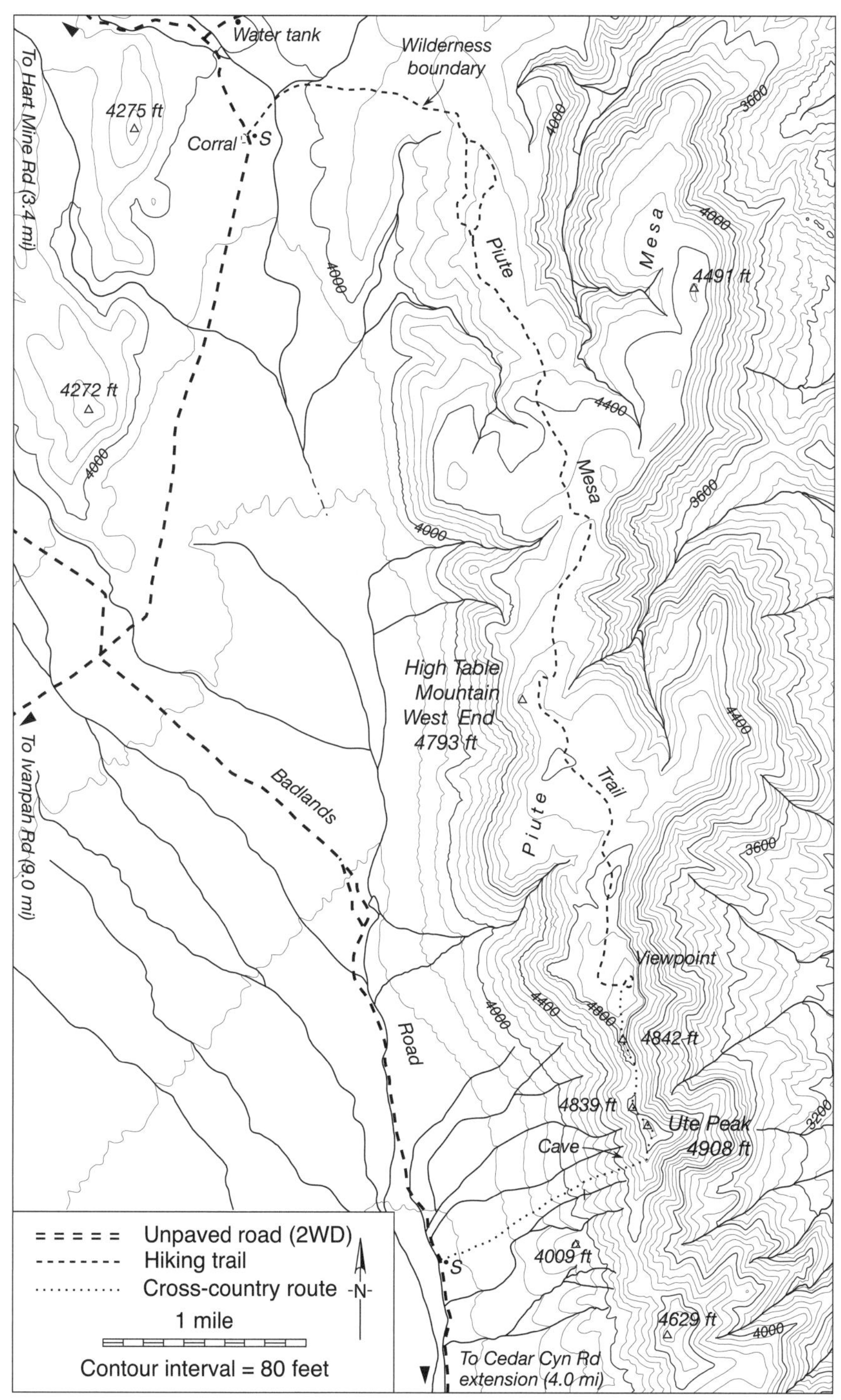
Water tank
Wilderness boundary
To Hart Mine Rd (3.4 mi)
4275 ft
Corral
S
4272 ft
Piute
Mesa
4491 ft
High Table Mountain West End 4793 ft
Badlands
To Ivanpah Rd (9.0 mi)
Piute
Trail
Viewpoint
Road
4842 ft
4839 ft
Ute Peak 4908 ft
Cave
4009 ft
4629 ft
To Cedar Cyn Rd extension (4.0 mi)
Unpaved road (2WD)
Hiking trail
Cross-country route
1 mile
N
Contour interval = 80 feet

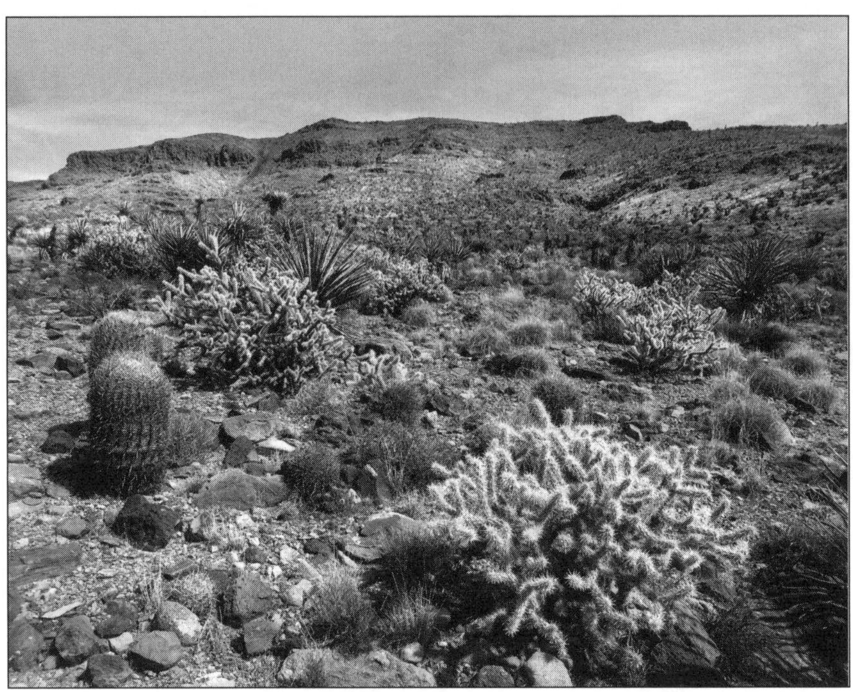

Cactus garden on the way to Ute Peak (left of center)

The Piute Mesa Trail offers a much more leisurely approach, gaining a comparable elevation in five times the distance. After 1 mile the road enters the Piute Range Wilderness and climbs a long gradual ramp to Piute Mesa, amid Mojave yucca, cacti, and small Joshua trees. At the start of the plateau the road skirts High Table Mountain West End, which commands excellent views over precipitous slopes into Lanfair Valley. From the Piute Valley viewpoint at the end of the road, it is 0.7 mile along the crest, over three low rocky spurs, to Ute Peak.

Either way, it is a wild and scenic climb in rarely visited territory. All around the plateau and summit, Piute Mesa drops in staggered staircases of weathered cliffs and tall taluses draped in dark volcanic rubble. The panorama embraces hundreds of square miles of lonesome open valleys. The closest ranges are pushed back to a colorless crown pegged to a distant horizon that straddles three states. The exception is the Castle Mountains, their long serrated skyline rising just a few miles north. The nearly constant views over this striking range alone make it well worth looping back down the trail and road—13.4 miles of wildness, secluded and silent, downhill almost the whole way.

■

FORT PIUTE

Briefly active in 1867–1868, Fort Piute was a military outpost that protected the U.S. mail and freight wagons crossing the desert along the Mojave Road. Isolated on the preserve's far-flung eastern edge, it is still today harder to reach by car than most places. The fort's partially reconstructed blockhouse overlooking luxuriant Piute Spring is one of the preserve's classics. The scenic hike from the fort up the Old Government Road gives access to a beautiful creek, rock art, wagon ruts, and a breathtaking climb on this historic route.

General Information
Road status: Roadless; high-clearance access road
Fort Piute: 0.2 mi, 30 ft up loop / very easy
Piute Spring loop: 1.3 mi, 190 ft up loop / easy
Old Gov't Road: 2.4 mi, 870 ft up, 270 ft down one way / easy–moderate
Main attractions: A historic fort, lush creek, historic trail
USGS 7.5' topo maps: Homer Mountain*, Signal Hill
Maps: pp. 425*, *393*

Location and Access

Fort Piute is near the preserve's eastern boundary, at the southeast corner of the Piute Range. To reach it from the east, drive Highway 95 11.9 miles north of the Goffs Road (or 4.6 miles south of the Nevada stateline) to the Mojave Road, marked by a rock cairn. Proceed west on this road 6.1 miles across Piute Valley to a north-south service road, then 1.1 miles west to the Metropolitan Water District (MWD) Road, paralleled by power lines. Continue west 1.9 miles on the Old Government Road to the gate at Fort Piute, just inside Piute Canyon. With a standard-clearance vehicle, you will likely be stopped by the bumpy Piute Wash crossing 2.2 miles from Highway 95. Past the service road it takes high clearance to negotiate rocks and wash crossings.

To access Fort Piute from the west, drive to the intersection of the Cedar Canyon Road and Ivanpah Road. Go 120 yards north on the Ivanpah Road and make a right on the eastern extension of the Cedar Canyon Road. Continue east 3.65 miles to a junction, and angle right at 45° onto the AT&T Cable Road. Follow it 6.1 miles to a junction at the foot of the Piute Range. To hike to Fort Piute, turn left, go 0.5 mile to a junction, and park; the track closed to vehicles on the right is the Old Government Road to the fort. To drive to Fort Piute, from the junction

Reconstructed ruins of Fort Piute (2007)

on the AT&T Cable Road continue east 3.9 miles, over a low pass, then down through the Piute Range to the MWD Road. Turn left and go 1.45 miles north. Turn left again and drive 1.9 miles to Fort Piute. The descent from Piute Pass is steep, canted, and it has loose rocks; it requires high clearance, and four-wheel drive in the uphill direction.

History: Redoubts and Indian Wars

In the 1850s, the ancient trail the desert people had blazed across the Mojave Desert over the centuries emerged as one of a very few practicable routes of travel between the Colorado River and the coast. To protect the U.S. mail service and freight wagons traveling on the Mojave Road from the natives, understandably upset by increasing encroachment on their lands, starting in 1866 the U.S. Army established a series of redoubts between Fort Mojave and Camp Cady. These small military camps were strategically located at the rare water sources along the road. The first one was set up at Rock Spring in late 1866. Fort Piute was built by the U.S. Infantry in December 1867. It was actually not a fort but a sub-post dependent on Fort Mojave, about 24 miles away along the Colorado River, and it was garrisoned by troops from Fort Mojave. Fort Piute had only a multiple-room stronghold protected by thick walls and rifle ports, a rock corral, and a small structure used either for a sentry, a cannon, or as a shelter. Up to 18 men occupied the site and escorted travelers across Indian lands. The outpost was also a relay station where the Overland Mail changed and rested its horses and mules. When the mail was re-routed further south in 1868, the outposts along the Mojave Road were abandoned. Fort Piute was deserted in May, just five months after it was erected.

Route Description

Fort Piute. After the long drive across arid Piute Valley, the green oasis spilling along Piute Canyon below the road is a refreshing sight. This is Piute Spring, home of the preserve's largest riparian system and longest flowing creek, both a quasi-miracle in this rainless country. The ruins of Fort Piute are a short walk from the end of the road. Recently restored to about a third of their original height, the ruins' thick stone walls outline a few rooms separated by narrow doorways. The walls were originally at least 6 feet tall and supported a wooden roof. The entrance is in the middle of the long right side. The central room it leads into was a corral. The room to the right, closest to the hills, was the sleeping quarters. The room to the left was used for storage and baking. The corral of loose stones below the blockhouse likely dates from the same era. The two structures were originally connected by two parallel walls to protect people walking between them.

Lower Piute Spring. The area's centerpiece is, however, not the fort but Piute Spring and the magical little stream that irrigates it. From the fort it is a short stroll down to the edge of it. In September 2004, a fire likely started by human negligence decimated 12 acres of this rare ecosystem. Since then, the vegetation has recolonized the canyon bottom quickly thanks to the flowing creek. An abundance of cottonwoods and willows now grow prolifically in regenerated soils.

In historic days, from Fort Piute the wagon road went right through the spring. Since then, the Piute Canyon Trail has been blazed along the canyon's low north rim to bypass the spring. Starting as a wide path just past the fort, it wanders lazily along a wide bench right above the tree tops. Its main attraction is the views of the vibrant oasis snaking in the trench-like canyon below, and Piute Creek sparkling in the sunlight. You are close enough to hear the water gurgling and the breeze brushing through the tree tops. In late fall and early winter, the low sunrays torching the canopy to a golden glow is one of this desert's strangest sights. In the summer, the spring's soft green foliage against the background of dark volcanic hills seems equally improba-

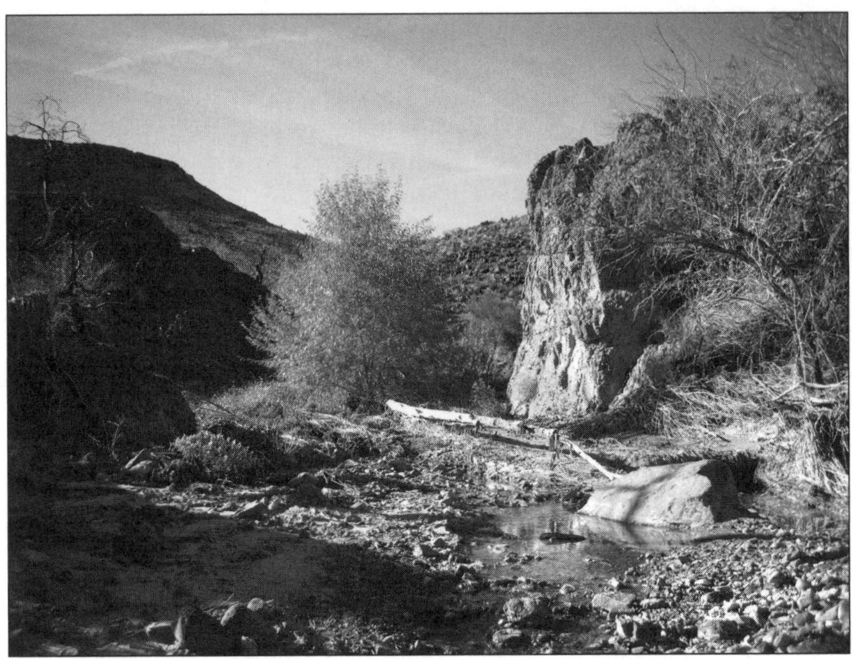

Cottonwoods and cliffs along Piute Creek at Old Government Road crossing

ble. Native Americans made good use of this wet canyon. The Whipple Expedition of 1854 reported irrigated fields in this area, perhaps the work of Mohave Indians or Southern Piute Indians, who subsisted more on agriculture than other cultures. Above the trail, the slope is covered with luminous cholla, tall barrel cactus, and red-clawed cottontop cactus, displayed as neatly as in a botanical garden.

After 0.6 mile the trail angles left and splits at an open fork in the canyon. Piute Canyon and the Piute Canyon Trail continue straight ahead; the fork on the left is Fort Piute Canyon. The other trail drops left 50 yards to the canyon floor. This crossing is particularly scenic. The creek flows along sandy beaches bordered by sedge, willows, and handsome red bluffs. Downstream, a tiny cascade drops into a deeper pool. It is common to see bighorn and coyote tracks by the water's edge, grass pressed to the ground by a flashflood, and in the winter sheets of ice—along with butterflies!

From the crossing you can return down through the spring. The old trail is still there, although a little bushwhacking may be necessary, or sidestepping on the more open south side of the spring vegetation. You might spot a frog, a desert iguana or a gecko, or blue dragonflies dancing over Piute Creek. Together with the upper part of the spring,

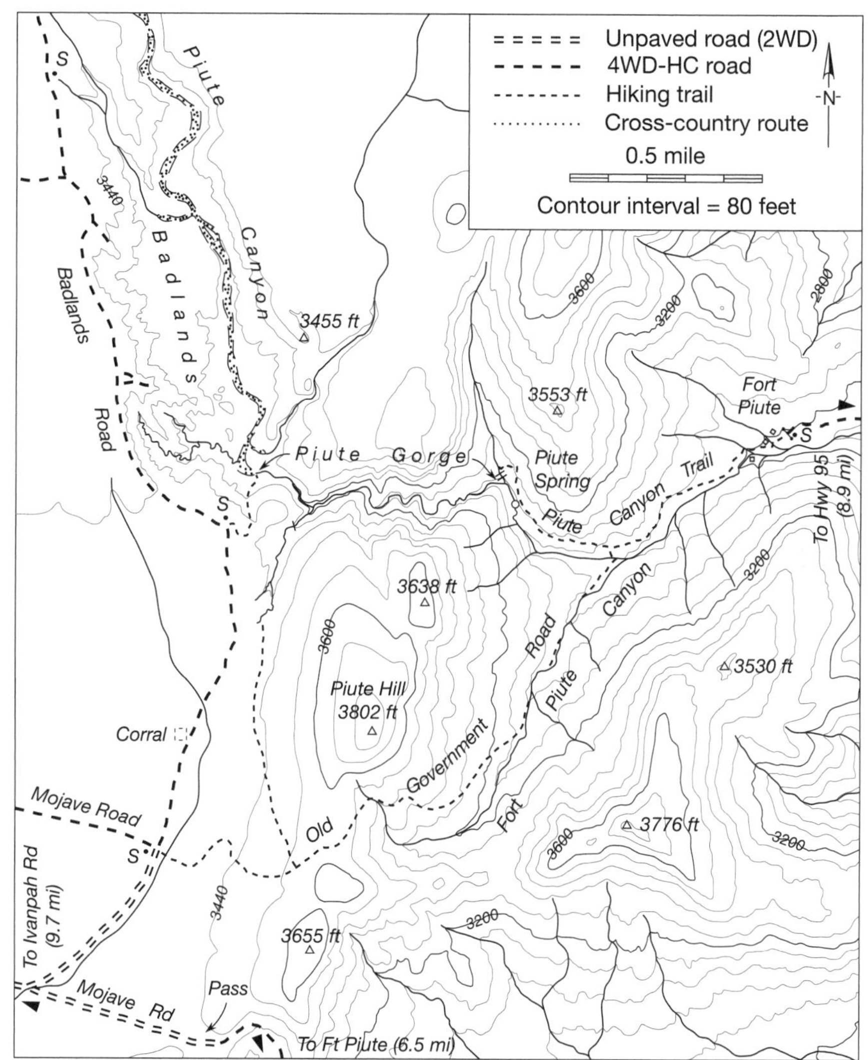

Fort Piute and Old Government Road

	Dist.(mi)	Elev.(ft)
End of road at Fort Piute	0.0	2,800
Fort Piute	0.05	2,830
Piute Creek crossing	0.65	2,880
Petroglyphs	~0.75	~2,920
Pass into Lanfair Valley	1.9	~3,585
Badlands Road at Mojave Road	2.4	3,400

upstream from the crossing, it is easily the most bucolic place in the preserve. Just before getting back to Fort Piute, there is a large walled enclosure on the south bank, possibly a former dwelling.

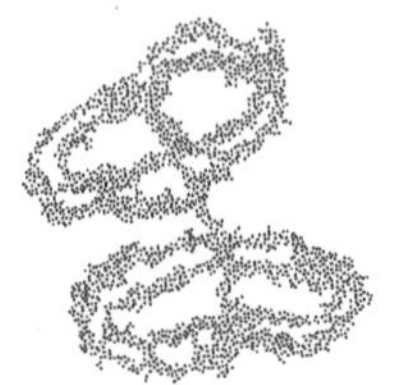
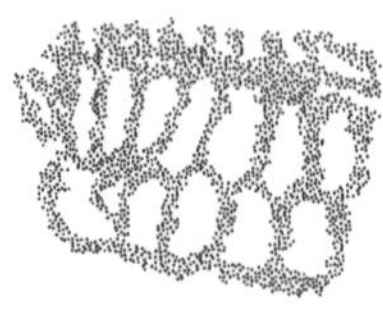

The Old Government Road. Alternatively, from the crossing you can walk the Old Government Road to the edge of Lanfair Valley. This beat-up one-lane road is one of the few original segments of the Mojave Road closed to vehicles. It starts on the south side of the wash, about 20 yards downstream from where the trail joins the wash. Soon after, a section of the historic road climbs over red bedrock; it still bears the deep parallel ruts ground by wagons over 150 years ago. Native Americans left their mark too, centuries earlier, in the form of fine petroglyphs pecked in the desert varnish of low basaltic boulders. Many figures are scattered shortly past the ruts, between the road and the canyon wash. The most unusual ones are a surprisingly realistic desert tortoise and tattoos wrapped around a pyramidal boulder.

Past the wagon ruts the road continues a little, disappears in the gravelly wash, reappears for a tenth of a mile on the west bank, and disappears again. Its erratic path suggests that in historic times, the spring extended into this wash and periodically forced the road out of it. After 0.5 mile, the road resumes on the right bank. From there it leaves the wash and climbs the steep flank of Piute Hill 0.6 mile to a pass into Lanfair Valley. This grade was said to be the most arduous on the entire Mojave Road. As you climb it you might ponder how it must have felt to struggle up this road in the 1860s, surrounded by alien cacti and hostile natives, with no other roads around, crossing unchartered territory fraught with danger, heading to an isolated coastal village of a few thousand souls. Most of us are no longer this courageous.

Although less than 200 feet above Lanfair Valley, the pass offers a superb view of this empty desert plain stretching out for miles into the stony heart of the preserve. On the west side, it is an easy descent on the well-constructed historic road to the Mojave Road at the foot of the range. Refer to *Piute Canyon* for optional return routes.

■

PIUTE CANYON

Piute Canyon holds impressive records. Of all the canyons in the preserve, it is one of the most colorful and narrowest. It is home to the preserve's only true gorge and largest badlands, to the lushest spring, and the most abundant creek. That so many attributes are concentrated in only a few square miles of an immense desert is a brilliant cosmic joke. Needless to say, this is a must.

General Information

Road status: Roadless; high-clearance access road
Piute Canyon Trail: 1.1 mi, 410 ft up, 210 ft down one way / easy–moder.
Badlands to Fort Piute: 3.5 mi, 770 ft up, 90 ft down one way / moderate
Piute Cyn–Fort Piute Cyn: 8.1 mi, 1,040 ft up loop / moderate–difficult
Main attractions: A dramatic volcanic gorge, badlands, creek, spring
USGS 7.5' topo maps: East of Grotto Hills, Signal Hill*, Homer Mtn*
Maps: pp. 425*, *393*

Location and Access

Piute Canyon is at the south end of the Piute Range, at the eastern edge of the preserve. It consists of three very different sections, the badlands in the upper canyon, the gorge in the mid canyon, and Piute Spring in the lower canyon. The upper and mid canyon are easiest to reach by car from the west by driving what I refer to as the Badlands Road, which parallels the western base of the Piute Range. From this road the canyon can be accessed on foot at three points, at the head of the badlands, at the head of the gorge via a short trail, or via the Old Government Trail, which connects to the lower canyon. These options can be combined to make a number of circuits and loops of various lengths throughout this area. Consult the map to get a better idea of the lay of the land and of your options. This section describes the downhill hike through the entire canyon. Alternatively, one can start from Fort Piute and hike up canyon (see *Fort Piute* for access).

To get to the Badlands Road, drive the Cedar Canyon Road to Lanfair. Go north 100 yards on the Ivanpah Road and make a right on the eastern extension of the Cedar Canyon Road. Drive west on this good primitive road 3.65 miles to a junction, and angle right at 45° onto the AT&T Cable Road. Follow it 6.1 miles to its junction with the Mojave Road, near the foot of the Piute Range. Make a left and drive 0.5 mile northeast to a junction, where the Mojave Road angles 90° to

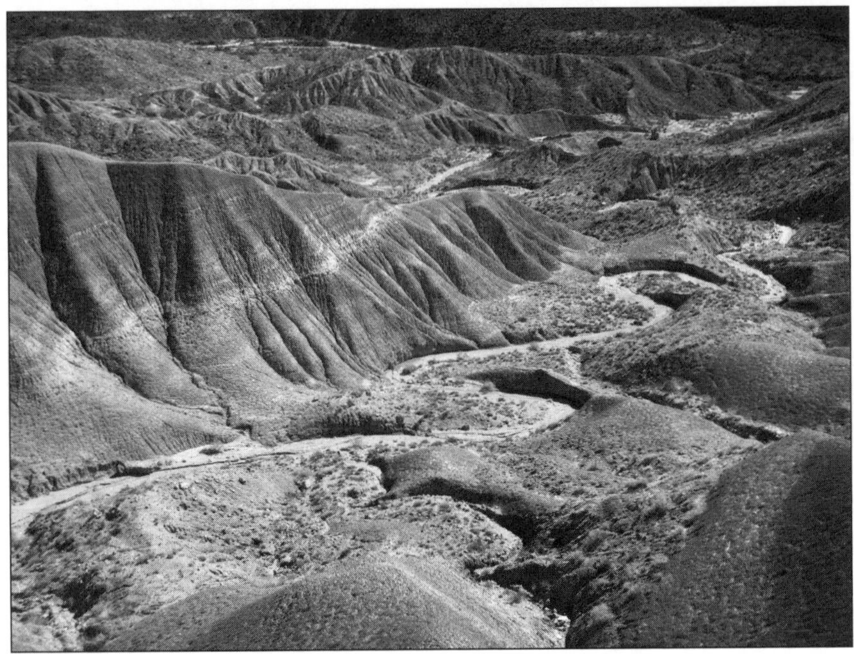

Badlands above the head of Piute Gorge

the left. Park at this junction if you want to hike the Old Government Trail: it starts a short distance up the hillside to the east. Otherwise continue straight on the Badlands Road 0.85 mile to a wide parking area on the right, overlooking the badlands. Park here if you want to hike directly into the gorge. The trail at the east end of the parking area drops in 0.25 mile to the head of the gorge. To hike the badlands, continue north on the Badlands Road 1.1 miles to a fork. A few short side roads along the way end at great overlooks over the badlands. *Do not hike into the canyon from the overlooks.* Badlands are very crumbly and heal extremely slowly, and walking on them would cause significant damage. Bear right at the fork, and park after 0.25 mile, in a right bend. A short walk to the southeast will take you to a ravine that drops into the badlands. This drive can be done with a standard-clearance vehicle, but it is long, and it is safer with a high-clearance vehicle.

Geology

Piute Canyon is a bit of a geological anomaly. Unlike most canyons, it does not drain a slope but cuts right through a mountain. This feat was possible because Lanfair Valley, on the west side of the Piute Range, is higher than Piute Valley on the east side (by about 800 feet), and the range between them is not very high. Comparatively little erosion was therefore needed to cut the gorge through the range down to the floor of Lanfair Valley. In the Pleistocene and possibly Pliocene, a small pluvial lake filled the shallow basin where Lanfair Valley abuts the southwestern corner of the Piute Range, uphill from the future location of the gorge. This lake might have assisted erosion of the gorge.

Since the geologic completion of the gorge, stream erosion has been carving down into the siltstone, claystone, and sandstone that were deposited at the bottom of the lake, resulting in the beautiful badlands in the upper part of Piute Canyon. Although not nearly as popular as the gorge and spring, they are as unique and impressive.

Route Description

The badlands. From the Badlands Road the ravine mentioned in the access section widens as it slices down through the sharp edge of the drainage, then it turns into a gulch framed by wrinkly slopes. At first only bits of the underlying siltstone poke through here and there. But as you progress downhill the slopes become more barren, until you are surrounded by the typical bright denuded hills of badlands. In 0.65 mile this smaller wash joins the main wash. (If you are planning to return this way, make a mental note of this fork, or you may miss your turn coming back up.) The larger naked hills visible down canyon are the heart of Piute Canyon's badlands. The wash eventually takes you right by them. Long, keen-edged buttresses of siltstone slope down gracefully from the canyon rim. Every surface is devoid of vegetation and deeply chiseled into smooth ridges. Pastel shades of white and cream grade into light ochres. When they bear leaves, the catclaw along the sandy wash seem incongruously green in this sterile land. To best appreciate this magnificent place, hike up the side canyon on the west side just before the gorge. For a few hundred yards its narrow wash snakes tightly through a surreal world of brilliant hills.

Please do your share to preserve these fragile badlands. Do not walk on hillsides or crests. Stay in washes, where you will leave fainter footprints that the next rain will erase.

Piute Gorge. Just below the badlands Piute Canyon makes a left bend, passes by the lower end of the short access trail that drops from the rim, and enters the gorge. The transformation is surprisingly sudden. One moment you are walking in a bright open landscape; the next you find yourself trapped in a corridor less than 100 feet wide, partly filled with shadows. For a mile, Piute Canyon remains a closed, tightly

Volcanic cliff along Piute Gorge

twisting gorge framed by 300-foot walls. The formations are bold fusions of reds, browns, and grays accented with black. We owe these unusually colorful displays to a series of volcanic eruptions that took place in the Miocene, across terrain that had already been devastated by the Peach Springs eruption 18.4 million years ago. This time the area was repeatedly smothered under thick layers of andesite, dacite, rhyolite flows, tuffs, and an intense episode of ash fall.

Such a concentration and diversity of fairly young extrusive rocks are uncommon. The ash flow outcrops in the purplish buttress at the mouth of the first side canyon. Perpendicular walls crammed with light-gray dacite cobbles alternate with crinkled cross-sections of volcanic breccia and tilted layers of red lava. All exposures are dark, angular, and rough, a befitting reflection of their cataclysmic genesis. Little vegetation tempers this stark mineral monopoly. Solitary catclaw and willow grow along the wash, tousled and dead-looking most of the year. Stiff barrel and cottontop cacti cling to the slopes, as do a few stern yucca. Except after a heavy downpour, when water gathers in ephemeral puddles in the sand, the land is utterly dry.

The high walls and tortuous wash effectively keep the gorge's many secrets hidden until the very last moment. Somewhere in there you will run across overhangs and caves, a high wall of black breccia, a peculiar gallery of balanced basalt boulders, and a gargantuan block sitting squarely in the wash. There are boulder occlusions, short narrows, slants, and low falls. At one of the narrows, stream erosion has polished the bedrock breccia into exquisite orange-hued mosaics veined with calcite crystals.

The gorge ends as abruptly as it begins: the canyon makes a sharp 90° right bend and opens up onto a straight corridor of sand. To proceed, either bypass the spring on the Piute Canyon Trail, or continue down the wash through the upper part of Piute Spring. Both routes converge at the Old Government Road 0.4 mile down canyon.

Piute Canyon Trail: Gorge to Piute Creek crossing. This old trail follows a low bench on the north side of the canyon, from the lower end of the gorge to Fort Piute. Its western segment is faint, and the west end of this segment is a little tricky to find. In the sharp right bend at the bottom of the gorge, a side canyon crossed by boulders takes off to the north. Along the first 100 yards, this side canyon is interrupted by three falls, all less than 20 feet high. It is easy to scramble up the first two. The third one, nearly vertical, is bypassed by a trail on the right. Just above this fall, climb the steep talus on the right about 15 feet to an outcrop of red lava. The Piute Canyon Trail starts here. It shoots straight up the steep slope in very tight and short wiggles. After 220 yards, it reaches a junction. Make a right on the lower fork (the upper fork soon loops back and joins it). The rest of the trail follows Piute Canyon's rim, about 150 feet above the wash.

This is a fun little trail, narrow and uneven, just elusive enough to pique one's interest. It commands forbidding views of the gorge's

Piute Canyon

	Dist.(mi)	Elev.(ft)
Badlands Road	0.0	3,485
Piute Canyon wash	0.65	3,290
Main side canyon in badlands	1.4	3,220
Foot of trail/start of gorge	1.5	~3,210
Trailhead at Badlands Road	(0.25)	3,420
Lower end of gorge/side cyn	2.45	3,020
Piute Spring (head)	2.55	2,980
Fort Piute Canyon	2.85	2,880
Fort Piute (via Piute Cyn Trail)	3.5	~2,830

twisted narrows. Further on, your attention will be constantly drawn to Piute Spring's canopy protruding from the canyon below. Scenic spreads of diamond cholla and barrel cactus thrive among volcanic cobbles and outcrops. You might spot the crisp petroglyph of an atlatl pecked on a flat boulder.

After 0.4 mile the trail reaches a fork. The trail on the right drops to Piute Creek, then continues across the creek up Fort Piute Canyon. The other fork, straight ahead, is the continuation of the Piute Canyon Trail to Fort Piute (0.6 mile). These two trails are described under *Fort Piute.*

Upper Piute Spring. From the lower end of the gorge it is a short walk to the head of Piute Spring—the preserve's lushest and wettest. It starts with tall clumps of arrowweed, then comes a grove of cattail and willow, and finally a dense forest from which rises the delicate sound of running water. Over the next 2.5 miles, Piute Canyon is a sinuous jungle of willow, catclaw, baccharis, honey mesquite, and cottonwood irrigated by a hefty creek. To minimize impact, walk on the more open sandy stretches on the left bank. Soon you will run into the remains of an old foot trail lined off and on with rocks. It is vague, overgrown, and discontinuous, but it will take you most of the way through to Fort Piute Canyon without bushwhacking.

This is a delightful hike, and perhaps the most unique in the preserve. You walk in the deep shade of ancient cottonwoods, through dappled light and green understories. Red-spotted toads and tadpoles, algae, watercress, blue dragonflies, and butterflies thrive in this tiny microcosm, all united by the lively creek. Their enduring survival in this fierce land strains the mind.

The trail eventually disappears after crossing to the right bank. Just a little further the creek squeezes through a shaded narrow passage in nicely polished reddish breccia. For a few very short tight twists it flows in a deeper channel livened by tiny gurgling cascades. It emerges just above the confluence with Fort Piute Canyon, at a scenic sand-filled opening bordered by handsome bluffs.

From this point there are several options to return. You can push on down canyon to Fort Piute, another 0.6 mile, either through the lower part of Piute Spring or on the Piute Canyon Trail. Alternatively, you can return on the Old Government Road, which will take you up Fort Piute Canyon over the low crest of the Piute Range and back to the Badlands Road and your starting point. These three routes are described under *Fort Piute.*

■

THE MOJAVE ROAD

Originally a foot trail to the coast blazed by indigenous tribes, converted into a wagon road in the 1850s, the Mojave Road is today a 130-mile four-wheel-drive recreational road that cuts clear across Mojave National Preserve. Most of it a one-lane track, this long historic road is ideal to experience the preserve's vastness and rich natural and human history. You will get to visit cool springs and military outposts, tackle rocky grades, sandy washes, and a salt flat, drive through sprawling Joshua tree woodlands dotted with cacti, and hike to many nearby natural wonders. Allow a few days for this once-in-a-lifetime trek, or sample it a little at a time, whenever the mood strikes for a dusty ride in the desert.

General Information

Road status: Mostly high-clearance road, with some 4WD stretches
Marl Mountains loop: 7.2 mi, 950 ft up loop / moderate–difficult
Main attraction: Driving a historic primitive road across the preserve
Maps: pp. *393**, 425, *221**, 397, *265**, *83**, 113, 117, 99, 95

Location and Access

The Mojave Road starts on the Fort Mojave Indian Reservation along the Colorado River at the extreme southern tip of Nevada. It ends 129 miles west near Camp Cady, east of Barstow. About 60% of it lies in Mojave National Preserve. This section describes the portion between Piute Valley near the California-Nevada border (14 miles west of its east end) and the head of Afton Canyon southwest of Baker (about 12 miles east of its west end). Some stretches are too narrow for vehicles to pass by each other, so I recommend driving it westbound, like Dennis Casebier does in *Mojave Road Guide*. The starting point is on Highway 95, 4.6 miles south of the Nevada stateline. Coming from the south, this is 11.9 miles north of the Goffs Road.

History: The High Road Through Hell

For centuries the indigenous inhabitants of the Mojave Desert navigated across their huge homeland on an extensive network of trails they had fashioned over time. One of the most important of these trails was the Mojave Trail. It crossed the desert from the Colorado River north of present-day Needles to the Pacific Coast, hopping from spring to far-apart spring to ease the perilous journey. We do not know which tribe or tribes created it. We do know that the Mohave Indians used it to travel as far as the coast and trade sea shells and other materials. They lived in villages scattered along the lower Colorado River, where they led a comparatively sedentary existence supported in part by agriculture. The Mojave Trail saw little traffic, so it is likely that they did not have exclusive rights to it. More nomadic tribes, like the Chemehuevi, likely used at least portions of it on their frequent hunting and gathering expeditions and seasonal migrations.

The natives had amicable relationships with the first travelers who came to their land. In the spring of 1776, Mohave Indian guides took Father Francisco Garcés, a member of Anza's second expedition to southern California, on the Mojave Trail all the way to Mission San Gabriel near Los Angeles. He was the first white man to travel on the trail. Fifty years later, American trapper Jedediah Smith was also shown the way on the ancient trail. But the friendly era ended soon after. Over the following year, the Mohave Indians encountered emigrants displaying hostile behavior, and they became defensive. When Smith returned in 1827, they killed half of his party. For the next 20 years, Anglo-Europeans traveled in increasing numbers through the Mojave Desert, including famous explorers Kit Carson and John Charles Fremont, and they too used Indian trails. By then the natives had realized that their very livelihood was threatened by newcomers. The remaining history of the Mojave Trail was continually molded by this strained relationship.

When the Southwest was acquired by the United States in 1848, the Mojave Desert was a blank spot on the map. The government sent out a series of surveyors to the desert, in part for scientific purposes, and mostly to identify a route for a railroad that would connect the country's coasts. In 1853–1854, the party led by Lt. Amiel Weeks Whipple was the first to bring wagons to the Mojave Trail as it crossed the desert to Los Angeles. In 1857, former Navy Lt. Edward F. Beale was given the difficult mission of blazing a wagon road across the region. Beale also took with him a herd of 25 camels with the mission to evaluate their effectiveness in the American deserts. The camels idea was not such a success, but Beale's crews did complete the road, in 1861. The wagon road crossed New Mexico and Arizona to the Colorado River, then continued westward along the old Mojave Trail.

The relationship with the natives worsened in August 1858, when they ambushed the first emigrants from the east on the new wagon road, wounding and killing many. In the spring of 1859, an army of 500 soldiers was sent to subdue the insurgents. After the natives capitulated, two infantries were left behind to build a fort named Fort

Mojave in the middle of their territory along the Colorado River. From 1859 to early 1861, wagons regularly crossed the desert on the Mojave Road to supply the fort and deliver the U.S. mail between Prescott, Arizona and San Bernardino. The Colorado River area was then safe from Indian depredations. The start of the Civil War in 1861 forced the army to abandon many of its outposts, including Fort Mojave.

The next influx of travelers on the Mojave Road were miners, prompted by the discovery of gold in the San Bernardino Mountains in 1860, then along the Colorado River in 1861. When Arizona was given territory status in 1863, many took the Mojave Road to the new territory's gold mines. By then the Southern Piute, Chemehuevi, and other tribes had become adept at ambushing small parties along the road. In response, the U.S. Army re-garrisoned Fort Mojave and sent soldiers to escort the U.S. mail. In 1866 and 1867, in order to divide the long route between Fort Mojave and Camp Cady into shorter, more manageable segments, it also deployed a string of outposts along the route, including at Rock Spring, Marl Spring, Piute Spring, and Soda Lake.

In 1868, the mail traffic was re-routed on the La Paz Road further south, and the outposts were abandoned. Civilians still kept the Mojave Road alive. The Civil War was over, and travel from the East Coast to California increased. Ranchers and homesteaders started settling in the Mojave Desert. The rich silver strikes on Clark Mountain, as well as in the New York and Providence mountains, also added traffic to the Mojave Road, as did stagecoach services.

The opening of the railroad in 1883 put an end to much of this activity. For safety reasons wagon masters preferred to follow the railroad, and rail became the main mode of travel across the desert. After the turn of the century, the Mojave Road slowly fell into disuse. The locals referred to it as the Old Government Road, and except for its eastern segment across Lanfair Valley, it became just a memory.

In the 1960s and 1970s, growing awareness of the desert's recreational values brought weekend explorers in jeeps to the old wagon road. In 1981, a group of volunteers called *Friends of the Mojave Road* repaired the decayed road and marked it with rock cairns. Their efforts paid off. Decades later, the Mojave Road has survived as an enduring link to the region's rich past, and a source of inspiration for visitors seeking a connection with the more primitive days of yore.

Route Description

The Mojave Road. On its long journey across the preserve, the Mojave Road crosses successively Piute Valley, the Piute Range, Lanfair Valley, the Mid Hills, and enters Kelso Valley. Then it circles around the Beale Mountains and Marl Mountains, skirts the cinder cones area, and finally descends to and crosses Soda Lake. West of the preserve it pushes on many more empty miles up the sandy bed of the Mojave River to Afton Canyon and eventually Camp Cady.

Patience is essential to discover this huge territory. Much of the Mojave Road is barely wide enough for vehicles to cross paths, so progress is slow. The scenery evolves equally slowly. Piute Valley, at the very start, is a good case in point: it is one immense bajada thickly covered with large creosote bush. The monotony is not broken until miles later, on the way up to the low pass over the Piute Range. Right by the side of the road, colorful gardens packed with Mojave yucca, staghorn cholla, and barrel cactus thrive among groves of orange volcanic pinnacles. When you crest the pass and stare down at the vastness of Lanfair Valley, you are confronted with another repetitive creosote-bush plain. It takes several more miles before the scenery changes again, where the valley metamorphoses into a beautiful forest of Joshua trees, one of the largest in the Mojave Desert. The trees are scarce and puny at first, but they quickly multiply and grow, and they will keep you company for the best part of the next 45 miles. Across most of Lanfair Valley, the mighty crest of the New York Mountains dominates the northern skyline. Their forested slopes stand in sharp contrast to the dark volcanic crags and mesas of Hackberry Mountain and the Woods Mountains to the south. As the road creeps up towards the Mid Hills and the massive chain of the Providence Mountains, cacti and yuccas join the scene in greater numbers. For miles their disheveled fluorescent heads bristle across the scenery in ever-changing compositions. At places, a fraction of a mile holds most of the region's many species. In the vicinity of colorful Pinto Mountain, the Mojave Road reaches its highest point, just high enough for a close look at evergreens.

The Joshua tree cover is thickest just on the west side of the Mid Hills, where the road winds down Cedar Canyon. But from there on down to Soda Lake and beyond, the greening process is reversed. The elevation drops, the soil gets drier, the vegetation gradually shrivels up from Joshua tree and cactus heaven to rabbitbrush, creosote bush, and saltbush. In this open terrain, at any one time there might be half a dozen mountain ranges in sight, sometimes twice this many. Each one adds its own signature presence, not always in proportion to its size. The Marl Mountains, a diminutive range easy to overlook, is likely to make an impression for its photogenic boulder fields and views of the Kelso Dunes. Just beyond this range, the Mojave Road passes by the Cima volcanic field, offering for several miles rare views of its classical

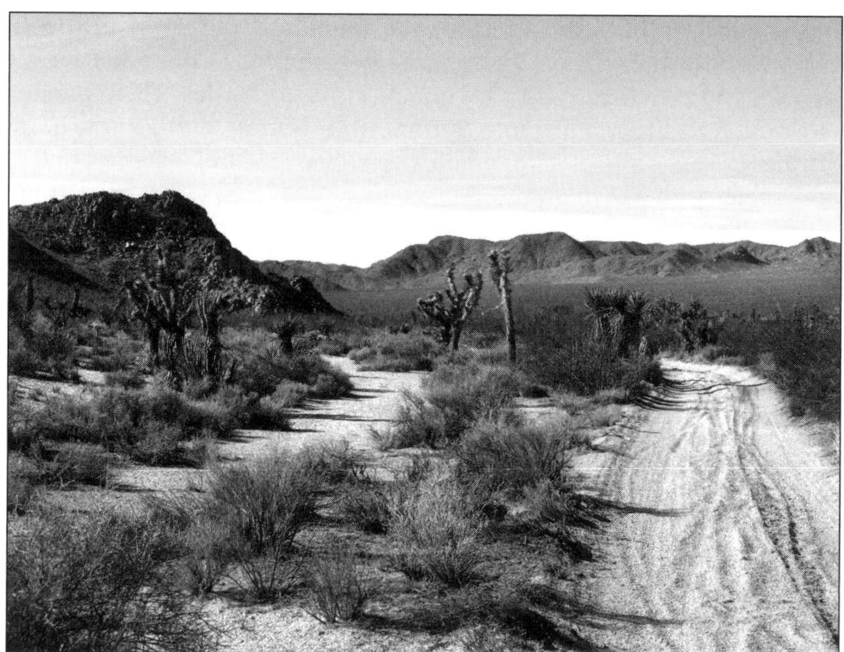

The Mojave Road near the Marl Mountains

volcanoes. There are more desolate ranges beyond—the precipitous Old Dad Mountain, the complex ridges of Cowhole Mountain, its sand-coated little sister, and the stark Soda Mountains. Ultimately, on Soda Lake's bright shore, the soil gets so caustic that even the hardiest plants cannot eke out a living. For several miles across the lake, the land turns to a lifeless playa of mud and salt.

Beyond the lake, the Mojave Road meets with the bleakest element yet. For the last 20 miles it meanders through a deep river of sand punctuated only with scant ghostly shrubs so parched they never seem to bear fresh leaves. This is not the Mojave Road's wildest stretch—most of it is inside the Rasor Off-Highway Vehicle Area, and the rest follows the Union Pacific Railroad—but it is the most challenging. You can bail by driving up the Rasor Road to the interstate, but you would be missing the best—Afton Canyon, also known as the Grand Canyon of the Mojave. For 6 miles the road meanders along the bottom of this narrower passage, where the Mojave River squeezes between striking badlands. Made of soft sedimentary rocks, the canyon walls have been deeply chiseled into amazingly colorful displays of spires and gullies. This is easily the most spectacular scenery along the entire Mojave Road. It ends with a bang at a rare flowing stretch of the Mojave River.

In the midst of this scorched land, this abundance of water nurtures a paradise of lush wetlands, by far the largest since the Colorado River.

The Mojave Road passes by numerous historic sites. There are the old military outposts at Piute Spring, Rock Spring, and Zzyzx. Marl Spring, once the site of a large mill, has a nice arrastre, watering holes, and a thick grove of mesquite. At Government Holes, two large cottonwoods lean gracefully over drifts of aromatic big sagebrush and an old-fashioned well that cattlemen used for decades. In the summer it is the shadiest spot for miles, and its leaky windmill gives off a little humidity and comfort. There are also ranches, corrals, water tanks, stone cabins, homesteads, rock art sites, and mills. To visit these sites in style, take with you a copy of Dennis Casebier's *Mojave Road Guide.* It provides the location and photographs of many of them, as well as a wealth of historical information.

Road conditions. As usual with desert roads, the physical condition of the Mojave Road varies significantly with the season and erosion. There can be snow. Storm washouts and flooded washes are not unheard of. It is hard to predict what you will find. Many segments of the Mojave Road can be driven with a standard-clearance vehicle. If you want to drive a couple of miles here and there, try it with care. For longer distances, a high-clearance vehicle is likely going to be needed.

Four-wheel drive is not generally necessary, but there are a few persistently bad spots that require it. The steep climb up the east side of the Piute Range (starting at mile ~11) is the first one. It is covered with loose sharp rocks, and at one point a crevasse slices half way through the road bed, on the precipice side. The short but abrupt grade down into Watson Wash (mile 31.1) is worse. It takes nerves of steel to nose down into this crooked chute so smooth that even with parking brakes on, a heavy vehicle will keep sliding down. At least this one is easy to bypass. The Soda Lake crossing is an even bigger challenge. For a few miles in the middle of the lake, the road is a wide swath of deep ruts in slippery mud. The crossing is often impracticable and closed in winter. The Mojave Road's supreme challenge, however, is sand. The first area is along the Cima volcanic field and Willow Wash, where the tracks are in soft sand for several miles. The worst is the long segment between Soda Lake and the head of Afton Canyon. Getting bogged down in this giant sand pit is remarkably easy. In upper Afton Canyon, just when you thought you were out of trouble, you will likely have to ford the Mojave River, which can be bumper deep... To be safe, tackle these challenging areas with at least one other vehicle. Experience in driving on wet terrains and sand is mandatory.

Hiking. Several areas along the Mojave Road offer excellent hiking opportunities. The classics are Piute Canyon, Rock Spring Canyon, the cinder cones, Cowhole Mountain, the Granites, and Zzyzx, all of which are described in this volume. There are also three original segments of the Old Government Road, now closed to motor vehicles, that can be hiked. The eastern one is cuts across the Piute Range along Fort Piute Canyon (see *Fort Piute*). The western segment connects the Mojave Road from the eastern edge of Soda Lake to Zzyzx, then south along the T & T berm to the Mojave Road west of the Granites (see *Zzyzx*).

The Mojave Road

	Dist.(mi)	Elev.(ft)
Highway 95	0.0	2,267
Piute Wash crossing	2.2	2,030
Metropolitan Water Dist. Rd	7.2	2,410
End of road at Fort Piute	(1.9)	2,800
Pass over Piute Range	12.1	~3,435
Jct with AT&T Cable Rd (right)	12.5	3,386
Jct with Badlands Road (left)	13.0	3,400
Ivanpah Road	23.6	4,098
Carruthers Canyon Road	27.5	4,465
Cedar Canyon Road (merges)	30.6	4,780
Rock Spring	31.8	4,775
Government Holes	34.0	5,050
Cedar Canyon Road (merges)	34.5	5,015
Highest point in Mojave Rd	36.5	5,166
Kelso-Cima Road	44.0	3,725
Marl Spring	52.3	3,885
Aiken Mine Road crossing	61.1	~3,135
Kelbaker Road	67.1	2,215
Brannigan Mine Road	70.9	1,655
Soda Lake (eastern shore)	78.3	945
Old Government Road	79.6	930
Travelers Monument	82.4	930
The Granites	83.7	935
Rasor Road	85.9	1,035
Shaw Pass	88.2	1,155
Afton Canyon (lower bridge)	98.0	1,237
Afton Canyon Campground	103.2	1,410
I-15 at Afton Road	106.8	1,765

The middle segment is the wildest. From Marl Spring the Old Government Road used to cut south along the Marl Mountains, then northwest across the range, until it was abandoned in 1859 because it was too rough. From the spring, the aging track vanishes in and out of washes for 1.3 miles. Just after it veers southwest, it splits off to the left as a faded spur, and ends in 1.2 miles at the edge of the wide gap in the mountains. The wild part is returning north through the gap, then up through Sheep Spring, a rare oasis of thick greenery in a narrow canyon. From there the Mojave Road offers an easy way back. This is a great, lonesome, off-beat loop, 7.2 miles for only 950 feet of elevation gain, in a wilderness peppered with boulders and Joshua trees.

The all-around best hiking area is Afton Canyon. Many exciting destinations are hidden among its colorful badlands. There are slot canyons, natural bridges, fluted falls, caves, and roadless bends in the Mojave River with flowing water and green oases, all of it in a stunning decor of tall wrinkled walls. The most impressive is the ore chute of an old mine hanging precariously in a crack way up an incline so sheer one feels compelled to check out how the miners got up there...

Logistics. Travelers on the Mojave Road and on the majority of the roads it crosses are rare. I drove on it many times and never encountered another party. If your vehicle gets immobilized, it might be a while before someone drives by and helps. Bring plenty of water and food in case you get stranded. Let someone know your itinerary.

The Mojave Road crosses many roads, and occasionally merges with or splits off from larger roads. Route finding at these junctions can be tricky. At most intersections the Mojave Road is marked with large rock cairns, so look for those systematically. However, the cairns alone are not enough. Take a detailed map with you. Without one, it is virtually impossible not to take a wrong turn somewhere and lose the road. The best available map is the National Geographic *Trails Illustrated Map*. The *Mojave Road Guide* also has very clear maps, and it provides essentially fool-proof step-by-step directions as well.

The average comfortable speed on the Mojave Road is somewhere around 10 miles per hour. If you did not stop anywhere, which would be a waste, it would take a very long day to drive all of it. If you visit the main roadside attractions, it can easily take two days. If you add a few short hikes, the tally can at least double. There are plenty of good spots to rest for the night. Like the emigrants who drove this road long ago, take it slowly. Only with a generous gift of time does one get to know a place well, even in the seemingly empty desert.

■

BIBLIOGRAPHY

Further Reading

Casebier, D. G. *Mojave Road Guide: An Adventure Through Time*. Essex, Ca.: Tales of the Mojave Road Publishing Company. Tales of the Mojave Road No. 22, 1999.

Casebier, D. G. *Fort Pah-Ute, California*. Norco, Ca.: Tales of the Mojave Road Publishing Company. Tales of the Mojave Road No. 4, 1974.

Duffield-Stoll, A. Q. *Zzyzx: History of an Oasis*. Desert Studies Contributed Series Number 65. Northridge, Ca.: Santa Susana Press, 1994.

Foster, L. *Adventuring in the California Desert*. Revised edition. San Francisco, Ca.: Sierra Club Books, 1997.

Hensher, A. *Abandoned Settlements of the Eastern Mojave*. Lake Oswego, Or.: Western Places 8, No. 3, 2007.

Ingram, S. *Cacti, Agaves, and Yuccas of California and Nevada*. Los Olivos, Ca.: Cachuma Press, 2008.

Knute, A. *Plants of the East Mojave: Mojave National Preserve*. Barstow, Ca.: Mojave River Valley Association, 2002.

Krist, J. *50 Best Short Hikes in California Deserts*. Berkeley, Ca.: Wilderness Press, 1995.

MacKay, P. *Mojave Desert Wildflowers: A Field Guide to Wildflowers, Trees, and Shrubs of the Mojave Desert, Including the Mojave National Preserve, Death Valley National Park, and Joshua Tree National Park*. Guilford, Ct.: The Globe Pequot Press, 2003.

Mitchell, J. *Keepers of the Caves*. Goffs, Ca.: Tales of the Mojave Road Publishing Company. Tales of the Mojave Road No. 23, 2003.

Rae, C. *East Mojave Desert: A Visitor's Guide*. Santa Barbara, Ca.: Olympus Press, 1992.

Sharp, M. M., and M. S. Moore. *Maruba, Homesteading in Lanfair Valley*. Goffs, Ca.: Tales of the Mojave Road Publishing Company. Tales of the Mojave Road No. 24, 2004.

Zdon, A. *Desert Summits: A Climbing and Hiking Guide to California and Southern Nevada*. Bishop, Ca.: Spotted Dog Press, Inc., 2000.

Sources: Books and Journals

Aubury, L. E. "The Copper Resources of California." *Cal. St. Mining Bureau Bull.* 50 (1908): 19–23, 325–340.

Busby, C. J., E. R. Schermer, and J. M. Mattinson. "Extensional Arc Setting and Ages of Middle Jurassic Eolianites, Cowhole Mountains (Eastern Mojave Desert Block, California)." *Geol. Soc. Am. Memoir* 195 (2002): 79–91.

Cardiff, S. W., and J. V. Remsen, Jr. "Breeding Avifaunas of the New York Mountains and Kingston Range: Islands of Conifers in the Mojave Desert of California." *Western Birds* 12 (1981): 73–86.

Chappell, G. "Railroads Around Mojave National Preserve." In *Old Ores: Mining History in the Eastern Mojave Desert.* R. E. Reynolds, Editor, Proc. of the 2005 Desert Symposium (2005): 41–48.

Cloudman, H. C., E. Huguenin, F. J. H. Merrill, and W. B. Tucker. "Part VI San Bernardino County—Tulare County." *Rept. XV of the State Mineralogist* 15 (1915–1916): 773–852.

Cowie S., P. Baird, and A. C. MacWilliams. *Mine Documentation in the Standard Mining District, Mojave National Preserve, California.* Western Archeological and Conservation Center, Tucson, Ariz.: Publications in Anthropology 88, 2006.

Crawford, J. J. *Thirteenth Rept. of the State Mineralogist* 13 (1894–1896): 230, 319–330, 606–609.

Dohrenwend, J. C., L. D. McFadden, B. D. Turrin, and S. G. Wells. "K-Ar Dating of the Cima Volcanic Field, Eastern Mojave Desert, California: Late Cenozoic Volcanic History and Landscape Evolution." *Geol.* 12, No. 3 (1984): 163–167.

Dohrenwend, J. C., and A. J. Parsons. "Pediments in Arid Environments." In *Geomorphology of Desert Environments*. Second edition. A. J. Parsons and A. D. Abrahams, Editors. Springer Science + Business Media B. V. Ch. 13 (2009): 377–412.

Dorr, E. P. Sworn Affidavit, *Cal. Mining J.* 10, No. 3 (1940): 37.

Eric, J. H. "Copper in California." *Cal. Div. of Mines and Geol. Bull.* 144 (1948): 298–299, 304, 307, 312, 314–315, 317.

Fiero, B. *Geology of the Great Basin*. Reno, Nev.: University of Nevada Press, 1986.

Fulton, R. "Evaporative Salt Production on Soda Dry Lake." In *Old Ores: Mining History in the Eastern Mojave Desert.* R. E. Reynolds, Editor, Proc. of the 2005 Desert Symposium (2005): 55–60.

Goldfarb, R. J., D. M. Miller, R. W. Simpson, D. B. Hoover, P. R. Moyle, J. E. Olson, and R. S. Gaps. "Mineral Resources of the Providence Mountains Wilderness Study Area, San Bernardino County, California." *U. S. Geol. Survey Bull.* 1712-D (1988): D1–D70.

Hazard, L., and J. T. Rotenberry. "Herpetofauna and Vegetation Survey of Cornfield Spring and Piute Spring, East Mojave Desert, California." In *Proc. of the East Mojave Desert Symposium*, Nat. Hist. Mus. of Los Angeles Co. Tech. Reports, No. 10 (1992): 69–73.

Hensher, A. "The Historical Mining Towns of the Eastern Mojave Desert." In *Old Ores: Mining History in the Eastern Mojave Desert.* R. E. Reynolds, Editor, Proc. of the 2005 Desert Symposium (2005): 28–40.

Hewett, D. F. "Geology and Mineral Resources of the Ivanpah Quadrangle, California and Nevada." *U. S. Geol. Survey Prof. Paper* 275 (1956).

Howard, K. A., J. E. Kilburn, R. W. Simpson, T. T. Fitzgibbon, D. E. Detra, G. L. Raines, and C. Sabine. "Mineral Resources of the Bristol/Granite Mountains Wilderness Study Area, San Bernardino County, California." *U. S. Geol. Survey Bull.* 1712-C (1987): C1–C18.

Jenkins, O. P. "Tabulation of Tungsten Deposits of California to Accompany Economic Mineral Map No. 4." *Cal. J. of Mines* and *Geol.* 38 (1942): 303–358.

Jones, C. C. "An Iron Deposit in the California Desert Region." *Engineering and Mining J.* 87, No. 16 (1909): 785–788.

Jones, C. C. "The Iron Ores of California and Possibilities of Smelting." *Am. Inst. Min. Eng. Trans.* 53 (1915): 306–311, 318–323.

Kerr, P. F. "Tungsten Mineralization in the United States." *Geol. Soc. Am. Mem.* 15 (1946): 164.

Kroeber, A. L. *Handbook of the Indians of California*. Bureau of American Ethnology Bulletin No. 78. Washington, D.C., 1925.

Laird, C. *The Chemehuevis*. Banning, Ca.: Malki Museum Press, 1976.

Laizure, C. M. "Elementary Placer Mining Methods and Gold-Saving Devices." *Rept. XXVIII of the State Mineralogist* 28 (1932): 112–204.

Lamey, C. A. "Vulcan Iron-Ore Deposit, San Bernardino County, California." *Cal. Div. Mines Bull.* 129 (1948): 87–95.

Lightfoot, K. G., and O. Parrish. *California Indians and their Environment: An Introduction*. Berkeley, Ca.: University of California Press, 2009.

Lindsay, J. F., D. R. Criswell, T. L. Criswell, and B. S. Criswell. "Sound-Producing Dune and Beach Sands." *Geol. Soc. Am. Bull.* 87 (1976): 463–473.

Lingenfelter, R. E. *Death Valley and the Amargosa: A Land of Illusion*. Berkeley, Ca.: University of California Press (1986): 135–142, 281–284, 381–387.

Lovich, J. E., and K. R. Beaman. "A History of Gila Monster (*Heloderma suspectum cinctum*) Records from California with Comments on Factors Affecting their Distribution." *Bull. Southern California Acad. Sci.* 106, No. 2 (2007): 39–58.

McCurry, M., D. R. Lux, and K. L. Mickus. "Neogene Structural Evolution of the Woods Mountains Volcanic Center, East Mojave National Scenic Area." *San Bernardino County Museum* A 42, No. 3 (1995): 75–80.

Meek, N. "Mojave River History from an Upstream Perspective." In *Breaking Up*. R. E. Reynolds, Editor, Proc. of the 2004 Desert Symposium (2004): 41–49.

Mickus, K. L., and M. McCurry. "Gravity and Aeromagnetic Constraints on the Structure of the Woods Mountains Volcanic Center, Southeastern California." *Bull. of Volcanology* 60, No. 7 (1999): 523–533.

Miller, D. A., J. G. Frisken, R. C. Jachens, and D. D. Gese. "Mineral Resources of the Castle Peaks Wilderness Study Area, San Bernardino County, California." *U. S. Geol. Survey Bull.* 1713-A (1986): A1–A17.

Miller, D. M., and J. L. Wooden. "Field Guide to Proterozoic Geology of the New York, Ivanpah, and Providence Mountains, California." *U. S. Geol. Survey Open-File Report* 94-674, 1994.

Myrick, D. F. *Railroads of Nevada and Eastern California. Volume II: The Southern Roads*. Reno, Nev.: University of Nevada Press, 1991.

Nadeau, R. *The Silver Seekers*. Santa Barbara, Ca.: Crest Publishers (1999): 119–132.

Nielson, J. E., J. G. Frisken, R. C. Jachens, and J. R. McDonnell, Jr. "Mineral Resources of the Fort Piute Wilderness Study Area, San Bernardino County, California." *U. S. Geol. Survey Bull.* 1713-C (1987): C1–C12.

Nielson, J. E., D. R. Lux, G. B. Dalrymple, and A. F. Glazner. "Age of the Peach Springs Tuff, Southeastern California and Western Arizona." *J. of Geophys. Res.* 95, No. B1 (1990): 571–580.

Novitsky-Evans, J. M. *Geology of the Cowhole Mountains, Southeastern California.* Houston, Texas, Rice University, Ph.D. thesis, 1978.

Partridge, J. F. "Tungsten Resources of California." *Cal. J. of Mines and Geol.* 37 (1941): 305–309.

Patchick, P. F. "A Geologist's Notes on the Ivanpah Mountains." *Desert Magazine* (May 1961): 8–11.

Pigati, J. S., and D. M. Miller. "Late Pleistocene Wetland Deposits at Valley Wells, Eastern Mojave Desert, California: Initial Results." In *Trough to Trough: The Colorado and the Salton Sea.* R. E. Reynolds, Editor, Proc. of the 2008 Desert Symposium (2008): 138–142.

Powers, A. "Gold or Just a Fever?" *Los Angeles Times,* September 11, 2006.

Reynolds, R. E. "Jurassic Tracks in California." In *Making Tracks—The Field Trip Guide.* R. E. Reynolds, Editor, Proc. of the 2006 Desert Symposium (2006): 19–24.

Reynolds, E. R., and T. Weasma. "California Dinosaur Tracks: Inventory and Management." In *Between the Basins: Exploring the Western Mojave and Southern Basin and Range Province.* R. E. Reynolds, Editor, Proc. of the 2002 Desert Symposium (2002): 15–18.

Sagstetter, B., and B. Sagstetter. *The Mining Camps Speak.* Denver, Co.: BenchMark Publishing of Colorado, 1998.

Sherer, L. M. *Bitterness Road—The Mojave: 1604 to 1860.* Menlo Park, Ca.: Ballena Press, 1994.

Sholtz, P., M. Bretz, and F. Nori. "Sound-Producing Sand Avalanches." *Contemp. Phys.* 38, No. 5 (1997): 329–342.

Stevens, C. H., and P. Stone. "The Pennsylvanian-Early Permian Bird Spring Carbonate Shelf, Southeastern California: Fusulinid Biostratigraphy, Paleographic Evolution, and Tectonic Implications." *Geol. Soc. Am. Spec. Papers* 429 (2007).

Stewart, K. M. "A Brief History of the Chemehuevi Indians." *Kiva* 34, No. 1 (1968): 9–27.

Storms, W. H. "San Bernardino County." *Eleventh Rept. of the State Mineralogist* 11 (1890-1892): 367–368.

Taylor, R. J. *Desert Wildflowers of North America.* Missoula, Mt.: Mountain Press Publishing Company, 1998.

Theodore, T. G. "Geology and Mineral Resources of the East Mojave National Scenic Area, San Bernardino County, California." *U. S. Geol. Survey Bull.* 2160 (2007).

Thomas, K., T. Keeler-Wolf, J. Franklin, and P. Stine. "Mojave Desert Ecosystem Program: Central Mojave Vegetation Database." Final Report, *USGS Science for a Changing World,* Sacramento, California, 2004.

Thompson, D. G. "The Mohave Desert Region, California." *U. S. Geol. Survey Water Supply Paper* 578 (1929): 679.

Tucker, W. B. "Los Angeles Field Division." *Rept. XVII of the State Mineralogist* 17 (1920): 333–374.

Tucker, W. B. "Los Angeles Field Division." *Rept. XX of the State Mineralogist* 20 (1924): 92–95, 196–200.

Tucker, W. B., and R. J. Sampson. "San Bernardino County." *Rept. XXVI of the State Mineralogist* 26 (1930): 202–325.

Tucker, W. B., and R. J. Sampson. "San Bernardino County." *Rept. XXVII of the State Mineralogist* 27 (1931): 262–401.

Tucker, W. B., and R. J. Sampson. "Current Mining Activity in Southern California." *Cal. J. of Mines and Geol.* 36 (1940): 53–81.

Tucker, W. B., and R. J. Sampson. "Recent Developments in the Tungsten Resources of California." *Cal. J. of Mines and Geol.* 37 (1941): 584–587.

Tucker, W. B., and R. J. Sampson. "Current Mining Activity in Southern California." *Cal. J. of Mines and Geol.* 39 (1943): 126–138.

Tucker, W. B., and R. J. Sampson. "Current Notes on Activity in the Strategic Minerals, Los Angeles Field District." *Cal. J. of Mines and Geol.* 39 (1943): 66–69.

Tucker, W. B., and R. J. Sampson. "Mineral Resources of San Bernardino County, California." *Cal. J. of Mines and Geol.* 39 (1943): 427–549.

Ver Planck, W. E. "History of Mining in Northeastern San Bernardino County," *State of Cal. Mineral Inform. Service* 14, No. 9, Sept. 1961.

Von Bernewitz, M. W. *Handbook for Prospectors and Operators of Small Mines.* Fourth edition. New York, NY: McGraw-Hill Book Company, Inc., 1943.

Vredenburgh, L. M. "Early Mines of Southern Clark Mountain, Northern Mescal Range and Ivanpah Mountains." In *Punctuated Chaos in the Northeastern Mojave Desert,* R. E. Reynolds and J. Reynolds, Editors, San Bernardino County Museum Assoc. Quarterly 43(1-2) (1996): 67-72.

Vredenburgh, L. "An Overview of Mining in the California Desert." In *Old Ores: Mining History in the Eastern Mojave Desert.* R. E. Reynolds, Editor, Proc. of the 2005 Desert Symposium (2005): 22–27.

Vredenburgh, L. M., G. L. Shumway, and R. D. Hartill. *Desert Fever: An Overview of Mining in the California Desert.* Canoga Park, Ca.: Living West Press, 1981.

Vriend, N. M., M. L. Hunt, R. W. Clayton, C. E. Brennen, K. S. Brantley, and A. Ruiz-Angulo. "Solving the Mystery of Booming Sand Dunes." *Geophys. Res. Lett.* 34, L16306 (2007).

Walker, J. D., and B. R. Wardlaw. "Implications of Paleozoic and Mesozoic Rocks in the Soda Mountains, Northeastern Mojave Desert, California, for Late Paleozoic and Mesozoic Cordilleran Orogenesis." *Geol. Soc. Am. Bull.* 101 (1989): 1574–1583.

Warren, C. N., and J. De Costa. "Dating Lake Mohave Artifacts and Beaches." *Am. Antiquity* 30, No. 2 (1964): 206–209.

Wilshire, H. G. "Geologic Map of the Cow Cove Quadrangle, San Bernardino County, California." *U. S. Geol. Survey Open-File Report* 92-179, 1992.

Wilshire, H. G., J. G. Frisken, R. C. Jachens, D. V. Prose, C. M. Rumsey, and A. B. McMahan. "Mineral Resources of the Cinder Cones Wilderness Study Area, San Bernardino County, California." *U. S. Geol. Survey Bull.* 1712-B (1987): B1–B13.

Wright, L. A., R. M. Stewart, T. E. Gay, Jr., and G. C. Hazenbush. "Mines and Mineral Deposits of San Bernardino County, California." *Cal. J. of Mines and Geology* 49, Nos. 1 and 2 (1953): 49–257.

Wright, L. A., R. M. Stewart, T. E. Gay, Jr., and G. C. Hazenbush. "Tabulate List of Mines and Mineral Deposits in San Bernardino County." *Cal. J. of Mines and Geology* 49, Nos. 1 and 2 (1953): 1–192.

Sources: Newspapers and Magazines

Calico Print, Calico, Ca. (1885–1886).

Citrograph, Redlands, Ca. (1887–1903).

Mining and Scientific Press, (August 1906): 130–131.

Mining Reporter (1899–1907).

Mining World, (February 6, 1906): 225–226.

The Mining And Metallurgical Journal, Los Angeles, Ca. (1897–1900).

■

INDEX OF DESTINATIONS

This section is a quick reference to the main destinations covered in this volume, categorized by types (e.g., canyons, peaks, etc.) and by activities (hiking, driving, backpacking, etc.). The categories titled "Botany," "Geology and minerals," and "History," which are extensive, have been limited to the most significant sites. Each entry is keyed to the main page (or occasionally two pages, or a range of pages) where it occurs in the book; the entry might continue in subsequent pages (which are not listed to conserve space). An asterisk marks a site that can be explored by car or by a short stroll from a car. In some instances, a portion of a site is reachable by car and has an asterisk (for example, the camp at the New Trail Mine), while another portion can only be reached on foot and has no asterisk (for example, the New Trail Mine). Entries in bold italic characters indicate the sites that are in my view the most outstanding.

Ghost towns, camps, and forts

Hiking trails (short)

Hiking trails (long)

INDEX

Regular numbers indicate entries in the text; italic numbers indicate entries in a map. In case of multiple text pages, boldface numbers are used to indicate the main entries.